THE OXFORD HANDBOOK OF
VALUE THEORY

THE OXFORD HANDBOOK OF
VALUE THEORY

Edited by
IWAO HIROSE
and
JONAS OLSON

UNIVERSITY PRESS

Oxford University Press is a department of the University of Oxford. It furthers
the University's objective of excellence in research, scholarship, and education
by publishing worldwide. Oxford is a registered trade mark of Oxford University
Press in the UK and certain other countries.

Published in the United States of America by Oxford University Press
198 Madison Avenue, New York, NY 10016, United States of America.

© Oxford University Press 2015

First issued as an Oxford University Press paperback, 2018

All rights reserved. No part of this publication may be reproduced, stored in
a retrieval system, or transmitted, in any form or by any means, without the
prior permission in writing of Oxford University Press, or as expressly permitted
by law, by license, or under terms agreed with the appropriate reproduction
rights organization. Inquiries concerning reproduction outside the scope of the
above should be sent to the Rights Department, Oxford University Press, at the
address above.

You must not circulate this work in any other form
and you must impose this same condition on any acquirer.

Library of Congress Cataloging-in-Publication Data
The Oxford handbook of value theory / edited by Iwao Hirose and Jonas Olson.
pages cm
Includes index.
ISBN 978-0-19-995930-3 (hardcover : alk. paper); 978-0-19-092702-8 (paperback : alk. paper)
1. Values. I. Hirose, Iwao. II. Olson, Jonas (College teacher)
BD232.O94 2015
121'.8—dc23
2014021185

Contents

Contributors — vii

Introduction to Value Theory — 1
Iwao Hirose and Jonas Olson

PART I FOUNDATIONS

1. Value and Normativity — 13
   Michael J. Zimmerman

2. Intrinsic and Extrinsic Value — 29
   Toni Rønnow-Rasmussen

3. Doubts about Intrinsic Value — 44
   Jonas Olson

4. Value and Desires — 60
   Graham Oddie

5. Value and Emotions — 80
   Christine Tappolet

6. Neutral and Relative Value — 96
   Garrett Cullity

7. Value and Time — 117
   Krister Bykvist

8. Monism and Pluralism about Value — 136
   Chris Heathwood

9. Prudential Value — 158
   Valerie Tiberius

10. Kantian Axiology and the Dualism of Practical Reason — 175
    Ralf M. Bader

PART II STRUCTURE

11. Value Incomparability and Incommensurability — 205
    RUTH CHANG

12. Value Superiority — 225
    GUSTAF ARRHENIUS AND WLODEK RABINOWICZ

13. General and Personal Good: Harsanyi's Contribution to the Theory of Value — 249
    JOHN BROOME

14. Theories of Value Aggregation: Utilitarianism, Egalitarianism, Prioritarianism — 267
    NILS HOLTUG

15. Organic Unities — 285
    ERIK CARLSON

16. Skepticism about Value Aggregation — 300
    IWAO HIROSE

PART III EXTENSIONS

17. Value and Cost-Benefit Analysis — 317
    MATTHEW D. ADLER

18. The Value of Health — 338
    DANIEL M. HAUSMAN

19. Freedom and Its Value — 356
    PRASANTA K. PATTANAIK AND YONGSHENG XU

20. Value in Nature — 381
    DAVID SCHMIDTZ

21. Population Axiology — 399
    M. A. ROBERTS

22. The Value of Existence — 424
    GUSTAF ARRHENIUS AND WLODEK RABINOWICZ

Index — 445

Contributors

Matthew D. Adler is Richard A. Horvitz Professor of Law and Professor of Economics, Philosophy, and Public Policy at Duke University, where he directs the Center for Law, Economics, and Public Policy.

Gustaf Arrhenius is Director of the Institute for Futures Studies, Professor of Practical Philosophy at Stockholm University and cochair of the Franco-Swedish Program in Economics and Philosophy at Collège d'études mondiales and the Swedish Collegium for Advanced Study (SCAS).

Ralf M. Bader is a Fellow of Merton College and a CUF Lecturer in the Department of Philosophy at the University of Oxford.

John Broome is Emeritus White's Professor of Moral Philosophy and a Fellow of Corpus Christi College at the University of Oxford, and an Adjunct Professor of Philosophy at the Australian National University.

Krister Bykvist is Professor of Practical Philosophy at Stockholm University.

Erik Carlson is Professor of Practical Philosophy at Uppsala University.

Ruth Chang is Professor of Philosophy at Rutgers University, New Brunswick.

Garrett Cullity is Hughes Professor of Philosophy at the University of Adelaide.

Daniel M. Hausman is Herbert A. Simon Professor of Philosophy at the University of Wisconsin–Madison.

Chris Heathwood is Associate Professor of Philosophy at the University of Colorado Boulder.

Iwao Hirose is Associate Professor at the Philosophy Department and the School of Environment, McGill University.

Nils Holtug is Director of the Centre for Advanced Migration Studies and Professor of Political Philosophy, University of Copenhagen.

Graham Oddie is Professor of Philosophy at the University of Colorado Boulder.

Jonas Olson is Docent (Associate Professor) of Practical Philosophy at Stockholm University.

Prasanta K. Pattanaik is Emeritus Professor of Economics at the University of California, Riverside.

Wlodek Rabinowicz is Emeritus Professor of Practical Philosophy at Lund University, Centennial Professor at London School of Economics, and Long-Term Fellow of the Swedish Collegium for Advanced Study (SCAS).

M. A. Roberts is Professor of Philosophy at the College of New Jersey.

Toni Rønnow-Rasmussen is Professor of Practical Philosophy at the Lund University.

David Schmidtz is Kendrick Professor of Philosophy and founding Director of the Center for Philosophy of Freedom at the University of Arizona.

Christine Tappolet is Professor of Philosophy at the Université de Montréal.

Valerie Tiberius is Professor of Philosophy at the University of Minnesota, Twin Cities.

Yongsheng Xu is Professor of Economics at Georgia State University, Atlanta, and a faculty affiliate at the Jean Beer Blumenfeld Center for Ethics at Georgia State University.

Michael J. Zimmerman is Professor of Philosophy at the University of North Carolina at Greensboro.

INTRODUCTION TO VALUE THEORY

IWAO HIROSE AND JONAS OLSON

I.1. What Is Value Theory?

VALUE theory, or axiology, concerns which things are good or bad, how good or bad they are, and, most fundamentally, what it is for a thing to be good or bad. Already this brief characterization of our topic raises a host of questions: What kind of value is in question? What kinds of things are or can be valuable? How can values be compared and measured? How does value theory bear on practical issues in ethics and other disciplines? These are all topics covered in this *Handbook*, the purpose of which is to offer a critical overview of the central topics in value theory that is both comprehensive and up to date.

As a philosophical discipline, value theory branches out in various directions. It overlaps partly with metaethics in that it investigates evaluative concepts and the nature of value. It also overlaps partly with normative ethics in that it studies what things are good or bad in themselves or as means; what things are good or bad *for* people; and how the value of outcomes relate to the moral rightness and wrongness of actions. Debates in value theory are sometimes closely associated with consequentialist theories of moral rightness and wrongness. Many consequentialist theories (e.g., classical utilitarianism) are based on some sort of value theory (for example, that happiness is the only thing of intrinsic value). But several prominent nonconsequentialist moral theories—such as Kantianism and W. D. Ross's theory of prima facie duties, to name only two examples—involve theories or principles about value. Value theory is thus not solely a concern for consequentialism and its advocates. Moreover, issues about value arise not only in philosophical disciplines that pertain directly to ethics, but also, for example, in epistemology, aesthetics, and philosophy of religion. This *Handbook*, however, focuses mainly on value theory as it pertains to ethics, broadly construed.[1]

Outside of philosophy, value theory branches out to economics. There are theories and conceptual distinctions in value theory that are highly relevant to economic theory and there are methods and results in economics that are useful in analyzing the formal structure of value. That the disciplines partially overlap has become clear in recent debates about topics such as expected utility theory, cost-benefit analyses, interpersonal comparisons of utility, and population ethics. These topics are all covered in this *Handbook*, and these chapters as well as some others are informed by economic theory.

The *Handbook* is divided into three main parts. The chapters in Part I ("Foundations") concern fundamental and interrelated issues about the nature of value and distinctions between kinds of value. The chapters in Part II ("Structure") concern formal properties of value that bear in particular on the possibilities of measuring and comparing value. The chapters in Part III ("Extensions") consider specific topics where questions of value are at the forefront. In the remainder of this introduction we briefly summarize each chapter and give some brief background.

I.2. FOUNDATIONS

One of the first questions to ask for philosophers thinking about value is how value fits into the broader theorizing about the normative. In the last two decades there has been considerable debate about the prospects of analyzing value in terms of concepts like reason, fittingness, or ought. In chapter 1 of this *Handbook*, Michael J. Zimmerman scrutinizes and contributes to this debate, which is still very much alive. Zimmerman draws a fundamental distinction between two families of concepts: the *evaluative* (which includes *goodness* and *badness*) and the *deontic* (which includes *rightness* and *wrongness*). He considers the possibilities of accounting for the one family of concepts in terms of some member or members of the other. After noting some merits and problems with each proposal, Zimmerman considers the prospects for a combined account.

One upshot of Zimmerman's chapter is that the kind of value most relevant to theorizing about value is *intrinsic* or *final* value. Roughly, for a thing to have intrinsic or final value is for it to be valuable in itself or as an end. Toni Rønnow-Rasmussen seeks in chapter 2 to clarify the notions of intrinsic and final value. He distinguishes between final intrinsic value and final extrinsic value in terms of supervenience, and he explores the relation between instrumental value and other kinds of nonfinal extrinsic value. He also examines the relevance of the intrinsic/extrinsic distinction to value theory.

It is not uncontroversial, however, that intrinsic value is central to theorizing about value and normativity. Some critics have doubted that there are things that have intrinsic value, and others have argued more radically that the concept makes no sense. Jonas Olson considers such doubts in chapter 3. Much of the skeptical debate about intrinsic value has targeted G. E. Moore's writings on the topic and drawn on P. T. Geach's classic article "Good and Evil" (1956). Olson takes as his point of departure Moore's central claims about intrinsic value and goes on to consider recent criticisms from Richard Kraut and Judith Jarvis Thomson, among others.

The next two chapters further explore the nature of value, and in particular its relation to desire and emotion. In chapter 4, Graham Oddie begins with the *Euthyphro*-like question whether things are good because we desire them or whether we desire things because they are good. Idealist theories endorse the former view and take values to be desire-dependent, while realist theories endorse the latter view and take them to be desire-independent. Oddie goes on to distinguish between different kinds of idealism and realism. Axiological realism is the view that the fittingness of desires is grounded in value. Oddie pays special attention to a version of axiological realism that takes desires to be appearances of value, and fittingness of desires to be a matter of correct representation of value.

At the outset of this introduction we characterized value theory as the discipline that deals with questions concerning what things are good or bad and what it is for a thing to be good or bad. Value theorists, however, are not exclusively concerned with "thin" evaluative notions, like goodness and badness. They also worry about so-called "thick" evaluative concepts, like courage and kindness, and about what Christine Tappolet in chapter 5 calls "affective concepts", such as admirability and disgustingness. Tappolet considers whether considerations in the theory of emotions can be used to illuminate the latter. She argues that they can and offers a plausible way of understanding what she calls "Value-Emotion Equivalences" (e.g., biconditionals like "X is admirable if and only if it is or would be fitting to admire X") that ties in with the perceptual theory of emotions. Tappolet also responds to the worry that affective concepts are not inherently evaluative after all.

The next two chapters discuss whether value is in various ways neutral or relative. In chapter 6, Garrett Cullity considers the question whether value is or can be relative to a person, or a valuer, such as an agent or an observer, and what it would be for value to be relative in this way. These questions have bearing on wider issues in normative ethics, particularly the question whether any coherent normative theory can be "consequentialized," that is, cast as a version of consequentialism. Cullity explores the promises and challenges for consequentializing normative theories and concludes that while versions of relative-value consequentialism are able to preserve the attractions of consequentialism, these theories are questionable on other grounds. In chapter 7, Krister Bykvist discusses temporal relativity and value. His leading questions concern the time of value and the value of time. More particularly, he asks first whether bearers of value always have temporal locations and whether value itself has temporal location, and secondly whether and in what ways temporal features—such as duration, temporal order, life periods, and tense—can be evaluatively relevant. As Bykvist shows, these questions have wide ramifications in normative theory, and they bear importantly on how to assess the goodness of lives and the badness of death.

The final three chapters in Part I remain at the foundational level of axiology but deal with more substantive issues. A historically prominent theory of what has value is hedonism. This is the view that all and only experiences of pleasure have (positive) intrinsic value. Hedonism is thus a monistic theory, and it is one of the theories discussed in chapter 8, in which Chris Heathwood considers monism and pluralism about value. Heathwood distinguishes between monism and pluralism with respect to what is good *for* people, what he calls "welfare," and with respect to intrinsic value, what he calls "value simpliciter." He draws several important distinctions between kinds of monism and pluralism, some of which are more radical than others, and considers what can be said for and against them. In chapter 9, Valerie Tiberius further explores the debate about the good for a person, that is, what is sometimes called "prudential value," or simply "welfare" or "well-being." Here too, hedonism is one of the prominent contenders. Tiberius's chapter provides guidance through this debate and argues that a good theory about prudential value should both explain why well-being—as the theory accounts for it—is good for the person whose well-being it is, and also what is good about well-being. In order to do so, theories about prudential value must steer a course between subjectivism and objectivism about well-being.

As we noted earlier, debates in value theory have often been associated with consequentialist theories in normative ethics, since such theories typically give normative rankings of actions in terms of their conduciveness to good outcomes. For reasons mentioned earlier, however, interest in axiology is not limited to consequentialism and its advocates. Chapter 10, by Ralf M. Bader, illustrates this. Kant famously held that the value of happiness is conditional and Bader argues that this feature of the value of happiness enables an integration of the fundamentally distinct values of morality and prudence. One highly attractive upshot of this integration is that it opens up a solution to Henry Sidgwick's famous problem of the dualism of practical reason, according to which acting morally and acting egoistically are equally rational although the requirements of morality and egoism often conflict (Sidgwick 1981 [1907]).

I.3. STRUCTURE

As becomes clear in Part I, there are many different types of values, and values may be possessed by different kinds of bearers. Substantial parts of value theory are concerned with consolidation of values borne by different people or entities, and with consolidation of different types of value. In this area of value theory, three issues are at the forefront. The first concerns how the relevant value is measured (*measurement*). The second is concerned with whether one type of value can be compared with another type, or whether the value possessed by one bearer can be compared with that possessed by another (*comparability*). The third is concerned with how different types of values, or values possessed by different individuals, are combined into a single numerical scale (*aggregation*). These issues are discussed in Part II, with special focus on comparability and aggregation.[2]

When we look at two different types of value bearers, there are cases in which it is difficult to determine which one is more valuable than the other. In value theory, this difficulty is usually understood in terms of either incomparability or incommensurability. These two terms are often not distinguished clearly and sometimes they are used interchangeably. In chapter 11, Ruth Chang offers a clear distinction between the two notions, and explains their importance. Two items are incommensurable just in case they cannot be put on the same scale of units of value. In contrast, two items are incomparable just in case they fail to stand in an evaluative comparative relation, such as being better than or worse than or as good as the other. According to this way of drawing the distinction, incomparability entails incommensurability but not vice versa. Chang further distinguishes incomparability from related phenomena such as parity, indeterminacy, and noncomparability. These precise distinctions, she shows, are important when value theory is put to use in the realm of practical reasoning.

Incommensurability must also be distinguished from discontinuity of value. In chapter 12, Gustaf Arrhenius and Wlodek Rabinowicz examine the latter. They first introduce two kinds of discontinuous value relations. The first is *strong superiority*: A is strongly superior to B if and only if *any* amount of A is better than any amount of B. The other is *weak superiority*: A is weakly superior to B if and only if *some* amount of A is better than any amount of B. They then proceed to examine the formal features of these two value relations. One of their major results is that if (1) some type of value bearer A is strongly or weakly superior to another type B, and (2) type B can be reached from type A by a long enough sequence of slight worsenings, then there must be two types of values C and D such that C is weakly superior to D although values of type C are only marginally greater than values of type D. This result, Arrhenius and Rabinowicz argue, casts doubt on the very notion of value superiority, or alternatively on the idea that superiority amounts to a radical difference in value.

As we said in section I.1, contemporary value theory stretches over various disciplines, and formal results in economics help to understand questions concerning the structure of value. There are some economists who have made fundamental contributions to value theory, and prominent among them is John C. Harsanyi. Harsanyi proved a groundbreaking theorem that extends the valuation of uncertain prospects for a single person to the valuation of distributions of good across people. His theorem is widely known, but not well understood, in philosophy. In chapter 13, John Broome reinterprets Harsanyi's theorem in philosophical parlance. Roughly, the theorem says that if the personal and general betterness relations satisfy the axioms of expected utility theory, and if the principle of personal good is true, then the general betterness relation can be represented by an expectational utility function that is the sum of expectational utility functions representing the personal betterness relations. This theorem is remarkable because if all premises in this theorem are accepted, then utilitarianism must be accepted. As Broome notes, one cannot reject the conclusion of the theorem unless one rejects one or more of its premises. Broome critically examines the arguments against the premises that rely on completeness, strong independence, and the principle of personal good.

Broome's chapter discusses the implications of Harsanyi's theorem for utilitarianism and prioritarianism. In chapter 14, Nils Holtug examines these two rival distributive principles, and in addition he considers egalitarianism and a lexicographic extension of the maximin rule (leximin). These four principles are not always clearly distinguished in the literature. Holtug analyzes these principles in terms of formal conditions—such as the Pareto principle, strong separability, and the Pigou-Dalton principle of transfer—and clarifies the differences between these principles. Furthermore, he highlights the main advantages and disadvantages of each principle.

Many distributive principles are additive. That is to say, for example, that general good is the (weighted or unweighted) sum of personal good. The additive form of distributive principles implies that, other things being equal, an increase in one person's good, or in one type of good, results in an increase in general good. However, the additive form of aggregation may be challenged. One ground for challenging additive aggregation is the idea of *organic unities*. In chapter 15, Erik Carlson attempts to identify what organic unities are, and what they imply. The idea of organic unities is usually associated with G. E. Moore, who provided two different definitions of organic unities (Moore 1993 [1903]: ch. 1). However, Carlson argues that both definitions fail to capture what Moore really had in mind, and that they are both inadequate in terms of measurement theory. Through a careful examination of other definitions of organic unities proposed by some of Moore's followers, Carlson identifies five criteria for organic unities and elucidates the relations between them.

The idea of organic unities does not imply that we cannot judge one outcome to be, all things considered, better or worse than another. It points merely to the inadequacy of a particular method of aggregating the values borne by different persons or entities. Recently, however, some philosophers have, more radically, challenged the very viability of aggregation of the values of different people's lives. Iwao Hirose critically examines the recent literature on skepticism about aggregation of value in chapter 16. He first provides a clear definition of interpersonal aggregation and elucidates its theoretical structure. He then argues against two types of objections to aggregation: *the argument from counterexamples* and *the argument from the separateness of persons*. One well-known challenge to nonaggregative views is that they are insensitive to the number of individuals who are affected by the choice of outcomes. This challenge has become known as the "number problem." Hirose surveys its literature and provides two nonaggregative solutions to the number problem.

I.4. Extensions

One of the salient features of value theory is that it goes beyond abstract philosophical analysis in that it has implications for substantive issues in practical contexts. Part III focuses on the philosophical problems that value theory raises in such contexts.

It is not an overstatement to say that almost all governmental and public decision-makings appeal implicitly or explicitly to some kinds of considerations about value. Value theory is used extensively in the theory and practice of cost-benefit analysis. Cost-benefit analysis is a method for comparing benefits and costs of, for example, a governmental project or policy. The theory of cost-benefit analysis rests on philosophically controversial assumptions. Matthew D. Adler focuses on two such assumptions in chapter 17. One is that costs and benefits are estimated on the basis of people's preferences, and cost-benefit analysis imposes idealizing rationality conditions on people's preferences (i.e., completeness, transitivity, continuity, strict increasement, independence and so on). Adler points out that almost all of these rationality conditions are questionable on normative and empirical grounds. Furthermore, preference-based accounts of well-being face numerous problems. The other assumption Adler takes up is that, following the tradition of new welfare economics,[3] cost-benefit analysis rules out interpersonal comparability of utility. Cost-benefit analysis instead appeals to some hypothetical compensation test such as the Kaldor-Hicks test, which does not require interpersonal comparison. Adler argues that hypothetical compensation tests are merely a criterion for efficiency, not the goodness of policies, and hence that compensation tests are morally justifiable only given a social welfare function that ranks possible outcomes and requires some sort of interpersonal comparability. It is somewhat ironical that, although cost-benefit analysis was motivated partly by doubts about interpersonal comparability, its moral justification requires interpersonal comparability.

When value theory is put to use in practical contexts, general problems of measurement often come to the fore. Take health policies, which are aimed to promote and protect the overall health of a population. In order to determine which policy or policies best promote the overall health of a population, we need to have a measure of health as the informational basis for designing health policies. Daniel M. Hausman points out fundamental difficulties in quantifying the value of health in chapter 18. Health is the absence of pathology. But health has no quantity or magnitude of its own. Health, then, must be measured by its value. However, Hausman points out a problem. Imagine that the physical and mental states of two individuals are qualitatively the same, and hence that their health states are the same. If health is measured by its value, their value must be the same. But the same health state has different values for them because of its differential effects on their respective well-being or opportunity. Hausman considers various ways to measure the value of token health states. He concludes, however, that the measurement of health is so complicated that health policies are bound to rely on rough indicators of the values of health states.

A similar problem arises in the context of the measurement of freedom. In the wake of nonwelfarist economic theory, many economists have examined the notion of freedom as an alternative informational basis for social choice. Although it is easy to say that increased freedom is desirable, it is not clear what "increased freedom" really amounts to. For example, it may be claimed that adding some options to a person's existing opportunity set does not increase her freedom if these additional options are of little importance to her. Thus, there is good reason to claim that freedom should be measured by the value of freedom, not by the number of options in the opportunity set. In chapter 19, Prasanta K. Pattanaik and Yongsheng Xu present and motivate various conditions for the measurement of freedom and its value that have been discussed extensively in welfare economics. They are inclined toward the idea that freedom should be measured by the value of freedom, rather than the opportunity set. However, they also point out many fundamental problems in measuring the value of freedom.

Health and freedom are typically thought of as constitutive parts of well-being. However, there are valuable things that are typically not thought of as constitutive parts of well-being. One example is the natural environment. Almost everyone agrees that the natural environment is valuable. But what kind of value does it have? In chapter 20, David Schmidtz argues that the kind of value at issue is a specific type of noninstrumental value that holds between a valued object and the subject who values it, such that the natural environment provides us with reasons to cherish it and treat it with respect. Schmidtz also examines two hotly debated topics in environmental value theory. One is the debate between individualists and holists, concerning whether things other than individual living things, for example, species and ecosystems, can have moral standing. The other is whether the realm of moral standing should be confined to humanity or how far beyond humanity it should extend. Schmidtz does not take sides in these debates. Nonetheless, he argues against species egalitarianism, which contends that all living things have equal moral standing.

Concern for deterioration of the environment has also been part of the motivation for value-theoretic approaches to questions concerning population size, which is the subject matter of chapters 21 and 22. In chapter 21, M. A. Roberts focuses on the recent literature on population axiology that Derek Parfit's celebrated "repugnant conclusion" has provoked. The repugnant conclusion is that "[f]or any possible population of at least ten billion people, all with a very high quality of life, there must be some much larger imaginable population whose existence, if other things are equal, would be better even though its members have lives that are barely worth living" (Parfit 1984: 388). Roberts considers two possible ways to avoid the repugnant conclusion. One is the "person-based" approach, which revises the standard interpretation of the person-affecting view in such a way that it escapes Parfit's nonidentity problem (Parfit 1984: ch. 16). The other is "pluralism." Pluralism holds that the relative moral goodness of two worlds is determined by (1) the sums of well-being, and (2) other values such as equality, human flourishing, and improvements in the plights of the least well-off, in those worlds. Roberts holds that the kinds of other values, mentioned in (2), help to avoid the repugnant conclusion.

Roberts's argument for the person-based approach is based on a disputable view about the value of existence, namely that a person's level of well-being is zero in any world in which she does not exist, and that, therefore, it can be better or worse for her to exist than not to exist at all. Some philosophers find such a view unacceptable because it seems that if a person's life is better for her than her nonexistence, her nonexistence would have been worse for her if she did not exist. But how can anything be better or worse for a person who does not exist? In chapter 22, Gustaf Arrhenius and Wlodek Rabinowicz agree with Roberts that it can be better or worse for a person to exist than not to exist. But they argue that it does not follow that nonexistence would have been better or worse for a person were she not to exist, and nor does it follow that people who do not exist should or could be assigned welfare levels. Arrhenius and Rabinowicz point out that their argument faces a general problem in value theory. That is, they need to assume that abstract states of affairs, and not just the obtaining of them, can be better or worse for a person. This may seem counterintuitive because the existence of such abstract states of affairs does not seem to make things better or worse for a person in any way. However, Arrhenius and Rabinowicz seek to explain why it is not in the end intolerably counterintuitive.

Acknowledgment

We would like to thank Joey van Weelden for proofreading and preparing the index.

Notes

1. Issues about value in the philosophy of religion and in aesthetics have been covered elsewhere in the Oxford Handbooks of Philosophy series; see Wainwright (2005) and Levinson (2005). For a recent discussion of issues about value in epistemology, see Pritchard, Millar, and Haddock (2010).
2. Since there are established monographs on measurement theory, this *Handbook* does not include a chapter specifically on measurement theory, The most important is Krantz et al. (1971). Roberts (1985) is more concise and accessible.
3. For a comprehensive survey of interpersonal comparability of utility in economics, see Hammond (1991).

References

Hammond, Peter J. (1991). "Interpersonal Comparisons of Utility: Why and How They Are and Should be Made." In Jon Elster and John E. Roemer (eds.), *Interpersonal Comparisons of Well-Being*. Cambridge: Cambridge University Press, 200–254.
Krantz, David H., R. Duncan Luce, Patrick Suppes, and Amos Tversky (1971). *Foundations of Measurement*, vol. 1. San Diego: Academic Press.
Levinson, J., ed. (2005). *The Oxford Handbook of Aesthetics*. New York: Oxford University Press.
Moore, G. E. (1993 [1903]). *Principia Ethica*, rev. ed., ed. T. Baldwin. Cambridge: Cambridge University Press.
Parfit, Derek (1984). *Reasons and Persons*. Oxford: Clarendon Press.
Pritchard, D., A. Millar, and A. Haddock (2010). *The Nature and Value of Knowledge: Three Investigations*. Oxford: Oxford University Press.
Roberts, Fred S. (1985). *Measurement Theory: With Applications to Decision-making, Utility, and the Social Sciences*. Cambridge: Cambridge University Press.
Sidgwick, H. (1981 [1907]). *The Methods of Ethics*, 7th ed., ed. J. Rawls. Indianapolis: Hackett Publishing.
Wainwright, W. J., ed. (2005). *The Oxford Handbook of Philosophy of Religion*. New York: Oxford University Press.

PART I
FOUNDATIONS

CHAPTER 1

VALUE AND NORMATIVITY

MICHAEL J. ZIMMERMAN

1.1. INTRODUCTION

MORAL philosophers and others who work on value theory often draw a distinction between two families of concepts: the *evaluative* and the *deontic*. The most prominent members of the first family are the concepts of goodness and badness. Prominent members of the second family are the concepts of rightness, wrongness, obligation, requirement, the concept of what there is a reason to do, and the concept of what ought to be done. There is an old and ongoing debate regarding what the distinction between the two families of concepts consists in; which concepts belong to which family; what the interrelations are between concepts that belong to the same family; and what the interrelations are between concepts that belong to different families. This chapter will be primarily concerned with the last of these questions.

First, though, we should attend to some distinctions. Consider the concept of goodness. (Similar considerations pertain to the concept of badness.) The word "good" that expresses this concept is used in a wide variety of ways. W. D. Ross draws a fundamental distinction between what he calls the *attributive* and the *predicative* uses of "good" (Ross 1930: ch. 3). The former use rests on the idea that what is good, in the relevant sense, is good relative to some kind. For example, someone may be a good singer but a bad pianist, a good plumber but a bad golfer, and so on. Judith Thomson has refined this idea, noting that it may be a mistake simply to say that someone is, for example, a good singer, since he may be good at singing folk songs but bad at singing opera (Thomson 1997). She therefore holds that, in the sense of "good" at issue, we should say that whatever is good is good *in some way* rather than *relative to some kind*. The key idea remains, though, that what is good in this sense is not good simpliciter but good relative to some standard. In contrast, the predicative use of "good" does not, according to Ross, involve such relativization. When we say, for example, that courage is good or that pleasure is good, we are not, Ross claims, saying that courage and pleasure are good relative to some standard but rather that they are good absolutely. In making this claim, Ross is endorsing the position taken by others before him, perhaps most notably by G. E. Moore, who, throughout his extensive discussions of goodness, rarely qualifies his use of the word "good" and, when he does qualify it, tends to do so in such terms as "good in itself" or "good as a means" (as at Moore 1903, 1993: § 15), which does not involve the kind of relativization involved with the attributive use of "good."

Everyone accepts that "good" can be used attributively. Some philosophers (such as Thomson and, before her, Peter Geach [1956]) deny that it can be used predicatively. We need not concern ourselves with this debate here, as long as we agree that it makes sense to claim, for example, that courage is good or that pleasure is good. But does it make sense to make such claims? It seems clear that it does, although determining precisely what is meant will require drawing yet further distinctions. Here I wish to bring two distinctions in particular to your attention. The first is one to which I just alluded: the distinction between what is good *in itself* and what is good *as a means*. Moore, for example, claims that pleasure (among other things) is indeed good—more particularly, that it is good in itself (Moore 1903, 1993: §§ 113 ff.). By this he means, roughly, that, whenever someone experiences pleasure, something good happens, regardless of what the source, or object, or context, or circumstances, or consequences of the pleasure might be. (Needless to say, this is a controversial claim.) Sometimes Moore expresses this idea by saying that pleasure is *intrinsically* good, since he holds that, when something is good in itself, its being so depends entirely on the intrinsic properties that it has (Moore 1922: 260; 1993: 286). This is a claim that has recently been disputed (Korsgaard 1983; Kagan 1998; Rabinowicz and Rønnow-Rasmussen 1999), and the more neutral term "*finally* good" has come to be used to express the idea that Moore and others have had in mind, the idea that something is good *for its own sake* rather than for the sake of something else to which it is in some way related. Final value is to be contrasted with nonfinal value, of which value as a means is a particular variety. To say that something is nonfinally good is to say that it is good in virtue of the final value of something to which it is in some way related; to say, more particularly, that something is good as a means is to say that it is good in virtue of the final value of something to which it is a means. For example, if pleasure is indeed finally good, then whatever is a means to pleasure (cooking a meal, say) will, insofar forth, be good as a means. (For further discussion of the issues raised in this paragraph, see chapter 2, on intrinsic and extrinsic value, in this volume.)

The second distinction, which cuts across the first, has to do with what is good *for a particular person* as opposed to what might be said to be good *for the world* (Feldman 2004: ch. 9). What is good for a person (in the intended sense) has to do with that person's welfare or well-being. If we assume that your being happy is finally good for you, then whatever contributes to your being happy (a certain regimen of diet and exercise, say) will, insofar forth, be nonfinally good for you. If your being happy makes me happy, then your being happy will also be good for me, but only nonfinally so; it is my happiness, not yours, that is finally good for me. However, it is also plausible to say that both your being happy and my being happy are finally good for the world—that the world is a better place the more happiness there is in it—so that whatever contributes to your or my happiness is, insofar forth, nonfinally good for the world. (Note that, although what is good for the world makes the world better, it is not the case that what is good for a person makes that person better. Rather, what is good for a person improves that person's welfare. For further discussion, see chapter 9, on prudential value, in this volume.)

There is a real roughness to what has just been said. That fact notwithstanding, let me now turn from evaluative to deontic distinctions. Just as "good" (and "bad") can be used in various ways, so too can "right" (and "wrong," and "ought," and so on). Suppose that you are faced with a difficult decision between options X, Y, and Z and come to me for advice. I give these options careful consideration and conclude, "The right thing for you to do is X." What do I mean? Well, there are a number of possibilities. I might mean that, morally speaking, you should do X. Or I might mean that, prudentially speaking (that is, as far as your own personal welfare is concerned), you should do X. Or I might mean that you should do X in light of some other kind of requirement (rational, perhaps, or aesthetic, or legal, or religious . . .). Again, determining precisely what is meant will require drawing distinctions such as these. But there is also another distinction that is pertinent here, that between requirements that have *normative force* and those that do not (Broome 2007). Suppose that, when I say that the right thing for you to do is X, what I mean, more particularly, is that doing X is what the law requires of you. And suppose that this is in fact the case. Do you then have a *good reason* to do X? Perhaps you do. If the law in question is morally well founded, then presumably you will have a *moral* reason to do X. Or if running afoul of the law puts you at risk of punishment, you will presumably have a *prudential* reason to do X. But does the law give you an *extra* reason to do X, one that *strengthens* the considerations in favor of doing X already provided by morality and prudence? Arguably not. If so, then, although moral requirements, prudential requirements, and perhaps other kinds of requirements have normative force, legal requirements as such do not.

Again, what has just been said needs considerable refinement, but at this point I will turn to the main question to be addressed in this chapter: is there any (interesting) relation between evaluative concepts ("the good") and deontic concepts ("the right")? There are two answers to this question that I will discuss. The first is that the right is to be accounted for in terms of the good; the second is that the good is to be accounted for in terms of the right.

1.2. Accounting for the Right in Terms of the Good

The idea that the right can be accounted for in terms of the good is probably most closely associated with the doctrine of consequentialism. The underlying theme of consequentialism, of which there are many varieties, is that the right thing to do is the best that one can do. Moore is one of the foremost proponents of consequentialism (although he does not refer to it by that name, which came into vogue only in the second half of the twentieth century). In an early work, he gives expression to this view as follows:

> [T]o assert that a certain line of conduct is, at a given time, absolutely right . . . is . . . to assert that more good or less evil will exist in the world, if it be adopted than if anything else be done instead. (Moore 1903: 25; 1993: 77)

There are a number of points to note about this statement. First, by "absolutely right" Moore means that which one is *morally* bound or obligated to do, all things considered (Moore 1903: 147; 1993: 197). Some other forms of consequentialism have to do with other kinds of rightness (such as what one should do from the prudential point of view). In the remainder of this section, I will, following Moore, deal exclusively with moral rightness. (Although Moore does not explicitly discuss what it is for some action to be merely *pro tanto* morally right as opposed to morally right *all things considered*, it may be that he would agree that an action is pro tanto morally right to the extent that it promotes good or prevents evil [Olson 2006; Orsi 2013].) Second, when talking about good and evil, Moore is concerned with what above I called *final* goodness and badness *for the world*.

Third, Moore's statement constitutes an *analysis* of the concept of all-things-considered moral rightness, in the same way in which the concept of a vixen may be analyzed by means of the statement that to assert that a certain animal is a vixen is to assert that it is a female fox. It is controversial just what is required for a successful analysis of this sort, but at least this much may be said: first, the concept being analyzed must be "broken down" into simpler concepts; second, the two assertions in question must be strictly equivalent, in the sense that, necessarily, one of them is true if and only if the other is also true; and third, anyone who rejects the analysis thereby betrays a failure to grasp the concept being analyzed.

In a later work, Moore gives a somewhat different statement of the view he embraces:

> [I]f we had to choose between two actions, one of which would have as its sole or total effects, an effect or set of effects, which we may call A, while the other would have as its sole or total effects, an effect or set of effects, which we may call B, then, *if* A [were intrinsically better than] B, it always would be our duty to choose the action which caused A rather than that which caused B. This . . . would be absolutely *always* true, *no matter what A and B might be like in other respects*. (Moore 2005[1912]: 27–28)

By "duty" Moore is once again referring to that which one is morally bound to do, all things considered. In this formulation, though, he explicitly says that what one is morally bound to do is to perform that action with the intrinsically (i.e., finally, for the world) best *effects* or consequences—hence the now popular characterization of this view as a version of "consequentialism."

There are two important differences between the two statements just quoted. First, whereas the first statement purports to provide an *analysis* of what it is to be morally bound to perform some action, the second merely claims that being so bound is *strictly equivalent* to the action in question being such that it would have consequences that were intrinsically better than those that any alternative action would have. This more modest second statement is surely the wiser of the two. As we will shortly see, there are many critics of consequentialism who claim that moral rightness is not exclusively concerned with the production of intrinsic value. According to the first statement, these critics would be guilty of conceptual confusion, of simply not understanding what it means to say that some action is morally right. The second statement has no such implication and allows for the possibility that both consequentialists and nonconsequentialists have an adequate grasp of the concept in question but disagree about what it takes, substantively, for an action to be morally right. (Moore gives his reasons for moving from the first statement to the second in Moore 1942: 558–59.)

The second difference between the two statements is this. Suppose that, if you were to perform some action X, then doing so would bring about a total set of consequences C. It is important to note that, unless we say that X would be a consequence of itself (which is a pretty odd way of talking, and certainly not what Moore has in mind when he talks of "effects"), the fact is that, if you were to perform X, it is not only C that would occur; for, obviously, X would occur too. Let us call the conjunction of X and C the "outcome" of X. Then the pertinent difference between the two statements can be put as follows. According to the first statement, the right action is that which would have the intrinsically best possible *outcome*, whereas, according to the second statement, the right action is that which would have the intrinsically best possible (total set of) *consequences*. Moore seems not to have noticed this difference between the two formulations of his view, but it was brought to his attention by C. D. Broad, who argued that the underlying idea that the right thing to do is the best that one can do is better captured by the first formulation than by the second; for, if it is the production of intrinsic value that determines whether an action is morally right, then not only the intrinsic value of C, but also that of X, factors into this determination (Broad 1942: 48–49). In his reply to Broad, Moore concedes this point (Moore 1942: 559–60). This concession, which seems appropriate, indicates that the term "consequentialism" is not particularly apt after all as a name for the view that Moore espouses. "Outcomism" might be better, but to my knowledge it is not a name that anyone has hitherto proposed.

There is reason to think that the shift from consequentialism to outcomism is not sufficient to capture the basic idea to which Moore seeks to give expression. This is a point that has come to light only relatively recently in the debate between so-called actualists and possibilists. Actualists are outcomists. They say, roughly, that the morally right thing to do is to perform that action which *would* have the intrinsically best possible outcome among those actions that one can perform (Goldman 1976; Sobel 1976; Jackson and Pargetter 1986; Goble 1993). Possibilists say something slightly but importantly different, namely, that the morally right thing to do is to perform that action which *could* have the intrinsically best possible outcome among those actions that one can perform (Goldman 1978; Greenspan 1978; Thomason 1981; Feldman 1986; Zimmerman 1996). The difference between the views makes a difference in certain cases in which one's own future behavior constitutes part of the outcome of one's action. Suppose, for example, that you have been invited to a memorial service for a highly regarded colleague of whom you have always been envious. The best thing you could do would be to accept the invitation and behave with all due decorum at the service. The worst thing you could do would be to accept the invitation and then misbehave at the service; better would be to decline the invitation and not show up at all. Suppose that, if you were to accept the invitation, your envy, though you *could* resist succumbing to it, *would* in fact get the better of you in such a way that you *would* misbehave at the ceremony. Under these circumstances, what would be the right thing for you to do, accept the invitation or decline it? There is no consensus among those committed to Moore's basic idea as to which is the correct verdict in this sort of case. Actualism implies that you ought to decline the invitation; for the world *would* be better if you did so than if you did not, since otherwise you would show up at the service and misbehave. Possibilism implies that you ought to accept the invitation, on the grounds that your declining it would be inconsistent with your doing the best you *could*, namely, accepting it and then behaving yourself with all due decorum.

Possibilists are, in a sense, internal critics of Moore, since they accept the basic idea underlying his view, but there are also many external critics, critics who claim that the right thing to do is not exclusively determined by the intrinsic value of any actual or possible outcome. The most common such criticism concerns the question whether the *end* justifies the *means*. According to Moore, it always does, in the sense that any action is morally acceptable as a means to some outcome as long as that outcome is the intrinsically best achievable under the circumstances. Very many people oppose this idea, holding that doing justice to others (and perhaps, also to oneself) requires respecting certain constraints on how one pursues a goal, no matter how good that goal may be. For example, killing one person to save five others from death is typically thought to be morally unacceptable because it constitutes a grave injustice to the one killed, even if it would be intrinsically better for the one to die and the five to live than for the one to live and the five to die, and even if there were no other means available to ensure that the five live. (Of course, this matter is controversial and not nearly as straightforward as it may at first appear.) Moore considers and rejects this criticism, but in the end his rebuttal simply rests on the claim that "[i]t seems . . . to be self-evident . . . that knowingly to do an action which would make the world, on the whole, really and truly *worse* than if we had acted differently, must always be wrong" (Moore 2005[1912]: 94). Unsurprisingly, this response has not silenced his critics; although some of these critics concede that consequentialism (or outcomism) is "compelling" (Foot 1985: 196), none of them agree that the claim to which Moore appeals is self-evident.

Another external criticism that Moore addresses concerns the role of *motives* in the determination of moral right and wrong. Some maintain that it is not possible to do the right thing if one is acting from a bad motive. Moore's response is to insist that motives have no bearing on whether an action is morally right or wrong, although they may well be relevant to other moral judgments, such as the judgment that someone is to be praised or blamed (Moore 2005[1912]: 95 ff.). This response is forced upon him by the consequentialism that he there embraces, since, if right and wrong are determined exclusively by the consequences of actions, and the motive of an action is, as seems plain, not one of its consequences, then right and wrong are not a function of motives. This response may not be required if one moves from consequentialism to outcomism, however, in that it might be argued that, when a person acts from one particular motive among others that he possesses, the manifestation of that motive counts as part of the outcome of his action. (It should be noted that the view that the intrinsic value of motives partly determines the intrinsic value of outcomes is quite distinct from the view, often referred to as "motive utilitarianism," that an action is morally right if and only if it is performed from motives that have or tend to have the best possible consequences or outcome [regarding which, see Adams 1976 for an early discussion].)

Yet another common criticism of Moore's view is that it is a mistake to focus on what consequences or outcome would or could *in fact* be achieved when determining what it is morally right or wrong to do; rather, what matters are the consequences or outcome *foreseeable* by the agent at the time of action. Moore addresses this criticism, too. Once again invoking the distinction between right and wrong, on the one hand, and praise and blame, on the other, he claims that, although what is foreseeable by the agent may be relevant to whether he is to be praised or blamed for what he eventually does, nonetheless what it is morally right or wrong for him to do turns on what in fact occurs as a result of his action (Moore 2005[1912]: 100–101). Discussion of this issue has recently been and continues to be quite vigorous. Some find Moore's response acceptable (Feldman 2006; Graham 2010), whereas others find it wanting (Ross 1939: ch. 7; Jackson 1991; Zimmerman 2008, 2014).

The move from consequentialism to outcomism might suggest that some form of reconciliation could be effected between Moore and his critics. I have already mentioned that someone who takes motives to be relevant to the determination of moral right and wrong might be brought into the outcomist fold. Consider, now, someone who claims that the end does not necessarily justify the means, and take the case of killing one to save five from death as an example. If the act of killing one person were itself finally bad to a sufficient degree, this might offset the final value of the continued lives of five other people in such a way that the outcome of killing the one would be finally worse than that of letting the five die and thus *not* be mandated by outcomism after all. But it is doubtful whether such a reconciliatory maneuver could be satisfactorily carried out in all cases, if only because there are cases in which one killing is not opposed to five lettings-die but rather to five killings, and yet many still find it intuitively plausible to claim that killing the one in order to save the five is morally impermissible. It should be noted, however, that there are some philosophers who are prepared to accept such judgments as this but who claim that, if certain "adjustments" are made in the name of justice, a form of outcomism can nonetheless be defended (Feldman 1995).

Even if a reconciliation between consequentialists and nonconsequentialists (or between outcomists and nonoutcomists) of the sort just mentioned turns out not to be feasible, there is reason to think that another sort of reconciliation is possible, one that is conducted at a more abstract level. The basic idea underlying consequentialism is, as noted above, that the right thing to do is the best that one can do, where "best" is understood to mean what is finally best for the world. This certainly seems to be at odds with what most nonconsequentialists want to say. A rights-theorist, for example, who addressed the one-versus-five case just mentioned might say that the reason that it is wrong for someone—you, say—to kill the one is that that person has a right against you that you not kill him, whereas the reason why it is not wrong for you to let the other five die is that (even if their dying would come about by way of their being killed by someone else, someone against whom they have a right that *he* not *kill them*) they do not have a right against *you* that you not *let them die*. But even such a view might be couched in terms of the claim that the right thing to do is the best that one can do. Perhaps "best" cannot be understood in terms of what is finally best for the world, but we might nonetheless say that, according to the rights-theorist, the right thing for *you* to do is what is "rights-best" as far as *you* are concerned. The idea here is simply that, whatever such a theorist declares the right thing to do to be and whatever his reason for so declaring it, his declaration would seem to indicate that the action in question is in *some* way superior to, better than, its alternatives. In general, *anyone* who says that, among options X, Y, and Z, X is the morally right thing to do would seem to be declaring X to be in *some* way better than either Y or Z. If this is indeed correct, then *any* substantive theory of what it is morally right to do can be cast in the same mold as Moore's theory. That is, although Moore's theory may have a different substantive *content* from that of some other competing theories (inasmuch as there are cases in which his theory declares something to be morally right that they declare to be morally wrong), these other theories can be seen to have the same formal *structure* as his: whatever is morally right is better (in *some* way—and it is here that the theories will differ as to just what way that is) than whatever is not morally right (Dreier 1993). In brief, we can say that *every* theory of moral right and wrong declares what is morally right to be *"deontically* better" than what is morally wrong; when theories differ as to what it *is* right or wrong to do, that is because they differ as to what renders one option deontically better than another. Of course, there are difficulties here, too. One difficulty has to do with so-called satisficing theories, according to which the right thing to do need only be "good enough" rather than best (Slote 1989). Another difficulty has to do with supererogation, that is, going above and beyond the call of duty. Supererogatory acts are typically thought of as being better than acts that are merely morally right; but, if what is right is best, it is hard to see how supererogation is possible. If these difficulties can be overcome, however, then perhaps the right *is* analyzable after all in terms of the good, as follows: to assert that an action is morally right, all things considered, is to assert that that action is deontically best (Zimmerman 1996). It might be claimed, however, that success in analyzing the right in this way is not tantamount to success in analyzing a deontic concept in terms of an evaluative concept. As noted in the opening paragraph, it is controversial which concepts belong to which family, and it is certainly arguable that the concept of what I have called deontic goodness does not belong wholly to the evaluative family.

1.3. Accounting for the Good in Terms of the Right

Just as some philosophers have sought to account for the right in terms of the good, so too some philosophers have sought to do the reverse. Some, indeed, contend that the good can be *analyzed* in terms of the right (a claim that, obviously, contradicts Moore's famous thesis that the concept of goodness cannot be analyzed in any terms [Moore 1903, 1993: §§ 6 ff.]). This is an idea that can be traced back at least to Franz Brentano (1969 [1889]), and it is one that has been endorsed by many others since (Broad 1930: 283; Ross 1939: 275–76; Ewing 1948; Chisholm 1986: ch. 5; Lemos 1994: ch. 1; Scanlon 1998: 95 ff.; Zimmerman 2001: ch. 4). It is an idea that is often referred to as the *fitting-attitude analysis* (or, for short, FA analysis) of value, in light of A. C. Ewing's use of the particular deontic term "fitting" when giving the following pithy formulation of the idea: "We may . . . define 'good' as 'fitting object of a pro attitude' " (Ewing 1948: 152). It is an idea whose plausibility is enhanced by the observation that our common way of speaking frequently appears to presuppose it. In English, for example, instead of saying that something is good, we often say that it is *valuable*, where to value something, in the relevant sense, is to have one of a variety of positive attitudes toward it, and the suffix "-able" expresses not simply the fact that the thing in question *can* be valued but that it is *right* or *fitting* (or *suitable* or *appropriate*. . .) to value it. And it is very easy to find more specific examples of this linguistic phenomenon that involve more specific attitudes. Consider, for example, the following terms: "admirable," "adorable," "commendable," "desirable," "estimable," "honorable," "likable," "lovable," "respectable," "venerable." There are of course similar examples involving negative attitudes (or, at least, the absence of positive attitudes), such as "abominable," "contemptible," "detestable," "dislikable," "execrable," "reprehensible," "undesirable," "unlikable," "unlovable." And there are further examples that involve some suffix other than "-able" or "-ible," such as "awesome" (and "loathsome"), "praiseworthy" (and "blameworthy"), "wonderful" (and "frightful"). Moreover, the FA analysis is flexible in two ways. First, it bridges the attributive-predicative divide. It makes sense to say, for example, both that Smith is a commendable golfer and that courage is commendable. Second, it can accommodate the distinction between final and nonfinal value. For example, a proponent of the analysis might say that to assert that something is finally good is to assert that it is fitting to value it for its own sake, whereas to assert that something is nonfinally good is to assert that it is fitting to value it for the sake of something else to which it is in some way related.

The FA analysis thus seems quite promising. Nonetheless, it faces a number of challenges. One challenge concerns the question *why* it is fitting to value something that is good. Suppose that Jones, a well-known philanthropist, has just made a large donation to a worthy cause. You tell me that you admire what he has done. I ask you why. You say, "I admire what he's done because it's admirable!"

"But why is it admirable?" I ask.

"Because it's good!" you reply.

Your answer seems sensible, although just what it means may not be altogether clear. However, *if* what it means is that the fact that what Jones did was good *grounds* or *explains* the fact that it was admirable, and *if* this is correct, then the FA analysis is in trouble; for it cannot be that something's being good is both the ground of its being valuable and the same thing as its being valuable. But those are big "ifs." Some philosophers accept them (Blanshard 1961: 284 ff.; compare also Ross 1939: 261–62), whereas others do not, claiming that what accounts for the admirability of Jones's behavior is not its goodness but rather its philanthropic nature, which is also what accounts for its goodness (Ewing 1948: 157, 172; Scanlon 1998: 95 ff. Scanlon characterizes this view as a "buck-passing account," in light of the fact that it passes the role of grounding the admirability of Jones's behavior from its goodness to some other feature of that behavior. The term has since become very popular). Notice, though, that, even if this challenge turns out to be successful, it impugns only the attempt to *analyze* the good in terms of the right; it leaves untouched the claim that there is a *strict equivalence* between something's being good and its being a fitting object of a pro attitude.

A second challenge to the FA analysis has to do with the question how, if at all, the concept of valuableness is itself to be analyzed. To see what is at issue here, consider an analogy. Suppose that you were to ask me what it is for something to be perceptible, and I were to propose this disjunctive list in response: for something to be perceptible is for it to be either visible, or audible, or tangible, or tastable, or smellable. This response would be unsatisfactory, for two reasons. First, it presupposes that there is no sixth (or seventh, or . . .) sense by means of which something might be perceived, a claim that may be true as a matter of fact but is certainly not true as a matter of necessity. Second, and more important, it overlooks the fact that the various items in the list have something in common. Suppose, for example, that someone were to propose extending the list as follows: or moveable, or submersible, or . . . Clearly, such an extension would be inappropriate, since neither moving nor submerging is a mode of perception. Perceptibility is precisely what unites visibility, audibility, and so on. Thus, if any analysis is in the offing at all, it would have to go the other way: for something to be visible is for it to be perceptible by means of seeing; for something to be audible is for it to be perceptible by means of hearing; and so on. For similar reasons, it would not be acceptable to say: for something to be valuable is for it to be admirable, or adorable, or commendable, and so on. If any analysis is in the offing, it would have to go the other way. But then we are faced with this question. What *is* it for something to be valuable, that is, for it to be such that it is a fitting object of a pro attitude? We cannot understand the concept of a pro attitude in terms of "either admiration, or adoration, or . . . ," so how are we to understand it? Should it be taken as a primitive notion, one that is itself not amenable to analysis? Well, perhaps. Another possibility is that there is some common, nonevaluative element that unites all pro attitudes. Again, perhaps so, but it is not obvious what this element might be. (Some pro attitudes, it seems, are conative but not affective, others affective but not conative, so that the element in question could not be either desire or emotion [Rabinowicz and Rønnow-Rasmussen 2004: 401].) Still another possibility is that the concept of a pro attitude is to be analyzed along the following lines: for someone to take a pro attitude toward something is for that person to have an attitude toward that thing that involves conceiving of it as something that is in some way good. *If* this analysis (or something like it) is correct, however, then the FA analysis is once again in trouble, since it would involve a vicious circularity; for it cannot be that the concept of goodness is to be analyzed in terms of the concept of a pro attitude, which is itself to be analyzed in terms of the concept of goodness (Ross 1939: 261–62; Rabinowicz and Rønnow-Rasmussen 2004: 401). Once again, though, even if this challenge to the analysis turns out to be successful, it leaves untouched the claim that there is a *strict equivalence* between something's being good and its being a fitting object of a pro attitude.

A third challenge to the FA analysis, however, does impugn this alleged strict equivalence. It concerns some familiar attributive uses of "good." We often make claims such as that so-and-so is a good liar or that such-and-such is a good garrote, and it is clear that these claims may be correct. But should we therefore infer that it is fitting to have some pro attitude toward the liar or the garrote? That is not at all clear (Brännmark 2008: 307–8). One reply is to insist that the liar or the garrote does warrant a favorable response: as far as liars or garrotes go, it is the good ones that merit preference. If this reply is to work, though, it must be qualified in some way, since there are obvious respects in which bad liars and bad garrotes are to be preferred to good ones. Another reply is to acknowledge that the FA analysis does not apply in such cases, but to maintain that that is because these cases involve an anomalous use of "good." If this reply is to work, some explanation of the alleged anomaly should be provided. A third reply is to concede that the FA analysis fails in such cases, even though they involve a standard use of "good," but to maintain that the analysis nonetheless applies to other cases. For this reply to be helpful, some principle of demarcation between the two sets of cases should be given. (Perhaps simply restricting the analysis to predicative uses of "good" would fit the bill.)

A fourth challenge concerns what has come to be called the wrong kind of reason (WKR) problem, in light of the fact that it is a challenge that was first directed at Thomas Scanlon's formulation of the analysis, in which the deontic term that is explicitly used is "reason" and which for present purposes may be put as follows: for something to be good is for it to be such that there is a reason to have a pro attitude toward it (Scanlon 1998: 97). The challenge is simply this: there are cases in which there is a reason to have a pro attitude toward something that is not good (Crisp 2000; D'Arms and Jacobson 2000; Rabinowicz and Rønnow-Rasmussen 2004). Here is a pertinent case. A (potent and believable) evil demon threatens to wreak havoc on the world unless you revere him; that would seem to provide you with a very good reason to revere him, even though he is evil, not good. This challenge to the FA analysis has spawned a voluminous literature, in which many different suggestions regarding how to distinguish between the "right" kind of reason (a kind that is indeed correlated with value) and the "wrong" kind of reason (of which the reason you have to revere the demon is an instance) have been proposed and criticized. One such suggestion is that the right kind of reason is provided by some property (or set of properties) of the *object* of the relevant pro attitude, whereas a reason that is provided by some property of the *attitude* itself is of the wrong kind (Parfit

2001). This has been criticized on the basis that, for any property of the first kind, there is a corresponding property of the second kind (Rabinowicz and Rønnow-Rasmussen 2004: 406). Another suggestion is that the right kind of reason is a reason to *have* the relevant pro attitude, whereas a reason to *promote* the attitude is of the wrong kind (Parfit 2001; Persson 2007; Skorupski 2007). This has been criticized on the basis that there is no justification for denying that a reason of the latter kind also constitutes a reason of the former kind (Rabinowicz and Rønnow-Rasmussen 2004: 412 ff.; Danielsson and Olson 2007: 513–14). Another suggestion is that the right kind of reason is one in which the properties of the object that provide a reason to have a pro attitude toward it *also* feature in the intentional content of that attitude (Rabinowicz and Rønnow-Rasmussen 2004: 414 ff.). This has been criticized on the basis that a reason of the wrong kind can be found that meets this condition (Rabinowicz and Rønnow-Rasmussen 2004: 419 ff.). Another suggestion is that the right kind of reason is one that must not make *reference* to the properties of the relevant pro attitude (Olson 2004). This, too, has been criticized on the basis that a reason of the wrong kind can be found that meets this condition (Rabinowicz and Rønnow-Rasmussen 2006). Another suggestion is that the right kind of reason is one that would remain even if the *benefits* of having the relevant pro attitude were absent (Lang 2008). Once again, this has been criticized on the basis that a reason of the wrong kind can be found that meets this condition (Olson 2009). Another suggestion is that the right kind of reason is a reason for the relevant pro attitude's *being correct* rather than a reason for *having* the attitude, in much the same way as the right kind of reason for believing something has to do with whether the belief would be correct rather than with whether a demon would wreak havoc if you failed to hold the belief (Danielsson and Olson 2007). One worry here has to do with whether the claim that an attitude such as reverence is correct can be understood without appealing to the goodness of the object revered; for, if not, then the FA analysis would once again involve a vicious circularity. Another suggestion is that the right kind of reason involves, more particularly, the object's being *worthy* of being the object of the relevant pro attitude; it seems mistaken to say, for example, that the demon is truly venerable, that is, *worthy* of veneration, even if there is a good reason of some kind to revere him (Rabinowicz and Rønnow-Rasmussen 2004: 422). One worry here is that, even if this solves the WKR problem, it may do so at the cost of undermining the attempt to analyze the good in terms of the right; for worthiness, it may be argued, is an evaluative rather than a deontic concept (Rabinowicz and Rønnow-Rasmussen 2004: 396). And still other suggestions for solving the WKR problem have been proposed and criticized.

A fifth challenge to the FA analysis concerns the question *for whom* and *to what degree* it is fitting to value something that is good. One much-discussed version of this challenge has to do with the fittingness of parental partiality. It is plausible to maintain that it is fitting for a parent to prefer the happiness of his own child to the equal, and equally good, happiness of a stranger; yet this judgment appears to conflict with the FA analysis—or, at least, with a natural extension of the analysis, according to which it is fitting to have the same pro attitude to the same degree toward objects that are equally good (Blanshard 1961: 287–88). Once again, many responses to this challenge have been suggested and criticized (for a detailed discussion, see Zimmerman 2011). In general, it seems clear what form such a response must take, if it is to accommodate both the claim that it is fitting for someone, S, to prefer x to y and the claim that x and y are equally good: first, there must be a way in which x is *better* than y relative to S, since only then could the FA analysis declare S's preferring x to y fitting; second, it must also be the case that it is fitting (either for S or for someone else or both) to take the same attitude to the same degree toward both x and y, since only then could the FA analysis declare x and y equally good in some way.

A final challenge to the FA analysis concerns so-called solitary goods (Bykvist 2009: 4 ff.). Such (alleged) goods consist in states of affairs that entail that there is no one in a position to take a relevant pro attitude (i.e., a pro attitude that it would be fitting to take) toward it. Suppose that happiness is good, and good in such a way that it is fitting to welcome it. Then, more particularly, the state of affairs of there being happy egrets is a good thing; so too, presumably, is the more complex state of affairs of there being happy egrets but no welcomers. The simpler state of affairs would appear to pose no problem for the FA analysis, but the more complex state of affairs, which is an example of a solitary good, may pose a problem. For, if to welcome a state of affairs entails that that state of affairs obtains, then welcoming the more complex state of affairs is logically impossible. Furthermore, if to welcome a state of affairs entails that one believes that that state of affairs obtains, then the pertinent belief regarding the more complex state of affairs would be necessarily false. In neither case would it seem plausible to say that welcoming the state of affairs is nonetheless fitting. Thus, unless this challenge can somehow be met, a proponent of the FA analysis must restrict the analysis to attitudes that are neither truth- nor belief-entailing, a restriction that might itself prove unwelcome, since it excludes a number of favorable responses (such as promoting what is good, or taking pleasure in what is good) to which proponents of the analysis have often appealed.

1.4. COMBINING THE ACCOUNTS

Attempting to account for the good in terms of the right was described above as the "reverse" of attempting to account for the right in terms of the good. However, this description, though natural, is potentially misleading, in that it might suggest that the two endeavors are incompatible with one another—that success in one "direction" would preclude success in the other. But that is not necessarily so. Certainly, if a particular sense of "good" is to be analyzed in terms of a particular sense of "right," then that same sense of "right" cannot be analyzed in terms of that same sense of "good," since combining the analyses would be viciously circular. But such circularity is avoided if either of the proposed accounts does not constitute an analysis (of the sort in question, one that involves "breaking down" a complex concept into simpler concepts) or if the senses of either "good" or "right" at issue are not the same in one account as in the other. In section 1.2, we began by looking at a proposal of Moore's, according to which the concept of *moral* rightness is to be analyzed in terms of the concept of final goodness for the world, and we ended by considering a proposal that this same concept of rightness is to be analyzed in terms of deontic goodness. Neither proposal is incompatible with the FA analysis, as long as "fitting" is not itself to be understood as expressing *moral* rightness. (Whether it should be so understood is a matter of debate. See Ewing 1948: 152; 1959: 90 ff.; Olson 2006, 2009; Orsi 2012; Zimmerman 2001: 89–90.) Thus there need be no inconsistency in accepting both the claim that the right can be accounted for in terms of the good and the claim that the good can be accounted for in terms of the right.

Acknowledgment

I am grateful to Jonas Olson for helpful comments on an earlier version of this chapter.

References

Adams, R. M. (1976). "Motive Utilitarianism." *Journal of Philosophy* 73: 467–81.
Blanshard, B. (1961). *Reason and Goodness*. London: George Allen and Unwin.
Brännmark, J. (2008). "Excellence and Means: On the Limits of Buck-Passing." *Journal of Value Inquiry* 42: 301–15.
Brentano, F. (1969 [1889]). *The Origin of Our Knowledge of Right and Wrong*. London: Routledge and Kegan Paul.
Broad, C. D. (1930). *Five Types of Ethical Theory*. London: Kegan Paul, Trench, Trubner.
Broad, C. D. (1942). "Certain Features in Moore's Ethical Doctrines." In P. A. Schilpp (ed.), *The Philosophy of G. E. Moore*. Evanston: Northwestern University Press, 43–67.
Broome, J. (2007). "Requirements." In T. Rønnow-Rasmussen et al. (eds.), *Hommage à Wlodek: Philosophical Papers Dedicated to Wlodek Rabinowicz*. www.fil.lu.se/hommageawlodek.
Bykvist, K. (2009). "No Good Fit: Why the Fitting Attitude Analysis of Value Fails." *Mind* 118: 1–30.
Chisholm, R. M. (1986). *Brentano and Intrinsic Value*. Cambridge: Cambridge University Press.
Crisp, R. (2000). Review of *Value . . . and What Follows* (by J. Kupperman). *Philosophy* 75: 458–62.
Danielsson, S., and J. Olson (2007). "Brentano and the Buck-Passers." *Mind* 116: 511–22.
D'Arms, J., and D. Jacobson (2000). "Sentiment and Value." *Ethics* 110: 722–48.
Dreier, J. (1993). "Structures of Normative Theories." *Monist* 76: 22–40.
Ewing, A. C. (1948). *The Definition of Good*. New York: Macmillan.
Ewing, A. C. (1959). *Second Thoughts in Moral Philosophy*. London: Routledge and Kegan Paul.
Feldman, F. (1986). *Doing the Best We Can*. Dordrecht: D. Reidel.
Feldman, F. (1995). "Adjusting Utility for Justice." *Philosophy and Phenomenological Research* 55: 567–85.
Feldman, F. (2004). *Pleasure and the Good Life*. Oxford: Clarendon Press.
Feldman, F. (2006). "Actual Utility, the Objection from Impracticality, and the Move to Expected Utility." *Philosophical Studies* 129: 49–79.

Foot, P. (1985). "Utilitarianism and the Virtues." *Mind* 94: 196–209.
Geach, P. (1956). "Good and Evil." *Analysis* 17: 33–42.
Goble, L. (1993). "The Logic of Obligation, 'Better' and 'Worse.'" *Philosophical Studies* 70: 133–63.
Goldman, H. S. (1976). "Dated Rightness and Moral Imperfection." *Philosophical Review* 85: 449–87.
Goldman, H. S. (1978). "Doing the Best One Can." In A. I. Goldman and J. Kim (eds.), *Values and Morals*. Dordrecht: D. Reidel, 185–214.
Graham, P. A. (2010). "In Defense of Objectivism about Moral Obligation." *Ethics* 121: 88–115.
Greenspan, P. S. (1978). "Oughts and Determinism: A Response to Goldman." *Philosophical Review* 87: 77–83.
Jackson, F. (1991). "Decision-Theoretic Consequentialism and the Nearest and Dearest Objection." *Ethics* 101: 461–82.
Jackson, F., and R. Pargetter (1986). "Oughts, Options, and Actualism." *Philosophical Review* 95: 233–55.
Kagan, S. (1998). "Rethinking Intrinsic Value." *Journal of Ethics* 2: 277–97.
Korsgaard, C. M. (1983). "Two Distinctions in Goodness." *Philosophical Review* 92: 169–95.
Lang, G. (2008). "The Right Kind of Solution to the Wrong Kind of Reason Problem." *Utilitas* 20: 472–89.
Lemos, N. (1994). *Intrinsic Value*. Cambridge: Cambridge University Press.
Moore, G. E. (1903). *Principia Ethica*. Cambridge: Cambridge University Press.
Moore, G. E. (1922). *Philosophical Studies*. London: Routledge and Kegan Paul.
Moore, G. E. (1942). "A Reply to My Critics." In P. A. Schilpp (ed.), *The Philosophy of G. E. Moore*. Evanston: Northwestern University, 535–677.
Moore, G. E. (1993). *Principia Ethica*. Rev. ed. Ed. Thomas Baldwin. Cambridge: Cambridge University Press.
Moore, G. E. (2005 [1912]). *Ethics*. Oxford: Clarendon Press.
Olson, J. (2004). "Buck-Passing and the Wrong Kind of Reasons." *Philosophical Quarterly* 54: 295–300.
Olson, J. (2006). "G. E. Moore on Goodness and Reasons." *Australasian Journal of Philosophy* 84: 525–34.
Olson, J. (2009). "The Wrong Kind of Solution to the Wrong Kind of Reason Problem." *Utilitas* 21: 225–32.
Orsi, F. (2013). "What's Wrong with Moorean Buck-Passing?" *Philosophical Studies* 164: 727–46.
Parfit, D. (2001). "Rationality and Reasons." In D. Egonsson et al. (eds.), *Exploring Practical Philosophy*. Aldershot: Ashgate, 17–39.
Persson, I. (2007). "Primary and Secondary Reasons." in T. Rønnow-Rasmussen et al. (eds.), *Hommage à Wlodek*. www.fil.lu.se/hommageawlodek.
Rabinowicz, W., and T. Rønnow-Rasmussen (1999). "A Distinction in Value: Intrinsic and for Its Own Sake." *Proceedings of the Aristotelian Society* 100: 33–52.
Rabinowicz, W., and T. Rønnow-Rasmussen (2004). "The Strike of the Demon." *Ethics* 114: 391–423.
Rabinowicz, W., and T. Rønnow-Rasmussen (2006). "Buck-Passing and the Right Kind of Reason." *Philosophical Quarterly* 56: 114–20.
Ross, W. D. (1930). *The Right and the Good*. Oxford: Clarendon Press.
Ross, W. D. (1939). *Foundations of Ethics*. Oxford: Oxford University Press.
Scanlon, T. M. (1998). *What We Owe to Each Other*. Cambridge: Harvard University Press.

Skorupski, J. (2007). "Buck-Passing about Goodness." In T. Rønnow-Rasmussen et al. (eds.), *Hommage à Wlodek*. www.fil.lu.se/hommageawlodek.

Slote, M. (1989). *Beyond Optimizing*. Cambridge: Harvard University Press.

Sobel, J. H. (1976). "Utilitarianism and Past and Future Mistakes." *Noûs* 10: 195–219.

Thomason, R. H. (1981). "Deontic Logic and the Role of Freedom in Moral Deliberation." In R. Hilpinen (ed.), *New Studies in Deontic Logic*. Dordrecht: D. Reidel, 177–86.

Thomson, J. J. (1997). "The Right and the Good." *Journal of Philosophy* 94: 273–98.

Zimmerman, M. J. (1996). *The Concept of Moral Obligation*. Cambridge: Cambridge University Press.

Zimmerman, M. J. (2001). *The Nature of Intrinsic Value*. Lanham: Rowman and Littlefield.

Zimmerman, M. J. (2008). *Living with Uncertainty*. Cambridge: Cambridge University Press.

Zimmerman, M. J. (2011). "Partiality and Intrinsic Value." *Mind* 120: 447–83.

Zimmerman, M. J. (2014). *Ignorance and Moral Obligation*. Oxford: Oxford University Press.

CHAPTER 2

INTRINSIC AND EXTRINSIC VALUE

TONI RØNNOW-RASMUSSEN

THE intrinsic/extrinsic distinction plays a central role in many philosophical discussions. Without a proper understanding of this distinction much of the recent debate about motivational reasons, mental content, and epistemic justification would be hard to understand. But perhaps no other subject is more closely associated with it than moral philosophy in general, and value theory in particular. The philosophical tradition which divides the value domain into what we nowadays describe as intrinsic and extrinsic values reaches back to antiquity. Generally much of the debate about the distinction has been substantive in character: the aim has been to determine which things are in fact intrinsically good or bad, and which things are good or bad merely as means. However, for the last one hundred years or so, with the birth and development of metaethics and formal axiology, philosophers have taken a growing interest in more formal issues. The distinction between intrinsic and extrinsic value has given rise to a batch of fundamental questions concerning the very nature, importance, and coherence of our value concepts.

The concept of intrinsic value has been glossed variously as what is *valuable for its own sake, in itself, on its own, in its own right*, as *an end*, or *as such*. By contrast, extrinsic value has been characterized mainly as what is valuable as a means, or for something else's sake. As a number of philosophers have pointed out, it is therefore likely that in the many works that deal with (particularly intrinsic) value, more than one concept, and hence more than one distinction, are relevant. In section 2.1, I will examine some recent accounts of the distinction between intrinsic and extrinsic value, and I will suggest that a minimal conception that combines two ideas has taxonomic advantages.[1] To argue this, however, in detail would require more space than I have here. My introductory remarks on this matter will therefore mainly serve another function; they will provide the background against which the further discussion of the two kinds of value will proceed.

Recent work has alerted us to the fact that the traditional way of explicating extrinsic value, as simply nonintrinsic value, leads to the conflation of a number of very different kinds of value. I shall reflect on this debate about varieties of extrinsic value in section 2.2. Finally, in section 2.3, I will consider some attacks on the notion of intrinsic value which in effect question either the very coherence of the intrinsic/extrinsic distinction or its role as a demarcation line between fundamental and nonfundamental value.

2.1. Final and Nonfinal Values

Always bearing in mind, then, that the label picks out more than one notion, I will use the shorthand "IE" to refer to the intrinsic/extrinsic distinction. Let us begin by asking how, historically, IE has been understood. A vivid tradition within Western value theory divides values according to what I shall refer to as the *Finality* sense (cf. Rabinowicz and Rønnow-Rasmussen 2000):

> (1) IE turns on what is valuable (and what is not valuable) for its own sake.

In *The Republic* Plato, for instance, distinguishes between different kinds of good, separating those that are valued for their own sake and those valued for the sake of something else (or in both ways).[2] A more recent way of dividing values departs from the idea that IE is about the difference in supervenient features. There is no consensus on the nature of the supervenience relation, but the following is a quite appealing approach: It is widely believed by realists and antirealists alike that values are properties which objects have in virtue of having other (natural) properties. This insight, which is often considered to be one of G. E. Moore's important contributions to value theory, supplies us with another approach to the distinction. While Moore described intrinsic value in various ways and sometimes used the formulation "for its own sake," he tended to home in on the question whether or not value depends on the properties internal to the value bearer.[3] On what I will refer to as the *Supervenience* sense,

> (2): IE turns on the nature of the value-making features of the value bearer; if a value depends exclusively on the bearer's internal properties it is intrinsic; otherwise it is extrinsic.

Understood in this way the distinction between intrinsic and extrinsic value might seem imminent. In a commonsensical way I suppose it is. Intrinsic value supervenes exclusively on internal features, extrinsic value on extrinsic features (or, to be more accurate, relational features that are external to the bearer of value). There are complications, though. First, (2) depends on the distinction between an object's internal and external features, and metaphysicians disagree as to how we should understand this distinction.[4] Value theorists tend to assume we have an intuitive grasp of what properties are internal or external. From a metaphysical point of view this assumption is not uncontroversial. Still, many present-day value theorists employ a method, building on a test proposed by Moore, which seemingly does not leave us totally in the dark. Moore's so-called isolation test requires us to consider things (as such) existing in absolute isolation. If things are assumed to exist in absolute isolation and yet the things' existence is considered to be good, we will have arrived at what what seems to us valuable in itself, on the basis of our having performed the isolation test (see Moore 1903: 187). In other words, by imagining the alleged value bearer as if it existed alone, we are able, Moore thought, to determine whether or not the object is intrinsically good. This test was supposed to make it possible to distinguish what is valuable in itself from what is either valuable for something else's sake or without value.[5]

Moore's thought experiment has been shown to be defective, though. Lemos (1994) convincingly argues that there could be bearers of intrinsic value that are incapable of existing alone. The fact of Smith's being happy is a case in point. This fact

> could not exist without Smith's existing. . . . Since it is necessarily false that Smith's being happy could be the only existing thing, this sort of ontological isolationism is not very clear or very helpful. (Lemos 1994: 37)

Shortcomings of the isolation test led Chisholm (1981), Lemos (1994), and Zimmerman (2001a: 132; cf. Bodanszky and Conee 1981) to amend it.[6] Common to their proposals is the idea that we should reflect on the supposedly valuable object, and then ask whether it is good, setting aside its consequences and without paying attention to any circumstances we believe it is or might be in. The demand that we contemplate the object in this way is not incoherent. It might be hard to comply with sometimes, but it does not ask the impossible of us. This amended test tells us, then, to consider the thing—whether or not we believe or imagine that it exists on its own—without reference to its context and what it brings in its train, and then to make an evaluative assessment. Lemos (1994: 10–11) refers to it as the "intentional isolation test," as opposed to Moore's ontological isolation test. If this kind of contemplation "leads" you to believe the thing is valuable, or good, then, assuming you really have managed to keep circumstances and consequences out of your contemplation, you will have arrived at what is valuable, or good, *in itself* or *for its own sake*. Or so the argument goes.

In one respect the intentional version is certainly an improvement on its ontological predecessor. But there are further complications. The custom of not distinguishing between value in itself and value for its own sake has, as we shall see in section 2.3, been questioned.[7] It has been argued that objects might be valuable for their own sake in virtue of relational properties that are not internal to the value bearer. If there is something to these complaints, determining the value of something with the help of the intentional version obviously becomes considerably more complicated. The intentional version might still be a catalyst that helps us trigger substantive evaluative reactions. However, we must now be on our guard; even the improved test may be doing more harm than good. The fact that we are not ready to ascribe goodness to something when we contemplate it in isolation is consistent with the fact that the object is valuable for its own sake.[8]

Such complexities notwithstanding, the supervenience approach helps us to structure our views in a fairly easy and helpful manner. In what follows I shall therefore take "extrinsic value" to refer to values that supervene on the value bearer's extrinsic (i.e., externally relational) properties, and I will refer to values accruing to an object in virtue of its internal features alone as "intrinsic." This will facilitate further discussion of the recent debates about intrinsic and extrinsic value.

We still need to consider an additional characterization of intrinsic value.[9] On what we might refer to as the *Derivation* sense,

> (3) IE turns on whether or not the value needs to be justified (by other values): if a value provides justification for other values *and* is not justified by any other value, it is intrinsic; and if it needs to be justified or is valuable in virtue of other things being valuable it is extrinsic (see e.g. Harold 2005).

Should we now conclude that values that depend on the circumstances are derivative, and that intrinsic values are nonderivative? As tempting as that might be, we need to tread carefully here. Consider the case of a valuable ring. The ring might be valuable only in virtue of the valuable diamond set in its clasp. Here the value of the ring is a function of the value of one of its parts; it derives from the value of the diamond.[10] It therefore appears to be a (conceptual) possibility that a derivatively valuable object gets its value from the value of its parts.[11]

Undeniably, the Supervenience sense of IE is important because it provides an important taxonomical tool in value theory. However, we also need the Finality sense. From a substantial point of view, it is at least possible for a unique painting to be valuable even if one of its value-making features is precisely its uniqueness. Building on such examples, a number of philosophers (see note 7) have suggested that what is valuable for its own sake, that is, what has final value, may well accrue to something in virtue of some of its externally relational properties—uniqueness being a bona fide case of a relational feature. In the remaining sections I will therefore assume there are two varieties of "value for its own sake." I will take this to be a *conceptually* interesting possibility. In line with this minimal conception of IE, which is based on (1) and (2), I shall refer to these values as two varieties of *final* value. The set of final values is then constituted by, on the one hand, intrinsic values (understood as the values something has in virtue of the bearer's internal features *alone*) and, on the other hand, final extrinsic values, that is, things that are valuable for their own sakes in virtue of at least some of the bearers' externally relational properties.

Other consideration may eventually lead us to dismiss the idea that anything as a matter of fact has final intrinsic or final extrinsic value. Later on in section 2.3 we shall consider some such considerations as well as some views that question that the notion of a final value is coherent. Meanwhile, here it is worth noting that there is a tradition in value theory that tends to understand alleged examples of final extrinsic value in terms of final intrinsic value. Bradley (2006) refers to this tradition as the Moorean view of intrinsic value. He takes Mooreans to endorse two core claims: that intrinsic values supervene on states of affairs, and that promotion is the proper response to such values. The second, "Kantian" tradition, considers what is intrinsically valuable to be something that accrues to concrete things. It is objects like persons rather than states of affairs that are the fundamental bearers of values, and the appropriate response is respect (rather than promotion).[12]

That intrinsic values are not supposed to be occasion-sensitive like extrinsic values is one of the cornerstones of a Moorean axiology (see Moore 1993 [1903]: 81). However, such a view certainly seems to overlook the obvious fact that if value supervenes on some contingent internal features, the object might lose its value; all it would take is for the object to lose those features that made it valuable in the first place. Mooreans generally agree that this appears to be so, but they insist the appearance is misleading. They tend (somewhat overconfidently, in my view) to handle the relevant counterexamples by arguing that they rest on a mistaken view of the bearer of value; once the correct bearer is identified, it should be evident whether it exemplifies final intrinsic or nonfinal extrinsic value. Suppose for instance you think that a historical object x is valuable for its own sake in virtue of its relation to some historically important figure. Mooreans might suggest that what you really mean by this is that the value accrues to a *state of affairs* (or a fact) to the effect that the object x that has this relation exists. Mooreans would then point out that this valuable state contains the relation as its component and so its value may be seen as *intrinsic*: the value of the state is based on the internal features of the state itself.

If all ascriptions of final extrinsic value can be reduced in this way, there is no reason to assume the existence of final values that are not intrinsic. This sort of response has been criticized, though. It has been argued that not all such reductions are reasonable. In some cases the reduction would put the cart before the horse: for example, a dress once owned by Princess Diana might be valuable for its own sake in virtue of having been owned by Princess Diana. However, the value of the dress does not seem explicable in terms of the value of the state (that Princess Dianna's dress exists); whatever value this state has, it does seem to derive from the value of the dress. (see Rabinowicz and Rønnow-Rasmussen 2000).[13]

Just what the fundamental bearers of final intrinsic or final extrinsic value are has been a much debated issue in value theory.[14] However, if we accept that attitudes may be appropriately or inappropriately directed to objects (in a wide sense), and that there are many kinds of appropriate responses (i.e., other than promoting or respecting), the endeavor to reduce every (concrete) thing-value to state-value, or vice versa, seems hard to defend.

The IE approach suggested here differs, if not in spirit, then in substance, from Korsgaard's much discussed proposal that we should not confuse the ways things have value with the ways we value things. For Korsgaard (1983, 1996), IE concerns the ways things have value. Intrinsic value is the value something has in itself; extrinsic value is the value a thing has from another "source." She contrasts the way we value things. We can value objects as ends or as having instrumental value regardless of the location of the source of value.

Korsgaard's position here is problematic. It has been argued that her notion of a "source" is ambiguous.[15] What she has in mind appears to be something other than the supervenience base of a valuable object—that is, those features, internal and/or external, that are the value-making properties of the object. Her "source" plays the role of what confers value to an object, or what constitutes the value of the object.[16] The question whether value requires such a source is fundamentally an issue about whether objectivism or subjectivism is correct. To answer it we need to adjudicate between theories that reject the idea that there is any need to talk about a subjective source once we have identified the value-making properties and the kind of subjectivism implying that we need to turn to the evaluator's (noncognitive) attitudes to understand why certain natural properties are value-making.

This is no place to explore the debate between subjectivists and objectivists.[17] Suffice it to say that, given the taxonomy suggested earlier (which can be accepted by both positions), intrinsic value and extrinsic final value become subcategories within final values, which is the more crucial concept in axiology and ethics.

Thus, an object's being finally valuable amounts to its being valuable for its own sake, either in virtue of the value bearer's purely internal features (intrinsic value) or because of some of its externally relational features. Should we then expect all nonfinal values to be extrinsic values?

It might seem reasonable. If something is valuable for something else's sake, it is not clear how it could have its value in virtue of its internal features alone. However, recently it has been argued that not even this is quite accurate; some nonfinal values possess value in virtue of only internal features. If that is correct, it follows that some nonfinal values are intrinsic in nature, and it will no longer be true that all intrinsic values are final values. As I will suggest in section 2.2, where I shall also consider some recent work on nonfinal extrinsic values, we should resist this radical position.

2.2. Varieties of Nonfinal (Extrinsic) Value

Among the nonfinal values, instrumental value—intuitively, the value attaching to a means to what is finally valuable—stands out as a bona fide example of what is not valuable for its own sake. Instrumental value has not received the same scrutiny as (final) intrinsic value. This is surprising, since it plays an important role in our evaluative outlook. Moreover, instrumental values are commonly introduced by philosophers to explain the very notion of intrinsic value. Beardsley (1965), in a classical paper, referred to this kind of explanation as the "dialectical demonstration of intrinsic value": if x derives its value from being a means to y, and y derives its value from being a means to z, and so on, we need at some point to put an end to this chain: we need to be able to refer to something that is valuable for its own sake and not for the sake of something else (of value). Beardsley was skeptical about this line of reasoning. It "projects a certain kind of ideal justification that cannot be completed if the series of means and ends has no last term" (7). But to demand this kind of ideal justification is excessive, he thought, since in other contexts we seem to be able to do without it.

Beardsley might be right in that we do not eventually need another kind of value in order to justify our claims about what has instrumental value. In fact, we might even take his skepticism a step further. The idea that instrumental value is a kind of value should not be simply assumed: the claim that something which leads to value is itself valuable has to be argued for (Rønnow-Rasmussen 2002).[18] However, suppose we set this issue aside. If instrumental value is carried by means, causes, or instruments (in a sufficiently general sense of these terms), and we can explain what means, causes, or instruments are without appealing to a value (or a noninstrumental value, at least), then it seems there is an opening for an analysis of instrumental value in which no reference to some other kind of value is made. The so-called fitting-attitude analysis of value (FA) provides answers both to the question what it is that makes an instrumental value into a value and to the question whether such a value can be analyzed without invoking a second kind of value. FA understands value in terms of a normative notion (e.g. fittingness or reason) and a pro or contra response (typically an attitude like a desire or preference) (see, e.g., Scanlon 1998; Rabinowicz and Rønnow-Rasmussen 2004).[19] It has also been pointed out that on one version of FA, x is instrumentally valuable if and only if there is a reason to favor x for the sake of something else, where the latter might, but need not, oblige us to refer to what is valuable for its own sake. Thus, FA has two advantages: first, it provides an account of what it is to be *valuable* as a means (i.e., being fitting or what there is reason to favor as a means); and second, it offers an analysis that does not require yet another value. Not all means are valuable on this account—only those that are either fitting to favor or such that we have the right kind of reason to favor.

Instrumental value is not, it seems, the only kind of nonfinal extrinsic value.[20] Kagan (1998: 109; Rønnow-Rasmussen 2002: 33) speaks of "symbolic value," that is, the value accruing to symbols. Bradley (1998: 110) discusses the related notion of a "signatory value," observing that "something could be good not because of what it causes or is a means to, but rather because of what it *signifies*."[21] And much earlier Lewis (1946) suggested that a constitutive part of a whole might have value even if it lacks instrumental or intrinsic value.

Very recently Dorsey (2012) has defended a quite radical view of instrumental values. He thinks such values might supervene on *dispositional* features that are genuine *internal* properties. Let us conclude this section by examining this last proposal.

Suppose we agree that dispositional properties[22] are genuine properties. Should we then say that instrumental values supervene on them? Perhaps. Certainly there is an ex ante usage of the phrase "instrumental value" that might suggest as much: we speak, for example, about the value of a hammer even if it has never been used as a hammer. Still, on an ex post usage it might make sense to confine the notion of instrumental value to objects which (de facto) have been means to something with (final) value. Conee underlines this de facto approach: "an event's instrumental value of any sort turns on only what would accompany it, not what it makes just likely" (1982: 353). Dorsey does not entirely reject the idea that his notion describes, not instrumental value, but rather what accrues to something that is disposed in a certain context to be a means to what has value. This kind of value would not, then, be the same as that which accrues to what *is* a means, in a certain context and in a certain world, to what is valuable. Indeed it might be argued that Dorsey is in the business of characterizing a merely potential value. On the other hand, I do not see why we should exclude from the outset the possibility that value accrues to potentiality. The real issue is rather what kind of value we are dealing with here.

Consider a new spare tire. This seems to have the kind of value which Dorsey has in mind. Granted that the value-making features of the tire are dispositional, Dorsey might therefore be right to think that he has refuted the view that all intrinsic value is final value. However, I think we should reject this conclusion. Suppose the tire is located in a climate so cold that the tire turns into something very fragile. Here it would no longer be "potentially" valuable (at least, not in the same way, and of course it is irrelevant that it might now come to have another instrumental value). But this suggests that the tire's value is in fact extrinsic. Should we therefore conclude that its dispositional features are, after all, not intrinsic features? Not necessarily. A perhaps more plausible suggestion is that the value does not supervene only on the internal features of the tire. It is rather a combination of internal dispositional features and some relational properties having to do with what a tire is capable of in a certain circumstance that has value. The value-making features would be dispositional (internal) features of the object, but also relational features of the world in which it is located.

2.3. The Coherence of IE

Recent discussions in formal value theory underscore the need to deepen our understanding of IE. The pivotal issue, one that reappears in all these discussions, is whether there is one, or more, or perhaps no kind of fundamental nonderivative goodness—the assumption being that intrinsic value is the more fundamental of the two kinds of value.

What I shall refer to as *Final Extrinsicalism*—the view that there are (at least) two kinds of final value, one intrinsic and the other extrinsic—challenges Final Intrinsicalism, which denies this, committing us instead to the view that there is only one final value, namely the intrinsic kind. The two positions do not exhaust the theoretical space open to us, but they are widely discussed and therefore deserve special attention.[23]

Examples abound which appear to be inconsistent with Final Intrinsicalism. Consider again the case of the rare stamp mentioned earlier. Rarity is an externally relational feature of the object, so if final value accrues to the stamp in virtue of it we seem to have a final extrinsic value, which means Final Intrinsicalism is seriously challenged.

An example provided by Jonathan Dancy adds considerable complexity to this picture. It concerns a joke that is funny only when the butt of the joke is present (Dancy 2004: 172). Space does not permit me to go into detail, but the general idea can be summarized as follows: objects are valuable in virtue of underlying properties, the value-making function of which appears to be conditional on the existence (or non-existence) of other properties that are not themselves value-makers. Thus, in this case the butt needs to be present, but his or her presence is not a funny-making feature of the story.

Contrast this with the earlier example about a dress that once belonged to Princess Diana, which might have final extrinsic value (Rabinowicz and Rønnow-Rasmussen 2000; cf. Kagan 1998; O'Neill 1992). Intuitively, the property of being Diana's dress is a value-maker, not merely a condition of the dress being valuable. Being at one time the property of a celebrity makes the object valuable. These examples, then, tell us different things. The presence of the butt does not make the story funny; it is rather a condition of the story's being funny.

Is the joke a case of intrinsic or final extrinsic value? It depends, I suppose, on whether we want to include in our definition of intrinsic and extrinsic conditions that enable properties to have a *value-making* function or disenable them from doing so. However, such an expansion would probably give rise to new boundary-drawing issues. It will therefore simplify matters greatly if we keep to the original idea that it is the nature of the value-making properties alone that determines whether a value is extrinsic or intrinsic. In accordance with this suggestion, the joke can be understood as carrying a special kind of intrinsic value—one that is conditional on some other features being present.[24] This is in keeping with the idea, maintained from the outset, that we should describe values as intrinsic or extrinsic depending on whether the value-makers are internally or externally relational features of the value bearer.[25]

Let us next turn our attention to a view that seems to challenge the coherence of the notion of final or intrinsic goodness. Consider the two following statements: "x is a good watch" and "pleasure is good." In the former case, "good" modifies a category (watches). It is an example of a so-called attributive use of "good." However, there seems also to be a predicative usage in which we express that something is (simply) good (where this is understood to typically express that the object is intrinsically good). In such examples, as, for instance, when we say that pleasure is good, "good" stands on its own.

One particularly persistent complaint against the idea that something can be simply good dates back to Peter Geach's seminal paper "Good and Evil" (1956). Geach argued that every meaningful use of "good" is attributive. Meaningful judgments of goodness are of the form "x is a good C," where C is a noun that picks out a kind, and where this is not the case, the relevant use of "good" is either nonsensical or capable of being reformulated in attributive terms. Geach maintained that "x is a good C" never meaningfully breaks down into "x is C *and* x is good (period)." For instance, "x is a good watch" cannot be understood as "x is a watch *and* x is good (period)."[26]

Value theorists disagree over whether Geach succeeded in showing that it is nonsensical to employ "good" predicatively to pick out the feature of simple goodness. For instance, Zimmerman (2001a) argues that we cannot dismiss intrinsic goodness just because "good, period" appears to be nonsensical.[27] Recently, Richard Kraut has joined ranks with the critics of intrinsic goodness (which he takes to be synonymous with absolute goodness, or what is "good, period"). Although he believes that we need not be committing some logical error when we predicate that something is good, period, he argues that we should nonetheless give up this notion. Once we realize that absolute goodness is not a normative property, "Positing such a property would do no evaluative work for us. It would be empty, practically speaking, to say that there is such a property but that nothing has it, or has had it, or ever will" (Kraut 2011: 8).[28]

Kraut's work is a contribution to the ongoing debate about how the relationship between "good, period" and "good-for" should be understood. It concerns primarily whether there are one or more kinds of noninstrumental value (goodness). While there is a general agreement that "good for" is used to describe what is valuable as a means, there is no consensus among value theorists about the noninstrumental usage of good-for. In recent years various attempts have been made to understand, or analyze, good-for in ways that either support (see, e.g., Regan 2004, 2003)[29] or challenge the Moorean dictum that there is just one fundamental kind of final goodness, namely absolute good, or (as Moore would also say) intrinsic good (see, e.g., Rosati 2008, Rønnow-Rasmussen 2011, 2013). If it is the case that neither *good, period*, nor *good-for* can be understood in terms of each other,[30] we face, it seems, not one but two versions of the IE distinction: one cast in terms of what is finally (noninstrumentally) good, period, and another cast in terms of what is finally (noninstrumentally) good-for. For the present, it is an open question whether the phrase "intrinsic value" in IE needs to be replaced with "intrinsic value-for," or complemented in some way, in order accurately to express the difference between what is fundamentally good and what is not.

Acknowledgments

A rewarding stay as a visiting fellow at CEPPA, St Andrews (Spring 2013) enabled me to enjoy my time writing this chapter. I thank Wlodek Rabinowicz for helpful comments on an early draft, and the editors of this volume, Iwao Hirose and Jonas Olson, for improvements to this chapter. My work on this chapter was supported by a grant from the Swedish Research Council.

Notes

1. See Feldman (1998), and Zimmerman (2010) for detailed discussion of the more prominent characterizations of "intrinsic value."
2. See Plato 1992: 357b–c. Plato distinguishes between goods that we desire for their own sake, goods that we desire both for their own sake and for the sake of their consequences, and finally goods that we desire only for their consequences. However, in contrast to many modern value theorists, Plato believed that we desire for its own sake what *directly benefits* us (367 b–e; references are due to Wlodek Rabinowicz, personal communication). The benefits Plato had in mind were things like virtue that constitute our final good but also

such things as sight and intelligence that partially cause our good. Sidgwick (1907 [1874]) famously interpreted Plato as making what is good for its own sake to be ultimately dependent on what is good for us (see note 32 below). For a different interpretation, see Brewer (2009: 200), who suggests that what Plato meant by saying that virtue is good for a person x is that virtue is a good (period) that is localized to x. On this view, the relational expression 'good-for' refers to a nonrelational goodness that is localized to a certain person.

3. See Moore (1922: 260). Note that although he believed that nothing can be good for its own sake unless it is intrinsically good, the converse, which is widely accepted by modern value theorists, was something that he dismissed in *Ethics* (1965 [1912]). There he claims that an object is good for its own sake only if all of its parts are intrinsically good. To illustrate, consider an intrinsically valuable painting. Suppose the canvass is not a valuable part of the painting. The painting would still be intrinsically good (beautiful), but it would not be good for its own sake but good for the sake of its good parts, e.g., its composition and color (cf. Moore 1965 [1912]: 30–32).

4. See, e.g., Humberstone (1996) for complications concerning the distinction between relational and nonrelational properties.

5. See *Principia Ethica*, p. 187. As is pointed out by Noah Lemos (1994), Moore is not the only one to propose such an isolation test. David Ross did so in *The Right and the Good* (1930: 68–69). According to Zimmerman (2001a), Richard Price made a similar claim in 'Review of the Principal Questions in Morals' (1887: 148).

6. Zimmerman shows that the ontological version is not only incoherent, but also misleading in certain cases. It can lead us to identify "certain states as parts of other states when they are in fact not parts of them at all" (Zimmerman 2001a: 141).

7. Beardsley (1965), Korsgaard (1983), Kagan (1998); O'Neill (1992); Rabinowicz and Rønnow-Rasmussen (2000) have argued that what is finally valuable need not be intrinsically valuable (in a Moorean sense).

8. As pointed out by Brännmark (2002), Kant suggested that we place the presumed bearer of value in different contexts to help us determine whether it is intrinsically valuable, i.e., valuable in any context. Recently Davison (2012) suggests that we imagine the reactions of a fully informed, properly functioning valuer; if he or she would not mind the annihilation of an alleged bearer of value, we should conclude that it has no value; and if he or she would mind, the value is intrinsic. The test is problematic, though. The fully informed valuer might not mind the annihilation of an object in virtue of its effects or because it is bad for something, which suggests that unless it is qualified it might rather be a test of what is valuable on balance.

9. There are other interpretations, but they are peripheral. In one, IE is associated with a distinction between trumping and nontrumping values (Frierson 2010); intrinsic values are then identified with the former, overriding values, and extrinsic ones with values that are, or might be, overridden by other values (for more on this, see Gustaf Arrhenius and Wlodek Rabinowicz's contribution in this volume, chapter 12). IE has also been read as a separator of instrumental and noninstrumental values: if a value accrues to a means, it is extrinsic; otherwise it is intrinsic. However, this division is too indiscriminate to be of any real use. Finally, in recent years IE has come to be seen as a way of indicating whether a value is perspective-neutral or perspective-relative (see Klocksiem 2011). There are also closely related value concepts. E.g., things have been characterized as having inherent value (Lewis 1946). Audi (2006) interprets this notion as follows: "something is inherently good provided that an appropriate experience of it is intrinsically good . . ., where

the range of appropriate experiences is limited to those that are responses to certain of its intrinsic properties" (86).
10. In the case of so-called organic unities there is no such obvious function between the value of the object and the value of the parts. On a common understanding the goodness or badness of these objects is greater or less than the goodness or badness that arises from the summation of the goodness or badness of their parts or constituents. The value of such objects is therefore not derivative in any straightforward way. For more on organic unities, see Erik Carlson's contribution to the volume, chapter 15.
11. The derivative/nonderivative value distinction raises more issues than I can pursue here. Matheson (2011) has recently argued that something might be a nonderivative value in one domain but derivative in another. I think there are more or less plausible ways to understand this idea, depending on whether we have in mind a pro tanto value (i.e. something that is valuable in one respect) or an all-things-considered value.
12. Note that Bradley recognizes that whether there are one, two, or more concepts of intrinsic value is in fact debatable. If we broaden the perspective of value to be not only about what should be promoted or respected, then it seems there are a great many other kinds of (attitudinal) responses, and accordingly, a great many value concepts. Later on we shall consider a value analysis that suggests this. This so-called fitting attitude analysis (FA) of value (see section 2.2 for more on FA) subsumes all these values under the concept of what is valuable for its own sake, i.e. final (intrinsic and extrinsic) value. The idea that there is a consequentialist response to value (promoting) and a deontological one (respecting) goes back to Pettit (1989).
13. Not all reduction maneuvers can be dismissed in this way, though. See Zimmerman (2001b). For a response, see Rabinowicz and Rønnow-Rasmussen (2003).
14. For a collection of work on the issue of the ontological categories of the *bearers* of intrinsic (final) value, see Rønnow-Rasmussen and Zimmerman (2005).
15. See Rabinowicz and Rønnow-Rasmussen (2000), Dancy (2004), and Hussein and Shah (2006). Cf. Langton (2007).
16. Korsgaard (1998: 63) repeats the idea that particular ends "have only extrinsic value, since their value depends on our own desires and interests in them and is conferred on them by our own rational choices."
17. See here Rabinowicz and Österberg (1996) and Rønnow-Rasmussen (2011). Intrinsic (but not extrinsic) value is sometimes thought to be an objective feature (cf. Langton 2007). But if what determines whether a value is intrinsic or extrinsic is whether or not it supervenes on internal features alone, subjectivists too may ascribe intrinsic value to objects.
18. For Moore (1993 [1903]: 24), instrumental value seems not to have been a kind of value: being instrumentally good was simply being a means to something good; it was not being good in virtue of being such a means. Cf. what he says about contributory value (Moore 1993 [1903]: 35). See also Lewis (1946: 384–85), who distinguishes what is instrumentally valuable from what is merely instrumental or useful.
19. On the so-called Buck-passing version of FA that is due to Scanlon (1998), it is the notion of a reason that is the deontic component. On this account, for an object to be good or valuable is for it to have properties that provide reasons to respond to it in various positive ways.
20. Conee (1982), and more recently Bradley (2013), have argued that an axiology should make room for a notion of *overall* instrumental value. Bradley expresses this kind of value in the following way: "Something is instrumentally good if and only of it causes things

to go better than they would have otherwise gone (for the world or for an individual); something is instrumentally bad if and only if it causes things to go worse than otherwise" (Bradley 2013: 1–2).

21. Signatory value has played an important role in recent discussions of the value of knowledge. See, e.g., Brown (2011).
22. Being soluble and being fragile are typical examples of dispositional properties.
23. A more restrictive version of extrinsicalism claims there is only extrinsic final value. This sort of view has not been taken up much in recent discussion, however.
24. Cf. Olson (2004), where intrinsicalism is distinguished from what the author calls "conditionalism."
25. In Dancy's terms, the distinction turns on the nature of the properties located in the "resultance base of value" (see Dancy 2004).
26. More recently this line of reasoning has been further developed by Thomson (2008).
27. For a defense of Geach, see Danielsson (2001).
28. For more on Kraut's view, see Jonas Olson's contribution to this volume, chapter 3.
29. For a criticism of Regan's view, see Rosati (2008). Cf. Hurka (1987, 2003).
30. Henry Sidgwick was an early advocate of this idea. In *Methods of Ethics* (1907 [1874]) he tried hard to come to grips with a value-dualistic approach. In fact, he thought that the fact that practical rationality has to choose between securing what is impersonally good (acting morally) or making sure you get what is good for you (acting only in your own self-interest) was something missing from ancient Greek ethics (see, e.g., Crisp 2004).

References

Audi, R. (2006 [2003]). "Intrinsic Value and Reasons for Action." In T. Horgan and M. Timmons (eds.), *Metaethics after Moore*. Oxford: Clarendon Press, 79–106.
Beardsley, M. C. (1965). "Intrinsic Value." *Philosophy and Phenomenological Research* 26: 1–17.
Bodanszky, E., and E. Conee. (1981). "Isolating Intrinsic Value." *Analysis* 41: 51–53.
Bradley, B. (1998). "Extrinsic Value." *Philosophical Studies* 91 (2): 109–26.
Bradley, B. (2006). "Two Concepts of Intrinsic Value." *Ethical Theory and Moral Practice* 9: 111–30.
Bradley, B. (2013). "Instrumental Value." In H. LaFollette (ed.), *The International Encyclopedia of Ethics*. Oxford: Blackwell.
Brännmark, J. (2002). "Morality and the Pursuit of Happiness: A Study in Kantian Ethics." Ph.D. diss., Lund University.
Brewer, T. (2009). *The Retrieval of Ethics*. New York: Oxford University Press.
Brown, C. (2011). "The Utility of Knowledge." *Erkenntnis* 77 (2): 155–65.
Conee, E. (1982). "Instrumental Value without Intrinsic Value?" *Philosophia* 11: 345–59.
Chisholm, R. M. (1981). "Defining Intrinsic Value." *Analysis* 41 (2): 99–100.
Crisp, R. (2004). "Sidgwick's Hedonism." In P. Bucolo, R. Crisp, and B. Schultz (eds.), *Proceedings of the World Congress on Henry Sidgwick: Happiness and Religion*. Catania: Universitatà degli Studi di Catania, Dimartimento di Scienze Umane, 104–57.
Dancy, J. (2004). *Ethics without Principles*. New York: Oxford University Press.
Danielsson, S. (2001). "On Geach on Good." In T. Rønnow-Rasmussen, B. Petersson, J. Josefsson, and D. Egonsson (eds.), (2007). *Hommage à Wlodek: Philosophical Papers Dedicated to Wlodek Rabinowicz*. www.fil.lu.se/hommageawlodek).

Davison, S. A. (2012). *On the Intrinsic Value of Everything.* New York: Continuum.
Dorsey, D. (2012). "Can Instrumental Value Be Intrinsic?" *Pacific Philosophical Quarterly* 93: 137–57.
Feldman, F. (1998). "Hyperventilating about Intrinsic Value." *Journal of Ethics* 2: 339–54.
Frierson, P. (2010). "Smithian Intrinsic Value." In V. Brown and S. Fleischacker (eds.), *The Philosophy of Adam Smith.* New York: Routledge, 231–49.
Geach, P. (1956). "Good and Evil." *Analysis* 17 (2): 33–42.
Harold, J. (2005). "Between Intrinsic and Extrinsic Value." *Journal of Social Philosophy* 36 (1): 85–105.
Humberstone, I. L. (1996). "Intrinsic/Extrinsic." *Synthese* 108: 205–67.
Hurka, T. (1987). "'Good' and 'Good for.'" *Mind* 96: 71–73.
Hurka, T. (2003). "Moore in the Middle." *Ethics* 113 (3): 599–628.
Hussein, N. J. Z., and N. Shah. (2006). "Misunderstanding Metaethics: Korsgaard's Rejection of Realism." In R. Shafer-Landau (ed.), *Oxford Studies in Metaethics,* vol. 1. Oxford: Clarendon Press, 265–94.
Kagan, S. (1998). "Rethinking Intrinsic Value." *Journal of Ethics* 2: 277–97.
Klocksiem, J. (2011). "Perspective-Neutral Intrinsic Value." *Pacific Philosophical Quarterly* 92: 323–37.
Korsgaard, C. (1983). "Two Distinctions in Goodness." *Philosophical Review* 92 (2): 169–95.
Korsgaard, C. (1998). "Motivation, Metaphysics, and the Value of the Self: A Reply to Ginsborg, Guyer and Schneewind." *Ethics* 109 (1): 49–66.
Korsgaard, C. (1996). *The Sources of Normativity.* New York: Cambridge University Press.
Kraut, R. (2011). *Against Absolute Goodness.* New York: Oxford University Press.
Langton, R. (2007). "Objective and Unconditioned Value." *Philosophical Review* 116 (2): 157–85.
Lemos, N. M. (1994). *Intrinsic Value: Concept and Warrant.* New York: Cambridge University Press.
Lewis, C. I. (1946). *An Analysis of Knowledge and Valuation.* Indianapolis: Open Court.
Matheson, D. (2011). "How to Be an Epistemic Value Pluralist." *Dialogue* 5: 391–405.
Moore, G. E. (1922). "The Conception of Intrinsic Value." In *Philosophical Studies.* New York: Harcourt, Brace, 253–74.
Moore, G. E. (1965 [1912]). *Ethics.* New York: Oxford University Press.
Moore, G. E. (1993 [1903]). *Principia Ethica,* rev. ed., ed. T. Baldwin. New York: Cambridge University Press.
O'Neill, J. (1992). "The Varieties of Intrinsic Value." *Monist* 75 (2): 119–37.
Olson, J. (2004). "Intrinsicalism and Conditionalism about Final Value." *Ethical Theory and Moral Practice* 7 (1): 31–52.
Pettit, P. (1989). "Consequentialism and Respect for Persons." *Ethics* 100 (1): 116–26.
Plato. (1992). *Republic.* Trans. G. M. A. Grube and C. D. C. Reeve. Indianapolis: Hackett.
Price, R. (1887). "A Review of the Principal Questions in Morals." In *British Moralists,* ed. L. A. Selby-Bigge, vol. 2. Oxford: Clarendon Press, 584–713.
Rabinowicz, W., and T. Rønnow-Rasmussen. (2000). "A Distinction in Value: Intrinsic and for Its Own Sake." *Proceedings of the Aristotelian Society* 100 (1): 33–51.
Rabinowicz, W., and T. Rønnow-Rasmussen. (2003). "Tropic of Value." *Philosophy and Phenomenological Research* 66 (2): 389–403.
Rabinowicz, W., and T. Rønnow-Rasmussen. (2004). "The Strike of the Demon: On Fitting Pro-attitudes." *Ethics* 14 (3): 391–423.

Rabinowicz, W., and J. Österberg. (1996). "Value Based on Preferences: On Two Interpretations of Preference Utilitarianism." *Economics and Philosophy* 12: 1–27.

Regan, D. H. (2003). "How to Be a Moorean." *Ethics* 113 (3): 651–77.

Regan, D. H. (2004). "Why Am I My Brother's Keeper?" In R. J. Wallace, P. Pettit, S. Scheffler, and M. Smith (eds.), *Reason and Value: Themes from the Moral Philosophy of Joseph Raz*. Oxford: Clarendon Press, 202–30.

Rønnow-Rasmussen, T. (2002). "Instrumental Values: Strong and Weak." *Ethical Theory and Moral Practice* 5 (1): 23–43.

Rønnow-Rasmussen, T. (2011). *Personal Value*. New York: Oxford University Press.

Rønnow-Rasmussen, T. (2013). "Good and Good-for." In H. LaFollette (ed.), *International Encyclopedia of Ethics*. Malden, MA: Wiley-Blackwell.

Rønnow-Rasmussen, T., and M. J. Zimmerman, eds. (2005). *Recent Work on Intrinsic Value*. Dordrecht: Springer.

Rosati, C. (2008). "Objectivism and Relational Good." *Social Philosophy and Politics* 5 (1): 314–49.

Ross, W. D. (1930). *The Right and The Good*. Oxford: Clarendon Press.

Scanlon, T. (1998). *What We Owe to Each Other*. Cambridge: Belknap Press of Harvard University Press.

Sidgwick, H. (1907 [1874]). *The Methods of Ethics*, 7th ed. London: Macmillan

Thomson, J. J. (2008). *Normativity*. Chicago: Open Court.

Zimmerman, M. J. (2001a). *The Nature of Intrinsic Value*. Lanham, MD: Rowman & Littlefield.

Zimmerman, M. J. (2001b). "Intrinsic Value and Individual Worth." In D. Egonsson, J. Josefsson, B. Petersson and T. Rønnow-Rasmussen (eds.), *Exploring Practical Philosophy: From Action to Values*. Aldershot: Ashgate, 123–138.

Zimmerman, M. J. (2010). "Intrinsic vs. Extrinsic Value." In Edward N. Zalta (ed.), *The Stanford Encyclopedia of Philosophy*, Winter 2010 ed. http://plato.stanford.edu/archives/win2010/entries/value-intrinsic-extrinsic/.

CHAPTER 3

DOUBTS ABOUT INTRINSIC VALUE

JONAS OLSON

3.1. INTRODUCTION: G. E. MOORE AND HIS CRITICS

It is often said that G. E. Moore's *Principia Ethica* set the agenda for the twentieth-century debate about metaethics and value theory.[1] While it is controversial how groundbreaking Moore's overall metaethical views really were, it is clear that in *Principia* and in later writings he made a number of innovative claims about intrinsic value that continue to attract a great deal of interest, both sympathetic and critical.[2] Nearly all of the last century's writings on intrinsic value take Moore's discussions as their point of departure.

Moore is also the foremost target of criticism of those who harbour doubts of various kinds about intrinsic value.[3] This chapter considers different kinds of recent doubts about intrinsic value, namely doubts about the fundamentality of intrinsic value (section 3.3); doubts about the property of intrinsic value (section 3.4); and doubts about the concept of intrinsic value (section 3.5). In order to understand these doubts and what motivates them we need first to survey some of the things Moore said about intrinsic value (section 3.2). Throughout the chapter, the focus is exclusively on arguments that target intrinsic value specifically. General arguments to the effect that there are no moral or evaluative properties or facts, or that no moral or evaluative judgements are true, will not be considered.

3.2. WHAT DID MOORE THINK ABOUT INTRINSIC VALUE?

Moore opens *Principia Ethica* with a discussion of the subject matter of ethics. According to Moore, we are typically in the business of making ethical judgements when we make claims that involve terms like "virtue," "vice," "duty," "right," "ought," "good," and "bad" (Moore 1993 [1903]: § 1, p. 53). The unifying feature of all such claims is that they all, or virtually all, concern human conduct. Ethics as a philosophical discipline is concerned with what good conduct is. Good conduct is a complex notion and since Moore states somewhat dogmatically that "we all know pretty well what conduct is," he infers that the important task in ethics is to determine what goodness is (Moore 1993 [1903]: § 2, p. 55).

Although Moore in *Principia* frequently uses the terms "good" and "goodness" without qualification, it is important to note that he does not have in mind some kind of generic goodness, but a particular kind of goodness, namely *intrinsic* goodness.[4] One important question in ethics concerns what is good as means, or good instrumentally. For a thing to be instrumentally good is for that thing to be conducive to things that are intrinsically good, so the more fundamental question in ethics concerns what things are intrinsically good.[5]

What is it, then, for a thing to be intrinsically good? As we shall see in section 3.5, the most radical kind of doubt about intrinsic goodness is that the very concept is confused and that it makes little or no sense to say of something that it is intrinsically good. According to two of Moore's suggestive remarks, for a thing to be intrinsically good is for it to be such that "it ought to exist for its own sake" (Moore 1993 [1903]: 34), or for it to be such that it would be good even if it were to exist in complete isolation (Moore 1993 [1903]: § 112, p. 236; cf. §§ 55, 57, pp. 145, 147). These suggestions are not meant as *analyses* of the concept of intrinsic goodness, however. In *Principia*, Moore famously held that the concept of intrinsic goodness is unanalyzable. Moore took conceptual analysis to be a matter of dividing the complex into simpler parts. Complex concepts, such as the concept of a horse, are analyzable, whereas simple or primitive concepts, such as yellow or intrinsic goodness, are unanalyzable (Moore 1993 [1903]: §§ 8–12, pp. 60–64).

In *Principia*, Moore also held that intrinsic goodness is the *sole* unanalyzable ethical concept: "That which is meant by '[intrinsically] good' is in fact, except its converse '[intrinsically] bad', the *only* simple object of thought which is peculiar to Ethics" (Moore 1993 [1903]: § 5, p. 57, Moore's emphasis). All other ethical concepts expressed by terms like "virtue," "vice," "duty," "right," and so on, are analyzable in terms of intrinsic goodness. According to the Moore of *Principia*:

> Our "duty" ... can only be defined as that action, which will cause more good to exist in the Universe than any possible alternative. And what is "right" or "morally permissible" only differs from this, as what will *not* cause *less* good than any possible alternative. (§89, p. 198, Moore's emphases)[6]

We thus arrive at two Moorean theses about the fundamentality of the concept of intrinsic goodness: First, it is unanalyzable. Second, it is the sole unanalyzable concept in ethics; all other ethical concepts are analyzable in terms of it. Let us call these two theses *Unanalyzability* and *Uniqueness*, respectively. Thus formulated, *Uniqueness* entails *Unanalyzability*, but not vice versa.[7]

Not only did Moore hold that the concept of intrinsic goodness is fundamental in the two ways just explained, he also held that it is nonnatural. According to Moore, a natural concept is a concept that the natural sciences (including psychology) deal with.[8] His argument here is the famous open question argument: for any object, X, and natural property, N, the question whether X, which has N, is also intrinsically good is significant or open. Had the concept of intrinsic goodness been a natural concept, however, there would have been some N such that the question whether X, which has N, is also intrinsically good is not open.

The open question argument is arguably one of the most extensively debated arguments in metaethics. We will not add to this debate here.[9] Let us note instead that from his claims about the *concept* of intrinsic goodness, Moore inferred parallel claims about the *property* of intrinsic goodness. Analyzable concepts pick out complex properties, whereas unanalyzable concepts pick out simple properties. The property of intrinsic goodness is thus a simple property. From the conclusion that the concept of intrinsic goodness is nonnatural, Moore inferred that the property of intrinsic goodness is also nonnatural. Here Moore relied on the synonymy criterion of property identity, according to which two terms pick out the same property if and only if they are synonymous. This criterion is fallacious, as is indicated by the example of "water" and "H_2O." These terms pick out the same substance although they are not synonymous.[10] Similarly, the terms "pleasant" and "intrinsically good" are not synonymous, but may still pick out one and the same natural property, namely that of being pleasant.

Moore might of course still be correct that the property of intrinsic goodness is nonnatural, although the open question argument fails to establish that conclusion. I will not here try to determine whether Moore's conclusion was correct, but we shall see in section 3.5 that some who have expressed doubts about intrinsic goodness have in fact been suspicious about nonnatural properties.[11]

Before we consider some doubts about intrinsic goodness, we shall take notice of two further Moorean innovations that have prompted doubts that are for the purposes of this chapter inessential. The first concerns the principle of organic unities. This is the idea that the parts of a complex whole may combine so as to give rise to a kind of holistic value, what Moore calls value *as a whole*, to the effect that "the value of such a whole bears no regular proportion to the sum of the values of its [proper] parts" (Moore 1993 [1903]: § 18, p. 79). Some friends of intrinsic value have accepted and developed the principle of organic unities (Lemos 1994: ch. 3), while others have rejected it (Zimmerman 2001: ch. 4).[12]

The second Moorean innovation to take notice of is *intrinsicalism*, that is, the idea that the intrinsic value of a thing depends, or supervenes, exclusively on properties intrinsic to that thing.[13] This view has been criticized by philosophers who think that the intrinsic value of a thing may partly depend on properties extrinsic to that thing.[14] For example, a dress might be valuable for its own sake, or as an end, on account of its property of having belonged to Princess Diana (Rabinowicz and Rønnow-Rasmussen 2000: 41). Some philosophers have argued that this calls for a conceptual reform, as the central concept turns out not to be that of intrinsic value, but that of *final* value. For a thing to have final value is for that thing to have value as an end, or to be valuable for its own sake, or to be such that it is fitting to value it for its own sake. Final value can be intrinsic or extrinsic, depending on whether the properties on which a thing's final value depends are extrinsic or intrinsic.[15]

Perhaps final value was the concept Moore had in mind all along and perhaps his view that all and only final values are intrinsic was due to his failure to consider certain pertinent examples. In that case all that might be called for is a terminological reform. Some authors, however, do not even agree that this much is called for. Michael Zimmerman agrees that the concept of interest is that of final value, but since he thinks that whatever has final value has it solely in virtue of its intrinsic properties, he sees no need to abandon the traditional term "intrinsic value" in favor of the less colloquial "final value."[16] For ease of presentation, I shall follow Zimmerman and most other participants of the debate and use the term "intrinsic value," but nothing substantial hangs on the terminological choice here.

To repeat, doubts about the principle of organic unities and about the thesis of intrinsicalism are inessential to our purposes. Participants in these debates agree, at least for the sake of argument, that the notion of intrinsic or final value makes sense, and that there is such a property that is important to ethical theorizing. In the coming sections we consider three kinds of doubts that are hostile to Moore's claims. We begin with the least serious one, which concerns the fundamentality of intrinsic value (section 3.3), and we proceed, via doubts about the property of intrinsic value (section 3.4), to the most serious one, which concerns the concept of intrinsic value (section 3.5).

3.3. Doubts about the Fundamentality of Intrinsic Value

If *Uniqueness* is correct, intrinsic value is in a straightforward way fundamental to ethics. Moore's version of *Uniqueness* renders what Michael Zimmerman calls *outcomism*—that is, the view that an action is right if and only if the total outcome it brings about is at least as intrinsically good as the total outcome that would have been brought about if any alternative action had been performed—*conceptually* true.[17] But as Moore came to realize, outcomism is a controversial normative view and denying it need not involve conceptual confusion. In *Ethics* (1963 [1912]), Moore therefore abandoned the view that all other ethical concepts are analyzable in terms of intrinsic value. He now held that at least some deontic concept, such as rightness, duty, or obligation, is unanalyzable too.

Post-*Principia* Moore rejected *Uniqueness* but still took intrinsic value to be central to ethics. Most importantly, Moore maintained that outcomism is true, although not conceptually true: certain claims about intrinsically good outcomes and certain claims about rightness, duty, or obligation are not equivalent in meaning, but equivalent in the sense that it is necessarily true that if an action, A, would bring about a total outcome that is intrinsically better than the total outcome of any alternative action, then A is uniquely right; there is a duty or obligation to perform A (Moore 1963 [1912]: 39).[18] This is not so by virtue of the meaning of "intrinsically better," "right," "duty," or "obligation," however. Rejection of *Uniqueness* thus reduces but does not eliminate the importance of intrinsic goodness to ethics.

Some of Moore's followers accepted nonnaturalism about intrinsic value but rejected *Uniqueness* as well as *Unanalyzability*. C. D. Broad and A. C. Ewing both suggested that intrinsic value is analyzable in terms of the ought of fittingness (Broad 1942; Ewing 1939, 1947). According to such a "fitting attitude analysis," for an object to be intrinsically good is for that object to be a fitting object of a pro-attitude.

Ewing advocated *Uniqueness* and *Unanalyzability* with respect to the ought of fittingness. He thus replaced Moorean intrinsic value with the ought of fittingness as the concept most fundamental and central to ethics.[19] Such a view may suggest that the concept of intrinsic value is ultimately eliminable from an ethical theory concerning what actions we ought to perform and what attitudes we ought to take up.[20]

While this may be so, our sole interest in ethical theorizing need not be to determine how we ought to act and what attitudes we ought to take up, and why we ought to do so. We may also be interested in comparing the intrinsic value of different scenarios, lives, characters, artworks, and so on. The fact that we sometimes do that in everyday thinking may be seen as sufficient reason to investigate whether the concept of intrinsic value is philosophically defensible, although it may not be essential for ethical theorizing.

Ewing was by no means an eliminativist about intrinsic value. He agreed with Moore that the question of how to analyze intrinsic value is crucial, perhaps even *the* crucial question in ethics, but he disagreed with Moore's considered view that it cannot be analyzed.[21] Several contemporary defenders of intrinsic value follow Ewing on this score (e.g., Lemos 1994; Zimmerman 2001).

A way of rehabilitating *Unanalyzability*—and possibly also *Uniqueness*—about intrinsic value, and a rationale for doing so, emerge when we consider a notorious problem that the fitting attitude analysis faces, namely the wrong kind of reason problem (Rabinowicz and Rønnow-Rasmussen 2004). The problem is in brief that there are scenarios in which we apparently ought to take up some pro-attitude toward an object, although this has no bearing on the intrinsic value of the object. One standard example of such a scenario involves an evil and powerful demon who threatens to wreak havoc unless we favor him for his own sake.[22] It seems that the fact that the demon has made the threat is a reason to favor him for his own sake, but it is not plausible that it follows from this that that the demon is intrinsically good. Ewing could respond that while it may be true that we ought to favor such a demon in some sense (perhaps a moral sense) of "ought," it is not true that we ought to favor him in the fittingness sense of "ought" (Danielsson and Olson 2007).[23]

How should we understand the fittingness sense of "ought," then? What is it for an attitude to be fitting? One suggestion is that for an attitude of a certain kind to an object of a certain kind to be fitting is for that attitude to be intrinsically good (Hurka 2003: 604). For example, a negative attitude to a malicious demon may be intrinsically good. Similarly, a pro-attitude to a life of virtue and happiness may be intrinsically good.[24] The view that *what it is* for an attitude to be fitting is for it to be intrinsically good suggests that fittingness is analyzable in terms of intrinsic value. In this way *Unanalyzability*—and possibly also *Uniqueness*—about intrinsic value may be rehabilitated. As we have seen, however, defenders of intrinsic value need not be concerned to rehabilitate those theses as long as rejection of them is not taken to support eliminativism about intrinsic value.

3.4. Doubts about the Property of Intrinsic Value

One kind of doubt about the property of intrinsic value has to do with its apparent normative redundancy. To see what the apparent normative redundancy of the property of intrinsic value amounts to, consider two examples: First, suppose that you suffer a painful toothache and that the pain is intrinsically bad. Plausibly, the fact that the toothache is painful is a reason for you to visit a dentist. But is it equally plausible that the fact that the pain is intrinsically bad is a further reason for you to visit a dentist?[25] Second, suppose that some resort is pleasant and that the pleasantness of a visit is intrinsically good. Plausibly, the fact that the resort is pleasant is a reason to visit it. But is it equally plausible that the fact that the pleasantness of a visit is intrinsically good is a further reason to visit?[26] The intuitive answer to both questions is no, and this suggests the general conclusion that "[intrinsic] value adds no reason to those generated by the ground for that value" (Dancy 2000: 164). It is in this sense that many think intrinsic value is normatively redundant.

The apparent normative redundancy of intrinsic value is often taken to support the view that intrinsic value reduces to reasons for attitudes and actions. But as we saw in the preceding section, advocates of such a reduction do not typically mean to cast doubt on the property of intrinsic value, but to propose a particular theory about the property.[27]

Other philosophers draw more radical conclusions. Richard Kraut has recently argued that the normative redundancy of intrinsic goodness suggests that "positing the existence of [intrinsic] goodness stands to ethical theory as positing the existence of phlogiston stands to physics" (2011: 27). Kraut uses the term "absolute goodness," but it is clear that his target of criticism is the property Moore took to be central to ethics, namely intrinsic goodness (see, e.g., Kraut 2011: 14–16).

The parallel between phlogiston and intrinsic goodness is supposed to be this: Phlogiston was thought to be a substance that causes material substances to combust and gets released during combustion. When Lavoisier and others demonstrated that combustion leaves no traces of phlogiston, and offered explanations of what combustion is that did not involve the notion of phlogiston, it became apparent that positing the existence of phlogiston is superfluous. Scientists eventually agreed that there is no such substance as phlogiston. Similarly, Kraut maintains that Moore took intrinsic value to be the one and only property that provides normative reasons for actions and attitudes. But the normative redundancy of intrinsic value demonstrates that for the purpose of specifying reason-giving properties, positing the existence of intrinsic value is superfluous. Just as scientists concluded that there is no such substance as phlogiston, moral philosophers should conclude that there is no such property as intrinsic value.

Kraut emphasizes that his doubts concern the *property* of intrinsic value. He does not doubt that there is a concept of intrinsic value and that it is coherent (Kraut 2011: 26–27). When scientists rejected phlogiston theory, they did not deny that the concept of phlogiston is coherent. What they denied was that there is something in the actual world that falls under the concept of phlogiston; they denied that the property of being phlogiston is instantiated in the actual world. Analogously, philosophers should not reject the concept of intrinsic value. They should hold that nothing in the actual world, and perhaps nothing in any possible world, falls under it, that is, that the property of being intrinsically valuable is not instantiated in the actual world, and perhaps instantiated in no possible world.

Kraut's doubt about intrinsic value is based on the premise that Moore and other proponents of the property of intrinsic value are committed to the view that intrinsic value is a (or *the*) reason-giving property. Is this premise correct? Let us focus on Moore. Recall that in *Principia Ethica*, Moore took intrinsic value to be the one and only primitive concept in ethics. According to this view, for there to be a reason to perform some action, A, is for A to be conducive to intrinsic goodness. Since intrinsic goodness is a supervenient property,[28] A is conducive to intrinsic goodness if and only if A is conducive to something that has the property of being intrinsically good; for example, pleasure. That A is conducive to intrinsic goodness *analytically implies* that there is a reason to perform A, and the reason to perform A is the fact in virtue of which A is conducive to intrinsic goodness, for example, the fact that A is conducive to pleasure. Following others, we can think of a reason for an action or attitude as a fact that counts in favor of, or pro tanto justifies, that action or attitude; not as the fact that that action or attitude is (pro tanto) justified (see, e.g., Scanlon 1998).

On Moore's *Principia* view, *what it is* for there to be reasons to perform an action, A, is for A to be conducive to intrinsic goodness; it is not the case that the fact that A is conducive to intrinsic goodness is a (or the) reason to perform A. Kraut's interpretation of Moore seems to be based on a conflation of the question of what it is for there to be a reason (i.e., the question of how the concept of a reason is to be analyzed) with the question of what the reasons are.[29] Moore's *Principia* view answers the former question in terms of intrinsic value, and the latter in terms of the natural features on which intrinsic value supervenes. Compare the structure of ideal observer theories. According to an ideal observer theory of normative reasons, what it is for there to be a reason for some agent to perform A is for it to be the case that an ideal observer would want that agent to perform A. On most such theories, however, the reason for the agent to perform A is not the fact that the ideal observer would want the agent to perform A, but the consideration(s) on account of which the ideal observer would want the agent to perform A.

Kraut is therefore twice wrong when he claims that according to Moore's view, "when an action has [the] property [of being conducive to intrinsic goodness], *that* is a reason to undertake it" and that "*this* is the only possible reason to perform any action" (2011: 5, emphases added). The only textual evidence that Kraut offers for his reading is Moore's claim that "[t]he only possible reason that can justify any action is that by it the greatest possible amount of what is good absolutely [i.e., intrinsically] should be realised" (1993: § 60, 153).[30] But the way to read this is that for an action to be justified (all things considered) is for that action to realize the greatest possible amount of intrinsic goodness, and what justifies the action is the fact that by it the greatest possible amount of, for example, pleasure, is realized. This is consistent both with Moore's general view in *Principia* and with the normative redundancy of intrinsic goodness.

According to Moore's post-*Principia* view, Uniqueness is false; it is not the case that intrinsic value is the property in terms of which all other normative properties are analyzable. However, there is a "two-way necessary" connection between, for example, an action's property of being obligatory and its being maximally conducive to intrinsic goodness; necessarily, if an action has one of these properties it also has the other.[31] Correlatively, there is a two-way necessary connection between an action's property of being such that there is reason perform it and an action's property of being conducive to intrinsic goodness.

But now note that the reason-giving relation is *asymmetrical* in the sense that an action's property of being such that there is reason perform that action depends on some base properties of the action, and those base properties of the action do *not* depend on the action having the property of being such that there is reason to perform it. On Moore's post-*Principia* view, the relation between an action's property of being such that there is reason to perform it and its property of being conducive to intrinsic goodness is *symmetrical*, so this relation is not the reason-giving relation.

Neither Moore's *Principia* view, nor his post-*Principia* view, is committed to the view that intrinsic value is a reason-giving property. There is simply no tension between the view that intrinsic value is normatively redundant, which in the light of the examples above may seem highly plausible, and the view that there is a property of intrinsic value.

One might still maintain that although there is no tension here, the normative redundancy of the property intrinsic goodness is a reason to reject it. But there may also be countervailing reasons to accept it. For example, we typically think that some things, such as food, clothes, and money, are good because they are means to what is good in itself, for example, pleasure, and because they are means to avoid what is bad in itself, for example, pain. Moreover, many have found it a compelling thought that it cannot be right to prefer a worse state of affairs to a better.[32] A plausible qualification of this thought is that it cannot be right to prefer an *intrinsically* worse state of affairs to one that is *intrinsically* better. Correlatively, one might find it compelling that there can be no reason to perform an action unless it leads to an intrinsically good outcome. In that case, if there are reasons for action, there is a property of intrinsic goodness.

Kraut's attempted analogy between phlogiston and intrinsic value breaks down in two respects. First, phlogiston was introduced in order to explain combustion. The discovery that phlogiston is superfluous in explaining combustion undermined the reason to believe that there is phlogiston, and we may add that the lack of observable effects of phlogiston is a positive reason to believe that there is no phlogiston.

In contrast, Moore did *not* hold, or was not committed to holding, that intrinsic value is a (or *the*) reason-giving property. The plausible claim that intrinsic value is normatively redundant therefore does not undermine the reason to believe that there is a property of intrinsic value. Second, there were no other, independent reasons to believe that there is phlogiston, in addition to its supposed significance in explaining combustion. In contrast, although intrinsic value is normatively redundant, there are reasons to believe that there is such a property, since, as we have seen, the thought that some things are valuable as means and others in themselves, is a common and intuitive one.

3.5. Doubts about the Concept of Intrinsic Value

There is a familiar distinction between attributive and predicative goodness. The term "good" is used in the attributive sense in statements like "X is a good knife (or car, or friend, or dog, or . . .)"; it is used in the predicative sense in statements like "Happiness (or knowledge, or friendship, or equality, or . . .) is good." W. D. Ross highlighted this distinction in his influential book *The Right and the Good* (1930) and he claimed that predicative goodness, and in particular intrinsic goodness, is most important to philosophy (2002 [1930]: 73).

In an article published a couple of decades later, Peter Geach argued that no sense can be made of predicative goodness (Geach 1956). The only kind of context in which "good" is used legitimately is in statements like "X is a good Y," where X is a particular object or a kind of object and Y is a kind of object whose function can be performed well or badly. On this view, what is good is always good relative to a kind, so the only kind of goodness that makes sense is what we may call good-of-a-kind. Since intrinsic goodness is supposedly not a good-of-a-kind, the conclusion is that the concept of intrinsic goodness makes no sense.

Geach's arguments have come under a lot of fire (see, e.g., Pigden 1990; Thomson 1997; Zimmerman 2001: ch. 2; 2004), and a pithy response to his conclusion, which many have quoted, is Panayot Butchvarov's observation that "millions have thought they understood Genesis 1:31: 'And God saw every thing he had made, and behold, it was very good' " (Butchvarov 1989: 17). Here "good" appears to be used predicatively. At the very least, there is no obvious reading on which what God had made was a good-of-a-kind.

The criticisms notwithstanding, Geach's conclusion has remained influential. According to the most persistent critic of intrinsic goodness in recent years, Judith Jarvis Thomson, Geach was quite right to reject Moorean intrinsic value, although the claim that we may legitimately call something good only when it is good relative to some kind is overstated. Just to give some of Thomson's examples, something may be good *to* look at (or listen to, or eat, or drink, or . . .); someone may be good *with* children (or with dogs, or . . .); someone may be good *in Hamlet* (the play), or *as* Hamlet (the Prince); and, perhaps most importantly, something may be good *for* people (or animals, or plants, or . . .) (Thomson 1997: 276). All of those are examples of things or persons being good in some way. Thomson's position is summed up in the slogan that *all goodness is goodness in a way*; there is no such thing as something's being "plain, pure good" (Thomson 2001: 19). This is in line with Geach's contention that "there is no such thing as being just good or bad" (Geach 1956: 34). Thomson could respond to Butchvarov's observation that what God saw according to Genesis 1:31 was that what he had created was good to look at, or perhaps more plausibly, that it was good for the alleged crown of his creation, namely human beings.[33]

Let us now pause to consider the relevance of Thomson's slogan and her rejection of plain, pure goodness, to the question of whether the concept of intrinsic goodness makes sense. We have already noted that Moore in *Principia* often talked about goodness unqualifiedly, and sometimes about "absolute goodness." That may suggest that what Moore had in mind was something like plain, pure goodness. It is clear, however, that the concept he had in mind, and the concept that he took to be central to ethics, was that of intrinsic value. We have also seen that Moore took the concept of intrinsic value to be unanalyzable. But this does not mean that there is nothing illuminating to be said about it. We have seen that according to Moore, for a thing to be intrinsically good is for it to be such that it would be good even if it were to exist in complete isolation. This is because the intrinsic goodness of a thing is the kind of goodness that depends exclusively on properties intrinsic to that thing (see, e.g., Moore 1993 [1903]: §§ 55, 57, 112; 1993 [1922]). Thomson might object that these accounts of what it is for something to be intrinsically good leave us no wiser since they involve what seems to be a reference to unqualified goodness.[34]

We have also seen that Moore suggested that that which is intrinsically good is such that it ought to exist for its own sake.[35] It is not immediately clear if and on what grounds Thomson would object to such a characterization of intrinsic goodness, for Thomson does not reject the idea of "just plain ought." In contrast to the question of what things are plainly and purely good, the question of what a person just plain ought to do is, according to Thomson, a genuine one (2001: 46).

There are at least two complaints that Thomson could make at this point. She might first respond that while the question of what a person just plain ought to *do* makes good sense, the question of what just plain ought to *be* or *exist* makes as little sense as the question of what is plainly and purely good. Second, Thomson might object that as long as Moore maintains that the concept of intrinsic goodness is unanalyzable, he cannot also maintain that *what it is* for a thing to be intrinsically good is for it to be such that it ought to exist for its own sake. We are thus still not sufficiently enlightened about what it is for something to be intrinsically good.

Both complaints are silenced if we reject Moore's doctrine of *Unanalyzability*. Consider, for instance, Ewing's analysis, according to which for a thing, X, to be intrinsically good is for X to be such that we (or anyone who is in a position to do so) ought, in the fittingness sense of "ought," to take up a pro-attitude toward X for X's own sake

(Ewing 1939; 1947). Or consider Michael Zimmerman's recent proposal that for X to be intrinsically good is for there to be an ethical requirement that one favor X for X's own sake (Zimmerman 2001: 25, 88–90).

It is not clear what Thomson's response to such a move would be. In a recent article she poses the question of what philosophers mean when they ask the question whether pleasure is (intrinsically) good and floats the hypothesis that they mean to ask whether we ought to seek pleasure (Thomson 2003: 94). Note that if we assume that to seek something is one way of taking up a pro-attitude toward it, then on views like Ewing's, the claim that pleasure is intrinsically good may well be analyzed as the claim that we ought to seek pleasure for its own sake.

Thomson goes on to ask, if what philosophers mean to ask when they ask whether pleasure is intrinsically good is indeed whether we ought to seek it (for its own sake),

> [t]hen why the devil don't they say that? There is a long story in the offing here. Told very short, the story says that they want their answer to be self-justifying. Wanting to know whether we ought to seek pleasure, they ask whether it's good because a "yes" would concurrently yield that we ought to seek it *and* seem to explain why. That's pretty cryptic; but I'm sure that something like it must be right. (Thomson 2003: 94, Thomson's emphasis)

That story may be about right in some cases. But it is clearly not right concerning all defenders of intrinsic goodness. Consider Ewing:

> It will be objected against me that it is only fitting to approve, or have a pro-attitude towards, what is good because we first know or believe it to be good and that, if we did not believe it to be good, there would be no ground for such an attitude, so that the attitude would not be fitting. The answer is that the ground lies not in some other ethical concept, goodness, but in the concrete, factual characteristics of what we pronounce good. Certain characteristics are such that the fitting response to what possesses them is a pro-attitude, and that is all there is to it. (1947: 172, cf. 157–58; 1959: 100).

On Ewing's view, then, the fact that pleasure is intrinsically good (if it is a fact) yields an affirmative answer to the question of whether we ought to seek pleasure, because what it is for something to be intrinsically good is for it to be such that we ought to approve of it, or take up pro-attitudes toward it (for example, seek it) for its own sake. The justifying explanation of why we ought to seek pleasure is, however, *not* that it is intrinsically good, but rather that the nature of pleasure makes it the case that the fitting response to pleasure is a pro-attitude.

This is not to say that views like Ewing's are without problems; we mentioned the notorious wrong kind of reason problem in section 3.3. But regardless of whether Ewing's view, or something like it, is ultimately correct, it suggests a way to make sense of the concept of intrinsic value.

Acknowledgments

An earlier version of this chapter was presented at a seminar at Stockholm University and at a workshop on Normativity and Attitudes at Université de Montréal. I thank the participants for helpful discussions. Special thanks to Karin Enflo, Sofia Jeppsson, Victor Moberger, Sarah Stroud, Frans Svensson, Torbjörn Tännsjö, and Jonathan Way, for valuable comments.

Notes

1. *Principia Ethica* was originally published in 1903. References to paragraph and page numbers are to the revised edition (1993).
2. For an informative discussion that places *Principia* in its historical context, see Hurka (2003).
3. A notion of intrinsic goodness is also present in Kant's work. According to Kant, a good will is "good in itself and, regarded for itself, is to be valued incomparably higher than all that could merely be brought about by it" (1997 [1785]: 8). In the twentieth century, however, criticisms of intrinsic value have focused heavily on Moore. Moore's views and criticisms of them will therefore be the topic of this chapter. See Ralf Bader's contribution to this volume, chapter 10, for a discussion of Kant's notion of intrinsic value.
4. In later writings, Moore was more careful to talk qualifiedly about *intrinsic* goodness, see, e.g., Moore 1963 [1912] and 1993 [1903]: 22. Note that for a thing to be intrinsically good is for that thing to have *positive* intrinsic value; for a thing to be intrinsically bad or evil is for that thing to have *negative* intrinsic value; and for a thing to be intrinsically neutral is for that thing to have *neutral* intrinsic value. In this chapter, we shall mostly be concerned with positive intrinsic value, i.e., intrinsic goodness.
5. Moore 1993 [1903]: §§ 15–17, pp. 72–78. "Thing" should here be understood not as "physical object," but as a placeholder for whatever entity can possess instrumental and intrinsic value, e.g., states of affairs, facts, acts, etc.
6. For similar definitions, see, e.g., § 17, pp. 76–77; § 101, pp. 216–17.
7. Alternatively, one could formulate *Uniqueness* in such a way that it does not entail *Unanalyzability*. One might take *Uniqueness* simply to be the thesis that all other ethical concepts are analyzable in terms of intrinsic goodness. The concept of intrinsic goodness may in its turn be analyzable in terms of, e.g., some psychological concept. As we shall see, however, this was clearly not Moore's view.
8. This is the view Moore settles for in the preface to the prospected but never published second edition of *Principia Ethica* (1993 [1903]: 13). In the book, Moore makes some attempts at defining the notion of a natural property (§ 26, pp. 91–93), which he, in the preface to the second edition, repudiates as "hopelessly confused" (1993 [1903]: 13).
9. For a recent discussion of what Moore got right and what he got wrong, see Gibbard 2003: ch. 2.
10. See Horgan and Timmons (1992) for further discussion of this point and its relevance to the open question argument.

11. For a contemporary defense of the view that the property of intrinsic goodness is nonnatural, see Oddie (2005).
12. See Erik Carlson's contribution to this volume, chapter 15, for further discussion about organic unities.
13. This idea is most clearly developed in Moore (1993 [1922]) and in the preface to the second edition (Moore 1993 [1903]).
14. Korsgaard 1983; Kagan 1998; Rabinowicz and Rønnow-Rasmussen 2000; Olson 2004. For a survey of this debate, see Toni Rønnow-Rasmussen's contribution to this volume, chapter 2.
15. Rabinowicz and Rønnow-Rasmussen (2000) suggest that intrinsic value is a subcategory of final value. But another possibility is that the intrinsic/extrinsic distinction cuts across the final/nonfinal distinction, so that there can be intrinsic and nonfinal value as well. See Moore (1963 [1912]) and Ewing (1947) for suggestions along these lines.
16. Zimmerman 2001: 25. See also the discussion in Zimmerman 2001: ch. 3. Kagan (1998) gives examples similar to Korsgaard's and Rabinowicz and Rønnow-Rasmussen's, but he does not advocate a terminological reform. According to Kagan, the intrinsic value of a thing may depend partly on its extrinsic properties.
17. See Michael Zimmerman's contribution to this volume, chapter 1.
18. Moore later said that suchlike claims are "'logically' equivalent" (1942: 599).
19. This is true of Ewing's (1939) and (1947). Ewing abandoned *Uniqueness* in his (1959).
20. See, e.g., Tännsjö (2010: 128–32), who recommends that talk of intrinsic goodness be eliminated from ethical theorizing. See also Crisp 2008: 261.
21. I say that this was Moore's *considered* view, because he did ponder the possibility that intrinsic goodness is analyzable in terms of rightness, see 1993 [1903]: 5; cf. 1942: 594–99.
22. See Rabinowicz and Rønnow-Rasmussen (2004) and Michael Zimmerman's contribution to this volume.
23. Ewing argued that the ought of fittingness is primitive and he suggested tentatively that the moral ought is analyzable in terms of the ought of fittingness. On Ewing's proposal, the claim that an agent ought morally to perform some action, A, is analyzable as the claim that if the agent does not perform A, he ought (in the fittingness sense) to be in that respect an object of the emotion of moral disapproval (1939: 14).
24. According to Hurka's "recursive" theory, there are a number of basic intrinsic goods and evils, and fitting attitudes to the basic intrinsic goods and evils are themselves intrinsically good (correspondingly, unfitting attitudes are intrinsically evil). Moreover, (un)fitting attitudes to the nonbasic intrinsic goods and evils are also intrinsically good (evil) (see Hurka 2001). Moore advocated a similar theory of value in the final chapter of *Principia Ethica*.
25. This example is in Dancy (2000).
26. This example is in Scanlon (1998).
27. See, for example, Scanlon's "buck-passing" account of intrinsic value (Scanlon 1998). See also Ewing (1947: ch. 5). The label "redundancy argument" was invented by Roger Crisp (2005). Crisp himself does not endorse the argument.
28. In a reply to C. D. Broad, Moore said that "I should never have thought of suggesting that [intrinsic] goodness was 'non-natural,' unless I had supposed that it was 'derivative' in the sense that, whenever a thing is good (in the sense in question [i.e., intrinsically]), its goodness (in Mr. Broad's words) 'depends on the presence of certain non-ethical characteristics' possessed by the thing in question: I have always supposed that it did so 'depend' in

the sense that, if a thing is good (in my sense, [i.e., intrinsically]), then that it is so *follows* from the fact that it possesses certain natural intrinsic properties, which are such that from the fact that it is good it does *not* follow conversely that it has those properties" (Moore 1942: 588, Moore's emphasis).
29. Kraut is not alone in making this conflation. See Olson (2006) for discussion.
30. It should be clear that Moore is here talking about justification *all things considered* as opposed to justification pro tanto.
31. Moore 1942: 599. In his *Ethics*, Moore holds that the claim that an action is a duty and the claim that it is maximally conducive to intrinsic goodness are "equivalent," but not identical in meaning (1963 [1912]: 39). Cf. Moore 1942: 608–11.
32. Foot 1985. Foot herself recognised the compellingness of the thought but went on to challenge it. Judith Jarvis Thomson finds the thought "deeply satisfying" (2001: 8), but, like Foot, she goes on to reject it. A. C. Ewing found it "hard to believe that it could ever be a duty deliberately to produce less good when we could produce more" (1947: 188) and claimed that it is a merit of his analysis of intrinsic goodness that it renders this principle acceptable in a way which is consistent with Ross's deontological theory (Ewing 1947: 188–89).
33. It is not clear, however, that Thomson's slogan accounts for all goodness attributions. For example, a retributivist might claim that the state of affairs that the virtuous are happy and the vicious unhappy is a good state of affairs, while the state of affairs that the virtuous are unhappy and the vicious happy is a bad state of affairs. The natural interpretation of this thought is that the first state of affairs is intrinsically good, whereas the latter is intrinsically bad. It is not clear that the goodness and badness in question are among the ways of being good and bad that Thomson's slogan recognizes. (See Zimmerman 2004: 548, for a similar point.) Perhaps Thomson could try responding that the only way to make sense of these claims is to take them to mean that we ought to promote the first state of affairs and that we ought to prevent the latter state of affairs from obtaining; see the discussion to follow in the main text about this possibility. However, in a recent article, Thomson takes a different tack. She is now impressed by the point that 'good' in statements like "That the virtuous are happy is good" seems to be used predicatively, so as to predicate the property of being intrinsically good of a state of affairs (Thomson 2010). The negative part of the view she now leans towards is that when 'good' is used predicatively, no property is attributed, and no proposition is expressed by the sentence in which the predicative 'good' is used. The positive part of the view is that a speaker who says that it is good that the virtuous are happy expresses a positive attitude to this fact; she is saying "Hurrah!" of the fact that the virtuous are happy (Thomson 2010: 762–64). In other words, Thomson leans towards expressivism. She calls the view "narrow expressivism" because it is only meant to be a view about predicative uses of 'good' (and related words). (Whether this makes for a narrower form of expressivism than standard versions of the view is far from clear.) Thomson's endorsement of the view is not wholehearted, however: "I don't think for a moment that Narrow Expressivism is clearly right, but I do think it very much worth taking seriously" (2010: 764).
34. Geach notes the use of 'good' that Moore et al. take to be central to ethics is one that ascribes a nonnatural property. But he complains that "nobody has ever given a coherent and understandable account of what it is for [a property] to be non-natural" (Geach 1956: 35). Perhaps Thomson's critique of Moore is also partly motivated by misgivings about nonnatural properties. But in that case, Geach's and Thomson's criticisms do not target intrinsic value specifically and therefore fall outside the scope of this chapter.

35. Moore 1993 [1903]: 33. Moore thought that the statements "X is intrinsically good" and "X ought to exist for its own sake" are equivalent, and in *Principia* he took the latter to be analyzable in terms of the former.

References

Broad, C. D. (1942). "Certain Features in Moore's Ethical Doctrines." In P. A. Schilpp (ed.), *The Philosophy of G. E. Moore*. Evanston, IL: Northwestern University Press, 41–68.
Butchvarov, P. (1989). *Skepticism in Ethics* (Bloomington: Indiana University Press.
Crisp, R. (2005). "Value, Reasons, and the Structure of Justification: How to Avoid Passing the Buck." *Analysis* 65: 80–85.
Crisp, R. (2008). "Goodness and Reasons: Accentuating the Negative." *Mind* 117: 257–65.
Dancy, J. (2000). "Should We Pass the Buck?" In A. O'Hear (ed.), *Philosophy, the Good, the True, and the Beautiful*. Cambridge: Cambridge University Press, 159–73.
Danielsson, S., and J. Olson (2007). "Brentano and the Buck-Passers." *Mind* 116: 511–22.
Ewing, A. C. (1939). "A Suggested Non-naturalistic Analysis of Good." *Mind* 39: 1–22.
Ewing, A. C. (1947). *The Definition of Good*. London: Routledge & Kegan Paul.
Ewing, A. C. (1959). *Second Thoughts in Moral Philosophy*. London: Routledge & Kegan Paul.
Foot, P. (1985). "Utilitarianism and the Virtues." *Mind* 94: 196–209.
Geach, P. T. (1956). "Good and Evil." *Analysis* 17: 33–42.
Gibbard, A. (2003). *Thinking How to Live*. Cambridge: Harvard University Press.
Horgan, T., and M. Timmons (1992). "Troubles for New Wave Moral Semantics: The Open Question Argument Revived." *Philosophical Papers* 21: 153–75.
Hurka, T. (2001). *Virtue, Vice, and Value*. Oxford: Oxford University Press.
Hurka, T. (2003). "Moore in the Middle." *Ethics* 113: 599–628.
Kagan, S. (1998). "Rethinking Intrinsic Value." *Journal of Ethics* 2: 277–97.
Kant, I. (1997 [1785]). *Groundwork of the Metaphysics of Morals*. Trans. and ed. M. Gregor. Cambridge: Cambridge University Press.
Korsgaard, C. M. (1983). "Two Distinctions in Goodness." *Philosophical Review* 92: 169–95.
Kraut, R. (2011). *Against Absolute Goodness*. New York: Oxford University Press.
Lemos, N. M. (1994). *Intrinsic Value: Concept and Warrant*. Cambridge: Cambridge University Press.
Moore, G. E. (1942). "A Reply to My Critics." In P. A. Schilpp (ed.), *The Philosophy of G. E. Moore*. Evanston, IL: Northwestern University Press, 533–677.
Moore, G. E. (1963 [1912]). *Ethics*. London: Oxford University Press.
Moore, G. E. (1993 [1903]). *Principia Ethica*, rev. ed., ed. T. Baldwin. Cambridge: Cambridge University Press..
Moore, G. E. (1993 [1922]). "The Conception of Intrinsic Value." In T. Baldwin (ed.), *Principia Ethica*. Cambridge: Cambridge University Press, 280–98.
Oddie, G. (2005). *"Value, Reality, and Desire"*. Oxford: Oxford University Press.
Olson, J. (2004). "Intrinsicalism and Conditionalism about Final Value." *Ethical Theory and Moral Practice* 7: 31–52.
Olson, J. (2006). "G. E. Moore on Goodness and Reasons." *Australasian Journal of Philosophy* 84: 525–34.
Pigden, C. (1990). "Geach on 'Good.'" *Philosophical Quarterly* 40: 129–54.

Rabinowicz, W., and T. Rønnow-Rasmussen (2000). "A Distinction in Value: Intrinsic and For Its Own Sake." *Proceedings of the Aristotelian Society* 100: 33–51.
Rabinowicz, W., and T. Rønnow-Rasmussen (2004). "The Strike of the Demon: On Fitting Pro-attitudes and Value." *Ethics* 114: 391–423.
Ross, W. D. (2002 [1930]). *The Right and the Good*. Ed. P. Stratton-Lake. Oxford: Clarendon Press.
Scanlon, T. M. (1998). *What We Owe to Each Other*. Cambridge: Harvard University Press.
Tännsjö, T. (2010). *From Reasons to Norms: On the Basic Question in Ethics*. Dordrecht: Springer.
Thomson, J. J. (1997). "The Right and the Good." *Journal of Philosophy* 94: 273–98.
Thomson, J. J. (2001). *Goodness and Advice*. Ed. A. Gutman. Princeton, NJ: Princeton University Press.
Thomson, J. J. (2003). "Reply to Sinnott-Armstrong." *Southern Journal of Philosophy* 41: 92–94.
Thomson, J. J. (2010). "Reply to Critics." *Analysis* 70: 753–64.
Zimmerman, M. J. (2001). *The Nature of Intrinsic Value*. Lanham, MD: Rowman & Littlefield.
Zimmerman, M. J. (2004). "Critical Notice of Judith Jarvis Thomson, *Goodness and Advice*." *Noûs* 38: 534–52.

CHAPTER 4

VALUE AND DESIRES

GRAHAM ODDIE

4.1. THE APPARENT MAGNETISM OF THE GOOD

> [In] the [pull] of the will and of love, appears the worth of everything to be sought or to be avoided, to be esteemed of greater or lesser value.
>
> Augustine (1982: 109)

We tend to be drawn to what's good and repelled by what's bad—or so it seems to each desiring being. This apparent magnetism of the good suggests a counterpart of the Euthyphro dilemma: are things good because we desire them or do we desire them because they are good? Call this the Dilemma.

Despite its suggestiveness, the Dilemma embraces a couple of problematic presuppositions: that some things really are valuable, and that there really is some important and interesting dependence relation between value and desire. But, accepting these presuppositions, the Dilemma does capture two broad and important positions:

1. There are values and facts about value, and what makes something valuable is the fact that it is desired. There are no antecedently existing, desire-independent values or value facts.
2. There are values and facts about value that exist independently of and antecedently to our desires. Things are not made valuable by facts about desire, but the valuable is what makes things desirable, or appropriate to desire.

Theories of the first sort are naturally classified as *idealist*, since they render value dependent on attitudes, in particular on desire and aversion. Those of the second sort are naturally classified as *realist*, since they posit attitude-independent values.[1]

We can distinguish two varieties of value idealism. Different individuals can and often do desire different things. Joe wants the Democrats to win the House, while Moe is deeply averse to that. If desire makes something valuable, and aversion makes it disvaluable, then it seems that a Democratic win is both good and bad. The obvious way for the idealist to remove the apparent conflict here is to relativize values to subjects. A Democratic win is *good for Joe*, and *bad for Moe*. Such values are not only desire-dependent but also *subject-relative* or *valuer-relative*.[2] Some idealists hold that all values are subjective-relative in this sense. This position will be called *subject-relative idealism*, or *subjectivism* for short.

A desire-dependent value need not be subject-relative. Something might have value not in virtue of some particular individual's desires, but rather in virtue of the distribution of desires overall. A state might be valuable just to the extent that it would satisfy desires generally—the more desires it satisfies the better. Such values would be desire-dependent but *subject-neutral*. The thesis that there are subject-neutral values but that they are all desire-dependent will be called *subject-neutral idealism*. Subject-neutrality embodies one aspect of objectivity.

The value realist holds that there are desire-independent values. The realist can embrace both subject-relative and subject-neutral values. Some states might be good for a particular subject, and be so independently of her desires. A subject's desires might be an unreliable guide to what would be good for her. And some things might be good for a subject but not contribute to subject-neutral value—value simpliciter. It might well be good for a villain to enjoy the fruits of his villainy, but his enjoyment of them isn't good simpliciter. One slot in the logical space should be reserved for theories that maintain that all goods are subject-relative and desire-independent.[3] Call this *subject-relative value realism*. (We need not give it a fully separate treatment here.)

The subject-neutral value realist holds that there are values that are neither desire-dependent nor subject-relative. Of course the subject-neutral value realist can also countenance subject-relative values of both the desire-dependent and desire-independent kind.

We can distinguish two varieties of value realism. Both hold that value is independent of the distribution of actual desires, but differ over what counts as fundamental. It is prima facie plausible that the good is what's *desirable*, in the normative sense that desire is the appropriate or required attitude to it. Alternatively, what is good is what's *valuable*, and the valuable is what it is appropriate to value. If to value a state of affairs is to desire it, then what is good is what it is appropriate to desire.

The *normative realist* takes normative facts about what desires are fitting or required to be fundamental. The *axiological realist*, by contrast, holds that the order of being is the opposite: that values and value facts are fundamental, and these are what explain and justify the normative facts about the fittingness of desires. An important variant of axiological realism, namely *representational realism*, holds that desires are appearances of value, and that the fittingness of a desire is simply a matter of accurate representation.

Many different kinds of entities are the subjects of evaluative judgments. While the objects of desire are often taken to be of a uniform category, desire is standardly taken to be a "propositional attitude," the objects of desire being either propositions or *states of affairs*. Many axiologists have also taken states of affairs to be the primary subjects of evaluative judgments (Chisholm 1986; Lemos 1994). In identifying the relation between value and desire, we will take the subjects of the value attributes we are interested in to be the same as the objects of desire: namely propositions or states of affairs.[4]

4.2. Idealism

4.2.1. Subject-Relative Desire-Dependent Values

Simple subject-relative idealism (or *subjectivism* for short) holds that state P is good for X if and only if (and because) X desires P. Since both value and desire come in degrees, a more accurate characterization of subjectivism is this: P is good for X exactly to the *extent* that (and because) X desires P. Similarly, P is *bad* for X exactly to the extent that (and because) X is averse to P (or desires $\neg P$).

Subjectivism has had no shortage of proponents. Hobbes (1962: 38), for example:

> But whatsoever is the object of any man's appetite or desire, that is it which he for his part calls "good"; and the object of his hate and aversion, "evil"; ... For these words ... "good," "evil" ... are ever used with relation to the person that uses them, there being nothing simply and absolutely so.

Von Ehrenfels (as cited by B. Smith 1994: 292):

> We do not desire things because we grasp in them some mystical, incomprehensible essence "value"; rather, we ascribe "value" to things because we desire them.

And, most recently, Goldman 2009: 13:

> Values exist only for and because of valuing beings, beings motivated to seek or avoid certain states of affairs ... the true value for a person of various objects or objectives is that which derives from coherent and informed sets of [desires].

There are, however, desires the satisfaction of which don't seem to create value, not even value for the desirer herself. These include, inter alia, desires that are *ill-informed, irrational, base, poorly cultivated, pointless, artificially aroused,* and *paradoxical*. (See Heathwood 2005.) Call such desires *defective*. If the satisfaction of a defective desire is not good for the desirer then subjectivism is false.

The subjectivist can disarm the defective desires objection in one of two ways. The standard strategy is to restrict value-generating power to desires that are *refined* or *idealized* in various ways. The other strategy is to stick to the simple view, and show that nothing really untoward follows from assuming that so-called defective desires confer subject-relative value on their objects.

Suppose Michael wants to please all and only those people who don't please themselves. This desire is defective because it is logically impossible for it to be satisfied. So given simple subjectivism, this desire guarantees that something bad for Michael will take place. The subjectivist may be unwilling to count such desires among those that are value-generating. One's desire set should be purged of desires that cannot, logically, be satisfied. Such desires are deemed to lack value-generating power.

Somewhat more realistically, there are contradictory combinations of desires. Warren, full of avarice, wants *to be the richest person alive*. But he is also a tiny bit compassionate, and, when he thinks about it for a moment, finds himself averse to *everyone else's being poorer than he is*. He desires the latter state of affairs not to be the case. Being logically challenged he doesn't realize that he cannot have one without the other. Does this mean that whichever of his two desires is satisfied, the state that satisfies it will be both good and bad (i.e., not good) for Warren? That seems wrong. Warren's desires are defective because, logically, they cannot be jointly satisfied. The subjectivist may deny that any of the desires in an irrational desire-set are value-generating. Warren's desire-set will have to made coherent before his desires can confer value on states.

Now consider Divided Kevin (a character loosely based on one from *The Office*). Being greedy, he wants to eat lots of fries, but, being sensible, he wants to stay slim and healthy. There is nothing incoherent in Divided Kevin's desire set. If the simple subjectivist is right, the best outcome for him would be the satisfaction of both desires. Unfortunately that can't happen given the way the world is structured, but that is not really a count against the value-generating power of his desires. It is the world that is at fault, not Divided Kevin.

Conflicted Kevin has the same desires but also believes that eating lashings of fries makes one fat. His desires, although not at odds with each other, are at odds with his beliefs. If his beliefs are true he cannot satisfy his desires. A subjectivist might require that for any of a subject's desires to be genuinely value-generating, they must be jointly realizable in the light of the desirer's beliefs. Only coherent *belief-desire* combinations generate value. So Conflicted Kevin's desires wouldn't be value-generating.

Suppose Deluded Kevin has been seduced by jealous rivals into believing that eating lots of fries is the very best diet for staying slim and healthy. Deluded Kevin's desires cohere with his beliefs. But there is something suboptimal about his belief-desire combination. If he satisfies his desire for fries he will become unhealthily obese. So satisfying his desire for fries doesn't seem good for him after all. Subjective idealists might demand more of one's belief-desire combination: to be genuinely value-generating one's desires must not only cohere with one's beliefs, one must be *well-informed*.

Suppose Greedy Kevin, like Conflicted Kevin, knows the relevant facts—that if he eats lots of fries he will get fat—and decides in the light of that to refine his desires by killing off his desire to stay thin and healthy. His belief-desire set is now coherent and well-informed and so it makes eating lashings of fries good for him, even though by so indulging himself he will become obese and unhealthy. He is very happy with this refinement.

The subjective idealist who requires only that one's desires be coherent and informed to generate value (Goldman 2009) will embrace this somewhat counterintuitive conclusion. There are no desire-independent constraints on subjective value, apart from the demands of coherence, good information, and means-ends rationality.

There are other ways in which a desire set can be internally problematic. Tormented Kevin is addicted to fries but hates his addiction. This is a second-order desire, a desire to not have, or to not satisfy, his first-order desires for fries. A subjective idealist might go on to restrict the value-generating desires to first-order desires that are backed up by second-order desires. According to this view, the only desires that generate value for you are those that you desire to have or desire to satisfy. The subjective idealist might demand quite a bit more of such second-order desires, stipulating that they generate value only if they would survive the test of full information and vivid imaginative engagement (see Lewis's contribution to Smith, Lewis, and Johnston 1989).

The refined subjective idealist thus begins with the subject's actual desires, whether or not they are defective, and changes them by means of some process of refinement into a set of acceptable value-generating desires.

Another way for the subjective idealist to go is to stick to the simple view, embrace the satisfaction of all actual desires as good for the desirer, and argue that this has no unhappy consequences. For example, the simple subjective idealist can maintain that it really is good for Deluded Kevin to eat fries. But it is also bad for him to get fat and unhealthy. If he eats the fries he will gain one, temporary good and lose another long-term good. If his desire to stay thin is stronger than his desire to eat fries, then eating the fries will still be intrinsically good for him, but it will bring in its wake a larger subject-relative evil. Eating fries is thus good for him *in itself*, but not good for him *all things considered*, because satisfying it will frustrate other desires that are weightier or more numerous or both (see Heathwood 2005).

Note that one can also embrace the goodness for Greedy Kevin of his eating fries and becoming unhealthily obese without accepting that his eating fries and becoming unhealthily obese is a good thing simpliciter. Facts about what is good for a desirer may not carry any implication for what is good in the subject-neutral sense. One who countenances subject-neutral value could say that eating fries is good for Greedy Kevin, while adding that his living like that makes the world a worse place overall. And a pure subjectivist will also deny that what's good for Kevin adds subject-neutral value to the world, because subjectivists deny there is any such thing.

Even if all defective desires can either be tamed or else refined away, there are two difficulties for subjectivism.

First, even though Greedy Kevin's desires are apparently self-destructive, their bad effects may be largely restricted to Kevin himself. Stalin's desires are another matter. Uncle Joe had remarkably coherent desires, excellent means-end reasoning, and a large cohort of individuals to keep him exceptionally well informed. As a consequence, he had a coherent, well-informed set of desires, and he achieved a very high degree of desire-satisfaction over the course of his life. So, according to both kinds of subjectivism, lots of really terrible states of affairs—millions of people starving, being imprisoned, dying of torture, and so on—were very good indeed for Uncle Joe. But his desires, and their satisfaction, also just seem bad *period*. The subjective idealist can of course deem their satisfaction bad for sundry others, but cannot deem them or their dissatisfaction bad *period* without countenancing values that are at least partly objective in being subject-neutral.

Second, it is well known that just as coherent desire sets belonging to a single individual undergird plausible subject-relative values, given a collection of coherent desirers, the subjective values they generate can be aggregated into what appear to be rather plausible subject-neutral values. To this possibility we now turn.

4.2.2. Subject-Neutral Values

Subject-neutral idealism posits value-attributes that, while desire-dependent, have at least one of the marks traditionally associated with objectivity: they apply to states of affairs simpliciter, rather than being relations between states and subjects.

Suppose that each desirer X in a group G is coherent. Then for each such there exists a credence function C_X and a desiredness function D_X which respectively represent X's degrees of belief and X's desires.[5] The possibility of representing coherent desire sets by cardinal belief and value functions is what formally underwrites the plausibility of subjectivism. The subjectivist can then identify the value of P for X—$V(X,P)$—with the value of one of the functions, D_X, that represent his desires, at the proposition P: $D_X(P)$.

But something analogous may well hold for desires considered collectively provided each member of the group has a coherent set. Let's suppose that for each individual X his coherent desire set underwrites the subject-relative and desire-dependent value of P for X—$V(X,P)$. Let us make three assumptions that a subjectivist might find hard to reject: first, that no state is better (simpliciter) than another unless it is better for someone; second, that if a state is not worse for anyone but is better for at least one person, then it is better simpliciter; and third, that value simpliciter, just like subjective value, obeys the principle of expectation (that the value of a state is the expected value of the outcomes of the state). Then it can be proved that subject-*neutral* value V_G just is the sum of the individual subject-relative values.[6] V_G yields the axiological component of a version of preference utilitarianism, a theory which posits desire-dependent subject-neutral values, that are the aggregation of subject-relative values. (The deontological component specifies what agents *ought to do* in the light of these values—but that is an additional element.) So, if the existence of suitable representations of coherent individual preferences underwrites the existence of subjective-relative desire-dependent values, then the existence of suitable aggregations of subjective values can also underwrite the existence of desire-dependent subject-neutral (i.e., partially objective) values.[7]

Mutatis mutandis if subjectivism is wrong in maintaining that the satisfaction of coherent individual desires necessarily generates subject-relative value for the desirers involved, then an idealism that aggregates subject-relative values into these subject-neutral values would simply multiply those errors. Even if the satisfaction of Stalin's coherent but intuitively bad desires are good for Stalin, counting their satisfaction in favor of overall value would skew subject-neutral value in favor of what are, intuitively speaking at least, very bad states. If mass suffering is bad then the mere fact that someone wants others to suffer en masse should not improve the value of a state in which mass suffering occurs. Far from enhancing the value of states, such desires detract from overall value.

The desires of a group might also be refined to remove these anomalous consequences. Just as second-order desires might play a role in refining or overriding first-order desires in the generation of subject-relative values, so too they might play a role in refining subject-neutral values. Suppose that each individual cares not only about herself, but also about certain others, to a greater or lesser degree. About some she cares a lot, about others very little or nothing at all. Within the spirit of idealism we could characterize such caring as a species of second-order desiring—X cares for Y just to the extent that X wants Y's desires to be satisfied. Someone who cared only about her own desire-satisfaction would be a pure egoist, and, fortunately, pure egoists are a rather rare breed.

One's first-order desires and one's second order-desires might be in tension. Suppose Romeo's first-order desires, his desires for this and that, are all satisfied, but Juliet's are all frustrated. If Romeo cares about Juliet he should take on board her dissatisfaction, at least a little, and revise his first-order desires in the light of his very own second-order desires and Juliet's first-order desires. Given that he really does care about Juliet, he should be at least a tiny bit dissatisfied that Juliet has such a high degree of frustration. And the same goes for Juliet. If she cares about Romeo's desire satisfaction then to that extent she should be a little bit satisfied that all his (initial) first-order desires are satisfied. If this process of refinement of first-order desires in the light of one's own second-order desires is modeled in a rather simple and obvious way, we get the following surprising result: given a rather weak condition of connectedness, if everyone continues revising her desires in the light of her *own* desires, then everyone's first-order desires will converge in the limit. We could identify these converging desires with the subject-neutral values that the set of initial subject-relative desires underwrite and generate (Oddie 2005: ch. 4).

What is the connectedness condition that guarantees convergence? Let us say there is a *chain of care* from individual X to individual Z if there is a sequence of individuals Y_1, Y_2, ..., Y_n such that X cares at least a little bit about Y_1, ... Y_i cares at least a little bit about Y_{i+1} ... and Y_n cares at least a little bit about Z. The group is *connected* if between any two individuals in the group there is a chain of care and at least one individual in the group cares at least a little about himself. For connectedness to obtain, no one has to start out caring for everyone else, or even very many others. In fact the condition can hold even if each individual only cares about one other.

So starting from conflicting desires a process of group desire-refinement, where each refines her desires in the light of her very own desires, will lead such a connected community of desirers to converge on subject-neutral values. In this way, the idealist can generate a map of quasi-objective value that ends up remarkably close to the kind of map of value favored by a realist.

The connectedness condition is weak but it is not trivial. For example, the existence of a single pure egoist—one who cares only about his own desire-satisfaction—in an otherwise connected group will force all desirers, in the limit, to converge on the egoist's desires. And if there are two pure egoists with different desires then there will be no resulting convergence to objective values at all. Rather, there will be convergence to competing subjective values—in which the egoists' desires receive disproportionate weight. Worse, if there are desirers who don't just fail to care for others but who positively hate others (i.e., desire their desire-dissatisfaction), then the process of refining first-order desires in the light of second-order desires typically produces no convergence to anything—either subject-relative or subject neutral (Oddie 2005: ch. 5).

We have here two different models of how objective values might emerge from, and be undergirded, by desires. The aggregation model relies on deriving subjective values from individual desires and agglomerating the subjective values in some way. The convergence model doesn't agglomerate subjective values, but rather utilizes a process of refinement of first-order desires in the light of each individual's second-order desires, to arrive at convergent limiting desires.

Unfortunately neither model can guarantee what most would think of as a desirable distribution of value over possible states. Namely, one that blocks the power of various defective desires—either at the first order (if there are any such) or at the second order (such as egoism and hatred)—from skewing subject-neutral values so generated.

To capture the common intuitions about value, not all desires can be value-generating or value-enhancing. In order to exclude defective first-order and second-order desires from skewing the overall distribution of value in the wrong direction, there have to be some desire-independent constraints on desires.

4.3. REALISM

The realist claims value is irreducible to actual desires. Consider something good, world peace say. If good it also seems desirable, in the normative sense. It seems fitting to desire something just to the extent that it is good and to be averse to it just to the extent that it is bad. But even within realism we hear a distant echo of the Euthyphro problem. Is something valuable because it is appropriate to desire it, or is it appropriate to desire it because it is valuable?

4.3.1. Normative Realism

Fitting attitude theorists take facts about the fittingness of desires to be fundamental, and use these to effect a reductive account of value—a reduction of the evaluative to normative facts about desires.

The idea, in its broadest outline, is that something is good if and only if, and because, it is fitting to *favor* it. Favoring can be any "pro-attitude," and different pro-attitudes may be appropriate to different kinds of entity.[8] In the case of the value of *states*, favoring is, or at least involves, desiring. Call this version of the *FA* approach, the *Fitting Desire* account.

C. D. Broad stated the theory, somewhat guardedly, in this way:

> I'm not sure that 'X is good' could not be defined as meaning that X is such that it would be a fitting object of desire to any mind which had an adequate idea of its non-ethical characteristics (Broad 1930: 283).

More succinctly:

Fitting Desire account of the good (FD)
P is good if and only if (and because) it is fitting or appropriate to desire P.

For the *FD* biconditionals to provide a reduction of the axiological to the normative, the notion of fittingness cannot itself be, or, involve an axiological concept. We cannot say, for example, that what it is for a desire for P to be fitting is just that it be *good* to desire P. However, the Fitting Desire account of the good could provide a reduction, without threat of circularity, provided fittingness is a *deontic* rather than an axiological concept. We can call this:

Deontic FD
It is fitting to desire P if and only if one *ought* to desire P.
or
It is fitting to desire P if and only if one has *most reason* to desire P.[9]

On the *FD* account there is a sense in which fitting desires generate value. But it differs from the idealist program in a crucial respect. The idealist thinks different desires can undergird different distributions of value. In general the realist doesn't think that different distributions of desires lead to different distributions of value.

There is however an area in which the occurrence of desires could well make a difference to value. For example, it might be good to have *fitting* desires. Is the having of fitting desires itself a good thing? That is certainly compatible with *FD*, but doesn't follow from it. However, one can clearly add the following plausible principle to *FD*:

Fitting Higher-Order Desires (FDH)
It is fitting to desire to desire P if and only if it is fitting to desire P.

From *FD* and *FDH* we can infer: it is *good* to desire P if and only if P is good.

So by combining *FD* and *FDH* we get the so-called *recursive account* of value, which has been recently been championed with interesting results by Hurka (2001). Note that there is no limit to the number of possible iterations of higher-order desiring, and so there may be no limit to the amount of additional value that accrues to such iterations. Perhaps to rein in a potential value explosion we need to add a constraint of diminishing returns for higher-order desiring.

Even though the *FD* account can allow that desiring generates value in this way, it also denies that all desires are value-generating or value-enhancing. It can thus sidestep the obvious objections to idealism. But it is not without its problems. The most famous of these is the *wrong kind of reason* (*WKR*) objection (Rabinowicz and Rønnow-Rasmussen: 2004). We can adapt the standard examples to fit with desire. Suppose there is a powerful, plausible, and malevolent demon who makes the following offer: if you desire anything other than the worst outcome he will ensure the worst outcome. But if you desire the worst outcome then he will ensure some much better outcome. Further, if you agree to desire the worst, he will make it the case that you do so desire. You have a high degree of belief in his abilities and his threat. What ought you to desire? What do you have most reason to desire? In these unenviable circumstances what you ought to desire, what you have most reason to desire, is the worst outcome. But then it follows from *Deontic FD* that the worst possible outcome is good.

The *FD* theorist might say that it is impossible to adopt that desire. You would adopt the desire for the worst only if you were averse to the worst, so your desire-set would become defective. But of course the demon may have a way of having the new desire *replace* your previous aversion, provided you agree. You would start out being averse to the worst, but in order to avoid the worst you would have to agree to the demon's replacing your aversion to the worst outcome with desiring the worst. Of course, if the demon stays true to his word, your newly adopted desire will in fact be frustrated. But that is a contingent fact—it is not a *necessarily* self-defeating desire, like Michael's desire to please all and only those who don't please themselves. (The demon might improbably go back on his word, for example.)

The *FD* theorist might say that your adopted desire does not really *fit* its object, even if it is the desire you have most reason to adopt in light of the demon's threat. Consider a closely related phenomenon. You might have most reason to adopt a clearly false belief under the demon's duress. He might demand that you *believe*, wholeheartedly and unreservedly, that he is the most perfect possible being, under threat of eternity in hell. There is a very clear sense in which that belief is not a fitting one. A belief represents things as being a certain way, and it is a defect of a belief that it is misrepresents things. Any attitude that represents its object as being a certain way seems not to be fitting if the object is very much not that way. The belief the demon is demanding you adopt may be the one you have most reason to get yourself to adopt, but it is incorrect. Things are not the way it represents them as being. Now suppose desires are states that also represent the world as being a certain way. Clearly the desire for P (unlike the belief that P) doesn't represent the world as being in a P-state. (Nor, contrary to a long tradition, does it represent the world as being in a $\neg P$-state.) But suppose the desire for P represents its object as *good*. If so, then a desire for the worst possible state would misrepresent its object very badly. To that extent it would not be fitting at all, even though it is the desire you have most reason to adopt.

This response is promising, but it is a substantial move away from the deontic notion of fittingness, and toward a *representational* notion of fittingness (Tappolet 2011). The representational notion presupposes that the value of states is up and running prior to the application of a notion of fittingness as representationally accurate. As such, it doesn't sit happily with the aim of reducing the axiological to the normative. We return to this below.

Another prominent objection to the *FD* account involves partiality (Ewing 1959; Oddie 2005; Olson 2009). The *FD* account entails that anyone who desires some state fittingly desires it just to the extent that it's good. And that yields:

The Isomorphic Response thesis

Any two subjects who respond fittingly to the same states have isomorphic sets of desires.

It follows that if *X* and *Y* have conflicting desires, then at least one of them has unfitting desires. That's implausible. Suppose that you are standing by the shore. Your daughter and some stranger's daughter are both out swimming, and as often happens in such situations, both have both been caught in a deadly rip. The lifeguard on duty can save at most one girl from drowning in the rip, so he has to choose. Suppose that neither girl's life has more subject-neutral value than the other's. Both drownings would be equally bad impartially considered. If *FD* is correct the only fitting response for both you and the stranger would be to be indifferent between the two outcomes. And yet even if one *judges* the two outcomes to be equally bad, surely it is permissible to desire that one's own daughter be the one who is saved. Surely how much one cares for someone can legitimately inform how much one desires her well-being?

The demand for impartial responses to value seems to miss something important about how we are differentially related to the various loci of value. The *FD* account, at least as it has been traditionally stated, appears to allow no room for such variation.[10]

4.3.2. Axiological Realism

The WKR objection shows that on normative construals of *fittingness* (the *most reason* construal, or the *obligatory* construal) it can be fitting to desire a state without its being good. If that is right then the FD biconditionals fails, and value cannot be grounded simply in the fittingness of desires.

While *FD* theorists have tried various maneuvers to avoid the *WKR* objection none has garnered widespread acceptance. This suggests that *FD* theorist might block the counterexamples by switching to a different notion of fittingness: namely, fittingness as *correctness*. But the best candidate for this is correctness of a representational state with respect to the object that it represents. In the case of desire, this would be tantamount to construing desiring *P* not simply as some kind of representation of *P* itself but rather as a representation of *P* as *good*. If this is right then a desire for the worst state would be a representation of the worst state as good. And clearly that representation misses its mark, disastrously, even if the having of such a desire would have everything else going for it.

A representational notion of fittingness will not serve the aim of reducing values to normative features of desires. First, the notion that something correctly represents a state as good presupposes antecedent states of goodness. Second, being representationally accurate is not *itself* a normative feature of a representational state. Belief states are representational states. It is sometimes claimed that truth is the norm of belief, which is generally cashed out in terms of a norm: that one *ought* to have all and only true beliefs. By that norm all who are undecided or have a false belief run afoul of epistemic norms. That seems harsh. Can only omniscient beings meet their epistemic obligations? (See Bykvist and Hattiangadi 2007.)

The representational realist maintains that there are some value facts that obtain independently of and prior to desires. She can also happily maintain that the obtaining of the value fact *that P is good* makes a representation of *P* as good *correct*. So desires could be fitting in this sense only if they were representations of value. And *desiring P* would be fitting when it is a *correct* representation—that is, *P* really is good. (This is in fact a first stab which will be refined below.)

Are desires representations of value, and if so what kind of representation are they?

There are both doxastic from nondoxastic representations. A representation that *P* is *doxastic* if having that representation entails having the belief that *P*. There are also nondoxastic representations. A visual experience of the pinkness of the rose is nondoxastic. One can have the visual experience without having that belief, or while believing the opposite. (One might have the visual experience but believe that one is looking at a white rose through rose-tinted glasses.) And one can also have the belief without having the visual experience (say, after the lights go out).

One can desire *P* without having the belief that *P* is good. And one can believe that *P* is good without desiring *P*. One's desires and one's beliefs about the good often come apart at both seams. So if desires are representations of the good they are nondoxastic representations. Perceptual appearances are nondoxastic representations of things. So one plausible thesis is that desires are *appearance-like*, rather than *belief-like*, representations of value. We will call this the *Value Appearance* thesis (*VA*): desires are appearances of value.[11]

Note that *VA* is independent of its converse: that appearances of value are all desires. For one thing entities other than states (e.g., buildings, works of art, persons, ecosystems, and so on) might be the subject of value judgments, but do not seem to be apt objects of desire. Other mental states—like the emotions of love, or appreciation, for example—might be appearances of value of other kinds of entity. It is certainly *compatible* with *VA* that all value appearances have some desiderative component, but it is not entailed by it.

That desires are appearances of value has an ancient pedigree. If we interpret the pull of the will along with the pull of love as desire, then Augustine, in the quote with which we began, is affirming not only that desires are appearances of value but that all value appearances are desiderative.[12]

More recently Denis Stampe (1987) writes:

> The view I shall take is this: Desire is a kind of perception. One who wants it to be the case that *P* perceives something that makes it seem to that person as if it would be good were it to be the case that *P*, and seem so in a way that is characteristic of perception. To desire something is to be in a kind of perceptual state, in which that thing seems good.[13]

That there are value appearances is undeniable. That desires are a kind of value appearance is perhaps not so obvious. Those who take a *purely* dispositional view of desire, for example, would presumably reject it.[14] What can be said in favor of it?

First, a direct argument in favor. In desiring *P* one experiences the *magnetism* of *P*. In desiring *P*, *P* presents itself as a state that is *to be welcomed, pursued, favored*, and so on. Now suppose that (necessarily, not contingently) the good *is* that which is *to be welcomed, pursued, favored*, and so on Then when one desires *P*, it seems to one that *P* is good (Oddie 2005: 55). This argument is subject to an intentionality objection. The fact that one experiences *P* as *A*, where *A* = *B*, may not entail that one experiences *P* as *B*, because one may be unaware that *A* = *B*. Even if it is analytic that *A* = *B*, one may not have the conceptual resources to grasp that. It is also vulnerable to the objection that the purported identity fails if the fitting attitude account fails.

Second, however, there are some abductive arguments in its favor. The thesis explains or accommodates various intuitively compelling features of value and desire including the following.

Any epistemically optimistic theory of value has to postulate some source of basic value data. If all one could know about value reduced to analytic truths (like the transitivity of the *better than* relation) then our knowledge of value would be thin indeed. For us to have epistemic access to value, there has to be something that plays the role of *value data*. Value appearances or value seemings would play such a role. If *desires* are value appearances then there would be a rich source of value data which is both perfectly familiar and not at all queer.

Even though one can believe that *P* is good without desiring *P*—and vice versa—there should still be some necessary connections between value beliefs and desires. *VA* delivers one such. Desires would stand to value beliefs as perceptual states stand to perceptual beliefs. They would give us prima facie, defeasible grounds for such beliefs. At the ground level our epistemic access to value must involve value appearances. So if *VA* is true, many, perhaps most, of our justified value beliefs would be connected to desires at the ground level. But the necessary connection would not be too tight. In particular we would have no reason to embrace the internalist thesis that value judgments entail desires.

VA can also explain the compatibility of acceptable partiality of desires with the existence of subject-neutral values. Appearances, unlike beliefs, are subject to perspectival effects. How things appear to one depends crucially on where one stands in relation to them, and legitimately so. For example, they look bigger the closer they are. Given our relative distance from the sun and the moon, there are occasions on which the moon (though much smaller) legitimately appears much bigger than the sun. If there is an analogous notion of distance in value space, and *VA* is true, then it should not be surprising that one can legitimately desire the less valuable state to the more valuable. And there is such a notion. One is closer in value space to the states of beings with whom one has deep emotional connections (one's nearest and dearest) so if *VA* is right, their weal and woe not only do, but *should* loom larger in our preferences than the weal and woe of distant strangers. Your daughter's drowning should *seem* worse to you than some stranger's drowning. (See Oddie 2005. See Gert 2010 for an attempt to accommodate this within the normative *FA*-program.) So the fittingness of perspectivally sensitive appearances is not *simply* a matter of the accuracy of the associated beliefs. It is also a matter of where in relation to the object the perceiver stands.

VA doesn't entail that desires are an infallible source of value knowledge. The desire for *P*, the simple appearance of the goodness of *P*, is *some* evidence that *P* is good, but, like all appearances, it is defeasible evidence. It is quite compatible with knowing that *P* is not good. Value appearances, like perceptual appearances, are subject to distortion, illusion, theory-ladenness, and are in any case highly perspectival by their very nature. This is how value looks now, from *this* idiosyncratic location in value space.

How, then, can I arrive at reasonable and reliable beliefs about subject-neutral values on the basis of admittedly defective and highly perspectival value experiences? First, my value experiences have to be integrated. I have to reconcile apparently conflicting value appearances with one another. Some will turn out to be inaccurate representations, some will turn out to be highly perspectival. And since lots of other beings also have value experiences, those too have to be somehow integrated and weighed in the balance as I attempt to construct an adequate theory of the subject-neutral value landscape. *VA* is thus compatible with a high degree of fallibilism in our value judgments.

VA is by no means the peculiar possession of the representational realist. And it is not just *compatible* with both versions of realism and both versions of idealism. If it is true these theories turn out to be instances of standard responses to the general question of the relation between experience and reality. All responses to the Dilemma can happily appropriate *VA*, though only the representational realist has need of it. Indeed, even those who reject the presuppositions of the Dilemma can appropriate it (see next section).

VA is a controversial thesis, and there are a number of powerful objections to it.

Human babies ("babes") and sundry nonhuman animals ("brutes") have desires. That newborn babe wants its mother's milk. Felix the cat wants to go outside. But it seems odd—to some at least—to say that it seems good to the human neonate to have its mother's milk, or that it seems good to Felix to go outside. Why? Perhaps to experience *P* one has to believe that *P*, or to be able to entertain the belief that *P*, and it is widely held that babes and brutes don't have beliefs. On this construal, the objection assumes that perceptual experiences are essentially doxastic, so it fails.

Still, even if value appearances aren't doxastic, wouldn't babes and brutes have to have the *concept* of goodness in order to *experience* the goodness of states? This construal of the objection is based on the following principle:

Concept Possession Principle (CPP)
To experience *P* one must possess the concepts necessary to grasp that *P* is the case.

It would follow that to experience *P's being good* one must possess the concept of goodness. Since babes and brutes clearly don't have that concept (or so it is assumed) they cannot have those experiences.

There are two main responses to this. One is to accept *CPP* and bite the bullet. Since babes and brutes don't possess the concept of goodness, and *CPP* is true, they don't really have desires. (This is effectively Stampe's response in his 1987.) They might have desire-like states but they cannot have *real* desires, or desires like ours. That's a big bullet to bite. The other is to deny *CPP* and embrace nonconceptual perceptual content. Babes and brutes do have desires, so they do have experiences of the goodness of things, but, since there is the possibility of nonconceptual content, they don't have to possess the concept of the good in order to do so. (A third and closely related response locates the goodness not in the *content* of the desiderative experience, but in the *mode* of presentation. To desire *P* is for *P* to appear to one in a certain way, the positive-value-presenting way.)[15]

Much of what we experience in perception does transcend our conceptual resources. Most of us have much richer musical experiences, for example, than our repertoire of musical concepts can handle. Concept formation presumably begins with nonconceptualized experience, on which our grasp of those concepts is based and out of which it evolves. (See Gärdenfors 2000.) Babes and brutes have many experiences for which they lack discriminating concepts (as we do). If this is right, babes and brutes could have experiences of the good without possessing a concept of goodness, at least in any objectionable sense.

A highly pedigreed thesis about desire, one which can be traced back to Plato, is that one can only desire what one does not have.

> Anyone ... who has a desire desires what is not at hand and not present, what he does not have, and what he is not, and that of which he is in need; for such are the objects of desire and love. (Plato *Symposium*, in Reeve 2012: 184)

As Jeffrey points out, this needs to be stated carefully:

> Socrates argues that ... to desire something is to be in want of it: you cannot desire what you already have. ... better to say that you cannot desire what you already think you have: one who believes that a proposition is true cannot desire that it be. (Jeffrey 1983: 62–63)

This thesis is explicitly incorporated into Jeffrey's version of subjective decision theory: if one fully believes *P* then one's degree of desire for *P* is identical to one's degree of desire for the tautology.

The same idea is also built into the dispositional-motivational theory of desire—that a desire just is a state that meshes with one's beliefs to cause actions. According to the dispositional theory, my desire for *P is* that mental state which, in conjunction with the belief that doing something A will bring about P, causes me to do A (*provided I am rational*). Clearly, if I already believe P obtains, then, at least if I am rational, there will be no such state that causes me to act to bring about P. I cannot be disposed to bring about P if I believe P to be the case already. So any desire must die as soon as the subject believes it to be satisfied, or even with the belief that it will be satisfied. Belief is the thief of desire.

It is clear that many states that we fully believe obtain seem good or bad. The situation I believe to obtain in Syria now seems very bad to me: VA, together with the fact I am averse to what's happening there, entails this. As I look out the window I see that it is another warm, sunny, dry day in Boulder today, and that also seems good to me: VA together with the fact that I want it to be that way, entails this. So if one cannot desire what one believes to be the case, then VA is false. Desires cannot be value appearances.

The realist who embraces VA must reject the thesis that one cannot desire what one believes to be the case, and along with that must reject both the dispositional theory of desire, and the representation of desire in subjective decision theory. However there are clear counterexamples to both. A convinced atheist might strongly prefer a universe empty of the Divine Being to one graced with God's existence, just as a devout theist might well have the reverse preference. So if desire and preferences go hand in hand—another tenet of subjective decision theory—then it is clear we have a rich set of desires concerning states we believe to be the case. Note also that a rational being can desire that God not exist (whether or not she believes that God exists) and not be at all motivated to try to do anything at all to make that the case, since it is impossible to do anything at all about it. One can have desires for, and preferences over, states that one knows cannot be influenced by whatever one can do. There are also *inactable desires*— desires on which it is impossible for the agent to act. Suppose Kevin wants Kelly to fall in love with him *without his doing anything whatsoever to make that happen*. It can be shown (Friedrich 2006) that such a desire cannot be successfully acted upon. But surely such a desire can exist.

The most telling objection to realism involves the reliability of desires as value data. For the idealist it is no accident that desires reveal at least part of the value landscape, since (roughly speaking) desires directly or indirectly *create* that landscape. But for the realist there is no such guaranteed link. If there is any systematic alignment between desires and value then for a realist that would be an entirely contingent matter.

If desires track the shape of the value landscape (at least the landscape in the neighborhood of the desirer) then that would either just be a matter of luck or it would be because the value landscape exerts some kind of influence on our desires. That not only seems rather farfetched, there is a challenging evolutionary debunking argument against the possibility of any such systematic causal influence (Street 2006). Presumably our preference structures have evolved the way they have because they were fitness-enhancing, not because they revealed the shape of some desire-independent value landscape.

Indeed it is difficult to see how desire-independent values could have any influence on our desires at all, since any such impact would require value facts to be part and parcel of the causal network. If naturalism about value is false (value facts are not reducible to purely natural facts) then the causal efficacy of value would appear to threaten a violation of the causal closure of the purely natural realm (see Bedke 2009). Here, however, there are a variety of strategies for the value realist analogous to those which a nonreductionist about the mental might deploy to reconcile the causal closure of the physical with the causal efficacy of the mental.[16]

4.4. Conclusion

The virtues of value idealism are evident. Idealists claim to make do without naturalistically unfriendly states. Furthermore, they render value epistemically accessible exactly to the extent that our desires are accessible. However, if not all actual desires are value-generating, if only appropriately refined or laundered desires will do the job, then the epistemic and metaphysical advantages start to fade. Epistemic access becomes more problematic the more refined desires have to be before they count as value-generating. And if the constraints on what desires count as value-generating cannot be legitimately squeezed out of actual desires, then the idealist would have to resort to desire-independent normative or evaluative facts.

The chief virtue of value realism is its ability to constrain the set of potentially value-generating desires, independently of contingent facts about the actual distribution of desires. The axiological realist can, in addition, supplement this with a story of our epistemic access to value through desire. The Value Appearance thesis yields an interesting account of how we might be justified in adopting value judgments (tentatively and fallibly) in the light of our desires taken as whole. But the metaphysical commitments of axiological realism are hefty, especially if the realist invokes causal connections between value and desire to explain how desires might track value.

The problems faced by those on both sides of the Dilemma might well lead one to question the underlying presuppositions: that there really are values and value facts, and that there is some interesting relation of dependence between value and desire. Value *antirealism* is the rejection of the first, existential presupposition, and it is a live option. Antirealists need not reject all interesting relations between value and desire. They can, and almost certainly will, hold that there is a pervasive *illusion* of value, and that this illusion of value is created and sustained, inter alia, by desires. Antirealism is compatible with the Value Appearance thesis, and in fact the latter immediately entails that if values don't exist then every desire is a value illusion.

Another possibility is the rejection of the second presupposition—that desires are the class of attitudes most relevant to the valuable. It is noteworthy here that Augustine, in the quote with which we began, mentions *love* alongside the pull of the will. The class of mental states which either reveal or create value may constitute a very much richer class of attitudes which includes emotions like love, of which desire is but one member.[17]

Notes

1. One might maintain that while value doesn't depend on desires, it is does depend on some other attitudes. But recall that we are accepting, for the moment, the two presuppositions of the Dilemma.
2. The more established term is *agent-relative*. However, the terminology of *agent*-relativity privileges the role of *agency* and *actions* in value theory. Value does not only have the function of guiding action and choice, and some values might exist without having any action-guiding relevance. I prefer a less loaded terminology. See Garrett Cullity's contribution to this volume "Neutral and Relative Value," chapter 6.
3. This seems to be the view of Geach (1956) and Thomson (2008)—that there is no coherent predicative notion of *goodness*, or relation of *better than*. There is only a subject-relative notion (what is good *for X*) and an attributive notion (*a good F*). See Pigden (1990) for a telling critique of this view. Kraut (2011) holds that the predicative notion makes sense but denies that there is corresponding property. See Jonas Olson's contribution to this volume, "Doubts about Intrinsic Value," chapter 3.
4. This is in fact a simplifying assumption that could profitably be relaxed. Most of the points discussed can be reformulated using a broader and much more natural conception of the objects of desire and subjects of value as *states* in the broader sense of *states of being*, i.e., *properties*. States of affairs can be captured as a special subset of these—properties such that if one thing has them everything does.
5. That is it say (confining ourselves for the moment to states of affairs):

    $C_X(P) > C_X(Q)$ iff X's degree of belief in P exceeds his degree of belief in Q;

    $C_X(P) = C_X(Q)$ iff X's degree of belief in P equals his degree of belief in Q;

    $D_X(P) > D_X(Q)$ if and only if X prefers P to Q.

    $D_X(P) = D_X(Q)$ if and only if X is indifferent between P and Q;

    The valuer's degrees of belief and desire jointly obey the expectation thesis. This last condition can be stated explicitly in decision-theoretic notation. Where $Q_1,...,Q_n$ is any partition of the set of states, we have, for all P: . The function D_X is u $D_X(P) = \sum_{i=1}^{n} D_X(Q_i)C_X(Q_i|P)$ nique up to linear transformation.
6. That is $V_G(P) = \sum_X V(X,P)$ See Harsanyi (1955) and Broome (1991). Of course all such proofs will involve contested assumptions, but so too do proofs of the representability of individual preferences.
7. See John Broome's contribution to this volume: "General and Personal Good: Harsanyi's Contribution to the Theory of Value," chapter 13.
8. Brentano (1889), Broad (1930), Ewing (1947) and (1959), McDowell (1985), Chisholm (1986), Lemos (1994), Mulligan (1998), Scanlon (1998), Dancy (2000), Tappolet (2000), D'Arms and Jacobson (2000), Johnston (2001), Zimmerman (2001), Skorupski (2010).
9. This reasons-based formulation is also due to Ewing 1959, but has been revived recently by Scanlon 1998.
10. There is a further class of objections to fitting attitude theories in general—namely, the solitary goods objection due to Bykvist (2009). But that objection hits favoring attitudes that are either *factive* (favoring *P* entails *P*) or *credal* (favoring P entails believing *P*). Desiring is neither factive nor credal. See Oddie (forthcoming).

11. *VA* is sometimes called the *Guise of the Good* thesis. However it should be noted that the latter often covers doxastic as well as nondoxastic variants. Davidson 1970 and Tenenbaum 2007 are best construed as doxastic versions of the thesis. *VA* is a nondoxastic variant of the Guise of the Good.
12. I owe this quotation to Simon Blackburn, who, somewhat perversely in my view, uses it to support his version of expressivism.
13. Johnston 2001 adopted a version of *VA* in his 2001. See also Oddie 2005 and Tenenbaum 2007.
14. See Smith 1994 for a definitive statement and defense of the dispositional/motivational theory of desire in the context of value.
15. I owe this insight to Federico Lauria (2014), who develops the rival deontic thesis that the desire that *P* is the presentation that *P* ought to be, where the oughtness lies in the mode of presentation of *P* and not in the content of the presentation.
16. See Oddie 2005 chapter 7 for one such.
17. See the entry to this volume by Christine Tappolet, "Value and Emotions," chapter 5.

References

Augustine (1982). "The Literal Meaning of Genesis." In J. Quasten, W. J. Burghardt, and T. C. Lawler (eds. and trans.), *Ancient Christian Writers*, vol. 1, book 4. New York: Newman Press.
Bedke, M. (2009). "Intuitive Non-naturalism meets Cosmic Coincidence." *Pacific Philosophical Quarterly* 90: 188–209.
Brentano, F. (1889). *Vom Ursprung sittlicher Erkenntnis*. Leipzig. Duncker & Humblot.
Chisholm, R. M. (1986). *Brentano and Intrinsic Value*. New York: Cambridge University Press.
Geach, P. T. (1956). "Good and Evil." *Analysis* 17 (2): 33–42.
Broad, C.D. (1930). *Five Types of Ethical Theory*. New York: Harcourt Brace.
Broome, J. (1991). *Weighing Goods, Equality, Uncertainty and Time*. New York: Blackwell.
Bykvist, K. (2009). "No Good Fit: Why the Fitting Attitude Analysis of Value Fails." *Mind* 118: 1–30.
Bykvist, K., and A. Hattiangadi. (2007). "Does Thought Imply Ought?" *Analysis* 67 (296): 277–85.
D'Arms, J., and D. Jacobson. (2000). "Sentiment and Value." *Ethics* 110: 722–48.
Davidson, D. (1970). "How Is Weakness of the Will Possible?" In Joel Feinberg (ed.), *Moral Concepts*. New York: Oxford University Press, 93–113.
Ewing, A. C. (1947). *The Definition of Good*. Westport, CT: Hyperion Press.
Ewing, A. C. (1959). *Second Thoughts in Moral Philosophy*. London: Routledge and Kegan Paul.
Friedrich, D. G. (2006). *An Affective Theory of Desire*. Ph.D. diss., Australian National University.
Gärdenfors, P. (2000). *Conceptual Spaces*. Cambridge: MIT Press.
Gert, J. (2010). "Color Constancy and the Color/Value Analogy." *Ethics* 121: 58–87.
Goldman, A. H. (2009). *Reasons from Within: Desires and Values*. New York: Oxford University Press.
Harsanyi, J. C. (1955). "Cardinal Welfare, Individualistic Ethics and Interpersonal Comparisons of Utility." *Journal of Political Economy* 63 (4): 309–21.
Heathwood, C. (2005). "The Problem of Defective Desires." *Australasian Journal of Philosophy* 83 (4): 487–504.

Hobbes, T. (1962), *Leviathan*, Michael Oakeshot (ed.), New York: Simon and Schuster.
Hurka, T. (2001). *Virtue, Vice, and Value* (Oxford University Press.
Jeffrey, R. (1983). *The Logic of Decision*. Chicago: University of Chicago Press.
Kraut, R. (2011). *Against Absolute Goodness*. New York: Oxford University Press.
Lemos, N. M. (1994). *Intrinsic Value: Concept and Warrant*. New York: Cambridge University Press.
Mulligan, K. (2010). "Emotions and Values." In P. Goldie (ed.), *Oxford Companion to the Philosophy of Emotions*. New York: Oxford University Press, 475–500.
Moore, G. E. (1903). *Principia Ethica*. New York: Cambridge University Press.
Mulligan, K. (1998). "From Appropriate Emotions to Values." *Monist* 81: 161–88.
Oddie, G. (2005). *Value, Reality and Desire*. New York: Oxford University Press.
Oddie, G. (Forthcoming). "Desire and the Fitting Attitude Theory of Value." In J. Deonna and F. Lauria (eds.), *The Nature of Desire*. New York: Oxford University Press.
Olson, J. (2009). "Fitting Attitude Analyses of Value and the Partiality Challenge." *Ethical Theory and Moral Practice* 12: 365–78.
Pigden, C. R. (1990). "Geach on 'Good.'" *Philosophical Quarterly* 40 (159): 129–54.
Plato. (2012). *A Plato Reader: Eight Essential Dialogues*. Ed. C. D. C. Reeve. Indianapolis: Hackett.
Rabinowicz, W., and T. Rønnow-Rasmussen. (2004). "The Strike of the Demon: On Fitting Pro-attitudes and Value." *Ethics* 114 (3): 391–423.
Scanlon, T. M. (1998). *What We Owe to Each Other*. Cambridge: Harvard University Press.
Skorupski, J. (2010). *The Domain of Reasons*. New York: Oxford University Press.
Smith, B. (1994). *Austrian Philosophy: The Legacy of Franz Brentano*. Chicago: Open Court.
Smith, M. (1994). *The Moral Problem*. Oxford: Blackwell.
Street, S. (2006). "A Darwinian Dilemma for Realist Theories of Value." *Philosophical Studies* 127 (1): 109–66.
Tappolet, C. (2000). *Emotions et valeurs*. Paris: Presses Universitaires de France.
Tappolet, C. (2011). "Values and Emotions: Neo-sentimentalism's Prospects." In Carla Bagnoli (ed.), *Morality and the Emotions*. New York: Oxford University Press, 117–34.
Tenenbaum, S. (2007). *Appearances of the Good: An Essay on the Nature of Practical Reason*. New York: Cambridge University Press.
Thomson, J. J. (2008). *Normativity*. Chicago: Open Court.
Smith, M., D. Lewis, and M. Johnston. (1989). "Dispositional Theories of Value." *Proceedings of the Aristotelian Society* 63: 89–174.
Zimmerman, M. J. (2001). *The Nature of Intrinsic Value*. Lanham, MD: Rowman & Littlefield.
Zimmerman, M. J. (2011). "Partiality and Intrinsic Value." *Mind* 120 (478): 447–83.

CHAPTER 5

VALUE AND EMOTIONS

CHRISTINE TAPPOLET

IF one thinks of the *admirable* and admiration, of the *shameful* and shame, or of the disgusting and disgust, it is difficult to deny that there must be close ties between values, on the one hand, and emotions, on the other hand. Because one can distinguish between evaluative concepts, evaluative judgments, evaluative properties and evaluative facts, and also because several types of relation can be envisaged, the question of what relation holds between values and emotions ramifies into several distinct questions.

Consider evaluative judgments. One option is to claim that such judgments are reducible to, constituted by, or identical to emotions.[1] This option has been attractive to proponents of noncognitivism, the view that evaluative, or more generally normative, judgments do not have the function of predicating evaluative properties and thus fail to be truth-assessable, or at least fail to be truth-assessable in any substantial way. As a view about judgments, noncognitivism is distinct from, but congenial to, two important but controversial doctrines in metaethics which consider emotions to be central to ethics: emotivism (or expressivism), the semantic thesis that the function of evaluative sentences is to express emotions (Stevenson 1937; Ayer 1952), and projectivism, the view that the evaluative is a projection of our emotions onto the world (Blackburn 1984).

In general, views such as noncognitivism, emotivism, and projectivism are premised on two assumptions about the nature of emotions: (*a*) emotions lack cognitive content; and (*b*) emotions are essentially motivational states, so that by establishing a link to emotion, the motivational power of evaluative judgments, sentences, or facts is supposed to be accounted for (see Ayer 1952, for instance). The recent consensus in emotion theory is that there is ground to question these assumptions and to adopt a broadly cognitive account of emotions.

Interestingly, one of the main accounts of emotions proposes an ontology of emotions that amounts to a mirror-image of noncognitivism. This view, judgmentalism, holds that emotions are, or necessarily require, evaluative judgments (Solomon 1976; Nussbaum 2001). Fear would thus be, or necessarily require, the judgment that what one fears is fearsome or dangerous. Another possibility is to posit causal relations between evaluative judgments and emotions. It is plausible to hold that emotions causally influence evaluative judgments, such as when your anger gets you to assess your opponent negatively. However, in at least some cases, it is clear that the causal relation goes the other way around: evaluative, or more generally normative, judgments play a causal role in the arousal of emotions. It should be noted that the two claims are not necessarily incompatible. For instance, your anger might be caused by the judgment that someone slighted you, but it might also influence how you assess that person. A further kind of relation lies at the level of epistemology. According to an influential account of emotions that stresses the analogies with sensory experiences, the so-called perceptual theory of emotions (Meinong 1972 [1917]; de Sousa 1987; Tappolet 2000; Goldie 2001), emotions would allow agents to be aware of evaluative properties in the same way as color experiences allow us to be aware of colors. On the basis of this, it has been claimed that emotions at least prima facie justify evaluative judgments. However, it has also been argued that, vice versa, evaluative judgments justify emotions, a claim that does not sit well together with the thesis that emotions are in a position to justify evaluative judgments.

These are but the bare outlines of the most striking relations that can be taken to hold between evaluative judgments and emotions. In this chapter, I want to focus on a distinct but related topic, that is, the relation between evaluative concepts and emotions. The central question addressed here is that of the relation between concepts such as *admirable* and *disgusting* and emotions such as admiration and disgust.

A suggestion that has been prominent in recent debates is that the relation between the evaluative and emotions can be expressed in the form of propositions like the following: something is admirable if and only if feeling admiration is appropriate in response to it, something is shameful if and only if shame is appropriate with respect to it, something is disgusting if and only if disgust is appropriate with respect to it.[2] Such propositions, which I shall call "value-emotion equivalences," raise the question of how to interpret them, something that needs to be settled before assessing their plausibility. A first question is how to read the biconditional. According to advocates of what has become known as fitting attitude analysis, the equivalences consist in conceptual analyses of the relevant evaluative concepts. But as we shall see, this is not the only possibility. Moreover, what needs to be specified is what the relevant kind of attitude is supposed to be and what it is for such an attitude to be appropriate. These issues will be discussed in section 5.1, the aim of which is to present a plausible version of the value-emotion equivalences. The following section turns to an important worry regarding value-emotion equivalences. In general, advocates of such equivalences assume that concepts such as *admirable* or *disgusting* are evaluative. However, in the light of debates about whether thick concepts are evaluative, it is reasonable to wonder whether concepts such as *admirable* or *shameful* really are evaluative concepts. This worry raises the deep question of what it is about evaluative concepts that makes them evaluative. Before turning to this issue, let us have a closer look at the alleged relation between evaluative concepts and emotions.

5.1. Value-Emotion Equivalences

As I said, it is difficult to deny that concepts such as *admirable, shameful,* or *disgusting*, which I will call "affective concepts" in order to be as neutral as possible with respect to the question whether such concepts are evaluative, have a tight connection to emotions. The foremost reason why this is so is simply because such concepts, of which there are a great many, are picked out by terms that are lexically connected to emotion terms. Thus, on the positive side, you have *admirable, hopeful, pride-worthy, lovable, respectable, awesome,* and *amusing*, whereas on the negative side, there are *shameful, disgusting, contemptible, embarrassing, fearsome, frightening,* and so on. Not all emotions have a lexically derived affective concept—consider anger or guilt, for instance—but many do, and when there is no natural language term, it is always possible to designate the relevant concept by a complex expression. Thus, things can be considered worthy of your anger or of your guilt.

A further point that attests to the intimacy of affective concepts and emotions is that on most accounts the formal objects of emotions are picked out by affective concepts. It is in terms of the formal objects of emotions that the appropriateness conditions of emotions are specified.[3] For example, most would agree that the admirable is the formal object of admiration, in the sense that an episode of admiration is appropriate on the condition that what you admire is genuinely admirable. Put in terms of concepts, one could say that the concept of the admirable picks out the formal object of, or sets the standard for, the emotion of admiration.

Finally, and relatedly, emotions and the properties that correspond to affective concepts, if there are such properties, share a number of structural traits:

a. *Degrees.* Both emotions and what can be called "affective properties" allow for degrees.[4] An interpretation of *Einstein on the Beach* can be more or less admirable, and of course, you can admire it more or less, with more or less intensity.
b. *Valence.* Both affective properties and emotions have valence. They are both divided into two groups, which are described as positive and negative. On the side of positive evaluative properties, you have being admirable, being pride-worthy, being lovable, and so on, while on the negative side, you have being despicable, shameful, disgusting, and so on. The same kind of polarity is found in emotions, which are standardly thought to divide into positive and negative emotions.[5] What is meant by positive and negative emotions can be quite different depending on the context, but in the sense in which joy is opposed to sadness or pride to shame, for instance, the distinction appears to mirror that between positive and negative evaluative concepts.
c. *Polarity.* A point that is closely related to the former is that many affective properties and many emotions form pairs of polar opposites. On the side of values, you have pairs such as admirable *versus* despicable, pride-worthy *versus* shameful, while on the side of emotions you have admiration *versus* spite, pride *versus* humility, love *versus* hate, and so on.

Given these different considerations, one has to acknowledge that affective concepts are by nature related to specific responses: they wear their response-dependence on their sleeves.[6] In fact, one might at first sight think that affective concepts and emotions are even more tightly connected than what would be true on the value-emotion equivalences. One might thus suggest that what holds is the simple biconditional, according to which something is admirable insofar as one admires it, and so on for the other affective concepts. Such a suggestion, which is sometimes called simple subjectivism (Rachels 1986: ch. 3), will not do, however. The reason is that, as most would agree, we sometimes admire what is not admirable. The commonly accepted amendment to simple subjectivism is to add the condition that emotions be fitting or appropriate. Thus, we arrive at value-emotion equivalences.

Consider the following biconditional:

(1) x is admirable if and only if feeling admiration is appropriate in response to x.

Before assessing the plausibility of such propositions, it is necessary to further specify them. There are three interdependent questions. The first question is how to understand the relation between the two sides of the "if and only if." The second question concerns the nature of the emotional response that is referred to. The last question is what is it for such a response to be appropriate or fitting? Let me consider these in turn.

The standard assumption, which as its name indicates is characteristic of fitting attitude analysis, is that (1) consists in an analysis of the concept *admirable*. The idea is that in what is assumed to be a strict equivalence, the concept is broken down into what are taken to be simpler conceptual elements, that is, the notion of a feeling of admiration and the notion of appropriateness. Moreover, the equivalence is taken to be a conceptual truth, so that the failure to accept it betrays a failure to fully grasp the concept (see Zimmerman, chapter 1 in this volume). But there are other ways to read (1). Thus, the biconditional could be held to be a contingent proposition that holds only in the actual world and which has to be established a posteriori. Another possibility is to read the biconditional as a possibly necessary, but substantial, normative or even moral proposition, so that what is admirable is what it is that we are normatively or morally required to admire. However, the most prominent alternative to fitting attitude analysis interpretation is to read it as a conceptual elucidation, as opposed to an analysis. The equivalence would be taken to be a necessarily true proposition, which expresses the thought that the concept *admirable* is conceptually connected to the concepts of admiration and of appropriateness, but none of the concepts would be considered to be more fundamental. On such a no-priority view, the grasp of these concepts would be interdependent.

A second important question is what kind of response is invoked in such equivalences. By contrast with Brentano (1889), who explicitly refers to love in his analysis of the concept *good*, fitting attitude analysis theorists have not restricted themselves to emotions (see Ewing 1947). Quite generally, it appears possible to plug into a putative analysis of evaluative concepts items as varied as evaluative judgments, conative states (such as desires), or even types of actions.[7] However, when considering affective concepts it appears difficult to avoid the reference to states that standardly count as emotions.

The follow-up question that arises is what kind of state emotions are. Depending on the account of emotion that is favored, very different versions of the values-emotion equivalence result, ranging from the more to the less plausible. Thus, if one takes emotions to be or necessarily require evaluative judgments, as the judgmental theory of emotions proposes, then we obtain the proposition that something is admirable if and only if judging that it is admirable is appropriate. In the most obvious of its interpretations, this proposition is true, but also viciously circular, so that it cannot be offered as an account of the concept *admirable*. The reason is that the very same concept is part of the content of the judgment mentioned in the right-hand side, so that possession of the concept to be accounted for is required to understand the proposition.[8] Fortunately, as will be made clear shortly, there are other theories of emotions on the market.

The third question is how to understand the notion of appropriateness. This simple question has proven particularly tricky. Answering it is crucial to avoid what has become known as the wrong kind of reason objection, because it was mainly targeted at versions of the fitting attitude analysis expressed in terms of reasons for attitudes.[9] In a nutshell, what poses a problem is that there can be a reason to feel an emotion toward something that fails to fall under the relevant affective concept. One can for example have prudential reason to feel admiration toward something that clearly fails to be admirable. Thus, the question is whether one can specify what the right kind of reasons are. In the same way, it can be appropriate to feel an emotion toward something that fails to fall under the relevant affective concept, so that the right kind of appropriateness needs to be specified.

Quite generally, there are two main ways to conceive of what it is to be appropriate for an emotion (see Tappolet 2011). The first is to take the concept to be normative or deontic. On this conception, an appropriate emotion is an emotion that ought to be felt, roughly. This is the standard account in the recent literature, but it is not the only one possible. On a different conception, appropriateness is a matter of correct representation. An appropriate emotion is an emotion that is correct from the epistemic point of view, in the sense that it represents things as they are, evaluatively speaking.[10]

An important virtue of such a representational account of appropriateness is that it makes the wrong kind of reason objection easy to handle. Since the appropriateness of an emotion is defined in terms of whether that emotion represents things as they are, evaluatively speaking, it is ruled out that feeling an emotion can be appropriate, in that sense, with respect to something that fails to fall under the relevant evaluative concept.[11] According to such an account, something is admirable if and only if this thing is such that feeling admiration is correct in response to it, and this is so only if it is admirable.

One might worry that such an account would not be illuminating enough to be of interest. It appears that what is proposed is simply that something is admirable just in case it is admirable, and so forth for the other affective concepts. However, there is reason to think that in spite of its circularity, the resulting equivalence is of interest. What it underlines is the crucial epistemic role that emotions play in our grasp of affective concepts. As David Wiggins (1987) suggested, the important point to keep in mind is that there is nothing more fundamental to appeal to than admiration when we try to find out whether or not something is admirable, and the same can be said about other affective concepts.

The main virtue of this representational interpretation of the value-emotion equivalence is that it is grounded on what is arguably a highly plausible account of emotions, the so-called perceptual theory of emotions, according to which emotions are perceptual experiences of a particular kind.[12] What is specific about emotions, compared to sensory perceptual experiences, is that they represent things as having evaluative properties. Thus, an emotion of admiration with respect to a friend will be correct just in case the friend is really admirable. An important point here is that on this account, emotions have representational, albeit not conceptually articulated, content. Emotions represent their object as having specific evaluative properties, that is, as fearsome or disgusting, and so forth, even though the agent who undergoes the emotion need not possess the relevant evaluative concepts (*fearsome, disgust*, etc.).[13]

It would take us too far to discuss the perceptual theory of emotions.[14] The only point I would like to make here is that what makes it attractive is that it steers a middle course between two opposed accounts of emotions, each of which has some plausibility, but both of which are ultimately unsatisfactory. At one end of the spectrum, there is the so-called feeling theory, according to which emotions consist in states, such as bodily sensations, that are characterized by the way they feel, but which have no representational content (James 1890; Lange 1885; Whiting 2011). At the other end of the spectrum lies the judgmental theory, according to which emotions are or necessarily involve conceptually articulated judgments, so that to fear something would amount to judging that the thing in question is fearsome (Solomon 1976; Nussbaum 2001). The main objections to the feeling theory are that it cannot take into account that emotions have intentional objects—we are afraid of a dog, angry at someone, and so on—and that it fails to make room for the fact that we assess emotions in terms of how they fit their object, such as when we say that it is inappropriate to feel fear at an innocuous spider. Apart from the fact that it does a poor job at accounting for the fact that emotions are felt states, what plagues the judgmental theory is that it is incompatible with the observation that one can undergo an emotion without possessing the relevant concepts—one can be afraid of something without possessing the concept of fearsomeness, for instance.[15]

In conclusion, it appears that one can spell out value-emotion equivalences that are not only plausible in themselves, but also that are well supported by emotion theory. There are a number of questions that need to be discussed to fully assess the proposed interpretation of the value-emotion equivalence. The focus here will be on a problem that raises the question of what it is for a concept to be evaluative.

5.2. Are Affective Concepts Evaluative?

Sentences like "Natacha's pizzicato is admirable" or "Pierre's attitude toward foreigners is disgusting" make it difficult to deny that affective terms are evaluative, in the sense that it is part of their meaning that they convey positive or negative evaluations.[16] What appears to be expressed by the first sentence is praise, while the second sentence appears to express stark criticism. Thus, on the assumption that what is true of terms also holds of concepts, it is natural to think that affective concepts like *admirable* and *disgusting* are inherently evaluative in the sense that a concept like *admirable* would by essence be a positive evaluative concept, while the opposite is true of *disgusting*.[17]

As has gone largely unnoticed, these claims can be challenged. As will be obvious if one considers affective concepts to be a subclass of thick concepts, the reason is that the considerations that are used to argue that so-called thick concepts, such as *courageous, generous*, or *cruel*, are not inherently evaluative, can easily be transposed to affective concepts.[18] It will be useful to first consider a distinct challenge to the claim that affective concepts are evaluative.

It can be agreed that being admirable is distinct from being admired, and being admirable is also distinct from being such as to cause admiration. What is admired, or what is such as to cause admiration, can be admirable but it need not be so. Given the analogy with concepts such as *bendable*, or *expansible*, in which the suffix "-able" or "-ible" expresses a possibility (what is bendable being what can be bent, and what is expansible being what can be expanded), one could suggest that *admirable, disgusting*, and so forth, can similarly be parsed as what *can* be admired, what *can* disgust, and so on. If so, concepts such as *admirable* or *disgusting* would not be evaluative. In reply, one could suggest that it is simply obvious that *admirable* and *disgusting* are evaluative, or indeed normative, concepts. Clearly, that reply will not convince someone who doubts that such concepts are evaluative. There is a plausible rejoinder to such doubts, however. It amounts to underlining that there is an important difference between *bendable* and *admirable* in that the fact that something is bendable does not entail anything about its goodness or badness, whereas that something is admirable seems to entail that it is good, or in fact good to a high degree, in at least one respect. Generally, it appears that when we describe things in affective terms we place them on scales that go from the best to the worst (pro tanto), or simply from better to worse (pro tanto). Being more or less admirable entails being more or less good at least in a certain respect, while being more or less disgusting entails being more or less bad at least in a certain respect.

However, that affective concepts are thus connected to *good* and *bad* is what can be challenged in the light of the discussion of thick concepts, a type of concept which is thought to be opposed to thin concepts.[19] Typical examples of thick concepts are *courageous, generous*, and *cruel*, whereas *good* and *bad* are typical examples of thin concepts.[20] While the former are thought to involve both an evaluative and a descriptive aspect, the latter are thought to be purely evaluative or normative. A question which has attracted a lot of attention is whether the two components of thick concepts can be disentangled into an evaluative (or normative) component and a descriptive component.[21] In order to show that the components can be disentangled, some, like Simon Blackburn (1992), have argued that thick concepts are not inherently evaluative, or more precisely, that on the assumption that thick concepts are by definition inherently evaluative, there are no such concepts. What is of interest here is not so much the entanglement issue as the question whether thick concepts are inherently evaluative.²² The variability argument that has been presented is based on evidence that suggests that thick terms are contextually variable in evaluative valence (see Väyrynen 2011). This is taken to show that the evaluations that thick terms and concepts are used to convey are not part of their meaning, but depend on context. Two kinds of examples have been and still are discussed. First, there are examples involving comparative locutions, such as "too tidy" and "too industrious" (Hare 1952: 121). What is suggested is that even though "tidy" and "industrious" as typically taken to convey positive evaluation, they have what appears to be literal uses in which they express criticism. In the second kind of example, unmodified thick evaluative terms or concepts appear to convey an evaluation that is opposite to the usual one, such as when we say, "Yes, cruel certainly, but that's just what made it such fun" (Hare 1981: 73), or "This year's carnival was not lewd. I hope it'll be lewd next year" (Väyrynen 2011: 8, who acknowledges Matti Eklund (personal communication)).

Now, the striking fact is that affective terms and concepts allow for the same kind of examples. One can say, "This person is too admirable to be really likeable" or "The Halloween outfit was not disgusting enough." In the first sentence, "admirable" appears to have changed its valence, for the sentence appears to convey criticism, while in the second sentence, "disgusting" appears to convey a positive evaluation. In the same way, one can say, "Yes, disgusting certainly, but that's just what made it such fun" or "This year's Halloween outfit was not really disgusting. I hope that it'll be disgusting next year." On the basis of such examples, it appears easy to argue that affective terms and concepts are not inherently evaluative.

The question is what to think of the variability argument. In fact, there are good reasons to resist the argument. A first point to note is that concepts like *good* and *bad*, whose status has not been questioned, allow for the same kind of examples. Thus, a wine can be said to be too good to be used for cooking (Väyrynen 2011: 7). And one can also have cases of simple predication, such as when one says, "Yes, bad certainly, but that's just what made it such fun," or "This year's performance of the conservative party was not bad. I hope that it'll be bad next year." Such examples should make us suspicious.

Let us first consider the cases involving comparatives. As Väyrynen (2011: 5–9) notes, the way modifiers such as *too* and *not . . . enough* behave in general explains how a concept may appear to flip its valence. What such constructions involve are implicit or explicit standards of comparison, and it is relative to such standards that the evaluative content of the whole expression can be understood. In Väyryen's words, "the standard for counting as satisfying *too F* or *not F enough*, is typically neither the same as the standard for satisfying *F* nor determined by the same factors" (2011: 7). For example, the standard for satisfying *loud* is clearly distinct from the standard for satisfying *not loud enough to keep the neighbors awake* or from that for satisfying *too loud to be safe for hearing*. An interesting point that this example brings to light is that *too* and *not . . . enough* can take a nonevaluative concept, such as *loud*, to form a complex evaluative concept. This bolsters the case against the variability argument, for there is no more reason to believe that *loud* becomes an evaluative concept in such a context than there is to believe that *tidy, industrious,* and so on change their valence.

What about the unmodified cases? A number of moves are available to defend the view that thick concepts are inherently evaluative. A first point to note, however, is that insofar as concepts and not only terms are concerned, it will not do to invoke the distinction between semantic meaning and speaker meaning.[23] The reason is that this distinction has no equivalent at the level of concepts. Thus, the suggestion that a term like "lewd" is used ironically, such as when the speaker mocks the sort of prudishness involved in the standard use of the term, cannot be transposed to the level of thoughts and concepts. But there are other moves open to the invariantist.

A reply that works at both levels is that which appeals to the distinction between predicative and attributive uses of terms and concepts.[24] Consider a typical predicative adjective, such as "green." When you say, "This is a green ball," what you say is "This is a ball and this is green," so that if something is a green ball, it follows that it is green. By contrast, an attributive adjective, such as "big" or "tall," functions as a predicate modifier. But when you say, "This is a big mouse," you obviously don't say, "This is a mouse and this is big." A big mouse need not be a big pet, and it is clearly not big qua mammal or animal. Now, evaluative terms and concepts appear to allow for both attributive and predicative uses. When you say that something is a good knife, this does not entail that it is good as such, for relative to a different kind of thing, such as being a weapon (compared with a gun, say) what you consider need not be good. In such cases, what is good is not good simpliciter but relative to a standard. In other cases, however, such as when we say that knowledge is good, there seem to be no such standards. When we say or judge that knowledge is good, we don't say or judge that knowledge is good qua F, while it could be bad qua G.[25]

With this in mind, let us return to the question whether thick terms and concepts are inherently evaluative or not. What can be suggested is that at least in some cases, apparent inversions are due to the attributivity of the term or concept. As Väyrynen (2011: 10) notes, being frugal qua college master might be a bad thing, while being frugal qua person might be a good thing. In the same way, being cruel or disgusting might be a good thing qua joke, for it might add to its amusingness, while being quite bad qua public address, say. It might be the case that relative to some standard, a term or concept has a fixed valence, such as when frugality is predicated of persons, but relative to other standards, the valence can shift (Väyrynen 2011: 11). The important point is that the variability in attributive uses does not entail that the concept itself is variable.

The example of the joke that is all the better for being cruel or disgusting indicates a second reply to the variability argument, one that uses G. E. Moore's principle of organic unities. According to Moore, "The value of a whole must not be assumed to be the same as the sum of the values of its parts" (1993 [1903]: 28). The idea is that if two elements are put together, the resulting whole may have either more or less intrinsic value than the states would have if they existed alone. Moreover, on a holistic interpretation of this principle, the parts retain their value when they are put together in a whole.[26] This idea can be put to work in reply to the variability argument as follows: being bad in some respect might add to the positive value of a whole, something which explains the apparent valence shift. For example, a joke that includes a dose of cruelty or disgustingness might be all the better for it.

A last reply to the variability argument that appears promising is to appeal to a particular kind of contextual enrichment. So-called free enrichment is a mechanism by which additional information is provided by the context, such as when "I have had supper" has to be interpreted as "I have had supper tonight" given the context.[27] The transposition to concepts is not straightforward, but one way to go is to consider what happens in cases of contextual enrichment that depend on specific concepts, such as indexicals. When I think that I am hungry, the context determines that it is I, Christine, who is hungry. In the same way, one could suggest that when it seems to me that I think that I have had supper, the context can be such that what I really think is that I have had supper tonight.

The suggestion, then, is that what explains the apparent variability is that what appears as a complete sentence or thought is in fact incomplete but gets filled in by the context. Thus, the sentence "He is frugal" might express a negative evaluation not because "frugal" is negatively valenced, but because the context is such that what is uttered or thought is negative, such as in "He is frugal to the extent of stinginess." In this example, what would be expressed is that the person is too frugal, so that it is not a surprise, given what we have seen above, that the sentence conveys a negative evaluation. The context might also provide a particular standard relative to which the standard valence of a term or concepts appears inverted. Thus, given a particular context, the sentence "He is frugal" might have to be understood as "He is a frugal college master." Thus, the reply that makes use of free enrichment reinforces the one that is based on the distinction between attributive and predicative uses.

If this is on the right lines, there are several explanations of the apparent variability in valence, some of which are cashed out in terms of mechanisms that work together, such as free enrichment and relativization to a standard. Of course, it cannot be excluded that some examples cannot be explained by the working of these mechanisms, but the onus lies with the advocate of the variability argument to make their case. As things stands, it is safe to assume that affective terms and concepts are inherently evaluative. It follows that value-emotion equivalences are not threatened by worries about the evaluative status of affective concepts.[28]

5.3. Conclusion

It is not only difficult to deny that affective concepts such as *admirable, shameful*, and *disgusting* are intimately related to emotions, but as we have seen, there are reasons to believe that such concepts are conceptually tied to emotion concepts. There are obvious lexical ties between the corresponding terms. Moreover, the formal objects of emotions are picked out by affective concepts. And finally, putative affective properties and emotions share important structural traits. According to a plausible suggestion, the relation between affective concepts and emotions can be expressed in the form of what I have called value-emotion equivalences, according to which something falls under an affective concept if and only if feeling the corresponding emotion is appropriate in response to that thing. As was underlined, there are quite different ways to read such biconditionals, and their plausibility varies depend on how they are understood. What I have argued is that the representational interpretation, according to which an appropriate emotion is one that is correct from the epistemic point of view, has the virtue of making the wrong kind of reason objection easy to handle. It is also well supported by what appears to be a plausible account of emotions, the perceptual theory of emotions, which underlines the analogies between emotions and sensory perceptual experiences.

An important worry is whether concepts such as *admirable* are genuinely evaluative. I have argued that even though the variability considerations that are used to argue that thick terms and concepts are not inherently evaluative can easily be transposed to the case of affective concepts, these considerations fail to show that such terms and concepts are only evaluative in the pragmatic sense that they have evaluative uses. The cases in which affective terms appear to have a different valence from the standard one can be explained in terms of a number of mechanisms, such as relativization to a standard and free enrichment, so that there is no need to abandon the intuitive claim that such terms and concepts are inherently evaluative.

Before I close, I would like to flag a further worry, which is related to the fact that some evaluative concepts, such as *courageous, generous,* or *good,* seem to lack close ties to emotions. This alleged fact raises doubts about the prospect of finding value-emotion equivalences for each and every evaluative concept. The question at stake is whether all evaluative concepts have a conceptual connection to emotion concepts. This is not the place to discuss this issue in any depth, but let me sketch a possible way to handle it.

In fact, the worry splits in two. First, it concerns thick concepts, that is, concepts such as *generous* and *courageous*, which, as we have seen, are thought to combine both a descriptive and an evaluative (or more generally normative) component. The question is whether value-emotion equivalences hold for such concepts, given that it is far from obvious that such concepts are as closely related to emotions as affective concepts are. This question is related to the difficult issue concerning the relation between the descriptive and the evaluative (or normative) component. Following John McDowell (1978, 1979), many deny that thick concepts can be analyzed or disentangled into two distinct components.[29] The reason this question is related to the worry about the generality of value-emotion equivalences is due to the fact that the most obvious way to relate thick concepts and emotion concepts is by spelling out the relation between thick concepts and affective concepts. The idea is that it is because of its connection to the admirable that the courageous and the generous are connected to admiration, for instance. The question is how exactly to spell out such an idea, but in principle it appears feasible to say that an action is courageous if and only if that action has specific natural properties, such being performed in spite of a perceived threat, in virtue of which it is admirable (see Tappolet 2004).

The second part of the worry concerns the most general evaluative concepts, such as *good* or *bad*. Such thin concepts also appear to lack an obvious connection to emotion concepts, something which is a problem for the claim that evaluative concepts are, quite generally, tied to emotion concepts. One might be tempted to postulate emotions that are tailored for the good and the bad, respectively. A difficulty with this proposal is that none of the known lists of emotion kinds, whether they are drawn from folk-theorizing, from philosophy, or from other fields, mention such emotions. A more plausible way to deal with this issue is to claim that *good* and *bad* are related to positive and negative emotions. Thus, one could suggest that something is good if and only if it makes positive emotions such as admiration, joy, or pride appropriate, whereas something is bad if and only it makes negative emotions such as contempt, sadness, or shame appropriate. To assess this proposal, the main question to address is what positive and negative emotions are. This is in fact a more difficult question than it might seem to be, because what might appear to be the most natural proposals (that is, proposals in terms of hedonic tone or in terms of motivation) face serious difficulties (See Teroni and Deonna 2012). In the end, it might be that what positive emotions have in common is that they are tied to positive evaluative concepts, while negative ones are tied to negative evaluative concepts. Whether this makes for too tight a circle is a good question. In any case, the hope of specifying what is characteristic of evaluative concepts, as opposed to nonevaluative concepts, in terms of their relation to emotion concepts depends on the possibility of generalizing value-emotion equivalences.

Acknowledgment

I am grateful to Jonas Olson for his helpful comments.

Notes

1. See Jesse Prinz (2007) for the claim that moral judgments are what he calls "sentiments," that is, dispositions to undergo a number of emotions, such as shame, guilt, and resentment.
2. As Zimmerman (chapter 1 in this volume) notes, such propositions can be traced back at least to Franz Brentano (1889), who wrote: "We call something good if the love that relates to it is correct. The good in the more general sense of the word is what has to be loved with correct love" (1889: 19). More recently, see, among others, Broad 1930; Ross 1930; Ewing 1947; Wiggins 1987 [1976]; McDowell 1985; Chisholm 1986; Lemos 1994; Anderson 1993; Scanlon 1998; D'Arms and Jacobson 2000; and Zimmerman 2001.
3. According to Kenny, who is responsible for introducing the concept in contemporary emotion theory, the formal object of a state is the object under that description which must apply to it if it is possible to be in this state with respect to it (1963: 132). He claims that the description of the formal object of an emotion involves a reference to belief: one has to believe that something is dangerous in order to feel fear. In recent times, however, it has become common to claim that the formal object of an emotion is a property. Thus, de Sousa writes that "[t]he formal object of fear—the norm defined by fear for its own appropriateness—is the Dangerous" (2002: 251). More generally, see Teroni 2007.
4. By contrast, the deontic does not appear to allow for degree—things are not, it seems, more or less obligatory or forbidden. See Hume 1978 [1739-40], III, vi: 530-31; Hare 1952: 152; and Mulligan 1998.

5. Surprise might be an exception here, since it is not clear whether it is a positive or a negative emotion. One possibility is to say that there are two kinds of surprise, one positive, and one negative. See Ortony, Clore, and Collins 1988.
6. Some, like Wright (1992) and Johnston (2001), only consider dispositional or projective accounts to be response-dependent. For a more liberal take on response-dependence see D'Arms and Jacobson (2000, n. 20).
7. See Oddie, chapter 4 in this volume) for desires, and Bykvist 2009 for a survey of the different possibilities.
8. See Peacocke (1992: 89) for the same type of suggestion with respect to perceptual concepts.
9. See D'Arms and Jacobson 2000; Rabinowicz and Rønnow-Rasmussen 2004; and Zimmerman, chapter 1 in this volume.
10. In Tappolet 2011, I argue that being appropriate, in that sense, is not normative.
11. This suggestion is close to Danielsson and Olson's claim that x is good means that x has properties that provide content-reasons to favor x, where content-reasons for an attitude are reasons for the correctness of the attitude, a notion which they claim is analogous to truth (2007).
12. See Meinong 1972 [1917]; de Sousa 1987, 2002; Tappolet 1995, 2000, 2012; Johnston 2001; and Prinz 2004, 2006; Deonna 2006; Döring 2007; Goldie 2009; and Tye 2008. For critical discussions, see Deonna and Teroni 2012; and Brady 2013.
13. For nonconceptual contents, see inter alia, Evans 1982 and Peacocke 1992.
14. For critical discussion, see Deonna and Teroni 2012; Brady 2013; Dokic and Lemaire, forthcoming.
15. The same problem arises for so-called quasi-judgmental theories, according to which the cognitive states are taken to be thoughts (Greenspan 1988) or construals (Roberts 2003).
16. I'll assume here that if a term or concept is inherently evaluative, it is also inherently valenced, but see Dancy 1995: 265 for the claim that thick terms and concepts are evaluative in their meaning, but yet contextually variable in valence. For discussion, see Väyrynen 2011:11–12
17. It is not clear that it makes sense to ask whether a concept, understood as a content component of mental states, is inherently evaluative, for by contrast with terms it is not clear that a concept can be evaluative in the weak sense of allowing for evaluative usages, given a particular context. Unlike a term, a concept does not change its meaning. For the sake of argument, I will abstract from this difference between terms and concepts.
18. The notion of thick concept has been introduced by Bernard Williams (1985: 128–30).
19. According to Williams, judgments involving thick concepts are supposed to be both action-guiding and world-guided, while thin concepts are deemed merely action-guiding and more general. The question of how exactly to characterize the distinction is debated. See Gibbard 1992; Dancy 1995; Scheffler 1987; Tappolet 2004; Elstein and Hurka 2009.
20. Deontic concepts such as *right*, *wrong*, and *ought* are also taken to be thin.
21. See Kirchin 2013b (6–7), as well as more generally, Kirchin 2013a.
22. In fact, this debate is confusing, for if advocates of disentangling hold that thick concepts can be split into thinly evaluative concepts and descriptive concepts they would seem to be committed to the view that thick concepts are inherently evaluative. I am grateful to Jonas Olson for underlining this point.
23. See Väyrynen 2011 for a discussion of this and of other strategies.
24. See Ross 1930: 65; Geach 1956; as well as Zimmerman, chapter 1 in this volume.

25. According to some, such as Geach (1956) and Thomson (1992), "good" has no predicative use, but as the knowledge example manifests, this is doubtful. See Olson, chapter 3 in this volume.
26. See Hurka 1998 for a distinction between this interpretation and a "conditionality interpretation," according to which parts change their value when they enter a whole. See also Carlson, chapter 15 in this volume.
27. See Récanati 2004: ch. 2. For an application to the case of thick concepts, see Väyrynen 2011: 13.
28. For a different take on this debate, see Väyrynen 2013 for a defense of a pragmatic conception according to which thick concepts are not evaluative in virtue of their content.
29. See Elstein and Hurka 2009 for critical discussion.

References

Anderson, E. (1993). *Value in Ethics and Economics*. Cambridge: Harvard University Press.
Ayer, A. J. (1952). *Language, Truth and Logic*. New York: Dover.
Blackburn, S. (1984). *Spreading the Word: Groundings in the Philosophy of Language*. Oxford: Clarendon Press.
Blackburn, S. (1992). "Morality and Thick Concepts: Through Thick and Thin." *Proceedings of the Aristotelian Society Supplementary Volume* 56: 285–99.
Brady, M. S. (2013). *Emotional Insight*. New York: Oxford University Press.
Brentano, F. K. O. (1889). *The Origin of Our Knowledge of Right and Wrong*. London: Routledge and Kegan Paul.
Broad, C. D. (1930). *Five Types of Ethical Theory*. London: Routledge and Kegan Paul.
Bykvist, K. (2009). "No Good Fit: Why the Fitting Attitude Analysis of Value Fails." *Mind* 118 (469): 1–30.
Chisholm, R. M. (1986). *Brentano and Intrinsic Value*. New York: Cambridge University Press.
Dancy, J. (1995). "In Defense of Thick Concepts." *Midwest Studies in Philosophy* 20 (1): 263–79.
Danielsson, S., and J. Olson. (2007). "Brentano and the Buck-Passers." *Mind* 116 (463): 511–22.
D'Arms, J., and D. Jacobson (2000). "Sentiment and Value." *Ethics* 110: 722–48.
Deonna, J. (2006). "Emotion, Perception and Perspective." *Dialectica* 60 (1): 29–46.
Deonna, J. and Teroni, F. (2012). *The Emotions: A Philosophical Introduction*. New York: Routledge.
De Sousa, R. (1987). *The Rationality of Emotion*. Cambridge: MIT Press.
De Sousa, R. (2002). "Emotional Truth." *Aristotelian Society Supplementary Volume* 76: 247–63.
Dokic, J., and S. Lemaire. (Forthcoming). "Are Emotions Perceptions of Values." *Canadian Journal of Philosophy*.
Döring, S. (2007). "Seeing What to Do: Affective Perception and Rational Motivation." *Dialectica* 61 (3): 361–94.
Elstein, D. Y., and T. Hurka. (2009). "From Thick to Thin: Two Moral Reduction Plans." *Canadian Journal of Philosophy* 39 (4): 515–35.
Evans, G. (1982). *The Varieties of Reference*. Oxford: Clarendon Press.
Ewing, A. C. (1947). *The Definition of Good*. London: Macmillan.
Geach, P. T. (1956). "Good and Evil." *Analysis* 17 (2): 33–42.
Gibbard, A. (1992). "Thick Concepts and Warrant for Feelings." *Proceedings of the Aristotelian Society Supplementary Volume* 66: 267–83.

Greenspan, P. S. (1988). *Emotions AND Reasons: An Inquiry into Emotional Justification.* London: Routledge.
Goldie, P. (2001). *The Emotions: A Philosophical Exploration.* New York: Oxford University Press.
Hare, R. M. (1952). *The Language of Morals.* Oxford: Clarendon Press.
Hare, R. M. (1981). *Moral Thinking.* Oxford: Clarendon Press.
Hume, D. (1978 [1739–40]). *A Treatise of Human Nature,* 2nd ed., ed. L. A. Selby-Bigge, with text rev. and variant readings by P. H. Nidditch. New York: Oxford University Press.
Hurka, T. (1998). "Two Kinds of Organic Unity." *Journal of Ethics* 2 (4): 299–320.
James, W. (1890). *The Principles of Psychology.* Cambridge: Harvard University Press.
Johnston, M. (2001). "The Authority of Affect." *Philosophy and Phenomenological Research* 63 (1): 181–214.
Kenny, A. (1963). *Action, Emotion and Will.* London: Routledge and Kegan Paul.
Kirchin, S., ed. (2013a). *Thick Concepts.* New York: Oxford University Press.
Kirchin, S. (2013b). "Introduction: Thick and Thin Concepts." In Simon Kirchin (ed.), *Thick Concepts.* New York: Oxford University Press, 1–19.
Lange, Carl Georg (1885). "Om Sindsbevaegelser: Et Psyki-fysiologisk Studie." Kjbenhavn: Jacob Lunds. In C. G. Lange and W. James (eds.) and I. A. Haupt (trans.), *The Emotions.* Baltimore: Williams and Wilkins, 33–92. Reprinted as "The Emotions," 1922.
Lemos, N. M. (1994). *Intrinsic Value: Concept and Warrant.* New York: Cambridge University Press.
McDowell, J. (1978). "Are Moral Requirements Hypothetical Imperatives?" *Proceedings of the Aristotelian Society Supplementary Volume* 52: 13–29.
McDowell, J. (1979). "Virtue and Reason." *Monist* 62 (3): 331–50.
McDowell, J. (1985). "Values and Secondary Qualities." In T. Honderich (ed.), *Morality and Objectivity: A Tribute to J.L. Mackie.* London: Routledge & Kegan Paul, 110–29.
Meinong, A. (1972 [1917]). *On Emotional Presentation.* Trans. M.-L. Schubert Kalsi. Evanston, IL: Northwestern University Press.
Moore, G. E. (1993 [1903]). *Principia Ethica,* rev. ed., ed. T. Baldwin. New York: Cambridge University Press.
Mulligan, K. (1998). "From Appropriate Emotions to Values." *Monist* 81: 161–88.
Nussbaum, M. C. (2001). *Upheavals of Thought: The Intelligence of Emotions.* New York: Cambridge University Press.
Ortony, A., G. Clore, and A. Collins. (1990). *The Cognitive Structure of Emotions.* New York: Cambridge University Press.
Peacocke, C. (1992). *A Study of Concepts.* Cambridge: MIT Press.
Prinz, J. J. (2004). *Gut Reactions: A Perceptual Theory of Emotion.* New York: Oxford University Press.
Prinz, J. J. (2006). "Is Emotion a Form of Perception?" *Canadian Journal of Philosophy* 36 (5): 137–60.
Prinz, J. J. (2007). *The Emotional Construction of Morals.* New York: Oxford University Press.
Rabinowicz W., and T. Rønnow-Rasmussen. (2004). "The Strike of the Demon: On Fitting Pro-attitudes and Value." *Ethics* 114 (3): 391–423.
Rachels, J., and S. Rachels. (1986). *The Elements of Moral Philosophy.* New York: McGraw-Hill.
Récanati, F. (2004). *Literal Meaning.* New York: Cambridge University Press.
Roberts, R. C. (2003). *Emotions: An Essay in Aid of Moral Psychology.* New York: Cambridge University Press.

Ross, W. D. (1930). *The Right and the Good.* New York: Oxford University Press.
Scanlon, T. (1998). *What We Owe to Each Other.* Cambridge: Belknap Press of Harvard University Press.
Scheffler, S. (1987). "Morality through Thick and Thin: A Critical Notice of Ethics and the Limits of Philosophy." *Philosophical Review* 96 (3): 411–34.
Solomon, R. C. (1976). *The Passions.* Garden City, NY: Anchor Press / Doubleday.
Stevenson, C. L. (1937). "The Emotive Meaning of Ethical Terms." *Mind* 46 (181): 14–31.
Tappolet, C. (1995). "The Sense and Reference of Evaluative Terms." In J. Biro and P. Kotatko (eds.), *Frege: Sense and Reference One Hundred Years Later.* Boston: Kluwer, 113–27.
Tappolet, C. (2000). *Emotions et valeurs.* Paris : Presses Universitaires de France.
Tappolet, C. (2004). "Through Thick and Thin: Good and Its Determinates." *Dialectica* 58 (2): 207–21.
Tappolet, C. (2011). "Values and Emotions: The Prospects of Neo-sentimentalism." In Carla Bagnoli (ed.), *Morality and the Emotions.* New York: Oxford University Press, 117–34.
Tappolet, C. (2012) "Emotions, Perceptions, and Emotional Illusions." In C. Calabi (ed.), *Perceptual Illusions: Philosophical and Psychological Essays* (Houndsmill: Palgrave-Macmillan, 207–24.
Tappolet, C. (Forthcoming). "The Normativity of Evaluative Concepts." In A. Reboul (ed.), *Mind, Values and Metaphysics: Philosophical Papers Dedicated to Kevin Mulligan.* Berlin: Springer.
Teroni, F. (2007). "Emotions and Formal Objects." *Dialectica* 61 (3): 395–415.
Thomson, J. J. (1992). "On Some Ways in Which a Thing Can Be Good." *Social Philosophy and Policy* 9: 96–117.
Tye, M. (2008). "The Experience of Emotion: An Intentionalist Theory." *Revue Internationale de Philosophie* 243: 25–50.
Väyrynen, P. (2011). "Thick Concepts and Variability." *Philosophers' Imprint* 11 (1): 1–17.
Väyrynen, P. (2013). *The Lewd, the Rude and the Nasty: A Study of Thick Concepts in Ethics.* New York: Oxford University Press.
Whiting, D. (2011). "The Feeling Theory of Emotion and the Object-Directed Emotions." *European Journal of Philosophy* 19 (2): 281–303.
Wiggins, D. (1987 [1976]). "Truth, Invention, and the Meaning of Life." In *Needs, Values, Truth.* Oxford: Blackwell, 87–138.
Wiggins, D. (1987). "A Sensible Subjectivism." In *Needs, Values, Truth: Essays in the Philosophy of Value.* Oxford: Blackwell, 185–214.
Williams, B. A. O. (1985). *Ethics and the Limits of Philosophy.* Cambridge: Harvard University Press.
Wright, C. (1992). *Truth and Objectivity.* Cambridge: Harvard University Press.
Zimmerman, M. J. (2001). *The Nature of Intrinsic Value.* Lanham, MD: Rowman & Littlefield).

CHAPTER 6

NEUTRAL AND RELATIVE VALUE

GARRETT CULLITY

AMONG normative reasons for action, a distinction is commonly made between the agent-relative and the agent-neutral. The fact that I have promised to pick you up from work is a reason for me to do that; the fact that bugging your phone would violate your privacy is a reason against it. The first of these is a fact about me, and a reason just for me; the second is not a fact about me, and a reason for everyone.

A distinction can also be drawn between relative and neutral attributions of value. Suppose my daughter and your son are competing for a job and my daughter gets it. Then it would make sense for us to react differently to the same event. It would make sense for me to think that what has happened is good and to celebrate it, but for you to think it is bad and be disappointed by it. If someone else, observing this difference, were to ask which of us is correct, the right response would be to reject the question: although our judgments differ, we are not really disagreeing. It is like the kind of difference-without-disagreement that there is when a positional judgment is relative to the perspective of an observer. When one card player says that the draw pile is on the left and the other says it is on the right, it is easy to explain how both can be speaking truly: the first is saying that it is on the left-relative-to-her, the second that it is on the right-relative-to-him. The parents' judgments seem to display the same difference-without-disagreement. The job news is good-relative-to-me and bad-relative-to-you. However, not all value judgments are like this. Is the pleasure that some people get from violent pornography good or bad? When you answer that question, you do seem to be disagreeing with someone who gives a different answer. The judgment you are making, of course, is a judgment *about* only some people—those who get this kind of pleasure. But is their getting it good or bad? Different answers to that question do seem to contradict each other.[1] They cannot be reconciled by relativizing them to the evaluator (Wallace 2010: 518).

That gives us a distinction between two kinds of value judgment. We can say that the first kind makes attributions of relative value, and the second neutral value. Examining the tenability of this distinction and enquiring about its significance is the topic of the chapter.

The parents in the example just given are not agents but interested observers, so the relativity of their value judgments is not agent-relativity. However, in the literature on relative value, the main focus of attention is on *agent*-relative value, because of the bearing this has on the possibilities open to a consequentialist ethical theory.

Consequentialism, as I shall understand it here, is the broad family of ethical theories whose common feature is the claim that the rightness of an action is fully determined by its relationship to an evaluative ranking of states of affairs ("determined," in the sense that this relationship is what *makes* an action right).[2] To fill out a particular theory in this family, one must specify the relevant relationship and the evaluative ranking. How broad a range of possibilities does that leave open? If its ranking of states of affairs is relativized to agents, some writers maintain, a consequentialist theory can accommodate much of the content of moral "common sense" (Sen 1982; Dreier 1993; Louise 2004; Portmore 2005, 2011). It can recognize constraints against performing certain bad kinds of actions, even when doing so will prevent more actions of the same type from being performed by others. If the rightness of my action depends on the value relative to me of the state of affairs it produces, and its being a state of affairs in which *I* torture someone makes it very bad relative to me, it could still be wrong for me to torture someone, even to prevent two tortures. A theory of this kind also allows my personal relationships and projects to bear directly on what it is right for me to do—so that it can be right to look after the welfare of my own children when with the same amount of effort and resources I could instead have benefited a larger number of other children more greatly. Indeed, it is sometimes suggested that any consistent set of opinions about right action can be consequentialized in this way—that for any such set of opinions, it is possible to construct a consequentialist theory that endorses them (Dreier 1993: 23; Louise 2004: 536).

I turn to this issue from section 6.3, examining the viability of relative-value consequentialist theories and some of the difficulties they face. But I begin with the prior question of how we should understand the notion of relative value itself.

6.1. Relative Value and "Good for"

The existence of relative goodness is controversial. More work is needed to defend and explain it than simply to offer examples like the one above, of the parents whose children are competing. An obvious first thought is that it is not really true that the parents are reacting to "the same event." What I judge to be good is my daughter's success; what you judge to be bad is your son's failure: so we are actually attributing value to different objects, and that explains how we are not disagreeing.

However, despite the availability of that reply, the example does seem to draw our attention to something that merits further examination. Suppose we change the example, so that our children are not competing. They are applying for different, equally good jobs, and both succeed. Now two good things have happened, as both of us should be able to see. Even if your son is a complete stranger to me, I should be able to appreciate that it is a good thing that this young person has got a job. It makes sense for me to respond positively to that fact. However, it doesn't make sense for me to respond as positively to your son's news as to my daughter's. It is fitting for me to celebrate her news, but not his. Her connection to me means that I properly value her success more highly. It's not just that I do happen to value it more highly: it is more valu*able*, for me.

But how exactly are we to explain the content of claims about relative value such as these? What is the relation between the property of being good-relative-to that is attributed in such remarks, and what we are talking about when we use the ordinary English word "good" (Schroeder 2007a: § 2)? Ordinary English does not appear to have a phrase that expresses the kind of relativity that advocates of relative value believe in. It does have the phrase "good for." But none of the three different meanings that that phrase can ordinarily have seems to attribute this kind of relative value. "Object O is good for person P" can mean (1) O benefits P or (2) O serves P's purposes or (3) O is good according to P. But none of these coincides with what advocates of relative value are claiming. Perhaps my daughter's success does benefit me or serve my purposes; but whether or not that is so, neither of those things need be what I am thinking when I think that her success is good. And nor is the claim that my daughter's success is good-relative-to-me simply equivalent to the claim that, according to me, my daughter's success is good. For one thing, that fails to distinguish the relative value of my daughter's success from the neutral value of your son's—for it is also true that, according to me, his success is good too. And for another, it does not allow for the possibility of failing to recognize something's relative value. If a depressive illness leaves me unmoved by my daughter's success, that could prevent it from being good according to me, but it would not remove its relative value: it would remain celebration-worthy by me. We need to say this in order to explain how my depression would be an impairment—a failure to respond fittingly to that good event.

Some writers express thoughts about relative value by using the metaphor of an evaluative "perspective"—thereby emphasizing the analogy with the perspective-relativity of positional judgments that we noticed above. But this metaphor calls for further explanation. It needs to be shown how it makes judgments of relative value distinct from "good for" judgments of type (3).

So we need a clearer explanation of what it is for value to be relative to a valuer. The most helpful way to do that is to pursue the thought that good things are those that are fittingly favored, and that what is fittingly favored depends on the favorer (Garcia 1986; Portmore 2007).

6.2. Goodness and Fittingness

That thought is central to a distinctive and long-standing tradition of theorizing about value. Within this tradition, good things are thought of as the fitting objects of favorable responses, and bad things of unfavorable ones.[3]

In approaching that tradition, the best way to think of "fittingness" is as a name for the relationship we assert between a response-type and its object when we use evaluative words containing suffixes like "-worthy," "-able," "-ful," "-some," or "-ing": "praiseworthy," "desirable," "shameful," "awesome," "boring."[4] Saying that an action is praiseworthy is equivalent, on this usage, to saying that it is a fitting object of praise—or, as we can also say, that it calls for praise.[5] When we say this, however, some caution is required. The words containing such suffixes are not always evaluative: if you say that an event is "boring," for example, you could be saying only that it causes boredom, and not that it is boredom-*worthy*. And if we use "fittingness" to express the latter, "-worthiness" relation, it has to be acknowledged that we are departing from ordinary speech, which more often uses "fittingness" to refer to all-things-considered appropriateness. An action can be praiseworthy without praise being all-things-considered appropriate (and vice versa).[6] Nor is "fittingness" a name for the relation of being-a-normative-reason-for: we can have reasons for praising people who are not praiseworthy.[7]

However, as long as these cautionary points are borne in mind, it can be plausibly claimed that good things are those that it is fitting to respond to favorably, and bad things unfavorably. Some writers (following Brentano and Ewing) have thought of this as a fitting-response *analysis* of value; others (following Moore) reject that further claim.[8] We need not take sides on that.[9] "Fittingness" can be used as a name for the relationship that positive and negative responses bear to good and bad things, respectively; and when it is, one can assert a connection between three groups of concepts: goodness and badness, favorable and unfavorable responses, and the relational concept of fittingness—leaving it open whether or not it is plausible to claim that any one of those concepts can be analyzed in terms of the other two.[10] Favorable and unfavorable responses, one can then add, take different forms—producing, protecting, appreciating, celebrating; avoidance, protest, dislike, grief—and this allows us to give content to the thought that there are different ways in which things can be good or bad: they can be the fitting objects of different responses of these two broad kinds (Ewing 1947: ch. 5; von Wright 1963; Anderson 1993: ch. 1; Gaus 1990: §§ 13–14; Scanlon 1998: ch. 2, § 3; Rescher 1969: ch. 2; Thomson 1992).

How does this help us to make sense of relative values? To appreciate this, we can notice that, at least sometimes, fittingness is a three-place relation. In ascertaining whether an object is desirable or an alternative choiceworthy, we often have to know who is the desirer or chooser. A plate of oysters or a ticket to a public dissection may be desirable for you but not for me, if you will enjoy these things and I will not. The difference in what we enjoy makes the possession of these objects desire-worthy for you but not for me. So in this kind of case, the fittingness relation is a relation between three things: an object, a response, and a responder. But if so, we have an interpretation for relative goodness. Whenever something is a fitting object of a positive response, it is good; but fittingness, when it is a three-place relation, is relative to a responder; so in those cases, goodness is relative to a responder.[11]

With this, we have a way of making sense of the earlier parental example. My relationship to my daughter makes celebration a fitting response for me to make to her success, but not for you: it is celebration-worthy-by-me, and in that way good relative to me. How should we express this? The only phrase we seem to have available in ordinary English is "good for me"; but as we saw above, that is already used to express claims of three different kinds, (1)–(3), none of which coincides with this one. In the interests of clarity, then, it seems better to introduce a new expression, "good$_{me}$," where O is good$_{me}$ whenever O is fittingly favored by me (where "fittingness" is a name for the relation identified above).

This supplies us with an answer to the challenge of explaining the relationship between relative value and ordinary uses of the word "good." It does not proceed by searching for an expression in ordinary English that can be unambiguously used to talk about that relation. But it does find a range of evaluative expressions in ordinary English whose suffixes express a relation that is instantiated whenever something is good or bad. It is by reference to the responder-relativity of that relation that we can explain the relativity of value.

6.3. Consequentialism and Relative Value

That supplies us with a plausible interpretation of claims about relative value. It does not yet tell us how to contrast it with neutral value—we will come to that in the next section. And notice that it does not require us to be attracted to consequentialism in order to have a case for recognizing relative value: rather, it suggests that wherever a fitting favorable or unfavorable response is responder-relative, we have relative value. But now, equipped with that thought, let us examine its application to consequentialism.

Why be attracted to consequentialism? The place to begin, I think, is with the "classical" view that treats the evaluative as prior to the normative: the goodness or badness that things have is the source of the reasons there are for us to respond to them in some ways but not others.[12] Something that makes this seem attractive is the recognitional structure of our experience of goodness. You can be struck by the goodness of a piece of music, or a landscape, or a noble gesture when you encounter them. When, noticing that, it occurs to you that you ought to pay attention to the music, or protect the landscape, or emulate the gesture, that seems to be a further thought. If you say that an object is good and that you ought to look after it, you have not repeated yourself: the second, normative remark has a recommending force that is not yet present in the first, evaluative one. And the evaluative status seems prior in the order of explanation. It makes sense for you to tell me that *because* the music is so good, I ought to listen to it.

This makes views on which the evaluative is prior to the normative attractive. However, not all such views are consequentialist. Consequentialist views are those that concentrate on one kind of value bearer—a state of affairs—and hold that the rightness of action depends on its relationship to the value of states of affairs. To be a consequentialist, you need not hold that states of affairs are the sole bearers of value. But you do need to hold that states of affairs can be evaluatively ranked, and that the rightness of an action is determined by the relationship it bears to an evaluative ranking of states of affairs.

Why make this further claim? One prominent answer appeals to the plausibility of the principle:

(P) If, given all the actions you could perform and all the ways the world could be as a result, you know that one action will produce the best result, all things considered, then it is permissible.

One might doubt the principle that if your action *will* produce the best result, then it is permissible (Dreier 1993: 24–25; Portmore 2005: 98–99; Schroeder 2007a: 279). When you are acting in conditions of ignorance, perhaps it can be impermissible to do what will actually produce the best result, because of the risk of producing a terrible one.[13] But such cases are eliminated when you *know* that your action will produce a top-ranked state of affairs. If you know that, of all the ways the world could be as a result of your acting (including all of the qualities your action will have), it will all things considered be best if you perform a given action, how could that action fail to be permissible?

Principle (P) does not entail consequentialism. But consequentialism is the natural way to formulate a general theory of right action that accommodates (P), and (P) looks plausible. So this seems to confer plausibility on consequentialism.

However, when a consequentialist theory adopts a ranking of states of affairs that is not relativized to anyone, this line of argument confronts a problem. If there are constraints on permissible action of the form mentioned earlier—constraints against performing certain bad kinds of actions, even when doing so will prevent more actions of the same type from being performed by others—then that undermines the attempt to argue from (P) to a nonrelative consequentialism. The point is often put this way. If the value of states of affairs is not relativized to anyone, then however large a contribution my bad action makes to the resulting state of the world, two such actions must make a contribution that is twice as great. So (P), and consequentialism, carry the implication that it is permissible to perform any action, no matter how bad, in order to stop two similar actions from being performed by others. That seems false, so both should be rejected.

On closer inspection, though, that is too quick. Suppose your action belongs to some bad act-type *T*, and the circumstances are such that the only way to prevent two other people from *T*ing is to perform an act of type *T* yourself. Then your action will have a feature that the other two do not have: it is an action of *T*ing-to-stop-two-other-people-from-*T*ing. So the value of the state of affairs produced by your action depends on how bad *that* feature is. An unrelativized axiology could contain the structural principle: for any bad act-type *T*, *T*ing-to-stop-two-other-people-from-*T*ing is more than twice as bad.[14] A consequentialist whose axiology was structured in that way could still say that your action is impermissible.[15]

So the problem is not actually that a consequentialist view with an unrelativized axiology cannot recognize constraints against performing actions of certain types: it can.

The problem is that its constraints would have to be accompanied by matching constraints on third parties that seem implausible. To see this, imagine the following scenario. I have decided to torture one person in order to prevent two others from being tortured; you can prevent me. So there are these two alternative states of affairs:

s_1
I don't torture A.
B and C are tortured.
You prevent me from torturing A.

s_2
I torture A.
B and C are not tortured.
You don't prevent me from torturing A.

Which ranks higher? The usual view that accepts constraints on torturing will want to say both that I should not torture A to prevent B and C from being tortured, and that you should not prevent me from torturing A. I shouldn't torture someone for the sake of minimizing the number of tortures; but nor should you intervene to stop me from doing that when you will thereby maximize the number of tortures. However, a consequentialist who says the first thing must assign a higher ranking to s_1; to say the second, she must assign a higher ranking to s_2. If her axiology is unrelativized, she cannot consistently do that.

A relative-value consequentialism avoids this problem. It holds that the rightness of my action is determined by the relationship it bears to an evaluative ranking$_{me}$ of states of affairs. We have seen how to interpret such relativized rankings. For s_1 to be higher ranked$_{me}$ while s_2 is higher ranked$_{you}$ is for s_1 to be fittingly preferred by me (because it is a state of affairs in which I do not torture) while s_2 is fittingly preferred by you (because it is a state of affairs in which you minimize the number of tortures, without torturing). So a view of this kind is able to recognize constraints that target agents and not potential interveners. At the same time, it can explain the attraction of (P). For when (P) is given a relative-value interpretation, there is a powerful supporting argument for it—one that draws on the connection between goodness and fitting responses. When something is good, it is fitting to respond to it favorably. The fitting response to a state of affairs with higher value is to prefer it: when one state of affairs has a higher value than another, it is preferable. But there is a tight connection between the fittingness of preference and that of choice. Suppose I face a choice between doing A and not doing A, and I know that, all things considered, the state of affairs that will result if I do A is preferable to any state of affairs in which I do not—where "the state of affairs that will result if I do A" is understood to include my doing A. Then A must, all things considered, be more choiceworthy than not-A. When my action is included in a top-ranked state of affairs, there is no state of affairs containing an alternative action that is preferable to it, so it is no less choiceworthy than any other action, so it must be permissible.[16] The upshot is an argument for relative-value consequentialism: it is the view that best accommodates and reconciles the plausibility of both principle (P) and the recognition of "common sense" moral constraints (Portmore 2011: ch. 7).

6.4. Relative and Neutral Goodness

So we have an interpretation of relative goodness, and an explanation of how it can be used to allow for the existence of constraints within a consequentialist theory. However, what remains to be explained is how we should interpret *neutral* goodness. There is an array of different possibilities to consider: the five main ones are these.

6.4.1. Nonindexation

We might try to explain the contrast between neutral and relative goodness as a distinction between two different kinds of fittingness relation. An object has relative goodness when it participates in a three-place fittingness relation with a favorable response and a responder. But there are also fittingness relations with no responder-place, it might be claimed; and neutral goodness is what is possessed by the objects of those. To illustrate this, consider praiseworthiness. To be praiseworthy is to have a kind of goodness: the kind you have when you are the fitting object of praise. But praiseworthiness does not seem to be relative to a responder in the same way as desirability. A plate of oysters may be more desirable for you than it is for me; and if your tastes change, then they will lose the desirability (for you) that they used to have. But praiseworthiness is not like that. The praiseworthiness of Mandela's achievement does not depend on any facts about any potential praiser. Praiseworthiness, one might say, is not praiseworthiness *for* anyone in particular; it is simply a two-place relation of fittingness between praise and its object.

That suggests a first account of the difference between neutral and relative value. As applied to the ranking of states of affairs, the thought would be this. State of affairs s_1 is better$_{me}$ than s_2: it is fittingly preferred by me. But now compare s_1 and s_2 with:

s_3
I don't torture A
B and C are not tortured.

State of affairs s_3 is better than s_1 and s_2, it might be claimed, without any indexation. It is preferable, but not preferable for anyone in particular: there is a fittingness relationship between these states of affairs and preference, but the relationship has no responder-place.

However, this first proposal causes problems for relative-value consequentialism. That makes the rightness of my action dependent on its relationship to an evaluative ranking$_{me}$ of states of affairs. But on this first proposal, s_3 is not better$_{me}$ than s_1 and s_2; it is just better than s_1 and s_2, without indexation. So a relative-value consequentialist who adopts this first proposal is unable to say that, when I can act to produce s_3 instead of either s_1 or s_2, it is right to do so. But surely that action *is* right. The relative-value consequentialist needs an interpretation of neutral value on which it can affect the rankings of states of affairs that determine the rightness of action. The first proposal is unable to do that (Smith 2003: 586; Wallace 2010: 522).

In looking for a better proposal, we might turn to the literature on agent-relative and agent-neutral reasons for help. Actually, that distinction is drawn in two different ways, and they provide models for two further proposals for drawing the corresponding distinction between values.

To see this, we can return to the opening pair of examples. The fact that I have promised to pick you up from work is a reason in its favor; the fact that bugging your phone would violate your privacy is a reason against it. I explained what makes the first reason agent-relative and the second agent-neutral by saying that the first is a fact about me, and a reason just for me; the second is not a fact about me, and a reason for everyone. But that gives us two different criteria for the distinction, and they do not coincide. One makes the distinction in terms of who has the reason: just me, or everyone (Parfit 1984: 143; Broome 2013: 66; Schroeder 2007b: 104). The other makes it in terms of the content of the reason: whether it contains a certain kind of reference to the agent (Nagel 1970: 90; Nagel 1986: 152–53; McNaughton and Rawling 1995; Skorupski 1995: 49; Skorupski 2010: 63–67). To see the difference, consider this: the fact that keeping one's promises treats the promisees with respect is a reason for keeping one's promises, whoever one is. This qualifies as an agent-neutral reason on the first way of drawing the distinction: it is a reason that everyone has.[17] But in the description of the reason, there is a reference to the agent, so on the second way of drawing the distinction it counts as agent-relative.

Since "agent-neutral" and "agent-relative" are philosophers' technical terms, we should not be drawn into a spurious debate over which of these rival ways of drawing the distinction is right, but simply recognize them both and not confuse them. They provide two further models for thinking about agent-neutral values.

6.4.2. Universalization

Taking the first way of thinking about agent-neutral reasons as our model, we get this suggestion:

O is neutrally good iff $\forall x(O \text{ is good}_x)$.

O is neutrally good just when it is fittingly favored by everyone. If we say this, we can sensibly allow for context-sensitivity in determining the domain over which we are quantifying. Thus, in applying consequentialism, we might sensibly take "everyone" to comprise all moral agents, thereby excluding the actions of young children from assessment as right or wrong.

This proposal avoids the problem with (1). Now, s_3's being agent-neutrally better than s_1 and s_2 does imply that it is better$_{me}$. So this second proposal does allow the relative-value consequentialist to hold that it is right for me (and anyone else) to produce s_3 in preference to either s_1 or s_2. However, it faces a new problem. We now have a view on which, whenever O is neutrally good, it must be good$_{me}$ (along with everyone else). But it then becomes impossible to make sense of the characteristic feature of constraints: that they apply in cases where one should do what produces a state of affairs that is agent-neutrally worse. The relative-value consequentialist is trying to find a treatment of cases which meet *that* description: she does so by saying that a state of affairs that is agent-neutrally worse can be agent-relatively better. But on this second proposal, nothing can meet that description. Nothing can be agent-neutrally worse without being agent-relatively worse (Schroeder 2007a: 293).

6.4.3. No Agent-Reference

So let us see what happens if we take the other way of thinking about agent-neutral reasons as our model. That defines an agent-neutral reason as one containing a certain kind of reference to the agent who has it. We need to be careful about formulating the parallel proposal for neutral goods. The strict parallel would be:

O is neutrally good iff O makes no reference to the responder for whom it is fitting to favor O.

But the only things that are capable of referring to anything are semantic items such as words and propositions, and the minds that use them. No other good things refer to anything. This problem is not so pressing for the definition of agent-neutral reasons on which this is modeled. The "facts" that constitute our reasons can credibly (if contestably) be treated as propositions, and the question whether they refer to the agent for whom they are reasons then makes sense. The corresponding question for most good things—including states of affairs—makes no sense.

So the right way to formulate this proposal is instead:

O is neutrally good iff the properties in virtue of which O is fittingly favored can be described without a reference to the responder for whom it is fitting to favor O.[18]

Thus, state of affairs s_1 has the property of including the torture of two people: that is a fitting object of my aversion, and since that property can be described without reference to me, it is a respect in which s_1 is neutrally bad. There is a property of s_2, on the other hand—namely, *my* perpetrating a torture—that makes it especially avoidance-worthy$_{me}$. Since that property cannot be described without reference to me, it is a respect in which s_2 has relative badness.

On this proposal, there will need to be a change in our definition of relative value. Goodness relative to x, on this proposal, is not defined as goodness$_x$. Rather, both neutral and relative goodness are kinds of goodness$_x$. Neutral goodness is the kind of goodness$_x$ that something has when the properties in virtue of which it is fittingly favored by x can be described without a reference to x; relative goodness is the kind it has when they cannot.

This proposal can now avoid the problems with (1) and (2). It improves on (1) by allowing that all goodness is goodness$_x$, and thus that agent-neutral goodness can have a bearing on what it is right to do. And it improves on (2) by allowing that a state of affairs can be agent-neutrally worse while, overall, being better$_{me}$. This is possible because, since it makes relative and neutral goodness into different kinds of goodness$_{me}$, it can allow for cases in which neutral badness$_{me}$ is outweighed by relative goodness$_{me}$.

However, now there is a new problem.[19] Consider cases of proper competition: a running-race, for example, which you and I are both striving to win. In a case of this kind, a thought one might have is: "Both competitors are equally deserving. Neutrally speaking, the best outcome would be if the race is a tie, and both get first prize." However, that thought might be conditional on both of us trying our hardest to win: only then, one might think, are we deserving of the prize. The thought, then, has the following structure: my winning is best$_{me}$ (it is fittingly preferred by me), your winning is best$_{you}$, but a tie is neutrally best. The problem is that it seems coherent to think that a thought of this form could be correct in a situation in which *everyone* is in proper competition. In a situation of that kind, the equal allocation of what we are competing for would be impartially best; but there would be no individual for which that allocation is preferable, so there would be no x for which that allocation is best$_x$. Maybe there is in fact no such situation: that does not matter. The problem is that a thought of that form seems coherent, but this third account of neutral goodness cannot allow its coherence. If there can be coherent thoughts about what is neutrally best that are not thoughts about what is best$_x$ for any individual x, then this third account must be rejected too.

6.4.4. The View from Nowhere

We can turn next to Sidgwick's famous remark that "the good of any one individual is of no more importance, from the point of view (if I may say so) of the Universe, than the good of any other" (Sidgwick 1981 [1907]: 382). This thought returns us to the metaphor of "points of view" or "perspectives": just as there is my own personal evaluative perspective, there is an impersonal, objective point of view—the "view from nowhere," as Nagel puts it, from which my special attachments are no more important than anyone else's (Nagel 1986, esp. ch. 8). One way of reading Sidgwick is as distinguishing between how important my welfare subjectively seems to me from my own self-absorbed point of view, and how important it objectively *is*. Read that way, he is rejecting the idea of relative value: there is just the objective truth about the value of my welfare, and erroneous subjective opinion about its value. However, there is another direction in which to take Sidgwick's thought—the direction in which Nagel takes it. This is that there are two different evaluative perspectives that we are capable of occupying: on the one hand, my own subjective perspective, the perspective internal to my own personal concerns; and on the other, an objective perspective from which I can see those concerns as only one set among others, in comparison to which it has no special claim to importance. And this suggests a fourth way of thinking about the contrast between relative and neutral value. It amounts to a contrast between what is good$_{me}$ and what is good$_{the\ universe}$, or good$_{nowhere}$.

But unfortunately, formulating the Sidgwick-Nagel thought in that way turns it into nonsense. When the metaphor of "points of view" is given the interpretation we found for it in section 6.2 above, the idea of something's being good$_{the\ universe}$ or good$_{nowhere}$ becomes unintelligible. Goodness$_x$ is what something has when it is the fitting object of x's favorable attitude. But nothing is the fitting object of the universe's or nowhere's favorable attitude. That makes no sense.

6.4.5. Impartiality

So let us try one further thought (Suikkanen 2009). Again, this comes with a pedigree—it has its sources in Adam Smith (2002 [1759]) and Mill (1998 [1861]: ch. 2). This is the thought that:

O is neutrally good iff O is good$_{impartial\ spectator}$.

This now allows us to give a coherent interpretation to the idea of evaluation from a perspective that is removed from every set of personal concerns. The idea of something's being the fitting object of an impartial spectator's favorable attitudes does make sense. We know what it is for a person to be impartial with respect to the members of some group: it is for her attitudes and actions to be unaffected by her own personal interests, preferences, and attachments. It can of course be questioned to what extent anyone actually succeeds in attaining that state. Perhaps it is an ideal that no one actually reaches. And the notion of a spectator who observes the entire state of the world and forms impartial attitudes about that is obviously an abstraction. But it is a coherent abstraction.

This proposal needs a further refinement. There are many ways of being impartial. Some of them are unjust, and others are monstrous: a judge who decides the outcome of a lawsuit by tossing a coin is acting impartially; so is a despot who inflicts suffering on people indiscriminately. Moreover, it seems to be a mistake to go looking for *the* form that morally good impartiality takes. It takes many different forms, depending on the context. If one is deciding the distribution of a good, then proper impartiality may involve attending to needs, or desert, or talent, or entitlement, depending on what is being distributed; if one is regulating an institution, it may mean confining one's attention to whether agreed procedures have been followed, independently of any of those factors.[20] "Proper impartiality" is many different things, not just one.

That helps us to deal with a worry that theories linking goodness to the responses of an impartial spectator standardly provoke. A spectator who was completely unmoved by anything could exhibit a kind of impartiality; but her attitudes would not be a reliable guide to what is good and bad. That is the wrong kind of impartiality. It is only if the spectator is *fittingly* impartial that good things will be the objects of her favorable responses—and fitting impartiality takes many context-dependent forms, not just one. The refinement we need, then, is this:

O is neutrally good iff O is good$_{\text{fittingly impartial spectator}}$.

On this proposal, we can then revert to the original idea that goodness relative to me is goodness$_{me}$.

This gives us a proposal for distinguishing neutral from relative value that now avoids the problems with the other four proposals we have considered. It has a coherent interpretation, unlike the fourth. Unlike the second and third, it does not imply that what is neutrally worse is worse$_{me}$. It avoids the problem for the third proposal by allowing for the possibility of a competition which every competitor fittingly prefers to win outright, but which a fittingly impartial spectator would prefer to end in a tie. And it improves on the second proposal by making sense of the thought that constraints apply in cases where one should do what produces a neutrally worse outcome. State of affairs s_1 is fittingly preferred by me over s_2, since it is a state in which I perpetrate a torture, but not by a fittingly impartial spectator, since it contains more tortures. Finally, unlike the first, this proposal can explain how the fact that s_3 is neutrally better than s_1 and s_2 can help to make it right for me to produce it. If a fittingly impartial spectator would prefer s_3 to both s_1 and s_2, and there is no fact about me that explains why it is fitting for my response to be any different from that of an impartial spectator, then it will be fitting for me to prefer the same thing.

Moreover, this fifth proposal gives the relative-value consequentialist something illuminating to say about the relationship of her view to traditional, neutral-value consequentialism. At the heart of traditional consequentialism is the thought that we can identify the moral point of view with the impartial point of view. Traditional welfarism, specifying this further, identifies moral impartiality with the impartial promotion of welfare, counting the welfare of each equally; traditional utilitarianism, going further still, identifies welfare with happiness. It is its identification of morality with impartiality that explains why traditional consequentialism sees right action as determined by its relationship to a *neutral*-valued ranking of states of affairs. However, the relative-value consequentialist is also equipped with a diagnosis of what is wrong with that traditional view: it is too limited. Morality sometimes requires impartiality (of various kinds) from us; but sometimes it does not. The personal relationships I bear to other people and projects, and the role that the actions I perform play in my biography, are relevant to how it is fitting for *me* to respond to the alternatives open to me.

So this last proposal does give us an illuminating and plausible way to distinguish neutral from relative value. It allows for a kind of consequentialism to be formulated that accommodates agent-relative moral requirements and permissions. It allows my own attachments and my relationship to my own agency to have moral significance, while retaining the attraction of a theory that is structured around the acceptance of principle (P).

6.5. Is Relative-Value Consequentialism Vacuous?

We have found a satisfactory way of formulating relative-value consequentialism. Should we believe it?

One kind of reaction to that question is that stretching "consequentialism" into this relative-value form deprives it of any distinctive content. This trivializes consequentialism, since it can now accommodate any moral opinion; so someone who believes relative-value consequentialism does not believe anything substantial at all.[21]

But that is wrong. There are some opinions about what is right and what is wrong that relative-value consequentialism, no matter how far we stretch it, will not accommodate—for example, that there are moral dilemmas in which all the alternatives open to you involve acting morally wrongly.

More significantly, even if relative-value consequentialism can accommodate a very broad range of opinions about which actions are right and wrong, it still makes distinctive and contentious claims about what determines their rightness or wrongness.[22] It embraces the classical view that the evaluative is determinatively prior to the normative. So it does not simply claim that the actions there are good moral reasons for a person to perform can be matched to a corresponding axiology; it claims that there are good moral reasons to perform it *because* of its relationship to what has value. Moreover, it goes further, in restricting the determining ground of the rightness of action to the value of states of affairs. This distinguishes it from other theories that embrace the classical view. For example, it differs from Elizabeth Anderson's "rational attitude theory," which sees the rightness of action as determined by whether it expresses a rational attitude to what has value (Anderson 1993: ch. 2; 1996: 539). Her theory accepts the classical view that the evaluative is determinatively prior to the normative, but it rejects consequentialism in making the rightness of action dependent on a proper responsiveness to bearers of value other than states of affairs, and in seeing the relevant forms of responsiveness to value as not restricted to promoting it.

So relative-value consequentialism is not trivial. All the same, it may seem unexplanatory. If its governing methodology is simply to consult intuitions about right action, and use those to construct its axiology, then it cannot offer us any help in guiding our normative thought. Unless there is some independent constraint on our axiology, it cannot help us to decide which normative opinions stand up to the demand for justification and which do not. The relative-value consequentialist is someone who simply reads his deontic opinions into the formulation of his axiology and then claims to find a justification for them there.

However, that criticism, too, seems unfair. The relative-value consequentialist need not adopt a methodology in which deontic intuitions are given a special privilege. Rather, it adopts the plausible principle (P)—a principle which, as we saw, is itself justified by the connection between fitting preference and choiceworthiness—as a constraint on the construction of a coherent ethical theory. It can then allow us to begin from independent considered judgments about both value and rightness, and invoke (P) to impose a constraint of coherence on the value- and rightness-judgments that can be reconciled with each other. This can allow it to adopt a sensible methodology that permits the mutual adjustment of judgments of both kinds in the search for a stable reflective equilibrium (Portmore 2007: 63–64).

6.6. Is Relative-Value Consequentialism Plausible?

However, although those two worries can be addressed, three further powerful challenges to relative-value consequentialism remain.

The first concerns the plausibility of its determination-claim. Often, it does indeed seem true that what *makes* an action right is its relationship to the value of its outcome. Administering an anesthetic can be right because it reduces pain, and less pain is better than more. However, the corresponding determination-claim is much more dubious when a relative-value consequentialist applies it to a moral constraint.

Recall: relative-value consequentialism claims that the rightness of my action is determined by its relationship to the goodness$_{me}$ of states of affairs, and explains goodness$_{me}$ via the biconditional:

O is good$_{me}$ if and only if O is fittingly favored by me.

This does not identify the property of being good$_{me}$ with the property of being fittingly favored by me: it just says that whenever something has one of those properties it has the other. However, we have no independent grasp of what goodness$_{me}$ is except through this biconditional: goodness$_{me}$ is to be understood as the property something has when it is fittingly favored by me. And this makes goodness$_{me}$ the wrong candidate to offer as the stopping point for determination-relations. Suppose we ask, in the torture example: Why is s_1 fittingly preferred by me to s_2? It will not do to answer that this is so because s_1 is better$_{me}$ than s_2, if our only grasp of what goodness$_{me}$ is relies on the biconditional above. But nor will it do, when asked why refusing to torture A is choiceworthy, to answer that this is so because s_1 is fittingly preferred by me to s_2. Rather, the determination-relations run the other way. What makes it fitting for me to prefer s_1 to s_2 is the choiceworthiness of the actions those states of affairs contain. State s_1 is preferable because s_2 includes my performing an action that there are strong reasons (reasons of respect for humanity, one might say) not to perform. And if (for that reason), it is fitting for me to prefer s_1 to s_2, *that* is why s_1 qualifies as better$_{me}$ than s_2. So the determination-relations run in the opposite direction to the one claimed by relative-value consequentialism.

The second worry concerns the restriction that relative-value consequentialism places on the value-bearers that determine rightness: it restricts these to *states of affairs*. It need not claim that states of affairs are the only bearers of goodness$_{me}$. That would be very implausible: if goodness$_{me}$ is what something has when it is the fitting object of my favorable attitudes, then surely there are many other kinds of things that have it: persons, physical objects, pieces of music, and so on. But relative-value consequentialism says that states of affairs are the only bearers of goodness$_{me}$ that determine rightness. That distinguishes it from other versions of the classical view (such as Anderson's, as we saw above). But that seems problematic in the following way.

In answering the question, "What makes it right for me not to torture A?" a nonconsequentialist version of the classical view can appeal to the value of the person A himself, in virtue of which it is fitting that I respond to A in a range of ways that amount to treating him with respect, which include not torturing him. Relative-value consequentialism cannot give that kind of answer. It must instead appeal to the value$_{me}$ of a state of affairs in which I do not torture. It is because the world's being one in which I do not torture has the property of goodness$_{me}$—the property in virtue of which that state of affairs is fittingly preferred by me—that it is right for me not to torture A. But that makes the determinants of rightness seem too self-regarding. It says that what matters morally is whether the world turns out to contain my performing a certain kind of action. But if rightness depends on a value$_{me}$-bearer, this is an implausible candidate to choose. It is more plausible to say that the wrongness of my torturing depends on the fittingness of respect for a person than on the fittingness of preference for the world's being one in which I do not torture.

A third worry is this. How can relative-value consequentialism avoid giving morally irrelevant personal attachments and projects a bearing on moral rightness? Again, consider achievement in a competitive pursuit. Suppose you and I are engaged in a race to discover the cure for cancer. If either of us succeeds, that will be neutrally good. But if I get there first, that will be good$_{me}$; if you do, that will be good$_{you}$. Surely that does not make it morally wrong for me to allow you to beat me to discovering the cure.

By itself, that need not be seen as a deep objection to relative-value consequentialism. It is an invitation to qualify the rightness-determining relationship in such a way that the higher ranking$_{me}$ of a state of affairs sometimes makes it morally right for me to produce it, but not always. However, the deeper worry it points to is this. It seems that there are several different determinants of whether a state of affairs is fittingly preferred by me. That it is a state in which my endeavors meet with success is one such determinant; that it includes my performing an action that is morally wrong is another. So the moral quality of my action, it seems, is one (but only one) of the various determinants of whether a state of affairs is fittingly preferred by me. Again, this suggests that the determination-relation runs in the opposite direction from the one claimed by consequentialism. The wrongness of certain actions makes it fitting for me to prefer states of affairs which do not include my performing those actions; it is not because it is fitting for me to prefer states of affairs that do not include certain actions that those actions are wrong.

So although relative-value consequentialism can be coherently formulated, there are reasons to be skeptical about it. It remains true that the earlier observations about the tight connection between preference and choice make principle (P) plausible:

If, given all the actions you could perform and all the ways the world could be as a result, you know that one action will produce the best result, all things considered, then it is permissible.

However, that should lead us to question just how much support the plausibility of (P) really does give to consequentialism. Consequentialism entails (P), but the converse is not true. (P) makes no claims about the determination-relation between value and rightness. So it is actually consistent with rejecting the classical view that the evaluative is determinatively prior to the normative altogether, let alone the more particular claims about the determination of rightness through promotion-relations to states of affairs that are distinctive of consequentialism.

6.7. Conclusion

This chapter has focused on the prospects for relative-value consequentialism, since it is an interest in those prospects that has given the stimulus to recent discussions of relative and neutral value. Critics sometimes suggest that relative-value consequentialism cannot be given a satisfactory formulation that retains what is supposed to be attractive about consequentialism. I have disagreed with that criticism, but have questioned the plausibility of this kind of theory on other grounds.

However, it should not be thought that if the prospects for relative-value consequentialism are poor, that should lead us to reject the distinction between relative and neutral value itself. We saw that this distinction can be defended independently of an interest in developing a theory of that kind. It requires only recognizing that the fittingness of responses to what has value can be responder-relative, and that is something we should accept whether we are consequentialists or not.

Acknowledgments

I am grateful to Antony Eagle, Iwao Hirose, and Jonas Olson for their helpful comments on an earlier draft.

Notes

1. Some philosophers seem committed to rejecting the intelligibility of goodness-judgments such as this one. See e.g. Thomson (1997); Kraut (2007); and, for further discussion, Olson, chapter 3 in this volume.
2. As I understand it, this concept of determination is normative, not metaphysical. It is the concept of "making right" that a realist and an antirealist can both deploy when they agree that (say) what makes it right to protect freedom of association is that it respects personal autonomy.
   Broader definitions of consequentialism are possible. The one in the text makes consequentialist theories into theories of the rightness of action. Others allow for independent ethical assessment of a range of other objects by evaluating their consequences (see Pettit and Smith 2000).
3. Brentano uses the term "correct" for the same relation. See Brentano (1969 [1889]: §§ 22, 23, 27, p. 74, and appendix 9, § 13); Chisholm (1986: ch. 5); also Chisholm (1976). The same thought is expressed as a claim about "appropriate" responses by Moore (1903: 204–5), Gaus (1990: § 6), and Zimmerman (2001: 199). For the source of this way of thinking, see Aristotle (NE: 1139a24–30).
4. "Response" needs to be understood broadly here, encompassing any orientational attitude or activity—so that acting to produce some not-yet-existing good state of affairs counts as a "response" to it.
5. Equivalent, and not an explanation of it. On this usage, the claim that a praiseworthy action is a fitting object of praise is not a substantive claim.
6. This is a source of some confusion in the "fitting-attitude" tradition of thinking about value. Ewing and Broad, for example, clearly think of judgments of "fittingness" as overall verdicts of appropriateness (Ewing 1947: 132–33; Broad 1930: 164–65, 219).
7. This is the so-called wrong kind of reason problem. For discussion, see Rabinowicz and Rønnow-Rasmussen (2004).
8. For difficulties with such analyses, see D'Arms and Jacobson (2000). For a proposed dispositional analysis of the fittingness-relation itself, see Smith (2003: 591–92).
9. Nor need we take sides on T. M. Scanlon's "buck-passing" view, that value properties do not themselves give us reasons (Scanlon 1998: 95–96).
10. In talking of "favorable" and "unfavorable" responses, we can simply rely here on our pretheoretical recognition of the range of ways in which actions, feelings, and other attitudes can amount to ways of being for or against their objects. (Contrast the more restrictive usage of Zimmerman 2001: 85–86.)
11. As Campbell Brown (2011: 762) points out, we could then represent our axiology as an ordered set of centered worlds.
12. In calling this "the classical view," I follow Raz (1999: 22). I do not mean the remark in the text to be read metaphysically—as claiming that value properties are properties that their bearers have prior to and independently of our responsiveness to them—although it is compatible with that further claim.
13. See Jackson (1981: 463), Parfit (2011: vol. 1, 159), and the discussion of "outcomism" in Zimmerman, chapter 1 in this volume.
14. Someone advancing this principle is committed to the measurement of value on a ratio, and not merely an interval scale.
15. "What if two other people will T-to-stop-two-others-from-Ting unless I do that?" Then that is covered by the same principle. Call that act-type U. Then I am still doing something

the others are not: *U*ing-to-stop-two-others-from-*U*ing. And the structural principle says that that is more than twice as bad.

16. That is not to say that whenever you *ought*, all things considered, to prefer a state of affairs including a given action, you ought, all things considered, to choose that action. Counterexamples to that can be devised by introducing "the wrong kind of reasons" for preference—reasons for preferring what is not preferable. If the eccentric billionaire imagined by Gregory Kavka (1983) offers me a million dollars for forming a preference to drink a toxin, whether or not I drink it, that would give me a good reason for the preference but not the choice. However, that would not be a case in which drinking it would be prefer*able*—preference-worthy—without being choiceworthy.
17. However, on this way of making the distinction, the particular reasons that are derivable from this are agent-relative. The fact that I have promised you to help to move your books is an agent-relative reason for me to help you move them—a reason that I have but others don't. For this approach, see Schroeder (2007b: 104).
18. This proposal is made by Michael Smith (2003: 588): "neutral goods are those properties in virtue of which things are good whose characterization requires no mention of the subject to whom the property of being good is a relation"; also Wallace (2010: 523).
19. It seems equally to be a problem for the second, universalization, view.
20. For further discussion, see Cullity (2013).
21. For the view that this is not an objection to relative-value consequentialism, but rather an argument for the inescapability of consequentialism, see Dreier (1993: 23) and Louise (2004: 534).
22. As I have defined it, it makes those claims. A weaker, biconditional definition is possible: one on which consequentialist theories of right action are theories of the form, "An action is right if and only if it bears relation *R* to evaluative ranking of states of affairs *S*." Then it would still be incorrect that this trivializes consequentialism, for the reasons given in the previous paragraph. But it would at least be arguable that any plausible moral theory can be given a relative-value consequentialist form, if it is arguable that moral dilemmas are implausible.

REFERENCES

Anderson, E. (1993). *Value in Ethics and Economics*. Cambridge: Harvard University Press.
Anderson, E. (1996). "Reasons, Attitudes and Values: Replies to Sturgeon and Piper." *Ethics* 106: 538–54.
Aristotle (1999). *Nicomachean Ethics*. Trans. T. Irwin. Indianapolis: Hackett.
Brentano, F. (1969 [1889]). *The Origin of Our Knowledge of Right and Wrong*. Trans. R. M. Chisolm and E. H. Schneewind. Ed. R. M. Chisolm. London: Routledge & Kegan Paul.
Broad, C. D. (1930). *Five Types of Ethical Theory*. London: Routledge & Kegan Paul.
Broome, J. (2013). *Rationality through Reasoning*. Malden, MA: Wiley-Blackwell.
Brown, C. (2011). "Consequentialize This." *Ethics* 121: 749–11.
Chisholm, R. M. (1976). "Brentano's Theory of Correct and Incorrect Emotion." In L. L. McAlister (ed.), *The Philosophy of Brentano*. London: Duckworth, 160–75.
Chisholm, R. M. (1986). *Brentano and Intrinsic Value*. Cambridge: Cambridge University Press.
Cullity, G. (2013). "Impartiality." In H. LaFollette (ed.), *The International Encyclopedia of Ethics*. Oxford: Wiley-Blackwell.

D'Arms, J., and D. Jacobson (2000). "Sentiment and Value." *Ethics* 110: 722–48.
Dreier, J. (1993). "Structures of Normative Theories." *Monist* 76: 22–40.
Ewing, A. C. (1947). *The Definition of Good*. New York: Macmillan.
Garcia, J. L. A. (1986). "Agent-Relativity and the Theory of Value." *Mind* 95: 242–45.
Gaus, G. (1990). *Value and Justification: The Foundations of Liberal Theory*. Cambridge: Cambridge University Press.
Jackson, F. (1981). "Decision-Theoretic Consequentialism and the Nearest and Dearest Objection." *Ethics* 101: 461–82.
Kavka, G. S. (1983). "The Toxin Puzzle." *Analysis* 43: 33–36.
Kraut, R. (2007). *What Is Good and Why: The Ethics of Well-Being*. Cambridge: Harvard University Press.
Louise, J. (2004). "Relativity of Value and the Consequentialist Umbrella." *Philosophical Quarterly* 54: 518–36.
McNaughton, D., and P. Rawling (1995). "Agent-Relativity and Terminological Inexactitudes." *Utilitas* 7: 319–25.
Mill, J. S. (1998 [1861]). *Utilitarianism*. Oxford: Oxford University Press.
Moore, G. E. (1903). *Principia Ethica* Cambridge: Cambridge University Press.
Nagel, T. (1970). *The Possibility of Altruism*. Oxford: Clarendon Press.
Nagel, T. (1986). *The View from Nowhere*. New York: Oxford University Press.
Parfit, D. (1984). *Reasons and Persons*. Oxford: Clarendon Press.
Parfit, D. (2011). *On What Matters*. Oxford: Clarendon Press.
Pettit, P., and M. Smith (2000). "Global Consequentialism." In E. M. B. Hooker, E. Mason, and D. E. Miller (eds.), *Morality, Rules, and Consequences: A Critical Reader*. Edinburgh: Edinburgh University Press, 121–33.
Portmore, D. W. (2005). "Combining Teleological Ethics with Evaluator Relativism: A Promising Result." *Pacific Philosophical Quarterly* 86: 95–113.
Portmore, D. W. (2007). "Consequentializing Moral Theories." *Pacific Philosophical Quarterly* 88: 39–73
Portmore, D. W. (2011). *Commonsense Consequentialism: Wherein Morality Meets Rationality*. New York: Oxford University Press.
Rabinowicz, W., and T. Rønnow-Rasmussen (2004). "Strike of the Demon: On Fitting Pro-attitudes and Value." *Ethics* 114: 391–423.
Raz, J. (1999). "Agency, Reason and the Good." In *Engaging Reason: On the Theory of Value and Action*. Oxford: Oxford University Press, 22–45.
Rescher, N. (1969). *Introduction to Value Theory*. Englewood Cliffs, NJ: Prentice-Hall.
Scanlon, T. M. (1998). *What We Owe to Each Other*. Cambridge: Harvard University Press.
Schroeder, M. (2007a). "Teleology, Agent-Relative Value, and 'Good.'" *Ethics* 117: 265–95.
Schroeder, M. (2007b). *Slaves of the Passions*. New York: Oxford University Press.
Sen, A. (1982). "Rights and Agency." *Philosophy and Public Affairs* 11: 3–39.
Sidgwick, H. (1981 [1907]). *The Methods of Ethics*. Indianapolis: Hackett.
Skorupski, J. (2010). *The Domain of Reasons*. Oxford: Oxford University Press.
Skorupski, J. (1995). "Agent-Neutrality, Consequentialism, Utilitarianism . . . A Terminological Note." *Utilitas* 7: 49–54.
Smith, A. (2002 [1759]). *The Theory of Moral Sentiments*. Cambridge: Cambridge University Press.
Smith, M. (2003). "Neutral and Relative Value after Moore." *Ethics* 113: 576–98.
Suikkanen, J. (2009). "Consequentialism, Constraints and the Good-Relative-to: A Reply to Mark Schroeder." *Journal of Ethics and Social Philosophy* 3: 1–9.

Thomson, J. J. (1992). "On Some Ways in Which a Thing Can Be Good." In E. F. Paul, F. D. Miller, and J. Paul (eds.), *The Good Life and the Human Good*. Cambridge: Cambridge University Press, 96–117.

Thomson, J. J. (1997). "The Right and the Good." *Journal of Philosophy* 94: 273–98.

von Wright, G. H. (1963). *The Varieties of Goodness*. London: Routledge & Kegan Paul.

Wallace, R. J. (2010). "Reasons, Values, and Agent-Relativity." *Dialectica* 64: 503–28.

Zimmerman, M. J. (2001). *The Nature of Intrinsic Value*. Lanham, MD: Rowman & Littlefield.

CHAPTER 7

VALUE AND TIME

KRISTER BYKVIST

WHAT is the time of value? What is the value of time? These are the two main questions considered in this chapter. Before we attempt to answer these questions we have to make them more precise. In fact, the first main question splits into two:

Does *what* has value always have a temporal location?

Does *value itself* have a temporal location?

The second main question asks whether *temporal features* themselves can be evaluatively relevant. In order to answer this question we need to determine which temporal features can be relevant for which kind of value. The temporal features I will discuss in this chapter are duration, temporal order (being before, simultaneous, after), life-periods (childhood, adulthood, old age), and tense (past, present, future). The kinds of value I have decided to focus on are well-being (good for, bad for, better for), intrinsic value (i.e., value in virtue of intrinsic features), final value (which some think is different form intrinsic value), virtues, and moral value of persons. There are of course many other kinds of value to consider, but this list captures some of the most important kinds of value discussed in moral philosophy.

In section 7.1, I shall discuss whether all good and bad things can be said to have a temporal location. In section 7.2, I shall discuss whether value itself has a temporal location, and my main focus will be on the temporal location of the badness of death. In section 7.3, I shall turn to the question of which temporal features, if any, are evaluatively relevant.

7.1. THE TIME OF WHAT HAS VALUE

Do all good and bad things have a temporal location? No doubt many valuable things do have determinate temporal locations. I feel pleasure *now*; so this is the time at which this good occurs. I achieved the feat of climbing the highest mountain *yesterday at noon*; so this was the moment at which that good occurred. Of course, not all goods and bad occur at particular moments; some occur during *periods* of time. The classical music concert and the performance of Shakespeare's *Romeo and Juliet* are examples of goods that take some time, and thus span over several moments. It seems also possible to have goods that are *temporally scattered*. Consider for instance a desire-based theory of well-being, according to which what is good for you is that there is a correspondence between your desires and the world. On this view, it is good for you that you desire p, and p obtains. Now suppose that you desire, now, that something will happen in the future, but that in the future you will lose this desire. When exactly does this correspondence occur? It seems wrong to say that it occurs now, since at this time the object of the desire has not yet occurred. But it also seems wrong to say that it occurs tomorrow, since at this time the desire is in the past. It seems better to say that it occurs at the *fusion* of today and tomorrow, that is, the smallest possibly discontinuous time that has today and tomorrow as parts. But then we have a temporally scattered good, since its occurrence is scattered over two distinct times.

Why does it matter whether good things have temporal locations? It matters if you want to (*a*) adopt a future-oriented morality, (*b*) avoid axiological double-counting, and (*c*) make sense of momentary well-being.

7.1.1. Future-Orientedness

The temporal location of goods matter if you are *future-oriented* in the sense that you are only concerned with making the future as good as possible (see Bergström 1966: 125). In order to decide which future is best to realize, you need to know which goods will occur in the future, so you need to know the exact temporal locations of goods. For example, if you assign value to the satisfaction of desires, you should care about a satisfaction only if both the desire and its object are in the future. If the desire is in the past and you can now only realize its object, then the satisfaction does not matter since it is not wholly part of the future. I will come back to this kind future-orientedness in section 7.3.4 and show that it can generate dynamic inconsistency if we also accept a certain kind of temporal organic unities.

7.1.2. Double-Counting

The temporal location of goods matters if you want to assess the total value of a temporally extended situation, for with no clear idea about the timings of the good you may be vulnerable to *double-counting* of goods. Suppose, for instance, that you are a hedonist and thus assign value only to pleasure. (This is only for illustration. The arguments below apply to many nonhedonist axiologies.) It seem fairly easy to determine when you feel pleasure, but in order to assess the positive value of the world you need to somehow aggregate the value of all pleasures in the world. The problem is that often when you feel pleasure during a certain interval you also feel pleasure at subintervals. In fact, the intensity of your pleasure during the whole interval might fluctuate drastically from one subinterval to another. It seems thus important to be able to track these changes of intensity when assessing the total value of the pleasure felt during the whole interval. To asses the value of the pleasure you feel during the whole interval, we need to make sure that we do not first count the value of the pleasure during one subinterval, then count the value of longer subinterval that *includes* the previous one. That would be to double-count the pleasure I felt during the first subinterval. How can we avoid this double-counting?

If pleasure were always felt at *instants*, we would have an obvious answer: just look at each instant and see how intense the pleasure is at that instant. The total value of the pleasure is then equal to (or at least proportionate to) the *integral* of the intensities of the pleasure at the infinite number of instants that make up the interval. However, it is not clear that it makes sense to talk about feeling pleasure at an instant, since an instant is a *durationless moment*. It seems plausible to assume that it takes some time to feel pleasure. Even if some pleasures are instantaneous, definitely not all are. For example, the pleasure I feel when I play the last few notes of my favorite tune takes some time, namely, the time it takes to play those notes. Or, more generally, if you want to assign value to the pleasure I *take* in doing something, then since the doing takes some time, the pleasure will also take some time. We thus need another solution.

One natural option is to look at each instance of pleasure and see how long it takes and how intense it is. The total value of the pleasure is then the duration times the intensity. Note that we do not need to assume that all pleasures have the same duration. But we need to stipulate that a new pleasure begins whenever there is a change in intensity of felt pleasure.

7.1.3. Momentary Well-Being

It is a platitude that you can be well off now, and you can be better off now than you used to be in the past. This talk about *momentary* well-being presupposes that we can temporally locate what has value for you, since, as Broome (2004: 101) points out, it seems plausible to assume that "how well off a person is at a time depends only on how things are for her at that time."

There is a family of well-being theories that seem to have problems with momentary well-being. According to this family, what has value for people are certain *correspondences* between attitudes and the world (see Bradley 2009: 11–18). This correspondence can be between pleasure-takings and the world, as some hedonists would claim. They would claim that what is good for a person is that the complex fact she takes pleasure in x, and x exists. But the correspondence could also be between desires and the world, as the desire-based theories of well-being mentioned above would claim: what is good for a person is that she desires x, and x obtains. The correspondence could also be between cognitive states and the world, for one could argue that what is good for a person is that she has true beliefs, that is, that she believes *p*, and *p* is true.

One could object to all these correspondence theories that they do not provide a plausible account of momentary well-being (see Bradley 2009: 21). To illustrate the problem, let us assume the desire-based theory of well-being (but any of the others would do as well). Suppose I desire, today at noon, that x happens tomorrow at noon, but when tomorrow comes I have lost this desire. If x happens tomorrow at noon, when does the satisfaction obtain? Not today at noon, because x has not happened yet. Not tomorrow at noon, since then the desire is lost. One may suggest as we did above that the best we can say is that the satisfaction obtains at the fusion of these two times. But this answer may seem unsatisfactory because it would then seem difficult for things to go well or badly for a person at any moment. At the moment at which I have the desire for x, x does not yet obtain and thus the satisfaction does not occur. Hence the satisfaction cannot be part of my momentary well-being at this moment. When the desired object x occurs, my desire is in the past, so the satisfaction does not occur then either. Hence the satisfaction cannot be part of my momentary well-being then either.

This verdict is misleading, however, because there is an obvious reply, at least if we can make sense of a *synchronic* desires, a desire we have at one time for something to happen at that very same time. Your momentary well-being at t is determined by the desires you have at t for a thing to happen at t. (Similar moves could be made on behalf of the other correspondence theories. You are well off at a moment, if you take pleasure, at this moment, in something that happens at the same moment; or if you believe, at this moment, that p when p obtains at this moment.)

However, Bradley (2009: 23) has recently argued that this way of making sense of momentary well-being is not plausible, for he thinks that whether or not a satisfaction of a desire counts as part of one's momentary well-being at a certain time does not always depend on whether the time of the desire and the time of the object overlap at this time. He bolsters this claim by using an example from Feinberg (1993: 181–82): a woman desires something, and in one case her desire is frustrated before she dies, in another case, it is frustrated shortly after her death. Bradley agrees with Feinberg that there is little reason to think that the woman's momentary well-being is different in the two cases.

This argument is not especially convincing. The example seems to trade on the fact that the woman would not *feel* any more frustration in the first case. So, the example seems more an objection to the idea that momentary well-being can be affected by changes that are not experienced by the subject than an objection to the idea that momentary well-being is only determined by the satisfactions of synchronic desires. Hedonists would of course insist that changes in momentary well-being must involve changes in experience. But a correspondence theory, such as the desire-based theory, would not accept this experience requirement.

More generally, if changes in momentary well-being need not involve changes in experience, and value for people is assigned to compound states of affairs of the form p at t and q at t^*, it is hard to see why it is so implausible to think that whether this state of affairs affects the momentary well-being at t depends on whether t is identical to t^*. Similar reasoning applies to the notion of momentary intrinsic value. Imagine an egalitarian theory that assigns positive intrinsic value to equality, no matter whether it is experienced or not, and no matter whether the inequality is between well-being at the same time or at different times. If we deny an experience requirement on momentary intrinsic value, why would it be implausible to say that whether a compound state of affairs of the form *I am happy at t and you are equally happy at t^** adds to the momentary value at t depends on whether t is identical to t^*? If the identity holds, perfect equality between us will occur at t, which will add value to t; if the identity does not hold, this equality will not obtain at t, and, consequently, its value cannot be added to the momentary value at t.

Similarly, if we deny an experience requirement on momentary well-being, why would it be implausible to think that whether a compound state of affairs of the form *I desire, at t, x and x obtains at t^** adds to my momentary well-being at t depends on whether t is identical to t^*? If the identity holds, a desire satisfaction will occur at t, which will add value to my momentary well-being at t; if the identity does not hold, this desire satisfaction will not occur at t, and thus its value cannot be added to my momentary well-being at t.

7.1.4. Atemporal Goods

So far, we have been discussing goods that can be given a temporal location. This is not to say that these locations are always determinate. For example, if it is good to be virtuous and I work hard toward this goal, *when exactly* do I become virtuous? There does not seem to be a clear cut-off point, since the notion of being virtuous is vague. A much more radical question is whether there are goods that have *no* temporal location at all, not even an indeterminate one. If abstract entities can be good, then we will have some candidates. Here is one. It is not uncommon to be told that certain theorems in logic or mathematics are elegant, simple, and even beautiful. If these features are seen as making the theorem good, then we have a case of something that is a good but which lacks a temporal location. Of course, the written-down version of the proof does exist in time, but many logicians and mathematicians would insist that what is elegant, simple, and beautiful is the abstract formal structure itself. After all, the written-down version might be messy and difficult to read because of an unnecessary complex formalism. Also, to say that these abstract goods occur *eternally, at all times*, sounds a bit strained. Indeed, it is often assumed that one important mark of abstract things is that they lack temporal location.

One option is to say that theorems are not purely abstract in this sense, for it does seem defensible to say that they started to exist when they were first proven. After that they have no determinate temporal location, so we can say they only exist *after* they have been proven. Whether this is the right move depends on difficult questions in metaphysics of logic and mathematics. Suffice it to say here that even on this account there is no way of finding a *determinate* temporal location of these abstract goods.

Other candidates for atemporal goods include divine individuals. For example, on one popular understanding of God, he (she, it?) is a necessary being who lacks temporal location. God exists outside time and but could not fail to exist. If God is good, which seems to be the standard assumption—in fact, he is often seen as the greatest being imaginable—then we would have an example of an atemporal good. Of course, there are obvious problems with this account of God. For instance, how could he interact with his temporally located creation if he stands outside time?

A very tentative conclusion after this short discussion is therefore that it does not seem easy to find clear examples of atemporal goods without taking a controversial stand in tricky metaphysical debates about abstract entities and divine beings.

One may wonder why it matters whether there are any atemporal goods. It does matter if you want to promote what is good and you think promotion involves *causally* bringing about things (which is a natural thought). Since causation is a relation between things in time—the cause *precedes* the effect—we cannot causally bring about atemporal goods. So, they would not be goods that we can promote in this sense.

Of course, there is another more permissive notion of promotion that could be invoked, namely, the notion of what we bring about in a *counterfactual* sense. In this permissive sense, you bring about something B by doing A just in case it holds that if you were to do A, B would be the case. All atemporal goods, no matter whether they are necessary or not, can be promoted in this sense. But it should be noted that this is a very inclusive sense of promotion. In this sense, I can bring about that 2 plus 2 equals 4, and that the dinosaurs once existed, which may seem like pretty strange abilities.

Even if atemporal goods could not be promoted in any plausible sense, so that they are irrelevant for what we should do, they could still be relevant for what we should *feel* or have *attitudes* about. Atemporal goods, like beautiful mathematical theorems and God (if he exists) can still be fitting objects of pro-attitudes.

7.2. The Time of Value: The Badness of Death

So far, we have been discussing the time of what has value. Now we turn to the question of whether value itself has a temporal location. It is tricky to spell out this distinction in natural language since when we say things like "This is good now," "That was not better before," it is not clear whether we are talking about the temporal location of what is good or the temporal location of value. Also, when we talk about the temporal location of value are we talking about the temporal location of evaluative *properties*, such as the property of being good? If so, the answer would be pretty straightforward. If one accepts that evaluative properties can exist without being exemplified, evaluative properties seem to be atemporal beings. They exist, but not at any time. It is more interesting to ask whether evaluative *facts*, the fact that something is good or bad, has a temporal location.

One natural way to approach this question is to compare it to the more general question of what it means to say that a fact has a temporal location. If facts are seen as exemplifications of properties, this question is typically understood as asking for the time at which the property is *exemplified*. It is not the time of the existence of the property, but the time of the exemplification of the property that we are after when we ask for the timing of facts.

A dismissive view on these matters would say that there is *no time* at which evaluative properties are exemplified. Evaluative properties are exemplified atemporally. It is true that *what* is good often have a determinate temporal location, but the exemplification of goodness does not itself have a temporal location.

A less dismissive view would say that the time of the exemplification of an evaluative property coincides with the *time of the object* that exemplifies the evaluative property. This account seems to be adequate for at least some exemplifications of evaluative properties. For example, the time of the exemplification of intrinsic goodness of the pleasant experience I have right now is simply the time of the pleasant experience. This seems to square fairly well with how we talk about the intrinsic value of pleasant experiences: "When is the pleasure I feel now intrinsically good? Well, it is intrinsically good *now*." When the pleasure has ceased it seems natural to say that it *was* intrinsically good, not that it *is* still intrinsically good.

Things are not so easy, however, if we turn to the debate about the badness of death. Here it seems like many philosophers do think that there is a genuine question to be asked about the timing of the badness of death, when the badness in question is understood as badness *for* the person who dies. They all agree that death itself can be temporally located, but they disagree about when death *is bad* for the person who dies. Indeed, there is a much-discussed updated version of Epicurus's argument that seems to show that death cannot be bad for a person (see, for instance, Bradley 2009: 73):

(1) Anything that is bad for a person must be bad for that person at a particular time.
(2) There is no time at which a person's death is bad for her.

So

(3) Death is not bad for a person.

Premises (1) and (2) talk about "bad for a person at a particular time," but, as I have said, the question is not about when the bad thing, death, occurs, but about the temporally location of badness itself. Premise (1) assumes that there is always such a temporal location for badness, and premise (2) says that there is no time at which death is bad.

Premise (2) is often argued for by pointing out that it does not seem plausible to say that your death is bad for you *before* you die, because that is too early. It is not plausible to say that death is bad for you *when* you are dead, because that is too late; there is then no you for whom it could be bad (it is assumed that you cease to exist when you die).

Bradley (2009: 73–111) has recently questioned this argument for (2). Bradley thinks that the badness of many illnesses and injuries is temporally locatable. He gives the example of his toe-stubbing that caused him to feel pain for a week. Bradley thinks it is obvious that his toe-stubbing was bad for him during this week. Now, Bradley concedes that death might be bad in timeless ways, but he insists that it is also bad in the way his toe-stubbing was bad, that is, in a timeful way. So he blocks the argument by rejecting premise (2) and starts looking for a suitable time for the badness of death.

In order to know what we are looking for we need to know what Bradley means by saying that his toe-stubbing was bad for him at a certain time (or during a certain period). It is tempting to understand him as saying that a harmful *effect* of the toe-stubbing occurred at this time (or period). As Bradley himself says about his toe-stubbing, "The duration of the harm is limited and, in principle, easily locatable" (Bradley 2009: 74). Note that "the harm" is here naturally understood as referring to the harmful effect, that is, the painful experiences. However, this is, in fact, not what Bradley has in mind, for he wants to deny that death has any intrinsically bad effects for the dead person. Later in the chapter (Bradley 2009: 88), it becomes clear that what he means by saying that his toe-stubbing was bad for him at a certain time is that his life would have been going better for him at this time had he not stubbed his toe. More exactly, Bradley means that his well-being at this time is lower than the well-being he would have enjoyed at this time, had he not stubbed his toe.

So, according to Bradley, to ask about the time of the badness of someone's death is to ask about the time of its *difference-making* badness, that is, the time at which the person is worse off because of her death. If her death is bad for her at a certain time, then her well-being at this time is lower than the well-being she would have enjoyed at this time, had she not died at this time.

Phrased in this way, the question seems to have an obvious answer: there is no time at which death is bad for you. At no time before your death are you worse off, because your death cannot make a difference to the well-being during your life. At no time at or after your death is death bad for you, because you have no well-being at all when you are dead. To avoid this conclusion, Bradley spends a lot of time defending the view that we do have a level of well-being even when we are dead and do not exist: We have *zero level* of well-being when we do not exist.

We see then that Bradley defines the timing of the badness of death in terms of the timing of the moments when we have lower well-being because of death. This means that in the end the timing of the badness of death—the timing of the fact that death is bad—is *reduced* to the timing of *what* has value for people. So, Bradley does not assume that there are irreducible timings of badness.

A general worry with Bradley's discussion of the time of the badness of death is that he seems to assume the principle that if something is bad in the difference-making sense—it would be better overall if it did not occur—then it must always make sense to ask *when* it is bad in this sense. But there are clear counterexamples to this principle. Suppose a music show would have been better if there had been an encore. Preventing the encore is bad in a difference-making sense, since it would make the show worse as a whole, but there is no future time at which the longer show with the encore is better than the shorter show without the encore. Of course, we can compare the moments of the longer show with the moments of the shorter one, but it does not make sense to compare the value of the future parts of the longer show with the value of the nonexistent future parts of the shorter show. No one would be tempted to assign zero value to the nonexistent future parts of the shorter show.

If this principle is not valid in general, why should we assume that it is valid in the case of the badness of death (especially if we then have to assume, very controversially, that we can have a level of well-being at times we do not exist)? This may lead us to rethink the first premise in Epicurus's argument.

This is not to say that the badness of death is in no way like the badness of stubbing your toe. Both your death and your toe-stubbing are bad in a difference-making sense. Both can be bad in the sense that they prevent you from enjoying goods. Your death can prevent you from enjoying a longer and good life. Your toe-stubbing can prevent you from enjoying some good activity, such as playing football. But it is only your toe-stubbing that has a difference-making sense of badness that can be temporally located. So, the badness of death is not exactly like the badness of toe-stubbing, which seems to be a welcome result.

7.3. THE VALUE OF TIME

It is now time to turn to the question of the value of time. It is pretty obvious that temporal features can have instrumental evaluative significance. For example, it is bad to get the medication when it is too late to cure the illness. The more interesting question is whether there are any *temporal features* that can be said to be evaluatively relevant *in themselves*?

7.3.1. Duration

One obvious candidate is duration. No one would claim that duration itself is valuable (it is even hard to know what that would mean), but most would accept that duration in itself makes a difference in value in the sense that the longer a good lasts, the better it is, and the longer a bad lasts, the worse it is.

One problem with this view is that it is not clear that it can be applied to all goods and bads. First of all, some goods and bads cannot be temporally extended. For example, it is not possible to extend achievements like reaching the peak of the highest mountain, becoming fully virtuous, or finishing your magnum opus. These goods are *punctual* in the sense that they essentially occur at an instant or a short moment.

Second, even if a good is temporally extendable, it may not be possible to extend it without it becoming less good. For example, I could extend the music performance by adding a few more songs. But even if each song is good, the whole performance may not be better because of loss in unity and coherence. Similarly, the movie could have been longer by adding a few good scenes, but the movie as a whole would have suffered because of a slack in the narrative structure.

A more radical challenge to the idea that duration is always evaluatively relevant is that one may wonder whether *experienced* duration is sometimes more important than objective duration. Suppose that you can choose between a painful operation that will take thirty minutes and one that will take forty minutes. Unfortunately, the shorter operation can only be done if you are given a medication that will cause you to feel as if it is takes a very long time (the medication will somehow slow down your experiential world). Is it so clear that the shorter one is better for you if you will experience the objectively shorter one as much longer?

Note that even if you deny that the longer a good lasts the better it is and the longer a bad lasts the worse it is you can still maintain that *more instances* of certain kind of good is better and more instances of a certain kind of bad is worse. It is important to distinguish between prolonging the duration of a particular good and creating more goods of the same kind. For example, even though we cannot extend a particular punctual good, we can make things better by creating more punctual goods of the same kind. For example, even though you cannot extend the particular good of becoming fully virtuous with respect to benevolence and generosity, you can make yourself a better person by becoming fully virtuous with respect to *other* particular virtues, such as honesty and bravery. Similarly, even though the movie cannot be extended with some more scenes without making it worse, you can create more value by making *more movies* of the same high quality.

7.3.2. Life-Periods

Do *life-periods* have intrinsic evaluative significance? It is pretty uncontroversial that the moral value of an activity or character trait may depend on the life period in which it occurs. As Slote (1983) has pointed out, some virtues are *period-relative*. Whether a certain character trait is a virtue may depend on in which period of a person's life the character trait is displayed. For example, innocence is a virtue for the young child but not for the adult, whereas prudence is a virtue for the adult, but not for the young child. Slote goes further and argues, more controversially, that achievements in one's childhood count for less than achievements in one's prime. This is controversial, for even if it is true that the aesthetic quality of my childhood drawings is much lower than the aesthetic quality of my mature paintings, it is not clear that my childhood achievement is less impressive *as an achievement*. To judge a childhood achievement we need to take into account the limited abilities of a child. A childhood drawing of a middling aesthetic quality may very well be a more impressive achievement than an aesthetically superior drawing by a mature artist who miserably fails to realize her great potentials in her drawing.

Another way life-periods can be relevant to value is when we assess the value of equality. One general approach to the value of equality is to look at the distribution of well-being and judge it to be better if it is less unequal. Now, this way of putting it does not decide what we are comparing the well-being of. One option—the most common one, we might add—is to compare the well-being of whole *lifetimes*. But one could argue that this is not the only relevant kind of well-being equality to take into consideration. We could also ask how people compare when it comes to their *corresponding life-periods* (see McKerlie 2013: 52–87). Even if, at the moment, young people are better off than old people one may think that this is not too bad, if the old people *had* the same level of well-being, when they were young, as the young people have today, and the young people today *will*, when they are old, have the same level of well-being as the old people have today. Why should we care about the current inequality between young and old if those who are now young will experience similar unhappiness in their final years and if those who are now elderly were themselves happy in their youth? One might of course endorse this distribution because one thinks that the lifetime well-being of the young and the old will be equal in this case and that this is what matters fundamentally. The sticking point is therefore whether it is better to transfer resources from one age-group to another *merely* to create equality between their corresponding life-periods, if this would also create inequality between their current lives as well as between their complete lives. It is doubtful that we are willing to make such transfers (see McKerlie 2013: 65).

7.3.3. Temporal Order

It is fairly uncontroversial that the *temporal order* of events—one event coming before, at the same time, or after another event—affects the overall value of a sequence of events. For example, an intimate relationship that starts poorly and ends well seems better than one that starts well and ends poorly. Indeed, some would argue that a whole life that starts poorly, gets progressively better, and ends well is better than a life that starts well, gets progressively worse, and ends poorly, even if the sum of momentary well-being is the same in the two lives.

Of course, we need to be careful when we reflect on these examples, for the person in the "uphill" life may take pleasure in the fact that her life has an "uphill" shape, and the person in the "downhill" life may take displeasure in the fact that her life has a "downhill" shape. If so, the amount of pleasure and displeasure will not be the same in the two lives. Many would insist, however, that if we control for these factors, we can see that the *overall shape* of the relationship or life makes a difference in overall value. What we have here, they would claim, is a temporal *organic unity*, a temporal whole whose overall value is not a sum of the values of its proper parts. (For more on organic unities, see Carlson's chapter 15 in this volume.)

A clearer case of a temporal organic unity would perhaps be artistic or athletic careers. It seems that artists or athletes who continue practising their art or sport way past their prime thereby decrease the overall value of their careers, even if their last performances are not bad. A relatively poor end to a fantastic career seems to decrease the overall value of the career. Hurka 2011: 179) suggests that the boxer Muhammad Ali's last fights, though clearly better an average boxing fight, were so below *his* own peak that they made his career less good.

Another case where the temporal order of events has been deemed morally important concerns the distribution of rewards, compensations, and punishments. It is common to think that it is good that people get what they deserve. If so, we need to know *when* they should get the thing they deserve. It is often assumed that a person cannot deserve to be punished before she has committed a crime, even if it is certain that she will commit the crime. Similarly, it is assumed that a person cannot deserve a reward before she has done what will merit the reward, even if it is certain that she will perform the relevant action. Finally, it is assumed that a person cannot deserve compensation for some misfortune before she has suffered the misfortune. More generally, the idea is that if S deserves x at t in virtue of the fact that S does or suffers something at t^*, then t^* cannot be later than t.

It is doubtful whether this general principle is true, however. As Feldman (1995) points out, it seems sensible to give benefits to dying children—a trip to Disneyland, for example—as a compensation for the painful death that will happen to them later. Similarly, soldiers who volunteer for suicide missions are often rewarded with honors before the mission. Of course, one could insist that it is the fact the children or the soldiers *will* die that justifies the rewards, and this is a fact that obtains in the present, but this move may sound a bit ad hoc.

Temporal order can also be relevant to the value of *equality*. An alternative to comparing the lifetime well-being of people when assessing the equality value of a distribution is to compare one person's well-being at a particular time with other people's well-being at the same time, so the comparison is always between *simultaneous* states of different lives. If I am born twenty-five years before you, the well-being of my middle age will be compared with the well-being of your youth, and if there is inequality, the distribution will be judged to be worse in one respect. This view is not without supporters, since it seems intuitive to say that what matters is that some are miserable *while* others flourish. Here is an example that may bring out the attractiveness of this view (McKerlie 2013: 64):

		T1	T2	T3	T4	T5	T6
Case I	A	8	8	2	2		
	B	2	2	8	8		
Case II	A	8	8	2	2		
	B			2	2	8	8

There does not seem to be any objectionable inequality in Case II. There is no inequality at any time and the lifetime well-beings of the different people A and B are perfectly equal. On the other hand, in Case I, there is inequality between A and B at every moment from T1 to T4.

The final and much more controversial example of the relevance of temporal order concerns the *discounting* of future benefits and harms. One way to spell this discounting out is to give less weight to benefits and harms that occur *later*; that is, to give more value to earlier benefits than later benefits and less disvalue to earlier harms than later harms. It is very doubtful whether this holds water, however. As Broome (2004: 71) points out, assuming that we should be more upset about worse things, this view implies that we should be more upset when we hear about some newly discovered disaster that happened long ago, in the Middle Ages say, than to hear about a contemporary disaster. It is also doubtful whether this view captures the original intuition about discounting the future. This intuition typically comes with bias against the past and for the present. In short, the intuition is that we should discount both backward and forward in time. On this view, what matters is not whether something is earlier or later than something else but whether it is past, present, or future. (I will come back to the relevance of tense in section 7.3.5.)

7.3.4. Historical Axiologies and Future-Orientedness

Some axiologies, *historical axiologies*, we may call them, accept temporal organic unities that satisfy the following condition:

> A temporal whole *A-and-B* (where *A* precedes *B*) is better than a temporal whole *A-and-C* (where *A* precedes *C*) and *B* is *worse* than *C*. (This is a violation of a monotonicity condition on value. For more on this condition on value, see Carlson's chapter on organic unities, chapter 15 in this volume.)

Here are some samples of such axiologies:

> *Retributivism*: crime followed by punishment is better than crime followed by no punishment but punishment in itself is worse than no punishment.
> *Cross-time egalitarianism*: The compound state of affairs of Jane's being happy, today, to degree 2 and John's being happy, tomorrow, to degree 2 is better than the compound state of affairs of Jane's being happy, today, to degree 2 and John's being happy, tomorrow, to degree 10, since there is inequality in the former but not in the latter. But John's being happy, tomorrow, to degree 2 is in itself worse than John's being happy, tomorrow, to degree 10.
> *Preferentialism*: All preference satisfactions are good, and all preference frustrations are bad. Preferring today to have a certain preference frustrated tomorrow and having this preference frustrated tomorrow (i.e., having a certain second-order preference satisfied) is better than preferring today to have the preference frustrated tomorrow and not having it frustrated tomorrow (i.e., having this second-order preference frustrated); but having this first-order preference frustrated is in itself worse than not having it frustrated. I assume here that the preferentialism in question is sensitive to the intensity of preferences so that satisfactions (frustrations) of stronger preferences are better (worse). I also assume here that the second-order preference is stronger than the first-order preference.

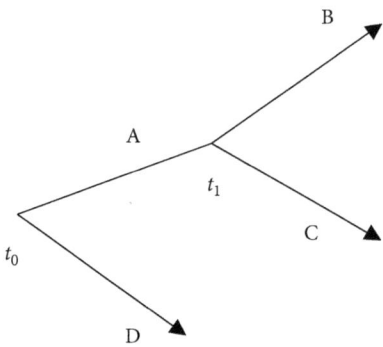

FIGURE 7.1 Dynamic Inconsistency

Historical axiologies face difficulties if they are combined with future-orientedness. They lead to *dynamic inconsistency* as the schematic example in figure 7.1 shows:

Assume a historical axiology so that A-and-B is better than both A-and-C and D, but that C is better than B. Then a future-oriented theory would tell the agent at t_0 to realize the future A-and-B. After the agent has realized A and moved to t_1, he is facing a choice between future B and future C. Since C is better than B and the past does not matter he should now realize C.

What is bad with this kind of dynamic inconsistency? One problem is that it makes it difficult for an agent to use this axiological theory as a *guide for action*. To see this, assume that in my example the agent knows that his theory tells him to do A-and-B at t_0 and C at t_1. If the agent is really committed to his theory and thus wants to do what it tells him to do not just today but also at any subsequent time, how is he supposed to decide what to do? He knows that if he does what the theory tells him to do at t_0 then he will not be able to do what the theory tells him to do at t_1. In other words, the agent seems to be trapped in a deliberative dilemma.

Can the future-oriented theories with historical axiologies avoid this problem? According to what has been dubbed the *sophisticated* approach, dynamically inconsistent theories suffer from a kind of myopia. (For more on the sophisticated approach, see Rabinowicz 1995.) When they single out the set of feasible options they do not take into consideration what the agent *will* or *would* do at future choice points. So, for instance, in my example, A-and-B is seen as a feasible option for the agent at t_0, even though he will not choose B when he reaches t_1 (assuming that he at t_1 does what he, from the standpoint of t_1, should do.) The sophisticated approach tells us to reconsider what is feasible in light of what the agent will do in the future. More exactly, the sophisticated approach assumes that the agent will do the right thing at the last choice point in each branch of the tree (and, given future-orientedness, what is the right thing to do at this point does not depend on the past relative to this point). This information is then used to determine what is feasible in the next-to-last choice in each branch. By working recursively backward in the tree we can determine what is feasible at the initial choice point. (For a more thorough characterization of this use of backward induction, see Rabinowicz 1995: 593–95.) So, in my example, A-and-B should no longer be considered feasible at t_0 since the agent is expected to deviate from this plan at t_1—remember that C is the best move at t_1. What remain as feasible options at t_0 are A-and-C and D, and whichever is better should be chosen. Thus no dynamic inconsistency is generated.

Is this a reasonable approach to take? It would be if the concept of feasibility employed were indeed the right one to adopt in the context of passing moral judgments on actions. But this is highly contentious. Recall that according to the sophisticated approach, A-and-B is not a feasible option at t_0 because if the agent were to start implementing this course of actions he would deviate from it later at t_1. But, clearly, this counterfactual truth cannot in itself decide the issue whether A-and-B is feasible in the sense proper for objective moral prescriptions. To see this more clearly, suppose it is true that if I were to go to the bank I would not withdraw money for Oxfam. Note that this does not entail that my failing to withdraw money would be a psychologically compulsive act or that refusing to withdraw money for Oxfam is a deep-rooted habit of mine. Now, if the counterfactual truth in itself showed that I cannot go to the bank and withdraw money for Oxfam, then given the principle that *ought implies can* it would follow that it is false that I ought to go to the bank and withdraw money for Oxfam. But, surely, this does not follow. It would make it absurdly easy to get off the moral hook.

A related and more general problem with the sophisticated approach is that it assumes that an ideal agent has views about what he will do in the future. It depicts the ideal agent as a *predictor* rather than a deliberator. The agent lets predictions of his future actions influence his deliberation. In this sense, he treats his future self as another person. Of course, this might be a justified attitude to take when the future self exists in the remote future and is radically different from the present one. But it is surely an odd attitude to take when the future self exists in the near future, two seconds ahead say, and shares the same psychological make-up.

In view of these difficulties one should seriously consider if it is worth the price to insist on the combination of future-orientedness and historical axiologies. If one adopts a historical axiology, it seems more sensible to care about the *total* state of the world rather than only the future. Why pretend that only the future matters when one knows that making the future better sometimes means making the world as a whole a worse place?

7.3.5. The Value of Tense

It is clear that we in fact are tense partial in the sense that we often care about the tensed features of certain benefits and harms. For example, we often give more weight to experiences in the near future than to experiences in the more distant future. In particular, we often try to postpone painful experiences even if this means that we will suffer more. For example, I cancel my dentist appointment today even if it will be more painful to fill my teeth in the future. Our bias is not just toward the immediate future. We discount the nearer future to a greater rate. This bias creates preference reversals, as the following example from Parfit (1992 [1984]: 159) shows:

> I decide that when, in five minutes time, I remove the plaster from my leg, I shall wrench it off at once, now preferring the prospect of a moment's agony to the long discomfort of easing the plaster off hair by hair. But when the moment comes I reverse my decision.

Not many would defend this bias as rationally or morally acceptable. Indeed, when we realize that we have this bias we often feel unease, especially since we realize that we will suffer more because of the bias: "Here I go again, easing of the plaster hair by hair. If only I could stick to my prior decision." The change of decision seems to be a kind of weakness of will or backsliding, which is often enabled by a failure to fully imagine the pain in the further future.

There is another time bias, however, that many think is rational, or at least not irrational, and that is our preference for having great pains *behind* us to having lesser pains *before* us. Consider the famous example from (Parfit 1992 [1984]: 165–66): You are in hospital for a surgery. Since you have to cooperate with the surgeons during operation, you can't have anesthetics. The operation is very painful but you will be given a pill that makes you forget about the operation. No bad side effects will come from the operation. Now suppose that you have just woken up in the hospital. Your nurse tells you that you either had an operation yesterday that was very painful and lasted for ten hours or that you will have an operation later today that will be very painful but only last for one hour. What would you prefer to be true? If you are like most people, you would prefer to have had the longer and more painful operation behind you, and, on the face of it, this does not seem irrational, even though, it is on the whole worse for you to have the longer operation rather than the shorter one.

It is important to note that our bias toward the future is not very robust. Imagine that you are comparing having one hundred hours of extreme torture behind you, which, fortunately, you will not remember, and will not leave any physical or psychological scars, or having one second of minor pain in front of you (a short moment of pain of a hang-nail, say). When the pains differ in this way we do not seem to have a clear preference for having the greater pain behind us. Indeed, when we bring in *other* people's suffering, the time bias is even weaker. Carlson (1995: 64) gives the following example. Suppose that you want a bar of chocolate, which will give you some pleasure, and that someone asks you which of the following situations you prefer: (*a*) the situation in which you enjoy the pleasure from eating the chocolate and a lot of other people suffer immensely in the past, or (*b*) the situation in which you do not enjoy this pleasure and the other people do not suffer in the past. Not many people would prefer (*a*) to (*b*), which is all good, since such a preference seems deeply immoral.

Furthermore, if we consider nonexperiential harms, things that are bad but not experienced, the time bias is weak or nonexistent. Compare having been ridiculed behind your back one hundred times in the past with the prospect of being ridiculed behind your back once later today. We seem not to have a clear preference for having the greater nonexperiential harm behind us (Brueckner and Fischer 1986). But then

Parfit's hospital example can at most show that it is not irrational or immoral to have a time bias concerning experiential harms when the past and the future harms do not differ too much.

The question now is whether this time bias can be expressed as a true evaluative claim: Is it *better* to have the greater past pain of the long operation behind you than to have the lesser future pain of the short operation before you? Here "better" could either be read as "impersonally better" or "better for." For my arguments, it does not matter which kind of betterness you have in mind. For ease of exposition, I shall use "great past pain" as short for "the greater past pain of the longer operation," and use "small future pain" as short for "the lesser future pain of the shorter operation." The question then is, more succinctly put, "Is great past pain and no small future pain better than small future pain and no past great pain?"

One might think that the answer is obviously no, for how can a scenario with *great* pain be better than one with *small* pain? After all, the greater a pain, the worse it is. But this reaction is based on a misunderstanding. We do not need to deny that greater pains are worse, *other things being equal*. And one could argue that other things are not equal here, since we are comparing a great *past* pain with a small *future* pain. There is a difference in tense to take into account.

One could wonder whether this means that we have to deny that the great past pain in the first scenario *would have been* worse than the future pain in the second scenario *would be*. Note that this comparison of value is both a *cross-time* and *cross-world*. We look at the past time of the first possible scenario, when the doctors are causing the person extreme pain, and assess the value, at that moment in that scenario, of the great pain, and then we look into the future time of the second scenario, when the person is undergoing a much less painful operation, and assess the value, at that moment in that scenario, of the small pain, and then, finally, we compare these two values. It seems reasonable to say that the badness of the pain at the past moment in the first scenario would be greater, since the intensity of the pain would be greater in the past moment of the first scenario than it would be in the future moment of the second scenario.

This worry also trades on a misunderstanding, however. We are not supposed to compare the *possible past* value of great past pain with the *possible future* value of small future pain, but the *present* value of the possible past great pain with the *present* value of the possible small future pain. What we want to know is whether the present badness of the possible past great pain is less than the present badness of the possible future small pain.

After these clarifications it is time to critically assess the target claim that it is better to have great past pain than small future pain.

One objection to this claim is that if we think that the present badness of a pain depends on its tense properties, whether it is past, present, or future, we are in fact saying that the value of a pain depends on features other than its *intrinsic* features. To be past, present, or future does not seem to be an intrinsic feature of a painful experience. If this is true, then we must deny that past great pain can be *intrinsically* better than small future pain. We must deny that past great pain can be, *in itself*, worse than small future pain.

There are two possible replies here. The first is to concede that great past pain cannot be intrinsically better than small future pain, but claim that it is mistake to think that intrinsic value is the same as final value. Intrinsic value is value in virtue of intrinsic features. Final value is value that is not derived from the value of anything else. There are putative examples of things that have final value but not intrinsic value. Think of a rare stamp (Kagan 1998: 277–97) or a dress that has belonged to Princess Diana (Rabinowicz and Rønnow-Rasmussen 1999: 33–52). The stamp has final value in virtue of being rare, which is not an intrinsic feature of the stamp. Similarly, Diana's dress has final value in virtue of having belonged to Diana, which is not an intrinsic feature of the dress.

The other reply is to accept that intrinsic value is the same as final value, but maintain that we need to be careful about how we define the *objects* of evaluation. When we say that the stamp has value, this is loose speaking. What we should say to be more precise is that the state of affairs *the stamp's being rare* has intrinsic value in virtue of including the property of being rare, but including such a property is an intrinsic feature of the state of affairs. So we do not have to deny the intrinsic value of the relevant states of affairs (for more on this general approach see Zimmerman 2001: 33–73). This approach can be applied to the past and future pains, as well. Instead of saying that the past pain is less bad because it is bad, we should say that the state of affairs *the great pain's being past* is less intrinsically bad, in virtue of including the tense property of being past.

A more serious objection to the target evaluative claim is that tense properties cannot be evaluatively relevant, for the simple reason that there are no such properties (or at least no such properties exemplified). Tense is only a feature of the way we *represent* the world, not a feature of the world itself. What we find in the world are times (and periods) and the relations of being earlier, being later, and being simultaneous. This is not the place to discuss these deep issues in the metaphysics of time. Here it suffices to note that we need not accept the existence of tense properties in order to take tense seriously. One option is to say that what we ascribe value to are nonperspectival facts or states of affairs under a *mode of presentation*, or under a *description*. The tenseless fact that I am in pain at t is bad under all descriptions, but it is less bad under the description "I *felt* pain at t," and more bad under the description "I *will* feel pain at t."

One problem with this option is that it does not seem to square with a more robust realism about values, according to which what has value has value no matter how you describe it or whether there are any descriptions around. (Nor does this option square well with the idea that we are talking about intrinsic value of facts, for whether a fact is represented in a certain way is not an intrinsic feature of it.)

Another option that avoids this problem is to insist that facts or states of affairs have value in themselves and not just under descriptions, but say that how much we *should care* about a state of affairs does not just depend on the value of the state of affairs but also on how they are represented. The fact that I feel pain at t is itself bad, independently of how you describe or represent this fact. But if you correctly represent this fact as "I *felt* pain at t" you have reason to care less about it than if you correctly represent it as "I *will* feel pain at t."

In order to apply this idea to the original hospital case, we also need to add the crucial assumption that even if great pain is worse than small pain, no matter when these pains occur, sometimes we have reason to care more about small pain just because we know that it is in the future and that the great pain is in the past. Hence, it is not better to have great pain behind us than small pain before us, but we have reason to care less about great pain, if we know that it is in the past and that small pain is in the future. Whether this, in the end, is an acceptable solution depends on, among other things, how value and reason to care are related. (See Zimmerman's chapter 1 in this volume, on the fitting attitude analysis of value.) Obviously, this move will not work if value is defined in terms of reason to care, but this so-called fitting attitude analysis of value has recently been the object of much criticism. But you can reject this analysis and still accept that there are strong links between values and reasons to care. For example, you can say that we always have *some* reason to care about what is bad, because it is bad, but how much we should care about it does not just depend on its degree of badness but also about whether we know it to be past, present, or future.

REFERENCES

Bergström, L. (1966). *The Alternatives and Consequences of Actions: An Essay on Certain Fundamental Notions in Teleological Ethics*. Stockholm: Almqvist & Wiksell.
Bradley, B. (2009). *Well-Being and Death*. New York: Oxford University Press.
Broome, J. (2004). *Weighing Lives*. New York: Oxford University Press.
Brueckner, A., and J. Fischer. (1986). "Why Is Death Bad?" *Philosophical Studies* 50: 213–23.
Carlson, E. (1995). *Consequentialism Reconsidered*. Boston: Kluwer.
Feinberg, J. (1993). "Harm to Others." In J. Fischer (ed.), *The Metaphysics of Death*. Stanford, CA: Stanford University Press, 171–90.
Feldman, F. (1995). "Desert: Reconsideration of Some Received Wisdom." *Mind* 104: 63–77.
Hurka, T. (2011). *The Best Things in Life: A Guide to What Really Matters*. New York: Oxford University Press.
Kagan, S. (1998). "Rethinking Intrinsic Value." *Journal of Ethics* 2: 277–98.
McKerlie, D. (2013). *Justice between the Young and the Old*. New York: Oxford University Press.
Parfit, D. (1992 [1984]). *Reasons and Persons*. New York: Oxford University Press.
Rabinowicz, W. (1995). "To Have One's Cake and Eat It Too: Sequential Choice and Expected-Utility Violations." *Journal of Philosophy* 92: 586–620.
Rabinowicz, W., and T. Rønnow-Rasmussen. (1999). "A Distinction in Value: Intrinsic and for Its Own Sake." *Proceedings of the Aristotelian Society* 100: 33–52.
Slote, M. (1983). *Goods and Virtues*. Oxford: Clarendon Press.
Zimmerman, M. (2001). *The Nature of Intrinsic Value*. Lanham, MD: Rowman & Littlefield.

CHAPTER 8

MONISM AND PLURALISM ABOUT VALUE

CHRIS HEATHWOOD

At the start of Plato's *Philebus*, Socrates sums up the two views that he and Protarchus will be discussing:

> Philebus says that the good for all animate beings consists in enjoyment, pleasure, delight, and whatever can be classed as consonant therewith, whereas our contention is that the good is not that, but . . . thought, intelligence, memory, and things akin to these, right opinion and true reasoning. (Plato 1958, 11b)

Philebus holds, in a word, that "pleasure is the good," Socrates that "knowledge is the good."[1] On each of these views, there is just *one* kind of good. Each is thus a form of *monism* about the good. A more ecumenical approach would allow that both pleasure and knowledge are good—and perhaps other things as well, such as love, beauty, and virtue. This is *pluralism* about the good.

This chapter explores some of the important facets of the contemporary debate between monism and pluralism in axiology. We will begin by explaining what value monism and pluralism are (section 8.1), and will then consider some important arguments bearing on the question (section 8.2).

Whether monism or pluralism is true may have implications for other areas of moral philosophy. For example, if pluralism is true, it may be more difficult to hold a reductionist metaethic about axiological properties. This is because goodness would then be "multiply realizable," which stands in the way of identifying it with any particular nonevaluative property. Susan Wolf (1992) argues that one kind of pluralism makes possible an attractive, moderate relativist metaethic that doesn't devolve into a troublingly expressivist or subjectivist one. Others believe that value pluralism supports a liberal political system in which there are strong protections for individual freedom.[2] Some forms of pluralism are also thought to have perplexing practical implications, for example, that in some situations none of our choices would be justified, or that in other situations, no matter what we do, there is reason to regret it. These we will discuss later.

8.1. What Are Axiological Monism and Pluralism?

One familiar kind of pluralism in moral philosophy holds that there are a plurality of basic *moral obligations*, such as those codified in the Ten Commandments or in W. D. Ross's list of prima facie duties (Ross 1988 [1930]: 19–22). This kind of pluralism competes with the monistic theories of moral obligation of Mill (1863), whose single fundamental creed is the principle of utility, and Kant (1997 [1785]), for whom the supreme principle of morality is the categorical imperative. But our topic here is not monism and pluralism about moral obligation but rather *axiology*, which studies not right and wrong but *good* and *bad*.

8.1.1. Axiological Preliminaries

We will be concerned with two axiological notions. One is the kind involved in Socrates's remarks above: judgments as to something's being good or bad *for us*. These include judgments as to someone's being well or badly off, being benefited or harmed, or having a good or a bad life. We will call these *welfare* judgments.[3]

We also make judgments as to some state of affairs or outcome being simply a good or a bad state of affairs or outcome. Unlike welfare judgments, these kinds of judgment are not explicitly relational: we are not saying that the state of affairs is good or bad *for* someone (although that is often also true, and in fact is often what makes it a good or a bad state of affairs); we are saying that it is simply a good or a bad situation. We can call these judgments of value simpliciter. They appear in ordinary language in remarks such as, "The situation in the Philippines is quite bad," and "It's a good thing that the forest didn't burn down."

Some judgments contain both axiological notions, as when it is claimed that it's a bad thing when the wicked are well off. Henry Sidgwick intuited the grander thought that "the good of any one individual is of no more importance, from the point of view (if I may say so) of the Universe, than the good of any other" (1907: 382). I'll stipulatively refer to welfare and value simpliciter as *axiological value*.

Axiological value should not be confused with moral value, a sort of value had paradigmatically by actions and agents, as when we speak of a "good deed" or a "bad man." Axiological judgments should also be distinguished from the following sorts of value judgment: "This is a good umbrella," "Thumbscrews are good for inflicting pain," "'Aubade' is a good poem," "Laticia is good at sudoku," and "Samuel Jackson was good in

Snakes on a Plane."⁴ Our focus is on the two concepts of axiological value, or "'the good' as this is often understood in philosophical discussion, . . . a notion of how it would be best for the world to go, or of what would be best for particular people" (Scanlon 1998: 79).

Another distinction in axiological value cuts across the distinction between welfare value and value simpliciter. This is the familiar distinction between *intrinsic value*, the value something has in itself or as an end, and *instrumental value*, which something has, for example, when it is a means to something with intrinsic value.⁵ It's good to have money, but having money is of course of no intrinsic benefit; if it couldn't get you anything else, it would not be worth having. Money is good insofar as having it can get you things of intrinsic value, such as, say, enjoyment (on Philebus's view) or intelligence (on Socrates's view).

In order to understand monism and pluralism, we also need to distinguish between two different ways in which a thing can be intrinsically good. Axiologists are primarily interested in discovering which things have what we can call *basic* intrinsic value, in contrast to *derivative* intrinsic value. A state of affairs has its intrinsic value *derivatively* when it has it in virtue of the intrinsic value (or values) of some more basic state of affairs (or states of affairs) of which it is composed or constituted. Perhaps the most familiar kind of entity with derivative intrinsic welfare value is a *life*. A person's life, if he is lucky, will be a good life for him. Its goodness for him will be intrinsic—it's not as if his life is good for him because of something further that it brings about for him. But its intrinsic value will be derivative, at least in part: it will be explained, at least in part, in terms of the intrinsic value of some of the components of that life, or some of the events that take place within it. And some such events will, in turn, have their intrinsic value basically or fundamentally—that is, not in virtue of values had by the more basic states that might compose them.⁶

When we are wondering whether monism or pluralism in axiology is true, we are wondering about value at the most fundamental level, that is, *basic, intrinsic* value. We are not wondering, for example, whether instrumental value is unitary or diverse, for it is uncontroversial that it is diverse. Even if just one kind of thing is intrinsically, basically good, for us and for the world, a plurality of different kinds of thing will tend to bring about this one kind of thing, and thus be of instrumental value.

8.1.2. Monism and Pluralism about Value Properties

We have drawn distinctions between several kinds of value: welfare, value simpliciter, moral value, and a number that we didn't label. Drawing these distinctions makes possible the first thing we might be monists or pluralists about: *value properties themselves*. In his contribution to this volume, Ralf Bader characterizes Kant as endorsing "Value Dualism" on the grounds that Kant "recognizes two distinct types of value, namely (1) moral value, and (2) prudential value" (Bader, chapter 10 in this volume). On this sort of pluralism, it's not that there is more than one morally good thing or more than one prudentially good thing (though that might also be true), it is that there is more than one value *topic*. I'll call this *pluralism about value properties*, or *value property pluralism*.[7] For value property pluralism to be true, it is not enough that we can draw distinctions in thought between the putative value properties of prudential value, value simpliciter, moral value, aesthetic value, and so on. The distinctions, or at least some of them, must be *irreducible*. That is, it must be that there is no single one of the value properties in terms of which all of the other value properties can be analyzed.

Taking into account all the evaluative categories, it would be surprising if value property monism were true. But *axiological* value property monism has a better chance of being true, since it attempts to reduce just two evaluative categories—our two axiological notions—down to one. G. E. Moore is attracted to this view (1903: § 59). Puzzled by the notion of welfare, Moore asks, "What, then, is meant by 'my own good'? In what sense can a thing be good *for me*?" He suggests that this just means "that my possession of it is good *simply*" (Moore 1903: 98). Moore is thus suggesting that we analyze welfare in terms of value simpliciter. This is one form of axiological value property monism.[8]

It is also possible to be an axiological property monist "in the other direction." That is, one might analyze intrinsic value simpliciter, a notion of which some are suspicious, in terms of welfare, about which skepticism is less common (this differential in perceived dubiousness is one motivation for such a reduction).[9] On this theory, to say that a state of affairs is intrinsically good simpliciter is just to say that it contains a positive balance of welfare.[10]

It is also possible to be an axiological property monist not because one thinks that an analysis of one axiological property in terms of the other is possible, but because one denies the very intelligibility of one of the notions, or at least denies that it has any instances. Thomas Hobbes (1991 [1651]: ch. 6) evidently rejects the notion of value simpliciter, holding that all value is value *for*.[11] Judith Thomson (2008) and Richard Kraut (2011) hold similar views today.[12] And in fact G. E. Moore is sometimes interpreted as being an eliminativist rather than a reductionist about welfare.

There is also the less parsimonious option. Henry Sidgwick, for instance, believes in both welfare and value simpliciter but does not appear to think that one is definable in terms of the other. This is connected to his well-known doctrine of the dualism of practical reason, a doctrine that troubled Sidgwick, due to its possible implications for practical decision-making (1907: 496–509; see also Bader, chapter 10 in this volume). We will discuss the practical implications of value property pluralism in section 8.2. To be sure, being a pluralist about axiological properties does not imply pluralism about which kinds of thing have each kind of value. Indeed, Sidgwick himself was a monist (what I below call a "substantive monist") about both welfare and value simpliciter (Sidgwick 1907: 3.14).

8.1.3. Substantive Monism and Pluralism

The core issue of monism versus pluralism in axiology is, for each axiological notion, whether to be a monist or a pluralist about it. To be a monist about it is to hold, to a first approximation, that there is just one kind of thing that has this kind of value, to be a pluralist that there is more than one such kind of thing. We can call these views *substantive* axiological monism and pluralism.[13]

8.1.3.1. *Substantive Monism about Welfare*

Welfare monism is, to a first approximation, the view that just one thing makes our lives better and just one thing makes our lives worse. The oldest and simplest such view is *hedonism*, the Phileban view in Plato's dialogue, which holds that pleasure is the one thing of ultimate benefit to us and pain the one thing of ultimate harm. Though hedonism about welfare is thought to be less popular than it used to be, it very much continues to be discussed, clarified, refined, and defended today, and is in any case an important starting point for theorizing about welfare (see Feldman 2003; Crisp 2006; Mendola 2006; Tännsjö 2007; and Bradley 2009: ch. 1). A similar and possibly even equivalent monistic theory claims that welfare is constituted by *happiness* (Sumner 1996; Feldman 2010).

Another well-known version of monism about welfare, probably more popular today, is *desire satisfactionism*, which holds that our lives are made better just when we get what we want (see Carson 2000; Heathwood 2005; Oddie, chapter 4 in this volume). Such a theory is often assumed by welfare economists, perhaps because it is thought to make welfare easier to measure (Sumner 1996: 113–22). Related monistic theories claim that welfare is constituted by the realization of our *aims* (Rawls 1971: 92–93, 417), or, alternatively, our *values* (Raibley 2010). Many such theories appeal not to our actual desires or aims but to our rational or idealized desires or aims.[14]

A third prominent general kind of welfare monism is *perfectionism*, which holds that what ultimately makes our lives worth living is developing those traits that are essential to and/or distinctive of us, or are simply virtues or excellences in their own right.[15] While many forms of welfare monism are *subjective* theories, in the rough sense that, according to them, our well-being consists not in what we get in life but in our attitudes about what we get, monism should not be confused with subjectivism. Perfectionism is an objective, or attitude-independent, welfare monism, as are some forms of hedonism.

8.1.3.2. *Substantive Pluralism about Welfare*

Substantive pluralism about welfare is, to a first approximation, the view that there are an irreducible plurality of basic goods (or bads) for us. The set is irreducible in the sense that nothing in the set is such that its value can be wholly explained by appeal to the value of other items in the set. In other words, each good must be put forth as both genuinely *intrinsic* and *basic*.

Although there is large overlap between the two views, pluralism about welfare should not be identified with "objective list theory" (Parfit 1984: 4). While subjective theories tend to be monist, we can imagine pluralist subjective theories, such as one that puts forth happiness, desire satisfaction, and aim achievement as its list of basic intrinsic goods. Also, if one-item lists are allowed, then objective list theories can be monistic. Hedonism is sometimes thought of as such a theory.

Which items tend to appear on pluralists' lists? Derek Parfit (though he does not commit to pluralism) mentions "the development of one's abilities, knowledge, and the awareness of true beauty" (Parfit 1984: 3). James Griffin's list comprises, roughly, accomplishment, autonomy, understanding, enjoyment, and deep personal relations (Griffin 1986: 67–68). Martha Nussbaum's list is longer still, including life, health, bodily integrity, emotional attachment, practical reason, affiliation, play, and more (Nussbaum 2000: 77–80).[16] Some forms of pluralism about welfare are pluralistic at least in part because they hold that holistic features of a person's life—such as whether the life generally improves over time, whether the life has variety, or whether tragedies early in life are redeemed by accomplishments later on—contribute directly to how good the life is (see Velleman 1991; Feldman 2004: ch. 6; Lemos 2010).

8.1.3.3. *Which Things Are Good versus What Makes Them Good*

A certain distinction in the theory of well-being is relevant to whether a theory is ultimately monistic or pluralistic. William Frankena suggests that a theory of welfare should answer not only the question of *which things* are good as ends for us but the question of *what makes* them good (Frankena 1973: ch. 5; see also Moore 2000: 78 and Crisp 2006: 622–23). In order to be truly monistic, a theory of welfare must have a monistic answer to the second question, the question of good-makers. The theory must claim that for all the things or states that are intrinsically good for us, they are all made good for us by the same single feature. A rational aim theorist might offer a list of what she takes the rational aims to be, or a perfectionist might offer a list of what he takes the human perfections to be. That these lists contain a plurality of items would not suffice to make their theories pluralistic. This is because, for each item, the fact that it is good would be explained in each case by the same one thing: its being a rational aim, or its being a human perfection. Truly pluralistic theories, by contrast, will typically hold that, for each good kind of thing on the list, it is, so to speak, its own good-maker. For example, the theory might say that not only are states of health intrinsically good states for us to be in, they are intrinsically good states for us to be in simply because they are states of health. To say that a good is its own good-maker is really just a way of saying that it is a *basic* intrinsic good.[17]

8.1.3.4. *Monism and Pluralism about Value Simpliciter*

Pluralism about value simpliciter is explicitly endorsed by G. E. Moore and W. D. Ross. Ross's list of goods is quadripartite: simplifying somewhat, it comprises virtuous disposition and action; deserved, innocent pleasure; the apportionment of pleasure and pain to the virtuous and vicious respectively; and knowledge (Ross 1988 [1930]: ch. 5). For Moore, the greatest goods are personal affection and the appreciation of what is beautiful (Moore 1903: § 113), but Moore also countenances the value of the mere existence of beautiful things (§ 50) and, with less conviction, of mere consciousness (§ 18). Ross explicitly denies that aesthetic enjoyment deserves its own place on the fundamental list. He regards it as a "a blend of pleasure with insight into the nature of the object that inspires it," and thus believes that its value is already fully accounted in his theory by the appearance of pleasure and knowledge on his list (Ross 1988 [1930]: 141).

Recent defenders of substantive pluralism about value simpliciter include Noah Lemos, whose list includes, among many of the items already receiving mention, "the flourishing of some forms of non-sentient life" (Lemos 1994: 99) and Robert Audi, who emphasizes, among other things, the intrinsic value of doing the right thing (Audi 2004). Substantive pluralism about value simpliciter is also a commitment of anyone who believes in the intrinsic, basic value of distributional goods, such as equality. Axiological egalitarians believe that although it matters how much total welfare an outcome contains, it also matters, in itself, how that welfare is distributed (see Holtug, chapter 14 in this volume).

8.1.4. Radical Pluralism: The Fragmentation of Axiological Value

We've yet to mention a third main kind of pluralism, one that is more radical—and consequently more philosophically interesting—than the views described thus far, but which is by no means a peripheral view among those who describe themselves as pluralists about value.[18] To understand the view, it helps to appreciate some of its motivations, so our discussion here will encroach on section 8.2's presentation of the arguments for the various theories. We'll consider a welfare value version of this more radical pluralism.

We begin with the substantive pluralist idea that several distinct kinds of thing—such as those appearing on the lists above—help to make our lives better. And we are impressed by two phenomena: (1) apparent *incomparability*, or how value comparisons between instances of the different goods don't always seem possible, even in principle; and (2) apparent *uncompensability*, or how losing out on an instance of one of the goods is sometimes not fully made up for by receiving a better instance of a different good. These thoughts may suggest that not even substantive pluralism is enough. For on substantive pluralism about welfare, the various good things all still have the same one kind of goodness, the one and only kind of welfare goodness that, on this view, there is. This common currency is thought to make substantive pluralism unable to accommodate the phenomena of incomparability and uncompensability. What is needed, it is thought, is the idea that each of the welfare goods is valuable *in its own way*. A loving relationship, for instance, has a loving-relationship-ish kind of welfare value, and a great achievement has a great-achievement-ish kind of welfare value. Aristotle may have had something like this in mind when he wrote, "the notions of honour and wisdom and pleasure, as being good, are different and distinct. Therefore, good is not a general term corresponding to a single Idea" (*Nicomachean Ethics* I.6, qtd. in Stocker 1990: 168).

This sort of pluralism combines the two earlier pluralisms. It is a substantive pluralism because it is not just a claim about what the value topics are; it advances substantive claims about which things in fact have value, saying that a plurality of different kinds of thing do. But it is also a kind of value property pluralism, since it holds that there are a plurality of different welfare value properties. Indeed, for each different kind of good thing, there may be a unique welfare value property that only it can have. We will call this view *radical pluralism*.[19]

Two issues concerning radical pluralism are worth thinking about further, though I have space only to mention them here. First, we should be open to the possibility that we might combine welfare value property pluralism with substantive welfare *monism*. Some have wondered whether comparability fails even on the theories ostensibly most friendly to it, such as hedonism. Franz Brentano (1902: 27) writes,

> how foolish would any one appear were he to assert that the pleasure he had in smoking a good cigar increased 127, or, let us say, 1077 times in intensity yielded a measure of the pleasure experienced by him in listening to a symphony of Beethoven or contemplating one of Raphael's madonnas!

A hedonist, the paradigm monist, might thus be tempted to say that the pleasures of cigar smoking make our lives better in a different way—in a cigar-smoking-pleasure kind of way—than do the pleasures of symphony-listening, which have symphony-listening-pleasure value. An instance of one of these goods might be thought to be incomparable to and uncompensable by an instance of the other. Such a theory, even if still in some sense a form of monism (since there is still just one overarching good-making property, *being pleasurable*), would also be a form of welfare value property pluralism.

The second issue concerning radical pluralism is that one might doubt the very coherence of the picture. As we have been discussing it, the goods that are each good in their own unique, sometimes incomparable, sometimes uncompensable, way all manage to make our lives better. That is, they are all welfare goods. Thus is there not still some general common currency of welfare value after all, standing in the way of incomparability and uncompensability? Or is the existence of the plurality of specific welfare value properties that the theory posits enough to deliver incomparability and uncompensability, despite the further existence of the generic welfare value property?

8.1.5. Further Problems in Understanding Substantive Monism and Pluralism

We have suggested that substantive monism is the view that there is just one intrinsically and basically good kind of thing and one intrinsically and basically bad kind of thing, while pluralism is the view that there is more than one of at least one of these kinds of thing. But there are problems with this characterization. One concerns how to individuate kinds. The problem works at both ends, by threatening to turn an intuitively monistic theory into pluralistic one, and threatening to turn an intuitively pluralistic theory into a monistic one.

Hedonists hold that pleasure is the good. But there are many kinds of pleasure. There are intellectual pleasures, aesthetic pleasures, gustatory pleasures, and so on. These are different kinds of thing. Thus is hedonism, the paradigmatic monistic axiology, in fact a form a pluralism, since it admits that many different kinds of thing are intrinsically, basically good? Indeed, Socrates's own description of hedonism as the view "that the good for all animate beings consists in enjoyment, pleasure, delight, and whatever can be classed as consonant therewith" might have made us wonder earlier whether it is really a monistic doctrine.

To see the problem at the other end, consider a pluralism on which both pleasure and knowledge are intrinsically, basically good. Here (perhaps) is a kind of thing: the kind *being an instance of either pleasure or knowledge*. The pleasure I experienced when drinking coffee this morning and the knowledge I acquired while reading the paper were both instances of this single good. Can this theory thus be understood to be a form of monism, since it holds, or can be understood as holding, that there is just one intrinsically and basically good kind of thing: *being an instance of either pleasure or knowledge*?

Perhaps we can resolve this problem by focusing not on the question *Which things are good?*, but, once again, on the question *What makes them good?* Consider my state of gustatory pleasure in sipping my morning coffee as well as your state of intellectual pleasure in completing a logic proof. Each of these states is intrinsically, basically good, according to hedonism. We can ask the hedonist, of each state, *What makes it good?* Although they are different kinds of state—one is a gustatory pleasure, the other an intellectual pleasure—I should think that the hedonist would give the same answer in each case, namely, *that it is a state of pleasure*. That is the reason, for each of these different kinds of state, that it is intrinsically, basically good.

But what about the following alternative explanation as to why my state of gustatory pleasure is intrinsically good: *that it is a state of gustatory pleasure*? Arguably, this would not be the correct explanation (or at least not the deepest or most basic correct explanation). It would be like saying that this state of affairs is intrinsically good *because it is a pleasure that occurred on a Tuesday*. The extra fact of its gustatory-ness or its Tuesday-ness in fact plays no role in explaining why the state is good, and thus is not, strictly speaking, a part of the explanation (or at least not part of the deepest explanation). If this is right, then this provides an account of why hedonism is a form of monism: it is a form of monism because, for each basically, intrinsically good thing, the reason (or at least the most basic reason) that it is basically, intrinsically good is the same one reason in each case: its being a state of pleasure.

The focus on good-making may also help in explaining why intuitively pluralistic theories are pluralistic. Consider again the view that both pleasure and knowledge are intrinsically basically good. Why, on this theory, is the pleasure I received when drinking coffee this morning intrinsically basically good? The answer, it would seem—or at least the deepest answer—is simply *that it is a state of pleasure*. The correct explanation would intuitively *not* be that the state is intrinsically basically good because *it is either a state of pleasure or a state of knowledge*. *It's being a pleasure* is in fact the explanation (or, again, at least the deepest explanation). Likewise for the knowledge I acquired while reading the paper: it is intrinsically basically good, on this theory, simply because it is an instance of knowledge. This axiological theory, then, is a form of pluralism because, according to it, for each basically, intrinsically good thing, there is more than one possible explanation of why it is basically intrinsically good: that it is a state of pleasure is one; that it is a state of knowledge is another.[20]

There are further classificatory puzzles that we don't have space to investigate. One concerns theories on which distinctions among the sub-kinds of a good kind are evaluatively relevant. For example, unlike simpler hedonists, J. S. Mill holds that pleasures of the intellect are intrinsically more valuable than equally intense and long-lasting pleasures of mere sensation (Mill 1863: ch. 2). Should this make Mill a pluralist? I don't know what the intuitive answer is (if there is one), but the account sketched above would presumably classify him as a monist, since presumably, for either an intellectual or a sensory pleasure, what makes it good on Mill's theory is simply *that it is a pleasure*, that is, the same one thing in each case.

8.2. Arguments for and against Monism and Pluralism

Since monism and pluralism about the same axiological notion are logically incompatible, arguments for one are necessarily arguments against the other. It is thus often arbitrary whether to describe a certain argument as an argument for (or against) pluralism as opposed to an argument against (or for) monism. Thus, in what follows, we'll simply enumerate and describe a number of arguments that bear on the topic.

8.2.1. The Straightforward Argument for Substantive Pluralism

The most straightforward, and perhaps the most common, reason to be a substantive pluralist is that there is reason to think that a certain kind of thing is intrinsically, basically good and also reason to think that a certain other kind of thing is intrinsically, basically good. Such arguments tend to appeal to basic intuitions about intrinsic value.

A nice illustration of the straightforward argument with respect to value simpliciter involves W. D. Ross's "two states of the universe" arguments (Ross 1988 [1930]: ch. 5). In one, Ross begins by aiming to show that virtuous action and disposition, such as the desire to relieve others from suffering, is intrinsically good. In support of this, Ross writes:

> It seems clear that we regard all such actions and dispositions as having value in themselves apart from any consequence. And if anyone is inclined to doubt this and

to think that, say, pleasure alone is intrinsically good, it seems to me enough to ask the question whether, of two states of the universe holding equal amounts of pleasure, we should really think no better of one in which the actions and dispositions of all the persons in it were thoroughly virtuous than of one in which they were highly vicious. (Ross 1988 [1930]: 134)

Next, Ross writes:

> It seems at first sight equally clear that pleasure is good in itself. Some will perhaps be helped to realize this if they make the corresponding supposition to that we have just made; if they suppose two states of the universe including equal amounts of virtue but the one including also widespread and intense pleasure and the other widespread and intense pain. (Ross 1988 [1930]: 135)

If these are sound arguments—and they certainly have intuitive appeal—then pluralism about value simpliciter is true.[21]

The straightforward argument is also advanced for welfare as well. In a recent paper Christopher Rice writes:

> Loving relationships ... are judged to be good for people *because* they involve reciprocal love. Similarly, meaningful knowledge is judged to be good for people *because* it involves appropriately justified beliefs about meaningful truths. (Rice 2013: 202)

Rice adds that we intuitively do *not* judge that these things are good for people merely because people have positive attitudes toward these things.

The straightforward argument is arguably stronger in the case of value simpliciter than in the case of welfare. For there is a certain widespread intuition about welfare that cuts against pluralism about welfare (because it supports subjectivism about welfare), whereas there is no corresponding intuition about value simpliciter. Peter Railton states the intuition about welfare in the following well-known passage:

> what is intrinsically valuable for a person must have a connection with what he would find in some degree compelling or attractive, at least if he were rational and aware. It would be an intolerably alienated conception of someone's good to imagine that it might fail in any such way to engage him. (Railton 1986: 9)

Another straightforward argument for pluralism about welfare appeals to Robert Nozick's famous "experience machine" thought experiment, in which we have the choice to live out the rest of our lives on a machine that feeds us convincing, pleasurable illusions (Nozick 1974: 42–45). Some people have the intuition that such a life, though more pleasant than a normal life, would be less good. This suggests that pleasure isn't the only good thing in life, and thus that pluralism about welfare is true.

However, there is an alternative, monist-friendly explanation of why the experience-machine life is less good: it contains less desire satisfaction. This explanation is monist-friendly because it is available to a desire satisfactionist. Some have argued, however, that the package of explanations on the topic provided by the pluralist is superior (Lin, forthcoming).[22]

If substantive pluralism does indeed do better justice to widely shared evaluative intuitions, as these arguments may suggest, then monists may reply by arguing that these intuitions should be rejected. One strategy is to argue for monism on other grounds (such as the arguments to be discussed below), and then to appeal to these premises to show that the anti-monistic intuitions must thus be mistaken. This would require that the premises in the pro-monistic arguments be more compelling than the anti-monistic intuitions. A more comprehensive case would include an error theory for these intuitions, or an explanation of why we would have them if they are false. Some monists have offered this. One kind of argument notes that it is a common mistake to attribute intrinsic value to highly reliable instrumental values (cf. Smart 1973). If we get pleasure or desire satisfaction whenever we gain new knowledge or appreciate great art, perhaps this causes us to judge, mistakenly, that knowledge and aesthetic appreciation are good in themselves. Another kind of error-theoretic argument claims that, for each of a number of putatively valuable things, it would be advantageous, evolutionarily or otherwise, to be disposed to believe that it has intrinsic value, even if it does not (Crisp 2006: 637–39). Such arguments must be approached by monists with caution, however, as they risk debunking all evaluative intuitions.

8.2.2. The Argument from the Explanatory Inadequacy of Substantive Pluralism

For much of what has been said so far in this chapter, we might wonder why we should even call attention to the categories of monism and pluralism in the first place. Shouldn't we just try to figure out which things are good in themselves and what makes them good? Of what philosophical significance is it whether the best theory turns out to be monistic or pluralistic? The answer is that a number of important arguments in axiology turn on precisely the issue of *how many* goods or good-makers there are, in relative abstraction from what the goods or good-makers happen to be. Thus we can be given reasons to be a monist or a pluralist relatively independently of the particular variety of monism or pluralism.

One such argument concerns the alleged explanatory inadequacy of substantive pluralism (Bradley 2009: 16; Schroeder 2012: § 2.2.1). Suppose that someone puts forth these as the basic goods: accomplishment, autonomy, understanding, enjoyment, and deep personal relations. The list seems random; a natural question is, Why these goods? If these five really are the basic, intrinsic goods, and no other candidate (virtue, self-respect, developing one's capacities, etc.) makes the list, shouldn't there be some explanation for this? If there isn't, then the theory fails to explain something that may intuitively need explaining. If there is an explanation for this, it would presumably come in the form of some criterion for inclusion on the list. Such a criterion would identify the feature that the things on the list have in virtue of which they make the list. In other words, it would be telling us the one thing that makes these things good. But then the theory, appealing as it does to a single good-making feature, would have become a form monism!

What to make of this argument? Perhaps it's possible for the true theory of welfare to be less explanatorily adequate (cf. Rice 2013: 205). If there really are an irreducible plurality of basic goods, then ipso facto the explanatory demand cannot be met. Perhaps, then, the demand is question-begging against pluralism. It might be rejoined that, surely, all else equal, the theory that leaves less unexplained is more likely to be true. The pluralist might accept this principle, but claim that not all else is equal, since pluralism better accounts for the phenomena (as reflected, for example, in the straightforward arguments above). To say this, however, is essentially to concede that pluralism has a feature that makes it less likely to be true. If that's right, then the argument from explanatory inadequacy would be a successful philosophical argument, which is not to say a decisive one.

But the pluralist may have a different reply available, a *tu quoque* reply. For we can pose the same question to the monist; we can ask her, *Why this one good?* If her single good (or single good-maker) really exhausts the list of basic goods (or good-makers), and no other candidate makes the list, shouldn't there likewise be some explanation for *that*? It's not clear that the monist will be able to answer this question any more easily than the pluralist can answer his. If so, and if the explanatory demand is just as reasonable when the good is unitary as when plural, then the explanatory adequacy argument for monism fails.[23]

8.2.3. The Argument from Uncompensability for Radical Pluralism

We caught a glimpse of the argument from uncompensability when we introduced radical pluralism above. The argument begins by calling our attention to a certain phenomenon: that in some choice situations, even when one knows that a certain option is the better option, something appealing or desirable remains about the worse option that isn't fully made up for, or compensated, by anything in the better option. As it is sometimes put, it is reasonable to regret your not getting the worse option, even though it is the worse option.

We can use a case of Michael Stocker's for illustration:

> Suppose we are trying to choose between lying on a beach and discussing philosophy—or more particularly, between the pleasure of the former and the gain in understanding from the latter. (Stocker 1990: 172)

Let's suppose that it would be a modest gain in understanding but quite a pleasant rest on the beach so that your day would go better for you if you were to lie on the beach than if you were to discuss philosophy. Still, there is something attractive about philosophical insight that is wholly missing from lazy sunbathing, so that you feel that you are sacrificing something.

Contrast this with a case in which one is choosing between, say, a medium-sized chocolate milkshake and a large chocolate milkshake.[24] Suppose it would be better to get the large milkshake. In this case, there is nothing in the medium-sized milkshake that is not made up for in the large. It would be senseless to have the sense that, in forgoing the smaller shake for the larger, one has missed out on something that is lacking in the large. Regret would be clearly irrational here. But regret does not seem so irrational in the earlier case.

What does this show? Some believe that it is evidence that a radical pluralism is true (Stocker 1990: ch. 6). On radical pluralism, if you choose the better option of lying on the beach, then, while you'll get a better day, your day will lack a certain kind of value—philosophical-understanding-value—a value property totally missing in the other option. This may explain why the regret, or the sense of having missed out on something, is reasonable. For this to be a successful argument for radical pluralism as against competing theories, it must add the further premise that competing theories cannot adequately explain why such feelings would be reasonable.

Is that further premise true? A substantive pluralism that countenances the basic value of both pleasure and understanding can certainly say, fully and literally, that there is something valuable in the worse option that is wholly absent from the better option, namely, understanding. So the question is whether, on substantive pluralism, that loss of understanding is compensated for by the (ex hypothesi more valuable) pleasure in the better option. For the argument for radical pluralism to work, the radical pluralist needs the answer to be, "Yes, substantive pluralism does imply that the loss of understanding is fully compensated for." In support of a yes answer, the radical pluralist may say that, on substantive pluralism, the choice is ultimately between two quantities of the same stuff: welfare. So just as it would be silly to regret not getting the small milkshake, so too would regret be silly in this case, if substantive pluralism is true. In support of a no answer, the substantive pluralist might advance a certain thesis about rational regret, to the effect that regret can be justified simply on the basis of the nature of the good thing itself that was missed out on—in this case the understanding itself. It need not have its own special value property; that it is a good thing and is a *different kind* of good thing is enough to make the regret for not having gotten it reasonable (cf. Hurka 1996). After all, what is worth getting and worth wanting isn't the *value property* but the valuable *thing*. So can't the valuable thing itself, rather than the value property, justify a certain attitude? Against this suggestion, the radical pluralist may insist that the less good valuable thing can justify regret only if it is *valuable in a different way* from the better option—that is, only if radical pluralism is true.

Interestingly, the argument from uncompensability seems to pose no special challenges for substantive monism beyond those it poses for substantive pluralism (cf. Hurka 1996). That is, considerations of uncompensability do not seem to favor substantive pluralism over substantive monism. It might be said that hedonistic substantive monism goes wrong in the case above because it fails to recognize the intrinsic value of understanding. That might be true, but such an argument has nothing to do with uncompensability; it is simply a version of the straightforward argument for pluralism (see section 8.2.1 above). To make the argument about substantive monism's ability to explain uncompensability, we can change the case, to one of comparing the pleasures of lying on the beach with the *pleasures* of discussing philosophy. But about such a case, it seems that whatever the substantive pluralist said above in attempting to justify the regret can be said by the substantive monist here. This is because the pleasures are so different: the pleasures of lazing on the beach are quite unlike the pleasures of discussing philosophy. Since both are good things, but are such different good things, the monist can attempt to explain the regret in just the way suggested above for the substantive pluralist.

Against the contention that considerations of uncompensability do not favor substantive pluralism over substantive monism, one might appeal to a case in which the pair of pleasures being compared are not so different in kind. But the more similar the pleasures become, the more the regret will seem irrational, as in the milkshake case. Notice, too, that if the traditional substantive monist feels that her explanation of the regret is not in the end successful, she can become a "radical monist"; that is, she can posit a plurality of value properties (lying-on-the-beach-pleasure-value, philosophical-discussion-pleasure-value, etc.), just as a substantive pluralist can (see section 8.1.4 above).

According to the reply to the uncompensability argument for radical pluralism that we have been considering, competing views can adequately explain the rationality of the regret. An alternative reply simply denies the rationality of the regret. If it really would give you a better day to lie on the beach, maybe regret would be childish or pathological. This reply can be bolstered by the observation that it is certainly rational to regret that one must choose between the two good things—that one can't have both. Perhaps when we have the thought that regret is rational in these cases, *that* is what we are thinking. But then these cases would provide no support for radical pluralism, since the competing views straightforwardly accommodate that thought (see Schaber 1999 and Klocksiem 2011).

Against this point, recall the milkshake case. Suppose that it is regrettable that we can't have *both* the medium and the large milkshake. The point above would seem to predict that we would have a tendency to confuse this regretability with regretability over not having chosen the smaller milkshake. That is, it predicts that we should have the intuition that after one has correctly chosen the large shake, it is rational to regret not having chosen the smaller one. But, as noted above, we don't have this intuition.

8.2.4. Comparability Arguments

Considerations related to value comparability have been appealed to both in support of and against pluralism. Both kinds of argument make use of the idea that there will be incomparability if, and only if, goods are plural. Incomparability occurs when there are two things that are both intrinsically, basically good, but (1) neither is better than the other and (2) nor are they equally good. They simply stand in no comparative evaluative relation at all.

Monists might use this against pluralists. They might claim that the incomparability implied by pluralism itself implies that justified choice between such goods is impossible. Because justified choice is always possible—it can never be that whatever you do, you do wrong—pluralism must be false. Pluralists, for their part, may use the idea against monists, claiming that incomparability is required to do justice to the complexity of our practical lives.

Why think that pluralism begets incomparability? First consider the following. Suppose yesterday you received both some enjoyment and some understanding. Suppose I ask, Which did you get more of, enjoyment or understanding? Plausibly, that question has no answer. It simply makes no sense to suppose that there might be more or less enjoyment in some situation than there is understanding (provided at least that there is some of each). That is like supposing that the speed of the earth might be greater than its size.

Next, notice that the analogous claim concerning things of the same kind seems to fail: it *does* make sense to think that there might be more or less enjoyment in some situation than there is enjoyment in some other situation. That two states of enjoyment are comparable in terms of quantity, while a state of enjoyment and a state of understanding are not, may suggest that the *values* of two states of enjoyment are comparable, while the *value* of a state of enjoyment and the *value* of a state of understanding are not. This is the main line of reasoning from pluralism to incomparability (Stocker 1990: 166–67).

But is this even true for every pair of enjoyments? What about Brentano's idea that it is absurd to suppose that the amount of enjoyment some person receives in listening to Beethoven might be greater, by some precise amount, than the enjoyment he receives in smoking a cigar? The failure of such relationships, which is sometimes called "incommensurability," does not in fact establish incomparability. Even if pleasures don't stand in these mathematical relations, it still might be that, for any two pleasures, either one is stronger than the other or they are equally strong. Furthermore, it is not even clear that Brentano's claims of incommensurability are true.[25]

There is another case to consider that's relevant to whether monistic theories are like pluralistic theories as regards comparability: comparing the good with the bad. Suppose yesterday you received some pleasure and some pain. Suppose I ask, Which did you get more of, pleasure or pain? Can that question be answered? There cannot be more or less pleasure than there is understanding in some situation, but can there be more or less pleasure than there is pain in some situation? For my part, I'm inclined to say yes; at the very least, I balk much less at a pleasure/pain comparison than at a pleasure/understanding comparison. Some theories of the nature of pleasure can even shed light on why. According to one such theory, pleasure is explained in terms of desire (see Spencer 1871: § 125; Brandt 1979: 38; Heathwood 2007). Roughly, pleasurable experiences are those we want to be occurring while they are occurring, and painful experiences are those we want not to be occurring while they are occurring. The comparability of pleasure and pain is then explained in terms of the comparability of the wanting involved in pleasure and the wanting involved in pain.

We have just been considering whether monism, too, might lead to value incomparability. Let's return to the argument that pluralism does. One way to resist this argument begins with the observation that if some state of enjoyment is good, there is intuitively a fact as to *how* good it is. The state of enjoyment won't just have value, it will have some specific quantity of value. And likewise for understanding: if some state of understanding has value, there will be some quantity of value that it, too, has. But then we have on our hands two quantities of the same one thing: value. And whenever one has two quantities of the same thing, it must be either that one quantity is greater or that they are equal.

This line of argument shows at most that *substantive* pluralism does not deliver incomparability, and so it points to why—repeating now a point from earlier—those pluralists who believe in incomparability are moved to be radical pluralists. If they are merely substantive pluralists, they hold that the various good things each participate in the same one kind of value, and thus open themselves to the argument of the previous paragraph. To obtain incomparability, they can become radical pluralists. They can hold that enjoyment has its own enjoyment-value, while understanding has understanding-value. Now, multiplying kinds of value in this way still may not guarantee incomparability, for there could still be some more generic value property—or "supervalue"—that subsumes the plurality of specific value properties. To secure incomparability, radical pluralism evidently needs to take an even more radical form, and hold that there is no such generic value property (if this is indeed a coherent view; see section 8.1.4 above).

A challenge for this form of radical pluralism—and more generally for the idea that pluralism implies incomparability—is "nominal-notable comparisons" (Chang 1997: 14). If understanding and pleasure are both basic goods, then surely it's better to understand Einstein's theory of relativity than it is to enjoy one lick of a lollipop. If that's right, then some instances of understanding and pleasure are comparable. If that's true, it may be difficult to sustain the thesis that not all are (which is not to deny that the answer to some questions of value comparison will be unknowable or vague).

Pluralists' attempts to secure incomparability may fail for yet another reason. It is commonly held that there is a connection between value and rational or fitting attitudes.[26] On one plausible-sounding view, if some state of affairs would be good, we have reason to want it to occur, and, moreover, to want it to occur to the degree that it is good. Chris Kelly argues from this to the impossibility of value incomparability—even granting the assumption that each good thing is good in its own way, that is, even on radical pluralism. If the plausible-sounding view above is true, then, claims Kelly, "Whether it is autonomy-value, pleasure-value, or beauty-value, if it is really value, the ideal desirer would, absent defeaters, want it" (Kelly 2008: 374). And the strength of her desire would indicate its degree of value. Since any two desires are comparable with respect to strength of desire, so too will the plurality of goods be comparable with respect to value.[27]

I will conclude by returning to the more radical pluralism. I suggested that it is the surest way to secure incomparability. But it is also then the surest way for pluralists to expose themselves to the monist charge that pluralism is incompatible with justified choice in some situations. Some radical pluralists want to resist this. They want to avoid any failures of justified choice while simultaneously avoiding positing a supervalue that would threaten incomparability. In this connection, Griffin speaks of "super-scales" (1986: 90), and Stocker of "higher-level synthesizing categories" (1990: 172). It is hard to tell whether they are doing anything other than introducing a value property under another name.

Perhaps one way to retain justified choice alongside incomparability is to hold that when one faces a choice between two incomparable outcomes, either choice is permissible. This corresponds to one interpretation of Sidgwick's dualism of practical reason. One might object to this thought on the grounds that to say that each option is justified is just to say that the options are equally good after all, and so to abandon incomparability. But that doesn't seem right, at least in our restricted context. Recall that we have restricted our discussion to axiological value. Even if, in a wider sense of "good"—such as one on which "good" just means choiceworthy—each option is equally good, this does not mean that they are equally good in terms of either value simpliciter or welfare (or in terms of, say, understanding-value and pleasure-value).

Other radical pluralists accept failures of justified choice.[28] This view corresponds to the other interpretation of Sidgwick's dualism of practical reason, on which, in Sidgwick's words,

> the Cosmos of Duty is thus really reduced to a Chaos: and the prolonged effort of the human intellect to frame a perfect ideal of rational conduct is seen to have been foredoomed to inevitable failure. (1874: 473)

Socrates and Protarchus, for their part, end the *Philebus* in agreement that a pluralistic view is best—that neither a life devoted solely to pleasure nor a life devoted solely to knowledge is "self-sufficient" (60d)—though they express no worries about comparing the goods. Indeed, they conclude that the best life will contain just the right mixture of these and other goods.

Acknowledgments

Thanks to Shane Gronholz, Iwao Hirose, Justin Klocksiem, Eden Lin, Graham Oddie, Jonas Olson, and Miles Tucker for helpful feedback on earlier drafts. Special thanks to Shane Gronholz for research assistance. Part of the work for this chapter was completed during a fellowship at the University Center for Human Values, Princeton University. I thank the Center for this support.

Notes

1. Or at least these are common ways of encapsulating the two views. In Frede's translation, for example, she titles this section of the dialogue, "The Introductory Challenge: Pleasure vs. Knowledge" (Plato 1993: 1). I have cheated a little here in that, as Socrates summarizes his view in the full passage, he leaves it open that pleasure might be somewhat good.
2. See Berlin 1966 and Galston 2002; Arneson 2009 disagrees.
3. See Tiberius, chapter 9 in this volume, for a discussion of the main theories of welfare.
4. For more on such judgments, see Olson, chapter 3 in this volume, section 3.5.
5. Some prefer the term "final value" over "intrinsic value" (see Rønnow-Rasmussen, chapter 2 in this volume; Kagan 1998; and Korsgaard 1983). I use "instrumental value" broadly, to include also the case in which something prevents something bad rather than causes something good.
6. See Harman 1967; Quinn 1974; and Feldman 2000 for more on basic intrinsic value.
7. Mason (2011: § 1.1) calls this "foundational pluralism," Rønnow-Rasmussen (2013) "goodness pluralism."
8. Contemporary sympathizers with the Moorean view include Donald Regan (2004); Guy Fletcher (2012); Kris McDaniel (2014). See also Rønnow-Rasmussen, chapter 2 in this volume.
9. See Olson, chapter 3 in this volume, for some discussion about skepticism about intrinsic value simpliciter.
10. Cf. Harsanyi's Theorem, which Broome (chapter 13 in this volume) summarizes as the view that "general utility can be treated as the total of personal utilities." See also Schroeder 2012: § 1.1.1.
11. See also Rand 1964: 16 and Rønnow-Rasmussen, chapter 2 in this volume.
12. See Olson, chapter 3 in this volume for further discussion of their views.
13. Mason (2011: § 1.1) calls them "normative" monism and pluralism.
14. E.g., Brandt 1972: 682 and Railton 1986: 16; Heathwood 2005 defends actual desires.
15. See Aristotle 1968; Hurka 1993; and Kraut 2007, though Hurka might deny that his theory is a theory of welfare as I have characterized the notion.
16. Even more recent lists can be found in Hurka 2011 (pleasure, knowledge, achievement, virtue, and friendship), Fletcher 2013 (achievement, friendship, happiness, pleasure, self-respect, and virtue) and Rice 2013 (loving relationships, meaningful knowledge, autonomy, achievement, and pleasure).
17. Hurka (1996: 560–61) assumes a similar understanding of the monism/pluralism distinction, and describes it as "standard" (564). See also Lin (forthcoming).
18. Proponents include Stocker (1990), Kekes (1993), and Anderson (1995).
19. Ben Bradley used this term for this sort of view in his comments on Elinor Mason's paper "The High Price of Pluralism," at the Fifth Annual Bellingham Summer Philosophy Conference, Western Washington University, August 2004.
20. Philosophers have not devoted much attention to the question of just what makes an axiology monistic or pluralistic. One exception is Fred Feldman (2004, ch. 8). Feldman's account of the monism/pluralism distinction is superficially different from the account sketched here, but it may share some deeper similarities. For accounts with considerable overlap to the one outlined here, see Tucker (n.d.) and Lin (forthcoming).
21. Ross's argument is a "bare-difference argument." On bare-difference arguments and on their connection to the additivity and separability of value, see Oddie 2001. On additivity

and separability, see also Broome, chapter 13 in this volume, and Carlson, chapter 15 in this volume.
22. In another interesting argument for welfare pluralism, Alex Sarch (2012) contends that the best way to incorporate an objective element into a theory of welfare is to make it pluralistic.
23. For further discussion, see Bradley 2014: 205–6.
24. This case is similar to the "inclusion cases" in Hurka 1996.
25. For more on incommensurability and its relation to incomparability, see Chang, chapter 11 in this volume.
26. See Brentano 1902; Broad 1930: 238; Ewing 1947: ch. 5. The argument in the text doesn't require the strong thesis that value is reducible to fitting attitudes, just that there is a necessary connection between them (as in, e.g., Zimmerman 2001: ch. 4).
27. For criticism of this argument, see Klocksiem 2011: 340–43 and Mason 2011: § 4.
28. See Mason 2011: § 4.4 for a list of such philosophers. See Chang, chapter 11 in this volume, for further discussion.

References

Anderson, E. (1995). *Value in Ethics and Economics*. Cambridge, MA: Harvard University Press.
Aristotle (1968). *Nicomachean Ethics*, rev. ed., tr. H. Rackham. Loeb Classical Library. Cambridge: Harvard University Press.
Arneson, R. (2009). "Value Pluralism Does Not Support Liberalism." *San Diego Law Review* 46: 925–40.
Audi, R. (2004). *The Good in the Right*. Princeton, NJ: Princeton University Press.
Berlin, I. (1966). *Two Concepts of Liberty*. Oxford: Clarendon Press.
Bradley, B. (2009). *Well-Being and Death*. Oxford: Oxford University Press.
Bradley, B. (2014). "Objective Theories of Well-Being." In B. Eggleston and D. Miller (eds.), *The Cambridge Companion to Utilitarianism*. Cambridge: Cambridge University Press, 220–38.
Brandt, R. (1972). "Rationality, Egoism, and Morality." *Journal of Philosophy* 69: 681–97.
Brandt, R. (1979). *A Theory of the Good and the Right*. Oxford: Clarendon Press.
Brentano, F. (1902). *The Origin of the Knowledge of Right and Wrong*. Westminster: Archibald Constable.
Broad, C. D. (1930). *Five Types of Ethical Theory*. London: Routledge & Kegan Paul.
Carson, T. (2000). *Value and the Good Life*. Notre Dame, IN: University of Notre Dame Press.
Chang, R. (1997). "Introduction." In R. Chang (ed.), *Incommensurability, Incomparability, and Practical Reason*. Cambridge: Harvard University Press, 1–34.
Crisp, R. (2006). "Hedonism Reconsidered." *Philosophy and Phenomenological Research* 73: 619–45.
Ewing, A. C. (1947). *The Definition of Good*. London: Macmillan.
Feldman, F. (2000). "Basic Intrinsic Value." *Philosophical Studies* 99: 319–46.
Feldman, F. (2004). *Pleasure and the Good Life*. Oxford: Oxford University Press.
Feldman, F. (2010). *What Is This Thing Called Happiness?* Oxford: Oxford University Press.
Fletcher, G. (2012). "The Locative Analysis of *Good For* Formulated and Defended." *Journal of Ethics & Social Philosophy* 6: 1–26.
Fletcher, G. (2013). "A Fresh Start for the Objective-List Theory of Well-Being." *Utilitas* 25: 206–20.

Frankena, W. (1973). *Ethics*, 2nd ed. Englewood Cliffs, NJ: Prentice Hall.
Galston, W. (2002). *Liberal Pluralism*. Cambridge: Cambridge University Press.
Griffin, J. (1986). *Well-Being*. Oxford: Clarendon Press.
Harman, G. (1967). "Toward a Theory of Intrinsic Value." *Journal of Philosophy* 64: 792–804.
Heathwood, C. (2005). "The Problem of Defective Desires." *Australasian Journal of Philosophy* 83: 487–504.
Heathwood, C. (2007). "The Reduction of Sensory Pleasure to Desire." *Philosophical Studies* 133: 23–44.
Hobbes, T. (1991 [1651]). *Leviathan*. Ed. Richard Tuck. New York: Cambridge University Press.
Hurka, T. (1993). *Perfectionism*. Oxford: Oxford University Press.
Hurka, T. (1996). "Monism, Pluralism and Rational Regret." *Ethics* 106: 555–75.
Hurka, T. (2011). *The Best Things in Life*. Oxford: Oxford University Press.
Kagan, S. (1998). "Rethinking Intrinsic Value." *Journal of Ethics* 2: 277–97.
Kant, I. (1997 [1785]). *Groundwork of the Metaphysics of Morals*. Trans. and ed. M. Gregor. Cambridge: Cambridge University Press.
Kekes, J. (1993). *The Morality of Pluralism*. Princeton, NJ: Princeton University Press.
Kelly, C. (2008). "The Impossibility of Incommensurable Values." *Philosophical Studies* 137: 369–72.
Klocksiem, J. (2011). "Moorean Pluralism as a Solution to the Incommensurability Problem." *Philosophical Studies* 153: 335–49.
Korsgaard, C. (1983). "Two Distinctions in Goodness." *Philosophical Review* 92: 169–95.
Kraut, R. (2007). *What Is Good and Why*. Cambridge: Harvard University Press.
Kraut, R. (2011). *Against Absolute Goodness*. Oxford: Oxford University Press.
Lemos, N. (1994). *Intrinsic Value*. Cambridge: Cambridge University Press.
Lemos N. (2010). "Summation, Variety, and Indeterminate Value." *Ethical Theory and Moral Practice* 13: 33–44.
Lin, E. (Forthcoming). "Pluralism about Well-Being." *Philosophical Perspectives*.
Mill, J. S. (1863). *Utilitarianism*. London: Parker, Son, and Bourne, West Strand.
Mason, E. (2011). "Value Pluralism." In E. Zalta (ed.), *The Stanford Encyclopedia of Philosophy*, Fall 2011 ed. http://plato.stanford.edu/archives/fall2011/entries/value-pluralism/.
McDaniel, K. (2014). "A Moorean View of the Value of Lives." *Pacific Philosophical Quarterly* 95: 23–46.
Mendola, J. (2006). "Intuitive Hedonism." *Philosophical Studies* 128: 441–77.
Moore, A. (2000). "Objective Human Goods." In R. Crisp and B. Hooker (eds.), *Well-Being and Morality*. Oxford: Oxford University Press, 75–89.
Moore, G. E. (1903). *Principia Ethica*. Cambridge: Cambridge University Press.
Nozick, R. (1974). *Anarchy, State, and Utopia*. New York: Basic Books.
Nussbaum, M. (2000). *Women and Human Development*. Cambridge: Cambridge University Press.
Oddie, G. (2001). "Axiological Atomism." *Australasian Journal of Philosophy* 79: 313–32.
Parfit, D. (1984). *Reasons and Persons*. Oxford: Clarendon Press.
Plato. (1958). *Plato's Examination of Pleasure: A Translation of the Philebus*. Tr. R. Hackworth. Cambridge: The University Press.
Plato (1993). *Philebus*. Tr. D. Frede. Indianapolis: Hackett.
Quinn, W. (1974). "Theories of Intrinsic Value." *American Philosophical Quarterly* 11: 123–32.
Raibley, J. (2010). "Well-Being and the Priority of Values." *Social Theory and Practice* 36: 593–620.
Railton, P. (1986). "Facts and Values." *Philosophical Topics* 14: 5–31.

Rand, A. (1964). *The Virtue of Selfishness*. New York: New American Library.
Rawls, J. (1971). *A Theory of Justice*. Cambridge: Harvard University Press.
Regan, D. (2004). "Why Am I My Brother's Keeper?" In R. Jay Wallace, P. Pettit, S. Scheffler, and M. Smith (eds.), *Reason and Value*. Oxford: Clarendon Press, 202–30.
Rice, C. (2013). "Defending the Objective List Theory of Well-Being." *Ratio* 26: 196–211.
Rønnow-Rasmussen, T. (2013). "Good and Good For." In H. LaFollette (ed.), *The International Encyclopedia of Ethics*. Hoboken, NJ: Wiley-Blackwell.
Ross, W. D. (1988 [1930]). *The Right and the Good*. Indianapolis, Ind.: Hackett.
Sarch, A. (2012). "Multi-Component Theories of Well-Being and Their Structure." *Pacific Philosophical Quarterly* 93: 439–71.
Scanlon, T. M. (1998). *What We Owe to Each Other*. Cambridge: Harvard University Press.
Schaber, P. (1999). "Value Pluralism: Some Problems." *Journal of Value Inquiry* 33: 71–78.
Schroeder, M. (2012). "Value Theory." In E. Zalta (ed.), *The Stanford Encyclopedia of Philosophy*, Summer 2012 ed. http://plato.stanford.edu/archives/sum2012/entries/value-theory/.
Sidgwick, H. (1874). *The Methods of Ethics*, 1st ed. London: Macmillan.
Sidgwick, H. (1907). *The Methods of Ethics*, 7th ed. London: Macmillan.
Smart, J. J. C., and B. Williams. (1973). *Utilitarianism: For and Against*. Cambridge: Cambridge University Press.
Spencer, H. (1871). *The Principles of Psychology*. New York: D. Appleton.
Stocker, M. (1990). *Plural and Conflicting Values*. Oxford: Clarendon Press.
Sumner, L. W. (1996). *Welfare, Happiness, and Ethics*. Oxford: Oxford University Press.
Tännsjö, T. (2007). "Narrow Hedonism." *Journal of Happiness Studies* 8: 79–98.
Thomson, J. (2008). *Normativity*. Chicago: Open Court.
Tucker, M. (n.d.). "Value Pluralisms." Unpublished.
Velleman, J. (1991). "Well-Being and Time." *Pacific Philosophical Quarterly* 72: 48–77.
Wolf, S. (1992). "Two Levels of Pluralism." *Ethics* 102: 785–98.
Zimmerman, M. (2001). *The Nature of Intrinsic Value*. Lanham, MD: Rowman & Littlefield.

Chapter 9

Prudential Value

Valerie Tiberius

9.1. Introduction

Prudential value is the *good for* a person. It is the kind of value we aim at when we are acting for another person's sake, trying to benefit him or her, or when we are deliberating about how to live so that our lives go well for us. Prudential value is often identified with well-being, so that well-being is not one prudential value among many, but instead the most general category of prudential value. This is how the terminology will be used in this chapter: prudential value or well-being is the good for a person in the broadest sense. We can also talk about the particular prudential goods that comprise well-being. Different theories of well-being have different implications for what these goods are, though there is a fair amount of agreement on important items. To say that we are taking "well-being" in its broadest sense is not to say that well-being is all-encompassing in terms of the items on the list of prudential goods; some theories of well-being have very short lists of (intrinsic) prudential goods. Whether well-being includes lots of goods or few is a question that will be answered by discovering the right *theory*. This chapter focuses on theories of well-being, rather than on specific prudential goods.

What makes for a good theory? A theory of prudential value or well-being should provide a systematic explanation for why the things that are good for a person are good for her. Ideally, a theory of prudential value will do this in a way that respects certain features of the target concept. First, well-being is good *for* the person whose well-being it is; a good theory must explain this special connection to the subject. As Wayne Sumner puts it, the "relativization of prudential value to the proprietor of the life in question is one of the deepest features of the language of welfare" (Sumner 1995: 770). Your well-being is good for you, it benefits you, it makes your life go well. This feature is what distinguishes well-being from other kinds of value such as moral or aesthetic value. Sumner goes on to argue that subjective theories of well-being—that is, theories that make well-being depend on the attitudes of the subject—offer the best explanation for the subject-relativity of well-being, but this should not be assumed at the outset.

Subjectivity in the sense of attitude dependence is not the same as subject-relativity; and it is the explanation of the latter that is our theoretical desideratum.

Second, well-being is *good* for the person whose well-being it is and a theory of the prudential good must have some explanation for why it is something worth aiming at or promoting, whether for ourselves or others. In other words, a theory of well-being should explain the normative significance of well-being.[1] This second criterion raises some large philosophical issues. What is it for something to have normative significance or to give us reasons for action? How do we establish that something is normative rather than merely liked or wanted? I will not venture a general answer to this question, but instead I will explain the answer that seems to be assumed in the literature on well-being. Here reflective equilibrium is the background methodology, and arguments for the normativity of well-being according to the proffered theory take the form of intuition pumps, examples, and case studies designed to show that the theory's notion of well-being is an ideal intuitively worth promoting. We show that our theory's conception of well-being is normative by demonstrating that it is the best fit (of all the available theories) with considered judgments about how a person's life can go better or worse.

Let's call these two criteria for evaluating the merits of theories of well-being *subject-relativity* and *normativity*. These two criteria often pull in different directions, as we can see with some examples. Imagine Dancing Diane, who is training hard to meet her goal of being a professional ballet dancer. The training is physically punishing and stressful, and because Diane is an anxious person, the training is taking a great toll on her health. But this is what she has always wanted to do and she is very satisfied with her life. Subjectively, Diane's life is going well. She is enjoying her life and doing what she wants to do. But Diane's friends and parents might worry that this isn't a good life for Diane. They might think she is mistaken about what is good for her and that a physically healthier lifestyle would be more valuable for her. Or, consider Recluse Rex, who doesn't want to have friends and who finds no joy whatsoever in socializing with other people. Perhaps Rex is an extreme introvert or he just vastly prefers his own company; whatever the reason, there is nothing Rex likes or wants about having friends and nothing he misses in not having them. Pulled by the subject-relativity of well-being, we might ask how it could possibly be good for such a person to associate with others on the assumption that he won't learn to enjoy it in the way the rest of us do. How could it be good for Rex to force him to make friends if it's never something he will endorse as part of his own good? On the other hand, there does seem to be something tragic about Rex's life, something that is part of a good human life that he is missing out on. If Rex were our child, we would likely feel sad that he turned out as he did. We are pulled in both directions.

In short, theories of prudential value or well-being are trying to capture two different aspects of the good for a person that are sometimes in tension and supported by different sets of intuitions. On the one hand, it seems like what is good for a person cannot be something alien to her. On the other hand, what is good for a person has to be something that the rest of us can see as corresponding to a compelling ideal of human life that isn't beholden to what a particular person might find alien. As we review the going theories of prudential value, we will see how they do at capturing these competing elements.

9.2. OBJECTIVE LIST AND EUDAIMONIST THEORIES

Objective list and eudaimonist theories reject the subjectivist claim mentioned above that the explanation for why something is good for a person makes essential reference to that person's attitudes. According to the objective list theory, a person's life goes well to the extent that it includes or instantiates certain objectively good things, and the goodness of these things for the person is not explained by her liking them, wanting them, being pleased or satisfied by them, or having any other subjective response (Arneson 1999; Finnis 2011). Different theorists have slightly different lists, but they tend to agree on items such as achievement, friendship, knowledge, and pleasure.

One problem with objective list theories is that they do not have an easy way to explain the subject-relativity of well-being. The idea that something could be good for a person even though she herself has no interest in it, doesn't enjoy, want, or care about it, has seemed wrongheaded to many. It is open to objective list theories to say that subject-relativity is not, in fact, a very important feature of well-being and that to say otherwise simply begs the question against the view. Guy Fletcher (2013) offers a different (and, in my view, more promising) response, which is that the items on the list constitutively include subjective attitudes (e.g., love and other-regarding concern are part of friendship), even though their goodness is not explained by our attitudes. Objective list theories have also been criticized for not offering a systematizing explanation for the list of goods; lists are not theories, the critic says. This objection raises a large question about the criteria of adequacy for normative theories. Fletcher (2013) argues that objective list theories are *enumerative* theories (not *explanatory* theories) that do not purport to explain why what's good for a person is good for her.

Eudaimonist theories are objective theories that do provide a systematic explanation for the goods that they take to comprise well-being; they are, therefore, both enumerative and explanatory. Such theories take what's good for a person to depend on human nature. In the background is a general assumption about judgments of the form x is *good for* y, according to which this sort of judgment is always made relative to the kind of thing that y is and what it is to be a good one of those. A good knife is a knife that cuts well, and so what is good for a knife is to be kept sharp. A good bee is one that performs its function in the hive, so what is good for a worker bee is whatever enables him to find pollen, and what is good for the queen bee is whatever enables her to produce lots more bees. A good lioness is one that can hunt her prey and feed her cubs, so what's good for a lioness is to have sharp teeth and powerful legs. So too what is good for a human being is to be good at whatever it is human beings are supposed to do, that is, what is good for humans is to fulfill our natural telos.

First and foremost, eudaimonist theories need to tell us what the human telos is. As is well known, Aristotle (the inspiration for these theories) took our telos to be rational activity in accordance with virtue. To live a good human life, on this view, is to live a life of virtuous activity because acting in accordance with the virtues is acting as excellent members of the rational and social kind of creature that we are. Aristotle seemed to take our human nature to be inherently evaluative, so that once you spell out what the good functioning of a human being qua human being is, you have answered the question of what kind of life is good for a human being. As we'll see, contemporary defenders of this idea rely more heavily on reflective equilibrium to explain the goodness of a paradigmatically human life.[2]

Martha Nussbaum is one such contemporary defender. She argues for what she calls the capabilities approach to human flourishing, according to which the good for a person is to be understood in terms of central human functions: life; bodily health; bodily integrity; senses, imagination, and thought; emotions; practical reason; affiliation; other species; play; and control over one's environment (Nussbaum 2001). People who have the capability to function along these dimensions—people who are able "to do and to be" what these central human functions highlight—are faring well.

Perhaps the most important contribution of the capabilities approach is actually to political philosophy and international development, where it provides an alternative to approaches centered on the distribution of resources or primary goods. But here we shall consider the capabilities approach as a theory of prudential good. To do so, it will help to remember our two theoretical criteria. How does Nussbaum argue for the normative significance of the central human functionings? Nussbaum is up front about the role of reflective equilibrium in her argument. She rejects the idea that the value of functionings is to be explained by an appeal to the intrinsic normativity of our biological nature and instead argues that these functionings are what constitute a good human life because they are the object of an overlapping consensus among people across the globe about what central human capacities make life go well for us.[3]

The fact that this list of capabilities is one we can all recognize as constitutive of good human life goes some way to addressing the criterion of subject-relativity. But it may not go far enough. Recluse Rex does not think his life is made better by the ability to affiliate with others, because he doesn't care about affiliation. Dancing Diane isn't too fussed about her long-term bodily health, but she nevertheless thinks her life is going well. Nussbaum's answer to the problem presented by such cases is to point out that because practical reasoning is a vitally important functioning for human beings, there is room for people to fulfill their functions in various different ways. Moreover, because what we ought to promote for others is the capability to function rather than functioning itself, the theory does not license forcing Rex to have friends or coercing Diane into giving up dancing. Both, according to the capabilities approach, are better off with the capability to affiliate and to be healthy, though they might make choices that give these ways of functioning low priority in their lives.

Richard Kraut is another Aristotelian philosopher who has developed a sophisticated eudaimonist approach to well-being. Kraut argues that truths about "good for" are "grounded in facts about our physical and psychological functioning" (Kraut 2009: 90) on the basis of the desirability of a unified interpretation of "good for" across different contexts. We know what we mean when we talk about what's good for plants;

other things equal, the case for what's good for people should be analogous. So, according to the view Kraut calls "developmentalism," what is good for us is determined by our nature: "A flourishing human being is one who possesses, develops, and enjoys the exercise of cognitive, affective, sensory, and social powers (no less than physical powers). Those, in broadest outline and roughly speaking, are the components of well-being" (2009: 137).

Kraut also relies on reflective equilibrium in order to defend this ideal as something worth pursuing. Unlike Nussbaum, however, whose political purposes lead her to seek actual consensus among people from different cultures, Kraut draws on intuitions about cases such as cases of what we want for our children and what we think is regrettable in a human life.[4] In a departure from Aristotle (at least on one standard interpretation), Kraut does not think nature plays any foundational role in the justification of his conception of flourishing. Nature is a unifying principle for our ideas about how life can go better or worse for plants, animals, and people, but it could have turned out otherwise and Kraut grants that some aspects of our nature (such as our destructive powers) should be rejected from the ideal of human flourishing.

Some of the intuitions Kraut relies on are intuitions about why impairments are bad for people even when the people in question don't know or don't care that they are impaired. According to Kraut, "Someone who is incapable of developing a love of literature and whose only mental pleasure is checkers is handicapped by a cognitive or linguistic disability. It would have been better for him had his powers been greater" (2009: 178). Kraut sees this as an advantage of his theory over desire theories, but we might wonder about the cost of accommodating these intuitions for the desideratum of subject-relativity. If Joe will never be able to understand and enjoy the literature he is missing, how could it be good for him, the person he is now, if he were able to appreciate it? How could Joe's life be less good for Joe in virtue of his missing out on something normal human beings do when he himself is incapable of doing it?

Kraut is not unmoved by the subject-relativity requirement. To accommodate it, he argues that it is not enough to possess and exercise our natural human capacities, we must also enjoy doing so if we are going to flourish. This goes some way toward accommodating subjectivist intuitions, but many have thought that eudaimonism still does not pay enough attention to the individual subject.

9.3. Hedonism

If enjoyment is so important, why not make enjoyment the central focus of a theory of well-being? This is what hedonists do. According to hedonism, what is good for a person is pleasure and the absence of pain. Unsurprisingly, the big debate among different hedonists is about the nature of pleasure. The two main views are the sensation theory (called the "internalist" theory of pleasure by Sumner [1996]) and the attitudinal (or "externalist") theory of pleasure. Jeremy Bentham had the former view, according to which pleasure is identified with a distinctive sensation that is shared by all pleasant experiences. The main current defender of the sensation theory is Roger Crisp. The attitudinal theory identifies pleasure with an attitude—"being pleased"—taken toward a state of affairs (Feldman 2004). On this view, what makes an experience or state of affairs pleasurable is that the person having the experience has a certain pro-attitude toward it: "a person takes attitudinal pleasure in some state of affairs if he enjoys it, is pleased about it, is glad that it is happening, is delighted by it" (Feldman 2004: 56).

The debate between these two views centers on two objections. On one hand, the "none such" objection to the sensation theory, which charges that there is no sensation that all pleasurable experiences have in common (think: eating chocolate, understanding a philosophical argument, having an orgasm). Crisp's solution to this problem is to hold that pleasure is best described as a "feeling tone" that is instantiated in different ways in different experiences although the tone is shared (Crisp 2006). The attitudinal theory isn't subject to this objection, because on this view what pleasures have in common is not something intrinsic to the experience. Rather, pleasures have in common that they are all the object of the pro-attitude "being pleased by." On the other hand, the "Killjoy objection" to the attitudinal theory charges that this theory takes the fun out of pleasure, since we can be glad to be in a state that doesn't feel good (e.g., I might be pleased that I feel guilty about doing something very bad because the guilt speaks well of my character) (Haybron 2008: 64). The sensation theory certainly preserves the pleasantness of pleasure.

In terms of explaining the normativity of well-being, the sensation theory might have the advantage. The idea that something's being enjoyable is "the only '*good-for*-making' property there is" is compelling; it is, after all, one of the basic ideas that fuels utilitarianism (Crisp 2006). When it comes to the subject-relativity of well-being, however, both theories have problems. This is because although hedonism seems like a subjective theory (since pleasure is a psychological state), it is much closer to an objective list theory with one item on the list: pleasure. Pleasure or enjoyment is good for us, on this view, whether we want it or not. This point has been made vividly by Nozick's (1974) "experience machine" thought experiment. Nozick asks us to imagine we have the option of being hooked up to a machine controlled by very trustworthy neuroscientists who will ensure that we have a more pleasant life attached to the machine than otherwise. We are also to imagine that others have a similar option, so we will not be causing other people harm by opting to hook up to the machine. Would we do it? Nozick says that many people would choose not to use the experience machine because we care about things other than pleasure—being in touch with reality, for example, or *doing* certain things rather than just thinking that we are. If this is true, it is evidence that we take our own good to consist in more than pleasure, and this means that hedonism does not respect our subjective point of view.

Hedonists have responded to the experience machine objection in different ways. Crisp argues that too much weight has been put on this one thought experiment and that, if we evaluate the theory as a whole, it still does well in reflective equilibrium. Feldman, the main proponent of the attitudinal theory of pleasure, takes the objection head on and suggests that those who find the intuition compelling may add a requirement of "truth-adjustedness" so that pleasures not based on false beliefs count more than deceptive pleasures. Finally, Chris Heathwood, taking Feldman's view a step further (and, in a way, taking the killjoy objection as pointing to a feature rather than a bug), argues that pleasure just is a preferred experience, which permits us to say that the false pleasures in the machine are not good for the person who does not prefer them (Heathwood 2007). Hedonism then becomes indistinguishable from one version of a desire satisfaction theory of well-being, to which we will now turn.

9.4. Desire Theories

According to desire or preference satisfaction theories of well-being, what is good for you is getting what you want. These theories are popular in philosophy and they dominate in economics. One reason for this is surely their ability to capture the sense in which well-being is subject-relative.[5] After all, the intuitions that sustain arguments against eudaimonist and hedonist theories are, by and large, intuitions about cases in which something is claimed to be good for someone despite the fact that she does not want it. Nevertheless, desire theories have many problems of their own. Because of the strong intuitive appeal of desire theories, arguments for them often take the form of responses to these objections.

One immediate objection to the view—that there are cases in which our desires obviously lead us to do things that are harmful—gave rise to idealized desire theories, the most frequently discussed version of which is the full information theory (or informed desire theory) of well-being. According to this theory, what is good for a person is not getting whatever she happens to want, but getting what she would want if she were fully informed of all the relevant nonnormative facts. An early version of this theory, Richard Brandt's, took full information to be defined in terms of exposure to cognitive psychotherapy, which aims to uncover the false beliefs that are at the basis of our desiderative and emotional states (Brandt 1979). Brandt's idea was that our actual desires would be improved by this exposure in such a way that their satisfaction would always be good for us. An attractive feature of this proposal is that it reduces the "good for" to a natural (though hypothetical) fact about our desires as they would be after a naturalistically described process. However, as David Velleman (1988) has pointed out, the theory does not guarantee that the resulting desires are ones it is intuitively good for us to satisfy: some pathological desires (such as a desire to avoid spiders at all costs) can survive cognitive psychotherapy.

Problems with Brandt's view caused those interested in defending the full information theory to revise their characterization of full information so that one counts as fully informed if one knows or appreciates all the facts (Railton 1986). Further, proponents of this view now tend to hold that what's good for a person is not getting what her fully informed self wants, but rather getting what her fully informed self would want her to want. So, according to Railton, "This seems to me an intuitively plausible account of what someone's non-moral good consists in: roughly, what he would want himself to seek if he knew what he were doing" (1986: 177). This way of thinking about full information theory has been called the advisor model, since it defines well-being in terms of the advice of your fully informed self.

The attempt to get "full information" right is an attempt to meet the normativity criterion. What is sought is a characterization of full information that makes the resulting desires line up with our intuitive ideas about what is good for people. But the result of this process led to a view that doesn't have a clear path to explaining the subject-relativity of well-being, which was supposed to be the desire theory's great advantage. The problem is that there could be a great distance between a person's actual self and her fully informed self, understood as above. It's not clear that shifting to the advisor model solves all the problems, given how alien the fully informed self might be to the actual self (see Rosati 1995 for an influential discussion). Indeed, the alien nature of the fully informed advisor creates problems for explanations of both subject-relativity and normativity: the farther the ideal is from actual people, the less likely well-being subjects will be motivated by the recommendations of their ideal selves and the less likely the results will be intuitively compelling examples of what is good for us.

Informed desire theories are still widely accepted. This might be because the difficulty of specifying what it is for a desire to be informed has been underappreciated. Economists tend to say that desires must be informed and rational, because they recognize that without "cleaning up" our desires, the preference satisfaction theory of well-being has wildly counterintuitive results (Harsanyi 1977). But economists have not engaged with the literature critical of full information theories in philosophy. On the other hand, perhaps the theory can tolerate an imprecise notion of what it is for a desire to be informed, or a scaled-back notion according to which a desire is informed as long as it is a desire for the actual object as it is (Sobel 2009).

Full information theories gained popularity because it seemed like a way of preserving the insights of desire theory while solving the problem that some desires are obviously bad for us to satisfy. Recently, though, actual desire theories have come up with their own solutions to this problem that obviate the need to move to idealized theories. Chris Heathwood, for example, has argued that an actual desire theory that focuses on the satisfaction of intrinsic desires can solve the problems that desire theories were thought to have (see Heathwood 2006, 2005). To see how this works, we can consider an example from Peter Railton's defense of an informed desire theory: Lonnie is traveling in a foreign country feeling sick. Because he feels bad, he craves a comforting glass of milk. Little does he know that he feels sick because he is dehydrated and drinking milk will make him feel worse. According to informed desire theory, what is good for Lonnie is what his fully informed self would want him to want, namely, clear liquids. But actual desire theory yields the same result if we focus on Lonnie's *intrinsic* desire to feel better. Lonnie desires to drink milk as a means to feeling better, which he desires for its own sake. Actual desire theory has intuitive results, according to Heathwood, as long as it takes only intrinsic desires to determine well-being.

The focus on intrinsic desires does not help much to solve other problems that have been raised for desire theories, however.[6] For instance, according to the problem of remote desires the desire theory of well-being is stuck with the unintuitive conclusion that the satisfaction of, say, the desire for a stranger whom you'll never see again to fare well, or the desire for peace in a country you read about but will never hear of again, is good for the person who has these desires. It is unintuitive that something so distant from you and your experience could affect your well-being. Similarly, desires for things to happen after you are dead have been thought to cause troubles for desire theory, since it seems implausible to think you could be better off after you are dead. There is also the problem of the prospectivity of desire, which is that it can turn out that we don't like what we wanted once we get it. Desire theories can insist that the satisfaction of a desire is only good for you if that desire persists in some fashion through the satisfaction of it. For example, if on Monday you desire to have a beer on Tuesday and you get a beer on Tuesday, the satisfaction of that desire is only good for you if your desire for beer on Tuesday persists until its satisfaction.

Actual desire theory lines up with intuitions about subject-relativity quite well, since our intrinsic desires are not likely to seem alien to us. As mentioned above, counterexamples to objective theories of well-being are often put in terms of a conflict between what is good for a person according to the theory and what the person wants. Thus desires are often taken to be the defining feature of subjectivity. The focus on intrinsic desires goes some way toward meeting the other desideratum of a theory of well-being, but many are dissatisfied with desire theory's ability to explain the normative significance of well-being. The problem is that we can want things—even intrinsically, and even when informed—that don't seem to be good for us: things that are base or degrading, things that are immoral, things that are trivial or silly, and so on. Those who have Aristotelian intuitions will balk at the verdict that it could be good for a person to satisfy his desire to spend his life eating Pop-Tarts while watching reruns of *Battlestar Gallactica*. If you think about the perspective of a parent wishing a good life for her child, it's not hard to sympathize with the Aristotelian.

Desire theorists have argued for solutions to this problem. Heathwood bites the bullet and points out that to say that satisfying a base or trivial desire is good for a person is not to say that it is good all things considered (Heathwood 2005). James Griffin argues for a hybrid version of desire theory according to which the goodness of satisfying desires is contingent on the value of the objects that are desired (Griffin 1986). Another option is to abandon desire as the marker of subjectivity and to look for a subject-relative theory that doesn't incur the same problems. We will consider some such options in the next section.

9.5. Other Internalist Theories

Internalist theories take well-being to be determined by features of the individual well-being subject.[7] Internalism about well-being is broader (and weaker) than subjectivism in that it does not specify which aspect of the individual is the defining feature. Subjectivism defines well-being in terms of the subject's attitudes (such as desires or judgments of life-satisfaction). An internalist theory could take well-being to be dependent on the individual nature of the well-being subject, where this nature is not exhausted by her attitudes. Subjective theories such as desire theories are one variety of internalist theory, but there are others. One place that desire theories seem to go wrong is in separating well-being from enjoyment or positive feelings. The absence of any effect on how a person feels is what's at issue in the problem of remote desires and the problem of prospectivity. One might say that desire theories preserve a link to the subject, but to the wrong part of the subject. Those who have thought along these lines, but who have rejected hedonism for being too narrow, have argued for alternative theories of well-being to the "big three" enumerated by Parfit: hedonism, objective list, and desire theories (Parfit 1984).

Wayne Sumner argues for the authentic happiness theory of well-being. Happiness is defined as life satisfaction, which is "a positive cognitive/affective response on the part of a subject to (some or all of) the conditions or circumstances of her life" (Sumner 1996: 156). Happiness consists in both judging that your life is going well overall and feeling good about it, and it is, according to Sumner, something about which we cannot be mistaken. But happiness by itself is not sufficient for well-being. Motivated by the problem of adaptive preferences, Sumner adds an authenticity constraint so that only if one's happiness is informed and autonomous is one faring well; we can, then, be mistaken about whether we are achieving well-being. In this context, the problem of adaptive preferences is that our desires can adapt to oppressive circumstances so that we no longer want much.[8] Similarly, our satisfaction with life can adapt so that we find a low standard of living with few opportunities quite satisfying. Sumner insists that the kind of happiness that has the status of well-being is happiness that has not resulted from oppression or coercion.

The authentic happiness theory provides philosophical foundation for the most widespread view about well-being in psychology, which takes life satisfaction to be the main component of subjective well-being (Diener 1984; Diener, Scollon, and Lucas 2003). This makes the theory important for those interested in interdisciplinary approaches to well-being and in ensuring that well-being is something that can be effectively measured. Indeed, life satisfaction measures are so common in psychology that any philosopher who is interested in the measurement of well-being ought to have something to say about how life satisfaction is (or is not) related to well-being.[9] The life satisfaction theory has attracted some criticism from philosophers, however. Dan Haybron argues against the life satisfaction theory of happiness, charging that insofar as we ever make such overall assessments of our lives, these assessments are necessarily perspectival and subject to arbitrary contextual influences (Haybron 2007). You might decide to be grateful for the life you have, and feel thereby satisfied with it, though things are not going terribly well for you in terms of the achievement of your aims. The charge here is that even informed and unmanipulated satisfaction with one's life can seem like something not worth having; this is a charge against the alleged value of well-being according to the life satisfaction theory.

Haybron offers a different theory of happiness, according to which happiness is a positive emotional state of "psychic flourishing," which includes a person's emotions and moods and her propensities to experience positive emotions and moods over time (Haybron 2008). Well-being, according to Haybron, is individual nature fulfillment, which includes happiness as a key component. This theory is eudaimonistic, but not in the way Aristotelian theories are, because it does not give any pride of place to an individual's nature qua member of his or her species. The hope of individualist eudaimonism is that it can capitalize on some of the same intuitions that fuel Aristotelian eudaimonist theories in order to explain the value of well-being and yet it will do better at capturing the subject-relativity of well-being by tying well-being to a person's own characteristics (and not forcing species based norms on people who differ from their typical conspecifics). After all, individualist eudaimonism has an explanation of what goes wrong in the life of a person lying blissfully in the experience machine or the person who wants nothing more than to watch television reruns. As long as there is something about the individual nature of these people that is not fulfilled, Haybron can explain why they are not achieving well-being despite their desires or satisfactions.

Connie Rosati's theory of what she calls "personal good" raises similar hopes. According to Rosati, what makes something good for a person is a reason-giving fit between it and the subject, akin to the fit between two people in a healthy romantic relationship. The things that are nonmorally good for a person "tend to support or not undermine an individual's sense of her own value, to enliven rather than enervate, to provide identity and direction, and to furnish self-supporting sources of internal motivation"; the property of "good for" is the second-order property of being such as to produce these features (Rosati 2006: 120). Rosati's theory explains the subject-relativity of the personal good in a way that naturally makes it clear what is good about it—why we would want it for our own child, why such a life would not be something to regret, and so on—by reference to the important relationship between activities that count as contributing to our personal good and features of the lives we intuitively think of as valuable for people (e.g., feeling alive, having self-esteem and direction).

Finally, theories that put values (rather than desires or satisfactions) at the center of the theory of well-being are also engaged in an effort to preserve subject-relativity while capturing some of the intuitive explanation of the normativity of well-being from objective theories. One way to put values at the center of the view is to return to the Aristotelian theory and posit objective values the pursuit of which constitutes the good for a person (see also Darwall 2004). In order to better capture the subject-relativity of well-being, however, an attractive possibility is to focus on what people value (as opposed to what is valuable independently of valuers). Value-based views have been developed by Raibley (2010) and Tiberius (2008), both of whom take valuing to be an attitude that comprises both judgment and emotional dispositions.

Value-based theories have advantages similar to those of desire theories when it comes to explaining the subject-relativity of well-being, because they identify well-being with the fulfillment or realization of the agent's subjectively important goals.[10] Indeed one might argue that they do better in this regard, since values are endorsed by subjects as the kinds of goals worth fulfilling and since people are more likely to identify themselves in terms of their values than in terms of their desires simpliciter. Value theories, then, can solve some of the problems for desire theories that have to do with the fact that we have desires we don't take to give us normative reasons (trivial desires, desires for remote objects, base or degrading desires). If valuing includes a cognitive component such that people do not *value* the trivial, the remote or the degrading (even though they have the desire), then value theories can rule out some of these counterexamples. The cognitive component of valuing might be an attitude of "taking the emotional pattern toward the valued object to be justified or normative" (Tiberius 2008) or it might be just the belief that the valued object is good for you (Dorsey 2012).

Of course it is still possible that there are people who not only want degrading, trivial, or immoral things but also value them. This seems to be true even if valuing is understood cognitively: it's possible for a person to believe that something degrading is good for her. So, value theories are not going to rule out the possibility of the flourishing pig or cad; these theories will not yield results that line up perfectly with Aristotelian eudaimonist theories. Individualist eudaimonism will not do so either, because it is possible that an individual's nature is such that the life of the pig or the cad is the one that "fits." Some have thought that this is a serious cost of internalist theories of well-being: they force us to admit that a person could be living well, achieving her own good, flourishing by the standard of the bright eye and the bushy coat, even though she is morally monstrous. We might call this the "Happy Hitler" objection. Those who propose internalist theories can point out that in the actual world, pigs and cads (let alone Hitlers) are not likely to be very happy for a variety of reasons. The internalist must bite the bullet at some point, though, and point out that there are other evaluations we can make of people and their lives besides prudential ones; Hitler *might* have achieved his own good, but he was still evil and worthy of every sort of moral condemnation.

Most of the theories we have considered in this section can be seen as attempting to steer a middle course through subjectivism and objectivism about well-being. The pressure to do this comes from the need to meet the two competing desiderata of subject-relativity and normativity. Exactly what is the right way to go—nature fulfillment, fit, or value—will depend on the details, and there is work to be done here. But theories that occupy a middle ground do seem to have an advantage, given the constraints on the concept. Obviously, what internalist theories cannot do is underwrite strong pronouncements about what is good for people independently of their individual features. The intuition that it would be better for the person who cannot appreciate literature to have had this capacity—that there is something to be regretted in a human life that does not contain the particular human pleasures that are typical for members of our species—does not have a natural home in internalist theories.

9.6. WELL-BEING IN CONTEXT

As Shelly Kagan (1992: 169) has argued, the dialectic about the proper understanding of well-being has a certain shape: "there is an attempt to push the limits of well-being outward, moving from a narrow to a broader conception; then comes the claim that the resulting notion is too broad, and so we must retreat to a narrower conception after all." Some internalist theories of well-being are, in these terms, broader than others, but none is so broad as to capture the Aristotelian ideal of a good human life, the one we would wish for our children. How much of a problem this is depends on what we expect our characterization of well-being to do. Some (such as Scanlon) think that well-being is a rather useless notion that has no real role to play in ethical theory. Others—welfarists (such as Sumner)—think it is the very center of ethical theory. Kagan's view is somewhere in the middle: if well-being must be narrow (confined to the subject's mind or body), then it will still be morally significant, but its significance may be reduced. Interesting work on the subject of well-being includes attempts to locate this concept in ethics, political philosophy, and public policy generally.[11]

T. M. Scanlon (1998) is a prominent skeptic about the importance of the concept of well-being. Scanlon argues that the concept is not a useful one for making personal or moral decisions, because the reasons for which things end up on the list of well-being ingredients are different from the reasons we care about these things. For example, according to the desire theory of well-being (which Scanlon seems to assume), friendship is good for us because we want it (or because we would want it if fully informed). But what makes friendships desirable for us is not the fact that they satisfy our desires. Rather, we care about particular friends because of their good qualities, our histories with them, and the pleasure we take in shared activities. In a life in which we have to make decisions about how to be a good friend, which friendships to keep, and so on, the reasons that are relevant to our decision-making do not have to do with what satisfies our desires. Scanlon's point is that a theory of well-being must provide a unifying explanation for the prudential goodness of the things that are good for us, but this unifying explanation is not what we refer to when we are making practical, ethical decisions about how to live our lives. According to Scanlon, "Well-being disappears when we focus on it, leaving only the values that make it up" (1998: 128–29).

One thing to notice about this objection to theorizing about well-being is that it could be turned on other ethical theories—why do we need a general theory of "good" or "right," when what we really need to do is to focus on the particular reasons for which things are good or right? Moreover, because the objection assumes a particular kind of theory of well-being, it's not clear that it generalizes to other theories. Rosati's personal fit theory, for example, does give us direction about what kinds of things it makes sense for us to pursue for what reasons. Understanding the concept as she does could help guide our choices by attuning us to thinking about what activities combine with what we are like to make us feel good about ourselves in a sustaining way. Enumerative theories like the objective list theories discussed earlier do not aim to provide a unifying explanation at all, and so do not seem to be subject to Scanlon's objection.

Others are skeptical about the promise for a *single* theory of well-being. Anna Alexandrova (2013) has argued that there is not a single target of theoretical investigation and that we require different theories for different practical purposes. Others have argued that we require different theories of well-being for different theoretical purposes (Fletcher 2009; Tiberius 2007). It is reasonable to worry that the deep and persistent divide between externalists and internalists indicates that we really have more than one concept here.

Consequentialists who think that well-being is the central notion for ethical theory—the good to be maximized by right action—are known as welfarists. Welfarism assumes that well-being is something we can measure, compare across persons, and increase. In part these assumptions require philosophical attention:[12] the wrong theory of well-being might make it incommensurable or otherwise unsuitable as a goal for beneficent action. Once we have a good theory of well-being in hand, however, questions about how well-being can be measured and promoted are in large part empirical. For those who are interested in the practical implications of well-being research, this recommends collaboration with psychologists, economists, and others who are working on devising good measurement tools and discovering ways of making well-being improvements. Fortunately, so-called positive psychology (also known as hedonic psychology) has been influenced by philosophy in the ways that it conceptualizes well-being, which means that there are analogues of philosophical theories in the empirical literature (Tiberius 2006). The role of well-being in public policy is receiving a good deal of attention recently and this research will benefit from the contributions of philosophers (see Bok 2010; Diener 2009; Hausman 2012; Layard 2005).

Acknowledgments

I would like to thank Guy Fletcher, David Schmidtz, and the editors, Jonas Olson and Iwao Hirose, for helpful feedback on previous drafts of this paper.

Notes

1. Here I follow those who think that explaining normativity is explaining reasons for action. See, e.g., Schroeder (2007). For those who are attracted to the buck-passing view about value, explaining the normativity of well-being amounts also to explaining why it is a value. For general discussion of normativity and value see Zimmerman, chapter 1 in this volume.

2. Though Aristotle's methodology does bear some similarity to reflective equilibrium according to Richard Kraut (2006).
3. See also Nussbaum (1992), and see Antony (2000) for an insightful critical discussion.
4. Intuitions about what we want for our children might be one species of intuitions of what we want for the sake of a person we care about. Stephen Darwall (2004) develops a meta-ethical theory called the rational care theory of welfare that puts this idea at the center.
5. Their popularity in economics has a lot to do with the way in which they lend themselves to objective measurement (or are taken to).
6. Indeed, it may not even help make desire theory intuitive, if one thinks that our intrinsic desires can be bad for us.
7. See Haybron 2008: 156–157; Kagan 1992; and Sumner 1996: 27–34 for discussions of these distinctions. I regret perpetuating another internalism/externalism distinction in ethics, and I would urge that we rename such theories "subject-dependent" theories (see Hall and Tiberius, forthcoming), but I will retain the usual terminology here.
8. The problem is pressed by the economist Amartya Sen (1987), who, along with Nussbaum, defends a capabilities approach to well-being. Nussbaum argues that it is an important advantage of the capabilities approach that it can make sense of the claim that the satisfaction of preferences adapted to oppression is not necessarily good for a person.
9. For one attempt to defend the life satisfaction theory in the context of empirical work see Tiberius and Plakias (2010).
10. For an internalist view that takes *goals* to be the key to understanding well-being see Keller (2009, 2004).
11. For a general discussion of welfarism see Keller (2009). See also the references in the last paragraph of this chapter.
12. See Chang, chapter 11, and Carlson, chapter 15, in this volume.

References

Alexandrova, A. (2013). "Doing Well in the Circumstances." *Journal of Moral Philosophy* 10: 307–28.
Antony, L. M. (2000). "Natures and Norms*." *Ethics* 111: 8–36.
Arneson, R. J. (1999). "Human Flourishing versus Desire Satisfaction." *Social Philosophy and Policy* 16: 113–42.
Bok, D. C. (2010). *The Politics of Happiness: What Government Can Learn from the New Research on Well-Being*. Princeton, NJ: Princeton University Press.
Brandt, R. B. (1979). *A Theory of the Good and the Right*. New York: Oxford University Press.
Crisp, R. (2006a). "Hedonism Reconsidered." *Philosophy and Phenomenological Research* 73: 619–45.
Crisp, R. (2006b). *Reasons and the Good*. New York: Oxford University Press.
Darwall, S. (2004). *Welfare and Rational Care*. Princeton, NJ: Princeton University Press.
Diener, E. (1984). "Subjective Well-Being." *Psychological Bulletin* 95: 542–75.
Diener, E. (2009). *Well-Being for Public Policy*. New York: Oxford University Press.
Diener, E., C. Napa Scollon, and R. E. Lucas. 2003. "The Evolving Concept of Subjective Well-Being: The Multifaceted Nature of Happiness." *Advances in Cell Aging and Gerontology* 15: 187–219.
Dorsey, D. (2012). "Subjectivism without Desire." *Philosophical Review* 121: 407–42.

Feldman, F. (2004). *Pleasure and the Good Life: Concerning the Nature, Varieties and Plausibility of Hedonism*. New York: Oxford University Press.
Finnis, J. (2011). *Natural Law and Natural Rights*. New York: Oxford University Press.
Fletcher, G. (2009). "Rejecting Well-Being Invariabilism." *Philosophical Papers* 38: 21–34.
Fletcher, G. (2013). "A Fresh Start for the Objective-List Theory of Well-Being." *Utilitas* 25 (2): 206–20.
Griffin, J. (1986). *Well-Being: Its Meaning. Measurement, and Moral Importance* Oxford: Clarendon Press.
Hall, A., and V. Tiberius. (Forthcoming). "Well-Being and Subject-Dependence." *Routledge Handbook of Philosophy of Well-Being*.
Harsanyi, J. C. (1977). "Morality and the Theory of Rational Behavior." *Social Research* 44: 623–56.
Hausman, D. M. (2012). *Preference, Value, Choice, and Welfare*. New York: Cambridge University Press.
Haybron, D. (2007). "Life Satisfaction, Ethical Reflection, and the Science of Happiness." *Journal of Happiness Studies* 8: 99–138.
Haybron, D. M. (2008). *The Pursuit of Unhappiness: The Elusive Psychology of Well-Being*. New York: Oxford University Press.
Heathwood, C. (2005). "The Problem of Defective Desires." *Australasian Journal of Philosophy* 83: 487–504.
Heathwood, C. (2006). "Desire Satisfactionism and Hedonism." *Philosophical Studies* 128: 539–63.
Heathwood, C. (2007). "The Reduction of Sensory Pleasure to Desire." *Philosophical Studies* 133: 23–44.
Kagan, S. (1992). "The Limits of Well-Being." *Social Philosophy and Policy* 9: 169–89.
Keller, S. (2004). "Welfare and the Achievement of Goals." *Philosophical Studies* 121: 27–41.
Keller, S. (2009a). "Welfare as Success." *Noûs* 43: 656–83.
Keller, S. (2009b). "Welfarism." *Philosophy Compass* 4: 82–95.
Kraut, R. (2006). "How to Justify Ethical Propositions: Aristotle's Method." In R. Kraut (ed.), *The Blackwell Guide to Aristotle's Nicomachean Ethics* Malden, MA: Blackwell, 76–95.
Kraut, R. (2009). *What Is Good and Why: The Ethics of Well-Being*. Cambridge: Harvard University Press.
Layard, R. (2005). *Happiness: Lessons form a New Science*. London: Penguin.
Nussbaum, M. C. (1992). "Human Functioning and Social Justice in Defense of Aristotelian Essentialism." *Political Theory* 20: 202–46.
Nussbaum, M. C. (2001). *Women and Human Development: The Capabilities Approach*. Cambridge: Cambridge University Press.
Parfit, D. (1984). *Reasons and Persons*. Oxford: Oxford University Press.
Raibley, J. (2010). "Well-Being and the Priority of Values." *Social Theory and Practice* 36: 593–620.
Railton, P. (1986). "Moral Realism." *Philosophical Review* 95: 163–207.
Rosati, C. S. (1995). "Persons, Perspectives, and Full Information Accounts of the Good." *Ethics* 105: 296–325.
Rosati, C. S. (2006). "Personal Good." In T. Horgan and M. Timmons (eds.), *Metaethics after Moore*. New York: Oxford University Press, 107–32.
Scanlon, T. M. (1998). *What We Owe to Each Other*. Cambridge: Belknap Press of Harvard University Press.

Schroeder, M. A. (2007). *Slaves of the Passions*. New York: Oxford University Press.
Sen, A. K. (1987). *On Ethics and Economics*. Oxford: Blackwell.
Sobel, D. (2009). "Subjectivism and Idealization." *Ethics* 119: 336–52.
Sumner, L. W. (1995). "The Subjectivity of Welfare." *Ethics* 105: 764–90.
Sumner, L. W. (1996). *Welfare, Happiness, and Ethics*. Oxford: Clarendon Press.
Tiberius, V. (2006). "Well-Being: Psychological Research for Philosophers." *Philosophy Compass* 1: 493–505.
Tiberius, V. (2007). "Substance and Procedure in Theories of Prudential Value." *Australasian Journal of Philosophy* 85: 373–91.
Tiberius, V. (2008). *The Reflective Life: Living Wisely with Our Limits*. New York: Oxford University Press.
Tiberius, V., and A. Plakias. (2010). "Well-Being." In J. Doris (ed.), *The Moral Psychology Handbook*. Oxford: Oxford University Press, 401–31.
Velleman, J. D. (1988). "Brandt's Definition of 'Good.'" *Philosophical Review* 97: 353–71.

CHAPTER 10

KANTIAN AXIOLOGY AND THE DUALISM OF PRACTICAL REASON

RALF M. BADER

10.1. Introduction

Whereas consequentialists rank states of affairs in terms of their axiological properties and then invoke maximizing, optimizing, or satisficing functions applied to the resulting evaluative orderings to provide an analysis or reduction of deontic notions, deontologists are not, in the first place, concerned with the states of affairs that are brought about but with the nature of the actions that agents perform, identifying various conditions that actions must satisfy as well as principles to which they must conform. The Kantian approach is a paradigm case of deontological ethics, providing a criterion of permissibility that actions (or, more precisely, maxims) must satisfy insofar as they must be in agreement with reason and hence be universalisable.

The deontological nature of the supreme principle of Kantian ethics has led many people to focus almost exclusively on issues about duty, universalization, autonomy, and dignity when engaging with Kantian ethics, resulting in the unfortunate situation that value-based considerations have been largely ignored and that Kant has been criticized for supposedly failing to appreciate the importance of happiness. All of this has happened despite the fact that Kant's ethical theory does not restrict itself to duty but contains a well-developed account of value that plays a central role in the overall theory and that recognizes the significance of happiness. After all, the *Groundwork* starts with the axiological claim that the only thing that is unconditionally good is the good will. Likewise, the highest good, which is meant to represent the culmination of Kant's ethical system, is an axiological notion that includes happiness.

This chapter provides an account of the Kantian theory of value, showing how the fundamentally heterogeneous values of morality and prudence can be integrated into a complete ordering by appealing to the conditionality of the value of happiness, which allows us to explain how the claims of prudence can be silenced by the claims of morality, thereby solving the Sidgwickian problem of the dualism of practical reason.[1]

10.2. Kantian Axiology

The key commitments of Kant's value theory are twofold: (1) it is a dualistic theory, and (2) it is a conditional value theory. These two commitments ensure that the axiology has the form of a multidimensional conditional value structure.

VALUE DUALISM

> The Kantian account is a dualistic account that recognizes two distinct types of value, namely (1) moral value, and (2) prudential value. These types of value are fundamentally heterogeneous and derive from different sources. This axiological dualism is tied up with the general duality between reason and sensibility that underlies all of Kantian philosophy. The Kantian system is predicated on the idea that we are finite rational creatures that have both a rational and a sensible side. In the practical realm, this dualism gives rise to two types of values, two types of normativity, and two types of imperatives. While each side of our nature has its own type of good, these different values are not on an equal footing. In particular, moral value is the supreme good, whereas prudential value is only a conditioned good.[2]

CONDITIONAL VALUE

> Kant is committed to the conditionality of the value of happiness. Happiness is something that is good and that is to be brought about.[3] Moreover, it is something that is intrinsically good, since the source of the value of happiness is intrinsic, that is, happiness is valuable in virtue of its intrinsic nonevaluative features. Yet, it is also something that is only conditionally good, since the value of happiness is subject to an extrinsic condition, thereby making it conditionally intrinsically valuable. This condition consists in having a good will, which is a matter of adopting the correct priority ordering by subordinating the pursuit of happiness to the requirements of morality. The fact that the source of value is intrinsic explains why happiness is to be valued for its own sake, whereas the fact that it is subject to an extrinsic condition explains why happiness is to be valued only when it is had by someone who has a good will. The conditionality of the value of happiness plays a crucial role in the Kantian system, since it allows us to make sense of the idea that prudence can be silenced when it conflicts with duty. Because of this conditioning relationship, morality ends up not merely outweighing or trumping the claims of happiness, but ensuring that happiness does not have any (intrinsic) value at all and hence does not even constitute a pro tanto

reason when it conflicts with morality. That is, when it conflicts with duty, happiness counts for nothing.[4]

By combining the supreme good and the conditioned good, to the extent that the condition of its value is satisfied, one ends up with the highest good, that is, with happiness in accordance with virtue. The degree to which one is virtuous, that is, has a good will, determines the degree to which one's happiness is good and to which one deserves being happy.[5]

Something that might seem puzzling is that Kant holds both that the good will is the only thing that is unconditionally good, and that humanity is something that is of infinite worth. Since one cannot identify the good will with humanity, and since one cannot hold that both are unconditionally good, one needs to find a way to make room for the significance of humanity. The solution to this puzzle consists in recognizing that the claim about the good will is an axiological claim, whereas the claim about humanity is not concerned with what is good and to be valued, but with what has a special type of moral status. In particular, to say that rational agents have dignity and infinite worth is to say that they have a certain status that needs to be respected, in the first place that they are not to be treated as mere means. Thus, although humanity plays an important role in Kantian ethics, it does not have a place in Kantian axiology. Discussions of the "value of humanity" are, accordingly, misleading and will be set aside for the purposes of this chapter.[6]

10.3. The Dualism of Practical Reason

The bifurcation of goodness into moral and prudential goodness, which lies at the core of the Kantian theory of value, seems to generate a problem, in that it leads to what Sidgwick described as the "dualism of practical reason." The problem is that the radical heterogeneity of these two types of value implies that they cannot be ordered or weighed up against each other. As a result, morality and prudence can generate conflicting requirements, without there being anything to settle the conflict between them and to privilege one over the other. This fragmentation of value thus seems to leave practical reason in an irresolvable conflict whenever prudence and morality require different actions, thereby threatening to undermine the coherence of practical reason and to reduce the cosmos of duty to chaos (see Sidgwick 1874: 473).[7]

Within a monistic framework, the notion of an overall evaluation can be understood straightforwardly, since it simply corresponds to an all-things-considered evaluation. There is one type of value, and one can evaluate how things stand with respect to that value when all things, that is, all relevant facts, are considered. When the evaluation is not restricted in any way, one arrives at an assessment that integrates all the relevant facts.

By contrast, problems arise in the case of pluralism. As soon as a plurality of different types of values is at issue, the question arises as to how they can be integrated into an overall assessment that is not restricted to a particular type of value, but that considers all the different values there are. As long as the different types of value point in the same direction and order alternatives in the same way, there are no problems. Yet, once they pull in opposing directions, one needs the values to be commensurable in order to make sense either of trade-offs or of lexical orderings and thereby arrive at a determinate ordering of the alternatives. The problem then is that, since values of different types are incommensurable,[8] the possibility of such assessments risks being undermined. This means that one can only say that one should ϕ on the basis of the evaluation in terms of value V_1, and that one should not-ϕ on the basis of value V_2. But one cannot say what one should do considering both types of value. In this way, one can be guided by one of the values at a time, but not by both of them at the same time. Moreover, there will be nothing to choose between these values, nothing to privilege one over the other. One cannot appeal to V_1 to establish that one should be guided by V_1 as that would be question-begging, and likewise for V_2. Nor does there seem to be anything that could integrate these values into an overall evaluation, thereby leaving the agent with conflicting requirements and the existential choice whether to follow value V_1 or V_2.

To avoid this predicament, it would seem that one needs an external standard that encompasses both of the values and orders them with respect to each other. In other words, it would seem that one needs another value, a super-value subsuming the conflicting values. One could then evaluate alternatives with respect to this super-value to arrive at an overall assessment that would integrate the component values and adjudicate the conflicts between them.

It might be suggested that instead of bringing in a super-value, one can simply appeal to lexical orderings and hold that morality is overriding, in the sense that it has lexical priority over prudence, that it trumps prudence.[9] This suggestion, however, is confused. A lexical ordering arises in a situation in which the betterness ordering is such that different goods are ordered in such a way that any quantity of one good outweighs any quantity of the other good. For there to be a lexical ordering, there must accordingly be some betterness relation that orders the different goods. This, however, implies that moral value and prudential value cannot be lexically ordered, unless there is a betterness relation encompassing both of them. This means that a further type of value subsuming both moral and prudential value, that is, a super-value, is required if they are to be lexically ordered. The lexical ordering view is hence not an alternative to the super-value proposal. Instead, it is simply an instance of the super-value view. That is, it is simply a particular way of ordering different goods with respect to the super-value, namely one whereby moral value cannot be traded off against prudential value since any amount of moral good is better than any amount of prudential good, where this betterness claim has to be understood in terms of super-betterness, that is, better with respect to the super-value.

Likewise, the idea that this problem can simply be settled by appealing to the notion of all-things-considered value is confused. The locution "all-things-considered" modifies a given type of value but is not itself a type of value. With respect to some value V we can either evaluate all things taken together and thereby arrive at a complete evaluation, or we can restrict the evaluation by only evaluating certain things and thereby arrive at a partial evaluation.[10] That is, we can either have an all-things-considered evaluation with respect to V, or a partial evaluation with respect to V that is restricted to particular dimensions and that only assesses something with respect to certain good-making features. However, there is no such thing as a special type of value: all-things-considered value.[11]

10.3.1. Formal Values

Thus, it looks like one needs a further value in order to adjudicate the conflict between prudence and morality, where this would have to be a super-value subsuming the conflicting values. This view has been criticized by Griffin, who has claimed that we do not need substantive values to deal with pluralism, that "we do not need a super-value to have a scale. It is enough to have the quantitative attribute 'value'" (Griffin 1986: 89, also see 32, 90–92).[12]

Griffin's suggestion, however, is problematic. Value pluralism implies that values come in different types and that "quantities" of value will consequently be in different units. These units need to be converted if different values are to be traded off against each other. As soon as one allows for the possibility of conflicts, there will have to be a relative ordering or weighting of the different values. The merely formal attribute "value," however, does not give us a relative weighting of the different types of value and does not enable us to convert the different units. Although it is possible to construct various formal values with stipulated trade-off ratios, for instance by means of a 0-1 normalization that can be used to bring about proportional satisfaction, any such merely formal value will not have any intrinsic significance but will only matter extrinsically, if at all. While it can be used for certain purposes, for example, for the purpose of adjudicating competitions and suchlike, insofar as such formal values can be introduced and employed in a stipulative manner, this only ensures that conventional, but not intrinsic, significance can attach to them.

There are two tasks that cannot be performed by merely formal values and for which substantive values need to be brought in. First, there is a need to specify which values count. Formal values can be constructed out of all kinds of "values," out of all dimensions along which things can be ranked. Yet, not all ranking-dimensions are significant and to be used. Accordingly, it needs to be determined which candidates are ruled in, and which ones are ruled out—which dimensions matter, and which ones do not. Second, it needs to be specified how to construct the metric along which the values are to be traded off against each other. There is an infinite number of possible ways of combining the values that count, and something needs to single out a determinate relative weighting, a particular way of combining them. One needs to give an account why one is to normalize the values in one way rather than another, why one is to assign one set of relative weightings rather than some other weightings. There is thus an urgent need for something that privileges one of the infinitely many candidate weightings and that makes one way of combining these values the right way. In short, what needs to be determined is (1) which values count, and (2) how much each value counts. It would seem that a substantive value is what settles these questions. Without it, one can only construct a merely stipulative metric that lacks any intrinsic significance.

While a natural way of normalizing consists in treating the minima of the different values as equivalent and likewise for their maxima, that is, a 0-1 normalization, there are also other ways of normalizing. For instance, one can treat the midpoint of one value as equivalent to the maximum of the other value. Both ways of normalizing and aggregating the values agree on all judgments that can be established by means of dominance reasoning, which means that both methods can claim to be responsive to the normative significance of the different values. Yet these methods diverge when trade-offs are at issue. The first normalization treats the values as counting equally (i.e., the complete (non)satisfaction of one value is as important as the complete (non)satisfaction of the other value), whereas the second normalization is such that one value counts twice as much as the other value.[13]

It might be thought that the 0-1 normalization is privileged over alternative normalizations since it is permutation-invariant, treating the component values impartially. This commitment to impartiality, however, amounts to a value judgment to the effect that the components are equally significant. Since the relative importance of the different values is precisely what is to be established, one cannot simply start out with the idea that morality and prudence count equally. Instead, it is a substantive matter how much the values count, how they are to be ordered and weighed up, and an impartial normalization needs to be justified and shown to be privileged over alternative normalizations. Impartiality, accordingly, cannot be presupposed, but has to be argued for.

Since the components themselves do not determine how they are to be put together, something further is required to end up with a particular relative weighting. Whatever fills this role and provides the weighting cannot purely derive its significance from the components but, instead, needs to have its own significance. It must have independent significance, and must hence be something substantive rather than merely formal. Otherwise, it would not be privileged since all the other possible ways of putting together the components (or, at least, all those satisfying a positive responsiveness condition) would be equally significant, given that they would derive their significance in the same way from the components. That is, every way of normalizing has the same derivative significance, because the components from which this significance is derived are the same. This means that these normalizations need to be differentiated in terms of something else, and that one method can be privileged over the others only if it has non-derivative significance. If no weighting were privileged, then there would be no reason to put the components together in one way rather than any other way, and the selection of a normalization would then be an arbitrary matter.

10.3.2. Substantive Values

In order to avoid the dualism of practical reason, it is necessary to find a way of integrating prudence and morality into a combined ordering. As we have seen, conflicts between different values cannot be resolved by means of a merely formal value. As a result, it looks like it is necessary to bring in a further standpoint and appeal to a substantive value that adjudicates conflicts by determining either an ordering of the component values or a relative weighting of them that allows for trade-offs. This line of thought has been defended by Chang, who has argued that the usual way of adjudicating conflicts between different values involves an appeal to a further value (a "covering value") that subsumes the conflicting values.

Covering values allow us to resolve certain conflicts. In particular, they can deal with conflicts that involve restrictions to different dimensions of one and the same value. Such comparisons involve a unique value V with respect to which different things are evaluated along different dimensions. The covering value allows us to integrate the partial evaluations that are restricted to particular good-making features. In this way, one can combine two evaluative dimensions $V|_{d_1}(x)$ and $V|_{d_2}(x)$ by appealing to value V of which they are both restrictions. Comparisons across different dimensions are thus unproblematic from the point of view of commensurability.[14] Values, reasons, and oughts that are recognized or generated from one and the same normative standpoint are commensurable and can be put together by means of a covering value corresponding to this standpoint.

For instance, one can accept an attenuated form of pluralism by holding that both equality and utility are good, in the sense that these are two different types of good-making features of a distribution, two different dimensions along which distributions can be good. This means that utility and equality are ranking-dimensions that are such that the value of the distribution is positively responsive to increases in these features. That is, if D_1 is more equal than D_2 (other things being equal), then D_1 is better than D_2. Likewise, if D_1 contains more utility than D_2 (other things being equal), then D_1 is better than D_2. When evaluating distributions, one can restrict the evaluation to these different dimensions, ordering distributions in terms of how good they are in virtue of their level of equality, or in terms of how good they are in virtue of their level of aggregate utility. In other words, one can restrict the evaluation to a certain dimension, that is, assess how good x is with respect to value V in virtue of its good-making features along dimension d. Rather than evaluating V(x), one only assesses $V|_d(x)$. The two restricted evaluations can be combined to yield an overall evaluation, that is, $V(D) = f(V|_E(D), V|_U(D))$. It is in this context that it makes sense to speak of an all-things-considered evaluation, since one can have an evaluation with respect to value V that is not restricted to a particular dimension, but that considers all dimensions.

While equality and utility are distinct types of things, the notion of betterness is the same in each case, namely moral betterness. In this way, unlike in the case of morality and prudence, the different dimensions do not correspond to different normative standpoints, but instead represent different dimensions along which something can be morally good. Accordingly, such a pluralist can hold that equality and utility both have the same type of value, namely moral value, and that they are hence commensurable. Trading off the different dimensions of moral value, for instance by trading off equality against utility, is thus analogous to trading off the different dimensions of hedonic value, for instance by trading off intensity of pleasure against duration of pleasure.

By contrast, covering values are inadequate when it comes to conflicts between different types of values that are incommensurable, such as the values of prudence and morality, and are hence unable to overcome the conflict involved in the dualism of practical reason.[15] Unlike in the case of attenuated versions of pluralism that merely involve different good-making features, a robust version of pluralism that is committed to there being different types of values has to deal with the problem of incommensurability. Pluralists of the robust variety recognize fundamentally different values because they countenance different evaluative standpoints from which things can be assessed and compared. These different values are not merely restrictions of one and the same value, but are independent and self-standing. Values, reasons, and oughts issuing from different standpoints are incommensurable and cannot be subsumed under a covering value. That is, one cannot combine values $V_a(x)$ and $V_b(x)$ by appealing to a further value V_c that has the others as parts.[16]

The suggestion that a covering value (which Chang has baptized "prumorality") can subsume moral and prudential values, which are fundamentally heterogeneous and which have independent significance, is problematic on a number of counts.

1. To begin with, if they were subsumable under a common covering value, then this would imply that their normative significance would be derivative. As Chang notes, "If a moral value in conflict with a prudential one is a component of some more comprehensive nameless value, then the normativity of morality in the face of conflict with prudence derives from the normativity of that nameless value.... It is in virtue of that nameless value that, in a particular case, a moral value has whatever normativity it does in the face of conflict with a prudential one" (Chang 2004b: 148). This type of derivativeness, however, would contradict both the independence and heterogeneity of the standpoints of morality and prudence.

   On the one hand, if they were derivative, then they would not be independent. Instead, the values would derive their normative force from the covering value that would subsume them, thereby making them dependent on that from which they would derive their significance. Values and oughts that are internally generated by a standpoint derive their normativity from this standpoint. A standpoint is thus independent if it gives rise to its own values and oughts. These values/oughts will be internal to the standpoint. They will not be derivative but will instead be generated and imbued with normativity in accordance with the standards of the particular standpoint. By contrast, independence does not hold in cases in which they are externally validated by another standpoint. When there is an external standard that validates the verdicts passed by different standpoints and makes it the case that they are binding and have normative significance, then the latter are dependent on the former. In such a scenario, normativity is not internal to the particular standpoints but derives from the external perspective, which makes it the case that these standpoints only have derivative significance.

   On the other hand, if they were derivative, then they would not be heterogeneous. Instead, they would involve the same type of normativity as the covering value from which they would derive their significance and would hence be homogeneous. Internally generated values, however, are ordered in terms of the standards pertaining to the particular standpoint from which they issue. This means that different types of values involve different types of normativity that are not reducible to each other. Different types of values that correspond to different points of view in this way involve different betterness relations and come in different units of value and hence cannot be ordered or traded off against each other.[17]

The independence and heterogeneity of the standpoints thus precludes any axiological comparability.

2. A covering value that could resolve the dualism of practical reason would have to correspond to some further standpoint above and beyond the standpoints of morality and prudence. It is, however, not at all clear what this further standpoint could be, how it would operate, and on what basis it would order the components. What is this further value meant to be? And what is its source of normativity? The radical heterogeneity of morality and prudence makes it difficult to see how they could be combined, without them being integrated in a merely disjunctive manner. Moreover, it is unclear how the further standpoint could combine them without threatening to undermine the idea that the categorical imperative is the supreme principle of practical reason, since this standpoint would seem to "dethrone morality" (Haji 1998), something that is completely anathema from a Kantian perspective.[18]

3. Even if there were a further standpoint and a further type of value, it would not be possible to subsume such heterogeneous and independent values thereunder without regenerating the original problem. All cases of conflicts that are adjudicated by subsuming the conflicting values under a covering value either involve not independent values but only restrictions of one and the same value, or they involve a stipulative combination that merely has conventional significance. Neither type of case provides insight as to how conflicts can be resolved when one is concerned with independent values that have intrinsic significance. In such conflict cases, a further value would not resolve but rather exacerbate the original problem. This is because one would then need an explanation as to why the further value is to take precedence over the component values, something that cannot be established by reference to this further standpoint, given that its authority is precisely what is in question.

It might be thought that by subsuming the other values, one can explain why the super-value is to be taken as being authoritative since any claims made by its components will already be accounted for, on the basis that they will be integrated into the claim of the super-value. Yet, as we saw in the discussion of different normalizations, this explanation does not work. This is because the relative strength of the components is a substantive matter that needs to be settled and that is not derivative from the contributions of the components. When there is a conflict between one of the component values and the super-value, that is, when comparing two situations whereby the latter involves a loss in the component value but a gain in the combined value, then the question arises as to why the latter is to be preferred over the former. This question cannot be answered by arguing that the claim of the component value is already included in that of the combined value, because the degree to which it is included therein is a function of the combined value and, as such, presupposes the authoritativeness of that value (with respect to the component value), yet this is precisely what is to be established. This means that the super-value proposal only works where the significance of the component values is entirely derivative, but that it is not applicable to independent values that are intrinsically significant. As a result, we can see that there does not seem to be a way for a super-value to incorporate the disparate values of prudence and morality in a way that does not simply raise the original problem again.

This means that substantive values can only integrate different evaluative dimensions into an overall evaluation, but they cannot integrate the different values of morality and prudence. There are no problems in subsuming different dimensions of evaluation under a covering value, since what are subsumed in that case are ranking-dimensions that are restrictions of one and the same value. It is, however, not possible to subsume morality and prudence, given that they are separate evaluative standpoints. These heterogeneous standpoints are independent, which precludes subsumption under a common covering value.

Chang has criticized robust pluralism by invoking nominal-notable comparisons. "In general, a notable moral act is better with respect to both morality and prudence than a nominal prudential one. There must therefore be a covering value in terms of which comparisons of moral and prudential merit proceed, one that has both moral and prudential values as components. . . . We cannot make a judgement about the relative importance of these considerations without there being some value, however indefinite, in terms of which the judgment proceeds" (Chang 1997: 32). The argument is thus that nominal-notable comparisons between moral and prudential values are possible. From this it follows that there are normative relations that hold among them, which is meant to imply the existence of a covering value and hence the falsity of robust pluralism.

This argument, however, does not succeed since it is possible for there to be normative relations between different values, without these values being subsumable under a common covering value. That is, not all normative relations presuppose the existence of a covering value. Although the heterogeneity and independence of the different standpoints preclude axiological relations between them, they do not rule out all normative relations. In particular, there is the normative relation of silencing, which does not presuppose comparability and does not proceed via a covering value, but can instead be established by appealing to conditional values.[19] In this way, it is possible to have normative relations without having a covering value and without having axiological comparability.

Silencing can thus account for the cases that show that there are normative relations between morality and prudence, in that it implies that we should go with morality rather than with prudence. In order to generate problems for the silencing account and undermine robust pluralism, one would require nominal-notable comparisons going in both directions. That is, one would also have to have cases in which the verdict would go in the other direction, such that one would have to give precedence to prudence over morality. If there were normative priority relations in both directions, such that morality would sometimes take precedence and prudence would take precedence on other occasions, then the normative relation between morality and prudence could not be one of silencing but could only be explained by a covering value. The existence of such cases, however, is far from clear, given the intuitiveness of some version or other of the overridingness thesis, and is incompatible with the Kantian commitment to the categorical imperative being the supreme principle of practical reason.

10.3.3. Conditional Values

Neither formal nor substantive values allow us to address conflicts between morality and prudence, and hence are insufficient by themselves to resolve the dualism of practical reason. Instead, the way out of this predicament deriving from value dualism lies in the other Kantian commitment, namely in the conditionality of the value of happiness. The commitment to conditionality allows us to avoid conflicts between morality and prudence, thereby avoiding situations in which practical reason is faced with incompatible requirements. It does so by making the claims of prudence conditional upon being compatible with having a good will, which implies that they are conditional upon being permissible, thereby allowing morality to silence prudence. That is, the claims corresponding to moral value, namely the claims of duty, silence those of prudence.[20]

When the action that makes one happy is impermissible, the condition of the value of happiness would be undermined by performing this action. Though happiness results from the action, no value is thereby realized. Since the action does not produce anything of prudential value, there is no prudential reason to perform it. That is, given that the normative force attaching to hypothetical imperatives derives from the value of the end that is to be realized, it follows that if the condition of the value of the end fails to be satisfied, then no value will result from the realization of the end, which implies that one does not have any reason to take the means. Because the value of happiness is conditional, the claims of prudence that are based on this value will also be conditional. In this way, the claims of prudence can be silenced by the requirements of duty.[21]

Since the account of silencing ensures that there are no conflicts among the different values, a complete ordering can be generated without bringing in any relative orderings or weightings. There is hence no need to bring in a further substantive value to adjudicate conflicts. Nor is there a need to normalize the different values in order to integrate them into a coherent ordering. Instead, given that one has a conditional value structure in place that precludes the possibility of conflicts between the different types of values, appealing to a formal value turns out to be sufficient, since, as we will see in the next section, the absence of conflicts ensures that the different values do not need to be normalized but can rather be integrated in a disjunctive manner.

Substantive values only need to be brought in to determine which values count. Since the significance of the formal value is derived entirely from the significance of its component values, one has to be working with ranking-dimensions that matter intrinsically. Unless the components are substantive values that have intrinsic significance, the formal value will be a mere construct that will lack significance. Once these intrinsically significant components are in place, one can disjunctively integrate them into a complete overall ordering, as long as there are no conflicts among the substantive values. The absence of conflicts thus allows us to use a formal value to combine a plurality of substantive values, without any need to bring in a further substantive value subsuming them.

According to the silencing account, it is not the case that the moral ought trumps the prudential ought (or that moral value is lexically prior to prudential value). Rather, the prudential ought is conditional on being morally permissible. That is, instead of its being the case that one ought to do what morality tells one rather than what prudence does, prudence only commands that one take the means required for realizing one's ends on condition of its being the case that doing so is compatible with morality.

Otherwise, if one were to accept an account on which morality trumps prudence, one would face the problem of explaining what type of "ought" is implicated in the claim that one ought to comply with the moral ought rather than with the prudential ought (in the same way that one would need to explain the problematic idea that there could be a "super-value" with respect to which moral and prudential value could be ordered). This ought cannot be a moral ought since what is at issue is precisely establishing that the moral ought is the one that is to be complied with. Hence saying that there is a moral ought to the effect that one ought to comply with the moral ought, rather than the prudential ought, just presupposes what is to be established. For obvious reasons, it cannot be a prudential ought either. But this leaves the proponent of the trumping interpretation in a difficult situation since there does not seem to be any third type of ought, any third type of normativity. There are only morality and prudence, and neither of them underwrites the requisite ought statement. Moreover, even if there were some further ought, one would end up with the problem of explaining why one ought to comply with this third ought rather than with one of the others. The original problem would in this way simply be replicated rather than resolved.

Accordingly, it is preferable to adopt the silencing rather than the trumping interpretation and hold that there is no need for an ought to the effect that one comply with the moral ought. The first-order moral ought is sufficient by itself since there cannot be any competing ought claim, given that the prudential ought is conditional upon its compatibility with morality. In this way, one can avoid conflicts among the different oughts/values and ensure a coherent overall ordering, without having to make trade-offs and without having to bring in a further standpoint or a further value. This is possible since the way in which moral and prudential oughts/values are normatively related and integrated into an overall evaluation is internal and not imposed by some external standard that stands above them.

10.4. UNINDEXED OUGHTS

The question as to what one ought to do, where this is not restricted to a particular normative standpoint or a particular type of value, but where this is construed in an unrestricted manner, is not to be understood in terms of some further independent ought, such as the "just plain ought" (see McLeod 2001), or the "ought simpliciter," or suchlike. Instead, this unindexed ought is a disjunctive ought that is constructed out of the moral and prudential oughts. More precisely, ought(ϕ) $=_{df}$ m-ought(ϕ) $\vee$ p-ought(ϕ). This construction provides us with a deflationary construal of unindexed ought claims, such that there are no substantive ought-facts above and beyond the moral and prudential oughts.

For this constructed notion to be coherent, there cannot be any conflicts among the constituent oughts. If a situation were to arise in which it was both the case that m-ought(ϕ) and that p-ought(not-ϕ),[22] then the constructed ought would yield both ought(ϕ) and ought(not-ϕ). The deflationary construal of the unindexed ought thus only generates a coherent ordering in circumstances in which there are no conflicts. The conditional value structure precludes the possibility of precisely such conflicts. Insofar as the prudential ought is conditional on not violating the moral requirements, there can never be conflicting moral and prudential oughts. This ensures that there is no need for a further substantive ought. Given that there is no need to appeal to a relative ordering or weighting of prudence and morality, there is no need for the disjunctive ought to have any normativity or significance above and beyond the normativity of the component oughts. All normative force derives from the components, such that the disjunctive ought merely summarizes these normative facts without having any normative force of its own. In this way, it will not be a substantive ought but will rather be a merely formal construction that can be construed in a deflationary manner.

It might be objected that the account of conditionality is not sufficient to avoid conflicts. In particular, one might be concerned that it is possible for two options, ϕ and ψ, to be both morally permissible, yet that ϕ is prudentially better whereas ψ is morally better, such that p-ought(ϕ) but m-ought(ψ), where ϕ-ing and ψ-ing are incompatible. Since the condition on the value of happiness consists in having a good will, not in being maximally morally good, it would appear that one situation can be morally better than another, without the condition failing to be satisfied in the latter case. If the prudential ordering of these two situations is the reverse, then a conflict between the two heterogeneous values would seem to arise that could not be resolved by appealing to the conditionality thesis, since, ex hypothesi, the condition is satisfied in each case. In other words, it would appear that there can be conflicts between morality and prudence within the realm of the permissible.[23]

In response, we can note that this apparent possibility is ruled out by the Kantian commitment to rigorism, which holds that the maxim of an action is either universalizable, in which case it is permissible and the agent has a good will, or that it fails to be universalizable, in which case it is impermissible and the agent has a bad will. There is no room for supererogation, no room for a moral ordering of permissible actions, and it is not possible for one good will to be better than another. Given these rigoristic commitments, it follows that whatever is morally good is equally good (from the point of view of morality) as anything else that is morally good, and that these alternatives can accordingly be ordered from a prudential point of view in a way that does not allow for any conflicts between prudence and morality.[24]

In the same way that we can make sense of an unindexed ought, an unindexed betterness relation can be constructed disjunctively out of moral and prudential value, without presupposing any substantive notion of overall betterness.

$$x > y =_{df} x >_m y \vee x >_p y$$

$$x = y =_{df} (x =_m y \vee x =_p y) \wedge \neg(x >_m y \vee x <_m y \vee x >_p y \vee x <_p y)$$

In this way, one can accept a deflationary reading of unindexed betterness claims. This can be done as long as there are no conflicting betterness judgments, since the disjunctive notion of betterness would fail to be asymmetric if there were to be conflicts and would hence not give us a coherent ordering. In other words, this notion is only coherent if there is never a situation in which both $x >_m y$ and $x <_p y$, or in which both $x <_m y$ and $x >_p y$.

This deflationary disjunctive account is not to be confused with a dominance principle, such as the Pareto principle, whereby $x > y$ iff $x \geq_m y \wedge x \geq_p y \wedge (x >_m y \vee x >_p y)$.[25]

First, dominance principles are best understood as being concerned with substantive values, not with formal values that are construed in a deflationary manner. In this sense, they are substantive bridge-principles that specify how one is to order value vectors in terms of their components (whereby these can either represent different types of values, or different locations of one and the same value).

Second, there is the important difference that dominance principles presuppose comparability. In particular, x and y must be comparable with respect to each value, if they are to be ordered on the basis of the dominance principle. If x is better than y with respect to one value, but not comparable with respect to another, then the dominance principle will not be applicable. In that case, x and y will be noncomparable with respect to the unindexed betterness relation based on the dominance principle. This is crucial since conditionality brings about noncomparability. If x is such that the condition of the value of happiness fails to be satisfied, then it will not have prudential value.[26] Accordingly, it will not be comparable with respect to an alternative that does have prudential value. This means that y will not be better than x, even though it is both the case that y is morally better than x and that y is not prudentially worse than x, on the basis that they are not comparable with respect to prudential value. What is required for the applicability of the dominance principle is not just that y not be prudentially worse than x, but that it be at least as prudentially good as x, which presupposes comparability. Dominance principles are thus inapplicable to dualistic conditional value structures and cannot be employed to arrive at a complete ordering. Whenever morality and prudence conflict, these principles make the options at issue noncomparable. This kind of incomplete ordering would not allow us to overcome the dualism of practical reason.

The problem is thus that if there are two types of value and one is conditional on the other, then one risks losing completeness due to noncomparability with respect to the conditional value when comparing a situation in which the condition is satisfied with one in which it fails to be satisfied. Since dominance principles require that a situation be at least as good as its alternatives with respect to each type of value, they thereby presuppose comparability along all dimensions of value, which is incompatible with the conditionality of value.

The disjunctive construal of the unindexed betterness relation, by contrast, does not have any difficulties in dealing with the noncomparability resulting from conditional values. This is because prudential considerations are completely side-stepped in conflict cases, ensuring that moral considerations by themselves determine how the unindexed betterness relation orders such conflicting alternatives. Prudence is silenced in the sense that prudential reasoning does not issue any verdict. When there are two alternatives, whereby one leads to greater happiness but is impermissible, then one has moral reason not to do it and there are no prudential reasons in its favor (i.e., there are no prudential reasons to commit an impermissible action that would have to be outweighed or trumped by the moral reasons speaking against committing that action). The permissible action, by contrast, has something speaking in its favor, namely being morally better. Accordingly, the only thing that can guide us in ordering these alternatives is morality.[27] When the condition fails to be satisfied, only the moral betterness relation will be defined, and it will consequently determine the disjunctive betterness relation.

The disjunctive account thus coincides with the dominance principle when the condition is satisfied and the alternatives are comparable with respect to all the values that are at issue, but diverges in the context of noncomparability with respect to the conditional component value. Whereas the dominance principle results in an incomplete ordering due to rendering such options noncomparable, the disjunctive account generates a complete ordering by ranking them in accordance with their moral ordering.

10.5. Incompleteness and Transitivity

An important objection to the proposed account is that the disjunctive notion of betterness might turn out to be nontransitive, in particular that it might fail to be acyclic and allow for situations in which $x > y_1 > \ldots y_n > x$. More precisely, the problem is that one might be able to put together incomplete component orderings in such a way that the unindexed betterness relation violates transitivity and allows for there to be betterness cycles. While it is in principle possible for failures of transitivity to arise in this manner, this can only occur under special conditions that cannot arise within the Kantian system.

Before specifying the conditions under which this can occur, it is necessary to clarify the notion of incompleteness. A value V is incomplete with respect to domain D if it is not the case that $\forall\, x,y \in D\ (x \geq_V y \vee x \leq_V y)$. We can distinguish two ways in which a value can be incomplete.

EXTERNAL INCOMPLETENESS

V can fail to order x and y on the basis that V is not applicable to x (and/or to y), that is, x stands in no V-betterness relations (x is not even equally V-good as itself). Here we are dealing with V having restricted applicability relative to D, rather than with the noncomparability of two bearers of V. That is, we are not dealing with an incomplete ordering of elements within V's betterness field, but with a situation in which V's field is a proper subset of D.

INTERNAL INCOMPLETENESS

V can fail to order x and y on the basis that, even though V is applicable to both x and y, no V-betterness relation holds between them, that is, these items are not V-ranked against certain alternatives. The items are value-apt and are both within V's betterness field, but they are not comparable. This happens, for instance, in the case of quasi-orderings generated by dominance principles. Here we are dealing either with incomparability that is due to a substantive failure of comparison, or with noncomparability that is due not to the inapplicability of value V, but due to a formal failure of the betterness relation.

Thus, we can distinguish cases in which x and y fail to be comparable with respect to value V, whereby (1) this failure is external to V's betterness field in that at least one of the items is not V-apt, and whereby (2) this failure is internal to V's betterness field in that each of the items is V-apt.

The notion of incompleteness that is relevant in the case of conditionality and silencing is the external one. This is because the failure of the satisfaction of the condition ensures that prudential value is not applicable and that the item in question consequently does not belong to the betterness field of prudential value. The conditionality of prudential value ensures that there will be items that stand in moral betterness relations, without standing in prudential betterness relations, that is, items that are not prudential-value-apt but that are moral-value-apt. In particular, impermissible options are not ordered by the prudential betterness relation since the condition is not satisfied, yet they are ordered by the moral betterness relation, insofar as they are all equally morally bad. As a result, the prudential betterness relation turns out to be incomplete with respect to the field of the disjunctive notion of betterness, where $D_V = \{x : \exists y\ xR_V y\}$ and where $xR_V y =_{df} x \geq_V y \vee x \leq_V y$, that is, $D_V = D_m \cup D_p$. Put differently, the unindexed betterness field will be incompletely ordered by the prudential betterness relation, that is, $\exists x, y \in D_V$, such that (i) $\neg(x >_p y)$, (ii) $\neg(x =_p y)$, and (iii) $\neg(x <_p y)$.

Externally incomplete orderings can be combined in a way that leads to violations of transitivity only if there are multiple incomplete values that have partially overlapping betterness fields.

1. Cycles can arise only if there are at least three incomplete values that have partially overlapping fields. The values need to be incomplete in different ways, allowing one to switch between different values that fail to be comparable as one goes through the cycle, and none of the values can have a field that is a subset of the other two fields, that is, $D_{V_1}\backslash D_{V_2} \neq \emptyset$, and $D_{V_1}\backslash D_{V_3} \neq \emptyset$, and likewise for V2 and V3. In that case there can be alternatives such that $x \in D_{V_1}, D_{V_2}, \notin D_{V_3}, y \in D_{V_2}, D_{V_3}, \notin D_{V_1}$, and $z \in D_{V_3}, D_{V_1}, \notin D_{V_2}$, which makes it possible for $x >_{V_2} y$, $y >_{V_3} z$, and $z >_{V_1} x$.
2. Transitivity can fail due to noncomparability, rather than due to acyclicity, that is, $x > y$, $y > z$ but $\neg(x > z)$ because x is noncomparable with z. This type of failure of transitivity arises when the disjunctive betterness relation is nontrichotomous, which requires there to be at least two partially overlapping incomplete values, that is, $D_{V_1}\backslash D_{V_2} \neq \emptyset$ and $D_{V_2}\backslash D_{V_1} \neq \emptyset$. This makes it possible that $x \in D_{V_1}, \notin D_{V_2}$, $y \in D_{V_1}, D_{V_2}$, and $z \in D_{V_2}, \notin D_{V_1}$, such that $x >_{V_1} y$, and $y >_{V_2} z$, without there being a value that contains both x and z in its betterness field, thereby rendering them noncomparable with respect to the unindexed betterness relation.

Accordingly, we can see that neither type of intransitivity can arise in the case of the Kantian axiological theory since there is only one incomplete value (whereby incompleteness is understood with respect to the field of the disjunctive betterness relation, rather than in terms of its own field). The completeness of the moral betterness relation ensures that there cannot be failures of transitivity resulting from noncomparability, since the unindexed notion is nontrichotomous only if each component ordering fails to rank the options in question.

Even if the theory were not dualistic but would include further types of value, no intransitivities could be generated because conditionality is understood in terms of nonmoral values being conditional on moral value, which precludes the possibility of combining the incomparabilities in the manner requisite for there being intransitivities. More precisely, the transitivity of the moral betterness relation ensures that betterness cycles could only arise in a situation in which all the options were ranked as equally good in terms of moral value, such that a cycle could then be generated in terms of the incomplete nonmoral values. However, since these other values are incomplete due to being conditional on moral value and since, as we have seen, the options have to be morally equivalent, it follows that all the other values would either be such that in a given situation the condition was satisfied in the case of each value, or that it would fail to be satisfied in the case of each value, thereby precluding the possibility of cycles.[28]

10.6. SILENCING VERSUS BRACKETING VERSUS CANCELING

The Kantian conditional value structure allows us to make sense of the idea that morality silences the claims of prudence. This section will compare the Kantian account with other ways in which prudence can be set aside and can fail to contribute to the balance of reasons, in particular with (1) the idea of bracketing (and the associated notion of an exclusionary reason) employed by Scanlon and Raz, (2) the phenomenon of canceling discussed by Nozick and Raz, as well as with (3) another (related) notion of silencing developed by McDowell.

BRACKETING

When a reason is bracketed, there is some consideration that constitutes a reason. This reason, however, is excluded from deliberation and does not contribute toward the balance of reasons. Exclusionary reasons (i.e., reasons for bracketing) make it the case that a certain value or reason is, in Chang's terminology, not at stake in the choice situation or the context of evaluation. The reason or value is then not relevant within the choice context and is accordingly to be excluded from deliberation. In this way, it has no effect on which reasons the agent is to comply with, or on how things are to be evaluated for the purpose of deliberation.[29]

By contrast, in the case of silencing, there is no reason. Instead of an existing reason being excluded, the relevant consideration fails to constitute a reason, on the basis that a certain condition fails to be satisfied, even though that very same consideration would have constituted a reason within a different context in which the condition was satisfied. The relevant consideration, accordingly, has no effect on what is to be done, not because its goodness is excluded and because the reason that it constitutes is bracketed, but because it has no goodness, because it does not constitute a reason.

CANCELING

The phenomenon of canceling (see Nozick 1968: § 7; Raz 1999: § 1.1) is similarly distinct from conditionality/silencing.[30] We can understand the mechanism underlying canceling as consisting in the removal of the ground. That is, when a reason or value is canceled, what happens is that the ground of the reason is removed. For instance, in the case of promises, releasing someone from a promise makes it the case that the reason is canceled, that is, the promisor no longer has reason to ϕ (nor does he have reason to not-ϕ). This phenomenon involves a modification of the supervenience base, that is, canceling makes it the case that the ground of the reason is no longer present.

As such, it is distinct from the idea that one needs to distinguish the source or ground of a reason from the conditions that must be satisfied for the consideration in question to constitute a reason. In the case of conditionality, it is possible for there to be no reason or value, even though the ground is present, since the condition fails to be satisfied. That is, a reason can be removed, without the ground being removed, by making it the case that the condition is no longer satisfied such that the ground no longer constitutes a reason, whereas canceling requires the ground to be removed if the reason is to be removed.

This difference can be illustrated by the fact that canceling, unlike silencing, is essentially a temporal phenomenon. Canceling involves a situation where at t_1 one has reason to ϕ, but then at t_2 the base is changed such that one no longer has reason to ϕ. Conditions, by contrast, can be simultaneous with the grounds. This ensures that silencing does not necessarily take the form of there being a reason at t_1 that is then silenced at t_2, since the conditions need to be satisfied for the relevant consideration to constitute a reason in the first place.

A further difference that distinguishes conditionality from canceling is that conditions come in two distinct forms, namely there can be both enablers (i.e., things the presence of (at least one of) which is required for something to be valuable) and disablers (i.e., things the absence of (all of) which is required for something to be valuable), whereas there does not seem to be an analogous distinction when it comes to canceling.

SILENCING

McDowell has made use of the notion of silencing in the context of virtue ethics. While there are some similarities between the view developed by McDowell and the Kantian theory, there are important differences separating these accounts. In particular, the Kantian understanding of silencing is entirely normative and does not have any impact on motivational questions. When the condition fails to be satisfied, happiness lacks value. Given that there is no value in becoming happy in such a situation, that is, in realizing the ends of prudence, it follows that the claims of prudence do not have any normative force and do not generate any reasons for action. Prudence, however, retains its motivational force when its commands are silenced, given that happiness is agreeable even when it is not valuable. This means that, even though there is no normative conflict (and hence no threat to the coherence of reason) when the claims of prudence are silenced, there is still a struggle between morality and prudence at the level of motivation. By contrast, according to McDowell, the fully virtuous person, unlike the merely continent person, is not in any way inclined to act on the basis of self-interest when doing so conflicts with virtue. In this sense, the motivational force of happiness is silenced on the McDowellian account along with its reason-giving force.

On the Kantian account, silencing is explained in terms of the conditionality of the value of happiness (which, in turn, is explained in terms of what it is for something to have value). McDowell, by contrast, lacks a theory of conditional value, which makes it difficult to see how he can provide a mechanism that explains silencing and by means of which prudential considerations fail to constitute reasons when they conflict with morality. Providing such a mechanism is a complicated matter since it has to resolve the tension in the idea that prudence is independent, yet can be silenced by morality. That is, it needs to reconcile a commitment to pluralism, which amounts to recognizing different standpoints that are meant to be independent of one another, with a commitment to silencing, which requires the standpoints to interact.

In particular, the problem is that, unless one has a theory of conditional value, one lacks the distinction between the ground of value and the condition of value. This distinction allows one to hold that prudence is independent, in the sense that it has its own source, its own ground, yet can be silenced on the basis that it is subject to extrinsic conditions. One can then make sense of a situation in which the ground is present but in which there is no value, due to the fact that the condition fails to be satisfied. In this way, one can separate out normative silencing from changing the nonnormative/nonevaluative grounds.

If this distinction is missing, one will instead have to make it the case that the ground is absent if the value is to be absent. This, however, is not really a form of silencing but is instead analogous to canceling, in that it operates at the level of the ground, rather than just operating at the level of value by making it the case that the condition fails to be satisfied.[31] Insofar as the notion of silencing presupposes that there is something that is present but that is prevented from constituting a reason, one needs the distinction between grounds and conditions, since it is only with reference to this distinction that one can make sense of the ground being present but silenced, on the basis of its being prevented from being valuable due to its condition being undermined.

One way of understanding McDowell's suggestion that prudence is silenced takes precisely the form of operating at the level of grounds and is based on the idea that for the fully virtuous person there is no pleasure in actions that conflict with the requirements of virtue, even though such a person would derive enjoyment from these very same actions were they not to conflict with virtue. The 'situational appreciation' of a virtuous person "is such as to insulate the attractions of competing courses of action from generating actual urges to pursue them" (McDowell 1996: 102; also see McDowell 1978: 27). There is no temptation because the agent does not have the relevant desires and hence would not derive any enjoyment from these actions. There is thus nothing that could motivate (= motivational silencing) and nothing that could be good (= normative silencing). On this account, the difference is not restricted to the evaluative level, but also affects the nonevaluative level. Motivational and nonmotivational silencing accordingly go hand in hand.

This means that for the fully virtuous person, it is not the case that prudence makes claims that are silenced and that fail to constitute reasons. Rather, prudence is prevented from making claims in the first place, insofar as considerations that would otherwise be attractive and on which claims of prudence would be based are set aside. In other words, rather than there being claims of prudence that lack normative force, prudence simply does not make claims. Silencing, on this account, does not amount to the claims of prudence failing to constitute reasons, but instead consists in prudence being prevented from making claims.

The two accounts thus provide different explanations as to why there is no reason to perform actions that conflict with the requirements of virtue/duty. The silencing account based on conditional value holds that, though the actions would make one happy (in the Kantian sense, not the eudaimonistic sense), this would have no value and hence no normative force. The McDowellian account of silencing holds that performing such actions would not make one happy, which means that, for the fully virtuous person, there will be harmony between desire and virtue, between prudence and morality. While the former involves merely the absence of value, the latter also involves the absence of the ground.

This type of harmony between prudence and morality would solve the dualism of practical reason for fully virtuous agents. What is unclear though is what happens in the case of persons that fail to be fully virtuous. While it is clear that there is no motivational silencing, that is, there is temptation and struggle, it is not clear whether there is meant to be normative silencing. On the one hand, if there is normative silencing, then it becomes rather difficult to see by what mechanism this could be explained. Silencing could be explained neither by holding that the ground is absent, since only in the case of the fully virtuous person (but not the merely continent person) is the desire absent, nor by holding that there is a condition on happiness being valuable that fails to be satisfied, since this presupposes a theory of conditional value. On the other hand, if there is no normative silencing, then the solution to the dualism of practical reason would be limited, in that it would only work if everyone were fully virtuous.[32]

The difference in mechanism leads to a difference in terms of how these accounts can make sense of the idea that morality can require us to make sacrifices and that doing what is commanded by morality may involve a genuine loss. It would seem that giving up happiness in order to comply with morality should classify as a sacrifice, and that it would be in some sense reasonable for the agent to regret having to set considerations of happiness aside. The problem is that if prudence is silenced and there is no reason to perform actions conflicting with virtue, then there is no loss. However, the idea that there is something to be regretted can be rendered intelligible on the conditional value account. In particular, one can hold that, rather than regretting having failed to take the impermissible option, which would be problematic since any resulting happiness would have lacked value and hence would have failed to constitute a genuine gain, what is to be regretted is not being able to realize the end in a permissible manner. That is, even though realizing the end would not be good if it were achieved impermissibly, it would constitute a genuine gain if it were achieved in a permissible manner. In this way, the agent can regret being required by the moral constraints to refrain from realizing an end that is such that its permissible realization would classify as a genuine gain. The agent has to give up something that is agreeable and that would be good were the condition of its value satisfied. Insofar as there is something that is agreeable, the nonevaluative ground is present, and it simply happens to be the case that the condition is not satisfied, as a result of which it fails to be good. The McDowellian account, however, cannot use this explanation since the removal of the ground ensures that there is nothing agreeable, nothing that is desired, and hence nothing that would be good.[33]

One further difference between the accounts regards the precise nature of the conditions under which prudence is silenced. The Kantian account has broader scope as a result of explaining normative silencing in terms of conditional values. More precisely, it involves silencing not just of the commands of prudence, but also silencing of prudential evaluations. This is due to the fact that the condition is not, in the first place, concerned with how happiness is acquired. This means that the condition is not characterized in terms of features of the action leading to happiness, in particular whether the action is permissible or impermissible. Instead, it is characterized in terms of features of the agent, in particular whether the agent has a good will or a bad will.[34] There is thus a difference between characterizing the condition in terms of, on the one hand, happiness not being impermissibly acquired, and, on the other, happiness being had by someone who has a good will. This is important since the Kantian can in this way also avoid conflicts between morality and prudence in evaluating states of affairs, and not only avoid conflicts in deliberating about how to act. In other words, conflicts are avoided when it comes not just to oughts, but also to betterness judgments involving states of the person.

For instance, when a person compares, not from a deliberative but rather from a purely evaluative perspective, a situation in which he or she is happy but has a bad will with a situation characterized by being unhappy but having a good will, the latter will be judged to be morally better. Given the Kantian account, the two situations will not be comparable from the point of view of prudential value, since the condition on happiness being valuable fails to be satisfied in the former case. Accordingly, conflicts are avoided and the unindexed betterness relation will rank the latter situation above the former. By contrast, an account that is specified in terms of features of actions, and that is based, not on a theory of conditional value, but on how a virtuous person deliberates, may well judge the former to be prudentially better than the latter (since one is not adopting a deliberative standpoint, and since, moreover, the happiness may have been acquired in a permissible manner, insofar as it might simply be the result of luck, or due to the actions of other people, rather than due to impermissible behavior on the part of the agent), thereby resulting in conflicting evaluations that cannot be integrated into a coherent ordering. If silencing is restricted to reasons for action, but does not apply to axiological evaluations, then it will only remove the conflict between prudential and moral oughts, but not the conflict between prudential and moral betterness orderings.

10.7. Conclusion

Thus, we have seen that the Kantian commitment to value dualism seems to invite the Sidgwickian problem of the dualism of practical reason, but that this predicament can be avoided by means of the Kantian conditionality thesis. Despite there not being any way of ordering or trading off moral and prudential value, due to the absence of a further standpoint that subsumes these fundamentally heterogeneous types of values and of which they could be understood as being mere restrictions, it is possible to have a complete ordering by employing a deflationary construal of the unindexed betterness relation. This is possible since the conditionality of the value of happiness ensures that there cannot be conflicts between prudence and morality and that, consequently, no trade-offs need to be made across the different types of values. Given that no conflicts can arise (whether at the level of deliberation or evaluation), a disjunctive construal of the unindexed betterness relation allows us to order all states of affairs in a coherent manner. In this way, it is possible to address the Sidgwickian dualism of practical reason by means of a Kantian dualist conditional value structure. Moreover, since the question as to what one ought to do, considering all the normative demands to which one is subject, requires either that these demands be commensurable, which presupposes monism, or that these demands never conflict, which can only be ensured in principle by means of conditional value structures, we can see that the Kantian understanding of silencing is the only way of rendering dualism coherent.

Acknowledgments

Thanks to Joachim Aufderheide, Ruth Chang, Bruce Chapman, and Roger Crisp as well as the editors of this volume for helpful discussions and comments.

Notes

1. The discussion will focus on systematic issues, leaving aside exegetical questions. Supporting textual evidence, as well as critiques of alternative interpretations, can be found in Bader, forthcoming, Bader, n.d. a, and Bader, n.d. b.
2. A further important difference concerns the direction of determination. Although in each case there is a commitment to a biconditional connecting values and reasons, in the case of morality the principle precedes the good (= autonomy), since the principle is a formal principle that is not based on value but on the form of the maxim, in particular on its

universalizability. By contrast, in the case of prudence the good precedes the principle (= heteronomy), since the principle is a material principle that is based on the value of the end that is to be achieved.

3. The goodness of happiness is restricted to the agent, in the sense that it only generates reasons for the person whose happiness it is (when that person has a good will). As such, it only generates prudential reasons, but not reasons of beneficence (which are instead based entirely on formal, rather than material, considerations, resulting from the nonuniversalizability of a maxim of nonbeneficence).
4. The notion of conditional intrinsic value is not to be confused with contextual final value (which construes the source of value as being extrinsic rather than intrinsic, and which does not recognize the hyperintensional distinction between sources and conditions), nor with the idea that the intrinsic value of a thing can be defeated by being part of a disvaluable organic unity (which only generates the result that the value of happiness is outweighed, but not that it is silenced).
5. The highest good is in this way a combination of two separate goods, whereby one is conditional on the other, and as such is not to be understood as an organic unity, i.e., the value of the highest good is entirely reducible to the value of its components and no value resides in the combination.
6. If one were to insist on talking about humanity having value, then this would have to be understood in terms of value that is to be respected, rather than in terms of value that is to be promoted, and as such would not belong to axiology proper.
7. The Sidgwickian predicament is here construed as a conflict between two different types of normativity, namely the conflict between the requirements of morality and the requirements of prudence (see McLeod 2000).
8. Incommensurability, which applies to values themselves, is to be distinguished from noncomparability, which applies to alternatives that are being ordered and evaluated, i.e., to value bearers. Values are incommensurable if there is no common standard of evaluation, i.e., no value subsuming them. This means that they involve different betterness relations and that the values come in different units (where this notion of "unit" is not restricted to cardinal scales but also applies to ordinal scales, in which case units are to be understood in terms of levels/ranks in the ordering), such that there is no way of trading off or ordering the values. If alternatives involve different incommensurable values, then it is not possible to compare these alternatives in a way that integrates the different values, rendering them noncomparable. Noncomparability, however, does not imply that the alternatives involve incommensurable values.
9. A number of people have interpreted Kant as holding that morality is lexically prior to prudence. For instance, Cummiskey 1989: 121. Similarly, Timmermann, though correctly interpreting Kant as defending a view on which morality silences prudence, mistakenly considers this as amounting to morality and prudence being lexically ordered (see Timmermann 2007: 169–70).
10. For instance, someone who takes the value of distributions to be a function both of how equal they are and of how much utility they contain, can restrict the evaluation and only assess distributions in terms of how good they are on the basis of the degree of equality they exhibit.
11. One can, of course, give the phrase "all-things-considered value" a stipulative meaning and use it as a placeholder to refer to a covering value that subsumes the different values being considered (see Chang 2004a: 2), in which case "all-things-considered value" is an alternative label for "super-value." Whereas construing all-things-considered evaluations

as unrestricted assessments is innocuous, the placeholder reading has substantive presuppositions, given that it requires the existence of the relevant covering values.
12. Likewise, it is has been suggested that the notion of "reason" can do the requisite work, i.e., that prudential and moral reasons can be compared in terms of their strength and that one simply has to evaluate as to which reason is stronger.
13. The need for substantive values is particularly clear when there are no minima and maxima, i.e., when one is dealing with unbounded value-functions. In order to normalize, one needs to pick reference points on the different scales and treat them as being equivalent. Given the absence of minima/maxima, no "natural" reference points are available, which highlights the substantive nature of their selection.
14. At any rate, they are unproblematic from a theoretical point of view—numerous difficulties may arise when it comes to making comparisons in practice.
15. The type of incommensurability that is due to differences in types of value is global, in the sense that no comparisons can be made between these values, which implies that the relation of comparability is an equivalence relation. As such, it is to be distinguished from the notion of incommensurability that involves local gaps that are due to there being different ways of integrating different dimensions, leaving one with an incomplete intersection quasi-ordering and a nontransitive relation of comparability.
16. At best, they can be combined in a purely stipulative manner. This, however, does not respect the independence and intrinsic significance of the values, and any resulting verdict will only have conventional but not intrinsic normativity, which implies that stipulative trade-off ratios cannot be brought in to adjudicate conflicts when it comes to substantive values that are independently significant.
17. Chang has suggested that the focus on there being different points of views can be seen to be a red herring once one distinguishes "between a value 'per se' and a value qua instance of a *type* of value" (Chang 2004b: 123). This appeal to the notion of a "value per se," however, seems to mirror the confusion that we diagnosed in the case of Griffin's suggestion that the quantitative attribute "value" suffices.
18. That there is no room for any further value in the Kantian system becomes particularly clear when one considers the relation between the good and the principle of volition. Either the principle precedes the good, in which case one is dealing with the one and only formal principle, namely the categorical imperative, or the good precedes the principle, in which case one is dealing with the one and only material principle, namely the pragmatic imperative.
19. It should be noted that there is no conflict between silencing and independence. This is because independence regards the source of normativity, which is compatible with there being external conditions, i.e., nonderivativeness does not imply unconditionality. On the Kantian account, prudence is independent in that it does not derive its normativity from any other source. Prudential value has its own source of normativity that is separate from that of morality.
20. The notion of silencing in fact presupposes the dualism. This is because values of the same type can only outweigh each other, in which case any difference between them will only be a matter of degree and not a matter of unconditional silencing. For silencing, one needs heterogeneous values that are connected via a conditioning relation.
21. If one is to trace silencing to its ultimate source, then this explanation of silencing in terms of conditional value needs to be supplemented with an account of the mechanism underlying the conditionality of the value of happiness. The fact that the value of happiness is

conditional on having a good will can be explained by appealing to the idea that for something to be good is for it to be an object of practical reason, together with the idea that a bad will is a will that is involved in a practical contradiction and as such cannot have any objects (see Bader, n.d. a).

22. Or p-ought(ψ), where ϕ-ing and ψ-ing are incompatible.
23. For instance, one might think that an imperfect duty, such as beneficence, allows for cases in which both the option of helping and the option of not helping are permissible, but where helping is morally better yet prudentially worse.
24. One question that naturally arises is how it is possible to make sense of the idea of degrees of virtue/moral goodness, which seems to be required for the idea that happiness is proportional to virtue in the highest good, i.e., that moral good and prudential good are proportionally distributed. Here, the answer is that, while rigorism implies that moral goodness is a binary matter within each choice context, one can aggregate the different contexts to determine the proportion of morally good choices the agent has made throughout his or her whole life and thereby arrive at a notion of virtue that construes it as an extensive magnitude that allows for degrees (see Bader, forthcoming).
25. This kind of principle can be weakened in two ways: (1) it can be specified merely as a sufficient and not also a necessary condition for x > y, and (2) one can require strict rather than only weak dominance, i.e., $x >_m y \wedge x >_p y$.
26. It is important to note that when the condition fails to be satisfied, happiness lacks value rather than having value to degree zero, i.e., its value will be undefined and as such not comparable.
27. If there are multiple permissible actions, then these actions can be ordered with respect to each other in terms of prudential value.
28. In the case of internal incompleteness, it is possible to generate cycles involving only two values. For instance, a cycle will result if $x >_{V_1} y$, $y >_{V_2} z$, $z >_{V_1} w$, $w >_{V_2} x$, whereby V1 does not rank x, y with respect to z, w, and V2 does not rank y, z with respect to w, x. Similarly, a nontransitive ordering due to noncomparability can arise in the context of internally incomplete component orderings even if they have the same betterness fields. For instance, transitivity will be violated insofar as x and z will not be ranked by the unindexed relation if $x >_{V_1} y$, $y >_{V_2} z$, whereby V1 does not rank x, y with respect to z, and V2 does not rank y, z with respect to x. However, neither the moral nor the prudential betterness ordering admits of internal incompleteness.
29. For Raz, excluded reasons can affect nondeliberative evaluations. "In fact it is better that the excluded reasons be conformed to. They are reasons for performing certain actions, and, other things being equal, the fact that they are excluded by an exclusionary reason merely means that they should not be complied with, not that they should not be conformed to. The best course is if they are indirectly obeyed, i.e. if the action they indicate is performed for some other, independent, reason" (Raz 1999: 185).
30. Nozick also discusses related notions of nullifying, destroying, dissolving, and invalidating.
31. It will differ from canceling by not being essentially diachronic, i.e., not the removal of a ground that is present at one point and then absent at some later time, but preventing the ground from being present in the first place.
32. This situation would be analogous to that considered by Sidgwick, whereby the dualism is overcome as a result of a divinely induced harmony.
33. It might be suggested that, although the virtuous person does not have to give up something that is agreeable, he has to give up something that would be agreeable, namely

having a certain desire. That is, rather than regretting that the desire cannot be satisfied in a permissible manner, he would be regretting that the situation was such that one could not (in a manner compatible with the requirements of virtue) have this desire. However, the desire in question should not be salient in any way to the fully virtuous person since its attractions are "isolated." There is hence no reason to regret not having this particular desire. There is nothing that would occasion this regret and that would single out this desire in particular. Moreover, purely counterfactual facts as to what the person would have desired had he not been morally constrained in this way are too remote and do not underwrite any actual regret but, at best, a disposition to regret.

34. The account takes features of the action into consideration in a derivative manner, insofar as acting impermissibly entails that the person has a bad will and that the condition on the value of happiness consequently fails to be satisfied.

References

Bader, R. M. (N.d. a). "Kant and the Conditional Intrinsic Value of Happiness."
Bader, R. M. (N.d. b). "Pragmatic Imperatives and the Value of Happiness."
Bader, R. M. (Forthcoming). "Kant's Theory of the Highest Good." In J. Aufderheide and R. M. Bader (eds.), *The Highest Good in Aristotle and Kant*. New York: Oxford University Press.
Chang, R. (1997). "Introduction." In R. Chang (ed.), *Incommensurability, Incomparability, and Practical Reason*. Cambridge: Harvard University Press, 1–34.
Chang, R. (2004a). "All Things Considered." *Philosophical Perspectives* 18: 1–22.
Chang, R. (2004b). "Putting Together Morality and Well-Being." In P. Baumann and M. Betzler (eds.), *Practical Conflicts: New Philosophical Essays*. New York: Cambridge University Press, 118–58.
Cummiskey, D. (1989). "Consequentialism, Egoism, and the Moral Law." *Philosophical Studies* 57: 111–34.
Griffin, J. (1986). *Well-Being: Its Meaning, Measurement, and Moral Importance* New York: Oxford University Press.
Haji, I. (1998). "On Morality's Dethronement." *Philosophical Papers* 27 (3): 161–80.
McDowell, J. (1978). "Are Moral Requirements Hypothetical Imperatives?" *Proceedings of the Aristotelian Society Supplementary Volume* 52: 13–29.
McDowell, J. (1996). "Incontinence and Practical Wisdom in Aristotle." In S. Lovibond and S. Williams (eds.), *Essays for David Wiggins: Identity, Truth, and Value*. New York: Oxford University Press, 95–112.
McLeod, O. (2000). "What Is Sidgwick's Dualism of Practical Reason?" *Pacific Philosophical Quarterly* 81: 273–90.
McLeod, O. (2001). "Just Plain 'Ought.'" *Journal of Ethics* 5: 269–91.
Nozick, R. (1968). "Moral Complications and Moral Structures." *Natural Law Forum* 13: 1–50.
Raz, J. (1999). *Practical Reason and Norms*, 2nd ed. New York: Oxford University Press.
Sidgwick, H. (1874). *The Methods of Ethics*. London: Macmillan.
Timmermann, J. (2007). "Simplicity and Authority: Reflections on Theory and Practice in Kant's Moral Philosophy." *Journal of Moral Philosophy* 4 (2): 167–82.

PART II
STRUCTURE

CHAPTER 11

VALUE INCOMPARABILITY AND INCOMMENSURABILITY

RUTH CHANG

WHAT is incomparability? What is incommensurability? How do they relate? And why are they important?

As we will see, incomparability, and not incommensurability, is the more important phenomenon, and so that will be our main focus here. This chapter examines what incomparability is and the relation between the incomparability of values and the incomparability of alternatives for choice (section 11.2), differentiates incomparability from the related phenomena of parity, indeterminacy, and noncomparability (section 11.3), and defends a view about practical justification that vindicates the importance of incomparability for understanding rational choice (section 11.4). But first we turn to incommensurability (section 11.1). What is it, what is its significance, and how is it related to incomparability?

11.1. INCOMMENSURABILITY AND INCOMPARABILITY

We start with a gloss of each phenomenon. Two items are *incommensurable* just in case they cannot be put on the same scale of units of value, that is, there is no cardinal unit of measure that can represent the value of both items. Two items are *incomparable* just in case they fail to stand in an evaluative comparative relation, such as being better than or worse than or equally as good as the other.

Incomparability is thought to be of greatest philosophical significance when holding between *alternatives for choice*. Suppose you are faced with a choice between two incomparable options, say, spending your annual bonus on a new car or donating the money to Oxfam. If the alternatives cannot be compared with respect to what matters in the choice between them, it seems that there can be no justified choice between them.

As many philosophers believe, you're justified in choosing one alternative over another only if it is better or as good as the other, and incomparability holds when it's false that they stand in any such comparative relation. Incomparability among alternatives, then, leads to a breakdown in practical reason. If incomparability is widespread, then what we do in most choice situations falls outside the scope of practical reason. This in turn has upshots for our understanding of paradigmatic human agency: instead of being Enlightenment creatures who act according to the dictates of reason, we lead our lives without the guidance of reason.

Incommensurability, by contrast, is thought to be of most philosophical significance when holding, not between alternatives for choice, but between *abstract values*.[1] (Values, as I am understanding them, include any evaluative abstracta, including obligations, rights, duties, utility, excellences, and so on, and are not limited to evaluative criteria, like pleasure, that can be aggregated by a cardinal unit of measure.)[2] If two values cannot be measured by a cardinal unit, they are incommensurable. This use of "incommensurability" derives from the Greek term *asummetros* used by Aristotle to refer to the Pythagorean discovery that the lengths of the diagonal and side of a unit square—1 and $\sqrt{2}$—could not be placed on a single scale of numbers (von Fritz 1945; Heath 1921). Because the Pythagoreans thought that all numbers were rational, they believed that $\sqrt{2}$ could not be put on the same scale as 1. Today, of course, we have the real numbers, which include both rational and irrational numbers, and so the Pythagoreans did not have a genuine case of incommensurability. Nevertheless, they gave birth to the idea that items could lack a shared cardinal measure.

The importance of the incommensurability of values lies primarily in axiology, not in the philosophy of practical reason. If values are incommensurable, then values cannot be represented by cardinally significant real numbers. There is no cardinal unit—such as dollars—in terms of which we can measure pleasure and scientific achievement. Any hope of being able to mathematically model values on the reals, as we might model quantities of mass or length, must be abandoned. And so certain crude ethical theories, such as traditional forms of utilitarianism that presuppose values can be cardinally represented by utiles, must also be rejected. But since no plausible ethical theory essentially relies on the commensurability of values, the importance of value incommensurability is limited.

There is a derivative upshot for practical reason. If the values that matter in the choice between buying a new car and donating to Oxfam—say, utility and fulfilling moral obligations—are incommensurable, then it would be a mistake to model the rationality of the choice by assuming that rationality is a matter of maximizing some cardinally significant unit of value. Thus the incommensurability of values undermines expected utility theory and cost benefit analysis, which presuppose the cardinal measurement of the value or the preferability of options. At best, these approaches must be understood as crude heuristics for rational choice. But since many thinkers have already rejected these models as problematic on other grounds, the importance of the incommensurability of values for practical reason is also limited.[3]

How do incommensurability—the failure to be measurable by a shared cardinal unit of value—and incomparability—the failure to be comparable—relate? Some philosophers have mistakenly assumed that the incommensurability of values entails the incomparability of those values or their bearers. Some, for example, have noted that if values cannot be put on a "single scale" on which they can be "measured, added, and balanced," then alternatives bearing them could not be compared, and rational choice between them would have to proceed not by a comparison of their merits but by some other means (e.g., Hart 1961; Anderson 1997: 55ff.; D'Agostino 2003), such as *phronesis*, that is, a judgment of practical wisdom (Nagel 1979: 131). But incommensurability does not entail incomparability—whether of values or their bearers.

Consider an example. Suppose, as is plausible, that there is no cardinally significant unit of measurement by which we can evaluate both the abstract values of justice and mercy—justice and mercy are incommensurable. It does not follow that justice is not better than mercy with respect to promoting a secure and legitimate polis or that mercy is not better than justice with respect to being godly. Values may be comparable even if they are incommensurable. Nor does it follow that bearers of those values cannot be compared. A state policy of proportional punishment is better than a meter maid's merciful act of not writing someone a parking ticket with respect to achieving political legitimacy for the state. Bearers of value may be comparable even if the values they bear are incommensurable.

Nor does the incommensurability of bearers of value entail their incomparability. Even if there is no cardinal unit, such as a utile or a dollar, in terms of which the value of buying a new car and of donating the money to Oxfam can be measured, it might nevertheless be true that, with respect to moral goodness, donating to Oxfam is better.[4]

While incommensurability does not entail incomparability, incomparability entails incommensurability. If there is no comparative relation that holds between two items, a fortiori, there is no cardinal unit of measurement by which the two might be compared. Being commensurable is simply *one way* in which items might be comparable, and so if items are incomparable, they are incommensurable. Thus while incommensurability does not entail incomparability, commensurability entails comparability, both for value bearers and for abstract values themselves.

It is unfortunate that "incommensurability" is sometimes used as a synonym for "incomparability" (Raz 1986; Anderson 1993), since, as we've seen, incommensurability does not entail incomparability let alone reduce to it. The reverse is not true; no one has, to my knowledge, used "incomparability" to refer to incommensurability, although, as we have seen, the incomparability of items entails their incommensurability. An explanation of this usage is that incomparability—the failure of comparability—and not incommensurability—the failure of cardinal measurability—is the more philosophically significant phenomenon.

11.2. What Is Incomparability?

We glossed incomparability as the failure of comparability. Here is a precise definition of incomparability.

Incomparability (def): Two items are incomparable if it is false that any positive, basic, binary value relation holds between them with respect to a covering consideration, "V."

This needs unpacking. A value relation is positive if it represents how items relate rather than how they fail to relate. So, for example, "x is better than y" says something about how x stands to y, while "x is not better than y" says only how x does not stand to y. "Is better than" is thus a positive value relation, while "is not better than" is not.

A set of value relations is basic if it exhausts the conceptual space of comparability between two items with respect to V. A value relation is "basic" if it is a member of a basic set. So, for example, "x is better than y" belongs to a basic set, while "x is better than y but only slightly worse than z" does not. Many thinkers have assumed that "better than," "worse than," and "equally good" form a basic set of value relations, and thus that if these relations fail to hold of two items with respect to V, the items are incomparable with respect to V. Call this the "Trichotomy Thesis." We will be returning to this thesis later.

A value relation is binary if it relates exactly two items with respect to V. So, for instance, "x is much better than y with respect to V than z is" would not be binary while "x is better than y with respect to V" would be.

Incomparability is the failure of any positive, basic, binary value relation to hold between two items *with respect to a covering consideration, V*. V is a variable for either a single consideration or multiple considerations—and here we will assume that a value or values play this role. If a comparison proceeds with respect to multiple values, v1, v2, v3, and so on, there is the question of how these values relate to one another. This is an important and controversial question at the intersection of axiology and the philosophy of practical reason that we can't address here.[5] For our purposes we will simply assume that v1, v2, v3 ... can stand in any relation, including mere conjunction. So if x and y are incomparable, they cannot be compared—with respect to some value or values, V. Later we'll see why V is aptly called a "covering" consideration.

To see why claims of incomparability must proceed relative to a covering consideration, consider claims of comparability. Two items are never comparable, simpliciter; they are always comparable in some respect or respects. Chalk is comparable with cheese in some respects—cheese tastes better. Apples are comparable with oranges in some respects—apples are worse with respect to preventing scurvy. Being comparable is a matter of there being a positive, basic, binary value relation that holds between items *with respect to V*. Saying that two items are comparable, simpliciter, expresses an incomplete thought—comparable in what respect or respects?[6] Note that the same goes for nonevaluative comparisons. A stick can't be greater than a billiard ball, simpliciter; it must be greater in some respect, such as mass or length.

As the negation of claims of comparability, claims of incomparability must have the same logical form. Two items are never incomparable, simpliciter, but only incomparable with respect to V. As we will see, failure to appreciate the fact that incomparability must proceed with respect to a covering consideration has led some philosophers to conflate incomparability with other, quite distinct, phenomena.

11.2.1. Of Values

Incomparability is the failure of any positive, basic, binary relation to hold between two items with respect to V. If the items being compared are abstract values, then the claim of incomparability is the claim that one value is incomparable with another value with respect to some V.

But what does it mean to say that one abstract value, such as happiness, is incomparable with another abstract value, such as gustatory pleasure, with respect to an abstract value, V, such as individual well-being?

Again, we can look to comparability for help. If one value is better than another with respect to V, it makes a greater contribution to V.[7] Or, equivalently for our purposes, having the one value makes a greater contribution to having (more of/a significant manifestation of) V than does having the other value. So if happiness is better than gustatory pleasure with respect to individual well-being, then having happiness goes further toward—makes a more significant contribution to—having a good life than does having gustatory pleasure. Crucially, this is to be understood as a purely abstract claim and not one about any particular instantiations of happiness or of gustatory pleasure.

We can go further. Suppose that happiness is better than gustatory pleasure with respect to well-being, that is, being happy contributes more to one's well-being than does having gustatory pleasure. How exactly are we to understand this claim? After all, not every instantiation of happiness contributes more to one's well-being than every instantiation of gustatory pleasure. The once-in-a-lifetime pleasure of a custom-prepared five-course meal at Daniel might, arguably, contribute more to one's well-being than the fleeting sense of happiness one has when the sun is shining and all seems well with the world. At least we want to leave open that possibility.

Comparisons between values in terms of their contribution to some V are themselves explained in terms of other comparative facts—facts about how *particular instantiations* of those values comparatively relate with respect to V across sets of possible background facts.[8] Happiness can be multiply instantiated—there is the happiness of achieving a lifelong goal, the happiness of winning the lottery, the happiness of feeling the sun on your face after spending all day working in the office. (If these examples strike you as problematic, substitute your own.) Comparisons of abstract values are explained in terms of comparisons of the multitude of instantiations of them with respect to V across a multitude of possible background facts.

A toy illustration will help. Suppose God wishes to determine the comparative contribution of happiness and gustatory pleasure to individual well-being. He starts by considering the well-being of an arbitrary individual—let's call her "Mary." Mary exists in many possible worlds. God picks out one possible world and asks, "Which would constitute a greater contribution to Mary's well-being in that world—adding to her life the happiness of a good romantic relationship or adding to her life the gustatory pleasure of her favorite dessert?" He concludes that the happiness would contribute more. He then moves onto the other instantiations of happiness and gustatory pleasure. For instance, he asks, "Which would constitute a greater contribution to Mary's well-being—adding to her life the happiness of getting birthday greetings from a distant acquaintance or adding to her life the gustatory pleasure of the best meal she will have in her lifetime?" He concludes that the gustatory pleasure would contribute more. He carries on in this fashion until he has gone through all the possible instantiations of happiness and gustatory pleasure, determining which instantiation makes the greatest contribution to Mary's well-being in the given possible world. After taking a coffee break, he then goes on to repeat the process for every other possible world. At the end of day, he has a set of comparative facts about every possible instantiation of the abstract values in question as to their relative contribution to Mary's individual well-being across every possible circumstance. (Since Mary is, by hypothesis, an arbitrary individual, he only has to ask these questions about Mary, but of course there will be variations in answer across actual individuals in the same circumstances). These facts are the "inputs" to the determination of the comparative relation between the abstract values of happiness and gustatory pleasure with respect to their contribution to making a good life. For convenience, we might call the determination of the comparative relation between abstract values a "value comparison function."

Now we don't have much of a handle on what this value comparison function could be (not to mention how to determine its inputs). But we can posit a general feature a plausible function must have that has significance for our thinking about the relation between the incomparability of values and the incomparability of value bearers.

Possible value comparison functions might be arrayed very roughly along a spectrum; at one end are the "super-permissive" functions according to which *any* incomparability among instantiations in any possible world yields the incomparability of the values themselves, while at the other end are the "super-restrictive" according to which all instantiations must be incomparable in order for the values themselves to be incomparable.[9] Super-restrictive functions are clearly implausible; surely values could be incomparable even if *some* of their instantiations were comparable. All we have to do is think of candidate cases of incomparable values and note that a very good or "notable" instantiation of one of them is plausibly comparable with a very bad or "nominal" instantiation of the other in at least one possible world. Moreover, as we'll see shortly, there is a further formal constraint on comparisons—that "V" "cover" the items being compared—which underwrites the plausibility that there will always be *some* instantiation of a value that is comparable with *some* instantiation of another value with respect to contribution to V. If this is right, then we can proceed on the fairly secure assumption that even if two abstract values are incomparable with respect to V, some of their instantiations may be comparable with respect to V.

This in turn has an important implication for the relation between the incomparability of values and the incomparability of their bearers. Although happiness may be incomparable with gustatory pleasure with respect to individual well-being, the happiness of achieving a worthwhile lifelong goal might well be comparable with the gustatory pleasure of a lukewarm cup of coffee with respect to contribution to individual well-being in at least some possible worlds. And although equality may be incomparable with fairness with respect to justice, particular instantiations of equality may be comparable with particular instantiations of fairness in the actual world, and so policies between which the US Congress has to choose that manifest those particular comparable instantiations may nevertheless be comparable with respect to justice. The upshot is that investigation of the incomparability of alternatives for choice can proceed independently of investigation of the incomparability of values. Progress in understanding the incomparability of alternatives for choice and its significance for practical reason is thus not held hostage to progress in the rather more difficult problem of understanding the incomparability of values.

Sometimes philosophers misleadingly speak of the "incomparability" (or "incommensurability") of values when what they have in mind is not their incomparability but their normative irreducibility. A value is normatively irreducible if there is no other value in terms of which it can be explained or accounted for. Values might come in different "types," where types are individuated by some formal or substantive feature that precludes different types of value from being contributors to some value. Perhaps some values are necessarily relativized to an individual—they are "personal values," while others are "impersonal" and not so relativized (Ronnow-Rasmussen 2011) and so personal and impersonal values cannot be understood as contributors to some common value. Or perhaps agent-relative values are, normatively speaking, irreducibly distinct from agent-neutral values and thus do not contribute to any common value. Or, as some have argued, moral values are normatively irreducible and distinct from prudential values (Copp 1997), or utility is irreducibly distinct from obligation (Nagel 1979: ch. 9).

However, the normative irreducibility of values should not be confused with their incomparability. The confusion arises because the covering consideration requirement has been overlooked: comparability and incomparability must proceed relative to some V. Normative irreducibility holds of two values when there is no V to which the values contribute—those values cannot be accounted for in terms of their contribution to V. Incomparability holds when comparison between the two values with respect to V fails. As we will see later, if two values are normatively irreducibly distinct, then they may be *non*comparable with respect to each and every value but if noncomparable, then they are neither comparable nor incomparable with respect to those values.

11.2.2. Of Bearers/Alternatives for Choice

Two value bearers are incomparable with respect to V just in case there is no positive, basic, binary relation that holds between them with respect to V.

Just as there is a value comparison function that determines whether values are comparable, there is a value bearer comparison function that determines the comparability or incomparability of bearers of value. The inputs of that function are comparisons of the instantiations of values manifested by each value bearer against a set of possible circumstances. Take, for example, two paintings, say da Vinci's *La Gioconda* and Picasso's *Guernica*. Suppose we attempt to compare them with respect to beauty. Each painting bears beauty by manifesting particular instantiations of beauty. Our value bearer comparison function takes each comparative fact about how the instantiations of beauty manifested by each painting compare with respect to their contribution to the abstract value of beauty in each possible world—that is, how comparatively beautiful they are in each possible world—and delivers as an output an abstract comparative fact about how beautiful the two paintings are across all possible worlds.

But many—perhaps all—abstract comparative facts about value bearers across all possible worlds are not properly the subject of philosophical investigation. This is because, while declarations that *La Gioconda* is more beautiful than *Guernica* in the abstract across all possible worlds may be appropriate at certain kinds of overintellectual dinner parties, they are silly and pointless (Anderson 1993, 1997). A comparison of the beauty of two paintings does have significance, however, when it is relativized to the actual world. Such comparisons are important when the alternatives are options for choice in the actual world, for example, when you are a museum curator deciding which of two paintings to include in an exhibition or a homeowner trying to decide which of two reproductions to hang on your living room wall. In thinking about the incomparability of bearers of value, then, we should focus our attention on bearers of value that are alternatives for choice in a choice situation in the actual world.

11.3. What Incomparability Is Not

11.3.1. Parity

A general question about incomparability concerns which relations constitute the basic set of value relations that exhaust the conceptual space of comparability between two items with respect to V. Most philosophers have assumed the Trichotomy Thesis, the claim that the trichotomy of relations, "better than," "worse than," and "equally good" (or an equivalent set), forms a basic set of value relations; if none of the trichotomy holds between two items with respect to V, it follows that they are incomparable with respect to V. Indeed, many thinkers have *defined* incomparability as the failure of these three relations to hold.

This is a mistake. Defining incomparability as the failure of the standard trichotomy of relations to hold builds into the concept of incomparability a substantive assumption about which relations exhaust the conceptual space of comparability between two items that is open to debate. And this substantive assumption is no part of the ordinary notion of incomparability.

Consider the following thought experiment. Suppose you are a trichotomist, believing that "better than," "worse than," and "equally good" exhaust the conceptual space of comparability between two items with respect to V. I, however, am a dichotomist, believing that "better than" and "worse than" exhaust the conceptual space of comparability between two items with respect to V. You present me with two qualitatively identical bowls of ice cream and ask me to compare them with respect to deliciousness. As a dichotomist, I confidently conclude that they are incomparable with respect to deliciousness; after all, they taste the same to me and since one doesn't taste better than the other, the two are incomparable in tastiness. As a trichotomist, you insist that if they taste the same to me, they are equally good with respect to tastiness. But I don't recognize this relation of being "equally good"; as a good dichotomist, I maintain that if one is neither better nor worse than the other, they cannot be compared.

This disagreement might simply be verbal; I might simply use "incomparable" to *mean* "neither better nor worse." But it might instead be substantive. I might have overlooked a possible basic relation of comparability, in which case you will give me substantive arguments that suggest I have. Those arguments might draw upon a shared understanding of comparability and incomparability according to which it is an open question which relations exhaust the conceptual space of comparability between two items. You might appeal to the idea of a positive fact that gives a relation that holds between two items in contrast to a negative fact that gives a relation that does not hold between two items and point out that being "equally good" is more like being "better than" than being incomparable, that is, not related by any positive fact. On the basis of this shared understanding of comparability, you might give me arguments for the existence of things being equally good. You might draw an analogy with nonevaluative comparisons, and point out that just as two sticks can be of equal length, they can be of equal value with respect to V. You might show what philosophical work the relation of being "equally good," as opposed to being incomparable, can do in practical reason. Or you might show how related concepts, such as commensurability support there being a relation of "equally good." One way two items can be commensurable is by being measured by the same number of cardinal units of value. Since commensurability entails comparability, this way of being commensurable entails a way of being comparable. In short, if we share a concept of comparability that does not have a set of basic value relations built into it, you can, in principle, convince me that there are three, not two, basic relations of comparability.

Our ordinary concept of comparability—and correspondingly of incomparability—leaves open which relations exhaust the conceptual space of comparability between two items with respect to a V. It thus leaves open the possibility that there is a *fourth* basic value relation beyond the standard trichotomy of "better than," "worse than," and "equally good," what I have elsewhere called "on a par" (Chang 2002). Indeed, it leaves open the possibility that there are many more basic relations of comparability (Rabinowicz 2008, 2012).

The point for our purposes is that parity—or some basic relation of comparability beyond the traditional trichotomy—should not be confused with incomparability. Just because two items are such that, with respect to V, neither is better than the other nor are they equally good, it does not necessarily follow that they are incomparable. They might be on a par. To distinguish cases of incomparability from parity, we need arguments, some of which I have given elsewhere (Chang 2002). But conceptually the two are easy to distinguish. Incomparability is the failure of any positive basic value relation to hold; parity is the holding of a particular basic value relation beyond the traditional trichotomy. As we'll see, the distinction between them is important for how we understand practical justification.

11.3.2. Indeterminacy

Another idea that can be easily confused with incomparability is semantic indeterminacy, in particular, vagueness.[10] Incomparability holds when it is *false* or determinately not the case that any positive, basic, binary value relation holds between the items with respect to V. Vagueness in comparability holds when it is *neither true nor false*, or indeterminate, that a positive, basic, binary value relation holds between the items with respect to V.

Indeterminacy in comparison is due to the vagueness of the concepts employed in the comparison, most plausibly the covering consideration, V. Take a nonevaluative comparison between Herbert and Henry with respect to baldness. "Baldness" is a vague predicate—it has indeterminate application to a range of hair profiles that, suppose, include those belonging to Herbert and Henry. Since it is indeterminate whether Herbert is bald and indeterminate whether Henry is bald, it could be indeterminate whether Henry is balder than Herbert, indeterminate whether Herbert is balder than Henry, indeterminate whether they are equally bald—one might have one more hair than the other, but the distribution of hairs might be such that they aren't determinately equally bald. The vagueness of V can thus be one source of vagueness in comparability.[11]

In the evaluative case, comparisons might be indeterminate if the concept V is vague. Take *happiness*, plausibly a vague term. It might be indeterminate whether Mary is happy and indeterminate whether John is happy, and thus perhaps indeterminate whether either is happier than the other or they are equally happy. It might also be indeterminate whether they are on a par with respect to happiness. If these four relations exhaust the conceptual space of comparability between two items with respect to V, then the comparative happiness of Mary and John is indeterminate. Indeterminacy holds when it's indeterminate which comparative relation holds between them. Incomparability holds, by contrast, when it is determinately the case that *no* positive relation does.

Some philosophers have argued that putative cases of incomparability are in fact cases of vagueness. The most well-known argument is by John Broome (Broome 1997).

Broome's argument is too complex to summarize here, but we can examine the central principle, the "collapsing principle," upon which the argument relies. According to the collapsing principle in its general form, "For any x and y, if it is more true that x is F-er than y than that y is F-er than x, then x is F-er than y" (Broome 1997: 77).

Broome's argument for the principle is as follows:[12]

> My only real argument [for the collapsing principle] is this: If it is false that y is F-er than x, and not false that x is F-er than y, then x has a clear advantage over y in respect of its F-ness. So it must be F-er than y. It takes only the slightest asymmetry to make it the case that one thing is F-er than another. One object is heavier than another if the scales tip ever so slightly toward it. (Broome 1997: 74)

The basic idea is that anything that tips the scales in favor of x being F-er than y, including its not being false that x is F-er than y while its being false that y is F-er than x, makes what might look like the fact that it's neither true nor false that x is F-er than y "collapse" into the fact that it's true that x is F-er than y.

But this principle has plausibility only if Fness—be it moral goodness, beauty, or justice—can be measured by cardinally significant real numbers—that is, if we have commensurability among bearers of Fness.[13] If bearers of Fness are commensurable, then arguably (but only arguably) any asymmetry in favor of x's being F-er than y might support a collapse in favor of its being true that x is F-er than y. If F-ness can be measured by cardinal units, then a slight asymmetry in favor of one comparative claim might conceivably "tip the scales" so that the claim is true where it might have seemed neither true nor false. But if F-ness isn't representable by cardinal units, the collapsing principle has little going for it. Any consideration in favor of x's being F-er than y need not translate into its being true that x is F-er than y. Since it's hard to believe that *all* values ("all" is needed for the argument to work) can be measured by cardinal units of value, the principle—and the more complex argument upon which it relies—can be rejected.

Thus we should insist not only that the phenomena of incomparability and of indeterminacy due to vagueness are conceptually distinct, but also that there seems to be no good reason to think that one phenomenon collapses into the other.

11.3.3. Noncomparability

Comparability and incomparability must proceed relative to some covering consideration, V. So far, we have said very little about this "V" other than that it can be a value or values which may be related in different ways. There is much to be said about which sorts of considerations can occupy the role of "V," but we don't have space to examine those issues here. Instead, I want to point out one feature of a consideration that disqualifies it from playing the role of V in particular claims of comparability and incomparability. This will help us to distinguish incomparability from a related phenomenon, *non*comparability.

Associated with each V is a term "V," such as "beauty," "justice," "well-being," "utility as a corkscrew," "tastiness," and so on. Each term has a domain of application, that is, there are certain items to which the term properly applies. So, for example, the number four and beauty, in virtue of being abstract, cannot be tasty. Abstract numbers and values, then, do not fall within the domain of application of "tasty." Failing to fall within the domain of application should not be confused with a term's failing to hold of an item. Abstract numbers are not the kind of thing that could be tasty. Lamps, buildings, and excrement are all things that could be tasty or not, and so they fall within the domain of application of "tasty"—it's just false that they are.

If we tried to compare the number four and beauty with respect to tastiness, we would fail: no positive, basic, binary value relation holds between them with respect to tastiness. But this failure is not the *substantive* failure of incomparability; it is rather a *formal* failure of comparability, *non*comparability.

If at least one of two items being compared fail to fall within the domain of the application of "V" in the context of an attempted comparison, then they are noncomparable with respect to V.[14] Put another way, if the covering consideration, V, fails to "cover" both items being compared, they will be noncomparable. But they can be neither comparable nor incomparable since the formal prerequisites for being eligible as either comparable are incomparable have not been met. Noncomparability holds when the formal conditions required for comparability or incomparability to be possible fail to hold. Being "covered" by the covering consideration—that is, falling within the domain of its associated term in the context of comparison—is one such formal condition. We already encountered another—that there be a covering consideration with respect to which the items are compared.

Thus, if one attempts to compare rotten eggs and the number nine with respect to tastiness, they are noncomparable with respect to tastiness. But if one attempts to compare them with respect to, say, which associated idea is more pleasant to think about, perhaps the number nine is better.

Noncomparability among alternatives for choice has little philosophical significance. This is because the distinction between formal and substantive failures of comparability tracks the distinction between genuine practical choice situations and gerrymandered or ersatz ones. Practical reason will never ask agents to compare rotten eggs and the number nine with respect to tastiness—there can never be a genuine choice situation in which one must choose between alternatives with respect to some consideration that fails to "cover" both of them in the context of comparison.[15] Practical reason guarantees that once what matters in a choice is determined, the alternatives will be bearers of what matters in the choice between them in that choice situation. By contrast, incomparability poses a serious threat to practical reason. To this threat we now turn.

11.4. Why Is Incomparability Important?

According to "comparativist" views of practical justification, the comparability of alternatives is a necessary condition for the possibility of a (objectively) justified choice between them in that choice situation (Chang 1997, forthcoming).[16] The incomparability of alternatives in a choice situation is important, then, because it blocks the possibility of a justified choice between them in that choice situation.

Those who reject comparativism tend to make assumptions about comparability that comparativists need not adopt. For example, some deny that the comparability of the alternatives is required for the possibility of justified choice because they conflate comparability with commensurability. Commensurability is not required, but comparability is (see Anderson 1997). Others think that comparativism presupposes a maximizing view of justification: if the comparability of alternatives is necessary for there to be a justified choice, this must be because justification is a matter of choosing what maximizes V (Stocker 1997). But comparability does not entail maximization; perhaps a justified choice is one that is good enough with respect to V, but being good enough relies on the comparability of the alternatives.

Although comparativism is widely accepted, arguments for it are thin on the ground. I will end this chapter by suggesting two arguments in its support. First, comparativism underwrites a deep and attractive way of connecting three basic phenomena of practical reason: values, reasons, and action. Comparativism provides a structure that holds together a wide-ranging, intuitive, and yet flexible view about how the fundamental phenomena of practical reason relate. Second, the main rival to comparativism, "maximalism," lacks intuitive support. As I will suggest, the most plausible justification for maximalism turns on conflating practical reason with its subdomains.

11.4.1. Value, Reasons, Action

Suppose you have to choose between two vacation getaways, and what matters in the choice is doing what makes your life go best. One vacation involves a solitary, rejuvenating retreat at an urban spa, while the other involves camping with friends in awe-inspiring wilderness. If the spa vacation will make your life go better, then you have most reason to choose it. If the spa vacation is worse, then you have less reason to choose it, and, other things equal, most reason to choose the camping trip. Here we have a tidy isomorphism among value and reasons and action: if one alternative is better with respect to the value that matters in the choice, then you have most reason to choose it, and if it is worse in value, then you have most reason to choose the other alternative.[17] If the vacations are equally good with respect to V, then you have sufficient reason to choose either. Being better in value maps onto having most reason to choose it; being worse in value maps onto having more reason to choose something else; being equal in value maps onto having sufficient reason to choose either alternative.

But we should distinguish different ways in which you might have sufficient reason to choose either of two alternatives. Following Edna Ullman-Margalit and Sidney Morgenbesser (1977), we might say that when you have sufficient reason to choose either of two equally good alternatives, you "pick" one. Picking is the arbitrary selection of an alternative on the basis of its value or the reasons that support it, but that value and those reasons don't support choosing it *over* the other alternative. We might reserve the term "choose" for the selection of one alternative *over* the other on the basis of values and reasons that support selecting it *over* the alternatives. Thus having most reason because one alternative is better than the other justifies choosing in this strict sense; having sufficient reason because the alternatives are equally good justifies picking. Crucially, when you pick, you act within the scope of practical reason. You pick rather than choose because you have equal reason to choose either, not because your reasons are silent as to what, all things considered, you should do.

What about cases of incomparability? If the vacations are incomparable with respect to what makes your life go best, then you have neither most reason to choose nor sufficient reason to pick either. Reasons have "run out"; they are silent on the question of whether you have most or sufficient reason to choose either alternative. Since you have neither most nor sufficient reason to select either, your selection in that choice situation cannot be within the scope of practical reason. Here we might say that you "plump" for one of the alternatives. Plumping, like picking, is arbitrary selection, but only the latter is action within the scope of practical reason. Plumping is appropriate when reasons have run out but not when they are evenly balanced. This is because plumping—action outside the scope of practical reason—is a correct response when reasons are silent on the question of what you should do, all things considered, but not when reasons tell you to pick, all things considered.[18]

If plumping is action outside the scope of practical reason, what kind of action is it? Perhaps plumping is an exercise of mere animal agency, as when, for example, you might plump between two meals after emerging from a long fast. You are unconcerned about taste, nutritiousness, and so on, but, like an animal acting instinctively, simply reach for the nearest sustenance. More plausibly, plumping might be an exercise of the existentialist agency that Sartre had in mind when he claimed that existence precedes essence (Sartre 2007). Selection between alternative ways of being, Sartre thought, was fundamental and not guided by reasons or values. When we plump, then, perhaps we act as existentialist agents, selecting one alternative over another in a normative void.[19] If incomparability is widespread, then it seems that the existentialists were largely right: we act not as rational agents guided by reasons but as radically free creatures unmoored by reasons or values.

Finally, if comparable alternatives can be neither better nor worse than one another and not equally good, if, for example, they can be "on a par," then there will be corresponding views about the reasons we have to act. I have suggested such a view elsewhere (see Chang 2013a). For present purposes, we should simply note that the isomorphic structure that comparativism provides among values, reasons, and action makes room for such views.

In sum, comparativism underwrites a deeply intuitive structure relating value, reasons, and action, given in the chart below.

Value	Reasons	Action
x is better than y	most reason to choose x	choose x
x is worse than y	most reason to choose y	choose y
x and y are equally good	sufficient reason to choose either x or y	pick x or pick y
x and y are on a par	??	??
x and y are incomparable	neither most reason to choose one nor sufficient reason to pick either–outside the scope of practical reason	plump for x or plump for y

11.4.2. Maximalism

But comparativism has an important rival, "maximalism." According to maximalism, in order for a choice to be justified, it need only be *not worse* than the other alternatives. An alternative is justified so long as it is a *maximal* alternative, that is, not worse than any of the others. And since being not worse is not a positive comparative relation, being maximal is compatible with being incomparable. Thus, if two items are incomparable, there is a justified choice between them. One is justified in choosing either since each alternative is *not worse* than the other. Maximalism is a noncomparativist view; it holds that the comparability of alternatives is not necessary for the possibility of a justified choice.

Maximalism is widely accepted by decision theorists and rational choice theorists but also, usually implicitly, by many moral philosophers (e.g., Raz 1999). It is a less stringent view of practical reason than comparativism since its standard for practical justification is significantly weaker: according to maximalism, to be justified an alternative need only be not worse than any other, while, according to comparativism, to be justified an alternative must be at least as good or comparable in some other way (e.g., on a par) with the other alternatives. Which standard should we accept?

We might look for an intuitive justification of the maximalist's key idea. A metaphor might help. Maximalism's key idea is that being not worse is sufficient for being justified. It holds, then, that so long as an alternative hasn't, as it were, been knocked out of the arena of reasons by an alternative supported by stronger reasons, it is a justified choice. This is a deeply intuitive idea and explains, I believe, why maximalism enjoys such widespread support.

This intuitive justification of maximalism, however, is one that the comparativist can also help herself to. We need to distinguish the ways in which an alternative can be "left standing" in the arena of reasons. One way is by the alternative being equally as good as the other. This case won't distinguish comparativism from maximalism since both allow that choice can be justified when alternatives are equally good. What distinguishes maximalism from comparativism is the thought that there can be a justified choice among alternatives that are incomparable. Comparativism denies this. So we need to narrow the intuitive appeal of maximalism by asking the following: why think that a choice can be justified if it is left standing in the arena of reasons by being incomparable with the other alternatives?

Put this way, the intuitive force of maximalism is less clear. If there is no comparative relation between two alternatives, why think you are justified in choosing either? After all, with respect to what matters in the choice between them, they cannot be compared. We might say that incomparable alternatives are not ones left standing in the arena of reasons; rather, they haven't even gained entry to it. Once we clearly identify where maximalism departs from comparativism, it seems that there is no justification for the former.

I'll end with a diagnosis for why maximalism appears to have intuitive appeal. I believe that maximalism's appeal involves conflating justification in a subdomain of practical reason with justification in the domain of practical reason itself.

Consider legal justification. The law has limited jurisdiction over intentional actions; it does not attempt to rule on the justification of any intentional action whatever but only those that fall within its purview. There are thus two ways in which an action can be legally justified: first, by falling within the law's jurisdiction and being substantively justified and, second, by falling outside of the law's jurisdiction but not running afoul of any of its prohibitions. Actions that fall outside of the law's jurisdiction are legally justified, as it were, as a matter of default. For example, the law does not have jurisdiction on how many times a day you are to brush your teeth. So long as your teeth-brushing activities don't violate any legal prohibition, what you do, teeth-brushing-wise, is legally justified as a matter of default. The same goes for any other subdomain of practical reason. The way you wear your hair is not within the jurisdiction of the rules of chess. Thus, so long as the way you wear your hair doesn't violate any rules of chess, your stylish bob is chess-justified as a matter of default.

The possibility of being justified as a matter of default by not falling within the jurisdiction of a practical subdomain explains, I believe, why some theorists have been attracted to the idea that a justified choice is possible among incomparables. Actions that do not fall within a subdomain of reasons might be considered incomparable with respect to what matters in the choice. Brushing your teeth three times a day might be thought to be incomparable with brushing your teeth two times a day with respect to conforming to the law.[20] If they are incomparable, they are not worse than one another with respect to one's legal duties, and one is legally justified in doing either. This is the kind of case in which it is plausible to think that justified choice might be possible between incomparable alternatives.

But justification by default is not an option in the domain of practical reason itself since practical reason by its very nature has jurisdiction over all intentional actions. So an action cannot be practically justified as a matter of default. Since a case in which a justified choice among incomparables is possible within a subdomain cannot arise within practical reason writ large, the rationale for the maximalist view according to which justified choice among incomparables is possible has no application. Comparativism, not maximalism, is thus the more plausible view of practical justification.[21]

Acknowledgments

Thanks to Iwao Hirose and Jonas Olson for helpful editorial comments.

Notes

1. For a survey of different phenomena that sometimes go under the label "the incommensurability of values" and their philosophical significance, see Chang 2009b and Hsieh 2008.
2. It is unfortunate that the term 'values' has, at least in some quarters, been co-opted to refer only to evaluative abstracta that admit of cardinally significant representation, ruling out, it is supposed, "deontic" considerations like duties. But the ordinary notion of 'values' is much broader and includes considerations like duties, rights, and excellences, like scientific achievement, which may not be so represented. See also Scanlon 1998: ch. 2 for a similar appeal to a broad, "ordinary" notion of values. Compare Zimmerman, chapter 1 in this volume.
3. Other reasons to reject such views point to the nature of intelligent deliberation (Richardson 2000) and the possibility of organic unities among values (Carlson, chapter 15 in this volume). See Adler, chapter 17 in this volume for a review of different forms of cost-benefit analysis.
4. See Schmidtz, chapter 20 in this volume for other examples of ranking incommensurable items.
5. For a defense of the idea that V represents a unity, see Chang 2004b; for debate about this idea in the context of conflicts between morality and prudence, see, e.g., Chang 2004a; Raz 1999; Bader, chapter 10 in this volume; Richardson 2004.
6. It would be a mistake to understand comparability as obtaining between two items just in case there is a single comparison that holds between them with respect to some or other V since this would make comparability a trivial phenomenon. Correspondingly, it would be a mistake to understand incomparability as holding so long as there is no V in terms of which the two items could be compared. I address this phenomenon, which is not of much philosophical significance, in the text below.
7. An important issue here is whether the contribution must be constitutive or whether it may be instrumental or, indeed, some other way in which one value may "contribute" to another. I leave these interesting, somewhat technical, issues aside.
8. This formulation allows the possibility that background facts make no difference to how the instantiations relate if comparisons of value instantiations with respect to V are not background-fact-sensitive.
9. I say roughly because some might think that incomparability among values does not require any incomparability as an input, a possibility that does not fit neatly on the mooted spectrum. I leave this possibility aside.
10. There is also the possibility of metaphysical indeterminacy, which may be one explanation of parity, but there is no space to discuss this kind of indeterminacy here (see Chang 2000: ch. 5).
11. This is not to say that the vagueness of V entails the indeterminacy of comparability with respect to V as in many cases it does not. Nor is this to say that the only way indeterminacy

in comparability can arise is by the vagueness of V. Other ways in which there could be vagueness in comparability is if there is vagueness in the comparative of V or in the unrelativized comparative, such as 'better than'.
12. For a more detailed examination and critique of Broome's argument, see Chang 2002: ch. 6. For an argument that parity is a form of vagueness, see Elson 2014.
13. Indeed, Broome supposes that evaluative properties can be represented by cardinally significant real numbers in other work. See Broome 1991, 2004.
14. For a defense of the condition that only one and not both items must fail to be covered, see Chang 1997a. I add the condition "in the context of an attempted comparison" because, as Ralf Bader pointed out to me in conversation, it is possible that two alternatives for choice could individually bear V but in the context of a comparison fail to bear V for the purposes of that comparison. I doubt there is any nonstipulated or nonartificial V that admits of this possibility, but I here leave open the possibility.
15. This formal condition might be considered a constraint on how we understand the values relevant to a choice situation. If one is tempted to think that a value that fails to cover an option is relevant to the choice situation, one has misunderstood the choice situation.
16. By "objective justification" I mean "supported by most objective reason" or "objectively rational" where the rationality is that of reasons, not mere norms such as structural norms governing movements of mind.
17. The appeal to an isomorphism allows for neutrality on the priority relations that might hold among values, reasons, and action.
18. We can leave aside the complication of alternative responses, most notably, abandoning that choice situation and moving to one that does not involve incomparable alternatives (Barcan Marcus 1980).
19. We might be able to act as quasi-existentialist agents if we plump on the basis of pro tanto reasons. This seems to be Joseph Raz's view (Raz 1997).
20. These options are not *non*comparable with respect to one's legal duties because they are actions that could in principle fall afoul of the law if, for example, you are a toothpaste model who owes your employer a duty to brush your teeth more than twice a day.
21. For a more detailed argument against maximalism, see Chang forthcoming.

References

Anderson, E. (1993). *Value in Ethics and Economics*. Cambridge: Harvard University Press.
Anderson, E. (1997). "Practical Reason and Incommensurable Goods." In Chang (ed.), Cambridge, MA: Harvard University Press.
Andreou, C. (2013). "Parity, Comparability, and Choice." Paper presented to the CREUM Ethics Center, University of Montreal, June.
Barcan Marcus, R. (1980). "Moral Dilemmas and Consistency." *Journal of Philosophy* 77 (3): 121–36.
Broome, J. (1991). *Weighing Goods*. Oxford: Blackwell.
Broome, J. (1997). "Is Incommensurability Vagueness?" In R. Chang (ed.), *Incommensurability, Incomparability and Practical Reason*. Cambridge: Harvard University Press, 67–89.
Broome, J. (2004). "Reasons." In R. J. Wallace, P. Pettit, S. Scheffler, and M. Smith (eds.), *Reason and Value: Themes from the Moral Philosophy of Joseph Raz*. Oxford: Oxford University Press, 28–55.

Chang, R. (1997a). "Introduction." In R. Chang (ed.), *Incommensurability, Incomparability and Practical Reason*. Cambridge: Harvard University Press, 1–34.

Chang, R., ed. (1997b). *Incommensurability, Incomparability and Practical Reason*. Cambridge: Harvard University Press.

Chang, R. (2000). *Making Comparisons Count*. New York: Routledge.

Chang, R. (2002). "The Possibility of Parity." *Ethics* 112: 659–88.

Chang, R. (2004a). "Putting Together Morality and Well-Being." In M. Betzler and P. Baumann (eds.), *Practical Conflicts*. Cambridge: Cambridge University Press, 118–58.

Chang, R. (2004b). "All Things Considered." *Philosophical Perspectives* 18: 1–22.

Chang, R. (2009a). "Voluntarist Reasons and the Sources of Normativity." In D. Sobel and S. Wall, *Reasons for Action*. New York: Cambridge University Press, 243–71.

Chang, R. (2009b). "Incommensurability (and Incomparability)." In H. LaFollette (ed.), *International Encyclopedia of Ethics*. Malden, MA: Blackwell.

Chang, R. (2013a). "Commitments, Reasons, and the Will." In R. Shafer-Landau (ed.), *Oxford Studies in Metaethics* 8: 74–113.

Chang, R. (2013b). "Grounding Practical Normativity: Going Hybrid." *Philosophical Studies* 164 (1): 163–87.

Chang, R. (2013c). "Are Hard Choices Cases of Incomparability?" *Philosophical Issues* 22 (1): 106–26.

Chang, R. (Forthcoming). "Comparativism." In B. McGuire and E. Lord (eds.), *Weighing Reasons*. Oxford University Press.

Copp, D. (1997). "The Ring of Gyges: Overridingness and the Unity of Reason." *Social Philosophy and Policy* 14: 86–106.

D'Agostino, F. (2003). *Incommensurability and Commensuration: The Common Denominator*. Burlington, VT: Ashgate.

Elson, L. (2014). "Heaps and Chains: Is the Chaining Argument for Parity a Sorites?" *Ethics* 124 (3): 557–71.

Foot, P. (1978). "Morality as a System of Hypothetical Imperatives." In *Virtues and Vices*. Oxford: Blackwell, 157–73.

Froding, B., and M. Peterson. (2012). "Virtuous Choice and Parity." *Ethical Theory and Moral Practice* 15 (1): 71–82.

Griffin, J. (1986). *Well-Being*. Oxford: Clarendon Press.

Hart, H. L. A. (1961). *The Concept of Law*. Oxford: Clarendon Press.

Heath, T. (1921). *A History of Greek Mathematics*. Oxford: Clarendon Press.

Hsieh, N. (2005). "Equality, Clumpiness and Incomparability." *Utilitas* 17 (2): 180–204.

Hsieh, N. (2008). "Incommensurable Values." In E. N. Zalta (ed.), *The Stanford Encyclopedia of Philosophy*, Fall 2008 ed. http://plato.stanford.edu/archives/fall2008/entries/value-incommensurable/.

Hurka, T. (1993). *Perfectionism*. Oxford: Oxford University Press.

Nagel, T. (1979). "The Fragmentation of Value." In *Mortal Questions*. New York: Cambridge University Press, 128–41.

Parfit, D. (1986). *Reasons and Persons*. Oxford: Oxford University Press.

Parfit, D. (N.d.). "Toward Theory X." Unpublished.

Rabinowicz, W. (2008). "Value Relations." *Theoria* 74: 18–41.

Rabinowicz, W. (2012). "Value Relations Revisited." *Economics and Philosophy* 28 (2): 133–64.

Raz, J. (1986). *The Morality of Freedom*. Oxford: Clarendon Press.

Raz, J. (1999). *Engaging Reason*. Oxford: Clarendon Press.

Richardson, H. (1994). *Practical Reasoning about Final Ends.* Cambridge: Cambridge University Press.

Richardson, H. (2000). "The Stupidity of the Cost-Benefit Standard." *Journal of Legal Studies* 29 (2): 971–1003.

Rønnow-Rasmussen, T. (2011). *Personal Value.* Oxford: Oxford University Press.

Sartre, J.-P. (2007). *Existentialism Is a Humanism.* Tr. Carol Macomber. Ed. J. Kulka. New Haven: Yale University Press.

Scanlon, T. (1998). *What We Owe to Each Other.* Cambridge: Belknap Press of Harvard University Press.

Sinnott-Armstrong, W. (1988). *Moral Dilemmas.* Oxford: Blackwell.

de Sousa, R. (1974). "The Good and the True." *Mind* 83: 534–51.

Stocker, M. (1997). "Abstract and Concrete Value: Plurality, Conflict, and Maximization." In R. Chang (ed.), *Incommensurability, Incomparability and Practical Reason.* Cambridge: Harvard University Press, 196–214.

Ullman-Margalit, E., and S. Morgenbesser. (1977). "Picking and Choosing." *Social Research* 44: 757–87.

von Fritz, K. (1945). "The Discovery of Incommensurability by Hippasus of Metapontum." *Annals of Mathematics* 46 (2): 242–64.

Williams, B. (1981). "Conflicts of Values." In *Moral Luck.* Cambridge: Cambridge University Press, 71–82.

CHAPTER 12

VALUE SUPERIORITY

GUSTAF ARRHENIUS AND WLODEK RABINOWICZ

12.1. INTRODUCTION

LET's say that A and B are two kinds of goods such that more of A or B is better than less. We are going to discuss the following two relations that can obtain between A and B:

Strong Superiority (roughly): Any amount of A is better than any amount of B.[1]
Weak Superiority (roughly): A sufficient amount of A is better than any amount of B.[2]

It is easy to find examples of these relations in the literature, sometimes under the labels "higher goods" or "discontinuity in value." For example, already in the nineteenth century Franz Brentano claimed that "[i]t is quite possible for there to be a class of goods which could be increased *ad indefinitum* but without exceeding a given finite good."[3] Likewise, W. D. Ross asserted that "[w]ith respect to pleasure and virtue, it seems to me much more likely to be the truth that *no* amount of pleasure is equal to any amount of virtue, that in fact virtue belongs to a higher order of value, beginning at a point higher on the scale of value than pleasure ever reaches" (Ross 1930: 150). Similar views have been proposed by, among others, Roger Crisp, Jonathan Glover, James Griffin, Rem Edwards, Noah Lemos, Derek Parfit, and John Skorupski.[4] Their lineage goes back to at least Francis Hutcheson in the early eighteenth century and John Stuart Mill in the mid-nineteenth century.[5]

Superiority in value can be contrasted with

The Archimedean Property of Value (roughly): This property holds for goods of kind B relative to goods of kind A if and only if for any amount of A there is some amount of B which is at least as good.

This is like the Archimedean property of the real numbers: For any positive numbers x and y, there is a natural number n such that $nx \geq y$. The Archimedean property seems to capture the way we usually think about the aggregation of goods. Let's say that you are considering two holiday packages. The first is a week in Stockholm, the other a week in Copenhagen. You have a preference for Stockholm. It is possible, however, to better the Copenhagen-package by adding some extra days. It seems plausible that there is such a bettering, other things being equal, that would reverse your preference in such a way that you would prefer the Copenhagen holiday. If Stockholm-days are taken as one kind of good (kind A) and Copenhagen-days as another kind of good (kind B), then this case is an illustration of the Archimedean Property of Value. One might think that this feature is a general property of goods, that all kinds of goods satisfy the Archimedean Property of Value. Weak Superiority is a denial of this claim. Strong Superiority entails Weak Superiority. They are thus both versions of what we call *non-Archimedeanism*.

Superiority and non-Archimedeanism are structural features that can be true of many kinds of orderings. We shall discuss some different ways in which these ideas can be applied to the aggregation of welfare. It is important to separate these different applications of the superiority idea, since they will yield quite distinctive views with varying intuitive support.

First, however, we shall describe some of the problems that have motivated the recent interest in non-Archimedeanism.

12.2. Intrapersonal and Interpersonal Repugnant Conclusions

During the last thirty years or so, non-Archimedeanism has again become popular in connection with theories of welfare and population ethics. What is the reason behind this renaissance? Derek Parfit has brought attention to a problem for classical Total Utilitarianism. This view tells us to maximize the welfare in the world and implies what Parfit calls the Repugnant Conclusion:

> *The Repugnant Conclusion*: For any population consisting of people with very high positive welfare, there is a better population in which everyone has a very low positive welfare, other things being equal.[6]

In figure 12.1, the width of each block represents the number of people, whereas the height represents their lifetime welfare. All the lives in the diagram have positive welfare, or, as we also could put it, all the people have lives worth living. The A-people have very high welfare, whereas the B-people have very low positive welfare. The reason for this could be that in the B-lives there are, to paraphrase Parfit, only enough ecstasies to just outweigh the agonies, or that the good things in those lives are of uniformly poor quality, for example, eating potatoes and listening to Muzak.[7] However, since there are

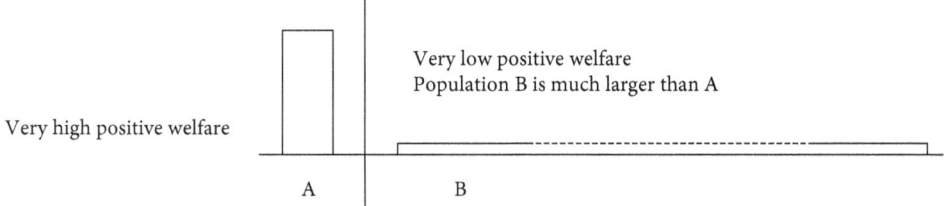

FIGURE 12.1 Repugnant Conclusion

many more people in B, the total sum of welfare in B is greater than in A. Hence, Total Utilitarianism ranks B as better than A—an example of the Repugnant Conclusion.[8]

A value maximizer could avoid this implication by invoking a form of non-Archimedeanism: She could claim that there is a number of lives with very high welfare, which is better than any number of lives with very low positive welfare, although the addition of more lives with very low positive welfare always makes a population better.

Figure 12.1 could also be taken to represent an intrapersonal version of the Repugnant Conclusion. The width of each block would then stand for the length of a life, and the height for the well-being at a certain time. For example, block A could represent a life of a hundred years in which every year is of a very high quality, and block B could stand for a much longer life in which every year is of very low quality.[9] If the B-life is long enough, then the total welfare of that life will be greater than that of the A-life and thus this life will be ranked as better by a maximizing theory of welfare. Again, this implication could be blocked by invoking a form of non-Archimedeanism. This is what Parfit suggests:

> I could live for another 100 years, all of an extremely high quality. Call this *the Century of Ecstasy*. I could instead live for ever, with a life that would always be barely worth living ... the only good things would be muzak and potatoes. Call this *the Drab Eternity*.—I claim that, though each day of the Drab Eternity would be worth living, the Century of Ecstasy would give me a better life.—Though each day of the Drab Eternity would have some value for me, *no* amount of this value could be as good for me as the Century of Ecstasy. (Parfit 1986: 161–64, emphasis in original)

Likewise, in his influential discussion of intrapersonal aggregation of welfare, James Griffin has proposed that there can be what he calls "discontinuity" among prudential values (welfare) of the form "enough of A outranks any amount of B" (this is what we call "Weak Superiority") (Griffin 1986: 85). Discontinuity entails, he explains

> the suspension of addition; ... we have a positive value that, no matter how often a certain amount is added to itself, cannot become greater than another positive value, and cannot, not because with piling up we get diminishing value or even disvalue ..., but because they are the sort of value that, even remaining constant, cannot add up to some other value.... [I]t is more plausible that, say, fifty years at a very high level of well-being—say, the level which makes possible satisfying personal relations,

some understanding of what makes life worth while, appreciation of great beauty, the chance to accomplish something with one's life—outranks any number of years at the level just barely living—say, the level at which none of the former values are possible and one is left with just enough surplus of simple pleasure over pain to go on with it. (Griffin 1986: 85–86)

We take it that most people find Griffin's and Parfit's examples rather persuasive. To establish whether the non-Archimedean idea involved in the examples is tenable, however, we need to spell it out in more detail and distinguish among its different versions.

12.3. Aggregation of Welfare and Non-Archimedeanism

Roughly, a person's welfare has to do with how well her life is going for her. To specify a person's welfare is to specify how good or bad her life is for her. Let's call those things that are good or bad for people "welfare components." Here are some components that have been proposed in the literature: pleasure or pain; satisfied or frustrated desires; autonomy or its absence; greater or lesser accomplishments; true or false beliefs; satisfying or dissatisfying personal relationships; experiences of beautiful or ugly objects, and so forth.

The kind of non-Archimedeanism expressed in the quotes above from Griffin and Parfit concerns the relationship between orderings of welfare components and the ordering of lives in respect to welfare. However, the route from welfare components to the welfare of lives can take different paths and, which is important, some form of non-Archimedean property can appear at different points along this path. Above, we only stated the Archimedean property for value, but we can of course also ascribe this property to other orderings, for example, the ordering of pleasures. Thus, we could order all experiences, including collections of experiences, in terms of how pleasurable they are (how much pleasure these experiences contain taken as a whole), that is, by the relation "is at least as pleasurable as." We could then ask whether this ordering is Archimedean. If it is, then for any two kinds of experiences A and B, and for any collection of experiences of kind A, there is some collection of experiences of kind B that is more pleasurable.

Even if the ordering of pleasures is Archimedean, we could still ask how such an ordering relates to the welfare of a life. We may assume that it is always better for a person to enjoy a greater amount of pleasure rather than less, as long as it is the same kind of pleasure in both cases.[10] However, we could ask whether for any kinds of pleasures A and B, and for any amount of pleasure of kind A, there is always some amount of pleasures of kind B which is *better* for a person. Here we are asking whether the Archimedean property applies to the contributive value of pleasure to the welfare of a life. And we might deny this. Hence, it is possible that the ordering of experiences by the relation "is at least as pleasurable as" is Archimedean despite the fact that the betterness ordering of pleasurable experiences is not.

On the other hand, we could question whether the very ordering of pleasure is Archimedean. We could start by looking at *atomic* experiences of pleasures, understood as the shortest possible experiences of pleasure that are the building blocks of all other experiences of pleasure. We could then investigate how the ordering of these atomic experiences relates to the ordering of all experiences, including collections of pleasurable experiences, in terms of the relation "is at least as pleasurable as." We could then ask whether for any two kinds of atomic experiences A and B, and for any collection of A-experiences, there is always some collection of B-experiences which, taken together, are *more pleasurable* (or, to put it differently, constitute a greater amount of pleasure). Here we are asking whether the non-Archimedean property appears in the aggregation of atomic pleasures to the overall pleasure in a life.

If non-Archimedeanism about pleasure is combined with the view "the more pleasure, the better," then it might be extensionally equivalent to non-Archimedeanism about the *value* of pleasure. Still, these two versions of non-Archimedeanism are different in an important way: If we hold that the non-Archimedean property appears in the ordering of pleasures, then it's still possible for us to claim that "the more pleasure, the better." This might be of importance for a hedonist who adheres to the classical utilitarian principle of maximization. One can accept this principle while still interpreting the ordering of pleasures in non-Archimedean terms and thus avoid some of the implications that are usually associated with classical utilitarianism, such as the Repugnant Conclusion and the like.

As we mentioned above, one can instead hold that the non-Archimedean property only appears in the betterness ordering of pleasure. The following quote from Mill might be read in this way:

> some *kinds* of pleasure are more desirable and valuable than others. It would be absurd that while, in estimating all other things, quality is considered as well as quantity, the estimation of pleasures should be supposed to depend on quantity alone.— Of two pleasures, if. . . . one of the two is, by those who are competently acquainted with both, placed so far above the other that they . . . would not resign it for any quantity of the other pleasure which their nature is capable of, we are justified in ascribing to the preferred enjoyment a superiority in quality, so far outweighing quantity as to render it, in comparison, of small account (Mill 1998: 56).

However, if one takes this view, then one cannot claim that "the more pleasure, the better." It is therefore on this reading somewhat surprising that Mill thought that the above position "is quite compatible with the principle of utility" (Mill 1998: 56), which he also sometimes refers to as "the Greatest Happiness Principle" (55). The latter label suggests that value tracks the quantity of pleasure.[11]

Riley (2008) defines standard ethical hedonism as the view that pleasure is the sole value and that it is "homogenous" in nature: there are no qualitatively different pleasures; the only differences concern duration and intensity. On this view, the ordering of pleasures is Archimedean. Riley claims that it is necessary for a standard hedonist to accept value additivity (which presupposes that the value ordering of pleasures also satisfies the Archimedean property).[12] As he puts it, "value additivity is built into the very meaning of standard hedonism." The crucial premise in his argument for this claim is as follows:

> one unit of pleasure contributes just as much positive intrinsic value as every other unit of pleasure does to the value of the whole pleasure comprised of the individual pleasures. (Riley 2008: 261)

This premise is ambiguous. In a given whole composed of pleasures, each unit of pleasure does contribute just as much to the value of the whole as every other unit. That's true: there are no relevant qualitative differences between pleasures on standard hedonism. Indeed, on that view, the value contribution of each unit of pleasure to a whole composed of n such units can be set to $1/n$-th of the value of the whole. However, it doesn't follow that a unit of pleasure has a fixed contributive value in the *marginalist* sense, that is, that it contributes the same amount of value to a whole to which it is added as any other unit contributes to the whole to which *it* is added. For example, the marginal contributive value of adding one unit of pleasure to a whole consisting of five units of pleasure doesn't have to be the same as the marginal value of adding one unit to a whole consisting of ten units of pleasure. Nothing in the definition of standard hedonism as given by Riley requires this, but this is what he needs for his argument for additivity to succeed. If the marginal contributive value of an additional unit can vary, then, in particular, its marginal contribution can decrease and converge down to zero as the number of units of pleasure goes to infinity. And then one can easily obtain a non-Archimedean effect insofar as the value of pleasure is concerned, if one, like Mill, goes beyond standard hedonism and allows for higher pleasures along with the lower ones. Even if lower pleasures are assumed to be homogeneous in nature, their aggregated value might never reach the value of a given collection of higher pleasures.

Indeed, to obtain non-Archimedean effects one doesn't need to move beyond standard hedonism. Thus, in the example discussed above, block A in figure 12.1 could represent a life of a hundred years in which every moment is very pleasurable, and block B could stand for a very long life in which every moment is pleasurable to a very low degree. However long the B-life is, it might be less valuable than the A-life (albeit it might very well contain a greater amount of pleasure). Pace Riley, this violation of the Archimedean property of value is perfectly compatible with standard hedonism. As we have seen, different kinds of pleasurable experiences are needed for a violation of the Archimedean property by the value ordering of pleasures. One might therefore ask how there can be such different kinds of pleasures given standard hedonism. The answer is simple: we can define kinds in terms of intensity of pleasures. In the example above, we can assume that moments of intense pleasure form the superior kind A and moments of low intensity pleasure form the inferior kind B.[13]

Non-Archimedeanism can appear not only in the ordering of personal value, that is, value for someone, but also in the ordering of impersonal value—value period. Thus, we can order populations of lives in terms of how good they are, that is, by the relation "is at least as good as." We can ask how welfare contributes to this impersonal value. Assume that we have an ordering of lives in terms of welfare. We could ask whether for any population consisting of people with very high positive welfare, there is a population of people with slightly positive welfare which is better. Here we are asking whether the Archimedean property holds for the contributive value of welfare to the value of populations. But we could also ask whether this property holds for the aggregation of individual welfare to the overall welfare of the population. If this property is violated at one of these steps, then we can still be maximizers of goodness but avoid the Repugnant Conclusion.

Of course, the non-Archimedean property could also apply to welfare components other than pleasure. Notably, it could hold *between* welfare components of different kinds. For example, one could hold that no amount of trivial pleasures can outweigh the loss of one's autonomy. This could be a view about how pleasure and autonomy contribute to welfare, or about how they contribute to the impersonal value of a life (its goodness period). The non-Archimedean property might also appear in the aggregation of welfarist and nonwelfarist goods into a measure of the value of actions, people, or lives. This seems to be what Ross had in mind in the passages we have quoted in the introduction and what Hutcheson had in mind when he wrote that "[t]he exercise of virtue for a short period... is of incomparably greater value than the most lasting sensual pleasure" (Hutcheson 1968 [1755]: 118).

Let's summarize this section. The non-Archimedean property can appear at different stages in the path from goods to welfare and to the value of people, lives, populations, worlds, and actions. It can appear in the contributive value of atomic experiences of pleasure to the pleasantness of aggregates of such experiences, in the contributive value of pleasure to the welfare of a life, in the contributive value of the welfare of lives to the value of populations and worlds, in the aggregation of welfarist and nonwelfarist goods into a measure of the value of actions, people, and lives, and so forth. Note that these possibilities are logically independent. For example, one could hold that "trivial" pleasures can always outweigh "high quality" pleasures when it comes to the welfare of a life but not when it comes to the contributive value of a life to the value of a population. One might think that a life with some amount of high-quality pleasures has a higher contributive value to a population than any number of lives with any amount of trivial pleasures, although the latter lives may have a higher degree of welfare.

12.4. THE GENERAL STRUCTURE OF SUPERIORITY IN VALUE

As we have seen above, Superiority and non-Archimedeanism are structural features that can be true of many kinds of orderings. In what follows, however, we are going to focus on superiority in value, and more specifically in goodness rather than in goodness for someone, but our results are applicable, mutatis mutandis, to other orderings as well. The relation "is at least as good as" that we shall focus on can be taken as a placeholder for other possible ordering relations, such as those that we have discussed above.

Thus, suppose a domain of objects is ordered by the relation "is at least as good as." Assume that this relation is a weak order, that is, transitive and complete in the domain under consideration. The completeness assumption, according to which all objects are ordered by the relation in question, is problematic, but we make it just for the sake of simplicity.[14] Assume that the domain is closed under concatenation, by which we mean the operation of forming mereological wholes out of any finite non-empty set of objects. Such wholes are themselves objects in the domain. We also take it that for any object e in the domain and for any number m, the domain contains a whole composed of m mutually nonoverlapping "e-objects," by which we mean objects of the same type as e. That two objects do not overlap means that they don't have any common parts. We take object *types* to be understood in such a way that any two representatives of the same type are equally good and interchangeable in every whole without influencing the value of the whole in question. Intuitively, we might think of objects of the same type as being identical in all value-relevant respects.[15] In what follows, statements such as "m e-objects are better than k e'-objects" should be read as claims about complex objects obtained by this kind of "same type"-concatenation: "A whole composed of m non-overlapping e-objects is better than a whole composed of k non-overlapping e'-objects."

It will also simplify matters if we suppose that all the objects in the domain are positively valuable, by which we mean that for any object e and any m, $m + 1$ e-objects are better than m e-objects. In other words, concatenating objects of the same type is value increasing. But we allow that the value of the objects in the domain may otherwise vary, and quite dramatically sometimes. Now we can define strong and weak superiority in a precise manner:

> *Strong Superiority*: An object e is *strongly superior* to an object e' if and only if e is better than any number of e'-objects.
> *Weak Superiority*: An object e is *weakly superior* to an object e' if and only if for some number m, m e-objects are better than any number of e'-objects.[16]

In other words, e is strongly superior to e' if it is better than any whole composed of e'-objects, however large. It is weakly superior to e' if a sufficient number of e-objects are jointly better that any whole composed of e'-objects, however large. Consequently, if e is weakly superior to e', then a whole composed of a sufficient number of e-objects is strongly superior to e'. Thus, the existence of weak superiorities entails the existence of strong superiorities in the domain, given closure under concatenation.

Both superiority and weak superiority involve violations of the Archimedean Property for betterness ordering:

> *The Archimedean Property of Value (exact formulation)*: For any object e and any positively valuable object e', there is a number k such that k e'-objects are at least as good as e.

Along with these two kinds of superiority relations between objects in the domain, we could define the corresponding relations between object *types*, one being that any object of a certain type is better than any number of objects of another type, and the other being that a sufficient number of objects of one type is better than any number of objects of another type. Since objects belonging to the same type are identical in all value-relevant respects, e is (weakly) superior to e' if and only if e's type is (weakly) superior to the type to which e' belongs. In what follows, however, we shall restrict our attention to superiority relations between objects.

A different perspective on superiority relations would involve thinking of objects as exhibiting various value-relevant *attributes*, each of which can be present in an object in varying degrees. As an example, think of an object as a possible outcome that can be characterized in terms of such value-relevant attributes as, say, (the levels of) achievement, satisfaction, freedom, and so on. We could then study superiority relations between attributes, rather than between objects themselves (or between object types). An attribute may be said to be superior to another attribute *relative* to an object e if and only if any improvement of e with respect to the former attribute is better than any change of e with respect to the latter attribute. Correspondingly, an attribute is weakly superior to another attribute relative to e if and only if some improvement of e with respect to the former attribute is better than any change of e with respect to the latter attribute. Apart from these superiority relations, which are relative to a specific object, one can also study global superiority relations between attributes, which hold relative to all objects. This is a plausible way of understanding views such as the one expressed by Ross in the passage quoted in the introduction, and the one expressed by Hutcheson in the quote in section 12.3. Such object-specific and global relations are discussed in Broome and Rabinowicz (2005), where it is shown that the results we are about to prove for superiority relations between objects in a large measure extend to the corresponding relationships between attributes.[17]

12.5. Strong Superiority without Abrupt Breaks

By a "decreasing sequence" $e_1, \ldots, e_n$, we shall in what follows mean a sequence of objects such that e_1 is better than e_2, e_2 is better than e_3, ..., and e_{n-1} is better than e_n. It is a common view that in a decreasing sequence in which the first element is strongly superior to the last one, some element must be strongly superior to its immediate successor. What often lies behind this view is the belief that e_1 can be strongly superior to e_n only if e_1 is *infinitely* better than e_n.[18] But if the latter is the case, then a decreasing sequence that starts with e_1 and ends with e_n must at some point involve an infinite drop in value. In other words, it must at some point reach an element e_i such that e_i is infinitely better than e_{i+1}. Which implies that e_i must be strongly superior to its immediate successor e_{i+1}.[19]

However, the claim that strong superiority between the first and the last element of the decreasing sequence implies strong superiority between some adjacent elements in the sequence is incorrect. At least, it is incorrect in all domains in which *weak superiority does not collapse into strong superiority*. More precisely, the following can easily be proved:

> *Observation 1*: Consider any two objects e and e' such that e is better than e'. If e is weakly superior to e', without being strongly superior to it, then the domain must contain a finite decreasing sequence of objects in which the first element is strongly superior to the last one, but no element is strongly superior to its immediate successor.

For the proof, see appendix 12.1.

12.6. Independence

While Observation 1 is provably true, it still seems somehow counterintuitive. Many people seem to have a strong intuition that a decreasing sequence in which the first element is strongly superior to the last one must contain an element that is strongly superior to its immediate successor.[20] As we have seen, the belief that seems to lie behind this intuition is that strong superiority in value requires infinite betterness. However, this assumption appears to rest on a presupposition that value is additive. If value is additive, then piling up the less valuable objects would sooner or later result in a whole that is at least as good as the strongly superior object, *unless* the value of that object is infinitely large by comparison. A similar presupposition of additivity seems to lurk, for example, behind the following statement of Jonathan Riley:

> Given the hedonist claim that happiness in the sense of pleasure (including the absence of pain) is the sole ultimate end and test of human conduct, there are only two logical possibilities: either qualitative differences [between pleasures] may be reduced to finite amounts of pleasure (for example, one unit of higher pleasure might be deemed equivalent to ten units of lower pleasure), in which case the quality/quantity distinction is epiphenomenal because pleasure is at bottom homogeneous stuff; or qualitative differences are equivalent to *infinite* quantitative differences, in which case pleasure is a heterogeneous phenomenon consisting of irreducibly plural kinds or dimensions arranged in a hierarchy. The second alternative is embodied in my interpretation. (Riley 1993: 292, our emphasis)

Riley's *tertium non datur* is apparently grounded in a belief that if a higher pleasure only has a finite value, then that value sooner or later would be reached, if we started piling up lower pleasures. This belief is correct if value additivity is assumed, but without such an assumption it is false.

To make room for strong superiority between the extrema of a decreasing sequence without strong superiority setting in at any point in the sequence, we must give up the infinitistic interpretation of superiority, which in turn requires giving up value additivity. We must allow that the aggregated value of several objects of the same type need not be the sum of the values each of them has on its own. That the value of a whole may differ from the sum of the values of its parts is of course an idea that should be familiar to post-Moorean value theorists.[21]

More precisely, we need to give up a condition of independence. If we want to have a sequence in which the first element is strongly superior to the last one, without any element in the sequence being strongly superior to its immediate successor, we must—as we shall see (cf. Observation 2 below)—reject the idea that the value of the whole has to be a monotonically increasing function of the value of its parts. That is, we must give up the *independence axiom* for the betterness ordering:

> *Independence*: An object e is at least as good as e' if and only if replacing e' by e in any whole results in a whole that is at least as good.[22]

Independence implies that the ordering of the contributions that different objects would make to the value of a given whole is context-independent. In other words, this ordering does not depend on the other parts the whole is composed of. Clearly, value additivity presupposes Independence.

With Independence, we could not have had strong superiority between the first and the last element of the sequence without strong superiority setting in at some point along the way.

> *Observation 2*: Suppose that the first element in a sequence $e_1, \ldots, e_n$ is strongly superior to the last one. Then, provided that "is at least as good as" is a complete and transitive relation on the domain under consideration, Independence implies that some element in the sequence is strongly superior to its immediate successor.

For the proof, see appendix 12.2.[23]

One can also prove that, with Independence, the distinction between weak and strong superiority cannot be upheld: the former collapses into the latter.

> *Observation 3*: Assume that "is at least as good as" is a transitive and complete relation which satisfies Independence. Then, for every e and e', if e is weakly superior to e', then e is strongly superior to e'.

Proof: Suppose, for *reductio*, that e is weakly but but not strongly superior to e'. Then, by Observaton 1, the domain contains a finite sequence in which the first element is strongly superior to the last one, but no element is strongly superior to its successor. But, by Observation 2, such a sequence cannot exist if Indepndence holds and "at least as good as" is a transitive and complete relation. (A direct proof of Observation 3, which does not rely on the two previous Observations, has been provided by Klint Jensen (2008); see Appendix 12.3.)

12.7. Giving Up Independence

What if we give up Independence? Then the following becomes possible: Suppose that when we start adding more and more valuable objects of the same type, the marginal value contribution of each extra object sooner or later starts to decrease, converging to zero.[24] If this decrease is sufficiently steep, then adding extra objects of the same type will never get us above a finite value limit: For any object e of a finite value, there will exist some finite value level v_e such that the aggregated value of an arbitrarily large number of e-objects is always lower than v_e. But then nothing excludes that a single object e' may be more valuable than any number of e-objects: All it takes is that the value of e' either equals or exceeds v_e.

The maneuver of letting the marginal value contribution of extra units of a given kind of good converge to zero is, of course, quite standard, even with respect to intrinsic values. In population axiology, it has been suggested as a way of avoiding the Repugnant Conclusion (cf. the discussion in section 12.2). To avoid this conclusion, we do not have to give up the welfarist idea that the value of the world is an aggregate of the welfare levels of its inhabitants. All we need is to assume that the aggregative operation is of an appropriate kind: Adding lives with positive but low welfare increases the value of a world but it will never increase that value beyond a certain finite limit.[25]

Given this convergence of value to finite limits, it is easy to account for the possibility of a decreasing sequence $e_1, \ldots, e_n$, in which (i) the first element is strongly superior to the last element, even though (ii) no element is strongly superior to the one that comes next.

As a simplest possible example, which for that reason is maximally artificial, assume that the sequence consists of three elements, e_1, e_2, e_3, with their values being, respectively, 5, 3, and 2. Suppose now, unrealistically, that the value contribution of extra objects of the same type rapidly decreases, from the very beginning, with each new contribution being half as large as the preceding one. Thus, for example, while the value of one e_3-object equals 2, the value of two such objects equals $2 + 1$, the value of three e_3-objects equals $2 + 1 + \frac{1}{2}$, and so on.

It is easy to see that for each object type, there is a finite value limit that cannot be exceeded by a whole composed of the objects of that type. That limit can be defined as the sum of the infinite sequence in which the first term equals the value of a single object of the type under consideration and each successive term stands for the value contribution obtained from adding another object of the same type. In the example, these limits have been chosen in such a way as to guarantee that the sequence satisfies the required conditions (i) and (ii). The value of the first element (5) exceeds the value limit for the last element $(2 + 1 + \frac{1}{2} + \ldots = 4)$. Consequently, the first element is strongly superior to the last one. But for each element in the sequence, its value is lower than the value limit for the next object in the sequence. That is, no element is strongly superior to the one that comes next. Thus, if convergence of same-type concatenation to an upper limit is allowed, it is logically possible to move from a strongly superior e_1 to an inferior e_n by a *gradually* decreasing sequence in which at no point there appears to occur a radical value loss.

Indeed, as has been proved by Klint Jensen (2008), convergence of same-type concatenation to an upper limit is a quite pervasive phenomenon. It holds for all objects that are weakly inferior to some objects in the domain provided that "is at least as good as" is a transitive and complete relation that divides the object domain into countably many of equivalence classes. It is a standard theorem of measurement theory that if the latter holds, then there exists a real-valued function V that represents "is at least as good as." That is, for all objects e and e', $V(e) \geq V(e')$ if and only if e is at least as good as e'. (Cf. Theorem 6.3 in Aleskerov, Boyssou, and Monjardet 2007: 206.) Now, consider any object e such that some object is weakly superior to e. Then the sequence $V(e)$, $V(2\ e\text{-objects})$, $V(3\ e\text{-objects})$,.... has an upper limit. For the proof of this observation (Observation 4), due to Klint Jensen (2008), see appendix 12.4.

12.8. WEAK SUPERIORITY IS DIFFERENT

We have seen that, in the absence of Independence, we can have strong superiority between the extrema of a decreasing sequence without strong superiority setting in at any point in the sequence. It is different with weak superiority. It can be shown, without assuming Independence, that any finite sequence whose first element is strongly superior to its last element must contain some element that is *weakly* superior to the one that comes next. In other words, in a sequence in which no element is even weakly superior to its immediate successor, the first element cannot be strongly superior to the last element.

This result can be strengthened. In a sequence in which no element is weakly superior to its immediate successor, the first element cannot even be *weakly* superior to the last element. More exactly, we can prove the following:

> *Observation 5*: Suppose that "is at least as good as" is a complete and transitive relation on the domain. Then, in any finite sequence of objects in which the first element is weakly superior to the last element, there exists at least one element that is weakly superior to its immediate successor.

To establish this observation, it is enough to prove the following lemma:

> *Lemma 1*: Suppose that "is at least as good as" is a weak order, that is, a complete and transitive relation on the domain. For any objects e, e', and e'', if e is weakly superior to e'', then e is weakly superior to e' or e' is weakly superior to e''.

Note: If "is at least as good as" is transitive and complete, then, by Lemma 1, the complement of weak superiority, that is, the relation of *not* being weakly superior, is transitive: If

e is not weakly superior to e' and e is not weakly superior to e'', then e is not weakly superior to e''. Since weak superiority by definition is asymmetric, its complement is a complete relation: e is not weakly superior to e' or e' is not weakly superior to e. Therefore, Lemma 1 implies that, given the transitivity and completeness of "is at least as good as," weak superiority is a so-called strict weak order, that is, a relation the complement of which weakly orders the object domain.

For the proof that Lemma 1 holds and that it entails Observation 5, see appendix 12.5.[26]

Observation 5 shows that weak superiority cannot obtain between the extrema of a finite sequence without setting in at some point in that sequence. Now, if the elements in a decreasing finite sequence are chosen in such a way that each consecutive element is only *marginally* worse than the immediately preceding one, then it might seem that no element will be weakly superior to the element that comes next.[27] But then, as we just have shown, the first element will not even be weakly superior to the last element in the sequence, however long such a sequence may be. This is surprising, since one would intuitively expect that a sufficiently long series of small worsenings can sooner or later result in an element that is radically worse than the point of departure.

One interpretation of our result is that we should give up this intuition and reject the existence of superiorities in the domain under consideration. We might want to deny that a sequence of small worsenings can ever yield an element that is radically worse than the original element. Since many examples of alleged superior goods do admit of series of gradual worsenings by means of which we end up with objects of very low value, this option puts into question the existence of genuine superiority relationships in the domain. On this view, alleged superiorities disappear upon reflection.

An alternative option is to accept that a series of small worsenings might sooner or later lead to things that are strongly inferior to points of departure and instead to revise our pre-reflexive idea of superiority. On this second interpretation, superiority need not imply a radical difference in value. Consider weak superiority first. If an object e' is only slightly worse than another object e, then e cannot presumably be strongly superior to e' (unless the decrease in marginal value that takes place in same-type concatenation of e' is extremely rapid). But, contrary to appearances, e might still be weakly superior to e', even though it is better only by a small margin.[28] A sufficient number of e-objects might, if conjoined, form a whole that is better than *any* whole composed of e'-objects. Indeed, on this alternative option, strong superiority need not be a radical difference in value either. While strong superiority does seem to require a considerable difference in value, this difference, as we have seen, need not be infinitely large: it can be scaled in a finite number of small steps. (For a further discussion, see Klint Jensen 2008.)

Of course, the first option might be more plausible in some domains, and the other in other domains. For example, we might find it counterintuitive that a sufficient number of pleasurable experiences of a certain intensity can make a whole that is better (or better for the subject) than any whole, *however large*, that consists of pleasurable experiences that are just *slightly* less intense. On the other hand, if some form of objective list theory of welfare is true, which might involve various perfectionist elements, then we might find it rather unproblematic that some outcomes can be strongly superior to others and that the latter can be reached from the former by sequences of small worsenings.

Appendix 12.1. Strong Superiority without Abrupt Breaks

Observation 1: Consider any two objects e and e' such that e is better than e'. If e is weakly superior to e', without being strongly superior to it, then the domain must contain a finite decreasing sequence of objects in which the first element is strongly superior to the last one, but no element is strongly superior to its immediate successor.

Proof: Suppose that e is better than and weakly superior to e', without being strongly superior to it. By the definition of weak superiority, there is some $m > 1$ such that m e-objects are better than any number of e'-objects. This means (cf. section 12.4 above) that the whole composed of m e-objects is strongly superior to e'. Now, consider the following sequence:

e_1 = the whole composed of m e-objects,
e_2 = the whole composed of $m - 1$ e-objects,
. . .
e_{m-1} = the whole composed of 2 e-objects
$e_m = e$,
$e_{m+1} = e'$.

The first object in this sequence is strongly superior to the last one. Furthermore, since "same type"-concatenation is value increasing and e is better than e', each element in the sequence is better than its immediate successor. Thus, the sequence is decreasing. At the same time, no element in the sequence is strongly superior to its immediate successor. In fact, as is easily seen, for all e_k such that $1 \leq k < m$, a whole composed of three e_{k+1} objects is better than e_k. (Such a whole consists of a larger number of e-objects than e_k and thus—by the assumption of value increasingness—must be better than e_k.) The remaining case to consider is when $k = m$, but that e_m is not strongly superior to e_{m+1} is true by hypothesis. Consequently, none of the objects in the sequence $e_1, \ldots, e_{m+1}$ is strongly superior to its immediate successor, despite the fact that e_1 is strongly superior to e_{m+1}. This completes the proof.

Appendix 12.2. The Importance of Independence: Abrupt Breaks

Weak Independence: If an object e is at least as good as e', then replacing e' by e in any whole results in a whole that is at least as good.

Observation 2: Suppose that the first element in a sequence $e_1, \ldots, e_n$ is strongly superior to the last one. If "is at least as good as" is a complete and transitive relation, Weak

Independence implies that some element in the sequence is strongly superior to its immediate successor.

> *Proof:* Suppose that e_1 is strongly superior to e_n. Assume, for *reductio*, that none of the elements e_i in the sequence ($i < n$) is strongly superior to its immediate successor. By completeness, this means that for every such e_i there is some number m_i such that the whole composed of m_i e_{i+1}-objects is at least as good as e_i. Now, start with e_1 and replace it by a whole w_2 composed of m_1 e_2-objects. By assumption, w_2 is at least as good as e_1. If we replace any e_2 in w_2 by m_2 e_3-objects, Weak Independence implies that the resulting whole is at least as good as w_2. We can in this way replace every e_2-object in w_2, one after another, by m_2 e_3-objects, until we reach a whole, w_3, that is composed of $(m_1 \times m_2)$ e_3-objects. By Weak Independence and the transitivity of "at least as good as"—relation w_3 is at least as good as w_2, and thus—again by transitivity—it is at least as good as e_1. Continuing in this way, from w_2 to w_3, from w_3 to w_4, and so on, using Weak Independence all the time, we finally reach a whole w_n that is composed of $(m_1 \times m_2 \times \ldots \times m_{n-1})$ e_n-objects. By transitivity, w_n is at least as good as e_1, which implies that e_1 is *not* strongly superior to e_n, contrary to the hypothesis.

Appendix 12.3. The Importance of Independence: Collapse

Independence: An object e is at least as good as e' if and only if replacing e' by e in any whole results in a whole that is at least as good.

Observation 3: Assume that "is at least as good as" is a transitive and complete relation which satisfies Independence. Then, for every e and e', if e is weakly superior to e', then e is strongly superior to e'.

> *Proof*, due to Klint Jensen (2008): Suppose that (i) e is weakly superior to e'. Assume for *reductio* that (ii) e is not strongly superior to e'. (i) means that for some m, m e-objects are better than any number of e'-objects. (ii) means that for some k, e is not better than k e'-objects. Since "is at least as good as" has been assumed to be a complete relation, it follows from (ii) that (iii) k e'-objects are at least as good as e. We now want to prove, by mathematical induction, that also for all $n > 1$, nk e'-objects are at least as good as n e-objects. It will then follow, given that "same type"-concatenation is value increasing, that $nk + 1$ e'-objects are better than n e-objects, for all $n > 1$, in contradiction to the claim made in (i). For the induction step, assume we have already established that $(n-1)k$ e'-objects are at least as good as $(n-1)$ e-objects. Then Independence implies that $(n-1)k$ e'-objects concatenated with e are at least as good as n e-objects. And, also by Independence, (iii) implies that nk e'-objects are at least as good as $(n-1)k$ e'-objects concatenated with e. Therefore, by the transitivity

of "at least as good as," nk e'-objects are at least as good as n e-objects. Which completes the proof.

APPENDIX 12.4. CONVERGENCE TO UPPER LIMITS

Observation 4: Suppose that "is at least as good as" is (i) a weak ordering that (ii) divides the object domain into a countable number of equivalence classes. Let V be a real-valued function that represents this ordering. (That such a function must exist given (i) and (ii) is a standard result in measurement theory.) Now, consider any object e such that some object in the domain is weakly superior to e. Then the sequence $V(e)$, $V(2\ e\text{-objects})$, $V(3\ e\text{-objects})$,.... has an upper limit.

> *Proof* (due to Klint Jensen 2008): Suppose that e' is weakly superior to e. Then there is some m such that $V(m\ e'\text{-objects}) > V(n\ e\text{-objects})$, for all n. Assume, for *reductio*, that the sequence $V(e)$, $V(2\ e\text{-objects})$, $V(3\ e\text{-objects})$, ... has no upper limit. This sequence is increasing, because we have assumed that same-type concatenation is value-increasing. But any unbounded increasing infinite value sequence approaches infinity. Therefore there must be some n, such that $V(n\ e\text{-objects})$ is greater than the finite value $V(m\ e'\text{-objects})$. This contradicts the hypothesis that e' is weakly superior to e.

APPENDIX 12.5. WEAK SUPERIORITY

Observation 5: Suppose that "is at least as good as" is a complete and transitive relation on the domain. Then, in any finite sequence of objects in which the first element is weakly superior to the last element, there exists at least one element that is weakly superior to its immediate successor.

> *Proof*: To establish this observation, it is enough to prove the following lemma:
> *Lemma 1*: Suppose that "is at least as good as" is a weak order, that is, a complete and transitive relation on the domain. For any objects e, e', and e'', if e is weakly superior to e'', e is weakly superior to e' or e' is weakly superior to e''.
> Observation 5 entails Lemma 1, since a triple e, e', e'' is an example of a finite object sequence. That Lemma 1 in its turn implies Observation 5 is easy to show. Suppose that "is at least as good as" is complete and transitive. Consider a sequence $e_1, \ldots, e_n$, in which e_1 is weakly superior to e_n. By Lemma 1, (i) e_1 is weakly superior to e_2, or (ii)

e_2 is weakly superior to e_n. If (i) holds, Observation 3 is established. If (ii) holds, then we consider the reduced sequence $e_2, \ldots, e_n$, and repeat the argument above. That is, either (iii) e_2 is weakly superior to e_3 or (iv) e_3 is weakly superior to e_n. If (iii), we are done, and if (iv), we consider the reduced sequence $e_3, \ldots, e_n$. Continuing in this way, we finally reach a two-membered sequence, e_{n-1}, e_n, and it is clear that Observation 5 trivially holds for such sequences.

It remains then to prove Lemma 1. Assume that (i) e is weakly superior to e'', but (ii) e is not weakly superior to e'. We need to show that, in such a case, e' is weakly superior to e''.

(i) means that there exists some number m such that

(1) m e-objects are better than any number of e''-objects.

(ii) implies that there is some number m' such that

(2) m e-objects are not better than m' e'-objects.

But then, given that "is at least as-good as" is a complete relation, (2) implies that

(3) m' e'-objects are at least as good as m e-objects.

By the transitivity of "is at least as good as," if one object is at least as good as another, which is better than some third object, then the first object is better than the third. Consequently, (3) and (1) imply that

(4) m' e'-objects are better than any number of e''-objects.

(4) implies that e' is weakly superior to e''. This completes our proof.

Appendix 12.6. Minimal Superiority

Definition 3: e is *minimally superior* to e' if and only if for some number m, there is no such k that k e'-objects are better than m e-objects.

Observation 6: Suppose that "is at least as good as" is a transitive relation. If the first element in a finite sequence of objects is minimally superior to the last one, there must exist some object in that sequence that is minimally superior to its immediate successor.

Proof: To establish Observation 6, we prove the following lemma:

Lemma 2: Suppose that "is at least as good as" is a transitive relation. For any objects e, e' and e'', if e is minimally superior to e'', then e is minimally superior to e' or e' is minimally superior to e''.

Lemma 2 is implied by Observation 6 and it implies Observation 6 in exactly the same way as Lemma 1 implies Observation 5 (see above, appendix 12.5). As for the proof of Lemma 2, it goes as follows:

Assume that (i) e is minimally superior to e'', but (ii) e is not minimally superior to e'. We want to show that, in such a case, e' is minimally superior to e''.

(i) means that there exists some number m such that

(1) for no number k, k e'-objects are better than m e-objects.

(ii) implies that there is some number k' such that

(2) $k'\,e'$-objects are better than $m\,e$-objects.

To prove that e' is minimally superior to e'', it is enough to establish that there is no such k that $k\,e''$-objects are better than $k'\,e'$-objects. Suppose, for *reductio*, that

(3) $k\,e''$-objects are better than $k'\,e'$-objects.

By the transitivity of "is at least as good as," the relation "is better than" is transitive as well. Therefore, (3) and (2) imply that

(4) $k\,e''$-objects are better than $m\,e$-objects.

But (4) contradicts (1), which concludes the proof.

Acknowledgments

This chapter draws on Arrhenius (2005) and Arrhenius and Rabinowicz (2005). We would like to thank John Broome, Erik Carlson, Roger Crisp, Iwao Hirose, Karsten Klint Jensen, and Jonas Olson for helpful comments. Thanks also to the Collège d'Études Mondiales and to the Swedish Collegium for Advanced Study for being such generous hosts during some of the time when this chapter was written and revised. Financial support from the Swedish Research Council as well as from Riksbankens Jubileumsfond and Fondation Maison des Sciences de l'Homme through the Franco-Swedish Program in Economics and Philosophy is gratefully acknowledged.

Notes

1. In Arrhenius & Rabinowicz (2005), this condition (or rather a version of it) is referred to simply as "Superiority."
2. The distinction between these two relations goes back to Griffin (1986), who refers to strong superiority as "trumping" ("*any* amount of *A*, however small, outranks *any* amount of *B*, however large," 83) and to weak superiority as "discontinuity" ("enough of *A* outranks any amount of *B*," 86).
3. Brentano (1969 [1907]): 158. If "finite good" here stands for a finite amount of a good, then this is just a statement of weak superiority. But if Brentano by a finite good means a good—a positively valuable object—whose *value* is finite, then he postulates more than just the existence of weak superiorities; he prefigures a more specific claim we are going to argue for in this chapter, namely the claim that superiority in value (whether weak or strong) does not require infinite betterness (see below, section 12.7).
4. See Crisp (1988: 188); 1992: 151; Glover (1977: 710; Griffin (1986: 85–86) Edwards (1979: 69–72); Lemos (1993); Parfit (1986: 161–64); Skorupski (1999: 94–101). See also Feit (2001), Klint Jensen (1996: 90–91); Portmore (1999); Riley (1993, 1999, 2008, 2009).
5. Hutcheson (1968 [1755]): 117–18); Hutcheson completed his treatise in 1738 but it was published posthumously in 1755; cf. Edwards 1979: 71); Mill (1998: 56). For another early source with a racist twist, see Rashdall (1907: 238–39). Newman (1885: 204), makes a similar claim about pain and sin. Hutcheson's pioneering position might be questioned. Brentano (1969 [1907]: 157) ascribes to Pascal the view that "there are classes of goods that can be ranked in

the following way: the smallest of any of the goods that are to be found in the higher class will always be superior to the totality of goods which are to be found in the lower class."

6. See Parfit (1984: 388). Our formulation is more general than Parfit's. The ceteris paribus clause is meant to rule out that the compared populations differ in any axiologically relevant aspect apart from individual welfare levels. Although it is through Parfit's writings that this "repugnant" implication of Total Utilitarianism has become widely discussed, the implication in question was already noted by Henry Sidgwick (1967 [1907]: 415), before the turn of the twentieth century. For other early sources of the Repugnant Conclusion, see Broad (1930: 249–50); McTaggart (1927: 452–53); and Narveson (1967).

7. See Parfit (1984: 388) and (1986: 148). For a discussion of different interpretations of the Repugnant Conclusion see Arrhenius (2000b, 2014) and Parfit (1984, 2014).

8. Notice that problems like this are not just problems for utilitarians or those committed to welfarism, the view that welfare is the only value that matters from the moral point of view. We have assumed that other axiologically relevant aspects are equal (cf. n. 6). Hence, other values and considerations are not relevant for the value comparison of populations A and B. Thus it is a problem for all moral theories according to which welfare matters at least when all other things are equal, which arguably is an adequacy condition for any moral theory.

9. There are other versions of the interpersonal case in which the compared lives may be equally long but one life contains some amount of A-goods and the other an arbitrarily large amount of B-goods, where some of the B-goods come more or less simultaneously. An example of the latter case is a life of a mediocre writer who receives appreciation from many enthusiastic readers, as compared with a life of a great writer who never gets a recognition.

10. When we say that, for example, one collection of experiences contains a greater *amount* of pleasure than another, we just mean that the former collection is more pleasurable than the other, i.e., comes higher on the "at least as pleasurable as"-ranking.

11. Roger Crisp has suggested to us that Mill might well have thought that value tracks pleasantness—the degree of pleasure—while interpreting this degree as a function not merely of the quantity of pleasure but also of its quality. This would make the quoted passage compatible with the Greatest Happiness Principle.

12. One way of stating value additivity is as follows. Let "o" stand for the operation of forming wholes (mereological sums). For any object e, let $V(e)$ be the value of e. Then, for all nonoverlapping objects e and e', $V(e \circ e') = V(e) + V(e')$. This formulation of additivity requires value to be measurable on at least a ratio scale. If we can only assume measurability on an interval scale, we need a bit more complicated formulation of additivity: For all objects e, e', and e'', if e doesn't overlap with either e' or e'', then $V(e \circ e'')-V(e') = V(e \circ e'')-V(e'')$. I.e., for every e, the size of e's value contribution to a whole in which it is a part is constant.

13. In fact, on this construction of kinds of pleasure, one might even want to claim that the A-life is not only more valuable but also more pleasurable than the B-life, however long the latter might be. This would mean that one accepts non-Archimedeanism about the ordering of pleasure and not just about the ordering of the value of pleasure.

14. For an account of the "is at least as good as"-relation, which analyzes it in terms of required preference-or-indifference and explains why this relation might well not be complete, see Rabinowicz (2008, 2012).

15. Object types should be distinguished from object *kinds*. Two wholes composed of objects of the same type can be said to be of the same kind. Thus, a whole composed of m e-objects is of the same kind as a whole composed of n e-objects, for any m, n, and e.

16. Note that, according to this definition, *e* may be weakly superior to *e′* even though *e′* is better than *e*. If this sounds unnatural, one might always add to the definition an additional requirement that *e* must be better than *e′* in order to be weakly superior to it. However, for simplicity's sake, we prefer to work with a more austere definition of weak superiority.
17. Can one also define superiority relations for values accruing to *states of affairs*? We are indebted to Iwao Hirose for alerting us to this question. At present, however, we don't see how this could be done, if it can be done at all.
18. Cf. Crisp (1992); Riley (1993, 1999); Parfit (1986). Riley (2008) also ascribes this view to Mill.
19. It does not really matter in the present context whether one takes strong superiority to require infinite or *lexical* betterness (for the latter interpretation, see Feit 2001). On the lexical view, a strongly superior object carries a value that is finite but belongs to a higher order than the value of an inferior object. These two constructions—the infinitistic and the lexical one—are closely related interpretations of the same idea. In particular, both imply that if the first element of the decreasing sequence is strongly superior to the last one, then at some point in the sequence, strong superiority relation must set in between the adjacent elements. Parenthetically, however, one should add that the infinitistic and the lexical interpretations of strong superiority are not equivalent. In fact, the former lends itself to some counterintuitive implications that the latter avoids. To see this, consider an object *e* that is strongly superior to some other object in the domain. On the lexical interpretation, there is no problem in requiring that same-type concatenation is value-increasing: two *e*-objects are better than one, three are better than two, and so on. But on the infinitistic interpretation, according to which the strongly superior *e* has an infinite value, it is difficult to understand how two *e*-objects can be more valuable than one.
20. Ryberg (2002: 419) claims that "[if] there is a discontinuity between the values ... at each end of the continuum [i.e., at each end of a descending sequence in which each successive element is only marginally worse than the preceding one], then at some point discontinuity must set in": at some point in the sequence there must be an element that is discontinuous with the one that immediately follows. From this claim, call it (R), he draws the conclusion that discontinuities don't exist, since it is counterintuitive to suppose that a discontinuity in value could exist between objects that only marginally differ in value. Unlike Griffin (1986), Ryberg by "discontinuity" means something like strong superiority: "According to the *discontinuity view* we can have a (lower) pleasure which, no matter how often a certain unit of it is added to itself, cannot become greater in value than a unit of another (higher) pleasure" (415). As Observation 1 shows, however, claim (R) is false on this interpretation. For a discussion of Ryberg's argument, see Rabinowicz (2003), who suggests that that the assumption of (R) is based on the fallacy of identifying superiority with "infinite betterness."
21. Cf. Moore (1993 [1903]: §§ 18–21 *et passim*). Moore was not the first philosopher to make this point. Another standard reference is Brentano (1969 [1889]). To be more precise, Moore does assume a form of additivity when he suggests that "the value on the whole" is the sum of (i) the values of the parts *plus* (ii) "the value of the whole, *as a whole*." (The latter may be either positive or negative.) But it can be argued that this form of additivity is a purely arithmetical construct. His "value of the whole, as a whole" could simply be interpreted as the arithmetical difference between "the value on the whole" and the sum of the values of the parts, independently considered. Moore himself points out that the value of a whole, as a whole, may be "expressed" as such a difference (1993 [1903]: § 129), but he seems

22. Qualification: If e'' is a whole in which e' is replaced by e, the restriction on the replacement is that e and e''-*minus*-e' are disjoint: No part of the former is a part of the latter.
23. Actually, for the proof of Observation 2, we do not need the full power of Independence. It is enough to assume the Independence holds from left to right, i.e., that replacing an object in a whole by another object that is at least as good always results in a whole that is at least as good. In appendix 12.2, we refer to this less demanding assumption as Weak Independence.
24. If Independence were to hold, such a decrease in marginal contributive value would not be possible. If e is more valuable than some object e', then—if Independence were to hold—adding yet another e to a whole that already contains many e-objects but no e'-object would still have to be more valuable than adding e'.
25. Cf. Parfit (1984: § 137, and Sider (1991). (Parfit's application of this idea to the value of populations comes from Hurka (1983).) However, neither Parfit nor Sider endorses this solution since it has other counterintuitive implications in population axiology. For a discussion, see Arrhenius (2000ab, 2014) and Arrhenius, Ryberg, and Tännsjö (2010).
26. The proof of Lemma 1 assumes that the relation "at least as good as" is complete, which is a rather exacting requirement. What if completeness is not assumed? Well, even in the absence of completeness, we can prove a variant of Observation 5.

> *Definition 3:* An object e is *minimally superior* to an object e' if and only if for some number m, no whole composed of e'-objects, however large, is better than m e-objects.
>
> *Observation 6:* Suppose that "is at least as good as" is a transitive relation. If the first element in a finite sequence of objects is minimally superior to the last element, then there must exist some element in that sequence that is minimally superior to its immediate successor.

For the proof, see appendix 12.6. For a similar result in the context of population axiology, see Arrhenius (2000b, 2014). Note that weak superiority entails minimal superiority, but not vice versa. Still, just as it is the case with these stronger relations, minimal superiority cannot obtain if "is at least as good as" has the Archimedean property.
27. Cf. the Quantity Condition discussed in Arrhenius (2000b, 2014), which captures this intuition in a population context. It is shown that this condition, together with some other weak conditions, implies the Repugnant Conclusion.
28. On this view, then, being weakly superior to an object is not sufficient for being much better than the object in question. (Indeed, as we have seen, an object might be weakly superior to another while being *worse* than the latter.) In fact, being weakly superior is not necessary for being much better either. It is easy to construct a case in which, in a descending sequence e, e', e'', (i) the value difference between the first element and the second one is larger than that between the second element and the third, (ii) the second element is weakly superior to the third, but (iii) the first element is not weakly superior to *any* of the elements that follow. While a sufficient number of e'-objects may be better than any number of e''-objects and e may be much better than e', there might still be no number of e-objects that cannot be outweighed by a sufficiently large number of e''-objects and by a sufficient number of e'-objects.

References

Aleskerov, F., D. Boyssou, and B. Monjardet. (2007). *Utility Maximization, Choice and Preference*, 2nd ed. Berlin: Springer.
Arrhenius, G. (2000a). "An Impossibility Theorem for Welfarist Axiologies." *Economics and Philosophy* 16: 247–66.
Arrhenius, G. (2000b). *Future Generations: A Challenge for Moral Theory*. F.D.-Diss. Uppsala: University Printers.
Arrhenius, G. (2005). "Superiority in Value." *Philosophical Studies* 123: 97–114.
Arrhenius, G. (2014). *Population Ethics*. Oxford: Oxford University Press, forthcoming.
Arrhenius, G., and W. Rabinowicz. (2005). "Millian Superiorities." *Utilitas* 17: 127–46.
Arrhenius G., J. Ryberg, and T. Tännsjö. (2010). "The Repugnant Conclusion." In E. N. Zalta (ed.), *The Stanford Encyclopedia of Philosophy*, Spring 2014 ed. http://plato.stanford.edu/archives/spr2014/entries/repugnant-conclusion/.
Brentano, F. (1969 [1889]). *The Origin of Our Knowledge of Right and Wrong*. Ed. R. M. Chisholm. New York: Routledge and Kegan Paul.
Brentano, F. (1969 [1907]). "Loving and Hating." Appendix to *The Origin of Our Knowledge of Right and Wrong*. Ed. R. M. Chisholm. New York: Routledge and Kegan Paul.
Broad, C. D. (1979 [1930]). *Five Types of Ethical Theory*. London: Routledge and Kegan Paul.
Broome, J., and W. Rabinowicz. (2005). "Superior Attributes." Appendix 3 to Arrhenius and Rabinowicz (2005), 140–46.
Crisp, R. (1988). "Ideal Utilitarianism: Theory and Practice." D.Phil. diss., University of Oxford.
Crisp, R. (1992). "Utilitarianism and the Life of Virtue." *Philosophical Quarterly* 42 (167): 139–60.
Edwards, R. B. (1979). *Pleasures and Pains: A Theory of Qualitative Hedonism*. Ithaca, NY: Cornell University Press.
Feit, N. (2001). "The Structure of Higher Goods." *Southern Journal of Philosophy* 39: 47–57.
Glover, J. (1977). *Causing Death and Saving Lives*. New York: Penguin.
Griffin, J. (1986). *Well-Being: Its Meaning, Measurement, and Moral Importance*. Oxford: Clarendon Press.
Hurka, T. M. (1983). "Value and Population Size." *Ethics* 93: 496–507.
Hutcheson, F. (1968 [1755]). *A System of Moral Philosophy*. Vol. 1. New York: Augustus M Kelley.
Klint Jensen, K. (1996). "Om afvejning af værdier." Ph.D. diss., University of Copenhagen.
Klint Jensen, K. (2008). "Millian Superiorities and the Repugnant Conclusion." *Utilitas* 20: 279–300.
Lemos, N. M. (1993). "Higher Goods and the Myth of Tithonus." *Journal of Philosophy* 90: 482–96.
McTaggart, J. M. E. (1927). *The Nature of Existence*. Cambridge: Cambridge University Press.
Mill, J. S. (1998 [1863]). *Utilitarianism*. Ed. Roger Crisp. Oxford: Oxford University Press.
Moore, G. M. (1993 [1903]). *Principia Ethica*, rev. ed., ed. T. Baldwin. Cambridge: Cambridge University Press.
Narveson, J. (1967). "Utilitarianism and New Generations." *Mind* 76: 62–72.
Newman, J. H. (1885). *Certain Difficulties Felt by Anglicans in Catholic Teaching*. Vol. 1. London: Longmans and Green.
Parfit, D. (1984). *Reasons and Persons*. Oxford: Clarendon Press.
Parfit, D. (1986). "Overpopulation and the Quality of Life." In P. Singer (ed.), *Applied Ethics*. Oxford: Oxford University Press, 145–64.
Parfit, D. (2014). "How We Can Avoid the Repugnant Conclusion." Photocopy.

Portmore, D. W. (1999). "Does the Total Principle Have Any Repugnant Implications?" *Ratio* 12: 80–98.

Rabinowicz, W. (2007). "Ryberg's Doubts about Higher and Lower Pleasures—Put to Rest?" *Ethical Theory and Moral Practice* 6: 231–37.

Rabinowicz, W. (2008). "Value Relations." *Theoria* 74: 18–49.

Rabinowicz, W. (2012). "Value Relations Revisited." *Economics and Philosophy* 28: 133–64.

Rashdall, H. (1907). *The Theory of Good and Evil: A Treatise on Moral Philosophy*, 2nd ed. Vol. 1. Oxford: Clarendon Press.

Riley, J. (1993). "On Quantities and Qualities of Pleasure." *Utilitas* 5: 291–300.

Riley, J. 1999). "Is Qualitative Hedonism Incoherent?" *Utilitas* 11: 347–58.

Riley, J. (2008). "Millian Qualitative Superiorities and Utilitarianism, Part I." *Utilitas* 20: 257–78.

Riley, J. (2009). "Millian Qualitative Superiorities and Utilitarianism, Part II." *Utilitas* 21: 127–43.

Ross, W. D. (1930). *The Right and the Good*. Oxford: Oxford University Press.

Ryberg, J. (2002). "Higher and Lower Pleasures—Doubts on Justification." *Ethical Theory and Moral Practice* 5: 415–29.

Sider, T. R. (1991). "Might Theory X Be a Theory of Diminishing Marginal Value?" *Analysis* 51 (4): 265–71.

Sidgwick, H. (1967 [1907]). *The Methods of Ethics*, 7th ed. London: Macmillan.

Skorupski, J. (1999). *Ethical Explorations*. Oxford: Oxford University Press.

CHAPTER 13

GENERAL AND PERSONAL GOOD

Harsanyi's Contribution to the Theory of Value

JOHN BROOME

13.1. Introduction

IN 1955, John Harsanyi published a singular contribution to the theory of value (Harsanyi 1955). He proved a theorem that links together the valuation of uncertain prospects for a single person and the valuation of distributions of good across people. The theorem's conclusion is important and remarkable; it is by no means obvious, and it requires some mathematics to uncover it. Perhaps as a consequence, philosophers of value have not always given this theorem the attention it deserves. This chapter describes and interprets the theorem, and explains its importance.

Harsanyi uses the language of economics, and he sets his argument in a framework that is generally taken for granted by economists but not widely accepted in philosophy. He assumes that each person's good consists in the satisfaction of her preferences. But his conclusion is about the relation between general good and the good of individual people. It is independent of particular assumptions about the nature of a person's good, and I shall present it in a way that does not depend on any such assumptions.[1]

13.2. The Theorem

An *outcome* is a state of affairs. Some outcomes are better than others: a relation of betterness holds among outcomes. For example, if the climate warms by two degrees, that is a better outcome than if it warms by three degrees.

A *prospect* is a number of possible outcomes, each having some degree of likelihood. Some prospects, too, are better than others, and a relation of betterness holds among them. Betterness among prospects is less fundamental than betterness among outcomes, because what ultimately matters is what actually happens, rather than what might happen. Betterness among prospects is therefore derivative, but it is genuine all the same. A prospect in which it is likely that global warming will stay below two degrees is better than one in which it is likely to go above two degrees.

Not only does betterness simpliciter hold among outcomes and prospects, so does betterness for particular people. It is true of each particular person that some outcomes and prospects are better for her than others. The prospect in which it is likely that global warming will go above two degrees is better for some people—perhaps some of those who live in Siberia—than the prospect in which it is likely to stay below two degrees. Let us say that *personal betterness relations* hold among outcomes and prospects. And let us distinguish the relation of betterness simpliciter by calling it the *general betterness relation*.

For the moment, let us assume that general betterness supervenes on personal betterness for people. That is to say, if neither of two prospects is personally better for anyone than the other, then neither is generally better than the other. Moreover, let us assume that this supervenience is positive. That is to say, if one of two prospects is personally better for someone than the other, and worse for no one, then it is generally better. I call this assumption of positive supervenience the *principle of personal good*. I shall question it in section 13.8.

The personal and general betterness relations have various structural properties. For one thing, they are orderings. Precisely, they are strict partial orderings, which means they are irreflexive and transitive. That is to say: nothing is better than itself, and if one prospect is better than another, which is better than a third, then the first is better than the third.

Next, let us go much further and assume that all these relations satisfy all the axioms of expected utility theory. (I shall question this assumption in sections 13.6 and 13.7.) Different versions of expected utility theory[2] have different axioms. But Harsanyi's Theorem can be proved within many versions, so it does not matter precisely which set of axioms we adopt.

A technical note: the axioms are generally specified for the relation "better than or equally as good as," whereas I take the primitive relation to be betterness. Equality of goodness may be defined in terms of betterness like this: "a is equally as good as b" means that neither a nor b is better than the other, and that any third thing c is better than a if and only if it is better than b. This definition has some consequences that may be questioned. One is that, if nothing is better than anything else, then everything is equally good. Nothing in this chapter turns on this choice of primitive, and I shall not discuss it further.

I shall adopt some technical terminology from expected utility theory. Take a set of prospects and outcomes on which there is a betterness relation. Take a function that assigns numbers to prospects and outcomes. The function is said to *represent* the betterness relation when the number it assigns to one prospect or outcome is greater than the number it assigns to another prospect or outcome if and only if the former is better than the latter. When a function represents a betterness relation, I call it a *utility function*, and I call the numbers it assigns to prospects and outcomes *utilities*. This defines exactly what I mean by these terms. Many economists use the word "utility" as a synonym for a person's "good," and this practice has recently been spreading among philosophers. It is not my meaning. A person's utilities are defined to represent the person's betterness *order*, not to represent the *quantity* of her good. The question of whether or not they also represent the quantity of her good is a substantive issue that will be considered in section 13.9.

Another piece of terminology: a utility function is said to be *expectational* when the utility it assigns to a prospect is the mathematical expectation of the utilities it assigns to the prospect's possible outcomes.

I have assumed the principle of personal good and I have assumed that both general betterness and personal betterness satisfy the axioms of expected utility theory. These assumptions together have a remarkable consequence. They imply that general betterness can be represented by a utility function that is the sum of utility functions that represent the personal betterness of each person. In brief, general utility can be treated as the total of personal utilities. In symbols:

$$U(x) = u_1(x) + u_2(x) + \ldots + u_n(x). \tag{*}$$

Here, x is a prospect or outcome, $U(x)$ is its general utility, and $u_1(x) \ldots u_n(x)$ are the personal utilities of all the people. Furthermore, all the utility functions are expectational.

This is Harsanyi's Theorem. Harsanyi's proof was built on Jacob Marschak's (1950) version of expected utility theory, which assumes there are objective chances. But the theorem is robust; it can also be proved in versions that allow for subjective credences.[3]

13.3. INTERPRETATION

What does this theorem tell us? The first thing is displayed on its face by formula (*): this formula has an additive structure. In technical language, it is *additively separable*. An outcome can be evaluated by first evaluating it from the point of view of each person separately, and then adding up the separate evaluations.

This is in itself an impressive conclusion. Addition is a very special operation. Philosophers sometimes take it to be the default mode of combining quantities together. They assume that, by default, a whole is the sum of its parts. When it is not, they think this needs some special explanation such as "organic unity" (see Carlson, chapter 15 in this volume). But when addition obtains, this too needs explanation. Why should the individual utility functions be combined by addition? None of the premises of Harsanyi's Theorem—neither the principle of personal good nor the axioms of expected utility theory—mentions addition. The additive structure arises from the mathematics, in a not very intuitive fashion.[4]

The debate between prioritarians and strict egalitarians about the value of equality is a debate about additive separability (see Holtug, chapter 14 in this volume). Strict egalitarians believe that general betterness depends partly on how people fare relative to each other. A strict egalitarian formula for general utility would contain some terms that embody comparisons between different people's situations. For example, it might contain some measure of the dispersion among individual utilities, such as their variance or the Gini coefficient. Being additively separable, formula (*) contains no such terms.

This does not immediately imply that the formula is opposed to strict egalitarianism. Each person's betterness relation might itself be influenced by the person's standing in comparison to other people. For example, suppose that in some outcome a person is worse off than other people who are no more deserving than her. This may be an unfairness she suffers. Suffering an unfairness is presumably bad for her, so it will influence her personal betterness relation, and will be registered in her own utility. Formula (*) does not rule that out. But it does rule out *communal* egalitarianism, which is the view that equality is a sort of good that belongs to the community as a whole rather than to the individual members of the community (Broome 1991: § 9.2). Harsanyi's Theorem is opposed to strict communal egalitarianism about good.

The second point of interpretation is more difficult. Start by concentrating on the utility function of one person—say the first, $u_1()$. Suppose some outcome a is better for this person than b, which is in turn better for her than c. Because the person's utility function represents her betterness, $u_1(a)$ is greater than $u_1(b)$, which is greater than $u_1(c)$. This is just to say that utilities represent the *order* of the person's good.

But there is more. Utilities are also assigned to prospects. Let us compare two particular prospects. One is the prospect that has a and c as possible outcomes, and gives them equal chances of one-half each. Call this prospect "Gamble." The second is a simple, "degenerate" prospect that has only one possible outcome, b. In this prospect b is certain; call it "Certainty." Suppose Gamble is better on balance for the person than Certainty. What does that tell us?

Gamble is better for the person than Certainty in one respect: it offers a one-half chance of the best outcome a, whereas Certainty offers only the less good b. Gamble is worse for the person than Certainty in another respect: it offers a one-half chance of the worst outcome c, whereas Certainty offers the better b. Whether Gamble is better or worse for the person on balance is determined by putting together the respect in which it is better with the respect in which it is worse. These respects are *aggregated*, we may say, which in this case means they are weighed against each other. The difference in goodness between a and b is weighed against the difference in goodness between b and c.

We are supposing Gamble is better on balance. This means that the difference in goodness between a and b counts for more in this aggregation—has a greater weight—than the difference in goodness between b and c. The fact that one prospect is better than the other tells us how differences in goodness weigh or count in this particular aggregation. The example is a simple one, but the point can be generalized. In general, the relation of betterness among prospects provides a basis for weighing up differences of goodness.

Moreover, utility measures how much these differences in goodness count. The example shows how. Since utility represents betterness and Gamble is better than Certainty, Gamble's utility is higher than Certainty's. Since utility is expectational, the utility of each prospect is the mathematical expectation of the utility of its outcomes. So the utility of Gamble is ½$u_1(a)$ + ½$u_1(c)$ and the utility of Certainty is $u_1(b)$. Since Gamble is better,

$$\tfrac{1}{2} u_1(a) + \tfrac{1}{2} u_1(c) > u_1(b).$$

That is to say:

$$u_1(a) - u_1(b) > u_1(b) - u_1(c).$$

The difference in utility between a and b is greater than the difference in utility between b and c. This represents the fact that the difference in goodness between a and b outweighs, or counts for more than, the difference in goodness between b and c.

Remember this is only how much these differences count in one particular sort of aggregation: aggregation in the context of uncertainty, where a prospect is evaluated from the point of view of a single person. The place of a prospect in the person's betterness ordering depends on aggregating together the different possible outcomes that make up the prospect. Utility measures how much differences in goodness count in this sort of intrapersonal aggregation. We may say it measures a sort of *contributory value* that an outcome has: the contribution the outcome makes to the value of a prospect.

Harsanyi's Theorem tells us about another, interpersonal sort of aggregation, where different people's goods are aggregated and weighed against each other. The formula (*) in Harsanyi's Theorem describes aggregation across people; it specifies how the good of different people goes together to make up general good.

For example, suppose the outcome d is better for the first person than another outcome e, whereas e is better for the second person than d. Assume that d and e are equally good for everyone else. In one respect, d is better than e—it is better for the first person—whereas in another respect e is better than d—it is better for the second person. Whether d or e is better on balance is determined by putting together the respect in which it is better with the respect in which it is worse. This is a matter of aggregating across people: of putting the first person's good together with the second's.

According to Harsanyi's Theorem, the result of this aggregation is given by the total of utilities. Outcome d is better than outcome e if its total utility is greater. That is to say, if

$$u_1(d) + u_2(d) > u_1(e) + u_2(e).$$

In other words, if

$$u_1(d) - u_1(e) > u_2(e) - u_2(d).$$

So d is better than e if the difference in the first person's utility between d and e is greater than the difference in the second person's utility between e and d. In general, differences in people's utility measure how much differences in people's good count in aggregating across people. Utility measures the contribution a person's good makes in this sort of aggregation.

This is the same utility as measures the contributory value of a person's good in aggregation under uncertainty. Harsanyi's Theorem links together the two sorts of aggregation. A person's good has the same contributory value in both. This is remarkable. On the face of it, aggregating under uncertainty and aggregating across people are quite different matters. Harsanyi showed they are linked, so long as the principle of personal good holds and both sorts of betterness satisfy the axioms of expected utility theory.

13.4. EXAMPLES: PRIORITARIANISM AND UTILITARIANISM

To illustrate the significance of this conclusion, let us imagine for a moment that we have some quantitative concept of a person's good: we attach meaning to quantities of good. Moreover, let us imagine that this meaning is portable between people, so we can say that a unit of good is equally good for each person. I shall consider in section 13.9 where this quantitative concept might come from; for the moment let us not question it.

Since utility represents betterness, the utility of an outcome is an increasing function of the outcome's goodness for the person. This means the graph of utility against good slopes upwards. Figures 13.1 and 13.2 show two different examples.

Suppose the graph curves downward, as it does in figure 13.1. Take a certainty of two units of good, and compare it with an uncertain prospect that has the same mathematical expectation of good: specifically, a gamble at equal odds between one unit of good and three units. The expected utility of the gamble is the average utility of one unit and three units; it is shown in the diagram. It is less than the utility of the certainty of two units. It follows that the gamble is worse than the certainty, even though its expected goodness is the same. The very uncertainty of the gamble counts against it. In a sense, uncertainty about good is a bad thing. Between any two prospects that have the same expectation of good, the one with less uncertainty is better. This is *risk aversion* about good, to use a common term. It is a consequence of the downward curvature of the utility graph.

Utility measures how much good counts in aggregation under uncertainty. The graph in figure 13.1 shows that an increase in good counts for more the less well off the person

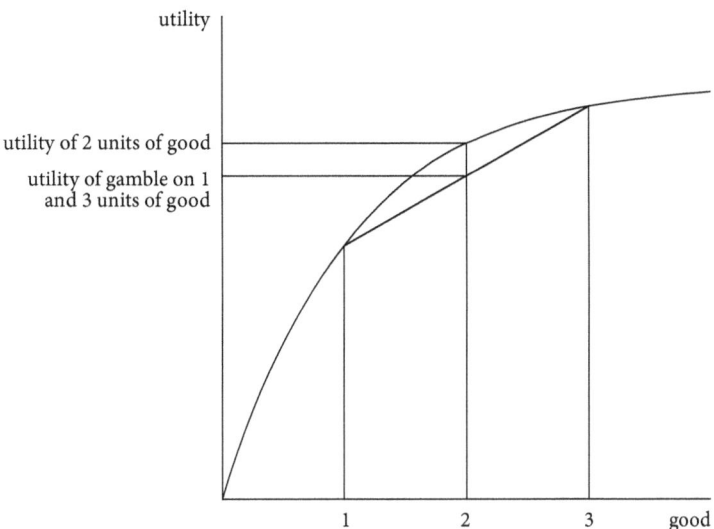

FIGURE 13.1 Risk Aversion and Prioritarianism

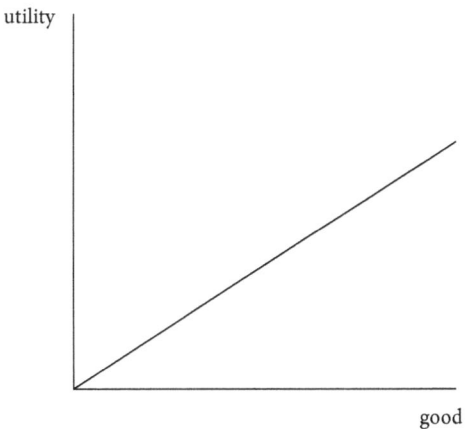

FIGURE 13.2 Risk Neutrality and Utilitarianism

is. A one-unit increase from one to two units counts for more than a one-unit increase from two to three units. Good has *diminishing marginal utility*, as economists say. It is this feature of the downward curvature that leads to risk-aversion about good.

Figure 13.1 shows the good of one person only. Now suppose that the relation between good and utility has the same curved shape for everyone. One implication is that risk aversion applies to everyone's good; this is a matter of intrapersonal aggregation under uncertainty. Harsanyi's Theorem tells us much more: it tells us that the same utilities also determine how good is interpersonally aggregated across people. The downward-curving shape of the utility function means that an increase of good counts for more the less well off the person is, in aggregation across people as well as in aggregation under uncertainty. Diminishing marginal utility applies to both sorts of aggregation.

Although I have assumed that the relation between utility and good has the same shape for everyone, I am not yet entitled to assume it is exactly the same relation for everyone. Utility can always be rescaled: if one function represents a person's betterness, so does any other function that is a positive multiple of that function. (The origin of the function can also be changed, but that fact makes no difference to the interpretation of Harsanyi's Theorem, and I shall ignore it.) So betterness can be represented by a family of functions, each a rescaling of the others. Harsanyi's Theorem says that, for each person, *one* utility function can be selected out of the family of functions that represents her betterness such that adding up these function across all the people gives us a utility function that represents general betterness. It does not say that the same function can be selected for each person.

However, we may supplement the theorem by assuming impartiality between people. Take a distribution of quantities of good across people, and imagine permuting the quantities among the people, so that the quantities remain the same, but some of them end up being possessed by different people. Impartiality is the claim that general good remains the same: what matters is quantities of personal good, not which particular people possess them. Impartiality implies that Harsanyi's Theorem selects the same utility function for each person. Given that, and given that the function shows diminishing marginal utility, the formula (*) in Harsanyi's Theorem is a *prioritarian* value function. It tells us that increasing the good of people who have more counts for less than increasing the good of people who have less.

A consequence of prioritarianism is that transferring a quantity of good from a better-off person to a less well-off person makes the world generally better. That is to say, for a given total of people's good, it is better that it is more rather than less equally distributed. Inequality is in this way a bad thing. For this reason, prioritarianism has traditionally been known among economists as *inequality aversion*. Harsanyi's Theorem tells us that prioritarianism or inequality aversion is tightly linked with risk aversion, provided the premises of the theorem hold. This is an important implication of the theorem.

Alternatively, the relation between a person's utility and her good might be linear rather than curved, as it is in figure 13.2. This implies *risk neutrality* about good. Given the supplementary assumption of impartiality, the formula (*) in Harsanyi's Theorem is then a *utilitarian* value function. It values the arithmetic total of people's good. Harsanyi's Theorem tightly links utilitarianism with risk neutrality.

13.5. Accepting or Rejecting the Conclusion

Many authors resist the tight link Harsanyi's Theorem makes between interpersonal aggregation across people and intrapersonal aggregation under uncertainty. There seems to be something wrong with "adopt[ing] for society as a whole the principle of rational choice for one man," as John Rawls (1971: 26–27) put it. Interpersonal aggregation is a moral matter, whereas intrapersonal aggregation is prudential. More specifically, interpersonal aggregation seems obviously to have an aspect of fairness that has no place in intrapersonal aggregation. This point has been made repeatedly in various ways by many authors from Peter Diamond (1967) to Michael Otsuka and Alex Voorhoeve (2009).

Nevertheless, the premises of Harsanyi's Theorem are plausible on the face of it, so the theorem constitutes a good argument for its conclusion. At least it sets a challenge to anyone who denies the link between interpersonal and intrapersonal aggregation, or more specifically the link between risk aversion and prioritarianism. She needs to identify which of the premises she rejects, and why. For example, when Otsuka and Voorhoeve (2009: 176) explicitly deny the conclusion of Harsanyi's Theorem by saying

> Some shift is justified in the priority we give to benefiting a person if she is very badly off rather than somewhat badly off when we move from the case of the isolated person to the interpersonal case,

they should also say which of the theorem's premises they deny.

It is not that the premises are unquestionable; several are open to objections. The significance of the theorem is not that its conclusion is indubitable. Its significance is to present us with a menu of options, of which we must select one. We may accept the theorem's conclusion, or we may choose one of its premises to reject.

My own view, set out in Broome (1991), is that we should accept the conclusion. This does not mean denying that interpersonal aggregation has an aspect of fairness that intrapersonal aggregation lacks. It means recognizing fairness as a personal good and unfairness as a personal harm. When a distribution of good among people is unfair in some way, this unfairness diminishes the good of individual people. The damage unfairness does to overall goodness appears in the damage it does to the good of individuals, not in the aggregation of good across people.

For example, insofar as it is a bad thing for good to be distributed unequally among people, it is bad because it is unfair to some people. It reduces those people's good. The badness of inequality is suffered by individuals; it is not some sort of communal badness. That is my account.

Philosophers sometimes think that inequality of good between people cannot itself reduce the good of people, because each person's goodness must first be determined in order to determine what inequality obtains between different people's good. But that is a fallacy. Each person's good and inequality between people's goods can be simultaneously determined. Here is a crude example taken from Broome (1991: 182). There are just two people, whose respective goods, g_1 and g_2, are given by

$$g_1 = \bar{g}_1 - \max\{0, \; \tfrac{1}{2}(g_2 - g_1)\}$$

and

$$g_2 = \bar{g}_2 - \max\{0,\ \tfrac{1}{2}(g_1 - g_2)\},$$

where $\bar{g}_1$ and $\bar{g}_2$ are their respective goods apart from the matter of inequality. If, say, $\bar{g}_1 = 2$ and $\bar{g}_2 = 3$, solving these equations shows that $g_1 = 1$ and $g_2 = 3$.

In that way, fairness can be made consistent with Harsanyi's Theorem.

13.6. Rejecting Completeness

Anyone who nevertheless still wants to reject the conclusion of Harsanyi's Theorem must choose which of the premises to reject. I shall next review the options.

The premise that personal betterness satisfies the axioms of expected utility theory is rarely questioned in this context. Expected utility theory has a strong intuitive attraction in its application to personal good and I shall raise no doubts about it here. However, its application to general good is different. In that application, there are special grounds for questioning the axioms of expected utility theory, and many authors reject one or another of them.

One axiom open to doubt is *completeness*, which says that, of any two prospects, either one is better than the other or they are equally good. This may be doubted on the grounds that the relative contributory values of different people's goods may not be fully determinate. When one of two outcomes is better than the other for one person and worse for another person, which of these outcomes is generally better will depend on the contributory value of one person's good relative to the other's. Many authors doubt that there is always a determinate result.

This is not necessarily a doubt about interpersonal comparability of good. The contributory value of good is not necessarily the same as good itself. Take two people who live very similar lives, but at different dates in history. It might be determinate that their lives are equally good, but not determinate what relative weight they have in determining general good. Some people believe in "discounting" good that comes later in time.[5] They would think the good of the later-living person counts for less. If they also think it is indeterminate what is the right rate of discount, they would think it indeterminate what relative contributory value the two lives possess. However, although this is a possible view, I know of no one who has adopted it. Doubts about completeness of the general betterness ordering arise much more commonly from doubts about the interpersonal comparability of good.

If the general betterness relation is incomplete, that does not necessarily vitiate Harsanyi's Theorem. It depends on how radical the incompleteness is. Some economists believe, or at least profess, that no comparisons at all can be made between the goods of different people: it is never true of two people that one is better off than the other.[6] If that were so, Harsanyi's Theorem would be completely empty. But if the incompleteness is less radical, the theorem can still have some significance.

It can still be applied in a supervaluationist manner. To explain how, I need first to reformulate the conclusion of Harsanyi's Theorem. I explained in section 13.4 that each person's betterness relation can be represented by a whole family of utility functions, each a rescaling of the others. The theorem says that there are functions, one for each person, that add up to a general utility function. The theorem itself picks the functions, we might say. But now I shall arbitrarily pick in advance one utility function for each person. Let these functions be $u_1()$, $u_2()$, and so on. Then the conclusion of the theorem, given the premises, is that general betterness can be represented by a weighted sum of these functions. There are positive weights a_2, a_3, and so on such that general utility is:

$$U(x) = u_1(x) + a_2 u_2(x) + a_3 u_3(x) + \ldots + a_n u_n(x).$$ (**)

(I have scaled the general utility function to make $a_1 = 1$.) This is the same theorem, presented in a different form.

Now, suppose the general betterness ordering is incomplete. Its gaps can be filled in. That is to say, so long as it satisfies the other axioms of expected utility theory, it can be extended to a complete ordering that satisfies all the axioms. Normally, there will be many different extensions of the ordering that have this property. One outcome or prospect is generally better than another if and only if it better according to every one of these extensions.

Harsanyi's Theorem applies to each one. The theorem tells us that, for each extension there will be weights a_2, a_3, and so on such that (**) is true. For each extension, each outcome or prospect x is assigned a general utility by the function $U(x)$, determined as a weighted sum of personal utilities through (**). One outcome or prospect is generally better than another if and only if it is better according to the general utility function determined by every extension.

If the indeterminacy is not great, the weights determined by the different extensions will not be very different from each other. Nor, therefore, will the general utilities determined for each extension through (**). Supervaluation would allow us still to think of overall general utilities, though they would be a bit indefinite. Some of the lessons I have drawn from the case where general betterness is complete will carry over. It will still be fair to say that personal utilities, which measure the contributory value of betterness in intrapersonal aggregation under uncertainty, also contribute to interpersonal aggregation.

So even if the general betterness ordering is incomplete to some extent, Harsanyi's Theorem still makes some link between intrapersonal and interpersonal aggregation. Giving up the assumption of completeness is therefore not a very effective strategy for someone who wishes to deny this link.

13.7. Rejecting Strong Independence

A second axiom open to doubt is known as the *strong independence axiom* or *sure-thing principle*. One part of this axiom is as follows. Suppose two different outcomes are equally as good as each other. Then a prospect that is a "mixture" of the two—leading to either one or the other of them—is equally as good as each of them.

Peter Diamond (1967) raised a powerful objection to this premise. He argued that it cannot recognize the sort of fairness that can sometimes be achieved by a random lottery. Suppose two people each have a claim to some valuable thing. Let it be to life-saving. Suppose each person is in mortal danger, and one can be saved but the other will die. Suppose their claims to being saved are equal. Fairness requires their equal claims to be equally satisfied. But that is impossible if one is saved, because the other will not be. It will normally be plainly wrong to save neither, but if one is saved some unfairness cannot be avoided. Nevertheless, a partial fairness can be achieved by holding a lottery: each claimant can be given the same chance of being saved. That is fairer than simply saving one or the other without a lottery.

One possible outcome is that the first claimant is saved. Another is that the second claimant is saved. Let us suppose these two outcomes are equally as good as each other. A lottery is a mixture that leads to either one or the other of these outcomes. So according to the strong independence axiom, it should be equally as good as each of the two possible outcomes. But it is actually better than both of them because it achieves a partial fairness, whereas saving one of the claimant's without holding a lottery does not achieve this sort of fairness. So the strong independence axiom is false. That is Diamond's argument.

It can be answered by treating fairness as a personal good and unfairness as a personal harm, in the way I recommended in section 13.5. The lottery leads to either one person's being saved or the other's being saved. But these outcomes are not exactly the ones that would be achieved by saving one or the other person without a lottery. If there is a lottery, the people are treated fairly to some extent. This is a good that is done them and it adds to their overall good. If there is no lottery, they do not have this good. So the lottery is not a mixture of the two outcomes in which there is no lottery. Therefore the strong independence axiom is not violated.

This response to Diamond is not universally accepted. I know of two different theories of value that are constructed by generalizing Diamond's objection. One comes from Larry Epstein and Uzi Segal (1992); the other from David McCarthy (2006). Both imply that a prospect that is a mixture of two equally good outcomes is always better than each of the outcomes. That is to say, they consistently reject the strong independence axiom. McCarthy's theory is a version of prioritarianism; he calls it *ex-ante prioritarianism*. It has the advantage of being immune to the strictures against prioritarianism that appear in section 13.9 below.

13.8. REJECTING THE PRINCIPLE OF PERSONAL GOOD

The most commonly questioned premise of Harsanyi's Theorem is the principle of personal good.

One reason to doubt it is that there are goods other than the good of people, and these must contribute to general good. The good of nonhuman animals is a clear example. It is also easy to take account of in the theorem. We have only to include nonhuman animals along with people, and extend the principle of personal good to make it a principle of personal and animal good. The theorem remains valid with this amendment. Other sorts of good can be accommodated in the same way: the good of ecological systems, for example, if it really exists.

Once extended in this way to include nonpersons, the principle of personal good can seem hard to doubt. Overall good surely depends in a positive way on the good of people, animals, and whatever else has a good that should be counted. However, the premise of Harsanyi's Theorem is that the principle applies to both outcomes and prospects. Several authors doubt it when applied to outcomes, even thought they accept it when applied to prospects.

An argument for applying the principle of personal good to prospects appears in Broome (1991: ch. 8). The arguments I have seen against doing so are indirect. They do not find an independent fault with the principle. Instead, they fault it because it joins with other assumptions to imply Harsanyi's Theorem. In this way, they are not as powerful as Diamond's objection to the sure-thing principle, because Diamond makes the independent objection I have described.

Wlodek Rabinowicz (2002) provides an example. He rejects the conclusion of Harsanyi's Theorem on the familiar grounds I mentioned in section 13.5, that interpersonal and intrapersonal aggregations of good are not as closely parallel as the theorem implies they are. He recognizes that one of the premises of the theorem consequently has to go. He finds the principle of personal good less secure than the others, so this is the one he rejects.

Marc Fleurbaey and Alex Voorhoeve (2013) argue in the same way. They start by rejecting the conclusion of Harsanyi's Theorem on the familiar grounds. Then they adopt a principle they call "the principle of full information," which is nothing other than the sure-thing principle or strong independence axiom.[7] This principle is perfectly consistent with the principle of personal good, so it cannot on its own constitute an objection to that principle. However, the sure thing principle (with the other axioms of expected utility theory), together with the principle of personal good, implies the conclusion of Harsanyi's Theorem; this is just Harsanyi's Theorem itself. So if the sure-thing principle (and the other axioms) are true, and the conclusion of Harsanyi's theorem is false, it follows that the principle of personal good is false. This is Fleurbaey and Voorhoeve's argument against it.

All these authors reject the principle of personal good only when it is applied to uncertain prospects. They accept it when it is applied to outcomes; presumably they find it too plausible there to reject it. This leaves them with a puzzle to deal with, as Rabinowicz (2002) recognizes. The outcomes that the principle applies to must contain no uncertainty; otherwise the same objection would recur for them. They will have to be fully specific possible worlds, with all details specified through all of history. We do not in practice encounter outcomes like that. The outcome of any act, or of anything that happens, is uncertain to some extent. Was the fine day's walking you enjoyed yesterday better than staying at home? Who knows? No doubt it was fun, but perhaps it triggered some small change in your body that will eventually take you to an early grave.

So the principle of personal good, which is so plausible, is left with no direct practical applications. This is not fatal to the argument, but it leaves work to be done if the principle is to be applied to outcomes and not prospects. We must be sure that our theory of value can be properly founded on outcomes of this sort that we do not encounter. Jeffrey's decision theory, for one, makes no distinction between prospects and outcomes. Indeed, Bolker's (1966) axiomatization of it is based on an "atomless" set of prospects, which contains no outcomes. So within this theory, a principle of personal good that applies to outcomes but not prospects cannot even be formulated.

13.9. UTILITY AND GOODNESS

To describe prioritarianism in section 13.4, I presumed we have a quantitative concept of a person's good. This is a big presumption, and we should not make it without some idea of how it might be satisfied. Where could this quantitative concept come from?

First, what do I mean when I call a concept *quantitative*? I mean that the degree to which something possesses the property denoted by the concept can be measured on what is called a "cardinal scale." This means in turn that differences between degrees can always be intelligibly compared.

Take some concept that has an intelligible comparative. For instance, take the concept of heaviness whose comparative is heavier than. Some things are heavier than others, which is to say that things differ in their degree of heaviness. The concept is quantitative if we can always make sense of comparisons between these differences: if we can always make sense of the claim that one difference is greater than another. Heaviness is quantitative if we can always make sense of the claim that the difference in heaviness between one thing A and another B is greater than the difference in heaviness between a third thing C and a fourth D (where A is heavier than B and C heavier than D). For heaviness we can indeed always make sense of this claim, so heaviness is quantitative. For heaviness, the claim means that, if A and D were put together on one pan of a pair of scales, they would outweigh B and C put together on the other pan. This is how differences in heaviness are comparable.

By contrast, our ordinary concept of hardness is not quantitative in this sense. It has the intelligible comparative harder than, but we cannot always make sense of comparisons of differences in hardness. Steel is harder than copper and oak is harder than pine, but we could not ordinarily make sense of the claim that the difference in hardness between copper and steel is greater than the difference in hardness between pine and oak.

A concept can sometimes be made quantitative by finding a way to make sense of comparisons of differences. When this is an innovation, it modifies the concept to make it a tighter, more precise one. Heaviness was presumably made quantitative and tightened up by the invention of scales. There are often alternative ways to make a concept quantitative. For purposes of science, various different scales of hardness have been developed, using different means for comparing differences. Each alternative provides a different quantitative concept of hardness.

What basis do we have for a quantitative concept of a person's good? How can we make sense of comparisons of differences in a person's good? I have already described one way in my example of Gamble and Certainty. The difference in goodness between outcomes a and b can be compared with the difference in goodness between c and d (where a is better than b and c better than d) by comparing the goodness of particular uncertain prospects. The goodness of a gamble at equal odds between a and d can be compared with the goodness of a gamble at equal odds between b and c. If the first is better than the second, the difference in goodness between a and b is greater than the difference in goodness between c and d.

That is not actually what I said when describing the example of Gamble and Certainty. I presented the example as a way of determining how much differences of goodness *count* in aggregation under uncertainty. I did not present the example as a way of making sense of differences in goodness themselves. I concluded that the difference in goodness between a and b counts for more than the difference in goodness between b and c. I did not conclude that the difference in goodness between a and b is greater than the difference in goodness between b and c. Why not?

Out of caution. Aggregation of differences under uncertainty is indeed one way to make sense of differences of goodness. So it can provide one quantitative concept of good. If we took this route, utility, which I defined to measure how much goodness counts, would actually be a measure of goodness itself. But there might be alternative, rival ways to make sense of differences, which would provide rival quantitative concepts of good. A case could be made for adopting the measure given by utility, but the case would be questionable if there was a rival.

For example, comparing differences in good for one person with differences in good for another person, in the process of aggregating good across people, might provide a rival scale. However, Harsanyi's Theorem tells us that the same utility functions as specify how good is aggregated under uncertainty also specify how good is aggregated across people. So, provided the premises of Harsanyi's Theorem hold, no rival scale arises from aggregation across people. This very much strengthens the case for taking utility to measure goodness itself. My own view is that the case is strong enough. We should treat utility as a scale of good. (See also Broome 2004: 86–91; Greaves, forthcoming; McCarthy 2006; Jensen 1995.)

Graphically, this means that the curved graph in figure 13.1 relating utility to goodness makes no sense. Since utility is nothing other than goodness itself, that graph has to be a straight line. One consequence is that risk aversion about good also makes no sense.

Another is that prioritarianism makes no sense if the premises of Harsanyi's Theorem hold. Prioritarianism relies on a distinction between a person's good and how much the person's good counts in aggregation between people. But given Harsanyi's Theorem and the identification of utility with good, no such distinction can be made.

I cannot rule out the existence of some other means to make sense of comparisons of differences that would be a genuine rival to utility as a measure of goodness. But at least a prioritarian who accepts the premises of Harsanyi's Theorem needs to explain what means she has in mind.

13.10. CONCLUSION

If utility does indeed measure goodness, then the formula (*), together with the supplementary assumption of impartiality mentioned in section 13.4, is the utilitarian theory of value. It says that general good is the total of the good of the people. Harsanyi's Theorem constitutes an argument for utilitarianism. His paper should be considered one of the founding documents of utilitarianism.

NOTES

1. My book *Weighing Goods* (Broome, 1991) is a fuller presentation.
2. For example, von Neumann and Morgenstern (1944), Marschak (1950), Savage (1954), Jeffrey (1965).
3. Mongin (1995) contains a proof within Savage's (1954) version. Broome (1990) contains a proof within the Bolker-Jeffrey version (Bolker, 1966, 1967; Jeffrey, 1965).
4. Interestingly, it arises from very different mathematical sources in different versions of the theorem. In Savage's decision theory, it follows from a theorem about "crosscutting separability," proved in Gorman (1968)—see the sketch proof in Broome (1991). In Jeffrey's decision theory, it follows from a theorem within measure theory, proved by Liapounoff (1940)—see the proof in Broome (1990). There must be a deep parallel in these theorems, but it is beyond my mathematical ability to identify it. Chapter 4 of Broome (1991) gives the most intuitive explanation of additivity that I can find.
5. This claim is implicit in a lot of economics, but few economists have made it explicitly. One who has is Arrow (1999).
6. For example, Arrow (1963: 9).

7. One part of the principle of full information as Fleurbaey and Voorhoeve state it is: "When one knows that, in every state of the world with positive probability, one is indifferent between two alternatives, then one should be indifferent between these alternatives." Compare the part of the strong independence axiom that I stated in section 13.7: "Suppose two different outcomes are equally as good as each other; then a prospect that is a 'mixture' of the two—leading to either one or the other of them—is equally as good as each of them." These are the same claim, differently worded.

REFERENCES

Arrow, K. J. (1963). *Social Choice and Individual Values*, 2nd ed. New Haven: Yale University Press.
Arrow, K. J. (1999). "Discounting, Morality, and Gaming." In P. R. Portney and J. P. Weyant (eds.), *Discounting and Intergenerational Equity*. New York: Resources for the Future, 13–21.
Bolker, E. D. (1966). "Functions Resembling Quotients of Measures." *Transactions of the American Mathematical Society* 124: 292–312.
Bolker, E. D. (1967). "A Simultaneous Axiomatization of Utility and Subjective Probability." *Philosophy of Science*, 34: 333–40.
Broome, J. (1990). "Bolker-Jeffrey Expected Utility Theory and Axiomatic Utilitarianism." *Review of Economic Studies* 57: 477–502.
Broome, J. (1991). *Weighing Goods: Equality, Uncertainty and Time*. Oxford: Blackwell.
Broome, J. (2004). *Weighing Lives*. New York: Oxford University Press.
Diamond, P. A. (1967). "Cardinal Welfare, Individualistic Ethics, and Interpersonal Comparisons of Utility: Comment." *Journal of Political Economy* 75: 765–66.
Epstein, L. G., and U. Segal (1992). "Quadratic Social Welfare Functions." *Journal of Political Economy* 100: 691–712.
Fleurbaey, M., and A. Voorhoeve (2013). "Decide as You Would with Full Information! An Argument against *Ex Ante* Pareto." In N. Eyal, S. Hurst, O. Norheim, and D. Wikler (eds.), *Inequalities in Health: Concepts, Measures and Ethics*. New York: Oxford University Press, 113–28.
Gorman, W. M. (1968). "The Structure of Utility Functions." *Review of Economic Studies* 35: 367–90.
Greaves, H. (Forthcoming) "Antiprioritarianism."
Harsanyi, J. C. (1955). "Cardinal Welfare, Individualistic Ethics, and Interpersonal Comparisons of Utility." *Journal of Political Economy* 63: 309–21.
Jeffrey, R. C. (1965). *The Logic of Decision*. New York: McGraw-Hill.
Jensen, K. K. (1995). "Measuring the Size of a Benefit and Its Moral Weight: On the Significance of John Broome's Interpersonal Addition Theorem." *Theoria* 61: 26–60.
Liapounoff, A. (1940). "Sur les fonctions-vecteurs complètement additives." *Bulletin of the Academy of Sciences of the USSR*, Ser. Math. 4: 465–78.
Marschak, J. (1950). "Rational Behavior, Uncertain Prospects, and Measurable Utility." *Econometrica* 18: 111–41.
McCarthy, D. (2006). "Utilitarianism and prioritarianism I." *Economics and Philosophy* 22: 1–29.
Mongin, P. (1995). "Consistent Bayesian aggregation." *Journal of Economic Theory* 66: 313–51.

Otsuka, M., and A. Voorhoeve (2009). "Why It Matters That Some Are Worse Off Than Others: An Argument against the Priority View." *Philosophy and Public Affairs* 37: 172–99.
Rabinowicz, W. (2002). "Prioritarianism for Prospects." *Utilitas* 14: 2–21.
Rawls, J. (1971). *A Theory of Justice*. Cambridge: Harvard University Press.
Savage, L. J. (1954). *The Foundations of Statistics*. New York: Wiley.
von Neumann, J., and O. Morgenstern. 1944. *Theory of Games and Economic Behavior*. Princeton, NJ: Princeton University press.

CHAPTER 14

THEORIES OF VALUE AGGREGATION

Utilitarianism, Egalitarianism, Prioritarianism

NILS HOLTUG

14.1. INTRODUCTION

CONCERNS about value aggregation are at the heart of moral and political philosophy. Consider, for example, Rawls's (1971: 27) complaint that classical utilitarianism does not take seriously the distinction between persons. Essentially, the complaint is that while it may be reasonable to aggregate according to a principle that weighs equal interests equally in cases of intrapersonal trade-off, this is not so in cases of interpersonal conflict because the satisfaction of one person's interests does not compensate another person for the frustration of hers.

My concern in the present chapter is with different principles of distributive justice and in particular the different accounts of aggregation to which they subscribe. However, the three principles I consider—utilitarianism, egalitarianism, and prioritarianism—differ not only regarding their accounts of aggregation, but may also do so regarding the units (or currencies) they aim to distribute. Thus, while utilitarianism (by definition) is concerned with the distribution of welfare and many egalitarians and prioritarians also take this to be the currency of justice, other proponents of the latter two positions claim that what matters is rather the distribution of resources (Dworkin 1981; Rawls 1971), capabilities (Sen 1980), access to advantage (Cohen 1989), or opportunities for welfare (Arneson 1989). In the following, I shall mostly remain neutral on what the appropriate currency is and shall simply use the term "advantage" (except when discussing utilitarianism, which by definition relies on the currency of welfare). "Advantage" may thus refer to any of these more specific currencies.

Furthermore, my concern is with axiology—and more particularly the value of outcomes—and not with other normative notions such as rightness or obligation.

Thus, my focus is on how the three distributive principles referred to above assess the value of outcomes and, more specifically, how they aggregate individual levels of advantage to reach such assessments. I shall therefore consider only axiological versions of these principles. Among other things, this means that they do not imply that a given act should be performed or a particular policy adopted. To illustrate, consider the case of a doctor who can save the lives of five patients, but only by killing an innocent and perfectly healthy bystander and distributing some of his organs to the five patients (Harman 1977: 3–4). While an axiological version of utilitarianism implies that, everything else being equal, it would be better for the doctor to redistribute the organs in this manner, this does not imply that she ought to do so. After all, axiological utilitarianism is compatible with, for example, an agent-relative constraint against killing the innocent.

My final introductory remark concerns the fact that the three principles discussed satisfy some rather strong impartiality requirements, including anonymity. Anonymity implies that the value of an outcome is not affected by a permutation of advantages over individuals who exist in that outcome. For example, it implies that in a two-individual case, (2, 1) and (1, 2) are equally good, where the first number denotes the first individual's advantage level and the second number denotes the second individual's level.

14.2. Utilitarianism

According to:

Axiological total utilitarianism: An outcome is noninstrumentally better, the higher the sum of individual advantages it contains.[1]

Formally, axiological total utilitarianism (henceforth: utilitarianism) can be represented by:

$$G = a_1 + a_2 + \ldots + a_n, \tag{1}$$

where a_1 represents the first individual's advantages, a_2 the second individual's advantages, and so on. The particular kind of advantages with which utilitarians are concerned is welfare. Thus, utilitarianism simply adds up individual welfare to reach a judgment about the overall value of an outcome.[2] Hence, it relies on an account of aggregation that has also turned into a utilitarian slogan, according to which "all interests count the same, weighted only for their strength." Claiming that equal interests are to count the same involves a substantial commitment to impartiality, and indeed utilitarians have sometimes aimed to derive utilitarianism from particular versions of this ideal (Hare 1981; Harsanyi 1982; Singer 1993).

There are two structural aspects of utilitarianism worth noting here. First, it satisfies the Pareto principle, according to which an outcome is better than another if it is better for some and worse for none, and two outcomes are equally good if they are equally good for everyone. Consider, for example, (10, 5) and (5, 5). Utilitarianism implies that an increase for an individual, holding others constant, always improves an outcome and hence that (10, 5) is better than (5, 5). Second, utilitarianism satisfies strong separability. A distributive principle generates a strongly separable ordering if and only if it implies that the ordering of the advantage level of any subset of individuals is independent of the levels of others (Broome 1991: 69). Strong separability, then, will not allow the advantages of unaffected individuals to affect the moral ordering. Consider the following four outcomes:

A = (2, 2, 2, 2, 2, 2, 2)   C = (2, 2, 1, 1, 1, 1, 1)
B = (4, 1, 2, 2, 2, 2, 2)   D = (4, 1, 1, 1, 1, 1, 1)

Strong separability implies that A is better than B if and only if C is better than D. This is because only the first two individuals are affected by a move from A to B and from C to D, and their advantages in A equal their advantages in C and their advantages in B equal their advantages in D. Utilitarianism does not allow the welfare of unaffected individuals to affect the ordering and implies that just as B is better than A, D is better than C.

A common complaint about utilitarianism is that it lacks sensitivity to distribution. For example, (9, 1) is held to be equal in value to (5, 5). In fact, this is also Rawls's (1971: 27) complaint, referred to above. Indeed, apart from objecting to utilitarian aggregation, Rawls also offers an account of what is wrong with it. Utilitarianism does not take seriously the distinction between persons since it offers a principle of aggregation that relies for its justifiability on intrapersonal compensation and then extends this principle to interpersonal cases (cf. Nagel 1970: 138; Nozick 1974: 32–33). Thus, where it may be prudent for me to choose a less severe pain now (say, by going to the dentist) to avoid a more severe pain later, because the prevention of the latter compensates me for the former, an individual is not similarly compensated for a harm by a benefit that accrues to *someone else*. And by being insensitive to compensation, utilitarianism in principle allows for highly unequal distributions, as illustrated by its indifference to (9, 1) and (5, 5).

A standard response to this objection is to point out that while utilitarianism may well lack sensitivity to distributions in principle, it will tend to favor equality in the distribution of resources such as income. This is because of the diminishing marginal utility of money (Brandt: 312–13; Hare 1981: 164–65). Thus, while an extra 100 dollars will make a big difference for someone who is poor, it will make less of a difference for someone who is rich and therefore, everything else being equal, utilitarianism will favor redistribution to the advantage of the poor. However, as critics have been eager to point out, this argument relies on the assumption that individuals have identical utility functions (Sen 1997: 16), that is, are equally good at transforming resources into welfare. But in fact, we have no reason to believe this to be the case. The reason why the argument relies on this assumption is that if, for a given level of income, some people are better at transforming an extra dollar into welfare than others, utilitarianism implies that it is better to transfer more money to them, everything else being equal. After all, utilitarianism will favor the outcome in which the total income is distributed such that each individual's marginal utility from the last earned dollar is equal.

Nevertheless, as the economist Abba Lerner (1944: 29–32) has shown, if in fact we do not have any knowledge about individual utility functions, expected welfare is maximized by an equal distribution of a fixed sum of income. Consider figure 14.1. The curves represent the marginal utilities of different incomes of two individuals, A and B. A's curve has the left-hand corner as its point of origin whereas B's curve has the right-hand corner. So where A starts at zero dollars in the left-hand corner, B starts at zero dollars in the right-hand corner. Because of diminishing marginal utility, A's curve slopes downward toward the right and B's curve downward toward the left. A and B have nonidentical curves and in fact, A is better at transforming money into welfare. The best distribution, in utilitarian terms, would be 150 dollars for A and 50 dollars for B, because this is where their diminishing marginal utilities are equal (and so the curves intersect). However, suppose we have no knowledge of their utility functions, except that they conform to the principle of diminishing marginal utility. If we divide the available sum of income equally, A and B will receive 100 dollars each, but now consider possible deviations from equality. If we give an extra 20 dollars to A, so that he receives 120 and B receives 80, the total welfare will increase because A is better at transforming income into welfare. In fact, the net gain will be the shaded area G (the difference between A's gain and B's loss). If, instead, we give the extra 20 dollars to B, the net loss will be the shaded area L. As we

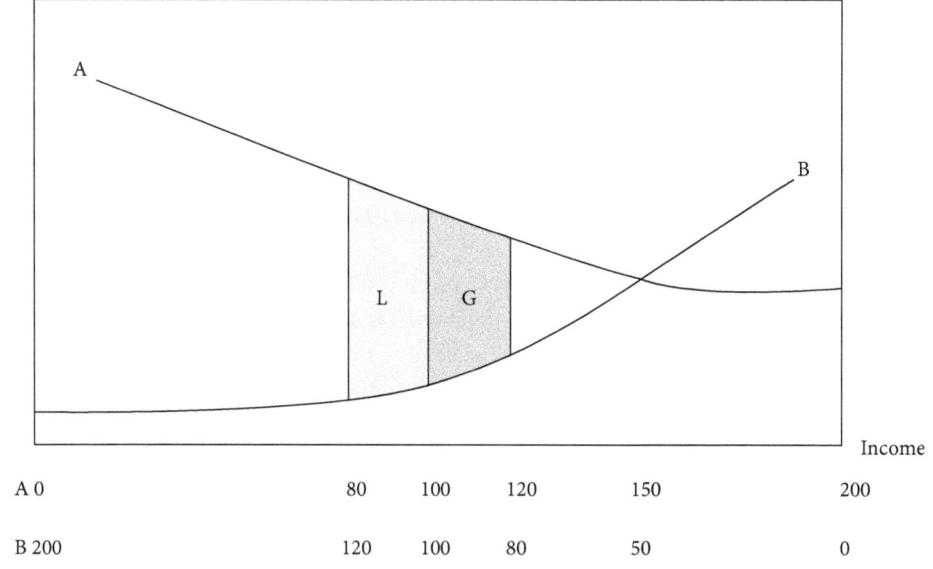

FIGURE 14.1 Marginal Utility

can see, the loss L from giving the extra 20 dollars to B is greater than the gain G from giving the extra 20 dollars to A. The point is that since we are assuming ignorance about the utility functions of A and B, we are equally likely to give the extra 20 dollars to A and B in our attempt to maximize welfare. And since the loss of giving it to B is greater than the gain of giving it to A, we maximize expected welfare by opting for an equal distribution of income.

This is a strong result, not least because while it does assume that individual utility functions satisfy the principle of diminishing marginal utility, it does not rely on interpersonal comparisons of welfare. And it establishes that a utilitarian social planner with no knowledge of individual utility functions would aim for an equal distribution of income, everything else being equal.

However, there are at least four reasons why this argument for monetary equality may not satisfy critics concerned with distribution. First, according to utilitarianism, lack of knowledge about individual utility functions should be seen as a cause for regret rather than celebrated as an equality-favoring tendency of the principle. That is, it would be better if the utilitarian planner *did* have access to individual utility functions because she could then promote total welfare by directing extra resources to those who are able to derive more welfare from them. So even if, in practice, utilitarianism may have a tendency toward monetary equality, it may be argued that this is for the wrong reason, where the right reason would (at least in part) appeal to an intrinsic concern for distribution.

The second reason some will object to the utilitarian argument for monetary equality is that a utilitarian planner may sometimes have information about individual utility functions where this information will in fact lead her to favor an unjustly unequal distribution of income. Consider, for example, Sen's (1997: 16–17) case of a disabled person who, due to a reduced range of opportunities, is less capable of transforming income into welfare than another, able-bodied individual is. Since welfare is maximized by equating the marginal utilities individuals derive from their income and since the disabled person's marginal utility from a given income is less than that of the able-bodied, utilitarianism implies that it is better to allocate less money to the former than to the latter. Thus, the disabled person is disadvantaged not only in terms of her disability but also in terms of income. Utilitarians may respond that, in realistic scenarios, the utility functions of the disabled will generally not differ in ways that would support allocating them less (Brandt 1979: 316–19), but others will want to press the point that this response relies on a highly contingent fact about human beings, at best.

The third reason one might be skeptical of the merits of the utilitarian argument for monetary equality is, precisely, that it is an argument (only) for *monetary* equality. If, as utilitarians maintain, welfare is what ultimately matters, then why care, at the most basic level, about the distribution of something else, such as income? If we are concerned with distribution and welfare is what matters, then arguably we should be concerned with the distribution of welfare, where monetary equality implies welfare equality only on the (dubious) assumption that individuals have identical utility functions. Of course, this argument does not establish that we *should* be concerned about distribution and so the distribution of welfare. The point is rather that if we do have a concern for distribution, which is after all the worry about utilitarianism that the argument for monetary equality is supposed to address, then it is not clear that a tendency toward monetary equality will be sufficient to meet our concern.

The final reason why some will find the utilitarian argument for monetary equality unsatisfactory is that even if utilitarianism does include a tendency toward such equality, it may nevertheless not strike the right balance between equality and efficiency. Consider, for example, leximin, according to which an outcome is better than another if it is better for the worst off individual, and if the worst off individual is equally well off in the two outcomes, the first outcome is better if it is better for the second worst off individual, and so on (for a precise definition, see Adler, chapter 17 in this volume). While both utilitarianism and leximin allow for efficiency-promoting incentives, they do not do so to the same extent. While utilitarianism allows for incentives leading to inequality whenever this maximizes total welfare, leximin allows for them only when they favor (or at least do not disfavor) those worse off than the beneficiaries of these incentives. Thus, unlike utilitarianism, leximin does not allow for trade-offs between the interests of the worse off and the better off. And some will want to argue that this strikes a better balance between equality and efficiency.

Rather than appeal to the tendency toward monetary equality as a way of capturing concerns about distribution, utilitarians may instead challenge the very argument intended to show that they do not take seriously the distinction between persons. As pointed out by David Brink (1993), this argument comes in two importantly different versions. According to the first, it is unacceptable to impose costs on an individual for which she is not compensated, where such costs are measured in nonmoral terms (for example, in terms of welfare). However, while this argument certainly rules out utilitarianism, it pretty much rules out any plausible distributive principle, even non-aggregative principles such as leximin and Rawls's own difference principle. After all, leximin will impose uncompensated costs on the better off whenever doing so will benefit the worst off.

According to the second version, it is unacceptable to impose *unjustified* costs on an individual for which she is not compensated. However, unless further qualified, this argument does not even rule out utilitarianism, as utilitarians may take "unjustified costs" to be costs that are not accompanied by equal benefits to others. Thus, we need a substantive account of "unjustified costs" and here distribution-sensitivists may argue for a moral asymmetry between costs that are imposed on the worse off and on the better off (Brink 1993: 259–64). Brink critically discusses nonaggregative such accounts (such as maximin), but the aggregative egalitarian and prioritarian views I discuss in later sections may also explain the asymmetry. Indeed, any view that satisfies the Pigou-Dalton principle of transfer may explain it, where this principle claims that if the sum of advantages remains constant, equality is increased by a transfer from a better-off individual to a worse-off individual, as long as their relative positions are not reversed.

14.3. EGALITARIANISM

While many find the lack of distribution-sensitivity in utilitarianism problematic, there are different accounts of why this is so. Egalitarians give one explanation, prioritarians another. The source of the problem, say (axiological) egalitarians, is that utilitarianism ignores the noninstrumental value of equality. When it comes to spelling out the content of egalitarianism, some theorists focus on orderings with respect to equality only (Holtug 2010: ch. 7; Parfit 2000 [1991]; Temkin 1993), whereas others focus on the overall (or all things considered) ordering (Broome, forthcoming; Fleurbaey, forthcoming). I shall say something about the latter approach later, but consider first:

Axiological egalitarianism. An outcome is in one respect noninstrumentally better, the more equal a distribution of individual advantages it includes.

Axiological egalitarianism (henceforth: egalitarianism) is a relational view in the sense that the moral value of an advantage to an individual depends on what levels other people are at (Parfit 2000 [1991]: 23; cf. Temkin 1993: 200). An increase in an individual's level from n to $n + 1$ noninstrumentally increases the value of an outcome in one respect if everyone else is at $n + 1$, but makes it in one respect noninstrumentally worse if everyone else is at n. Furthermore, by valuing equality noninstrumentally egalitarians distinguish themselves from, for example, utilitarians, who value (monetary) equality instrumentally only.

Now, there are various ways of measuring inequality, but it is arguable that the Pigou-Dalton principle restricts the range of views that may qualify as egalitarian. Thus, redistributions that decrease the difference between any two individuals are improvements, everything else being equal.

One way of justifying an egalitarian ordering of outcomes is simply to appeal to the noninstrumental value of equality (or disvalue of inequality; I do not distinguish here).[3] Another is to appeal to the outcome of a choice under ideal circumstances, for example behind a veil of ignorance (Rawls 1971). And a third is to propose a claim-within-outcome account of fairness, according to which outcomes are ordered in terms of how individuals fare relative to each other in each of them, more specifically as regards their claims to an equal share of advantages (Temkin 1993).

The reason why egalitarianism, as characterized above, orders outcomes in one respect only is that equality needs to be supplemented with a concern for efficiency. Otherwise (1, 1) would as good a distribution as (10, 10)—both outcomes contain perfect equality. Many egalitarians hold that the overall social ordering should satisfy the Pareto principle. And indeed, Paretian egalitarianism has the attractive implication that all things considered, it will never be better to level down, that is, to increase equality by lowering the level of the better off to the level of the worse off, as in the move from (10, 5) to (5, 5). In the following, I shall only consider combinations of equality and efficiency that satisfy the Pareto principle and I shall refer to this class of views simply as "Paretian egalitarianism." Thus, whereas egalitarianism orders outcomes in one respect only (namely, with respect to equality), Paretian egalitarianism is sensitive to both equality and efficiency and so may order outcomes all things considered.

Unlike leximin, egalitarianism is quite compatible with aggregation. Leximin rules out aggregation because it implies that increases to a worse-off individual can never be counterbalanced by increases to a better-off individual (or group of such individuals). Egalitarianism, on the other hand, may well allow for trade-offs between different individuals. Compare (1, 10, 10) and (2, 2, 10). Using the language of complaints, the first individual in the first outcome has a greater complaint than each of the first and the second individual in the second outcome, and for this reason leximin considers (2, 2, 10) better than (1, 10, 10). However, egalitarians may well want to aggregate the first and the second individuals' complaints in the second outcome and hold that their aggregate complaint is greater, suggesting that (1, 10, 10) is more equal than (2, 2, 10). But note that insofar as egalitarianism allows for trade-offs, the range of such allowable trade-offs will be determined by the particular measure of inequality assumed. Nevertheless, whatever the measure, egalitarianism will differ from utilitarianism in rejecting any trade-off that violates the Pigou-Dalton principle, as does the claim that (5, 5) is no better than (9, 1).

When it comes to trade-offs where equality conflicts with efficiency, Paretian egalitarians may disagree internally about the ordering of outcomes, depending on how much significance they attach to efficiency. Thus, Paretian egalitarians may disagree about whether, for example, (3, 3) is better than (9, 1). However, I shall assume that just like egalitarianism, Paretian egalitarianism must satisfy the Pigou-Dalton principle to qualify as a member of the egalitarian family.

It may be suggested that the above characterization of egalitarianism is too minimal in that it says very little about the overall ranking of outcomes (Fleurbaey, forthcoming: 2–3). This is because it focuses only on equality. Of course, Paretian egalitarianism says more, but not all egalitarians are Paretian egalitarians and in any case Paretian egalitarianism too may be criticized for insufficiently narrowing the scope of possible orderings. Indeed, besides Paretian egalitarianism, leximin and prioritarianism also satisfy both the Pigou-Dalton principle and the Pareto principle. Thus, precisely to distinguish the overall egalitarian and prioritarian orderings, John Broome (forthcoming: 2–3) has suggested that whereas the prioritarian ordering satisfies strong separability, the egalitarian ordering does not. Compare again outcomes A–D. Because A has a property C does not, namely that of being equal, the egalitarian overall ordering may imply that while A is better than B, D is better than C, thus violating strong separability. Furthermore, the denial of strong separability is a way of making sense of the idea that equality is a relational value, where the contribution of an individual's advantage level to the value of an outcome depends on the shares of others.

Whether or not we should impose such a further constraint on the overall egalitarian ordering, arguably, the minimal characterization provided by egalitarianism is in fact sufficient to distinguish this view from prioritarianism and to do so in a principled and significant manner. While this characterization is compatible with a wide variety of overall orderings, it nevertheless commits egalitarians, including Paretian egalitarians, to a particular *reason*, or partial reason, for endorsing a given overall ordering. That is, egalitarians will endorse a given such ordering at least in part because they take more equal outcomes to be noninstrumentally better than less equal outcomes. And while it may be the effects of the overall ordering that are felt by people insofar as it is implemented in policies, the reasons or justification for implementing it are no less important in political philosophy than the ordering itself, suggesting that it may indeed be appropriate to draw even fundamental distinctions, such as that between egalitarianism and prioritarianism, in terms of reasons.

The significance of the minimal characterization lies not least in the fact that it renders egalitarianism vulnerable to the leveling down objection. Compare (10, 5) and (5, 5). While egalitarians may reasonably claim that (10, 5) is certainly better all things considered—after all, this is implied by Paretian egalitarianism—they are nevertheless committed to the claim that (5, 5) is *in one respect* noninstrumentally better. After all, (5, 5) is more equal than (10, 5). But how can (5, 5) be in any respect better, when it is better for no one, not even the worse off? This is the leveling down objection (Parfit 2000 [1991]: 17).

I believe that there are two sources from which this objection derives its force (Holtug 2010: 181–88). Cases of leveling down may suggest that the concerns that have motivated us to be egalitarians in the first place are not really captured by egalitarianism. Thus, arguably at least part of what motivates such a concern is a concern for the worse off. However, (5, 5) does not make the worse off better off, merely the better off worse off. To further bring out this point, compare (10, 5) and (0, 0). According to egalitarianism, (0, 0) is in one respect noninstrumentally better, but in (0, 0) the worse off are actually even worse off than in (10, 5). Finally, on the assumption that welfare is the currency of justice and "0" is the level where life ceases to be worth living, egalitarianism implies that even (−10, −10) is in one respect noninstrumentally better than (10, 5), although everyone suffers terribly in the former outcome. Egalitarianism, then, does not really respond to our concern for the worse off.

The other source from which the leveling down objection derives its force is the idea that our axiology should take a person-affecting form. Roughly speaking, what this means in the present context is that an outcome cannot be in any respect better (worse) than another if there is no one for whom it is better (worse). This principle ties moral improvements to improvements in welfare, and its support for the leveling down objection is most easily seen if we take welfare to be the currency of justice. The principle then straightforwardly implies that (5, 5) cannot in any respect be better than (10, 5). But even if we assume a different currency, for example, resources, it lends support to the leveling down objection. While leveling down the resources of the better off to the level of the worse off will often be in the interest of the worse off (for example, because this tends to weaken hierarchical relations and improve their political power), presumably this will not be the case in the move from (10, 5) to (0, 0). In such cases, leveling down resources benefits no one, not even the worse off.

However, Larry Temkin (1993: ch. 9) has argued that the person-affecting principle is dubious and so cannot be used to support the leveling down objection. First, this principle gets us into trouble when applied to various issues in population ethics, such as the nonidentity problem (see also Hausman, chapter 18 in the present volume, on population axiology). Suppose either of two individuals may come into existence, and that the first individual, *a*, will have an advantage level of 5 and the second individual, *b*, a level of 10. Suppose also that *a* is caused to exist. Implausibly, the person-affecting principle rules out that this can be in any respect worse than if *b* had come into existence instead, because there is no one for whom it is worse (*b* does not exist). Second, such a person-affecting principle may rule out a great many moral ideals from our axiology, including, for example, autonomy and desert. After all, presumably we can have value-increases in autonomy or desert in the absence of increases in welfare (depending, of course, on exactly what we take welfare to consist in).

Nevertheless, in response to Temkin's first worry about the person-affecting principle, it has been argued that it should be replaced with a wide person-affecting principle, according to which, roughly, an outcome cannot be better (worse) than another in any respect if, were it to come about, there is no one for whom it would be better (worse), and were the other outcome to come about, there is no one for whom this outcome would be worse (better) (Holtug 2010: 186). This principle is compatible with claiming that it is (morally) worse if *a* comes about, since if *b* were to come about, this would be better for *b*. Furthermore, this principle supports the leveling down objection because there is no one for whom (5, 5) is better or (10, 5) is worse, and this is so irrespective of which of these outcomes come about.

In response to Temkin's second worry about the person-affecting principle, some critics have argued that the wide person-affecting principle may well capture the moral ideals that are worth preserving in our axiology (Holtug 2003), and others have modified the person-affecting principle to include various nonwelfarist ideals (Doran 2001).

While some egalitarians have responded to the leveling down objection by simply biting the bullet and accepting the implication that leveling down is in one respect better (Temkin 1993: 282), others have developed their egalitarian views in ways that may seem to avoid this objection, for example by claiming that equality is a person-affecting value (Broome 1991: 180–82; Hirose 2015: ch. 3), or that the value of equality is conditional on increases in welfare (Mason 2001), or that it is conditional on a scheme of cooperation to the mutual advantage of all (Norman 1998). I critically discuss these and other egalitarian attempts to avoid the leveling down objection in Holtug (2007; 2010: ch. 7).

14.4. PRIORITARIANISM

Whereas egalitarianism provides one analysis of what (if anything) is troubling about the lack of distribution-sensitivity in utilitarianism, prioritarianism provides another.

Axiological prioritarianism. An outcome is noninstrumentally better, the larger the sum of weighted individual advantages it contains, where advantages are weighted such that they gain a greater value, the worse off the individual is to whom they accrue.

More formally, axiological prioritarianism (henceforth: prioritarianism) can be represented as follows:

$$G = f(a_1) + f(a_2) + \ldots + f(a_n), \qquad (2)$$

where f is an increasing and strictly concave function of individual advantages. Thus, advantages gradually decrease in moral value the higher the level at which they fall, as illustrated in figure 14.2.

The prioritarian function is somewhat similar to utilitarianism, but instead of being an additive function of unweighted individual advantages, it is an additive function of *weighted* such advantages. According to prioritarians, then, what is troubling about the lack of distribution-sensitivity in utilitarianism is that utilitarianism does not give priority to the worse off. Where utilitarians believe that the moral value of an increase to an individual depends only on the size of the increase, prioritarians believe that it also depends on how well off the recipient would otherwise be.

Whereas both egalitarianism and prioritarianism satisfy the Pigou-Dalton principle and so consider distribution significant, they do so for different reasons. Parfit (2000 [1991]: 23) characterizes the main difference between these principles as a difference of relationality. More specifically, where egalitarianism is relational, prioritarianism is not. According to prioritarianism, the moral value of a further advantage to an individual depends only on the size of the advantage and on how well off she would otherwise be—the levels of others do not come into the picture. This difference is captured by my account of the relational aspect of egalitarianism above. According to egalitarianism, an increase in an individual's level of advantages from n to $n + 1$ noninstrumentally increases the value of an outcome in one respect if everyone else is at $n + 1$, but makes it in one respect noninstrumentally worse if everyone else is at n. According to prioritarianism, on the other hand, it is insignificant whether others are at n or $n + 1$; the moral value of the increase is the same in either case.

Egalitarianism orders outcomes in one respect only. But if, like Broome, we consider the violation of strong separability a requirement for the overall egalitarian ordering, this ordering will also differ from that of prioritarianism in a manner that reflects a difference regarding relationality. This is because prioritarianism satisfies strong

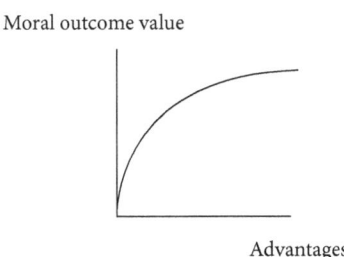

FIGURE 14.2 Diminishing Marginal Moral Value of Welfare

separability. It does not allow the ranking of two outcomes to be affected by unaffected individuals.

Note that where I have characterized egalitarianism as a view that orders outcomes in one respect only, I have characterized prioritarianism as a view that orders outcomes all things considered. This is because, unlike equality, giving priority to the worse off can be our only distributive concern. Thus, the prioritarian function straightforwardly satisfies the Pareto principle (where this implies, among other things, that equality at higher levels is preferred to equality at lower levels). Note also that this implies that, unless we follow Broome in imposing further conditions on the egalitarian overall ordering of outcomes, we may find Pareto egalitarians and prioritarians in agreement about that ordering (Tungodden 2003: 30–31). This, however, does not imply that egalitarians and prioritarians hold identical views. Only egalitarians are committed to the particular (partial) reason for endorsing that ordering captured by egalitarianism. And as we have seen, this is a reason that invites the leveling down objection.

Like prioritarianism, leximin gives priority to the worse off, and so it may be considered whether leximin is in fact a version of the former view, albeit an extreme version in that it gives lexical priority to the interests of the very worst off. According to the characterization I have given above, it is not. While leximin satisfies the Pigou-Dalton principle, the Pareto principle and strong separability, it differs from prioritarianism in two respects (Hirose 2015: 95-98). First, since it does not allow for trade-offs between the worse off and the better off, it is not a strictly concave function. Second, leximin is relational in a sense in which prioritarianism is not. Prioritarianism implies that the moral value of an additional unit to an individual depends only on that individual's own level of advantages. Leximin, on the other hand, implies that it depends on that individual's relative position, that is, whether she is worst off, second worst off, and so on.

As in the case of egalitarianism, the prioritarian ordering of outcomes may be justified in different ways. One is to appeal simply to the noninstrumental value of giving priority to the worse off. I have elsewhere suggested that prioritarians may ascribe noninstrumental value to compound states of affairs, each consisting of the state that an advantage of a certain size befalls an individual and the state that this individual is at a particular level of advantages, where this value increases when the size of the advantage increases but decreases when the advantage level increases (Holtug 2010: 204). Another is to appeal to the outcome of a choice under ideal circumstances, for example behind a veil of ignorance. And a third is to appeal to claims to advantages. Thus, Matthew Adler (2012: 365) argues that prioritarianism can be justified on the basis of a claim-across-outcome approach, according to which individuals have claims vis-à-vis pairs of outcomes, where such claims depend on their levels of advantages in each. More specifically, he argues that this approach supports an ordering that satisfies the Pareto principle, the Pigou-Dalton principle, and strong separability.

There is an issue of how to settle the weights, giving priority to the worse off, in the prioritarian function. Thus, prioritarianism can be described as occupying an intermediate position between utilitarianism and leximin, where utilitarianism gives no priority to the worse off and leximin gives lexical priority to the very worst off.

Prioritarians find both these extremes excessive, but obviously there is plenty of room in between, including weightings that approach utilitarianism in giving almost no priority to the worse off and weightings that approach leximin in making increases to the very worst off next to impossible to outweigh. Generally, prioritarians have suggested that the weights need to be settled intuitively (Parfit 2000 [1991]: 20), possibly through a procedure of achieving reflective equilibrium. Some may suggest that settling weights in this manner is too arbitrary, or unprincipled. But note first that even if the exact weights need to be settled intuitively, this is compatible with the existence of principled arguments for why certain classes of prioritarian functions are to be preferred over others (for example, Adler [2012: 383–99] argues that we have reason to favor an Atkinson social welfare function, but we may equally imagine arguments for more restrictive conditions). Second, note that it may be impossible to avoid intuitive weightings when developing a precise distributive principle. Thus, the utilitarian weighting, assigning equal weight to all equal increases in welfare, is no less in need of justification than the prioritarian weighting, and nor is the Paretian egalitarian weighting of equality and efficiency.

Above, I pointed out that prioritarianism differs from egalitarianism in not being vulnerable to the leveling down objection. In fact, many prioritarians consider this a reason to favor the former principle. Consider again (10, 5) and (5, 5). Prioritarianism does not imply that (5, 5) is in any respect better. After all, this principle values only increases in advantages, where these are weighted according to the advantage level of the recipient, and in the move from (10, 5) to (5, 5) there are no such increases. Furthermore, prioritarianism accommodates both of the concerns from which the leveling down objection derives its force. First, it is explicitly concerned with the fate of the worse off. And second, it satisfies the wide person-affecting principle referred to above. It implies that increases (decreases) in outcome value are always tied to increases (decreases) in individual advantages.

Nevertheless, it has been argued that upon closer scrutiny, the leveling down objection cannot be used to distinguish prioritarianism from egalitarianism (Broome 2002; Fleurbaey, forthcoming: 13; Persson 2008). In one version, the argument is this. It can be shown that the prioritarian ordering can be represented by:

$$G = T - I, \qquad (3)$$

where T is total advantages and I is a measure of the badness of inequality (Broome 2002). Here, decreases in I imply increases in G, everything else being equal. In the move from (10, 5) to (5, 5) both T and I decrease, but whereas the decrease in T lowers G, the decrease in I *increases* G. In other words, the decrease in the badness of inequality improves the outcome in one respect. But if prioritarians are committed to the claim that the move from (10, 5) to (5, 5) is in one respect better, then they are vulnerable to the leveling down objection after all.

However, arguably, one cannot derive such a judgment about the value commitments of prioritarians merely from the fact that the prioritarian function can be split into these two components, giving rise to an extensionally equivalent ordering (Holtug 2010: 209–18). To illustrate, consider that the utilitarian function may be expressed as:

$$G = n \times A, \qquad (4)$$

where n refers to the number of individuals and A to their average welfare. Although increases in A do increase G, everything else being equal, clearly this does not mean that (total) utilitarians are committed to the claim that increases in average welfare make outcomes in one respect better. After all, that would imply that $(-10, -9)$ is in one respect better than $(-10, *)$, where "*" refers to the fact that the second individual does not exist in the second outcome, and surely (total) utilitarians claim no such thing.

Furthermore, consider the possible specification of the prioritarian value commitments referred to above. According to this specification, prioritarians ascribe noninstrumental value to compound states of affairs, consisting in states of increases in advantages and states of advantage levels at which they fall. Since the move from $(10, 5)$ to $(5, 5)$ does not involve the creation of any additional such compound states, this move holds none of what prioritarians noninstrumentally value. Accordingly, prioritarians are not committed to the claim that leveling down is in one respect better and may simply deny that (3) says anything interesting about their value commitments.

Where prioritarians have argued that (only) egalitarianism is vulnerable to the leveling down objection, some egalitarians have recently argued that prioritarianism does not really capture the separateness of persons (Otsuka and Voorhoeve 2009). Consider the following pair of cases. In the first, *one-person case*, Adrian will either develop a slight impairment or (equiprobably) a very severe impairment. Both impairments can be treated but the treatment for the slight impairment would give rise to a slightly greater benefit for Adrian. In the second, *two-person case*, Bill will develop the slight impairment and Caroline the severe impairment, and the treatment of Bill would give rise to a slightly greater benefit. According to Otsuka and Voorhoeve, prioritarianism implies that Adrian should be treated for the very severe impairment (because if he turns out to have this impairment, he will be worse off) and Caroline should be treated rather than Bill—where this combination of claims fails to respect the difference between intra- and interpersonal trade-offs. Elaborating on their original account, Otsuka argues that the separateness of persons is violated in two respects. First, prioritarianism is insensitive to the existence of a prudential justification in (only) the one-person case, according to which the treatment of the less severe impairment can be justified to Adrian by pointing out that this treatment would maximize his expected advantage (Otsuka 2012: 368). After all, prioritarianism implies that he should not receive this treatment. Second, prioritarianism is insensitive to the introduction of competing claims of different individuals since when we go from the one-person to the two-person case, it does not provide an additional reason to provide the treatment for the severe impairment, stemming from the fact that Caroline is *worse off than* Bill (Otsuka 2012: 371).

Now, as pointed out in section 14.2, there are different versions of the separateness of persons, where the prioritarian version claims that it is unacceptable to impose unjustified costs on an individual for which she is not compensated, where "unjustified costs" are costs that cannot be justified with reference to the prioritarian weighting function. Naturally, prioritarianism satisfies the separateness of persons in this sense, which explains why for example (5, 5) is better than (9, 1) (cf. Porter 2012).

Nevertheless, let us consider the two respects in which Otsuka considers prioritarianism incompatible with the separateness of persons. And while it is not as straightforward as they suggest, let us assume for the sake of argument Otsuka and Voorhoeve's claim that prioritarianism implies that it is better to treat Adrian for the more severe impairment. Regarding the insensitivity of prioritarianism to competing claims, a couple of responses seem to be available to prioritarians. First, keeping in mind the distinction between different kinds of justification of distributive principles mentioned above, presumably some will be unimpressed by the merits of a claim-based approach and will invoke, for example, a value-based justification of prioritarianism, pointing out that this account implies a symmetrical treatment of one-person and two-person cases. That is, if distributions are to be justified on the basis of values and the moral value of an advantage depends only on its size and the level at which it falls, there is no basis for saying that the presence of competing claims in the second case introduces an asymmetry in our moral assessment of the two cases.

Second, prioritarians may emphasize that we should be careful not to conflate the distinction between claim-based and non-claim-based accounts, and between relational and nonrelational accounts, of fairness. Thus, prioritarians who are attracted to a claim-based account may invoke the distinction made earlier between claim-within-outcome and claim-across-outcome conceptions and argue that the latter is more plausible and, unlike the former, does not involve a commitment to relational justice present only in cases involving different individuals. Indeed, while Otsuka (2012: 370–71) appeals to Thomas Nagel's claim-based account of fairness, Adler (2012: 329–37) has argued that Nagel's account is best viewed as a claim-across-outcome account, not a claim-within-outcome account. Furthermore, according to Adler, the former account is more plausible in that it can be used to justify the Pareto principle and, in fact, it is a premise in his argument for why we should support prioritarianism rather than egalitarianism.

As regards Otsuka's point that prioritarianism ignores the significance of prudential justification, prioritarians may point out that this has nothing in particular to do with one-person versus two-person cases. Consider a version of the two-person case in which we may either provide a treatment for the more or the less severe impairment, where both Bill and Caroline face a 50 percent chance of developing the slight impairment, a 50 percent chance of developing the more severe impairment, and where they will not develop the same condition. In this case, a prudential justification can be given to both Bill and Caroline for providing the slightly more beneficial treatment for the less severe impairment. Thus, insensitivity to prudential justification is not a problem to which prioritarianism is uniquely vulnerable in virtue of, unlike egalitarianism, applying to one-person outcomes. After all, egalitarianism does not attach any significance to prudential justification and, indeed, does not distinguish between this new case and the original version of the two-person case—in both it recommends minimizing inequality and so opting for the treatment for the severe impairment. Furthermore, prioritarians may argue that it is not prioritarianism's symmetrical, but Otsuka's asymmetrical, treatment of the one-person case and this new version of the two-person case that is implausible (Parfit 2012: 413–16; cf. Otsuka 2012: 373–74). After all, this new version is simply an extension of the one-person case in which a second individual faces the same possible outcomes and probabilities as the first person. This extension may not seem to make different responses to the cases appropriate.

14.5. Worries about Aggregation

There are different dimensions in which distributive views may aggregate. Two of the most important are advantage levels and numbers of individuals. We aggregate across advantage levels if we claim that a benefit to a worse-off individual can be outweighed by a (sufficiently large) benefit to a better-off individual. And we aggregate across numbers of individuals if we claim that a benefit to one individual can be outweighed by (equal) benefits to each of two or more individuals. Some of the most troubling cases of aggregation involve both kinds. So consider a case in which, by imposing a large loss on a worse-off individual, we can ensure small gains for a large number of better-off individuals. Both utilitarianism and prioritarianism imply that if only *enough* individuals benefit, benefits to them outweigh the benefit to the worse-off individual, no matter (1) how small the benefits to the better-off individuals, (2) how large the benefit to the worse-off individual, (3) how well off the better-off individuals are, and (4) how badly off the worse-off individual is. Furthermore, some versions of Paretian egalitarianism also imply this (depending on how much weight is assigned to efficiency). Intuitively, then, it may seem that these distributive principles do not give enough priority to the worse off.

Such cases may seem to suggest that leximin offers a more plausible account, since it refuses to aggregate in this way. Thus, it implies that it is better to benefit the worse-off individual, because he has lexical priority over the rest. However, the nonaggregative tenets of leximin may in fact seem too excessive (McKerlie 1994). Consider first levels. Because it gives lexical priority to the worst off, it implies that an arbitrarily small benefit to the worst off individual outweighs an arbitrarily large benefit to the second-worst off, even though the latter may be only marginally better off. Then consider numbers. Leximin implies that a small benefit to the worst off individual outweighs great benefits to an arbitrarily large number of second-worst off individuals.

It may therefore seem as if a principle less aggregative than utilitarianism, prioritarianism and (some versions of) Paretian egalitarianism, but more aggregative than leximin is called for. However, attempts to develop such principles face a number of difficulties (Fleurbaey, Tungodden, and Vallentyne 2008), and so it is not clear that aggregation across levels and numbers poses a conclusive objection to principles that exhibit these features. Furthermore, it may be worth recalling that prioritarianism can be rendered arbitrarily close to leximin as regards giving priority to the worst off, as indeed may Paretian egalitarianism. (See also chapter 17 in this volume, by Matthew Adler, for a much more detailed account of the worries about aggregation considered in this section.)

Acknowledgments

For comments on an earlier version of the chapter, I would like to thank Nir Eyal, Iwao Hirose, Kasper Lippert-Rasmussen, Jonas Olson, Alex Voorhoeve, and participants at a workshop on political philosophy at Roskilde University, 2013.

Notes

1. What I here refer to as "noninstrumental" value, others refer to as "intrinsic" or "final" value. It is the value something has for its own sake, rather than because it tends to produce some other value.
2. Since, in the present chapter, I am concerned only with fixed populations, I can ignore average utilitarianism since in this domain its implications do not differ from those of total utilitarianism.
3. However, for a good argument for preferring a characterization that assigns disvalue to inequality, see Persson (2001: 31).

References

Adler, M. (2012). *Well-Being and Fair Distribution: Beyond Cost-Benefit Analysis*. Oxford: Oxford University Press.
Arneson, R. J. (1989). "Equality and Equal Opportunity for Welfare." *Philosophical Studies* 56 (1): 77–93.
Brandt, R. (1979). *A Theory of the Good and the Right*. Oxford: Clarendon Press.
Brink, D. (1993). "The Separateness of Persons, Distributive Norms, and Moral Theory." In R. G. Frey and C. W. Morris (eds.), *Value, Welfare and Morality*. Cambridge: Cambridge University Press, 252–89.
Broome, J. (1991). *Weighing Goods*. Oxford: Basil Blackwell.
Broome, J. (2002). "Respects and Leveling Down." http://users.ox.ac.uk/~sfop0060/pdf/respects%20and%20levelling%20down.pdf.
Broome, J. (Forthcoming). "Equality versus Priority: A Useful Distinction." In D. Wikler and C. J. L. Murray (eds.), *"Goodness" and "Fairness": Ethical Issues in Health Resource Allocation*. Geneva: World Health Organization.
Cohen, G. A. (1989). "On the Currency of Egalitarian Justice." *Ethics* 99: 906–44.
Doran, B. (2001). "Reconsidering the Levelling Down Objection against Egalitarianism." *Utilitas* 13 (1): 65–85.

Dworkin, R. (1981). "What Is Equality? Part 2: Equality of Resources." *Philosophy and Public Affairs* 10 (4): 283–345.
Fleurbaey, M. (Forthcoming). "Equality versus Priority: How Relevant Is the Distinction?" In D. Wickler and C. J. L. Murray (eds.), *"Goodness" and "Fairness": Ethical Issues in Health Resource Allocation*. Geneva: World Health Organization.
Fleurbaey, M., B. Tungodden, and P. Vallentyne. (2008). "On the Possibility of Non-aggregative Priority for the Worst Off." *Social Philosophy and Policy* 26 (1): 255–85.
Hare, R. (1981). *Moral Thinking*. Oxford: Clarendon Press.
Harman, G. (1977). *The Nature of Morality*. New York: Oxford University Press.
Harsanyi, J. C. (1982). "Morality and the Theory of Rational Behaviour." In A. Sen and B. Williams (eds.), *Utilitarianism and Beyond*. Cambridge: Cambridge University Press.
Hirose, I. (2015). *Egalitarianism*. London: Routledge.
Holtug, N. (2003). "Good for Whom?" *Theoria* 69 (1–2): 4–20.
Holtug, N. (2007). "A Note on Conditional Egalitarianism." *Economics and Philosophy* 23 (1): 45–63.
Holtug, N. (2010). *Persons, Interests, and Justice*. Oxford: Oxford University Press.
Lerner, A. (1944). *The Economics of Control*. New York: Macmillan.
Mason, A. (2001). "Egalitarianism and the Levelling Down Objection." *Analysis* 61 (3): 246–54.
McKerlie, D. (1994). "Equality and Priority." *Utilitas* 6 (1): 25–42.
Nagel, T. (1970). *The Possibility of Altruism*. New York: Oxford University Press.
Norman, R. (1998). "The Social Basis of Equality." In A. Mason (ed.), *Ideals of Equality*. Oxford: Blackwell, 37–51.
Nozick, R. (1974). *Anarchy, State, and Utopia*. New York: Basic Books.
Otsuka, M. (2012). "Prioritarianism and the Separateness of Persons." *Utilitas* 24 (3): 365–80.
Otsuka, M., and A. Voorhoeve. (2009). "Why It Matters That Some Are Worse Off Than Others: An Argument against the Priority View." *Philosophy and Public Affairs* 37 (2): 171–99.
Parfit, D. (2000 [1991]). *Equality or Priority?* The Lindley Lecture, University of Kansas. Reprinted in M. Clayton and A. Williams (eds.), *The Ideal of Equality*. Basingstoke: Macmillan, 81–125.
Parfit, D. (2012). "Another Defence of the Priority View." *Utilitas* 24 (3): 399–440.
Persson, I. (2001). "Equality, Priority and Person-Affecting Value." *Ethical Theory and Moral Practice* 4 (1): 23–39.
Persson, I. (2008). "Why Levelling Down Could Be Worse for Prioritarianism Than for Egalitarianism." *Ethical Theory and Moral Practice* 11 (3): 295–303.
Porter, T. (2012). "In Defence of the Priority View." *Utilitas* 24 (3): 197–206.
Rawls, J. (1971). *A Theory of Justice*. Cambridge: Belknap Press of Harvard University Press.
Sen, A. (1980). "Equality of What?" In S. McMurrin (ed.), *Tanner Lectures on Human Values*. Cambridge: Cambridge University Press, 353–69.
Sen, A. (1997). *On Economic Inequality*, 2nd ed. Oxford: Clarendon Press.
Singer, P. (1993). *Practical Ethics*. Cambridge: Cambridge University Press.
Temkin, L. (1993a). *Inequality*. New York: Oxford University Press.
Tungodden, B. (2003). "The Value of Equality." *Economics and Philosophy* 19 (1): 1–44.

CHAPTER 15

ORGANIC UNITIES

ERIK CARLSON

15.1. G. E. Moore's Notion of an Organic Unity

THE starting point of the discussion of organic unities in contemporary value theory is G. E. Moore's *Principia Ethica*, published in 1903.[1] Because of its great influence, it is appropriate to quote in full the passage where Moore introduces the concept of an organic unity:

> There is . . . a vast number of different things, each of which has intrinsic value; there are also very many which are positively bad; and there is a still larger class of things, which appear to be indifferent. But a thing belonging to any of these three classes may occur as part of a whole, which includes among its other parts other things belonging both to the same and to the other two classes; and these wholes, as such, may also have intrinsic value. The paradox, to which it is necessary to call attention, is that *the value of such a whole bears no regular proportion to the sum of the values of its parts*. It is certain that a good thing may exist in such a relation to another good thing that the value of the whole thus formed is immensely greater than the sum of the values of the two good things. It is certain that a whole formed of a good thing and an indifferent thing may have immensely greater value than that good thing itself possesses. It is certain that two bad things or a bad thing and an indifferent thing may form a whole much worse than the sum of badness of its parts. And it seems as if indifferent things may also be the sole constituents of a whole which has great value, either positive or negative. Whether the addition of a bad thing to a good whole may increase the positive value of the whole, or the addition of a bad thing to a bad may produce a whole having positive value, may seem more doubtful; but it is, at least, possible, and this possibility must be taken into account in our ethical investigations. However we may decide particular questions, the principle is clear. *The value of a whole must not be assumed to be the same as the sum of the values of its parts.* (Moore 1903: 27–28; italics in the original)

Moore goes on to point out that there is no established name for this "peculiar relation between part and whole," and proposes the term "organic" to denote the relation, and "organic unity" or "organic whole" to denote a whole of the relevant kind. Thus, he states that he shall use the term "organic" "to denote the fact that a whole has an intrinsic value different in amount from the sum of the values of its parts" (Moore 1903: 36).

One of Moore's favorite examples of an organic unity is being conscious of a beautiful object:

> It seems to be true that to be conscious of a beautiful object is a thing of great intrinsic value; whereas the same object, if no one be conscious of it, has certainly comparatively little value. . . . But the consciousness of a beautiful object is certainly a whole of some sort in which we can distinguish as parts the object on the one hand and the being conscious on the other. . . . [And] mere consciousness does not always confer great value upon the whole of which it forms a part. (Moore 1903: 28)

Another example employed by Moore is retributive punishment. This consists of two parts, namely, the crime committed and the punishment suffered. Each of these parts is bad, according to Moore, but their combination is good "as a whole," since it means that justice is carried out.[2]

As is evident from the above quotations, Moore regards his principle of organic unities as a thesis about *intrinsic* value. Intrinsic value, in Moore's sense, supervenes solely on the intrinsic properties of its bearers. If a thing has *final* value, that is, value *for its own sake*, or *as an end*, this value is always, Moore holds, intrinsic. (See Moore 1922b: 260.) A number of philosophers have argued, in opposition to Moore, that final value may supervene on extrinsic properties of its bearers, and is hence another category than intrinsic value. (See, e.g., Korsgaard 1983, or Rabinowicz and Rønnow-Rasmussen 1999.) This issue has important ramifications for how to best understand the notion of an organic unity, and we will return to it in section 15.4. Until then, let us go along with Moore's assumption that intrinsic value is the relevant category of value.

Moore does not say much about how the terms "part" and "whole" should be understood. If we are to get as clear as possible about his principle of organic unities, some discussion of this is necessary. First, it is clear that by "part," Moore means *proper* part. He would not claim that a whole is an organic unity whenever its value is not equal or proportional to the sum of the values of its proper parts *plus* the value of the whole itself.

Second, a "whole" should presumably be understood as a value bearer that has at least one proper part that is itself a value bearer.[3] That is to say, at least one part is either intrinsically good, intrinsically bad, or intrinsically neutral.[4] Without this restriction, any value bearer that is made up solely of parts lacking intrinsic value would be an organic unity. This is hardly what Moore intends. His calling the principle of organic unities a "paradox" indicates that it is not merely the claim that intrinsic value is an emergent property, requiring a certain degree of complexity in its bearers (cf. Zimmerman 2001: 136).

Third, the exact sense in which one bearer of intrinsic value can be a part of another probably depends on what kinds of entities have intrinsic value in general.[5] Since this question cannot be discussed here, let us simply assume that there is some way of concatenating value bearers into more complex value bearers, that is, wholes or unities. Let ○ denote this operation of concatenation. Thus, $a \circ b$ denotes a complex value bearer, having a and b as parts.[6] If all value bearers are states of affairs, ○ can perhaps be identified with conjunction, or somehow defined in terms of entailment.[7] If, for example, material objects can also be value bearers, ○ might be mereological fusion.

Fourth, Moore should be understood as claiming that there are wholes whose value does not equal, or is not even proportional to, the sum of the values of the members of a partition of the whole into *jointly exhaustive* and *mutually exclusive* parts. Consider a simple form of hedonism, assigning intrinsic value to states of affairs, understanding ○ as conjunction, and claiming that the intrinsic value of a state equals the amount of net pleasure it contains. Suppose that Alf, Beth, and Cecil all feel pleasure (to a certain degree at a certain time), and let a = *Alf feels pleasure*, b = *Beth feels pleasure*, and c = *Cecil feels pleasure*. The value of the complex state $a \circ b \circ c$ is then, according to this form of hedonism, equal to the sum of the values of a, b, and c. Since $a \circ b$, $a \circ c$, and $b \circ c$ are also proper parts of $a \circ b \circ c$, summing the values of *all* proper parts of the latter state would yield the wrong answer, as regards its value.[8] Surely, the fact that the value of $a \circ b \circ c$ does not equal the sum of the values of all its proper parts does not show that it is an organic unity.

As can be gathered from the first quotation above, Moore vacillates between two nonequivalent definitions of organicity. According to the first definition, a whole is organic if and only if its value is not *proportional* to the sum of the values of its parts. Let us call this definition the "nonproportionality definition." According to the second definition, which we may label the "nonidentity definition," a whole is organic if and only if its value is not *identical* to the sum of the values of its parts.[9] Assuming that Moore uses "proportional" in its standard mathematical sense, the nonproportionality definition can be more precisely expressed as follows: there is no numerical constant $k \neq 0$, such that, for any whole W, the intrinsic value of W equals kS_W, where S_W is the sum of the values of W's proper parts.[10]

Organicity according to Moore's nonproportionality definition implies organicity according to his nonidentity definition, but not conversely. It seems that only the definiens of the nonidentity definition is consistent with all the purported instances of organicity listed by Moore in the first quoted passage. His first example is that "a good thing may exist in such a relation to another good thing that the value of the whole thus formed is immensely greater than the sum of the values of the two good things." This does not imply organicity in the nonproportionality sense. If the value of a whole were always a million times, say, greater than the sum of the values of its parts, it would still be proportional to this sum.[11]

This may suggest that the nonidentity definition better captures Moore's intentions. But this is doubtful. He regards it as a consequence of the principle of organic unities that a whole can be improved by the omission of a good part:

> It follows from [the principle of organic unities] that, though in order to obtain the greatest possible sum of values in its parts, the Ideal [i.e., the best state of things

conceivable] would necessarily contain all the things which have intrinsic value in any degree, yet the whole which contained all these parts might not be so valuable as some other whole, from which certain positive goods were omitted. (Moore 1903: 184)

This is clearly not possible if there is a natural number n, such that the value of a whole is always n times greater than the sum of the values of its parts. Hence, the definiens of the nonidentity definition appears not to state a sufficient condition for organicity, as Moore himself conceives of this notion.

Moore thus seems to contradict himself. First, he claims that if the value of a whole is very much greater than the sum of the values of its parts, this whole is an organic unity. Second, he claims that if a whole is an organic unity, it is not necessarily made better by the addition of a good part. The mutual inconsistency of these claims can be seen by assuming, again, an axiological principle to the effect that the value of any possible whole is a million times the sum of the values of its parts. Given this principle, Moore's first claim implies, for any given whole, that it is an organic unity, while his second claim implies that it is not.

There may be more charitable interpretations of Moore's claims. Perhaps he just means that both claims are true of any *plausible* axiology that contains organic unities. (The axiological principle assumed in the last paragraph is surely not very plausible.) There is, however, an even more fundamental problem with Moore's definitions. A statement to the effect that the value of a certain thing is, or is not, equal or proportional to the sum of the values of certain other things is meaningful only if value can be measured on a ratio scale.[12] An ordinal, or even an interval scale, is not sufficient.[13] Paradigm examples of ratio scale measurement, such as measurement of length and mass, are also examples of "additive" measurement, in the sense that the value of a whole *is* always represented as the sum of the values of its parts. This presupposes an operation of concatenation that is structurally similar to the arithmetical operation of addition. Letting $\gtrsim$ and $\sim$ denote the relations "at least as F as" and "equally F as," where F is the property measured, the following three conditions must hold, for all items a, b, and c:

Monotonicity: $a \gtrsim b$ if and only if $a \circ c \gtrsim b \circ c$ if and only if $c \circ a \gtrsim c \circ b$.
Associativity: $a \circ (b \circ c) \sim (a \circ b) \circ c$.
Commutativity: $a \circ b \sim b \circ a$.[14]

If $\gtrsim$ is a transitive and complete relation, and an "Archimedean" condition is satisfied, the listed conditions imply that there is a real-valued function f, such that, for all a and b, (1) $f(a) \geq f(b)$ if and only if $a \gtrsim b$, and (2) $f(a \circ b) = f(a) + f(b)$ (see Krantz et al. 2007: 73–74). Further, another function g satisfies properties (1) and (2) if and only if g is a "similarity transformation" of f; that is, there is a real number $x > 0$, such that, for all a, $g(a) = xf(a)$. This is the defining characteristic of a ratio scale.

Hence, if the relations "at least as intrinsically good as" and "equal in intrinsic value to" satisfy monotonicity, associativity, and commutativity, it is not unlikely that intrinsic value is measurable on a ratio scale. It would then be meaningful to compare the value of a whole to the sum of the values of its parts. But this would also imply that the value of the whole is identical to this sum, and hence that there are no organic unities, according to Moore's definitions. On the other hand, if the conditions in question are not satisfied, intrinsic value cannot be measured on an additive ratio scale. If not, Moore's definitions of an organic unity threaten to make no sense, since the value of a whole cannot meaningfully be compared to the sum of the values of its parts. This indicates that Moore's principle of organic unities is either false or meaningless.[15]

On the face of it, there are fairly strong grounds for concluding that meaninglessness is the right verdict. Many plausible axiologies violate monotonicity. To borrow a case from Roderick Chisholm, exemplifying a principle he calls *bonum variationis*, suppose that a and c are two identical beautiful paintings, and that b is a beautiful piece of music. Suppose also that the intrinsic value of contemplating a is at least equal to the intrinsic value of contemplating b. It nevertheless seems plausible that the whole consisting in the contemplation of b and c is intrinsically better than the whole consisting in the contemplation of a and c. Intuitively, the fact that $b \circ c$ offers more *variation* than $a \circ c$ is important. In Chisholm's words, "other things being equal, it is better to combine two dissimilar goods than to combine two similar goods" (Chisholm 1986: 70–71).

Another putative counterexample to monotonicity is given by Sven Danielsson. The whole consisting of Alf's committing a crime and Alf being punished may be intrinsically better (less bad) than the whole made up of Beth's committing the crime and Alf being punished, even if Alf's committing the crime is, in itself, equal in value to Beth's committing the crime (Danielsson 1997: 32).[16] It is not hard to multiply examples.

If the concatenation operation involves a temporal or causal relation, plausible counterexamples to associativity and commutativity can also be found. Suppose that $a \circ b$ implies that a is succeeded in time by b, and consider the principle, called *bonum progressionis* by Chisholm, that a whole consisting of a less good thing, a, followed in time by a better thing, b, is intrinsically better than the whole consisting of b followed by a (Chisholm 1986: 71). Thus, letting $>$ symbolize "intrinsically strictly better than," $a \circ b > b \circ a$, which violates commutativity. Or consider retributive punishment again. It would be a plausible claim that the positive value of such punishment presupposes that the crime precedes the punishment in time. For a third example, assume that $a \circ b$ is defined as "a put on top of b." The aesthetic value of $a \circ b$ may then be very different from that of $b \circ a$, if a is a porcelain vase, and b is a slab of marble.

Concerning associativity, suppose that parentheses indicate the temporal order of concatenation. Simultaneously contemplating a painting, a, and a piece of music b, and later contemplating another piece of music, c, may be intrinsically better than simultaneously contemplating b and c, and then contemplating a. Or, as anyone who has tried to thicken a sauce knows, mixing flour and butter, and then adding some milk, is apt to yield a result that differs at least in culinary value from that of adding flour to a mixture of milk and butter.

If violations of monotonicity, in particular, are pervasive, there would seem to be little connection between the ordering of things, in terms of intrinsic value, and the concatenation operation. Since not all ratio scales are based on concatenation,[17] it is still conceivable that a ratio scale for intrinsic value can be obtained. As far as I know, however, nobody has advanced any reason to believe that this is so. It would be very remarkable if a structure essentially involving a concatenation operation were to yield a ratio scale, for reasons having nothing to do with this operation.[18] And more particular reasons for doubt are not hard to find. A standard real-number ratio scale requires, for example, that all items are comparable in terms of intrinsic value, and that no items are lexicographically superior to any other items. These assumptions have been denied by a great number of value theorists.[19]

15.2. Moore's Additivity Principle

Let us for the moment assume, however, that Moore's principle of organic unities is meaningful and true. Suppose, thus, that intrinsic values can be meaningfully summed, but that the value of a whole sometimes differs from the sum of the values of its proper parts. Many philosophers have, understandably, taken this to entail that intrinsic value is not subject to additive measurement. This seems not to be Moore's view, however. He claims that the intrinsic value of a whole is "equivalent to the sum of the value which it possesses *as a whole, together with* the intrinsic values which may belong to any of its parts" (1903: 214; Moore's italics). "Value as a whole" Moore defines as "[t]hat value which arises solely *from the combination* of two or more things" (1903: 215; Moore's italics). That is to say, if something has value as a whole, this is due to a holistic effect, which confers on the thing in question a certain value that cannot be reduced to the values of its proper parts. Thus, for example, Moore holds that

> [i]f it is true that the combined existence of two evils may yet constitute a less evil than would be constituted by the existence of either singly, it is plain that this can only be because there arises from the combination a positive good which is greater than the *difference* between the sum of the two evils and the demerit of either singly: this positive good would then be the value of the whole, *as a whole*. (1903: 215; italics in the original)

Assuming that intrinsic values can be meaningfully added, Moore's additivity principle would be trivial if "value as a whole" were simply treated as synonymous to "the difference between a thing's total intrinsic value and the sum of the intrinsic values of its parts." But the passages quoted in the previous paragraph indicate that Moore takes a thing's value as a whole to be a genuine instance of intrinsic value.[20] Thus interpreted, his additivity principle appears to be a substantial claim about the aggregation of intrinsic value. Since it presupposes the meaningfulness of summing intrinsic values, however, the principle is problematic for the same reasons that Moore's definitions of an organic unity are problematic.

Sven Danielsson has provided an interesting attempt to rescue Moore's additivity principle, in the face of organic unities. Danielsson notes that there is a close affinity between Moore's notion of intrinsic value as a whole, and the frequently discussed notion of *basic* intrinsic value.[21] Intuitively, a thing's basic intrinsic value is that part of its intrinsic value which is not derived from any of its proper parts. Utilizing the notion of basic value, Danielsson conjectures that an additive ratio scale for intrinsic value can under certain conditions be obtained, even if the monotonicity condition does not hold in general. His suggestion is that a thing's intrinsic value equals the sum of the *basic* intrinsic values of its (proper or improper) parts (Danielsson 1997: 33). As Danielsson acknowledges, however, quite strong structural assumptions have to be made in order to derive a ratio scale representation. These assumptions are not true in every plausible axiology.

15.3. Alternative Definitions of an Organic Unity

As we have seen, Moore's definitions of an organic unity make doubtful sense. Moreover, they do not seem to capture the notion of organicity he has in mind, even assuming that we can meaningfully sum intrinsic values. For example, his definitions do not imply that a whole can be made better by removing a good part, although he explicitly states that this follows from the principle of organic unities. Although most value theorists who have discussed organic unities have accepted one of Moore's definitions, a number of authors have suggested definitions of organicity that do not rely on a "sum" of values. Let us look at a few such proposals, and try to discern some underlying ideas.

Lewis White Beck suggests the following "refinement" of Moore's principle of organic unities: "The rank order of valuableness of any two things may vary according to the value of the wholes of which they are parts, and this variation in choiceworthiness is the sole criterion of the reality of an objective whole of values" (Beck 1941: 10; in the original, the whole sentence is italicized).

C. D. Broad claims that the principle of organic unities can be stated as follows: (1) It may be a good- or bad-making property of a whole, $a \circ b$, that it consists of a and b interrelated in a certain order by a certain relation R. (2) It may be a good- or bad-making characteristic of a that it stands in R to b. (3) It may be a good- or bad-making characteristic of b that it stands in the converse of R to a (Broad 1985: 256).

Chisholm defines a *mixed whole* as a whole that either has both good and bad parts, or is neutral and has either a good or a bad part. A whole is *unmixed* if and only if it is not mixed. A whole is an *organic unity* if and only if it is either (1) mixed and has no unmixed parts such that it falls in value between them, or (2) unmixed and has a good part that is better than it or a bad part that is worse than it (Chisholm 1986: 75).

This definition of an organic unity is problematic, since the definiens is not satisfied by some types of wholes which Chisholm himself takes to be organic unities (see Lemos 1994: 198–99). Consider again the *bonum variationis* case of the two identical paintings, a and c, and the piece of music, b. The whole consisting of the contemplation of b and c is unmixed and has no good part that is better than it (nor a bad part that is worse than it). Hence it is not an organic unity, according to Chisholm's definition.

Peter Vallentyne suggests that an axiology is organic if and only if it implies that "the relative ranking of two states of affairs may depend on the parts that they have in common" (Vallentyne 1988: 95). In a similar vein, I have myself proposed that an axiology should be defined as organic if and only if it violates monotonicity (Carlson 1997a: 57).

Noah Lemos, finally, finds a satisfactory definition of organicity elusive, but believes that, inter alia, the following conditions hold: (1) if an intrinsically bad whole has only good or neutral parts, then it is an organic unity; (2) if an intrinsically good whole has only bad or neutral parts, then it is an organic unity; (3) if two wholes have the same parts but differ in intrinsic value, then at least one of the wholes is an organic unity (Lemos 1998: 324).

On the basis of the cited suggestions, several putative criteria of organicity can be distinguished. Four such criteria will be discussed in the remainder of this section, and a fifth one in the next section. The first criterion, corresponding roughly to Broad's first clause and to Lemos's last clause, is that the "order" or "arrangement" of the parts within a whole may affect the value of the whole. A natural interpretation of this claim is that associativity or commutativity, or both, fail to hold:

First criterion for organicity: Associativity or commutativity is false.

The second criterion is that monotonicity fails to hold, implying that a whole may be improved by replacing a better part by a worse part:

Second criterion for organicity: Monotonicity is false.

This is my own earlier definition, and it is very similar to Vallentyne's. Furthermore, it is at least hinted at by Chisholm's definition.

The third criterion does not correspond exactly to any of the cited suggestions, but it expresses, I believe, an intuitive notion of organicity or value holism. Let S be a set of value bearers that are atomic, in the sense of not being concatenations of other value bearers. Further, let $S\circ$ be the superset of S containing the members of S and all their concatenations.[22] Assume also that the value differences between the elements of S can be at least partially ordered, and let the "value status" of a value bearer denote whether it is good, bad, or neutral. The third criterion is as follows:

Third criterion for organicity: The value ordering of S∘ is not a function only of the value ordering of S, the ordering of the value differences in S, and the respective value status of the members of S.

The fourth criterion is the idea expressed by Lemos's first two clauses:

Fourth criterion for organicity: A whole can be good (bad) although it has no good (bad) proper part.

The first three criteria, at least, are logically independent of each other. It is possible for an axiology to satisfy any one of these criteria without satisfying the other two, as well as to satisfy any two of the criteria without satisfying the third. To see that the first two criteria may hold in the absence of the third, consider an axiology according to which "antiassociativity": $a \circ (b \circ c) > (a \circ b) \circ c$, and "antimonotonicity": $a > b$ if and only if $b \circ c > a \circ c$, generally hold. The entire value ordering may then be determined by the ordering of the atomic value bearers (together with their value status and the ordering of the value differences), although monotonicity and associativity both fail to hold.

To see that the third criterion may hold in the absence of the first two, note that if $a > b > c > d$, the conjunction of monotonicity, associativity, and commutativity is not sufficient to determine the value relation between $a \circ d$ and $b \circ c$. This is so even if we add information about the ordering of the value differences between the atomic value bearers, and about their value status.

Whether the fourth criterion is logically independent of the first three depends on disputed issues concerning the logical connections between the monadic value properties of goodness, badness, and neutrality, on the one hand, and the dyadic betterness relation, on the other.

I surmise that all value theorists would agree that an axiology which satisfies the first three of the above criteria is properly called organic. Hence, the conjunction of these criteria may be regarded as a sufficient condition of organicity. Furthermore, any *plausible* axiology fulfilling the fourth criterion also fulfills the second. To see this, suppose that $a \circ b$ is good, while a and b are neutral or bad. Hence, for any neutral thing c, $c \gtrsim a$. If monotonicity holds, therefore, $c \circ b \gtrsim a \circ b$. This means that there is a neutral or bad thing, namely, b, such that *any* whole consisting of this thing and a neutral thing is good.[23] This is quite implausible, to put it mildly. Similarly, it is a safe conjecture that any plausible axiology that satisfies one of the first two criteria also satisfies the third. It seems that very strange principles, such as "antiassociativity" or "antimonotonicity," are required for an axiology to violate the third criterion if it satisfies either of the first two.

This suggests that the fourth criterion, at least, is by itself sufficient for organicity. I would hold that this is true also of the second criterion. The sufficiency of the first and the third criteria appears somewhat more disputable. Are any of the four criteria *necessary* for organicity? As we shall now see, there is reason to doubt this, at least if we are prepared to question the Moorean view of intrinsic value.

15.4. CONTEXTUALISM VERSUS MOOREAN HOLISM

The fifth and final criterion for organicity we shall discern corresponds, at least roughly, to Beck's definition, and to Broad's last two clauses:

Fifth criterion for organicity: The value of a part may depend on its relations to other parts of the whole.[24]

As we noted in section 15.1, Moore thought that all final value is intrinsic value, in the sense of supervening solely on intrinsic properties of its bearers. This view is occasionally, and for obvious reasons, called "intrinsicalism." The fifth criterion is incompatible with intrinsicalism. It presupposes the opposing view, which we may label "nonintrinsicalism," claiming that a thing's final value may supervene partly on its extrinsic properties. *Pace* Beck and Broad, nonintrinsicality is not a *necessary* condition for organicity. It is surely consistent to claim, with Moore, that the final value of a part stays the same no matter what whole it enters into, and define organicity in terms of one or more of the first four criteria we discussed (or some other criterion).

Nor is it entirely plausible, I think, to regard nonintrinsicality as *sufficient* for organicity. Some instances of nonintrinsicality do not seem to exemplify the kind of holism involved in an intuitive notion of organicity. Consider an axiology according to which Leonardo da Vinci's pen is finally good because it has belonged to a universal genius. This does not seem to imply that this axiology is organic. Similarly for the view that some rare items have final value because of their rarity. On this view, a rare stamp may be finally valuable on the condition that there are very few other stamps of the same kind. It is doubtful whether this should be regarded as a case of organicity.

Nonintrinsicalists typically explain organicity in terms of a thing's final value varying with the whole or context it is a part of (see Hurka 1998; Olson 2004). The examples in the last paragraph suggest that not every case of context-dependence is a case of organicity. Although Leonardo's pen would not be finally good in a context where it has not belonged to Leonardo, it is questionable whether the actual context, involving the pen and the fact about its past ownership, constitutes an organic unity. Similarly, it is unclear whether the rare stamp, in combination with the fact that there are few others like it, make up an organic unity. It may be suggested that the reason why these cases are not examples of organic unities is that they involve only one value bearer, and therefore do not exemplify "wholes" in the relevant sense. But this cannot, it seems, be the whole explanation. It is just as doubtful whether the concatenation of Leonardo's pen and the rare stamp, together with the conjunctive fact that the pen has belonged to Leonardo and the stamp is rare, is an organic unity.[25]

Hence, if the nonintrinsicalist is to provide an explication of organicity in terms of the context-dependence of final value, he must either find a way to distinguish between relevant and irrelevant kinds of context-dependence, or make plausible that the examples I have found dubious are, after all, cases of organicity. If either of these strategies is workable, nonintrinsicalism opens up a way of understanding organicity, which need not appeal to criteria like the four we distinguished in the last section. Let "contextualism" denote this view, and let "Moorean holism" refer to the conjunction of intrinsicalism and acceptance of organic unities.[26] If contextualism is true, organicity is compatible with the conditions for additive ratio-scale measurement being satisfied in each specific context, or possible world. This means that organicity may hold although the value of a whole always equals the sum of the values of its parts, in a given context.

To illustrate the difference between Moorean holism and contextualism, we may once again make use of Chisholm's *bonum variationis* case. According to the Moorean holist, the value of the contemplation of a, b, and c, respectively, is the same no matter in what context it takes place. Hence, if the contemplation of b and c is better than the contemplation of a and c, this must be because the former has a value as a whole, not attributable to either of its parts, which the latter lacks. The contextualist, on the other hand, would claim that the contemplation of c is better if it takes place in the context of also contemplating b than if it occurs in the context of also contemplating a.

There is a fairly extensive debate about the respective merits of Moorean holism and contextualism,[27] and I shall not here try to determine which is the more plausible view. There is also an intermediate position, according to which some organic unities are best understood in the contextualist fashion, whereas Moorean holism is more adequate in other cases (see Hurka 1998).

15.5. ARE THERE ORGANIC UNITIES?

It appears that most philosophers discussing the issue have accepted the existence of organic unities, in either the Moorean holist or the contextualist version. As we have seen, alleged examples of organic unities abound. Moreover, on certain views about what kinds of entities can have intrinsic value, commitment to organic unities may seem difficult to avoid, irrespective of the details of one's substantial axiology. Material objects perhaps furnish the clearest examples. Suppose that the *Mona Lisa* is finally good, due to its aesthetic qualities. Is the left half of the *Mona Lisa* also finally good? If so, what about the upper left quarter? And so on. Assuming intrinsicalism, it is hardly plausible to claim that every square millimeter of the painting has aesthetic qualities that make it finally good. Hence, it seems that there must be at least one (proper or improper) part of the painting that is finally good although it has no finally good proper parts.[28] The fourth criterion for organicity is thus satisfied, and, if the axiology is otherwise plausible, so is the second criterion. A nonintrinsicalist may instead claim that every part of the painting *is* finally good, but only given the actual arrangement of the parts, making up the masterful portrait. If so, the fifth criterion for organicity is fulfilled. Analogous arguments can, it seems, be made concerning most ascriptions of final value to material objects. In general, it is not plausible to maintain that every tiny part of a valuable object is itself valuable, at least not independently of context.[29]

However, this type of argument rests on a presumption that can be denied. As stated in section 15.1, the principle of organic unities should be understood as applying only to wholes having at least one proper part that is a *value bearer*. Hence, the argument in the last paragraph presupposes that every part of the *Mona Lisa* is a value bearer, even though some parts may have neutral value. It could be maintained, however, that parts below a certain size are not value bearers at all, and hence do not even have neutral value. If so, they are not "parts" in the sense relevant to the principle of organic unities.

A parallel strategy is employed by Michael Zimmerman, in a subtle defense of an additive version of intrinsicalism (Zimmerman 2001: ch. 5). Zimmerman assigns final value only to concrete states of individual objects. He rebuts alleged examples of organic unities by claiming that many allegedly value-bearing states are in fact "evaluatively inadequate," in the sense of not being sufficiently rich or complex to have intrinsic value. Several philosophers have, for example, regarded instances of "pleasure in the bad" as organic unities. The state a = *Alf is pleased at Beth's pain* is, on this view, intrinsically bad, although it contains an intrinsically good part, namely, b = *Alf is pleased*, and no intrinsically bad proper part. (That Beth is in pain is, arguably, not a part of a, since Alf's belief that Beth is in pain may be false.) Zimmerman claims, however, that b is evaluatively inadequate, and that a, if it is indeed intrinsically bad, need not therefore be regarded as an organic unity. Other putative organic unities can, he believes, be handled in a similar way, by appealing to evaluative inadequacy. Repudiating organic unities, Zimmerman argues that intrinsic value can probably be measured on an additive ratio scale.

Zimmerman's view has met with criticism,[30] and I shall not here try to assess its merits. Arguably, examples such as the *bonum variationis* case are less easily rebutted by invoking evaluatively inadequate states. Zimmerman's proposal may nevertheless embody the most plausible general strategy for denying the existence of organic unities.

Acknowledgments

I am grateful to Sven Danielsson, Iwao Hirose, and Jonas Olson for helpful comments and discussion. Drafts of this chapter were presented at a seminar at Uppsala University, and at a workshop on the island of Reichenau, arranged by the University of Constance. On both occasions, the participants provided useful suggestions. Special thanks to Christoph Fehige, who also gave me written comments.

Notes

1. Arguably, Moore's principle of organic unities was anticipated by Franz Brentano, in writings from the 1890s. See Chisholm 1986: 69–70; and Rønnow-Rasmussen and Zimmerman 2005: xxxii.
2. See Moore 1903: 214. This view does not commit Moore to the implausible claim that the whole consisting of the crime and the punishment is good "on the whole." That is to say, this whole need not make the world better than it would have been if neither the crime nor the punishment had occurred. The distinction between value "as a whole" and "on the whole" is expounded in section 15.2.
3. It may seem that we should demand that a whole have at least *two* value bearers as proper parts. However, this would exclude some often cited examples of organic unities, such as the "pleasure in the bad" case mentioned in section 15.5.
4. I here assume, for the sake of simplicity, that every bearer of intrinsic value is either good, bad, or neutral. Actually, I think a case can be made for the existence also of evaluatively "indeterminate" value bearers. (See Carlson 1997a.)
5. Moore does not explicitly address this question in *Principia*, but he attributes intrinsic value to entities of diverse kinds, such as physical objects, experiences, and entities made up of a physical object and someone's awareness of it. He seems later to have changed his views on this matter. In the early 1920s, he writes: "One thing, I think, is clear about intrinsic value . . . namely that it is only actual occurrences, actual states of things over a certain period of time—not such things as men, or characters, or material things, that can have any intrinsic value at all" (Moore 1922a: 327).
6. We need not assume that ○ is closed in the set of value bearers, so that, for *all* value bearers a and b, $a \circ b$ is a value bearer. Furthermore, if there are organic unities with only one proper part that is a value bearer, we should perhaps allow some entities that are not value bearers to be concatenated with value bearers. Otherwise, some organic unities are not concatenations.
7. The entailment approach is adopted by, among others Chisholm 1986: 73; Lemos 1994: 33–34; and, with important modifications, Zimmerman 2001: 55.
8. Michael Zimmerman (2001: 155) believes that an appeal to "basic" intrinsic value (see section 15.2) is necessary in order to solve this problem of "overcounting." The partition idea provides a simpler solution. A complication arises, however, from the fact that any whole with more than two proper parts can be partitioned in several different ways. Suppose that the value of each of three value bearers a, b, and c is 5 (according to some unit of measurement), that the value of $a \circ b$ is 0, and that the value of $a \circ b \circ c$ is 15. Then $a \circ b \circ c$ should presumably be classified as an organic unity (as should $a \circ b$), although its value equals the sum of the values of the parts contained in the partition $\{a, b, c\}$. The reason why $a \circ b \circ c$ is nevertheless an organic unity is that there is another partition, viz. $\{a \circ b, c\}$, for which this additive property does not hold.
9. Although the nonproportionality definition (Moore 1903: 27) seems superseded by the nonidentity definition (1903: 28, 36), it reappears in *Principia*'s final chapter (1903: 184).
10. If inverse proportionality is also to be excluded, we should add the requirement that there is no constant $r \neq 0$, such that, for all wholes W, the intrinsic value of W equals r / S_W.
11. Possibly, Moore intends "immensely greater" to signify a literally infinite value difference, so that, for every natural number n, the whole is better than an object whose value is n times the sum of the values of its parts. In that case, the value of the whole would not be

proportional, in the usual sense, to this sum. There is nothing in Moore's discussion, however, that supports this rather far-fetched interpretation.
12. For an explanation of the measurement-theoretical notion of meaningfulness, or "uniqueness", see, e.g., Roberts 2009: ch. 2.
13. Another possible interpretation of Moore's principle of organic unities is that the value of a whole is not any numerical function of the values of its parts. For this claim, or its denial, to make sense, intrinsic value must be measurable on at least an interval scale. This construal of Moore's principle is therefore also problematic.
14. The latter two conditions are sometimes called "weak associativity" and "weak commutativity," since they do not require that $a \circ (b \circ c) = (a \circ b) \circ c$, or that $a \circ b = b \circ a$, respectively.
15. Moore cannot be blamed for being unaware of this problem, since the theory of measurement was still in its infancy when *Principia Ethica* was written. An early critic of Moore's definitions is Lewis White Beck, who claims that "the concept of 'sum of values' is meaningless," since "values like degrees of temperature . . . are ordinal numbers with no corresponding cardinal significance" (1941: 9). Beck gives no hint, however, why values cannot have "cardinal significance." (Incidentally, he is wrong in claiming that temperature is measured only on an ordinal scale.)
16. As noted above, the combination of crime and punishment is one of Moore's examples of organic unities.
17. The Kelvin temperature scale, which has a fixed zero point, is one exception.
18. There are nonassociative and noncommutative concatenation structures with ratio scale representations that are nonadditive; i.e., $f(a \circ b) = f(a) + f(b)$ does not hold in general (see Luce et al. 2007, chs. 19–20). However, these structures all satisfy monotonicity.
19. However, see Carlson 2008, 2010, 2011, for suggestions how to define nonstandard ratio scales for orders involving incomparability and lexicality.
20. He is, however, not entirely clear on this point. Zimmerman (2001: 160–61) interprets Moore as proposing the trivializing conception of value as a whole.
21. For discussions of basic intrinsic value, see, e.g., Feldman 2000; and Zimmerman 2001: ch. 5.
22. If there are no atomic value bearers, we can suppose the members of S to be atomic relative to S∘, in the sense that if a and b are in S, then $a \circ b$ is in S∘, and if c is in S∘, there is no d, such that $c \circ d$ is in S.
23. Assuming that all neutral things are equal in value, and that anything that is at least as good as some good thing is itself good.
24. What Beck explicitly says is that the value relation between two things may depend on the *value* of the whole of which they are parts. Given that value supervenes on nonevaluative properties, however, this implies dependence on the nonevaluative properties of the whole.
25. Moreover, as mentioned in note 3, there may be reasons for acknowledging organic unities which have only one proper part that is a value bearer.
26. Cf. the distinction between "conditionality" and "holism," in Hurka 1998: 300–301.
27. For an excellent overview, and a resourceful defense of contextualism (or "conditionalism" in Olson's terminology), see Olson 2004.
28. I here ignore putative problems of vagueness.
29. There may of course be exceptions. If a piece of kryptonite is finally valuable simply because it is made of kryptonite, every part of the piece (at least down to the atomic level) is presumably also finally valuable.

30. See Lemos 1998: §§ 3, 5; Hurka 1998: 317–18; 2001, chs. 1, 5; and Olson 2004: 39 n. 26. Zimmerman responds to Lemos's and Hurka's criticism in his (2001).

References

Beck. L. W. (1941). "The Formal Properties of Ethical Wholes." *Journal of Philosophy* 38: 5–15.
Broad, C. D. (1985). *Ethics*. Ed. C. Lewy. Dordrecht: Martinus Nijhoff.
Carlson, E. (1997a). "The Intrinsic Value of Non-basic States of Affairs." *Philosophical Studies* 85: 95–107.
Carlson, E. (1997b). "A Note on Moore's Organic Unities." *Journal of Value Inquiry* 31: 55–59.
Carlson, E. (2008). "Extensive Measurement with Incomparability." *Journal of Mathematical Psychology* 52: 250–59.
Carlson, E. (2010). "Generalized Extensive Measurement for Lexicographic Orders." *Journal of Mathematical Psychology* 54: 345–51.
Carlson, E. (2011). "Non-Archimedean Extensive Measurement with Incomparability." *Mathematical Social Sciences* 62: 71–76.
Chisholm, R. M. (1986). *Brentano and Intrinsic Value*. Cambridge: Cambridge University Press.
Danielsson, S. (1997). "Harman's Equation and the Additivity of Intrinsic Value." In L. Lindahl, P. Needham, and R. Sliwinski (eds.), *For Good Measure: Philosophical Essays Dedicated to Jan Odelstad on the Occasion of His Fiftieth Birthday*. Uppsala: Department of Philosophy, University of Uppsala, 23–34.
Feldman, F. (2000). "Basic Intrinsic Value." *Philosophical Studies* 99: 319–46.
Hurka, T. (1998). "Two Kinds of Organic Unity." *Journal of Ethics* 2: 299–320.
Hurka, T. (2001). *Virtue, Vice, and Value*. New York: Oxford University Press.
Korsgaard, C. M. (1983). "Two Distinctions in Goodness." *Philosophical Review* 92: 169–95.
Krantz, D. H., D. Luce, P. Suppes, and A. Tversky. (2007). *Foundations of Measurement*. Vol. 1. Mineola, NY: Dover.
Lemos, N. (1994). *Intrinsic Value*. Cambridge: Cambridge University Press.
Lemos, N. (1998). "Organic Unities." *Journal of Ethics* 2: 321–37.
Luce, D., D. H. Krantz, P. Suppes, and A. Tversky. (2007). *Foundations of Measurement*. Vol. 3. Mineola, NY: Dover.
Moore, G. E. (1903). *Principia Ethica*. Cambridge: Cambridge University Press.
Moore, G. E. (1922a). "The Nature of Moral Philosophy." In *Philosophical Studies*. London: Routledge and Kegan Paul, 310–39.
Moore, G. E. (1922b). "The Conception of Intrinsic Value." In *Philosophical Studies*. London: Routledge and Kegan Paul, 253–75.
Olson, J. (2004). "Intrinsicalism and Conditionalism about Final Value." *Ethical Theory and Moral Practice* 7: 31–52.
Rabinowicz, W., and T. Rønnow-Rasmussen. (1999). "A Distinction in Value: Intrinsic and For Its Own Sake." *Proceedings of the Aristotelian Society* 100: 33–51.
Roberts, F. (2009). *Measurement Theory*. Cambridge: Cambridge University Press.
Rønnow-Rasmussen, T., and M. J. Zimmerman, eds. (2005). *Recent Work on Intrinsic Value*. Dordrecht: Springer.
Vallentyne, P. (1988). "Teleology, Consequentialism, and the Past." *Journal of Value Inquiry* 22: 89–101.
Zimmerman, M. J. (2001). *The Nature of Intrinsic Value*. Lanham, MD: Rowman and Littlefield.

CHAPTER 16

SKEPTICISM ABOUT VALUE AGGREGATION

IWAO HIROSE

16.1. Introduction

According to some ethical theories, the gains for some individuals can be balanced against the losses for other individuals to determine the relative goodness of states of affairs. I call it *interpersonal aggregation* or *aggregation* for short. Aggregation is an essential feature of utilitarianism and other consequentialist theories. For example, classical utilitarianism adds up the numerical value of people's pleasure and aims to bring about the state of affairs in which the sum of pleasure is maximized.

Critics of utilitarianism often reject aggregation and attempt to contrast their proposed theory with utilitarianism. For example, John Rawls (1971) eliminates any aggregative element from his theory of justice, which he claims to be a clear alternative to utilitarianism. Thomas Nagel (1979) and T. M. Scanlon (1982, 1998) also emphasize that their theories are nonaggregative. Thus, skepticism about aggregation is often conceived as one of the important motivations for, and an essential feature of, nonutilitarian ethical theories.

It is true that some alleged implications of aggregation are counterintuitive. One such implication is that, according to aggregative principles, a state of affairs can be made strictly better by, for example, harvesting organs from a healthy person's body without her consent and transplanting them to five needy patients in life-threatening conditions. Admittedly, this implication is counterintuitive. For critics of utilitarianism, to permit aggregation is to permit carving up a healthy person for the sake of benefiting others. They seem to think that we cannot avoid this kind of counterintuitive implication unless aggregation is eliminated.

The purpose of this chapter is to review the recent debate concerning aggregation. Section 16.2 gives a clear definition of aggregation and interpersonal aggregation. Section 16.3 discusses the counterexamples to aggregation. Section 16.4 examines the objection on the basis of the separateness of persons. Section 16.5 considers two other grounds for rejecting aggregation: the arguments from organic unities and skepticism about "better, simpliciter." Section 16.6 introduces the nonaggregative theories of Nagel and Scanlon, and points out that these theories encounter what has become known as the number problem in the recent literature. Section 16.7 considers two nonaggregative arguments that avoid the number problem.

16.2. THE GENERAL DEFINITION OF AGGREGATION

Here is the most general definition of aggregation. Aggregation occurs when the members in nonsingleton sets of morally relevant factors are combined into a numerical value that represents the relation of these sets. First, suppose the F-er relation defined on sets of n morally relevant factors.

Relation: $(a_1, a_2, \ldots, a_n)$ is at least as F as $(a'_1, a'_2, \ldots, a'_n)$, where F is some normative property, for example, good, morally important, morally justifiable, morally weighty, and so on.

Let us assume that the F-er relation is reflexive, transitive, and complete and hence that the F-er relation constitutes an F-ordering. The morally relevant factors in each set may be well-being, welfare, happiness, pleasure, income, resources, primary social goods, capability to function, claims, reasons, and so on. Aggregation implies that there exists a real-valued function that represents the F-ordering.

Aggregation: $(a_1, a_2, \ldots, a_n)$ is at least as F as $(a'_1, a'_2, \ldots, a'_n)$ if and only if $f(a_1, a_2, \ldots, a_n) \geq f(a'_1, a'_2, \ldots, a'_n)$, where $f()$ is strictly increasing in its arguments.

Function $f()$ should be increasing in its arguments because, other things being equal, the increase of one factor should make the value of the combined features strictly greater.

This is the most general definition of aggregation for the following reasons. First, it does not commit to any particular view concerning what subscripted indices indicate. If these indices indicate the mutually exclusive and jointly exhaustive temporal parts of a person's complete life, then it is *intrapersonal aggregation*. If indices indicate people, then it is interpersonal aggregation. Furthermore, there might be what might be called *extended interpersonal aggregation*. By extended interpersonal aggregation, I mean that we aggregate not only the morally relevant factors owned by different individuals, but also other morally relevant factors that cannot be dispersed to individuals, for example, the value of natural environment, the value of biodiversity, aesthetic value, (arguably) the value of equality, and so on.

Second, it is not committed to any particular account of morally relevant factors. Utilitarianism, for example, takes pleasure and pain to be the only morally relevant factor. Similarly, welfarism takes human well-being to be the only morally relevant factor. Some reason-based theories might balance the reasons owned by different individuals. The abovementioned definition is neutral between different accounts of morally relevant factors.

Third, it is not committed to any particular view concerning what the F-er relation stands for. The F-er relation is typically the betterness relation in axiology. But it does not need to be so. The F-er relation may stand for "is morally more important than," "is morally weightier than," and so on. Therefore, the abovementioned definition includes any ethical principles that represent the ranking of sets of morally relevant factors by real-valued functions.

Fourth, $f()$ is not confined to the additive function. Utilitarianism takes the goodness of a state of affairs to be a sum of the numerical value of people's pleasure. Yet the function may be the multiplication of the numerical value of morally relevant factors. The only restriction is that $f()$ should be strictly increasing.

The definition of aggregation I offered above covers different types of aggregation. In what follows, however, I will concentrate on interpersonal aggregation of well-being. This means that (a) subscripted indices indicate people, (b) morally relevant factors are people's well-being, and (c) the F-er relation indicates the betterness relation, that is, "is at least as good as." This definition of interpersonal aggregation includes four basic features. The first is $f()$ is symmetric. The symmetric function just implies that $f(a_1, a_2, ..., a_n) = f(a_2, a_1, ..., a_n) = ... = f(a_n, ..., a_2, a_1)$. In other words, permutations of personal identities do not alter the relative goodness of alternatives. This feature is sometimes conceived as a condition of *impartiality*. In the case of intrapersonal aggregation, the function may not be symmetric. To see this, partition a person's lifetime into three equally long temporal parts. Compare two courses of her life, (1, 2, 3) and (3, 2, 1), where parentheses show the level of well-being at period 1, period 2, and period 3 respectively. If the intrapersonal aggregation function, $f()$, is symmetric, $f(1,2, 3) = f(3, 2, 1)$. That is, the two courses of life are equally good. However, it may be argued that (1, 2, 3) is better than (3, 2, 1) because the former is an upward life whereas the latter is a downward life. Thus, a plausible form of intrapersonal aggregation may not satisfy symmetry (Velleman 1991). The second feature is that interpersonal aggregation demands some sort of *interpersonal comparability* of people's well-being. For utilitarianism, it suffices to compare the unit of different people's well-being. Other aggregative principles such as prioritarianism require both unit comparability and level comparability. The third is *Pareto*. Pareto holds that if one alternative is better for some person than another alternative, and if it is no worse for any person, then it is better than the other. Pareto underlies the idea that function $f()$ is strictly increasing in its arguments. The fourth is *continuity*. One way to express continuity is that, for all a_i, the upper contour set $\{a_j \mid a_j \text{ is at least as good as } a_i\}$ and the lower contour set $\{a_j \mid a_i \text{ is at least as good as } a_j\}$ are both closed.[1]

As I said earlier, utilitarianism obviously implies interpersonal aggregation. It is also the case that prioritarianism implies it. Prioritarianism in value theory holds that a state $(w_1, w_2, \ldots, w_n)$ is at least as good as $(w'_1, w'_2, \ldots, w'_n)$ if and only if $g(w_1) + g(w_2) + \ldots + g(w_n) \geq g(w'_1) + g(w'_2) + \ldots + g(w'_n)$, where w_i is the numerical value of well-being of person i and $g()$ is some increasing, strictly concave function. In other words, on prioritarianism, the relative goodness of states of affairs is represented by the weighted sum of well-being where the weights are strictly positive but diminish as the absolute level of well-being gets higher.

Given the theoretical structure of aggregation, we can see why some distributive principles are nonaggregative. Take maximin. According to maximin, the relative goodness of states of affairs is determined solely by the well-being level of the worst off. More precisely, maximin holds that a state of affairs $x = (w_1, w_2, \ldots, w_n)$ is at least as good as another state of affairs $y = (w'_1, w'_2, \ldots, w'_n)$ if and only if $\min(w_1, w_2, \ldots, w_n) \geq \min(w'_1, w'_2, \ldots, w'_n)$. The maximin function is not strictly increasing in its arguments. Nor does it satisfy Pareto. This is why maximin is nonaggregative. Take another example, leximin. Leximin first compares the worst off across alternatives and, if the worst off are at the same level, compares the second worst off, and so on. More precisely, leximin holds that for all $x = (w_1, w_2, \ldots, w_n)$ and $y = (w'_1, w'_2, \ldots, w'_n)$, if there exists a position k in $N = \{1, 2, 3, \ldots, n\}$ such that: (1) the well-being level in k is strictly higher in x than y; and (2) the well-being level of every position $j < k$ is the same in x as in y, then x is strictly better than y. Otherwise, x and y are equally good. Leximin is a discontinuous ordering. It does not satisfy continuity, and hence cannot be represented in functional form. This is why leximin is nonaggregative.

To be precise, aggregation is not synonymous with utilitarianism or consequentialism. Many egalitarian principles such as prioritarianism and some versions of telic egalitarianism are aggregative, but not utilitarian in a strict sense. Utilitarianism requires aggregation (i.e., summing-up), but not vice versa. Aggregation is not confined to consequentialism, either. Some consequentialist principles such as one based on maximin or leximin do not combine the good of different individuals, thus being nonaggregative. Some nonconsequentialist principles such as the reason-based ethical theory may well combine the reasons owned by different individuals in order to determine the rightness or wrongness of an action, thus being aggregative.

To put this important point in perspective, consider the case of the survival lottery (Harris 1975). In the survival lottery, all individuals are assigned a number. Then, one individual is drawn out of lottery, and his or her organs are harvested and transplanted in two or more needy patients, who would die if they did not receive a new organ. Many people find the survival lottery to be unacceptable. There are at least two separate issues in the survival lottery. One issue is about consequentialism. The other is about aggregation. On one reading of this discussion, the case of the survival lottery shows the unacceptability of aggregation. According to this reading, we should reject aggregation because we cannot avoid the survival lottery unless we reject aggregation. On this reading, the issues of aggregation and consequentialism are conflated. If we accept aggregation, it may be the case that saving the lives of two or more patients is better than the death of one individual. However, from this, it does not follow that it is right to adopt the survival lottery. Of course, if we accept both aggregation and consequentialism, it does follow. But one can accept aggregation but reject consequentialism and accept some deontic constraints. He or she can say that it is wrong to adopt the survival lottery because it violates a certain deontological constraint (e.g., treating a person merely as a means). Thus, advocates of aggregation are not necessarily committed to the survival lottery. Aggregation of benefits is confined to the axiological domain, and should be distinguished from consequentialism.

16.3. Objection from Counterexamples

The first type of objection is to claim that aggregation is unacceptable because some of its implications are simply counterintuitive or obviously wrong. An example is Larry Temkin's *Lollipops for Life Case* (Temkin 2009). Compare two alternative universes: (a) a large number of people each would receive many licks of lollipops over the course of their lives, and one innocent person would suffer unbearable agony for fifty years; and (b) a large number of people each would receive one less lick of a lollipop over the course of their lives, and the innocent person would be spared the agony and instead live a full, rich life. According to Temkin, most people firmly believe that (b) is better than (a), no matter how many people would get the one extra lollipop lick, whereas classical utilitarianism and other aggregative principles are committed to rejecting such a belief. From this, Temkin claims that aggregation is implausible and unacceptable.

Three questions can be raised. First, what follows? For the sake of argument, let us agree that (b) is better than (a). Aggregation skeptics seem to derive one of two theses. One is what I call the *strong thesis*. The strong thesis contends that aggregation should be rejected altogether. The other is the *weak thesis*. The weak thesis contends that aggregation should be rejected in some cases, but not in other cases. The weak thesis does not reject aggregation altogether, but merely constrains the cases where aggregation is permitted. If (b) is better than (a) and all aggregative principles judge (a) is better than (b), then it is not controversial to conclude that aggregation is unacceptable in the Lollipops for Life Case. The weak thesis follows from the judgment that (b) is better than (a). In contrast, the strong thesis does not follow. Even if it is agreed that (b) is better than (a) in the Lollipops for Life Case, aggregation may well be perfectly plausible in other cases. We cannot claim that we should reject aggregation altogether because it is implausible in the Lollipops for Life Case. Therefore, the objection to aggregation on the basis of counterexample is limited in its scope.

The second question is related to the first question. Is it plausible to appeal to counterexamples? For the sake of argument, let us suppose that aggregation is counterintuitive in the Lollipops for Life Case. Yet aggregation may appear perfectly acceptable or even desirable in other cases. In such cases, nonaggregative principles appear counterintuitive. Imagine that we are faced with a choice between saving the life of one individual and sparing a hundred individuals from losing a leg. Many people would find it counterintuitive to save the life of one individual and let a hundred individuals lose their leg. In the context of aggregation, counterexamples work in both directions. They work in favor of aggregation, and against aggregation. Thus, the appeal to counterexamples does not establish a conclusive case against aggregation.

The third question is this. Is the Lollipops for Life Case counterintuitive because of aggregation? In the Lollipops for Life Case, there is an important assumption that should be made explicit. That is, an additional lollipop lick is a morally nontrivial benefit. In order for the Lollipops for Life Case to work as a counterexample against aggregation, an additional lollipop lick must be a morally nontrivial benefit. If a lollipop lick is morally trivial, there is no aggregation of morally relevant factors in the Lollipops for Life Case. Some people might think that choosing (a) in the Lollipops for Life Case is counterintuitive for reasons other than aggregation. They may think that a lollipop lick is a morally trivial benefit and should not be taken into account when it comes to moral judgment. Other people may be critics of hedonism: pleasure is not a good in the first place. Nonetheless, they may well accept aggregation of other types of benefits such as capability to function. Thus, the implausibility of choosing (a) does not explain or justify the implausibility of aggregation.

Often, counterexamples to aggregation contain several hidden assumptions. Consider T. M. Scanlon's much-discussed *World Cup Case* (Scanlon 1998: 235). Imagine that Jones is receiving extremely painful electrical shocks due to an accident in the transmitter room of a television station. We cannot rescue him without suspending the transmission of a World Cup match for fifteen minutes, which millions of people are watching. Should we rescue Jones now or wait until the match is over? According to Scanlon, aggregative principles judge that the small enjoyment for a large number of World Cup viewers outweighs Jones's severe pain, and that (when aggregative principles are combined with consequentialism) it is right to continue the transmission. Scanlon, however, thinks that it is right to rescue Jones now.

In addition to the issue concerning whether the enjoyment of each World Cup viewer is morally nontrivial, there are three assumptions that should be made explicit. First, it must be assumed that no World Cup viewer is as badly off as Jones. If hundreds of World Cup viewers were worse off than Jones, some people would judge that it is better to continue the transmission. In this case, this example does not work. Second, it must be assumed that we are located far from the transmitter room. If I were in front of Jones, I would adopt the rule of rescue and suspend the transmission: I would not care about the World Cup viewers, no matter how many World Cup viewers might have heart attacks. Even if I adopt the rule of rescue, this does not mean that I reject aggregation. Third, the victim is clearly identified. We all know that the victim of the accident is Jones. We can easily imagine his painful face, screaming voice, the color of blood, and the tears of his family members. In contrast, the World Cup viewers are presented as the nameless masses. Generally, many people consistently exhibit cognitive bias toward an identified victim over a statistical victim.[2] In the World Cup Case, it is not surprising even if people show bias toward Jones over the masses. If we agree with Scanlon's claim on the basis of this cognitive bias, then the World Cup Case cannot be seen as a counterexample to aggregation.

Objections based on counterexamples are often based on implicit assumptions, cognitive bias, and/or implausible inference. Thus, those objections do not seem to undermine aggregation.

16.4. OBJECTION FROM THE SEPARATENESS OF PERSONS

Some critics of aggregation might appeal to the notion of the *separateness of persons*. That is to say, aggregation should be rejected because aggregative principles do not take the separateness of person seriously. Rawls (1971) first used this notion when he criticized classical utilitarianism. Other critics of utilitarianism also appealed to the notion of the separateness of persons (Gauthier 1963; Nagel 1970; and Nozick 1974). In this section, I will consider whether the notion of the separateness of persons can ground the objection to aggregation.

At the outset, let me clarify one important point. Rawls used the notion of the separateness of persons to criticize classical utilitarianism, but not other principles. More precisely, he criticized the "[r]easoning which balances the gains and losses of different persons as if they were one person" (Rawls 1971: 28). According to Rawls's diagnosis, classical utilitarianism appeals to the perspective of the impartial and sympathetic spectator, who treats the trade-off among different persons as if it were the intrapersonal trade-off for the spectator. From the perspective of the impartial spectator, a loss to one person, no matter how large, can be justified for the sake of a greater gain to others as if the loss and gain occurred within the course of the impartial spectator's life. Rawls then finds it problematic that reasoning which balances the gains and losses of different persons as if they were one person does not take the separateness of persons seriously. This means that Rawls did not claim that other forms of utilitarianism such as average utilitarianism do not take the separateness of persons seriously. Needless to say, Rawls criticizes average utilitarianism. But he does not criticize it on the basis of the separateness of persons. Given that there is a surprising contrast between classical utilitarianism and average utilitarianism, he criticizes average utilitarianism for different reasons (e.g., the heuristic assumptions in the original position, stability, self-respect, and the strains of commitment).

There is a problem in Rawls's attempt to criticize classical utilitarianism with an appeal to the separateness of persons (Hirose 2013). It is not clear at all why the separateness of persons is so important. Rawls does not explain why the separateness of persons is important. Probably, for Rawls, its importance is so obvious that he does not need to prove or argue for it. However, friends of Parfit's reductionism would claim that the fact that different people live different lives is not as important as Rawls thinks, and that there is no rational or moral ground for treating interpersonal and intrapersonal trade-offs differently. Contrary to Rawls, the moral importance of the separateness of persons is not obvious at all.

I have emphasized that Rawls appealed to the separateness of persons to criticize the "[r]easoning which balances the gains and losses for different persons as if they were one person" in classical utilitarianism. However, some people understand the separateness of persons in a broader sense. For example, Nozick (1974: 228–29) criticizes Rawls's difference principle on the basis of the separateness of persons: Since the difference principle is based on the pooling of natural talents of different people, the difference principle does not seem to take the separateness of persons seriously. I will not discuss which interpretation is the best one. For the present purpose, I will concentrate on one particular interpretation. The interpretation I will consider is focused on one implication of classical utilitarianism. As Rawls (1971: 29) puts it, one implication of classical utilitarianism is that "there is no reason in principle why the greater gains of some should not compensate for the lesser losses of others; or more importantly, why the violation of the liberty of a few might not be made right by the greater good shared by many." This implication is also an implication of aggregation. According to this interpretation, whenever there is an interpersonal trade-off, the separateness of persons is not taken seriously, regardless of whether such a trade-off is made possible from the perspective of an impartial spectator. Let us call this interpretation the *wider account* of the separateness of persons because it is quite different from Rawls's restricted interpretation.

The wider account may be challenged in several ways. First, nonaggregative principles may take the separateness of persons seriously, but may not take every person seriously. Take maximin, for instance. Maximin judges the relative goodness of states of affairs solely by the level of the worst off. Whatever happens to the non-worst off people, maximin is not concerned with their state unless one of them becomes the worst off. From this, it might be argued that nonaggregative principles do not take every person seriously, and that this feature is worse than not taking the separateness of persons seriously. Second, it is highly debatable whether aggregative principles do not take the separateness of persons seriously in any sense. Take classical utilitarianism. Parfit suggests one sense in which the separateness of persons supports classical utilitarianism.

> Sidgwick believed that this fact [i.e., the separateness of persons] is the foundation of the Self-interest Theory about rationality. If what is fundamental is that we are different persons, each with his own life to lead, this supports the claim that the supremely rational ultimate aim, for each person, is that his own life go as well as possible. (Parfit 1984: 329)

It is not my intention to claim that Parfit's interpretation of the separateness of persons in Sidgwick's theory is correct or better than the wider account. My point is just that there are different senses in which the notion of the separateness of persons can be understood. Aggregation skeptics should not baldly assert aggregation should be rejected on the basis of the separateness of persons unless they establish the wider account is more plausible than other interpretations. If the notion of the separateness of persons is invoked as a feature that aggregation always undermines, then that is simply a statement of a moral view, not an argument or ground for that moral view. What aggregation skeptics with the wider account have to do is to explain why the separateness of persons is so important and to establish that the wider account is more plausible than other interpretations of the separateness of persons.

16.5. Two Other Arguments

There are two other arguments against aggregation. The first is the argument from *organic unities*. The other is skepticism about "better, simpliciter." These arguments are discussed in other chapters of this volume.[3] So I will discuss them briefly.

Generally speaking, the idea of organic unities rejects that the value of a whole is a sum total of the value of its parts. In the context of interpersonal aggregation, it rejects that the goodness of a state of affairs is a sum total of people's well-being. The idea of organic unities does not necessarily claim that the goodness of people's well-being cannot be combined into an objective value. That is, it does not deny a real-valued function that represents the relative goodness of states of affairs. However, it claims that the real-valued function lacks the features that aggregation possesses. The value function $f()$ in aggregation has two features. One is that $f()$ is symmetric. The other is $f()$ is strictly increasing in its arguments. The idea of organic unities contends that the value function is either nonsymmetrical or nonincreasing or both. That is, the value function in organic unities lacks constraints on the value function, no matter how we characterize an individual's good.

First, let me explain the nonsymmetrical feature. Compare two three-person situations: (1, 2, 3) and (3, 2, 1). The brackets show the state of persons 1, 2, and 3 respectively. In this comparison, symmetry holds that $f(1, 2, 3)=f(3, 2, 1)$. However, there might be an argument against such a claim. For example, it might be argued that $f(1, 2, 3) > f(3, 2, 1)$. A possible explanation is this. Suppose that persons 1 and 2 are partners and form one household, and that person 3 forms a one-person household. If we care for equality of household well-being, we might claim that $f(1, 2, 3) > f(3, 2, 1)$, thus violating symmetry among individual well-being. To this claim, defenders of aggregation would argue that the idea of organic unities is inconsistent with aggregation of individual well-being, but consistent with aggregation of household well-being. The idea of organic unities, then, goes further. There are many other ways, in which a person's well-being interacts with other people's well-being. The interactions between people's well-being are irreducibly complex, and hence there is no principled way to preserve the symmetry.

A similar point can be made about the nonincreasing feature. Compare two states of affairs: (5, 1, 1) and (1, 1, 1). Again, the brackets show the well-being level of persons 1, 2, and 3 respectively. The strict increasingness of aggregation claims that $f(10, 1, 1)>f(1, 1, 1)$. In contrast, the idea of organic unities may well claim that $f(10, 1, 1)<f(1, 1, 1)$ because, for

example, there is an enormous inequality in (10, 1, 1) whereas there is a perfect equality in (1, 1, 1). To this claim, defenders of aggregation would argue that the disvalue of inequality can be dispersed among the worse-off individuals as a negative part of their personal good, and hence that aggregation of personal good, which consists in the value of individual well-being and the disvalue of inequality, can support the judgment that $f(10, 1, 1) < f(1, 1, 1)$.[4] Advocates of organic unities would, however, claim that the evaluation of a well-being distribution is irreducibly complicated, and hence that we cannot estimate the overall good of a state of affairs in a way that is consistent with the strict increasingness.

The last type of argument against aggregation is skepticism about "better, simpliciter" (see Anscombe 1967; Foot 1985; Lübbe 2008; and Thomson 2008). The idea of organic unities does not disagree that one state is, all things considered, better or worse than another. In contrast, skepticism about "better, simpliciter" contends that it does not make sense to say that one state is, all things considered, better or worse than another. The talk about better or worse makes sense only in the cases where "better or worse" is attributed to particular persons. That is, it makes perfect sense to say that a three-person state (10, 1, 1) is better for person 1 than another state (1, 1, 1), but not that (10, 1, 1) is better than (1, 1, 1).

Obviously, skepticism about "better, simpliciter" rejects Pareto. Pareto claims that if one alternative is better for some person than another alternative, and if it is no worse for any person, then it is better than the other. But skepticism about "better, simpliciter" does not support the consequent in Pareto. Skepticism also rejects impartiality. Impartiality claims that permutations of personal identities do not alter the relative goodness of alternatives. But skepticism refuses any talk about the relative goodness of states of affairs. Even more surprisingly, skepticism rejects interpersonal comparability. Compare my feeling a small pain for one minute and your feeling a severe pain for one hour. The only thing skepticism about "better, simpliciter" asserts is that a small pain is bad for me, and that a severe pain is bad for you. Skepticism does not say that your severe pain is worse than my small pain. The main claim of skepticism about "better, simpliciter" may appear counterintuitive in its own light. It also exhibits many counterintuitive implications in various contexts such as the number problem, which I will discuss in the following section.

16.6. Nonaggregative Theories

There are several notable nonaggregative theories. I shall concentrate on two theories. The first is Thomas Nagel's unanimity through pairwise comparisons (Nagel 1979). Whenever there is conflict of interests, no state of affairs is completely acceptable to everyone. Nagel's unanimity attempts to identify the state that is "least unacceptable to the person to whom is it most unacceptable." To identify the outcome that is least unacceptable from each person's point of view, Nagel puts forward the process of pairwise comparisons. Take a pair of individuals who will be affected by our distributive judgment. Compare the possible gains and losses of these two individuals. The state where the maximum loss for each person is minimized is the less unacceptable one. Perform the same comparison for every pair of individuals affected. By doing so, we can identify the least unacceptable state, considered from each person's view separately. For example, consider two states of affairs, A and B.

A: (1, 9, 9, 9, 9, 9)
B: (8, 7, 7, 7, 7, 7)

First, compare persons 1 and 2. If A is chosen, there will be 7 units of loss for person 1, and 2 units of gain for person 2. According to Nagel's pairwise comparison, the degree of unacceptability from the perspective of person 1 is greater than the degree of unacceptability from the perspective of person 2, simply because the possible loss for person 1 is greater than that for person 2. From the perspective of person 1, B is less unacceptable. Therefore, B is the state that is less unacceptable from the perspectives of persons 1 and 2 separately. The same reasoning and judgment both apply to the pairwise comparisons between person 1 and each one of persons 3, 4, and 5. Thus, B remains less unacceptable than A. Nagel's unanimity then concludes that B is less unacceptable than A. Nagel's unanimity is nonaggregative because B remains less unacceptable than A, no matter how many people would benefit from choosing A.

The second theory is T. M. Scanlon's contractualism (Scanlon 1982, 1998). According to his contractualism, an act is wrong when and because it is disallowed by principles that nobody could reasonably reject from individual standpoints. If there is one person who has reasonable grounds for rejecting a principle, this principle cannot serve as the basis of our ethical judgment, even if it benefits many other people. Whether or not a principle can be rejected does not depend on a sum total or average of people's well-being, or on the number of people who benefit from adopting this principle. It depends solely on the reasons a particular person has in a particular context. This feature of Scanlon's contractualism is called the *individualist restriction*. This individualist restriction serves as the basis for rejecting and constraining aggregative reasoning. For example, consider what Scanlon's contractualism implies in the abovementioned comparison of A and B. Scanlon's contractualism would claim that person 1 has a legitimate reason to object to principles that would choose A, no matter how many people would benefit from adopting these principles: principles that would choose B are the principles that nobody could reasonably reject from individual standpoints. Thus, Scanlon's contractualism is non-aggregative.

The nonaggregative feature of these theories encounters the *number problem*. Imagine that the lives of six individuals, situated in two separate locations, are in danger, but that we cannot reach the two locations in time. There are five individuals in one location and one in the other. The choice is between (a) saving the lives of five individuals and letting the one individual die and (b) saving the life of the one individual and letting the five individuals die. For the sake of argument, assume that there are no morally relevant differences among these six individuals. Call this example the *rescue case*. What is the right course of action in the rescue case? Aggregative theories have a straightforward answer and explanation. The answer is that it is right to save the lives of the five individuals. The explanation is this. Saving the life of an individual is good. The combined good of saving the lives of the five is strictly greater than the good of saving the life of one. There is no violation of a deontological constraint in saving the lives of the five. Thus, it is right to save the lives of the five.

John Taurek (1977), an aggregation skeptic, disagrees. He claims that it is right to flip a fair coin and give an equal chance of being saved to each of the six individuals.[5] According to Taurek, it does not make sense to say that saving five lives is better, simpliciter, than saving one life. The loss of a life is just bad for the person who loses that life. Taurek thinks that the coin-toss best captures his belief that each person's life should be respected equally.

Many people, including many aggregation skeptics, find Taurek's claim to be counterintuitive, and think that it is right to save the lives of the five. However, it seems that aggregation skeptics must agree with Taurek's coin-toss if they reject aggregation. How can aggregation skeptics justify the case for saving the five outright without an appeal to aggregation? This is the number problem, posed for aggregation skeptics.

Consider what Nagel's unanimity implies in the rescue case. There are two possible outcomes: (a) the lives of the five are saved and the life of the one is lost, and (b) the lives of the five are lost and the life of the one is saved. Given that the size of the possible loss is the same for every individual, (a) and (b) are just as acceptable. Therefore, Nagel's unanimity would be indifferent between (a) and (b). But this is counterintuitive to many people, including many aggregation skeptics.

Scanlon attempts to offer a solution to the number problem from the perspective of his contractualism (Scanlon 1998: 229–41). First, imagine that the choice is between saving one life and saving another life. In this case, the coin-flip is the principle that nobody could reasonably reject. Now imagine that four strangers are added to one side and the choice becomes between saving one life and saving five lives. If you still flip a fair coin, you would give no positive recognition to the presence of four additional strangers. Nevertheless, this would be reasonably objected to by each of the four additional strangers. By choosing to save the five strangers, we certainly recognize the presence of four additional strangers. Thus, saving the lives of the five is the principle that nobody could reasonably reject from each person's standpoint. This is Scanlon's *tie-breaking argument*.

Scanlon's tie-breaking argument can be challenged. For the sake of argument, let us agree with the process of reasoning behind his argument. Suppose that the choice is between saving the lives of five strangers and the lives of two different strangers. If the choice were between saving the lives of five and the life of one, following Scanlon's tie-breaking argument, saving the five is the principle that nobody could reasonably reject. Now imagine that one different stranger is added to the side of the one. If we still choose to save the five lives, the presence of one additional stranger does not make any difference about what we should do. The additional stranger does not receive any positive recognition for his claim to being saved, and therefore, we can reasonably reject the principle of saving the greater number. Thus, Scanlon's argument does not establish the case for saving the greater number of individuals.[6]

16.7. Two Nonaggregative Solutions to the Number Problem

Although Scanlon's argument is unsuccessful, there are two successful arguments that can justify the case for saving the lives of the five without an appeal to aggregation. The first argument is the *argument for best outcomes* (Hirose 2001; Kamm 1993). This argument appeals to two premises that I have already introduced. The first premise is impartiality. The second is Pareto. These two premises are the essential features of aggregation. But the argument for best outcomes does not require continuity.

Now, compare three alternatives, which show the states of three persons.

C: (saved, dead, dead)
D: (dead, saved, dead)
E: (dead, saved, saved)

By impartiality, C is just as good as D. By Pareto, E is better than D. Consequently, E is better than C. Thus, saving the two is better than saving the one. By continuing the same process for comparisons between saving n persons and $(n-1)$ persons, we can conclude that saving more is better than saving fewer. There is no violation of a deontic constraint in saving the greater number. Therefore, it is right to save the greater number.

To confirm that this argument is nonaggregative, consider the comparison of A and B in the previous section. In this comparison, the conjunction of impartiality and Pareto does not claim that A is strictly better than B. Actually, it does not tell us anything. This is because no permutations of personal identities can make a Pareto-superior state. That is, A and B are Pareto-incomparable. Impartiality and Pareto can give a solution only when there are equivalent states of individuals across different alternatives. Otherwise, impartiality and Pareto are silent. In the comparison of A and B, there are no equivalent states of individuals across different alternatives. Thus, the conjunction of impartiality and Pareto is nonaggregative. To be precise, aggregation implies impartiality and Pareto, but not vice versa.

The second argument is the *probabilistic argument* (Schelling 2006). This argument appeals to rational choice behind a veil of ignorance, which Rawls employs. But it does not assume that people are self-interested: They can be other-regarding. The argument runs as follows. If it is unknown who is in which group, anyone I want to save—myself, my spouse, my child, my friend, or someone who is especially deserving of rescue—is more likely to be in the group of the five. The probability that he or she is on the side of five individuals is 5/6, whereas the probability that he or she is on the other side is

1/6. Thus, saving the greater number of individuals is a better bet. This must be the case for everyone else. Therefore, in this hypothetical situation, everyone would agree to the general principle of saving the group of five individuals insofar as the number of individuals is the only difference. Thus, the probability argument concludes that the rule of saving the greater number would be unanimously agreed upon as a general principle

The probabilistic argument works only when the size of loss is the same for everyone. The argument appeals only to the likelihood of being in each location. To make it possible, the size of the loss to each individual must be equal. The probabilistic argument does not tell us when the size of the loss is different among the six individuals. Consider the comparison of A and B again. The likelihood alone cannot tell us which alternative is more desirable than the other. To determine the relative desirability of A and B, we need to estimate the expected good of each alternative. But the probabilistic argument does not say anything about the expected good of alternatives. It merely considers the likelihood. Thus, the probabilistic argument is clearly nonaggregative.

The probabilistic argument may offer good news to skeptics of "better, simpliciter." The probabilistic argument does not include any judgment about the relative goodness of states of affairs. It only appeals to the likelihood from each person's perspective. It is not clear whether "better, simpliciter" skeptics are willing to accept the probabilistic argument. But nothing in the probabilistic argument goes against skepticism about "better, simpliciter."

In this section, I examined two nonaggregative arguments for saving the greater number in the rescue case. These arguments work only in the cases where the level of harm is the same. When the level of harm is different from one person to another, these arguments do not say anything. Therefore, the scope of these arguments is very limited.

Notes

1. See Arrhenius-Rabinowicz on continuity and discontinuity, chapter 12 in this volume.
2. See Jenni and Loewenstein (1997) and Schelling (1984). Holtug (2010: 237) suggests an example, in which he neutralizes this bias in the World Cup Case, and calls it the *Distributed World Cup Case*.
3. For organic unities, see Carlson's chapter 15 in this volume. For skepticism about "better, simpliciter," see Cullity, chapter 6, Rønnow-Rasmussen, chapter 2, and Zimmerman, chapter 1 in this volume.
4. See Broome (1991) and Broome's chapter 13 in this volume. To illustrate Broome's point in this context, (10, 1, 1) can be redescribed as $(10, 1-d, 1-d)$, where d denotes the disvalue of inequality owed to the persons 2 and 3. The judgment that (1, 1, 1) is strictly better than (10, 1, 1) implies that $(1 + 1 + 1) > (10 + 1 - d + 1 - d)$. This means that (10, 1, 1) is strictly better than (1, 1, 1) if $d > 4.5$.
5. For the detailed analysis of Taurek's argument, see Hirose (2014); Kamm (1993); and Lawlor (2006).
6. Otsuka (2000) points out that Scanlon's tie-breaking argument is aggregative. According to Otsuka, it compares the claim of group of individuals because the claim of additional

individuals tips the balance only when it is presented together with that of the individual in the one-to-one hypothetical case.

References

Anscombe, G. E. M. (1967). "Who Is Wronged? Philippa Foot on Double Effect: One Point." *Oxford Review* 5: 16–17.
Broome, J. (1991). *Weighing Goods: Equality, Uncertainty and Time.* Oxford: Blackwell.
Foot, P. (1985). "Utilitarianism and the Virtues." *Mind* 94: 196–209.
Gauthier, D. P. (1963). *Practical Reasoning.* Oxford: Clarendon Press.
Harris, J. (1975). "The Survival Lottery." *Philosophy* 50: 81–87.
Hirose, I. (2001). "Saving the Greater Number without Combining Claims." *Analysis*, 61: 341–42.
Hirose, I. (2013). "Aggregation and the Separateness of Persons." *Utilitas* 25: 182–205.
Hirose, I. (2014). *Moral Aggregation.* New York: Oxford University Press.
Holtug, N. (2010). *Persons, Interests, and Justice.* Oxford: Oxford University Press.
Jenni, K., and G. Loewenstein (1997). "Explaining the Identifiable Victim Effect." *Journal of Risk and Uncertainty* 14: 235–57.
Kamm, F. M. (1993). *Morality, Mortality.* Vol. 1: *Death and Whom to Save from It.* New York: Oxford University Press.
Lawlor, R. (2006). "Taurek, Numbers and Probabilities." *Ethical Theory and Moral Practice* 9: 149–66.
Lübbe, W. (2008). "Taurek's No Worse Claim." *Philosophy and Public Affairs* 36: 69–85.
Nagel, T. (1979). "Equality." In *Mortal Questions.* New York: Cambridge University Press, 106–27.
Nagel, T. (1970). *The Possibility of Altruism.* Princeton, NJ: Princeton University Press.
Nozick, R. (1974). *Anarchy, State, and Utopia.* Oxford: Basic Books.
Otsuka, M. (2000). "Scanlon and the Claims of the Many Versus the One." *Analysis* 60: 288–93.
Parfit, D. (1984). *Reasons and Persons.* Oxford: Clarendon Press.
Rawls, J. (1971). *A Theory of Justice.* Cambridge: Harvard University Press.
Scanlon, T. M. (1982). "Contractualism and Utilitarianism." in A. K. Sen and B. Williams (eds.), *Utilitarianism and Beyond.* Cambridge: Cambridge University Press, 103–28.
Scanlon, T. M. (1998). *What We Owe to Each Other.* Cambridge: Belknap Press of Harvard University Press.
Schelling, T. C. (1984). "The Life You Save May be Your Own." In *Choice and Consequence.* Cambridge: Harvard University Press, 113–46.
Schelling, T. C. (2006). "Should Numbers Determine Whom to Save?" In *The Strategies of Commitment.* Cambridge: Harvard University Press, 140–46.
Taurek, J. (1977). "Should the Numbers Count?" *Philosophy and Public Affairs* 6: 293–316.
Temkin, L. S. (2009). "Aggregation within Lives." *Social Philosophy and Policy* 26: 1–29.
Thomson, J. J. (2008). *Normativity.* Chicago: Open Court.
Velleman, D. (1991). "Well-Being and Time." *Pacific Philosophical Quarterly* 72: 48–77.

PART III
EXTENSIONS

CHAPTER 17

VALUE AND COST-BENEFIT ANALYSIS

MATTHEW D. ADLER

17.1. INTRODUCTION

COST-BENEFIT analysis (CBA) is a methodology for evaluating governmental policies that is widely used by governments and scholars (Adler and Posner 2006). A "policy" is here used to mean any choice that a governmental official or body might have occasion to consider: enacting a statute, issuing a regulation, building infrastructure, and so on. Let **A** be a choice situation that government faces at some time. **A** is a set of possible actions, and a policy *a* is a member of such a set. (I will use "government" as a shorthand for either an individual official, such as the head of a regulatory agency, or an official body, such as a legislature.) Policy-evaluation methodologies, such as CBA, are generic frameworks for determining the best choice or choices in any given situation **A**.

CBA can be traced as far back as a 1772 letter from Benjamin Franklin to Joseph Priestly (Wiener 2013). However, its modern intellectual home is in economics. CBA became prominent following the paradigm shift that occurred in the 1930s and 1940s, the rise of the so-called "new welfare economics" (Chipman 2008; Chipman and Moore 1978; Little 1957). Important subliteratures within contemporary economics revolve around CBA. (These are synthesized in Freeman 2003 and Just, Hueth, and Schmitz 2004; see also Harberger and Jenkins 2002; Layard and Glaister 1994.) For the last thirty years, CBA has been the linchpin of the system of "regulatory review" in the United States, used by a powerful oversight body to screen all new regulations. Broadly similar regimes of regulatory impact assessment, incorporating CBA, have also existed for decades in Australia, Canada, and the UK, and more recently have spread to the EU, its member states, and the developing world (Kirkpatrick 2006; Renda 2011; Wiener 2007, 2013).

Why on earth would a philosophical handbook on value theory include a chapter about CBA? CBA is a dominant methodology for *evaluating* government policies: it determines the *best* choice in a given situation and indeed (as we shall see) provides a complete *betterness* ranking of choices, such that for any a and a^* in **A** either one is better than the other or the two are equally good. Economists, specifically, tend to orient their evaluations around *well-being*. The evaluative branch of economics is known as *welfare economics*, and properly so. Economists tend to assume that goodness supervenes on (human) well-being. Evaluative economics thus implicates *prudential value*—goodness *for* individuals. CBA, as part of evaluative economics, necessarily embodies certain views about prudential value. And those views end up having practical influence just because CBA does. (See Hausman and McPherson 2006, generally discussing the normative premises of welfare economics.)

This chapter first describes CBA. As will emerge, CBA is defined in terms of individual *preferences*. CBA ranks choices by summing monetary equivalents, with each individual's monetary equivalent for a choice in turn reflecting her preferences as between that choice and the status quo.

CBA thus (on one interpretation) adopts the account of prudential value which is pervasive in evaluative/welfare economics, namely the preference-based (or desire-based) view. Many philosophers also endorse this view, in some form. However, preferentialists about well-being continue to debate the specific content of a preference-based view. It is therefore important to attend to the specific conditions on preference that CBA imposes, or fails to impose. The chapter considers two such families of conditions: rationality conditions, and nonremoteness conditions. As part of the discussion of rationality conditions, the chapter also addresses the related problem of inferring monetary equivalents. Should CBA practitioners make such inferences by looking to behavioral evidence (even though individuals in actual behavior fail to satisfy CBA's rationality conditions on preferences)? To surveys?

A second cluster of topics addressed by the chapter revolves around interpersonal comparability. The "new welfare economics" was characterized by a skepticism about interpersonal comparability, and by an embrace of the normative criterion of Kaldor-Hicks efficiency. CBA, in turn, was justified as a practicable tool for implementing Kaldor-Hicks efficiency. But the Kaldor-Hicks defense of CBA turns out to be problematic. An alternative justification for CBA appeals to "social welfare functions." This justification is more persuasive—for those persuaded that a preference-based account of prudential value can be reconciled with interpersonal comparability.

An objection to the view of CBA generally taken in this chapter is that CBA's orientation around preferences does *not* involve a preference-based view of individual well-being. Someone's preferences embody what she aims at, as a free agent—how she chooses to shape the world—and her aims need not correspond to the maximization of her well-being (Sen 1995: 56). In turn, on the "agency" interpretation of CBA, this methodology is concerned to measure the extent to which individuals have realized their preferences (via monetary equivalents), and *not* the level of individuals' well-being.

The "agency" interpretation is supported by *some* language that economists use (for example, the language of "consumer sovereignty"; see Waldfogel 2005); but there is also plenty of evidence for the well-being interpretation, as a reading of what those engaged in CBA see themselves as doing. CBA, again, is part of so-called "welfare economics," and many in this field quite clearly equate well-being and preference-satisfaction (Hausman and McPherson 2006; for a textbook statement, see, e.g., Mas-Collel, Whinston, and Green 1995: 80–87). Both readings of CBA are worth examining—but not here. As befits a handbook on value theory, this chapter sees CBA as a methodology centered on a particular account of *prudential value*, the preference-based account. The picture to be presented here is that preferences figure in CBA because of the nexus between preferences and individual well-being. CBA *operationalizes* the preference account of prudential value—transmuting that account into a very general framework for providing guidance to government about its choices.

17.2. WHAT IS CBA?

Here, I describe the textbook approach to CBA (Boadway and Bruce 1984; Freeman 2003; Just, Hueth, and Schmitz 2004; Mas-Collel, Whinston, and Green 1995, ch. 3). This framework (like any decision-analysis tool) may end up being simplified in governmental or scholarly applications.

CBA evaluates choices in light of outcomes. An outcome is a partly specified possible world: a partial description of how the world might turn out. "Outcomes" are in turn usually thought of by economists as lists of individual attribute bundles—one bundle for each person in the population. With x an outcome, $x = (\mathbf{M}_1(x), \mathbf{M}_2(x), \ldots, \mathbf{M}_N(x))$, with $\mathbf{M}_i(x)$ the bundle of individual i in outcome x.[1]

What is contained in these bundles? CBA revolves around "money," and so a bundle must at least specify how much "money" the person has. "Money" is useful because it can be expended on markets. Finally, CBA has been applied to policies that affect "non-market" attributes, such as health or environmental quality; these, too, may be part of someone's bundle.

More precisely, let $\mathbf{p}$ be the prices of marketed goods in some outcome x. Let c_i be individual i's "consumption" in x: her total expenditure on marketed goods. Let $\mathbf{h}_i$ be the totality of her nonmarket attributes in x. Then $\mathbf{M}_i(x) = (c_i, \mathbf{p}, \mathbf{h}_i)$. Call this type of bundle a "consumption-specified" bundle.

CBA assumes that each individual has her own "utility" function: a mathematical function allowing for the assignment of numbers to bundles. Strictly, each individual i is seen to have *two* kinds of utility functions: a "direct" utility function $u_i(.)$ and an "indirect" (or derived) utility function $v_i(.)$. The "argument" (input) for the direct utility function is not a consumption-specified bundle, but a slightly different type of bundle—call it a "commodity-specified" bundle. Denote this as $\mathbf{B}_i$. $\mathbf{B}_i$, a commodity-specified bundle held by individual i, takes the form $(\mathbf{q}_i, \mathbf{h}_i)$, with $\mathbf{q}_i$ the list of marketed goods and services consumed by i, and $\mathbf{h}_i$ (as above) nonmarket attributes. It is here that preferences come into the picture. Individual i is supposed to have a well-behaved preference ranking, R_i, of commodity-specified bundles. "$\mathbf{B}_i\, R_i\, \mathbf{B}_i^*$" means that individual i weakly prefers bundle $\mathbf{B}_i$ to bundle $\mathbf{B}_i^*$. The direct utility function $u_i(.)$ is a mathematical representation of R_i. $u_i(\mathbf{B}_i) \geq u_i(\mathbf{B}_i^*)$ iff $\mathbf{B}_i\, R_i\, \mathbf{B}_i^*$.

Someone's *indirect* utility function for consumption-specified bundles is derived from her direct utility function as follows: $v_i(\mathbf{M}_i) = v_i(c_i, \mathbf{p}, \mathbf{h}_i)$ is the *maximum* value of direct utility that is achievable by individual i, given a total consumption amount of c_i, with nonmarket attributes $\mathbf{h}_i$, and facing market prices $\mathbf{p}$.

The apparatus of twin utility functions, indirect and direct, is needed by CBA because "money" (consumption) is a *summary* indicator, reflecting the totality of goods and services that money can buy. CBA measures policies' well-being impacts in terms of *money*, but individuals do not have fundamental preferences for money per se—rather for what money buys.

How does CBA use the apparatus of individual utility functions to evaluate policy choices? Assume, first, that government is choosing under conditions of certainty. Each choice in $\mathbf{A}$ leads, for sure, to one outcome. Thus $\mathbf{A} = \{x, y, z, \ldots\}$. Let s be the status quo outcome: what would result were government to do nothing. c_i^x indicates the consumption of individual i in outcome x; $\mathbf{p}^x$ the prices in x, and so forth. For each outcome, an individual can be assigned a *monetary equivalent*. Individual i's monetary equivalent for x ("$ME_i(x)$") is the change to i's status quo consumption which would just suffice to make her indifferent between the status quo and x. In terms of the indirect utility function:

$$ME_i(x) = \Delta c \text{ such that: } v_i\left(c_i^s + \Delta c, \mathbf{p}^s, \mathbf{h}_i^s\right) = v_i\left(c_i^x, \mathbf{p}^x, \mathbf{h}_i^x\right).$$

This monetary equivalent is also sometimes referred to as a "willingness to pay" or "willingness to accept" amount. Imagine that Sue is in a position to bargain with government about whether the status quo or some alternative outcome x should obtain. Imagine, first, that Sue would prefer the status quo. Then her monetary equivalent for x is (negative one times) the maximum amount she would be willing to pay (in the status quo), in exchange for government ensuring that the status quo rather than x obtains. Imagine, now, that Sue would prefer outcome x. Then her monetary equivalent for x is the minimum payment she would accept from government (in the status quo), in exchange for her agreement that the status quo rather than outcome x may obtain.

CBA's rule for ranking outcomes is just to sum monetary equivalents. Outcome x is socially at least as good as outcome y iff the sum of monetary equivalents for x is at least as large as the sum of monetary equivalents for y. This rule obviously yields a complete and transitive ranking of outcomes.[2] The best outcome or outcomes is the one with the largest sum of monetary equivalents; CBA's guidance is to pick any one of those.

This rule, moreover, satisfies the Pareto principle: if at least one individual's indirect utility is greater in x than y, and everyone else's is no smaller, CBA assigns x a greater sum of monetary equivalents than y.[3] There are variations of the rule just stated that fail to yield a complete and transitive ranking of outcomes; or that do so but fail the Pareto principle; and so the rule just described is plausibly the most attractive version of CBA (Adler 2012: 92–98).

CBA's rule can be readily extended to the case of risk, where each a is a probability distribution over outcomes. Now, each individual is supposed to have a ranking of *lotteries* of commodity-specified bundles that conforms to the axioms of "expected utility" (EU) theory. Individual i's direct utility function, $u_i(.)$, is still a function of commodity-specified bundles. It still takes the form $u_i(\mathbf{B}_i)$. And $u_i(.)$ still has a corresponding indirect utility function $v_i(.)$ over consumption-specified bundles (the maximum value of $u_i(.)$ reachable with that consumption-specified bundle). But $u_i(.)$ is now supposed to be an EU utility function, namely one that provides an *expectational* representation of these lottery preferences (Gilboa 2009; Kreps 1988; Mas-Collel, Whinston, and Green 1995: ch. 6). Individual i weakly prefers lottery L over commodity-specified bundles to lottery L^* iff the expected $u_i(.)$ value associated with L is at least as large as the expected $u_i(.)$ value associated with L^*.

From $u_i(.)$ and the corresponding $v_i(.)$, we can define a monetary equivalent $\mathrm{ME}_i(a)$ for each *action* in A. (I omit the technical details of the construction of $\mathrm{ME}_i(a)$, which are not relevant for a basic understanding of CBA, or for the philosophical issues to be addressed here.) CBA's ranking of actions just corresponds to the sum of monetary equivalents for each.

17.3. CBA, Rationality Conditions on Preferences, and the Inference of Monetary Equivalents

In its apparatus of utility functions and monetary equivalents, CBA imposes a variety of rationality conditions on preferences. These can be grouped into three categories. The first are conditions that arise even without risk in the picture, and that ensure the existence of $u_i(.)$, $v_i(.)$, and monetary equivalents. In order for $u_i(.)$ and thus $v_i(.)$ to exist, individual i's ranking of commodity-specified bundles must be *complete and transitive*. Moreover, if the set of commodity-specified bundles is uncountably infinite, the existence of $u_i(.)$ and thus $v_i(.)$ may require i's ranking of these bundles to be *continuous*. (On preferences and utility, see Kreps 1988; Mas-Collel, Whinston, and Green 1995: chs. 1, 3). Finally, in order for monetary equivalents to exist for every choice situation and be unique, $v_i(.)$ as a function of consumption must be strictly increasing in consumption, and must also have a sufficient range.[4]

The second category of rationality conditions are those that arise with risk in the picture, and that are necessary for the existence of an EU utility function $u_i(.)$. These well-known conditions have been much discussed in the literature on expected utility theory. In particular, individual i's ranking of lotteries over commodity-specified bundles must satisfy an "independence" constraint, which says that if i weakly prefers lottery L to L^* she must weakly prefer a mixture with probability p of L and probability

$(1-p)$ of a third lottery L', to a mixture with the same probabilities of L^* and L' (Gilboa 2009: ch. 8; Kreps 1988; Mas-Collel, Whinston, and Green 1995: ch. 6).

The third rationality condition is implicit in the definition of indirect utility $v_i(.)$. Recall that the indirect utility of a given consumption-specified bundle, $v_i(\mathbf{M}_i) = v_i(c_i, \mathbf{p}, \mathbf{h}_i)$, is the maximum direct utility which individual i could achieve, given prices $\mathbf{p}$, a total budget for expenditure (consumption) of c_i, and nonmarket attributes $\mathbf{h}_i$. CBA then takes $v_i(.)$ as an indicator of i's well-being with consumption-specified bundles. But $v_i(.)$ is a genuine such indicator *only if i is a rational maximizer of his preferences*. We are assuming that $u_i(.)$ captures i's preferences over commodity-specified bundles. If so, and if i is rational, he will expend a given budget to maximize the extent to which those preferences are satisfied, that is, to maximize $u_i(.)$. But if i is characterized by familiar failures of means-end rationality—akrasia, failures of calculation, satisficing behavior—he might use his resources imperfectly and end up with less direct utility $u_i(.)$ than is feasible with $(c_i, \mathbf{p}, \mathbf{h}_i)$.

Preferentialists about well-being often impose idealizing conditions on preferences, including rationality conditions (see generally Adler 2012: ch. 3, reviewing literature on well-being). Idealizing conditions can take two generic forms, which for the moment I'll discuss together. (I) *A requirement on hypothetical preferences*. Individual i is at least as well off with x as y iff i would weakly prefer x under hypothetical conditions H, and those hypothetical preferences satisfy conditions C. (II) *A requirement on actual preferences*. Individual i is at least as well off with x as y iff i weakly prefers x to y, and those preferences satisfy conditions C.

We can now ask whether the rationality conditions imposed by CBA on preferences are appropriate components of C (in either generic form). Is this the right account of preference-based prudential value? The answer to this question is not obvious, but preferentialists might plausibly answer no. Some have argued that CBA takes insufficient account of the "incommensurability" of goods (see sources reviewed in Adler 1998). This amounts to a challenge to one or another rationality condition in the first category set out above. The "incommensurability" critique might be a challenge to the assumption of a complete ranking of bundles. Perhaps some pairs of bundles are noncomparable: Individual i neither prefers one bundle to the other, nor is indifferent. Alternatively, the "incommensurability" critique might be a challenge to the continuity condition. Lexicographic preferences (Mas-Collel, Whinston, and Green 1995: 46–50) violate continuity. Finally, and most simply, it might challenge the premise of a $v_i(.)$ that is strictly increasing in consumption and that has "sufficient range" (see above). Perhaps there are some losses to nonmarket goods that no amount of consumption could repair.

Challenges to EU theory as an evaluative account (as an appropriate component of conditions C) challenge the second group of rationality conditions. Here, we should be careful—some who "challenge" EU theory may doubt its predictive ability without disputing its status as a component of C.[5] Still, such a challenge is possible. For example, Maurice Allais doubted "independence" as a requirement on the rational ranking of lotteries (Allais 1979).[6]

An important topic (for those who doubt CBA's rationality requirements as components of C) is whether a CBA-like procedure might be constructed even if some of these requirements are relaxed. Research on this topic is in its infancy (Bernheim and Rangel 2009).

A different set of issues arises for those who *endorse* CBA's rationality conditions as *evaluative* conditions. Much research in "behavioral economics" suggests that individuals frequently violate various of the conditions in the three categories I have described (Camerer, Lowenstein, and Rabin 2004; Kahneman and Tversky 2000; Kahneman 2011). Even the simplest requirement of a complete and transitive ranking of bundles is violated by "loss averse" behavior, whereby individuals frame changes to their attributes as losses or gains from an arbitrary reference point. Violations of EU theory are well known. Kahneman's prospect theory, and descendants, are an attempt to provide a non-EU theory of choice under risk that better fits observed behavior.

Here, the choice between the two generic forms for conditions C becomes important. If CBA's rationality conditions take form (II), a requirement on actual preferences, then the failure of those conditions yields some incomparability in prudential value—and if the failures are widespread (as appears to be the case) the extent of such incomparability will be large.[7] Under (II), if i has actual preferences for x over y, but those preferences fall short of C in some way, then presumably i is neither better off in x than y, nor worse off, nor equally well off.

This implication can be avoided by shifting to form (I). Presumably the hypothetical conditions are those of good information, deliberation, calm thought, and so on. So CBA now says: individual i's utility functions $u_i(.)$ and $v_i(.)$, and therewith his monetary equivalents, reflect the preferences over commodity-specified bundles that individual i *would have*, were he to reflect with good information, and so forth, and arrive at preferences that are complete, transitive, and otherwise meet CBA's rationality conditions. But there remains the question of inference. If individual i in actual behavior falls short of C, how can we infer these hypothetical $u_i(.)$ and $v_i(.)$ functions and the monetary equivalents they yield?

Both "revealed preference" (behavioral) evidence and "stated preference" (survey) evidence are used by some CBA practitioners to infer monetary equivalents (Bateman and Willis 2001; Champ, Boyle, and Brown 2003; Freeman 2003). The details of these methods, and their pros and cons, constitute a massive topic that I cannot pursue here—except to note that individual departures from rationality are one important aspect of the topic. If form (I) is adopted, and if individuals in their day-to-day behavior do indeed regularly fail to satisfy CBA's rationality conditions, surveys would seem to be the preferred method for estimating monetary equivalents. Survey respondents can be given good information and can be "debiased" (encouraged to think rationally). However, many economists remain critical of the stated-preference method (see Carson, Flores, and Meade 2001, surveying criticisms); and some of these criticisms are relevant even given form (I). Survey respondents (since not acting on their responses) may have little incentive to do the hard deliberational work needed to process the information provided and to arrive at a ranking of bundles that they seriously endorse. Surveys may not be "incentive compatible," that is, survey respondents may have an incentive to misstate their preferences. Finally, surveys are expensive.

Let me conclude by returning to the special rationality condition implicit in the definition of indirect utility. One way to handle the fact that individuals do not use their resources to maximize their preferences (certainly not their hypothetical preferences, and not even their actual preferences) is to define $v_i(.)$ so as to take account of actual failures of rationality. This is most straightforward using form (I) for conditions C. Utility function $u_i(.)$ is a numerical representation of the preferences that individual i would have, under idealized conditions. With form (I), utility $u_i(.)$ is a numerical representation of individual i's well-being with a given commodity-specified bundle—whether or not $u_i(.)$ tracks i's actual preferences. In turn, $v_i(.)$ for a consumption-specified bundle can be defined as the $u_i(.)$ level that individual i would attain, given i's actual behavioral dispositions. Such a definition of $v_i(.)$, together with form (I), means that $v_i(.)$ is a valid representation of the well-being that i (given his behavioral characteristics) actually reaps from consumption-specified bundles.

17.4. CBA AND "REMOTENESS"

Virtually all philosophers attracted to a preference-based view of well-being agree that some preferences concern states of affairs that are too "remote" from the preference-holder to make a difference to her well-being (Adler 2012: ch. 3). This is the lesson of Parfit's famous "stranger" example (Parfit 1987: 494). If I have a conversation with a stranger whom I will never see again, learn in the course of the conversation that he has a terrible disease, and form a preference that the disease be cured, then if the stranger *is* later cured—unbeknownst to me—my preference has been satisfied. But surely in this case the stranger's return to health doesn't improve *my* well-being. There needs to be some closer link to my life—for example, that the stranger is cured *and I learn about it and feel happy*, or that the person whose cure I prefer is not a stranger but rather my friend or relative.

Preferentialists continue to debate how to restrict preferences so as to solve the remoteness problem. Perhaps the preferred state of affairs must be some mental state of the preference-holder (her feeling happy, etc.). Perhaps it must be some mental state of hers *or* some condition of her physical body. Perhaps it must be a state the occurrence of which entails her existence. Perhaps the holder must be in a condition of self-sympathy (Adler 2012: ch. 3; Darwall 2002; Kagan 1992; Overvold 1982). No consensus solution to this difficult problem has emerged. But at least philosophers recognize the problem!

No parallel discussion within economics has occurred. Some areas of economics do limit the arguments for individuals' preferences. For example, in traditional optimal tax theory, each individual is seen as having preferences over her own consumption and her own leisure (Kaplow 2008); in health economics, the preferences are over health and consumption (Rey and Rochet 2004). But the motivation for such limitation, where it occurs, seems to be the enhanced tractability of simplified models of preferences—not a concern to solve the remoteness problem.

How does this impinge on CBA specifically? Not surprisingly, CBA practitioners calculate monetary equivalents for bundles of attributes that—on some solutions to the remoteness problem—are too remote to be welfare-relevant. The diversity of solutions to the problem makes this unsurprising. More interestingly, CBA practitioners also sometimes take account of attributes that—on *every* plausible solution—are too remote. A good example is "existence values" in the context of environmental CBA (Champ, Boyle, and Brown 2003; Freeman 2003: ch. 5). The sheer existence of an ecosystem in a nondegraded state is seen as a benefit to someone who prefers nondegradation, a benefit that is appropriately assigned a monetary equivalent—no less so than the benefit consisting of the ecosystem's "use value" to individuals who physically interact with it. But someone's preference regarding distant ecosystems (presumably a moral preference for a nondegraded environment), as opposed to a preference for feeling good about a distant ecosystem, or having a nondegraded ecosystem to use, seems no more welfare-relevant than the preference in Parfit's "stranger" case.

However, CBA can be refined to screen out existence values, and otherwise to take account of the remoteness problem. The preferentialist can add her preferred specification of the nonremoteness condition (whatever it might be) to the rationality requirements on preferences that CBA imposes. I noted earlier that *deleting* one of those rationality requirements (such as completeness) may threaten the existence of $u_i(.)$, $v_i(.)$, and monetary equivalents. By contrast, *adding* a requirement (such as nonremoteness) will not have this worrying effect. To be sure, adding the nonremoteness requirement *does* further complicate inference, since individuals in their behavior or in answering surveys may be acting on preferences that do not qualify as nonremote.

17.5. CBA and Interpersonal Comparisons

As already mentioned, the rise of CBA was connected to intellectual movements in economics that were skeptical about interpersonal comparisons (Robbins 1935, 1938; Hicks 1939; Kaldor 1939).[8] What, exactly, are the presuppositions of CBA regarding interpersonal comparability? A distinction is often drawn between interpersonal comparisons of well-being levels and interpersonal comparisons of well-being differences; but for my purposes here the two can be discussed in tandem.

First: Whatever the facts may be about interpersonal comparisons, CBA is not sensitive to such facts. Relatedly, CBA is consistent with the absence of interpersonal comparability.

As a preliminary matter, we need to define some terms. A function $f(.)$ operating on real numbers is "increasing" iff $s > r$ implies $f(s) > f(r)$. A function $f(.)$ operating on real numbers is a "positive affine" function iff $f(s) = as + b$, with a positive. (Note that positive affine functions are increasing.) Direct utility function $u_i^*(.)$ is an "increasing transformation" of utility function $u_i(.)$ iff there exists an increasing function $f_i(.)$ such that $u_i^*(\mathbf{B}_i) = f_i(u_i(\mathbf{B}_i))$ for all bundles $\mathbf{B}_i$. Direct utility function $u_i^*(.)$ is a "positive affine transformation" of $u_i(.)$ iff there exists a positive affine function $f_i(.)$ such that $u_i^*(\mathbf{B}_i) = f_i(u_i(\mathbf{B}_i))$ for all $\mathbf{B}_i$.

Note that if $u_i^*(.)$ is an increasing transformation of $u_i(.)$, then the indirect utility function $v_i^*(.)$ corresponding to $u_i^*(.)$ is an increasing transformation of the indirect utility function $v_i(.)$ corresponding to $u_i(.)$. This is also true for positive affine transformations. And both are true not only for the traditional definition of indirect utility, but also for the behaviorally inflected definition suggested at the end of the discussion earlier of rationality.

Now we can discuss interpersonal comparisons. Begin by taking risk out of the picture. If so, individual i's utility function $u_i(.)$ need only be *ordinal*. That is, CBA permits $u_i(.)$ to be replaced by an increasing transformation $u_i^*(.)$ Note that if $u_i(.)$ represents i's preferences R_i over commodity-specified bundles, and $u_i^*(.)$ is an increasing transformation of $u_i(.)$, then $u_i^*(.)$ also represents R_i.[9]

Moreover the indirect utility function $v_i(.)$ corresponding to $u_i(.)$, and the indirect utility function $v_i^*(.)$ corresponding to $u_i^*(.)$, will generate identical rankings of consumption-specified bundles: $v_i(\mathbf{M}_i) \geq v_i(\mathbf{M}_i^+)$ iff $v_i^*(\mathbf{M}_i) \geq v_i^*(\mathbf{M}_i^+)$. Thus monetary equivalents calculated using $v_i(.)$ and $v_i^*(.)$ will be identical.

Consider the list of indirect utility functions $v_1(.), v_2(.), \ldots, v_N(.)$, one for each of the N members of the population, corresponding to their direct utility functions $u_1(.), u_2(), \ldots, u_N(.)$. Consider now the list $v_1^*(.), v_2^*(.), \ldots, v_N^*(.)$, each corresponding to a $u_i^*(.)$ that is an increasing transformation of $u_i(.)$. Thus each $v_i^*(.)$ is an increasing transformation of $v_i(.)$. Assume, to begin, that there *are* true facts regarding interpersonal comparisons, and that (as it happens) the first list mirrors these facts. $v_i(x) \geq v_j(y)$[10] iff individual i's level of well-being in x is at least as large as individual j's level of well-being in y. $v_i(x) - v_j(y) \geq v_k(z) - v_l(w)$ iff the difference between the well-being of individual i in x and individual j in y is at least as large as the difference between the well-being of individual k in z and individual l in w.

The second list of utility functions may *not* mirror these facts. It need *not* be the case that $v_i^*(x) \geq v_j^*(y)$ iff individual i's level of well-being in x is at least as large as individual j's level of well-being in y. And it need *not* be the case that $v_i^*(x) - v_j^*(y) \geq v_k^*(z) - v_l^*(w)$ iff the difference between the well-being of individual i in x and individual j in y is at least as large as the difference between the well-being of individual k in z and individual l in w. (See note 11 for an example.)[11] But this is irrelevant for purposes of CBA. $u_i(.)$ and $u_i^*(.)$ are equally good representations of i's preferences, and the corresponding $v_i(.)$ and $v_i^*(.)$ will generate identical monetary equivalents.

Assume now that the skeptic about interpersonal comparisons is correct. There are no facts about interpersonal level and difference comparisons. Thus it cannot be said that $v_1(.), \ldots, v_N(.)$ is better or worse than $v_1^*(.), \ldots, v_N^*(.)$ in mirroring the interpersonal facts.. Such parity between the two lists of utility functions does not trouble

CBA, because CBA calculates the same monetary equivalents, regardless of which list is used.

Consider now the case of risk. If so, $u_i(.)$ is an EU function and is *cardinal* rather than ordinal. It is a well-known feature of EU theory that if $u_i(.)$ expectationally represents i's preferences over lotteries, and $u_i^*(.)$ does as well, then $u_i^*(.)$ must be a positive affine transformation of $u_i(.)$.

However, even if $u_i(.)$ is cardinal, the same conclusions as above hold true. Consider the list of indirect utility functions $v_1(.), v_2(.), \ldots, v_N(.)$, one for each of the N members of the population, each corresponding to one $u_i(.)$. Consider now the list $v_1^*(.), v_2^*(.), \ldots, v_N^*(.)$, where each $v_i^*(.)$ is a positive affine transformation of $v_i(.)$. It is *still* quite possible that the first list represents the true facts regarding interpersonal well-being comparisons while the second does not. (See note 12 for an example.)[12] But both lists generate the very same monetary equivalents,[13] and thus the superior informational content of the first list qua interpersonal comparisons is irrelevant to CBA. Conversely, the skeptical position—that facts about interpersonal comparisons are not better reflected by one or the other list, since there are no such facts—does not undermine CBA, because CBA is invariant to which list is used.

Second. CBA is consistent with interpersonal comparability, just as it is consistent with the absence of interpersonal comparability. CBA does not presuppose that the new welfare economists were *correct* in denying interpersonal comparability. This is immediate from the prior analysis. CBA is invariant between the lists $v_1(.), \ldots, v_N(.)$ and $v_1^*(.), \ldots, v_N^*(.)$, if each utility function in one list is an increasing or positive affine transformation of the corresponding utility function in the other—but this invariance is perfectly consistent with there being facts about interpersonal comparisons that one of these lists mirrors while the other does not.

Third. Developing an account of interpersonal comparisons poses a genuine challenge for preferentialists. The new welfare economists may have been wrong in denying interpersonal comparability; but they were correct, at least, in grasping that there is a real puzzle here. The basis for interpersonal comparisons, *given* preferentialism about well-being, is far from clear.

Space limitations prevent a detailed discussion of the issue. The key problems are twofold. First, individuals (even under idealized conditions) can have different preferences. I may prefer bundle (**q, h**) to bundle (**q*, h***), while you may have the opposite preference. Second, interpersonal comparisons should be consistent with the intrapersonal comparisons implied by individuals' (idealized) preferences. If $v_i(.)$ is such that $v_i(x) \geq v_i(y)$, then x is at least as good for i as y; and the preferentialist account of interpersonal comparisons is constrained by this intrapersonal fact.[14]

Given these twin constraints, it follows that interpersonal comparisons must take account not only of individuals' attributes, but of their preferences. Assume that in outcome x individual 1 has (consumption-specified) bundle **M** and individual 2 has bundle **M***, while in outcome y their holdings are reversed. Moreover, individual i's indirect utility function $v_i(.)$ assigns a greater value to **M** than **M***; individual 2 has different preferences, and her indirect utility function $v_2(.)$ assigns a greater value to **M*** than **M**. Thus the well-being of individual 1 in x is greater than the well-being of individual 1 in y, and the well-being of individual 2 in x is greater than the well-being of individual 2 in y. If we now insist that the interpersonal comparisons of individual 1 in either outcome to individual 2 in either outcome are just a function of which bundles the two have, we will have an intransitivity.

John Harsanyi's concept of "extended preferences" provides the building blocks for an account of interpersonal comparisons sensitive to individual preferences as well as attributes (Harsanyi 1977: ch. 4; Adler 2012: ch. 3; 2014; forthcoming a). Call an "extended bundle" a combination of an ordinary bundle **B**, and a preference structure R. Then someone's extended preferences are rankings of extended bundles. Moreover, Harsanyi proposes the following consistency condition: If preference structure R is such as to prefer bundle **B** to bundle **B***, anyone's extended preferences should rank extended bundle (**B**, R) above extended bundle (**B***, R). If $h(.)$ is an "extended" utility function representing these extended preferences, $h(\mathbf{B}, R)$ *might* be taken as the well-being level of an individual with bundle **B** and preferences R. Note how this consistency condition will work to satisfy the second constraint mentioned two paragraphs above. If some individual i has preferences R_i such that she prefers x to y, $h(.)$ will assign her a larger number in x by virtue of the consistency condition.

While the concept of "extended preferences" is an important one, it must be refined in many ways to yield a viable account of interpersonal comparisons. Among other things, individuals can have different extended preferences. The problem of the diversity of preferences recurs at this level.

17.6. Kaldor-Hicks Efficiency

To see the difficulties in justifying CBA with reference to Kaldor-Hicks efficiency, I will focus on the simplified case in which government is choosing under conditions of certainty. It is quite complex to specify the Kaldor-Hicks test for the choice among policies that are probability distributions across outcomes. Leaving that aside, the substantive difficulties affecting the certainty case (to be discussed in a moment) clearly will carry over to the more realistic case of choice under uncertainty.

The Kaldor-Hicks criterion (in the certainty case) is a criterion for ranking outcomes. Strictly speaking, the outcomes must specify the marketed goods that individuals purchase (their commodity-specified bundles), and not merely their consumption in the aggregate. And the criterion is intended as a supplement to the criterion of Pareto efficiency,[15] which says: if at least some strictly prefer outcome x to outcome y, and everyone else is indifferent, then x is a better outcome than y.

Assume that x and y are not ranked by the Pareto criterion (they are "Pareto-noncomparable"). Some strictly prefer x to y (the "winners" in x), while others strictly prefer y to x (the "losers" in x). x is *Kaldor-Hicks* efficient relative to y iff: there exists a costless redistribution of the goods that individuals hold in x, from the winners in x to the losers in x, creating x^+, which is Pareto superior to y. (For discussions of this criterion and variations, see Blackorby and Donaldson 1990; Boadway and Bruce 1984: chs. 3, 9; Chipman 2008; Chipman and Moore 1978. It originates with Hicks 1939; Kaldor 1939; and Hotelling 1938).

The standard defense of CBA—for those who endorse this methodology and are skeptical about interpersonal comparisons—is to appeal to the combination of Pareto and Kaldor-Hicks efficiency (Freeman 2003: 87–90; Just, Hueth, and Schmitz 2004: ch. 1; Mishan 1988: ch. 25). The standard defense says something like: x is ranked by the CBA test above y iff x is either Pareto efficient or Kaldor-Hicks efficient relative to y. Note that CBA *does* prefer Pareto-efficient outcomes. And, intuitively, it *does* seem to track Kaldor-Hicks efficiency in ranking Pareto-noncomparable outcomes. If the sum of monetary equivalents for x, calculated with respect to some status quo, is greater than the sum of monetary equivalents for y, then intuitively the winners in x relative to y would seem to have more than enough goods to compensate the losers. Moreover, note that the Kaldor-Hicks test (like CBA itself) does not presuppose interpersonal comparability.

One, technical, difficulty with this defense is that CBA and the Kaldor-Hicks test can actually diverge in ranking Pareto-noncomparable outcomes. This divergence has been discussed under the heading of the "Boadway paradox" (Blackorby and Donaldson 1990; Boadway 1974; Boadway and Bruce 1984: ch. 9).[16]

Leaving that aside, there are serious difficulties with the Kaldor-Hicks defense of CBA which concern the Kaldor-Hicks criterion itself.

One set of difficulties is formal. The betterness relation is asymmetric and transitive. If x is strictly better than y, then y is not strictly better than x. If x is strictly better than y, and y is strictly better than z, then x is strictly better than z. However, it turns out to be possible that each of two outcomes is Kaldor-Hicks superior to the other. (There exists a hypothetical redistribution in x from the winners in x to the losers in x, yielding a x^+ Pareto superior to y; *and* there exists a hypothetical redistribution in y from the winners in y to the losers in y, yielding a y^+ Pareto superior to x; Scitovsky 1941.) This so-called "Scitovsky" paradox might be solved via a double test, stipulating that x is better than y iff x is Kaldor-Hicks efficient relative to y and y is not Kaldor-Hicks efficient relative to x. But the double test, it emerges, can generate intransitivities (Gorman 1955).

A second set of difficulties is substantive. Assume that x and y are Pareto-noncomparable, and that the Kaldor-Hicks test (indeed the double test) points to x.

How does this constitute a normative *argument* for x? Although x *could* be transformed via costless redistribution into x^+, Pareto superior to y, in outcome x that redistribution has not occurred. Moreover, costless redistribution is infeasible given the tax mechanisms available to government (which inevitably have administrative costs, some rate of noncompliance, etc.). If x were to occur and government were then to engage in some form of taxation in an attempt to compensate the losers (relative to y), the result would not be x^+ but x^{++}, which might well not be Pareto superior to y. But even leaving this aside—even assuming that x^+ is feasibly reachable from x—how does the Pareto efficiency of x^+ relative to y establish that x (not merely x^+) is better than y? (Sen 1979).

Pretty clearly, then, it is problematic to think of the Kaldor-Hicks test as grounding a relation of moral betterness (or any other kind of betterness) between outcomes. If x is Kaldor-Hicks efficient relative to y, it does not follow that x is morally better than y, or better in any other sense. (And by extension, it would be problematic to see that test as grounding a relation of moral betterness between choices.)

Alternatively, the Kaldor-Hicks test is sometimes defended not as the criterion of betterness, but as a decision procedure which, in the long run, yields Pareto-superior outcomes (Graham 2008: 414–19). If government repeatedly makes choices that are Kaldor-Hicks efficient (by repeatedly using CBA), everyone will be better off. However, it seems exceedingly unlikely that the repeated use of the Kaldor-Hicks test is Pareto efficient in the long run *relative to the long-run use of all plausible competitor procedures* (for example, the long-run use of social welfare functions that give special priority to the poor), and not merely Pareto efficient relative to governmental inaction.

17.7. SOCIAL WELFARE FUNCTIONS

Social welfare functions (SWFs), like CBA, employ the apparatus of utility functions. But the information is used somewhat differently. CBA assigns each outcome a list of monetary equivalents relative to the status quo, and then compares two outcomes by summing these monetary equivalents. The SWF approach, by contrast, ranks two outcomes by direct comparison of the lists of individual utilities corresponding to the outcomes. An exemplary SWF is the utilitarian SWF, which simply sums utilities: x at least as good as y iff $v_1(x) + v_2(x) + \ldots + v_N(x) \geq v_1(y) + v_2(y) + \ldots + v_N(y)$. An equity-regarding variation on this is the "prioritarian" SWF, which sums utilities transformed by a concave function. (On SWFs, see generally Adler 2012 and also sources cited therein.)

By contrast with CBA, the SWF approach *does* presuppose interpersonal comparability (Bossert and Weymark 2004). This can be seen with the utilitarian SWF, although the point is quite general. Let $v_1(.), \ldots, v_N(.)$ be a list of individual utility functions. Let $v_1^*(.), \ldots, v_N^*(.)$ be increasing or positive affine transformations thereof. Then (as we have seen) CBA will be invariant to which list is used, but the utilitarian SWF will not be.[17]

Some SWFs correspond to moral views with considerable philosophical support—the utilitarian SWF to utilitarianism, the prioritarian SWF to prioritarianism—and such SWFs (by contrast with the Kaldor-Hicks test) *are* therefore a plausible basis for identifying morally better or worse outcomes. But how is this relevant to the justification of CBA?

Interestingly, a modified version of CBA sums monetary equivalents multiplied by distributive weights. This modified version has been discussed in scholarly work and, to a limited extent, used by government (Boadway and Bruce 1984: 271–81; Drèze and Stern 1987; HM Treasury 2003: 91–94; Little and Mirrlees 1994; Johansson-Stenman 2005; Ray 1984; Squire and van der Tak 1975). In the case of choice under certainty, with

s the status quo, the weighting factor assigned to individual i—call it $w_i(s)$—is multiplied by her monetary equivalent for each outcome x in the choice situation, $ME_i(x)$. The rule that distributively weighted CBA uses for ranking outcomes is: x is at least as good as y iff the sum of $w_i(s) \times ME_i(x)$ is at least as large as the sum of $w_i(s) \times ME_i(y)$. If all the outcomes are relatively "small" variations around the status quo, this rule—with appropriate weighting factors—approximates the ranking of the outcomes by an SWF.

For example, the utilitarian SWF can be approximated with a weighting factor $w_i(s)$ equaling the marginal utility of consumption for individual i, given his attributes in the status quo s. The consumption change that equilibrates the difference between s and x, that is, $ME_i(x)$, is converted into a well-being change by multiplying with this marginal-utility factor. This approach generalizes to the prioritarian SWF: now, the weighting factor reflects both the marginal utility of consumption and the marginal moral value of well-being itself (a value which, for prioritarians, is not constant). The distributive-weighting approach also generalizes, to some extent, to choice under uncertainty (Adler, forthcoming b).

Insofar as the SWF generating distributive weights *is* a plausible criterion for the moral goodness of choices and outcomes, distributively weighted CBA is also a plausible approximate criterion of moral goodness. And CBA *without* distributive weights can in turn be seen as an approximate such criterion in the very special case where everyone's weights are equal (in the case of the utilitarian SWF, for example, where everyone's marginal consumption utility in the status quo is equal).

The calculation of distributive weights (and the assessment whether we're confronting the special case where everyone's weights are equal) *does* depend upon facts about interpersonal comparisons. Assume that the marginal utility of consumption for individual 1, and thus $w_1(s)$, is calculated using utility function $v_1(.)$; for individual 2 using $v_2(.)$; and so forth. This can yield a different set of weighting factors, and a different ranking of outcomes, than if we use $v_1^*(.)$, $v_2^*(.)$, and so forth to calculate the weighting factors—with each $v_i^*(.)$ either an increasing or a positive affine transformation of the corresponding $v_i(.)$. Facts about each individual's preferences—the facts equally well reflected in $v_i(.)$ and $v_i^*(.)$—are not sufficient to justify the choice between these lists. What *would* justify the choice are facts about interpersonal comparisons.

Of course, the sensitivity of distributively weighted CBA to interpersonal comparisons is hardly surprising. Again, the distributive weighting technique is just an approximation to the direct application of SWFs to rank outcomes or choices. And such direct application (as illustrated in note 17) is sensitive to the choice between $v_i(.)$ and $v_i^*(.)$.

Still, there is a real irony here. Doubts about interpersonal comparability led to the new welfare economics and the Kaldor-Hicks test; and CBA became widely accepted in economics and, then, governmental practice in this intellectual milieu. But the Kaldor-Hicks criterion does not state a plausible criterion for the goodness of policies. If we want to justify CBA, we'll have to do so with reference to SWFs, and thus show how interpersonal comparisons are indeed possible. The justification of CBA presupposes the very thing that those who popularized CBA wanted to reject.

Notes

1. My presentation will sometimes use functional notation and/or subscripts, as here, and sometimes omit these where clear from context or otherwise unnecessary.
2. "Complete and transitive ranking" is used, here, as a synonym for a complete quasiordering. A quasiordering R on some set (here, the set $\mathbf{A}$ of choices, $\mathbf{A} = \{a, b, \ldots\}$) is a binary relation between elements of that set which is (1) reflexive ($a\,R\,a$ for all elements of $\mathbf{A}$); and (2) transitive ($a\,R\,b$ and $b\,R\,c$ implies $a\,R\,c$). From any such R we can define relations I and P, as follows: $a\,I\,b$ iff $a\,R\,b$ and $b\,R\,a$; $a\,P\,b$ iff $a\,R\,b$ and not $b\,R\,a$. Note that R, I, and P have the features, respectively, of the "at least as good as," "equally good as," and "strictly better than" relations.

    To say that a quasiordering R is *complete* means: for every two items in the set, either the first bears the R relation to the second, or the second to the first, or both.

    Now consider the case under discussion in the text, where $\mathbf{A} = \{x, y, \ldots\}$. Let the sum of monetary equivalents define a relation R^{CBA} between outcomes, as follows: $x\,R^{CBA}\,y$ iff $\sum_{i=1}^{N} ME_i(x) \geq \sum_{i=1}^{N} ME_i(y)$. R^{CBA} is clearly a complete quasiordering of the elements of $\mathbf{A}$.
3. Strictly, this satisfies the Pareto principle on the assumption that individuals expend their consumption so as to maximize direct utility. See below, discussing the rationality condition implicit in the definition of indirect utility.
4. Assume that $v_i(.)$ is not strictly increasing in consumption. Specifically, there is some pair $\Delta c \neq \Delta c^*$ such that: $v_i(c_i^s + \Delta c, \mathbf{p}^s, \mathbf{h}_i^s) = v_i(c_i^s + \Delta c^*, \mathbf{p}^s, \mathbf{h}_i^s)$. Now consider the case in which individual i has bundle $(c_i^x, \mathbf{p}^x, \mathbf{h}_i^x)$ in outcome x, and $v_i(c_i^s + \Delta c, \mathbf{p}^s, \mathbf{h}_i^s) = v_i(c_i^x, \mathbf{p}^x, \mathbf{h}_i^x)$. It follows that $ME_i(x)$ is not unique, since Δc^* also satisfies the condition $v_i(c_i^s + \Delta c^*, \mathbf{p}^s, \mathbf{h}_i^s) = v_i(c_i^x, \mathbf{p}^x, \mathbf{h}_i^x)$.

    By "sufficient range," I mean that the range of utility levels achievable in the status quo, by varying status quo consumption, must be large enough to include the utility associated with any bundle. (For example, if in the status quo individual i has good health, and in some other outcome she has poor health, then there is some sufficiently small consumption amount which—paired with good health—will give her the same utility as poor health combined with any consumption amount.) This is just to say that for any $(c_i^x, \mathbf{p}^x, \mathbf{h}_i^x)$, there is *some* Δc such that $v_i(c_i^s + \Delta c, \mathbf{p}^s, \mathbf{h}_i^s) = v_i(c_i^x, \mathbf{p}^x, \mathbf{h}_i^x)$. If no such Δc exists, then $ME_i(x)$ is not defined, let alone unique.
5. For example, Amos Tversky and Daniel Kahneman once wrote this about prospect theory: "[It] departs from the tradition that assumes the rationality of economic agents; it is proposed as a descriptive, not a normative, theory" (Tversky and Kahneman 2000: 65). Chris Starmer, in a comprehensive review of non-EU models, stresses: "My focus will be on *descriptive* as opposed to *normative* issues" (Starmer 2004: 105).
6. In general, Kahneman's current scholarship stresses the virtues of both fast, "System 1" decision-making (including prospect-theoretic choice) and slower, "System 2," approaches (Kahneman 2011).
7. Some incomparability is not problematic; but an account of prudential value that yields *widespread* incomparability would be.
8. It is well beyond the scope of this chapter to trace the intellectual history of challenges to interpersonal well-being comparisons. Suffice it to say that two quite different kinds of objection can be discerned. One such challenge asserts that interpersonal comparisons are normative or evaluative, rather than purely scientific. Social scientists, as such, have no basis for saying that one person is better off than a second. A second challenge

asserts that, even understood as normative or evaluative, interpersonal comparisons are problematic.

The first challenge has force: The concept of *well-being*, insofar as it figures in moral theory, *is* an evaluative or normative concept, rather than one which scientists (as such) require. But note that *intrapersonal* well-being comparisons are no more scientific than interpersonal ones.

The analysis to follow focuses, instead, on the second challenge, which I will express as follows: whatever the normative/value facts might be, there are no true facts regarding interpersonal well-being comparisons. For this challenge to be interesting (rather than one aspect of a general moral skepticism), it should be framed as follows: although there *are* some normative/value facts, those do not include facts regarding the comparative well-being of different persons. The challenge thus presupposes a metaethical framework that allows for the existence of some normative/value facts. (The extent to which various frameworks allow *that* is, in turn, a contested issue in metaethics. Cognitivist frameworks surely do so; but so too may frameworks that are hybrids of cognitivism and expressivism, or even straight expressivist approaches, depending on what is meant by a "fact.")

The preferentialist about well-being *may* have an adequate answer to the second challenge; but the challenge needs to be taken seriously. The answer is hardly obvious. See below.

9. With $u_i^*(.)$ an increasing transformation of $u_i(.)$, the proposition $\mathbf{B}_i \, R_i \, \mathbf{B}_i^+$ iff $u_i(\mathbf{B}_i) \geq u_i(\mathbf{B}_i^+)$ logically implies the proposition $\mathbf{B}_i \, R_i \, \mathbf{B}_i^+$ iff $u_i^*(\mathbf{B}_i) \geq u_i^*(\mathbf{B}_i^+)$.

10. As a shorthand, I will use "$v_i(x)$" to mean "$v_i(\mathbf{M}_i(x))$," with $\mathbf{M}_i(x)$ the consumption-specified bundle of individual i in x.

11. Assume that individuals i and j each strictly prefer x to y to z to w, while individuals k and l strictly prefer z to w to x to y. Then individual i's preference is represented by the utility function $v_i(.)$ such that $v_i(x) = 4$, $v_i(y) = 3$, $v_i(z) = 2$, $v_i(w) = 1$; individual j's preference is represented by the utility function $v_j(.)$ which assigns the same numbers as $v_i(.)$; individual k's preference is represented by the utility function $v_k(.)$ such that $v_k(z) = 9$; $v_k(w) = 8.5$; $v_k(x) = 5$; $v_k(y) = 3$; and individual l's preference is represented by the utility function $v_l(.)$ which assigns the same numbers as $v_k(.)$. But now consider $v_i^*(.)$ defined as two times $v_i(.)$; $v_j^*(.)$ defined as $v_j(.)$ squared; $v_k^*(.)$ defined as $v_k(.) + 1$; and $v_l^*(.)$ defined as the square root of $v_l(.)$. Note that each $v^*(.)$ is an increasing transformation of the corresponding $v(.)$. However $v_i(x) > v_j(y)$, i.e., $4 > 3$, while $v_i^*(x) < v_j^*(y)$, i.e., $8 < 9$. Similarly, $v_i(x) - v_j(y) > v_k(z) - v_l(w)$, i.e., $4 - 3 > 9 - 8.5$; but $v_i^*(x) - v_j^*(y) < v_k^*(z) - v_l^*(w)$, i.e., $8 - 9 < 10 - \sqrt{8.5}$.

12. Let $v_i(x) = 4$ and $v_i(y) = 3$, with $v_j(.)$ the same function. Let $v_i^*(.) = 3v_i(.) + 4$, while $v_j^*(.) = 20v_j(.) + 11$. Note that each $v^*(.)$ is a positive affine transformation of the corresponding $v(.)$, but the a and b factors are *different* as between i and j. Note also that $v_i(x) > v_j(y)$, i.e., $4 > 3$, but $v_i^*(x) < v_j^*(y)$, i.e., $16 < 71$.

13. Because risk is now in the picture, the monetary equivalents are of the form $\text{ME}_i(a)$: the monetary equivalent of individual i for action a, a probability distribution across outcomes. Let $u_i(.)$ and $u_i^*(.)$ be EU utility functions both representing i's preferences with respect to lotteries over commodity-specified bundles—with $v_i(.)$ and $v_i^*(.)$ the corresponding indirect utility functions. The $\text{ME}_i(a)$ values will be the same regardless of whether we use $v_i(.)$ or $v_i^*(.)$ to calculate them.

14. A third difficulty is that attribute bundles may not be universally "shareable" (Adler 2012: ch. 3; 2014; forthcoming a). Depending on how outcomes are specified (and thus the types of attributes that are included in the bundles), there may be bundles that some but not all individuals can possess. (For example, bundles might describe genetic makeup,

but a given individual will not—on one theory of personal identity—be able to acquire a genetic makeup radically different from her actual genes.)
Note that *if* individuals (under idealized conditions) had the same preferences, and *if* bundles were universally shareable, facts about interpersonal comparisons could be readily analyzed as follows: everyone is better off with (**q**, **h**) than (**q***, **h***) iff everyone (under ideal conditions) prefers having (**q**, **h**) to having (**q***, **h***).

15. Here, I use "Pareto efficiency" as a synonym for "Pareto superiority," so as to preserve a semantic parallel with "Kaldor Hicks efficiency."
16. The extant literature on the Boadway paradox involves multiple consumption goods and differences in equilibrium prices between the outcomes being compared. But an easier case to consider involves a single consumption good and a single nonmarket attribute (e.g., health). As already explained, the version of CBA that achieves a complete, transitive, and Pareto-respecting ranking of outcomes sums monetary equivalents *in the status quo* (Adler 2012: 92–98). But clearly, if the nonmarket attribute changes the marginal utility of consumption, the fact that outcome x has a greater sum of monetary equivalents than y (given individuals' marginal utilities of consumption in the status quo) does not entail that a redistribution of consumption *in outcome x* is possible which makes everyone better off in x than y.
17. Assume that there are two individuals in the population, i and j, and that $v_i(x) = 7$, $v_i(y) = 10$, $v_j(x) = 6$, $v_j(y) = 2$. Using these utility functions, the utilitarian SWF ranks x above y: $7 + 6 > 10 + 2$. But let $v_i^*(.) = 5v_i(.)$, and $v_j^*(.) = 3v_j(.)$, so that each $v^*(.)$ is a positive affine (and hence also increasing) transformation of the corresponding $v(.)$. Using the new utility functions, the utilitarian SWF ranks y above x: $35 + 18 < 50 + 6$.

References

Adler, M. D. (1998). "Incommensurability and Cost-Benefit Analysis." *University of Pennsylvania Law Review* 146: 1371–418.
Adler, M. D. (2012). *Well-Being and Fair Distribution: Beyond Cost-Benefit Analysis.* Oxford: Oxford University Press.
Adler, M. D. (2014). "Extended Preferences and Interpersonal Comparisons." *Economics and Philosophy* 30: 123–62.
Adler, M. D. (Forthcoming a). "Extended Preferences." In M.D. Adler and M. Fleurbaey (eds.), *Oxford Handbook of Well-Being and Public Policy*. Oxford: Oxford University Press.
Adler, M. D. (Forthcoming b). "Cost-Benefit Analysis and Distributional Weights." *Review of Environmental Economics and Policy*.
Adler, M. D., and E. Posner. (2006). *New Foundations of Cost-Benefit Analysis.* Cambridge: Harvard University Press.
Allais, M. (1979). "The Foundations of a Positive Theory of Choice Involving Risk and a Criticism of the Postulates and Axioms of the American School." In M. Allais and O. Hagen (eds.), *Expected Utility Hypotheses and the Allais Paradox*. Boston: D. Reidel, 27–145.
Bateman, I. J., and K. G. Willis. (2001). *Valuing Environmental Preferences: Theory and Practice of the Contingent Valuation Method in the U.S., E.U., and Developing Countries.* Oxford: Oxford University Press.
Bernheim, B. D., and A. Rangel. (2009). "Beyond Revealed Preference: Choice-Theoretic Foundations for Behavioral Welfare Economics." *Quarterly Journal of Economics* 124: 51–103.

Blackorby, C., and D. Donaldson. (1990). "A Review Article: The Case against the Use of the Sum of Compensating Variations in Cost-Benefit Analysis." *Canadian Journal of Economics* 23: 471–94.

Boadway, R. (1974). "The Welfare Foundations of Cost-Benefit Analysis." *Economic Journal* 84: 926–39.

Boadway, R., and N. Bruce. (1984). *Welfare Economics*. Oxford: Basil Blackwell.

Bossert, W., and J. A. Weymark. (2004). "Utility in Social Choice." In S. Barberà, P. J. Hammond, and C. Seidl (eds.), *Handbook of Utility Theory*. Boston: Kluwer, vol. 2: 1099–177.

Camerer, C., G. Lowenstein, and M. Rabin. (2004). *Advances in Behavioral Economics*. New York: Russell Sage.

Carson, R. T., N. E. Flores, and N. F. Meade. (2001). "Contingent Valuation: Controversies and Evidence." *Environmental and Resource Economics* 19: 173–210.

Champ, P. A., K. J. Boyle, and T. C. Brown. (2003). *A Primer on Nonmarket Valuation*. Boston: Kluwer.

Chipman, J. S. (2008). "Compensation Principle." In S.N. Durlauf and L. E. Blume (eds.), *The New Palgrave Dictionary of Economics*, 2nd ed. London: Palgrave Macmillan, vol. 2: 38–48.

Chipman, J. S., and J. C. Moore. (1978). "The New Welfare Economics 1939–1974." *International Economic Review* 19: 547–84.

Darwall, S. L. (2002). *Welfare and Rational Care*. Princeton: Princeton University Press.

Drèze, J., and N. Stern. (1987). "The Theory of Cost-Benefit Analysis." In A. Auerbach and M. Feldstein (eds.), *Handbook of Public Economics*. New York: North-Holland, vol. 2: 909–89.

Freeman, A. M. (2003). *The Measurement of Environmental and Resource Values: Theory and Methods*, 2nd ed. Washington, DC: Resources for the Future.

Gilboa, I. (2009). *Theory of Decision under Uncertainty*. Cambridge: Cambridge University Press.

Gorman, W. M. (1955). "The Intransitivity of Certain Criteria Used in Welfare Economics." *Oxford Economic Papers* 7: 25–35.

Graham, J. D. (2008). "Saving Lives through Administrative Law and Economics." *University of Pennsylvania Law Review* 157: 395–540.

Harberger, A. C., and G. P. Jenkins. (2002). *Cost-Benefit Analysis*. Northampton, MA: Edward Elgar.

Harsanyi, J. C. (1977). *Rational Behavior and Bargaining in Games and Social Situations*. Cambridge: Cambridge University Press.

Hausman, D. M., and M. S. McPherson. (2006). *Economic Analysis, Moral Philosophy, and Public Policy*, 2nd ed. Cambridge: Cambridge University Press.

Hicks, J. R. (1939). "The Foundations of Welfare Economics." *Economic Journal* 49: 696–712.

HM Treasury. (2003). *The Green Book: Appraisal and Evaluation in Central. Government*. London: TSO.

Hotelling, H. (1938). "The General Welfare in Relation to Problems of Taxation and Railway and Utility Rates." *Econometrica* 6: 242–49.

Johansson-Stenman, O. (2005). "Distributional Weights in Cost-Benefit Analysis: Should We Forget about Them?" *Land Economics* 81: 337–52.

Just, R. E., D. L. Hueth, and A. Schmitz. (2004). *The Welfare Economics of Public Policy: A Practical Approach to Project and Policy Evaluation*. Northampton, MA: Edward Elgar.

Kagan, S. (1992). "The Limits of Well-Being." *Social Philosophy and Policy* 9: 169–89.

Kahneman, D. (2011). *Thinking, Fast and Slow*. New York: Farrar, Straus and Giroux.

Kahneman, D., and A. Tversky. (2000). *Choices, Values, and Frames*. New York: Russell Sage.

Kaldor, N. (1939). "Welfare Propositions of Economics and Interpersonal Comparisons of Utility." *Economic Journal* 49: 549–52.

Kaplow, L. (2008). *The Theory of Taxation and Public Economics*. Princeton: Princeton University Press.

Kirkpatrick, C. (2006). "Regulatory Impact Assessment." In M. Crew and D. Parker (eds.), *International Handbook on Economic Regulation*. Northampton, MA: Edward Elgar, 232–54.

Kreps, D. M. (1988). *Notes on the Theory of Choice*. Boulder, CO: Westview Press.

Layard, R., and S. Glaister, eds. (1994). *Cost-Benefit Analysis*, 2nd ed. Cambridge: Cambridge University Press.

Little, I. M. D. (1957). *A Critique of Welfare Economics*, 2nd ed. Oxford: Oxford University Press.

Little, I. M. D., and J. A. Mirrlees. (1994). "The Costs and Benefits of Analysis: Project Appraisal and Planning Twenty Years On." In R. Layard and S. Glaister (eds.), *Cost-Benefit Analysis*, 2nd ed. Cambridge: Cambridge University Press, 199–231.

Mas-Collel, A., M. D. Whinston, and J. R. Green. (1995). *Microeconomic Theory*. Oxford: Oxford University Press.

Mishan, E. J. (1988). *Cost-Benefit Analysis: An Informal Introduction*, 4th ed. Boston: Unwin Hyman.

Overvold, M. C. (1982). "Self-Interest and Getting What You Want." In H. B. Miller and W. H. Williams (eds.), *The Limits of Utilitarianism*. Minneapolis: University of Minnesota Press, 186–94.

Parfit, D. (1987). *Reasons and Persons*. Oxford: Clarendon Press.

Ray, A. (1984). *Cost-Benefit Analysis: Issues and Methodologies*. Baltimore: Johns Hopkins University Press.

Renda, A. (2011). *Law and Economics in the RIA World*. Cambridge: Intersentia.

Rey, B., and J. C. Rochet. (2004). "Health and Wealth: How Do They Affect Individual Preferences?" *Geneva Papers on Risk and Insurance Theory* 29: 43–54.

Robbins, L. (1935). *An Essay on the Nature and Significance of Economic Science*, 2nd ed. London: Macmillan.

Robbins, L. (1938). "Interpersonal Comparisons of Utility: A Comment." *Economic Journal* 48: 635–41.

Scitovsky, T. (1941). "A Note on Welfare Propositions in Economics." *Review of Economic Studies* 9: 77–88.

Sen, A. (1979). "The Welfare Basis of Real Income Comparisons." *Journal of Economic Literature* 17: 1–45.

Sen, A. (1995). *Inequality Reexamined*. New York: Russell Sage.

Squire, L., and H. van der Tak. (1975). *Economic Analysis of Projects*. Baltimore: Johns Hopkins University Press.

Starmer, C. (2004). "Developments in Nonexpected-Utility Theory: The Hunt for a Descriptive Theory of Choice under Risk." In C. F. Camerer, G. Loewenstein, and M. Rabin (eds.), *Advances in Behavioral Economics*. New York: Russell Sage, 104–47.

Tversky, A., and D. Kahneman. (2000). "Advances in Prospect Theory: Cumulative Representation of Uncertainty." In D. Kahneman and A. Tversky (eds.), *Choices, Values, and Frames*. New York: Russell Sage, 44–65.

Waldfogel, J. (2005). "Does Consumer Irrationality Trump Consumer Sovereignty?" *Review of Economics and Statistics* 87: 691–96.

Wiener, J. B. (2007). "Better Regulation in Europe." In J. Holder and C. O'Cinneide (eds.), *Current Legal Problems 2006*. Oxford: Oxford University Press, 447–518.

Wiener, J. B. (2013). "The Diffusion of Regulatory Oversight." In M. A. Livermore and R. L. Revesz (eds.), *The Globalization of Cost-Benefit Analysis in Environmental Policy*. Oxford: Oxford University Press, 123–41.

CHAPTER 18

THE VALUE OF HEALTH

DANIEL M. HAUSMAN

This chapter will be concerned exclusively with the value of human health. In particular, I shall be concerned with the value of a person's health *to* that person, with the ways in which health is *good for* people. One important way in which health is good for a person is if health contributes to that person's well-being. But I shall not assume that the only way that health can be good for someone is through its bearing on well-being. Health may, for example, also contribute to freedom and independence, or it may constitute a personal good of its own kind.

It is uncontroversial that health is extremely valuable. Every culture values health highly, even as cultures disagree on details concerning what constitutes health. Health is not, however, always good for people. Those German men who were too unhealthy to serve in the Nazi armies were fortunate to miss out on the Eastern Front. Yet exceptions such as this one do not impugn the generalization that health is usually very good for people.

One obvious explanation of this generalization is that a minimal level of health is required for action, consciousness, and life itself. Without some minimal level of health, nothing else can make people's lives go well. Health beyond what is required for life and basic functioning is also of great value. Why? Three immediate answers come to mind, all of which are correct as far as they go. First, health is an extremely important cause of well-being. But this answer tells us little until we have some account of how health contributes to well-being. A second quick answer is that people value health. But this claim, true as it is, does not tell us much without an account of health that explains and justifies the value that people place on health. A third answer is that health promotes other values such as opportunity and autonomy. But again one must ask how health does so.

To understand the value of health, one needs to clarify what health is. That will be the task of the first two sections. Section 18.3 begins the task of explaining what constitutes *better* health and whether health has a scalar value, and section 18.4 considers whether preferences can serve as measures of better health, as is assumed by most of those working on health measurement. Section 18.5 addresses the question of whether a measurable scalar value can be assigned to health, and section 18.6 assesses three accounts of the value of health. Section 18.7 concludes.

18.1. EVALUATIVE VIEWS OF HEALTH

There is a large literature concerning the concept of health. Most of it takes health to be the absence of physical or mental disease or impairment. Although I shall take for granted this negative characterization of health, it is not uncontested. In 1947, the World Health Organization famously defined health as "a state of complete physical, mental and social well-being and not merely the absence of disease or infirmity" (1948: 100). But this definition conflates health and well-being, and, without ever explicitly repudiating it, the World Health Organization itself relies on narrower characterizations of health. Lennart Nordenfelt defends a positive "holistic" view of health as a second-order ability to realize one's goals (2000: 79–81). Carol Ryff has written extensively on positive health, which she identifies primarily with possessing purpose in life and quality relations with other people, although in her view other goods such as self-esteem and mastery are closely connected. She writes, "Positive health is ultimately about engagement in living" (Ryff and Singer 1998: 10).

Rather than interpreting those who see health as well-being (or a generalized ability to realize one's goals or as engagement with living) as disagreeing about the properties of some single thing called "health," I think these contrasting claims reveal that there are multiple notions of health. According to the broad concept of health I shall discuss—health as the absence of pathology—which is the concept employed by pathologists and physiologists, health depends on the functioning of the parts and processes within people's bodies and minds. Although being Jewish was likely to be fatal condition if one lived in Eastern Europe in the early 1940s, it was not itself a physical or mental pathology (though some Nazis mistakenly believed otherwise). Even those who maintain that there is a great deal more to health than what is "within the skin" can recognize a "negative" notion of health as the absence of pathology.

Having in this way limited the notion of health under discussion, controversies remain concerning what constitutes pathology. The many detailed accounts are of two general kinds: naturalist and evaluative. According to evaluative views, it is part of the concept of health that it is good for an organism, and our evaluative standards—particularly concerning well-being—help to define health. It might appear that evaluative theorists are obviously right.[1] Whether something is a disease apparently depends on whether it is bad for an organism in ordinary environments.[2] Tristram Engelhardt provides a memorable example of the way in which values have affected disease classification in his discussion of the history of masturbation, which for a couple of centuries was widely regarded as a disease in Europe and the United States (Engelhardt 1974). Consensus was never complete, and there were disputes about whether masturbation is a physical or a mental disease and about whether masturbation is a cause of disease rather than a disease itself. But much of the medical community regarded it as a medical disorder, and doctors prescribed treatments ranging from opium, cold baths, and visits to prostitutes for men to clitoridectomies for women. It is obvious in retrospect and was obvious at the time that moral judgment influenced disease classification. Tissot's influential mid-eighteenth-century treatise asserts, "We have seen that masturbation is more pernicious than excessive intercourse with females. Those who believe in a special providence account for it by a special ordinance of the Deity to punish this crime" (1758; quoted in Engelhardt 1974: 239).

Engelhardt sums up as follows:

> Insofar as a vice is taken to be a deviation from an ideal of human perfection, or "well-being," it can be translated into disease language.... The shift is from an explicitly ethical language to a language of natural teleology. To be ill is to fail to realize the perfection of an ideal type; to be sick is to be defective rather than to be evil.... The notion of the "deviant" structures the concept of disease providing a purpose and direction for explanation and for action, that is, for diagnosis and prognosis, and for therapy. A "disease entity" operates as a conceptual form organizing phenomena in a fashion deemed useful for certain goals. The goals, though, involve choice by man and are not objective facts, data "given" by nature. They are ideals imputed to nature. (Engelhardt 1974: 247–48)

Engelhardt concludes that health is the absence of defect or deviance, where defect and deviance are evaluative notions that depend on views of well-being, perfection, virtue, and duty.

It is, however, questionable whether the case of masturbation supports an evaluative view of health such as Engelhardt's (Boorse 1997: 72–78). Whether historical claims concerning attitudes toward masturbation are true depends on what people in the nineteenth century believed and why they believed what they did, rather than the definition of health. *If* one believes that masturbation involves physical or mental states that are bad for people, then according to the evaluative theorist, one ought to believe masturbation is a disease. Thus evaluative theorists regard nineteenth-century physicians as justified in their belief that masturbation (as an activity that issues from and causes harmful physical or mental states) is a disease, *given* their belief that masturbation is bad for people. The naturalist in contrast denies that harmful physical and mental states are automatically diseases and that diseases must be harmful. In some circumstances heresy is a fatal mental condition and flat feet a life-saving escape from the draft. Yet flat feet are pathological, while heresy may be healthy.

There has, of course, been a huge change in values concerning masturbation, and that change in values has been both a cause and an effect of a change in attitudes toward whether masturbation is a disease. But when one looks more closely, it turns out that the claim that masturbation is a disease was not defended by normative condemnation. The case rested instead on a long list of false assertions about the effects of masturbation on the functioning of other organ systems and about the mechanisms through which masturbation had these effects. Those false assertions were no doubt often motivated by moral objections to masturbation, but the causal connections show only that moral commitments can cause people to make false factual claims, not that morality defines pathology. The effects of masturbation were supposed to derive from debilitation caused by the loss of semen. But the loss of semen is not debilitating and has few effects on other organ systems. Masturbation does not result in the loss of more semen than intercourse, which was held to be harmless (apart from the risks of venereal disease), and some other theory had to be concocted to generate a mechanism whereby female masturbation diminished the functioning of body parts. Whether via the loss of semen or in some other way, masturbation does not cause stomach aches, epilepsy, blindness, deafness, vertigo, heart irregularities, or rickets—all of which were alleged to be its effects. If masturbation had these effects, then masturbation would be a disease or a cause of disease such as anorexia or cutting oneself. To the extent that those who regarded masturbation as a disease felt it incumbent on them to show that it had other physiological consequences than a morally condemnable self-induced orgasm, they seem to be repudiating rather than presupposing the view that Engelhardt defends. They apparently did not believe that it was sufficient to point out that masturbation is "a deviation from an ideal of human perfection."

Even though those who regarded masturbation as a disease were not content to point out that it was a normative defect, Engelhardt might still be right. Why shouldn't someone who regards masturbation as a defect regard masturbators as sick, just as most Americans are inclined to regard necrophiliacs as sick?[3] If God or evolution designed our sexuality exclusively to lead us to seek intercourse with living members of the opposite sex, then there is a malfunction in those who masturbate or have homosexual encounters or have intercourse with animals or cadavers, just as there is a malfunction in those who prefer a meal of mouse droppings to a decent dinner. (But notice that this thought shifts from a view of disease as morally, prudentially, or aesthetically bad to a view of disease as malfunction.)

Evaluative theorists maintain that it is a conceptual truth that health matters to what people value (see, for example, Cooper 2002; Engelhardt 1974; Reznek 1987). Poor health is supposedly an automatic excuse for certain behavior, a justification for sympathy and the provision of care, and something that diminishes overall well-being. But these claims appear to be false.[4] For example, infertility in young adults is unquestionably pathological. It is a failure of the reproductive system to do what it is designed to do. It may justify medical treatment. Yet many people seek infertility, at least temporarily. Women who are reversibly infertile because they are taking birth-control pills (and by virtue of lacking normal capacities thus not fully healthy) or men who have had vasectomies after having fathered as many children as they want are typically not worse off all things considered. They do not have a condition requiring medical treatment or excusing behavior that would ordinarily be condemned, and their condition does not call for sympathy or care from others.

An evaluative theorist has three possible ways of conceding that apparently better health can be worse for a person. First, even if circumstances are such that better health in a particular regard has harmful consequences, it might still be better in other respects. Second, evaluative theorists might question whether the physical and mental states that people take to be healthy are, regardless of the circumstances, always in fact healthy.

On this view, premenopausal women who are sexually active and want to avoid pregnancy are healthier if infertile, because infertility is better for them than fertility, while infertility is unhealthy in those premenopausal women in whom it is involuntary and unsought. A third possibility for the evaluative theorist is to maintain that it is a conceptual truth that states of better health are *typically or usually* better for people rather than invariably so. Cases in which it is better to be less healthy do not constitute counterexamples to these loose conceptual connections.

These three ways in which the evaluative theorist can meet the challenge posed by cases in which it seems that it is worse to be healthier, leave one wondering how substantial the disagreements between evaluative and nonevaluative views of health actually are. On the first alternative, it is a conceptual truth that setting aside their consequences (which may in unusual cases be harmful) states of better health are better for people. Most nonevaluative theorists agree that apart from unusual circumstances, better health is typically better. So the disagreement turns on whether it is a conceptual or contingent truth that health is a good thing. If evaluative theorists protect their claim in the second way by labeling physical and mental states that serve people's purposes as states of better health regardless of the functional deficiencies they may involve, then it seems that the evaluative theorist is concerned with a different notion of health than the one that is employed in pathology and physiology. The disagreement collapses into an argument about how to use the word "health." With the proper translation manual, it is questionable whether the evaluative theorist is asserting anything that the nonevaluative theorist denies. On the third alternative, it is also doubtful whether any important disagreement remains between evaluative and nonevaluative or naturalistic views of health. The evaluative theorist maintains that it is a conceptual truth that good health is generally good for people. The naturalist agrees that good health is generally good for people, but denies that this is a conceptual truth. What is at issue?

Perhaps the source of disagreement lies in the independent characterization of health that the naturalist provides and to which we shall now turn. Notice that evaluative views of health make it difficult to see how the term "health" can be used univocally to refer to states of people, animals, plants, or (more debatably) ecosystems. Health is usually a very good thing both intrinsically and instrumentally, and an evaluative view is defensible. But, as we have seen, to mount a successful defense of a conceptual connection between health and benefit requires some fancy footwork.

18.2. Naturalistic Views of Health

The leading nonevaluative "naturalistic" view of health is Christopher Boorse's biostatistical view (1977, 1987, 1997; see also Wakefield 1992 and Hausman 2012a). In Boorse's view, a pathology obtains when the functioning of parts or processes of the body or mind is appreciably less efficient than what is statistically normal in the relevant reference class in typical environments. Boorse defends a goal-contribution view of functions, whereby the function of a part of a directively organized system consists of the contribution that the part makes to how well or how probably the system achieves its goals. A directively organized system is one that shows resilience in the pursuit of its goals, where that resilience is explained by the structure of the system. Central goals of human beings, like other living things, are survival and reproduction. These goals are not determined by moral or prudential considerations. They are instead enforced by evolution. The functions of parts of human beings are the contributions those parts make to survival or reproduction or to the achievement of narrower goals of particular subsystems to which the parts belong. The functioning of the parts of people is healthy when it is not much below the median level of functional efficiency in a typical environment for the relevant reference class. Reference classes are narrower than whole populations, because unimpaired capacities of male and female and of different age groups differ. Infertility is not pathological in seventy-year-old women, and men who are unable to breastfeed have no disease.

Figure 18.1, drawn by Boorse (1987: 370 and 1997: 8),[5] helps clarify the view. Although Boorse draws what looks roughly like a normal distribution, there is no reason why the distribution of functional efficiency should be symmetrical, single-peaked, or continuous. There might be a small number of discrete levels. Median functional efficiency (which in a skewed distribution could be less than or greater than the mode) defines what is statistically normal.

Although the median in the distribution of levels of functional efficiency (in a typical environment) determines a benchmark, the distribution plays no further role in locating the line between pathological and healthy part function. Among the levels of functional efficiency that are lower than the median level, the level of functioning (as determined by the contribution the part makes to the goal-achievement of the systems to which the part belongs) determines whether functional efficiency is adequate and hence healthy or not. Functional efficiency that is "significantly" worse than the median level is pathological. Although functional efficiency is a matter of how *well* a part is functioning and is thus an evaluative notion, the standards of good functioning depend on a part's contribution to the systems to which it belongs and ultimately to survival and reproduction. Considerations of well-being, aesthetics, and virtue are irrelevant.

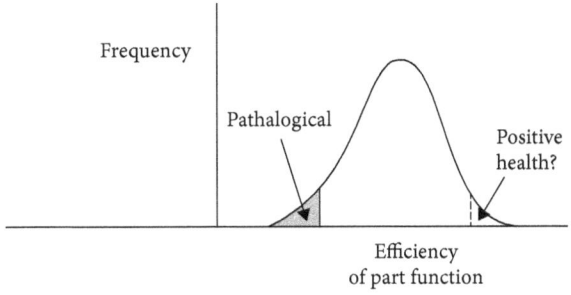

FIGURE 18.1 The Biostatistical Theory

In denying that there is any conceptual connection between health and well-being or other human values, naturalistic theories need not maintain that the relationship between health and well-being is solely instrumental. Health states may also be constituents of well-being, but whether certain levels of functional efficiency contribute to or constitute elements of well-being or other human values in specific environments is a separate question from their contribution to system goals and ultimately survival or reproduction.

18.3. Why Is It Better to Be Healthier?

What is it that makes it better to be healthier? To answer this question, more needs to be said about what it is to be healthier. This turns out to be trickier than it might at first appear, because pathology and health are multidimensional. One person may be in pain, another suffering a cognitive deficiency, a third unable to see. How are these different health states to be compared? To impose some order and to value these health states, health economists have constructed *health state classifications* and have then assigned values to the health states so classified.[6] Unlike someone's health, which depends not just on her instantaneous physical and mental states, but on their trajectories through time, health economists take a person's health state to be a snapshot at a moment, without reference to past or future. Just as the distance an object travels over an interval is the time integral of its instantaneous velocity, so a person's health during a period is the time integral of the person's health states. So, for example, the health state now of a woman with a symptomless cancer that will kill her in a few weeks could be little different from the health state of someone in full health. The fact that her health (as opposed to her instantaneous health state) is very poor shows up in her expected trajectory through increasingly terrible health states. Once one has classified the instantaneous health states, one can define people's health in terms of actual or expected trajectories through these health states. The classification of health states is fundamental to this way of describing people's health. For an example, the Health Utilities Index distinguishes eight "dimensions" of health: vision, hearing, speech, ambulation, dexterity, emotion, cognition, and pain, and distinguishes five or six levels of severity of deficiencies along each dimension, for a total of 972,000 health states.

As health-classification systems such as the Health Utilities Index recognize, people's health states are multidimensional. In this regard health states are analogous to consumption bundles in consumer choice theory. A person's consumption bundle consists of quantities of fruits, fish, water, wine, haircuts, home heating, and so forth, and though one bundle of commodities and services may cost more than another or provide an individual with greater happiness, there is no way to say that one bundle of commodities is literally larger than another, apart from the special case of dominance in which one bundle contains at least as much of each commodity as another and more of some commodities. Although Mitt Romney is much richer than most readers of this volume and consumes a more expensive bundle of commodities, as a Mormon, his beer consumption is probably much lower than that of an average college student. The bundle of commodities he consumes is probably neither literally larger nor smaller than the bundles of commodities and services consumed by different readers of this essay.

Just as one person's commodity bundle is often neither larger nor smaller than the commodity bundle of another, so it is frequently the case that one person has no larger or smaller quantity of health than another. One can compare how happy people are in various health states or what their median income is or how much on average they prefer one health state to another, but there is no way to say that Jack has literally *more health* than George, unless Jack's health state dominates George's—that is, unless Jack's health state is no worse than George's along any dimension and better along at least one dimension. It is tempting to suppose that one might make comparisons in terms of something like "overall functioning," but this is an illusion.[7] How is one to judge whether Jack, who has a very limited short-term memory, is healthier than Jane, who needs a walker to get around, or Jessica, who is very hard of hearing? What evidence bears on this question?

The relation "is at least as healthy as" is massively *incomplete*: most health states cannot be compared in their quantity or magnitude of health. It is not just that we cannot tell: there is no truth condition for the claim that one set of functional deficiencies constitutes a greater quantity or magnitude of health than another, unless the former dominates the latter. There is no such thing as a quantity or magnitude of health, just as there is no such thing as the "size" of a commodity bundle.

But, of course, we compare people's health all the time. If Jack is bedridden, senile, and deaf but has good vision, he seems to be clearly less healthy than George, who is color-blind, but otherwise healthy. Health comparisons such as this one are, I suggest, in fact comparisons of the *value* of different health states, of how good different health states are. When we say that one person is healthier than another, we usually mean that the first person's health is *better*. Similarly, when we say that Mitt Romney has more goods than the typical steelworker, we mean that his goods are more expensive or that most people would gladly trade the steelworker's bundle of commodities for Romney's. Though one person rarely possesses literally more or less health than another, it is often the case that one person's health is better or worse than another's.

Rather than finding a basis for the value of health in clarifying the measure of health, we have found that there is no measure of health apart from its value. So we might as well ask directly: what is it for one person's health to be *better* than another's or for someone's health to be better at one time than at another? One finds different answers in the literature. Norman Daniels cashes out the value of health in terms of opportunity (1985, 2007). In his view, someone's health at t is better than their health at t' (or than someone else's health at some time) if he or she has greater access to the normal opportunity range for someone of that age and sex in that social position and with those talents. Paul Dolan disagrees. He maintains that the value of a health state consists in the quality of subjective experience it involves (Dolan and Kahneman 2008). John Broome (2002: 94) and Dan Brock (2002: 117) assert that how good someone's health is is a matter of the contribution that their health makes to their well-being either as cause or component. The health measure in use in England and some other European countries takes the value of health to be a component of well-being, which health economists call "health-related quality of life." In practice, health economists usually take one health state to be better than another if and only if people *prefer* the former to the latter, regardless of the reasons for the preference.

None of these views seems satisfactory. The value of health cannot be cashed out entirely in terms of opportunities. Subjective experience is also important, whether or not it affects opportunities. But opportunity and capacities are important: health cannot be measured entirely in terms of subjective experience either. Subjective experiences are often good indicators of our health—indeed one can conjecture that the evolutionary point of many of our feelings is precisely to indicate what states of our bodies are healthy or diseased. But if our evidence is faulty or we have nervous, cognitive, or affective disabilities, our subjective experience may be excellent when our health is poor. Those with congenital analgesia (an inability to feel pain) are not in better health than those who feel pain.

Nor does the measure of health consist in its bearing on well-being. People with disabilities such as deafness who have coped successfully with their disability may be as well off as people without any disabilities. Whether deafness is a disability does not depend on whether it diminishes the quality of life. It sounds more plausible to maintain that the value of health consists in *health-related* quality of life, but I suspect that this view appears to be more plausible mainly because it is unclear what health-related quality of life is. What would it mean to say of someone who is deaf and is living an excellent life that her "health-related quality of life" is worse than someone who can hear? As John Broome has argued (2002), there is no way to decompose someone's well-being into some set of components, with a subset constituted or caused by the person's health. For example, as Allotey and coauthors (2003) vividly document, the extent to which paraplegia diminishes the quality of life differs dramatically depending on whether one confronts social, natural, and technological circumstances like those in Australia or like those in Cameroon.

18.4. Preferences and the Value of Health

What about preferences? Do they enable health economists to value health states sensibly? Economists do not typically define what they mean by preferences, and when they do offer definitions, they often make indefensible claims that are inconsistent with their own practices. In *Preference, Value, Choice and Welfare* (2012), I argue that the interpretation of preferences that best fits the practice of economists takes preferences to be subjective total comparative evaluations. What this means is the following:

1. Preferences are *subjective states* that combine with beliefs to explain choices. They cannot be defined by behavior. Even in the simplest case in which Sally faces a

choice between just two alternatives, x and y, one cannot infer that she prefers x over y from her choice of x without making assumptions about her beliefs. If Sally mistakenly believes that the choice is between x and some alternative other than y, then she might choose x from the set {x, y} despite preferring y to x.

2. Preferences are *comparative evaluations*. To prefer x to y is to judge how good x is in some regard as compared to y. To say that Sally prefers x is elliptical. If Sally prefers x, she must prefer x to something else.
3. Third, preferences are *total* comparative evaluations—that is, comparative evaluations with respect to every factor that the individual considers to be relevant. Unlike everyday language where people regard factors such as duties as competing with preferences in determining choices, economists take preferences to encompass every factor influencing choices other than beliefs and constraints.
4. Fourth, as total *comparative evaluations*, preferences are cognitively demanding. Like judgments, they may be well or poorly supported and correct or incorrect.

On this understanding of preferences, there are strong reasons to deny that one health state H is better than another, H', if and only if people prefer H to H'. First, people might prefer H to H', despite believing that H' was a state of better health. For example, a manic-depressive may prefer not to treat her disease, because of what she is able to achieve during manic periods, without believing that she is in better health when not medicated.

Health economists might respond that cases in which people judge that H' is a better health state than H but prefer H are unusual and may be ignored. Though not *defining* what it is for one health state to be better than another, perhaps preferences are reliable *indicators* of how good or bad health is. But it is questionable whether preferences are reliable indicators of health, because people's preferences among health states are likely to be mistaken. When economists measure people's preferences among flavors of ice cream or makes of cars, they are asking people for their comparative evaluations of alternatives that the respondents understand well, that they have had ample opportunity to consider, and concerning which they have a great deal of information. When, in contrast, health economists ask people to express their preferences among health states, they are asking people to appraise unfamiliar alternatives concerning which respondents typically have no secure preferences at all.

This concern about the reliability of survey respondent's comparative evaluations is not just a theoretical qualm. Consider, for example, the "quality weights" that are assigned to health states as classified by the EQ-5D, a health classification system used in Europe, including by the National Institute for Health and Clinical Excellence in England (which uses these weights to determine whether treatments are sufficiently cost-effective to be paid for by the National Health Service). The EQ-5D has five dimensions along which health states vary: mobility, self-care, usual activities, pain/discomfort, and anxiety/depression. Along each dimension, there are three levels: no problems, moderate problems, and severe problems. There are thus 3^5, or 243 distinguishable health states, to which "quality weights" are assigned. Death is assigned a quality weight of zero, and 1 is assigned to full health—that is, to no problems along any of the five dimensions. Apart from a few health states that may be worse than death, health states have some value between zero and 1. To assign values or "quality weights," members of the population are asked questions such as the following:

> Suppose that you faced a choice between (a) ten years of life remaining in health state 11112 (that is, with no problems on any of the dimensions of health except for moderate anxiety/depression) or (b) eight years of life with no problems on any of the dimensions of health. Which would you prefer?

This is not a choice that people have previously faced. It is far from well defined. What constitutes a "moderate" problem of anxiety or depression? If one actually faced such a choice—perhaps if one were faced with a choice of whether to take an antianxiety drug that would shorten one's life by two years—it would be an extremely important choice that would demand serious reflection. One would want to know more about how disabling the anxiety or the depression would be. Exactly what counts as "moderate" anxiety or depression? Would one still be able to work, to live independently? How would it affect one's social life or one's income? What sort of burdens would it impose on one's family and friends? To make a serious total comparative evaluation of these two alternatives—eight years in full health versus ten years with moderate anxiety or depression—one would need to gather a great deal of information and deliberate with care.

In fact, when those surveyed are asked whether they would prefer eight years in full health to ten years with moderate anxiety, they answer in a few seconds. What cognitive processes enable them to give immediate answers to questions that are unfamiliar, not well defined, and extremely difficult? They are probably substituting some easier question for the incredibly difficult question they have been asked (Kahneman 2011). Why should one take their answers as good measures of the value of health states? These problems with surveys have no easy solution. Rational survey respondents are never going to invest the effort that is required in order to have settled and well-supported preferences among alternatives such as these.[8]

These reasons to deny that H is a better state of health than H' if and only if people prefer H to H' raise a further question: Why defer to the judgment of survey respondents concerning the values of health states rather than making the judgment oneself? Unable themselves to figure out how to value health states, health economists instead elicit the views of people whose off-the-cuff answers show that they have not grappled seriously with the problems.

So the proposal to measure the values of health states by preferences fares no better than the proposals to measure the values of health states by opportunity, feelings, or well-being. The preferences people express should not be taken seriously as comparative evaluations to which they are committed. One should also wonder why, when faced with the difficult problem of providing a comparative evaluation of the health states defined by the EQ-5D, health economists should rely on the judgments of laypeople who know less about the health states and have had less opportunity to think about them.

18.5. Do Health States Have Values?

Regardless of whether one holds an evaluative or a naturalistic view of health, there is a serious additional problem with the proposal to measure health in terms of the value of health. If two individuals are in the same physical and mental state, then their health is the same. If their health is the same, then any acceptable measure of their health must assign the same number to their health. If health is measured by its value, then if health states are the same, their value must be the same. But the same health state has different values for different people in different environments. Being unable to walk is a devastating blow if one lives in an impoverished swampy or mountainous country with few paved roads. Its impact on well-being or opportunity is far less serious in a wealthy country with wheelchair-accessible transportation and buildings. A strained tendon that most people would find trivial may cost a violinist her career. If, as these examples illustrate, the same health states often have different values, then their values cannot be measures of health. But it is only in terms of their values that health states are generally comparable. So it appears that health is not measurable at all!

There is a way out of this conundrum (Hausman 2012b). One can distinguish between *token* health states—that is the health state of a particular individual at a particular time and place—and kinds or *types* of health states. The argument above shows that the values of tokens of the same type differ depending on the environment and the values and interests of individuals. Rather than concluding that kinds of health states have no single value, one can instead assign to health state types either the average value of their tokens weighted by the frequency of different circumstances or the value of their tokens in some "standard" context.

If the value of token health states were uniformly extremely sensitive both to the environment and to individual interests, there would be little point to considering their weighted average or the token value in some standard context, because these would tell us little about the values of the actual token health states. Fortunately the values of many token health states are not widely dispersed. A broken toe is a very serious injury to some dancers and athletes, but it has much the same value to a large majority of the population. A migraine headache is pretty much just as miserable whether one is walking through a rainforest or skiing across frozen tundra, whether one is a doctor, a dogcatcher, or a dockworker. But it is questionable whether average or standard values will serve all the purposes for which health measures are designed.

If the values of health state types are the values of tokens in some "standard" environment or averages of the values of tokens, then our inquiry into the value of health leads us to inquire about what constitutes or determines the value of token health states. That value depends jointly on the "within-the-skin" functioning of parts and processes as described by some system of health state classification, on the individual's specific environment—cultural, technological, biological, and geographical, and on the interests and values of the individual.

18.6. VALUING TOKEN HEALTH STATES

What makes a token health state better or worse? What constitutes its value? There are three main answers in the literature. Philosophers have argued that the value of health lies in its contribution to well-being, to opportunity, or to capability. Defenders of these three accounts take them as competing, but it is possible to regard the value of health as arising from some combination of its bearing on all three.

18.6.1. Health and Well-Being

Health obviously contributes to well-being, and minimal levels of health are a necessary condition to possessing a life worth living. Most health economists probably see the value of health as deriving from its contribution to well-being. Though they measure the value of health in terms of preferences, they implicitly take greater preference satisfaction to indicate greater well-being. Some philosophers such as Brock (2002) and Broome (2002) have also defended the view that the value of health lies in its bearing on well-being.

Yet, as already argued, health does not always contribute to well-being. Health improvements are not necessarily improvements in well-being both because of perverse environments such as wars, which may reward health deficiencies, and because certain disabilities, such as deafness, need not limit an individual's overall prospects of living well, despite limiting the variety of good lives that are open to them.

There are two responses to these objections. First, those who find the value of health in its contribution to well-being might argue that even if overall well-being is not necessarily lowered by poor health, the health-related *aspect* of well-being—the "health-related quality of life"—is diminished. This response seems merely to paper over the difficulty without seriously addressing it. Second, one might concede that poor health does not always diminish well-being, while insisting that it typically does, and that one is consequently justified in measuring the value of a health state by its bearing on well-being.

It is sensible to maintain that better health generally improves well-being, but health has value even when it does not promote well-being. Even if losing one's hearing does not make one worse off, it is a loss of something of value. A further problem with locating the value of health in its contribution to well-being is that it is no easier to understand or measure well-being than it is to understand or measure health. For the same reasons that one cannot identify the value of health with the quality of mental states, one cannot identify well-being with the quality of mental states. For many of the same reasons that preference satisfaction does not constitute health, it does not constitute well-being either. Like health, well-being is multidimensional, and assigning a scalar measure (for example, in terms of preferences or subjective experience) is problematic.

At the end of the day, one can still say that it is usually the case that those whose health is better are, other things being equal, better off, and if their health is much better, then, other things being equal, they are usually much better off. But these platitudes are not very informative.

18.6.2. Health and Opportunity

As Norman Daniels has argued, health is critical for opportunity. Indeed one way to understand how impairments such as deafness, blindness, or paraplegia can count as disabilities, even when they do not diminish well-being, is to point out their consequences for opportunity. Regardless of the social accommodations society may provide, those who are blind cannot be bus drivers and those who cannot walk cannot be Navy Seals.

The value of health is not exclusively a matter of the bearing of health on occupational opportunities, and Daniels never intended to make such a claim. He uses "opportunity" in a broader sense as the range of valuable activities and experiences available to individuals. Even though poor health may not limit the occupational opportunities of someone who is past a mandatory retirement age, it may limit her opportunities for social interactions, recreation, or enjoyment.

One could stretch the notion of opportunity still further than Daniels does, so that physical or mental states that do not limit activities also count as limiting opportunities, such as opportunities to be free of pain, to avoid anxiety, or to have normal sensory or cognitive functioning. Unless we are to stretch opportunity all the way to include these, Daniels's account of the value of health will not be adequate. Bouts of pain constitute health deficits regardless of whether they affect opportunities for activities. But if (unlike Daniels) one stretches opportunity so as to include opportunities not to be in pain, then the account is uninformative. It says that health states are bad insofar as they involve subnormal part functioning—that is to say that health states are bad insofar as they are unhealthy.

18.6.3. Health and Capability

Amartya Sen's proposal (1992, 1993; Robeyns 2005) to conceptualize what is of value to human beings in terms of various kinds of functioning (which he takes to be activities as well as states of affairs) and in terms of capabilities (which he takes to be sets of functionings that are available to people) has had a significant influence on contemporary thinking concerning health and its value. Health is one of the ten central human capabilities that Martha Nussbaum identifies (2000). Jennifer Prah Ruger argues that what is of value is not just health but "health capability," which consists of both health and the capability to pursue health (2010). Sridhar Venkatapuram (2011) argues that health is a "meta-capability"—a capability to acquire other capabilities—and that its value derives from the value of those capabilities, which is in part a matter of freedom and in part a matter of the value of the functionings that the capabilities make possible. Without using the language of capabilities, I have argued elsewhere that the value of health states depends jointly on the feelings they entail and on the activities they permit (Hausman 2010).

Unlike the claims that the value of health states consists in their bearing on well-being or in their consequences for opportunity, the claim that the value of health states depends on the capabilities they imply or, in my variant (Hausman, 2015), on the feelings and activity limitations they involve seems to be true. But one may reasonably question whether it is useful. Sen offers no way to evaluate functionings or capabilities except when capability sets are nested or all relevant evaluative criteria point in the same direction. Indeed he is skeptical about both the possibility and the desirability of scalar measures, which he believes lead people to overlook the complexities of evaluating ways of being and acting. Such skepticism is reasonable, and it may be that the best answer to the question "What is the value of health?" is to insist that health has many different values for different people in different circumstances. But Sen's skepticism does not respond to the practical need for measures that will help identify the diseases and risks that most diminish health or that will guide the allocation of health-related resources. That practical need does not demand a single context-independent measure of health, but it does demand some function from contexts to health state values, and Sen is skeptical about even such a context-sensitive measure.

18.7. CONCLUSIONS

The thrust of this discussion should be discouraging to those, like the staff at the Institute for Health Metrics and Evaluation, who seek to generate summary measures of population health and to measure the burden of different diseases, accidents, and risk factors. It is similarly unhelpful to others, like those at the National Institute for Health and Clinical Excellence in England, who need a scalar measure of the health benefits of alternative treatments in order to determine their cost effectiveness. But Sen has good reason to be skeptical of scalar measures of capabilities because all of the existing systems that purport to measure health or the burden of disease have serious flaws.

The questions that the Institute for Health Metrics and Evaluation address are important and real: how large a contribution to ill health do different diseases, injuries, and risk factors make? Without a scalar measure of health, one can only look at rough indicators, such as the contribution different diseases make to premature mortality. Similarly, within the constraints set by considerations of fairness, if the United Kingdom wants to allocate healthcare resources so as to improve health as much as possible, it apparently needs a scalar measure of health.

What is needed for health measurement or scalar evaluation is unfortunately not necessarily forthcoming. There is no good way to put the many values of different health states on a single scale that will serve all the purposes for which a generic health measure is intended. Those concerned to measure health have to make do with rough indicators of the values of health states.

Philosophers who are not concerned to measure health need not be discouraged by the incompleteness of health comparisons or the difficulties of locating health states along some single scale. If the concern is to understand the values of health rather than to measure health, no scalar unit is required. Neither is there any need for complete comparisons. Health states differ in many ways and have different values. Some health states may have aesthetic values. Consider upright posture or a clear speaking voice. The values of some states of mental health are akin to the values of traditional virtues such as courage or moderation. Other health deficiencies, both physical and mental, are unpleasant in a variety of ways. Others undermine the possibilities of undertaking various activities or pursuing certain objectives. These variegated values are real and palpable, even if there is no good way to put them all on any single scale.

Acknowledgments

I have had a great deal of help thinking through the issues in this chapter from many people over a long period of time. I am particularly indebted to Andrew Altman, Christopher Boorse, Dan Brock, Norm Fost, Paul Kelleher, Elselijn Kingma, Peter Schwartz, Russ Shafer-Landau, Alan Sidelle, and Reuben Stern.

Notes

1. That is Dominic Murphy's view. He assumes that everyone concedes that part of what defines a disease is harm (2009) and that the debate between "objectivists" and "constructivists" (neither of whom accepts a naturalistic view) turns on whether objective malfunction is a necessary condition for the existence of disease or pathology.
2. By an "ordinary" environment, I mean to rule out environments like the Nazi wartime draft or the systematic slaughter of Jews, in which traits that usually enhance well-being and opportunity or that are irrelevant to them can be very harmful.
3. According to the fourth edition of *Diagnostic and Statistical Manual of the American Psychiatric Association*, necrophilia is not a mental disorder unless it causes distress to the individual or harm to others. Earlier versions of the *DSM* did classify it as a disorder. What constitutes a mental disorder is much more controversial than what constitutes a physical disorder. Some societies have approved of intercourse with the dead under certain circumstances.
4. One central desideratum for an account of the concept of health is that it conform to the judgments of pathologists and physiologists. Their judgments are, however, fallible, and some are more central and more firmly held than others. So an account of the concept of health may conflict with some of the claims physiologists or pathologists make. This essay does not document its uncontroversial claims about their views.

5. Boorse accidentally mislabels the axes.
6. The methods employed in the global burden of disease studies carried out by the World Health Organization (2000) and the Institute for Heath Metrics and Evaluation (Murray et al. 2012–13) are somewhat different, but the differences are not material to the issues in this chapter.
7. One might resist this claim by arguing that fitness permits one to compare health states. But comparisons of fitness are not comparisons of health, if for no other reason than the much greater importance of reproduction to fitness than to health.
8. In addition there are systematic differences in the way individuals value health states, with those with experience of disabilities such as deafness judging them to be far less bad than those without those disabilities. So at least one of these groups has to be mistaken in their valuations. There is no good reason to believe that the values gleaned from preference surveys are correct.

References

Allotey, P., D. Reidpath, A. Kouamé, and R. Cummins. (2003). "The DALY, Context and the Determinants of the Severity of Disease: An Exploratory Comparison of Paraplegia in Australia and Cameroon." *Social Science and Medicine* 57: 949–58.

American Psychiatric Association. (2000). *Diagnostic and Statistical Manual of the American Psychiatric Association IV*. Arlington, VA: American Psychiatric Association.

Boorse, C. (1977). "Health as a Theoretical Concept." *Philosophy of Science* 44: 542–73.

Boorse, C. (1987). "Concepts of Health." In D. VanDeVeer and T. Regan (eds.), *Health Care Ethics: An Introduction*. Philadelphia: Temple University Press, 359–93.

Boorse, C. (1997). "A Rebuttal on Health." In J. M. Humber and R. F. Almeder (eds.), *What Is Disease?* Totowa, NJ: Humana Press, 1–134.

Brock, D. (2002). "The Separability of Health and Well-Being." In C. Murray, J. Salomon, C. Mathers, and A. Lopez (eds.), *Summary Measures of Population Health: Concepts, Ethics, Measurement and Applications*. Geneva: World Health Organization, 115–20.

Broome, J. (2002). "Measuring the Burden of Disease by Aggregating Well-Being." In C. Murray, J. Salomon, C. Mathers, and A. Lopez (eds.), *Summary Measures of Population Health: Concepts, Ethics, Measurement and Applications*. Geneva: World Health Organization, 91–113.

Cookson, R. (2005). "QALYs and the Capability Approach." *Health Economics* 14: 817–829.

Cooper, R. (2002). "Disease." *Studies in History and Philosophy of Biological and Biomedical Science* 33: 263–82.

Daniels, N. (1985). *Just Health Care*. Cambridge: Cambridge University Press.

Daniels, N. (2007). *Just Health*. Cambridge: Cambridge University Press.

Dolan, P., and D. Kahneman. (2008). "Interpretations of Utility and Their Implications for the Valuation of Health." *Economic Journal* 118: 215–34.

Engelhardt, H. T. (1974). "The Disease of Masturbation: Values and the Concept of Disease." *Bulletin of the History of Medicine* 48: 234–48.

Hausman, D. (2010). "Valuing Health: A New Proposal." *Health Economics* 19: 280–96.

Hausman, D. (2012a). "Health, Naturalism, and Functional Efficiency." *Philosophy of Science* 79: 519–41.

Hausman, D. (2012b). "Health, Well-Being and Measuring the Burden of Disease." *Population Health Metrics* 10: 1–7.

Hausman, D. (2012c). *Preference, Value, Choice and Welfare.* Cambridge: Cambridge University Press.

Hausman, D. (2015). *Valuing Health: Well-Being, Freedom, and Suffering.* New York: Oxford University Press.

Kahneman, D. (2011). *Thinking, Fast and Slow.* New York: Farrar, Straus and Giroux.

Murray, C., et al. (2012–13). "The Global Burden of Disease Study 2010." *The Lancet* 380 (9859): 2053–260.

Murphy, D. (2009). "Concepts of Disease and Health." In E. N. Zalta (ed.), *Stanford Encyclopedia of Philosophy*, Summer 2009 ed. http://plato.stanford.edu/archives/sum2009/entries/health-disease/.

Nordenfelt, L. (1987). *On the Nature of Health: An Action-Theoretic Approach.* Dordrecht: Reidel.

Nordenfelt, L. (2000). *Action, Ability and Health: Essays in the Philosophy of Action and Welfare.* Dordrecht: Kluwer.

Nussbaum, M. (2000). *Women and Human Development: The Capabilities Approach.* Cambridge: Cambridge University Press.

Prah Ruger, J. (2010). *Health and Social Justice.* Oxford: Oxford University Press.

Reznek, L. (1987). *The Nature of Disease.* London: Routledge and Kegan Paul.

Robeyns, I. (2005). "The Capability Approach: A Theoretical Survey." *Journal of Human Development* 6: 93–114.

Ryff, C., and B. Singer. (1998). "The Contours of Positive Human Health." *Psychological Inquiry* 9: 1–28.

Sen, A. (1992). *Inequality Reexamined.* Oxford: Clarendon Press.

Sen, A. (1993). "Capability and Well-Being." In M. Nussbaum and A. Sen (eds.), *The Quality of Life.* Oxford: Clarendon Press, 30–53.

Venkatapuram, S. (2011). *Health Justice: An Argument from the Capabilities Approach.* London: Polity Press.

Wakefield, J. (1992). "The Concept of Mental Disorder: On the Boundary between Biological Facts and Social Values." *American Psychologist* 47: 373–88.

World Health Organization. (1948). "Preamble to the Constitution of the World Health Organization." *Official Records of the World Health Organization*, no. 2. Geneva: World Health Organization.

Chapter 19

Freedom and Its Value

Prasanta K. Pattanaik and Yongsheng Xu

19.1. Introduction

Freedom constitutes one of the central concepts in political philosophy. Though it has received relatively less attention from economists, not only does one of the arguments that economists have often offered in support of the market mechanism run in terms of the individual freedom the markets promote (see, e.g., Hayek 1944; Friedman 1962), but the recent literature on the functioning and capability approach to well-being,[1] which has received much attention from economists, as well as philosophers, also emphasizes the role of freedom as an essential component of the well-being of an individual.

There are many complex issues that arise in connection with the notion of freedom of an individual and its value. In this chapter, we shall be concerned with four of them:

1. What do we mean when we say that an individual is free in some respect?
2. Why is freedom of any type valuable?
3. Can we compare two situations in terms of the freedom that a person enjoys? Further, can we compare the freedoms enjoyed by two different persons?
4. Can one compare the value of freedom that a person enjoys in one situation with the value of freedom that the same person or a different person enjoys in another situation?

Note that all these questions are about the freedom of individuals as distinct from the freedom of groups of individuals. In real life, we often talk about the freedom of groups of individuals as well as the freedom of individuals. Thus, one may ask whether some society *P* enjoys greater freedom of some type than some other society *Q*. In this chapter, however, we shall concentrate on the notion of freedom of a given individual, which, in many ways, is a simpler notion than the notion of freedom of a group of individuals.

The plan of the rest of the chapter is as follows. In section 19.2, we discuss the notion of freedom. Section 19.3 discusses the instrumental as well as intrinsic value of freedom.

In section 19.4, we consider the problem of measuring, at least ordinally,[2] the amount of freedom that a person enjoys in alternative situations and also the problem of interpersonal comparisons of freedom. Section 19.4 also takes up the issue of how one may compare the value of freedom that a given person enjoys in one situation with the value of freedom enjoyed by either the same person or a different person in another situation. Section 19.5 discusses some issues relating to the concept of an individual's opportunity set in a world of interdependent individuals. We conclude in section 19.6.

19.2. The Concept of Freedom

In this section, we seek to clarify some aspects of the notion of freedom.

19.2.1. MacCallum's (1967) Conceptual Framework

MacCallum's (1967) analysis of the concept of freedom provides a convenient starting point for us, though eventually we use a formal structure that is somewhat different from MacCallum's. MacCallum (1967) suggests that, when thinking about the freedom of an individual, i, one has in mind, explicitly or implicitly, a scheme of the following type:

(2.1) i is free from—to do/be/ have—,

where the first blank space is filled with a specification of some constraints and the second blank space is filled with a specification of actions, states of being, or "outcomes." Thus, we talk about i being free from illness to study, i being free from legal restrictions to travel abroad, i being free from financial constraints to attend college, and so on.

19.2.2. Freedom to Do/Be/Have What?

One constituent of MacCallum's scheme refers to the thing or things that the individual is free to do/be/have. We shall call those things the *options* under consideration and we shall refer to the individual's freedom to do/be/have those things as the individual's freedom to choose the relevant options. How we specify the options will depend on the specific context. Thus, we may be interested only in the individual's freedom to criticize the government or only in the individual's freedom in matters of religion, or in both these freedoms. Clearly, the options have to be specified differently in these different contexts. Even if we are interested in just the individual's freedom to criticize the government, depending on our context we may be interested in the individual's freedom to criticize the government in general, in which case we may like to specify the options simply as "criticize the government" and "do not criticize the government," or we may be interested in the individual's freedom to criticize the government in specific forums, in which case we may like to specify the options as "criticize the government in public lectures or newspapers," "do not criticize the government in public lectures or newspapers," and so on. For the sake of convenience, the context under consideration will be called the *focus context*.

Suppose we are interested in the individuals' freedom to read a specific newspaper, r. If we say that an individual is free to read r, do we necessarily imply that the individual is also free not to read it? In ordinary speech, when we say that an individual is free to read r, we usually imply that the individual is also free not to read it. But, if that is indeed the intention, then it will be more explicit to say that the individual is free to read r and also not to read it, that is, the individual is free to choose either of the two elements in the set, {reading the newspaper under consideration, not reading the newspaper under consideration}, which may be called the *opportunity set*. On the other hand, if, given the constraints of the individual, she has to read the specific newspaper and no other newspaper, then one way of saying it would be to say that the opportunity set of the individual is the singleton set, {reading r}.

Is the concept of an individual's freedom to do/be a necessarily linked to her preferences/values? When we say that an individual is free from certain constraints to do or be a, does it necessarily imply that she prefers to do a or values doing a? It is possible to argue that, at an intuitive level, there does not seem to be any such necessary connection between a person's freedom to do a and her desire to do a. It is not an awkward use of our language of freedom if we say that a person is free from financial and other constraints to study in a university, but she hates the idea of attending a university. Oppenheim (1981: 74) writes,

> we must be careful not to confuse the degree of an actor's freedom with the degree of value he attaches to his freedom. The degree of my freedom is a function of the possibilities left open to me, but does not depend on whether these do or do not include actions I desire to perform.

If one can say that individual i is free to do a without any presupposition that i prefers or values doing a, can one also say that i is free to do a when no one—neither i nor anybody else—desires or values doing a? Again, one can argue that whether i or other people desire or value doing a may be a relevant consideration in deciding whether i's freedom to do a is worth anything to i, but there does not seem to be any compelling reason to build into the notion of i's freedom to do a the consideration of whether any one desires to do a or values doing a. It is, however, important to note that many scholars do not agree with this. Berlin (1969: 130), for example, writes,

> The extent of my freedom seems to depend on (a) how many possibilities are open to me . . . ; (b) how easy or difficult each of these possibilities is to actualize; (c) how important in my plan of life, given my character and circumstances, these possibilities are when compared with each other; (d) how far they are closed and open by

deliberate human acts; (e) what value not merely the agent, but the general sentiments of the society in which he lives, puts on the various possibilities.

Given items (c) and (e) in Berlin's list, Oppenheim's position clearly differs from Berlin's. Sen (1991, 1992, 1993) has also forcefully argued that judgments about how much freedom a person enjoys must take into account the individual's preferences regarding the options available to her. We shall take up this point again a little later.

Often, we are concerned with the freedom of an individual to do several different things, and we talk about these different dimensions of freedom separately by making statements of the following type: "i is free to do a," "i is free to do a'," etc., where a and a' may refer to very different types of doings. Such statements need to be interpreted carefully. They should not be taken as necessarily implying that the constraints under consideration leave the individual free to do simultaneously a and a'. The laws of California do not prevent a suitably qualified person from taking up a teaching position in the University of California. Nor do they prevent such a person from accepting an expensive gift from a student of the University of California. But the laws do not permit a person to be a teacher in the University of California and to accept an expensive gift from a student of the University of California at the same time. Similarly, if we say that an individual is free from income constraints to educate her child and she is also free from income constraints to spend money on eating out, expensive clothes, and so on, it may leave it unclear whether the individual is free from income constraints to educate her child and simultaneously to spend money on eating out and expensive clothes. To avoid possible misunderstanding and to make the intention explicit, it is better to specify what, given the relevant constraints, i may be free or unfree to do, as mutually exclusive "bundles" or vectors of specifications for different types of doings/beings; we shall call such vectors *action vectors*.[3] Thus, in our first example, misunderstanding can be avoided by specifying the (mutually exclusive) alternatives as x = (hold a teaching position in the university of California, do not accept expensive gifts from any student of the University of California), y = (do not hold a teaching position in the University of California, do not accept expensive gifts from a student of the University of California), z = (do not hold a teaching position in the University of California, accept an expensive gift from a student of the University of California), and w = (hold a teaching position in the University of California, accept an expensive gift from a student of the University of California), and saying that a person is free from legal constraints to choose any of the (mutually exclusive) vectors in the opportunity set $\{x,y,z\}$ but is not free from legal constraints to choose w. The freedom of the individual in our second example can be precisely articulated in a similar fashion. In general, when one wants to consider several different types of freedom to do/be different things, it is much more explicit and unambiguous if one talks about the freedom to have a bundle of doings and beings rather than talking separately about the freedom to do/be these different things. This is true though in ordinary language we often do talk separately about one's freedoms to do different things.

Is it enough to specify the options facing an individual simply as action vectors or should one also incorporate in the specification of an option a description of the outcome that results from the action vector? Note that there are three distinct ways in which an option may be conceived, namely, as an action vector only, as an outcome only, or as an action vector together with the outcome that may result from the action vector.[4] Which particular conception one uses will depend on one's purpose and the relevant context. In many cases, however, the conception of an option simply as an action vector can be problematic. Suppose one is concerned with an individual's freedom to criticize the government. Even in a dictatorial regime, an individual can always choose to criticize the government. When one says that an individual living under a dictatorial regime is not free from political and legal constraints to criticize the government, what one has in mind are the dire consequences (death, imprisonment, torture, etc.) that follow if the individual chooses to criticize the government under such a regime. In such cases, a specification of the options in terms of the relevant action(s) without any specification of the consequence or outcome can be less than revealing. Also, whenever one is concerned with the value of the freedom that an individual may have to do/be certain things, it may be important to know what will be the outcome if the individual chooses a particular action vector. Of course, if the choice of an action vector leads to exactly one outcome,[5] then specifying the action vector will indirectly specify the outcome, but, even in such cases, it may be helpful to put in the specification of an option an explicit description of the outcome in addition to a description of the action vector. What about thinking of an option simply as an outcome without any reference to actions? Sometimes, intuitively, the actions may be indistinguishable from their outcomes. Thus, when one talks about an individual's freedom from financial constraints to eat nutritious food, to get medical help for illness, and to enjoy some leisure, the actions of eating nutritious food, getting medical help for illness, and enjoying leisure can also be thought of as outcomes. But, in general, when actions and outcomes are intuitively distinct, actions may have intrinsic value of their own; in that case, if one is concerned with the value of freedom, it may be desirable to think of options as a specification of an action vector together with a specification of the outcome that results from the actions.

Given an individual i whose freedom is under consideration, let X be the set of all mutually exclusive options x, such that i's freedom or unfreedom to choose x is of interest to us in our focus context and x is known to be physically or technologically feasible at the relevant point of time; we shall call X the *universal set of options*. What exactly do we mean by an option known to be physically or technologically feasible at the relevant point of time? We use an example to illustrate our meaning. Suppose we want to compare the freedom of a person in the year 1800 with respect to alternative modes of travel with the freedom, with respect to the mode of travel, of another person in the year 2000. Then, for the purpose of assessing the freedom of the person living in 1800, the universal set of options will include travel on foot, travel by horse, travel by a horse-drawn carriage, and so on, but will not include travel by car or travel by air since travel by car and air travel were not technologically feasible options in 1800. In contrast, the universal set of options appropriate for assessing the freedom of an individual living in 2000 should include travel by car and air travel.

In any given situation, not all the options in X will be available to the individual to choose. Which options in X will be available to the individual for choice will depend on the set of specific constraints actually facing her.

19.2.3. Freedom from What?

Consider now the constraints from which the agent may be free to do or be something. It may be useful to clarify here several aspects of the notion of constraints which may leave an individual free or unfree to choose an element of X. Note that, to some extent, the distinction between what constitutes or does not constitute a constraint often depends on one's judgment. Is an individual's strong aversion to hard work a constraint that makes her unfree to take up employment? Many people would not think so, though they may not hesitate to regard someone's obsessive fear of flying as a constraint that leaves the person unfree to undertake air travel.

Constraints may be of many different types and, in any given context, one may not be interested in all types of constraints. Following Feinberg (1973) one can broadly classify constraints into *external* constraints, that is, constraints which lie outside the body and mind of the agent under consideration, and *internal* constraints, that is, constraints which originate in the body or the mind of the agent. Thus, someone may not be free from external constraints imposed by the laws of her country to travel abroad or to join a trade union. Alternatively, someone may not be free from the internal constraint of obsessive fear of flying to go abroad; also, someone may not be free from the internal constraint of physical handicaps imposed by nature to play football. So far as external constraints are concerned, one may distinguish between external constraints that can be attributed to specific human agents (an individual, a group of individuals, the state, and so on) and those external constraints (e.g., an individual's lack of financial resources because of unemployment in a depression), which arise from the general institutions of the economy or the society. The freedom from constraints imposed by identifiable human agents has sometimes been called "negative freedom," while the freedom from constraints (e.g., lack of financial resources) arising from general economic institutions and internal constraints (e.g., the lack of physical strength, skill, or education) has sometimes been called "positive freedom."[6]

There is no compelling reason why one should necessarily consider all possible constraints at the same time. For some purposes, one may like to consider only the constraints imposed on an individual by identifiable human agents (freedom from such constraints is what has sometimes been called social freedom) (see Oppenheim 1981); in some other cases, one may be interested in the individual's freedom from restrictions imposed by the state only; and so on.

There are some constraints which may make an individual completely unable to do/be something. If i has lost both his legs, then there is no way in which i can play football.

But sometimes there are constraints which do not completely prevent a person from doing/being something; instead, these constraints render the individual incapable of doing/being something without being penalized or punished for doing/being that (or, at least without facing some risk of being penalized or punished for doing that). Thus, suppose there is a law which says that, if an individual i is caught picking somebody's pocket, then i will be imprisoned for sixty days. Then we would intuitively feel that the laws make i unfree to pick anybody's pocket. But this does not imply that i is unable to pick anybody's pocket. It is just that i is unable to pick anybody's pocket without taking some risk, say, 25 percent chance of imprisonment for sixty days. As we noted in section 19.2.2, one way of talking about freedom/unfreedom in such cases will be to build the penalty specification into the description of the individual's options. Thus, one can say that, given the legal constraints, i is free to choose one of the two options in the following opportunity set: {(do not pick anybody's pocket and do not face any risk of being penalized for picking anybody's pocket) and (pick someone's pocket and face the risky prospect where there is 75 percent chance of increasing wealth by some amount without incurring any penalty and 25 percent chance of being imprisoned for sixty days)}.

Suppose we are interested in an individual's freedom or unfreedom to choose the mutually exclusive options in some suitably specified X. Let $C = \{c_1, \ldots, c_m\}$ be the set of all conceivable constraints. At any given time, the individual will be faced with a subset of the set of all constraints; we shall denote this subset by C^*. As we noted earlier, the type of freedom we may be interested in need not necessarily be the individual's freedom from all the constraints that she actually faces: in a specific context, we may be interested only in the individual's freedom from constraints belonging to some nonempty subset, C', of C^*, the set of all constraints to which the individual is actually subject. Let h be a function, which, for every subset C' of C, specifies a non-empty subset $h(C')$ of X, such that, $h(\emptyset) = X$, and, for all non-empty subsets C^1 and C^2 of C, if $C^1 \subseteq C^2$, then $h(C^2) \subseteq h(C^1)$. We interpret the function h as follows:

(2.2) for every nonempty subset C' of C, the individual would not be able to choose any element of $X - h(C')$ whenever she faced all the constraints in C' (possibly, along with other constraints);

and

(2.3) for every nonempty subset C' of C, if the constraints in C' were the only ones that the individual under consideration faced, then she would be able to choose any element of $A = h(C')$.

Note that, saying that an individual is free from the constraints in C' to choose any element in the set $h(C')$, does not necessarily imply that the individual has the *ability* to choose every element of $h(C')$, unless the individual does not face any constraint outside C'. When one says that i is free from financial problems to pursue her education in a university, one is not saying anything about whether there may or may not be other constraints, such as the limited intellectual abilities of *i*, which can prevent *i* from going for university education.

In the recent literature on the measurement of freedom and the value of freedom, freedom has often been modeled as an individual's actual ability to choose one of several available options. Given this perspective, very often the formal analysis is exclusively focused on the set of all options *x*, such that the individual is able to choose *x* if she wishes to do so, and the constraints are omitted from the analysis altogether. This does not cause any serious misunderstanding if the constraints under consideration are the set of all constraints that the individual faces. If, however, we are concerned with a particular proper subset, C' of the set of all constraints that the individual faces (for example, C' may be only the political and legal constraints that the individual actually faces), then the interpretation of $h(C')$ needs to be as the set of all options that the individual would be able to choose if the constraints in C' were the only constraints faced by the individual. Consider the case of a woman who lives in a society where laws do not permit a woman from attending the university, who is too poor to afford university education, and who also lacks intellectual abilities required for university education. In this case there are three different constraints each of which is sufficient to prevent the woman from going to the university. Now suppose the legal constraint is removed. So far as the woman's actual ability to go to the university is concerned, there has been no change: as before, she is still unable to go to the university. One can, however, plausibly say that her freedom from legal restrictions to go to the university has increased since she would have been able to go the university had the resource and intellectual constraints been absent. For every subset C' of C, $h(C')$ will be called the *opportunity set* defined by the constraints in C' and will be interpreted as the set of all options in X that the individual will be able to choose if she was subject only to constraints in C'.

19.2.4. Contingent Freedom

One further point may be noted here. Some freedoms may be contingent on the occurrence or continuation of some event. Thus, when we say that people are free from legal constraints to criticize the state, it is possible that there is a suppressed qualifying phrase here, namely, the phrase "provided it is not a time of war." The contingent nature of the agent's freedom in such cases is typically recognized, and, if the event on which the freedom is contingent is not already explicitly specified, a little probing uncovers it easily. It is, however, important to recognize that there may be cases where the contingent nature of the freedom under consideration may be somewhat more subtle: the occurrence or continuation of an event, on which certain types of freedom of individuals in a society are contingent, may itself depend on how the individuals in the society choose to exercise their freedoms. This often happens in "economic" contexts, where the exercise of a particular type of freedom requires scarce resources. An individual's freedom from budget constraints to buy a given commodity bundle is a case in point. Suppose, at the prevailing prices everybody in the economy is able to buy commodity bundle *a* but suppose most people are actually buying commodity bundle *b*, which, as compared to *a*, contains less of oranges and more of some other commodities. It seems consistent with our ordinary language to say that everybody is free from budgetary constraints to buy *a* though most people are actually choosing to buy *b*. If, however, a sufficiently large number of people seek to exercise this freedom by choosing to buy the bundle *a*, the price of oranges may rise sharply and many people may not be able to buy *a*. Thus, the freedom of each individual to buy *a* may be contingent on the prices remaining the same, which, in turn, may be contingent on the circumstance that not too many people seek to use their present freedom to buy the bundle *a*. We shall return to this point in section 19.5.

19.3. The Value of Freedom

Why is individual freedom valuable? Or, to restate the question in the language of comparisons, why is more freedom more valuable, at least in some cases? For the sake of simplicity, let us assume that the set, X, of all possible options for the individual is fixed and we are considering two alternative sets of constraints, corresponding to which the opportunity sets are, A and B, respectively. Suppose $A \subset B$. Then we suppose that most people would say that the freedom of an individual increases (or, at least does not decrease) when her opportunity set changes from A to B. Why may such expansion of the individual's opportunity set be valuable? Increased freedom may be viewed solely as an instrument for achieving a more preferred/valued option or outcome (we shall call this the *instrumental value* of freedom). On the other hand, one may argue that increased individual freedom has a value apart from what option or outcome the individual can actually achieve with such increased freedom (we shall call this the *intrinsic value* of freedom).[7] In either case, one can consider the value of an individual's freedom as assessed by the individual himself (we shall call this *self-assessment* of the value of freedom) or the value of an individual's freedom as assessed by some other agent, such as an external evaluator, the community, and so on (we shall call such assessment *external assessment* of the value of freedom). The two types of assessment need not necessarily coincide.

19.3.1. The Instrumental Value of Freedom

It is possible to argue that the value of an individual's freedom to choose from a given opportunity set A is determined exclusively by the value of the most valued option in the set A, so that an opportunity set A offers more valuable freedom to the individual than another opportunity set B if and only if the most highly valued option in A is more valuable than the most highly valued option in B. But how does one determine the relative value, that is, ranking, of the different options in X? There are various possibilities here. The ranking[8] of the options in X may be:

(i) the individual's utility-based ranking of the options, where utility is interpreted as preference satisfaction or desire fulfillment;
(ii) the ranking of options reflecting the individual's considered judgment or evaluation of the options in terms of what she values[9] rather than what she prefers;
(iii) the ranking of the options in X in terms of standards widely accepted in the community to which the individual belongs.

Irrespective of whether one takes route (i), (ii), or (iii), by identifying the value of an opportunity set with the value of the highest-ranking option in the opportunity set, one would be taking an instrumental view of the value of freedom. The nature of such instrumentality, however, differs as between the three cases. In case (ii), the value of freedom depends exclusively on the utility of the utility-maximizing option in the opportunity set. This is analogous to the notion of indirect utility in economic theory. In economic theory the consumer is assumed to have a utility function, which assigns (ordinal) utility numbers to the consumption bundles that she can conceivably consume (these numbers simply represent the consumer's preference ordering over the conceivable consumption bundles) (see Debreu 1959). The indirect utility of the consumer corresponding to a given level of wealth and a given vector of prices is defined to be the utility of the bundle that she prefers most in her budget set, that is, the set of consumption bundles available to her given her wealth and the prices. In case (ii) also the value of freedom is determined exclusively by the highest ranking option in the opportunity set, but the ranking under consideration is the individual's ranking based on her considered judgments rather than her preferences. Case (iii) differs from the first two cases since the ranking of options used here is based on consensus in the community to which the individual belongs.

A somewhat different reason why freedom may have an instrumental value is the uncertainty regarding the individual's future preferences or evaluation of options. Consider a given opportunity set, A. Suppose x is the uniquely best option in A, defined by the individual's present preference ordering, R, over X. Why should an individual, who is concerned only with the desirability of the option that she actually chooses, be concerned about whether or not the options in $A - \{x\}$ are actually available? One reason can be that she is not sure whether R will continue to be her future preferences. If she thinks that her future preferences may be either R or R' and x' is the R'-greatest element in A (recall that x is the R-greatest element in A), then the continued availability of x' as well as x will be important for the satisfaction of her uncertain future preferences (see, for example, Koopmans 1962; Kreps 1979; Arrow 1995; and Barberà and Grodal 2011). The uncertainty of the individual regarding her future preferences may be probabilistic in nature or it may take less precise form without exact probabilities. In either case, given the uncertainty about future preferences, the availability of the other options in A

in addition to x, the individual's currently most preferred option in A, may be important for her. Thus, more freedom may be valuable because of the extra flexibility that it provides for the realization of an option that may be more preferred or valued in terms of the individual's future preference or evaluation function (this is what Kreps [1979] calls "preference for flexibility" and Feinberg [1973] calls "dispositional" freedom).

19.3.2. The Intrinsic Value of Freedom

For J. S. Mill (1962 [1859]), the value of freedom went beyond what freedom allowed the individual to achieve in terms of satisfaction of her already given preferences over options or in terms of the evaluative criteria by which she might judge the options. Freedom was valuable to Mill primarily because, without freedom, an individual could not develop her individual identity itself. For Mill, "free development of individuality is one of the leading essentials of well-being; . . . it is not only a coordinate element with all that is designated by the terms civilization, instruction, education, culture, but is itself a necessary part and condition of all those things" (Mill 1962 [1859]: ch. 3, par. 2), and Mill believed that development of individuality was possible only if the individual was free to make her choices. Mill (1962 [1859]: ch. 3, par. 3) argued, "The human faculties of perception, judgment, discriminative feeling, mental activity, and even moral preference, are exercised only in making a choice." Thus, for Mill, an individual's freedom to choose is valuable because it is in the process of making choices that the individual develops her own preferences and judgments, and, hence, her personality itself. Jones and Sugden (1982: 59) put Mill's notion with admirable clarity:

> To suppose that the act of choice requires the exercise of mental power is to suppose that the chooser is in some considerable measure an autonomous agent; whatever he chooses, he might have chosen something else. . . . What makes significant choice possible is that preferences are not just part of a person's physiology or psychology like the colour of his eyes or a tendency to depression. Given a person's psychology, and given the situation in which he finds himself, there remain different preferences that he could hold, and he has to decide which is right for him.

Mill's notion of the individual deciding what preferences/judgments she would have is similar to Kant's (2005 [1785]) idea of an individual choosing her own preferences "autonomously"; for Kant, an individual chooses her preferences autonomously when she forms her preferences according to some principle that is not solely derived from nature or social and economic convention and that the individual gives to herself.

Mill's idea of an individual's preferences and judgments being formed through the course of making choices from different sets of options is very different from the idea, usual in economics, of choices being made on the basis of already given preferences. The value of freedom extolled by Mill is an intrinsic value of freedom rather than the value of freedom as an instrument to go up higher in one's given utility-based ranking of options or some other given evaluative scale for the options.

19.4. THE MEASUREMENT OF FREEDOM AND ITS VALUE

19.4.1. Some General Conceptual Issues Relating to the Measurement of Freedom and Its Value

In this section, we discuss the problem of measuring (1) the degrees or "amounts" of freedom that individuals enjoy in alternative situations; and (2) the values of these different degrees or amounts of freedom. We will be concerned with ordinal measurement so that measurement will basically take the form of comparisons, such as "individual i has more freedom in situation α than she has in situation β" (ordinal comparison of degrees of freedom for a given person), "individual i has more freedom in situation α than individual j has in situation β" (ordinal interpersonal comparison of degrees of freedom), and "the freedom that i enjoys in situation α is more valuable than the freedom that j enjoys in situation β" (ordinal interpersonal comparison of the value of freedom). We would like to clarify two conceptual issues that arise here.

First, can one talk about more freedom or less freedom without referring to the values of the freedoms being compared (irrespective of whether the comparison is for a given person or across persons)? Intuitively, it is not clear to us why the notion of how much freedom an individual enjoys has to be dependent on the notion of the value of that freedom. Consider situation α where the constraints that you face are such that you have only two alternative options with respect to the choice of a dessert: eating a good apple and not eating anything for dessert. Now consider situation β, such that you have exactly three options, eating a good apple, not eating any dessert, and eating a rotten apple. Will it be completely absurd for you to say, "I have greater freedom in situation β than in situation α, but this extra freedom is not worth anything to me since neither I nor anybody in my society nor any reasonable person anywhere would choose to eat a rotten apple if the options of eating an apple or not eating anything for dessert are open"? We do not think so, but, as in the case of many other aspects relating to the concept of freedom and its value, the intuition of different people may differ considerably here (see sections 19.4.3 and 19.4.4 below).

Second, in the recent literature on the measurement of freedom and its value, often there has been a tendency to focus exclusively on the options that an individual is actually *able to choose* without any explicit reference to the constraints, the implicit assumption being that we are concerned with all the constraints, external and internal, that the individual actually faces. Given this exclusive focus on the options that the individual is able to choose without any consideration of the specific constraints that the individual faces, it will be natural to say that, if the opportunity set defined by the set of all constraints actually faced by the individual is the same in two situations, then the individual enjoys the same degree of freedom in the two situations. This, however, may be problematic from an intuitive point of view. Consider two situations, α and β. In α, individual *i*, who is a woman, has the resources and the intellectual ability required to study in a university but is unable to join the university because there is a law which says that women cannot study in a university. In situation β, *i* has the intellectual ability to go to a university and there is no gender-specific law that prevents *i* from studying in a university, but *i* is too poor to afford university education. In both situations, *i* is unable to study in a university, but *i* as well as many other people may, with some justification, feel that *i*'s unfreedom in situation α is much worse (in terms of value) than *i*'s unfreedom in situation β since the source of *i*'s unfreedom in situation α is an affront to *i*'s dignity as a human being. Taking this position will, of course, imply that the negative value of unfreedom cannot be assessed only by considering the opportunity set; one has also to consider the constraints underlying the opportunity set.

In the subsequent sections, we give an account of some contributions to the recent literature on the measurement of freedom and its value. So, despite the caveat in the preceding paragraph, we shall use the formal framework adopted in these contributions and assume that the assessment of freedom and/or its value in a given situation is to be done exclusively on the basis of the opportunity set, $h(C^*)$, defined by the set, C^*, of all constraints that the individual actually faces. Given this assumption, the comparison of freedom (resp., value of freedom) for a given person in alternative situations or interpersonal comparison of freedom (resp., value of freedom) amounts to a comparison of different nonempty subsets, A, B, and so on, of the universal set of options, where each such subset A is interpreted as the opportunity set defined by the set of all constraints that the individual actually faces in some situation α (this, of course, implies that A is the set of all options x such that the individual is able to choose x in situation α).

19.4.2. The Cardinality Rule for Assessing Freedom and Its Limitations

To develop our intuition about the amount of freedom offered by various opportunity sets, we consider some simple cases first. Suppose you live ten miles away from your workplace and the only transport option available to you to get to your workplace is to take Bus 19. Note that, in this case, you have no other choice but to take Bus 19 if you want to go to your workplace. In a way, to get to your workplace, you are compelled to take Bus 19 and have no freedom. This intuition can be generalized to the following axiom, which was discussed independently by Jones and Sugden (1982) and Pattanaik and Xu (1990):

(4.1) Any singleton opportunity set offers an individual zero freedom, and consequently, any two singleton opportunity sets offer the same amount of freedom to an individual.

Suppose a commuting train line will be added and will run from where you live to your workplace starting next year, while Bus 19 will continue to operate as usual. Will the added commuting train service increase your freedom? The answer seems to be affirmative: this expansion of the initial singleton opportunity set leads to the increase in an individual's freedom. Indeed, we can extend this intuition to the following axiom, which was proposed by Pattanaik and Xu (1990):

(4.2) The addition of a distinct alternative to a singleton opportunity set increases an individual's freedom.

While the above two axioms capture our intuition about freedom in simple cases, the next axiom attempts to articulate our intuition on freedom from a different perspective when two opportunity sets are enlarged respectively by adding to each a common alternative that is currently not present in the two opportunity sets. Suppose that initially we have compared the freedoms of two individuals, i and j, to choose their modes of transport to their respective workplaces and have concluded that individual i having the opportunity set A enjoys more freedom than individual j with the opportunity set B. Suppose now that a new mode of transport, car pool, which was not initially available to either i or j becomes available to both the individuals. How does this change our comparison of freedoms enjoyed by i and j? Our initial intuition seems to suggest that this should not change our earlier conclusion, that is, we should continue to regard i as enjoying more freedom than individual j: the comparison of freedoms offered by two opportunity sets should remain unaffected by the addition of a new option to each of the two initial opportunity sets if the new option did not belong to either of those two initial opportunity sets. Generalizing this intuition, we have the following axiom (see Pattanaik and Xu 1990 for a formal statement):

(4.3) The comparison of freedoms offered by two opportunity sets A and B is exactly analogous to the comparison of freedoms offered by the opportunity sets $A \cup \{x\}$ and $B \cup \{x\}$ as long as the option x does not belong to either A or B.

Each axiom above has its initial appeal. The combination of them, however, produces the following result (see Pattanaik and Xu 1990 for a formal statement and the proof):

(4.4) A reflexive and transitive freedom ranking, which ranks all possible finite opportunity sets, satisfies (4.1), (4.2), and (4.3) if and only if it is such that, an opportunity set A offers at least as much freedom as another opportunity set B just in the case that the number of options contained in A is at least as great as the number of options contained in B.[10]

The rule that ranks opportunity sets in terms of freedom on the basis of cardinalities of those opportunity sets may be called the *simple cardinality rule*. It may be argued that this rule is a naive and unsatisfactory rule for assessing degrees of freedom offered by opportunity sets. Then the message of (4.4) is that the three initially intuitively plausible axioms lead us to a naive rule for assessing degrees of freedom offered by various opportunity sets. Though (4.1), (4.2) and (4.3) have their initial plausibility, it may be argued that the apparent intuitive appeal of some of these properties must be rather doubtful.

Consider (4.3) first. Suppose we are considering opportunity sets that consist of alternative modes of transport. We may believe that the two opportunity sets {gray train} and {gray car} offer the same amount of freedom. At the same time, we may also believe that the opportunity set {gray train, red car} offers more freedom than the opportunity set {gray car, red car}, the reason being that traveling by a red car is vastly different from traveling by a gray train, while travelling by a red car is very similar to traveling by a gray car. In that case, our ranking of opportunity sets will violate (4.3). The example illustrates the failure of (4.3) to take into account information about the "similarity" or "closeness" that the different options may have to each other. Such information may be an important consideration for the assessment of degrees of freedom offered by various opportunity sets. Section 19.4.4 below discusses alternative ways of introducing notions of closeness or similarity of alternatives and methods of assessing freedom that take into account such similarity.

The intuitive appeals of the axioms of (4.1) and (4.2) have also been questioned in the literature on the ground that they fail to take into account the preference information about the alternatives. For example, Sen (1990, 1991) argues that if an alternative x is strictly preferred to another alternative y, then the opportunity set $\{x\}$ offers more freedom than the opportunity set $\{y\}$. This is because, according to Sen (1990, 1991), the evaluation of an individual's freedom depends crucially on how the individual values the alternatives contained in the opportunity sets. The acceptance of Sen's position would, of course, violate (4.1). The argument could be carried further (see Sen 1990, 1991) to say that the opportunity set {living a good life, being beheaded at dawn} offers the same degree of freedom as the opportunity set {living a good life}. Since the option "being beheaded at dawn" is far inferior to the option "living a good life", the addition of the option "being beheaded at dawn" to the opportunity set {living a good life} will not increase freedom. Note that the ranking [{living a good life, being beheaded at dawn} offering the same amount of freedom as {living a good life}] violates (4.2). It seems to us that the intuition underlying these objections to (4.1) and (4.2) have more to do with the measurement of the value of freedom than with the measurement of freedom. The consideration of the quality of available options (as determined by the individual's preferences or her considered judgments or by some other criterion) seems to be essential for assessing the value of freedom rather than the assessment of the degree of freedom.

To some extent, the distinction between the value of freedom and the degree or extent of freedom that we are suggesting is a semantic issue. Suppose we ignore the distinction and accept the position that an opportunity set A offers at least as much freedom to an individual as an opportunity set B if and only if the freedom offered by A is at least as valuable as the freedom offered by B. How do we then go about measuring freedom (or, equivalently under our assumption, the value of freedom)? This is what we discuss in sections 19.4.3 and 19.4.4.

19.4.3. The Value of Freedom

The framework discussed in section 19.4.2 rules out any role of the quality of options in the opportunity set in judgments about freedom. Sen (1990, 1991) and other writers such as Foster (1992) and Puppe (1996) have raised important objections to such a framework, and have argued for a framework that takes into account the quality of options in opportunity sets in assessing an individual's freedom. Assume that there is a given ordering, R, which ranks the options in terms of their "quality." Presently, we shall consider the exact intuitive content of this given quality-based ranking of the options. But, if we are given such a given "quality-based" ordering of options, then one way of incorporating that information into the ranking of opportunity sets in terms of the degrees of freedom they offer will be to specify the freedom ranking of opportunity sets as follows:

(4.5) An opportunity set A offers at least as much freedom as another opportunity set B if and only if, in terms of the ordering R, the highest ranking option in A ranks at least as high as the highest ranking option in B.

If option y ranks strictly higher than option x in terms of the ordering R, then, under the rule (4.5), $\{y\}$ will offer more freedom than $\{x\}$ and the same amount of freedom as $\{x, y\}$, and, therefore, the ranking rule given by (4.5) will violate both (4.1) and (4.2).

R can have alternative interpretations. As noted in section 19.3, one can take R to be the utility-based ordering of the individual where utility is interpreted as the satisfaction of the individual's current preferences, whatever such preferences may be. Given this interpretation of R, the freedom ranking defined by (4.5) will reflect the instrumental value of freedom as a means to go up higher in the utility scale. The idea of linking freedom and preference satisfaction can be traced back to Hobbes (1952 [1651]), who writes: "a *freeman* is he that, in those things which by his strength and wit he is able to do, is not hindered to do what he has a will to" (*Leviathan*, ch. 21, "Of the Liberty of Subjects," par. 2).

R can also be interpreted as an ordering of options based on the individual's considered judgments (rather than whatever preferences the individual may have), or as an ordering based on some consensus in the individual's community regarding the value of the options. As we discussed in section 19.3.1, the analysis of the instrumental value of freedom can also be extended to a framework where freedom is valued for its role in satisfying the individual's uncertain future preferences.

We now turn to the intrinsic value of freedom discussed in section 19.3.2. For this purpose, we consider the following example,[11] where, to start with, laws permit women to join the army but a specific woman, i, who currently has no intention of joining the army, attaches probability zero to the possibility that she would like to join the army in the future. Suppose the government proposes a change in the law that will prevent women from joining the army. If the freedom offered by an opportunity set is judged exclusively by the most preferred option in the opportunity set, then the change in the law will not affect the freedom of i. Also, since i attaches zero probability to her desiring to join the army in the future, there is no flexibility-based argument for saying that the change in the law will affect her freedom. Yet many people would feel that the change in the law would reduce i's freedom. One possible reason for this may be that, though i does not want to join the army and does not believe that she will actually want to join the army in the future, i can imagine herself as preferring to join the army. From this perspective, the value of i's freedom is to be assessed neither on the basis of a historically given preferences that the individual may have currently nor on the basis of the preference orderings that may have some positive probability of being assigned to her by nature as her future preference ordering, but on the basis of a *reference* set of preference orderings interpreted as the set of alternative preferences that she can imagine herself as having. Recalling Mill's notion of the value of freedom of choice in terms of the opportunity such freedom provides to the individual to develop her own preferences and personality (see section 19.3), one can say that, in the process of deliberating about her choices, the individual actively decides which of the orderings in the reference set she would have.

There can be other interpretations of the reference set of orderings. One can think of the reference set not as the set of alternative orderings that the individual can think of herself as having, but as the set of all orderings that a "reasonable person" may have in the objective circumstances of the individual i under consideration. In the context of our example above, a reasonable person in i's objective circumstances, that is, a reasonable person who is a woman, may strictly prefer joining the army to not joining the army, just as a reasonable woman may have exactly the opposite preference. When the reference set of orderings is given this interpretation, one can think of the individual as choosing for herself one of the orderings that a reasonable person in her objective circumstances may have. Going back to Sen's example of eating a good apple, no apple, or a rotten apple, one can argue that the reason why Sen's argument that adding the option of eating a rotten apple to the other two options (eating a bad apple and not eating any dessert) does not increase the individual's freedom seems convincing is not so much that the individual does not prefer eating a rotten apple to the other two options or that the individual will never prefer eating a rotten apple to eating a good apple and eating no apple in the future, but that no reasonable person will prefer eating a rotten apple to eating a good apple and eating no apple. The view that the value of i's freedom is to be assessed with reference to the set of all orderings that reasonable people can have in i's objective circumstances naturally raises the issue of how one specifies the notion of "reasonableness." It seems to us that this will be determined by the values prevailing in the society to which the individual under consideration belongs. It may be worth giving an example of how the idea of a reasonable person's preferences can be used to determine the appeal of an axiom such as (4.2). Suppose the agent, i, starts with an opportunity set $\{x\}$, where he has to choose x. Now suppose we add y to his initial opportunity set so that the new opportunity set is $\{x, y\}$. Does the new opportunity set, $\{x, y\}$, offer the individual more freedom? The answer to this question may depend on one's intuition about what the preferences of a reasonable person in i's community may be when placed in i's objective circumstances. If, in i's objective circumstances, every reasonable person belonging to i's community would prefers x to y, then one may believe that $\{x, y\}$ does not offer any more freedom than $\{x\}$. If, on the other hand, some such reasonable people prefer x to y and some other reasonable persons would prefer y to x then one may be willing to say that $\{x, y\}$ offers more freedom to i than $\{x\}$.

To see how the notion of a reference set of orderings can be used to analyze the ranking of opportunity sets in terms of freedom, the reader may like to consult, among others, Jones and Sugden (1982), Sugden (1985), Foster (2011), and Pattanaik and Xu (1998). Jones and Sugden (1982) and Pattanaik and Xu (1998) specifically interpret the orderings in the reference set as the preference ordering that reasonable people may have. This is also one of the interpretations that Sugden (1985) considers, but Foster (2011) does not use this specific interpretation.

19.4.4. Diversity and the Value of Freedom

As discussed in section 19.4.2, the cardinality rule neglects all information regarding the similarity that may exist among various alternatives in an opportunity set. Consider the example in section 19.4.2, involving alternative modes of transport. When ranking the two opportunity sets, {gray train, red car} and {gray car, red car} in terms of the freedom offered by them, one may feel that the former set offers more freedom than the latter since, as modes of transport, gray car and red car are very similar while gray train and red car are quite different. Consider another example. Suppose a and b are leftist parties; c is a centralist party; and d, e, f, and g are all rightist parties with only slightly different platforms. Then, in ranking the opportunity sets $\{a, c, f\}$ and $\{d, e, f, g\}$, one may like to take into consideration the fact that the diversity of political platforms offered by the opportunity set $\{a, c, f\}$ is greater than that offered by the opportunity set $\{d, e, f, g\}$, even though the latter opportunity set has more political parties in it than the former opportunity set, and, as a result, one may rank the set $\{a, c, f\}$ higher than the set $\{d, e, f, g\}$ in terms of freedom. If we think that the extent to which the alternatives in the set under consideration are similar to each other should enter our judgment about the degree of freedom offered by that set, then we need first to find a way to interpret the notion of similarity in this context and subsequently to incorporate this notion of similarity into our judgment about the freedom-based ranking of various opportunity sets. There are alternative ways of formulating the notion of similarity. For example, we can start with an ordinal distance function d to capture the comparison of the degree of the similarity (or dissimilarity) between any two options with the degree of the similarity (or dissimilarity) between two other alternatives in the set. For example, when we say that the degree of the similarity between a gray train and a red car is less than the degree of the similarity between a gray car and a red car, we can use an ordinal distance function d, such that $d(\text{gray train, red car}) > d(\text{gray car, red car})$. Likewise, when we say that the two political parties, g and e, are more similar to each other than another two political parties, a and e, an ordinal distance function d can be used to capture this comparison: $d(a,e) > d(g,e)$. In general, we can define an ordinal distance function d with the following interpretation: for all options x, y, z, w, $d(x,y) > d(z,w)$ indicates that the degree of similarity between x and y is less than the degree of similarity between z and w, and $d(x,y) = d(z,w)$ indicates that the degree of similarity between x and y is the same as the degree of similarity between z and w. Since d is a distance function, naturally, we can require that $d(x,x) = 0$ for all x in X, and $d(x,y) = d(y,x) \geq 0$ for all x, y in X. Equipped with this ordinal distance function d, we can then examine the problem of ranking opportunity sets in terms of freedom and make a connection between the value of freedom offered by an opportunity set and the notion of similarity among alternatives in the opportunity set. For example, axiom (4.1), discussed in section 19.4.2, seems to be a reasonable property in this context. As for (4.2), if two alternatives x, y are "exactly similar" to each other so that $d(x,y) = 0$, then, intuitively, $\{x, y\}$ and $\{x\}$ and $\{y\}$ all offer the same amount of freedom; if, however, x, y are not exactly similar to each other, then it is reasonable to say that $\{x, y\}$ offers more freedom than either $\{x\}$ or $\{y\}$. Indeed, one can use the given ordinal distance function to investigate various intuitions about ranking opportunity sets in terms of freedom. For specific analysis incorporating the notion of similarity, see the contributions by Pattanaik and Xu (2000, 2008), van Hees (2004), and Bervoets and Gravel (2007).

One can also start with a cardinal distance function and examine its implications for the ranking of opportunity sets in terms of freedom. Interested readers may refer to the contributions by Weitzman (1992), Nehring and Puppe (2002), Weikard (2002), and Gustafsson (2010) for explorations along this line.[12]

19.4.5. Interpersonal Comparisons of Individual Freedom

How to make interpersonal comparisons of individual freedom? If freedom is assessed using the simple cardinality rule, interpersonal comparisons of freedom are intuitively somewhat straightforward. However, when the assessment of freedom is based on the quality of options or a reference set of orderings, interpersonal comparisons of freedom become more difficult. In this context, we may be prepared to say that

(4.6) when two opportunity sets A and B are such that $B \subset A$, whoever has A enjoys at least as much freedom as whoever has B,

but otherwise there is no clear intuition to make a comparison of freedom enjoyed by two individuals. On the other hand, we may want to allow some, perhaps minimal, self-assessment by individuals of their own freedoms, based on their own "values." In that case, the following condition would seem attractive:

(4.7) For some opportunity sets C and D, for some distinct individuals i and j, C offers more freedom to i than D, but D offers more freedom to j than C.

We shall call the requirements (4.6) and (4.7) *dominance* and *minimal self-assessment*, respectively. Minimal self-assessment follows as a simple consequence when the measurement of freedom of a given individual in different situations is based on a given "quality-based" ordering of options of that individual and the orderings of different individuals happen to be different. Even when freedom is evaluated based on a (common) reference set of orderings, minimal self-assessment is plausible if we allow different individuals to weigh the orderings in the reference set differently in their assessments of their own freedoms. When we seek to make interpersonal comparisons of freedom in addition to comparisons of freedom of a given individual in different situations, dominance and minimal self-assessment as discussed above lead to difficulties if freedom rankings are required to be "minimally continuous." See Pattanaik and Xu (2007) for a detailed discussion of these difficulties.

19.5. THE CONCEPT OF AN OPPORTUNITY SET

Much of the recent literature on freedom in economics treats the options in an individual's opportunity set as *outcomes* that are available to the individual (see Pattanaik and Xu 2009 for a review). The individual's freedom is thus viewed as the ability to choose any of the mutually exclusive outcomes in the opportunity set. For example, in the competitive market economy, if an outcome for a competitive consumer is thought of as his consumption bundle, then his opportunity set is given by his budget set and his freedom is seen to be the opportunity of choosing any consumption bundle from his budget set. Similarly, in the functioning-capability approach to human well-being (Sen 1985, 1987; Nussbaum 1988), where an individual's well-being is captured by his *achieved functioning*[13] *bundle* as well as his *capability set*, that is, the set of possible functioning bundles available for him to choose, an individual's opportunity set is his capability set and the freedom of the individual is viewed as the opportunity to choose any one of the functioning bundles contained in his capability set. In section 19.2.2, we have indicated two other possibilities: one can also think of each option in the opportunity set as an action vector available to the individual or as a specification of an action vector and the corresponding outcome.

In a world in which there is a one-to-one relation between an outcome and an action vector, the distinction between these alternative conceptions of an opportunity set seems not to matter. This is because, in such a world, when we think of the individual as choosing an action plan, we can also think of her as choosing the outcome corresponding to that particular action plan, and vice versa. In the absence of such a one-to-one relation between outcomes and action plans, each of the three conceptions of an option is likely to run into problems. If the opportunity set is conceived as the set of action vectors available to the individual under consideration, it may well be the case that the individual can have many action vectors available to her, but, whatever action vector she chooses, the outcome is the same. It would then make little sense to claim that the individual enjoys much freedom; after all, a major reason for valuing freedom to choose actions is that such choice of actions can influence the final outcome. On the other hand, if the options in the opportunity are conceived either as outcomes or as combinations of action vectors and outcomes, it raises the issue of whether or not the individual can actually choose an outcome in a world with many individuals. In such a context, the outcome often depends on the action vectors chosen by other individuals as well as the action vector adopted by the individual under consideration, and no single individual is in a position to control or choose the final outcome. A few examples may clarify the point. An ill-paid worker may have the freedom to join a strike, but whether he will lose his job or get a pay raise may depend on the number of other similarly ill-paid workers in the same firm joining the strike. Despite antidiscrimination laws, the supervisors in a firm may be discriminating against women, and an individual female employee may have the freedom to report the matter to appropriate authorities, but the final outcome of such complaint may depend on whether other employees will come forward to give evidence, and how thoroughly the authorities conduct the investigation. A person has the freedom to interact with her friends, but the amount of interaction cannot be just determined by the person herself; it will also depend on how much her friends want to interact with her. A fisherman has the freedom to go out to the unregulated, common lake to catch fish, but the number of fish that he can catch depends on his effort and time as well as the number of other fishermen in the area catching fish. In general, the outcome is typically a result of strategic interactions among the individuals: it is determined by the action vector adopted by the individual under consideration together with the action vectors chosen by other individuals. In all such cases, the conception of an individual's freedom as either her ability to choose one of several outcomes or her ability to choose one of several action vector-outcome combinations would seem to be conceptually problematic. This problem has been discussed in several related contexts (see, for example, Basu 1987; Basu and López-Calva 2011; Pattanaik and Xu 2009, 2012; Pattanaik 1994; Bervoets 2009; Tadenuma and Xu 2010).

One important case of the absence of strategic interaction in economics is the classical perfectly competitive economy with a "very" large number of consumers and producers. In such a setting, given the competitive equilibrium prices, it is natural to think of consumption bundles as the outcomes for the consumer and the consumer's opportunity as her budget set, that is, the set of all consumption bundles x such that the value of x at the equilibrium prices does not exceed the consumer's income. The intuition is that, though the consumer actually chooses her consumption bundle figuring in the competitive equilibrium, she could have chosen any other consumption bundle in her budget set without affecting the competitive equilibrium prices because of the very large number of consumers. Even here, the notion of a consumer's freedom as the freedom to choose any consumption bundle in her budget set generates some amount of conceptual tension, since we know that if a large enough proportion of consumers simultaneously seek to exercise their freedom to choose any consumption bundle from their respective budget sets, then, as explained in section 19.2.4, they may end up in a situation where the freedom that they thought they had turns out to be illusory.

Faced with the problem of interdependence among the individuals discussed above, how do we formulate the notion of an opportunity set? With the help of game theoretic models, Pattanaik and Xu (2009, 2012) have made attempts to visualize opportunity sets in a world of interdependence among the individuals; interested readers may want to refer to Pattanaik and Xu (2009, 2012).

Acknowledgments

For helpful comments, we are grateful to Wulf Gaertner and Iwao Hirose.

Notes

1. For some foundational contributions to this approach, see Sen (1985, 1987) and Nussbaum (1988, 2000).
2. Ordinal measurement of something, say, *a*, involves comparisons, such as "more of *a*," "less of *a*," or "the same amount of *a*"; the questions of "more by how much" or "less by how much" are not relevant when measurement is simply ordinal.
3. Not doing or being something is also regarded as an action according to proponents of the doctrine of acts and omissions in ethics.
4. It is possible to think of outcomes in broad terms so as to include a description of the relevant actions. In this chapter, however, we are using the term "outcome" in a narrower and more common sense, so that it does not necessarily include a description of the individual's actions.
5. In section 19.5, we discuss an important case, where this may not hold.
6. See Berlin (1958). See also Feinberg's (1973: 12) distinction between negative constraints, such as the lack of financial resources, strength, and education, and positive constraints, such as a law imposing a penalty for criticizing the government; Feinberg defines positive freedom as the absence of what he calls negative constraints and negative freedom as the absence of what he calls positive constraints.
7. Urmee Khan has pointed out to us that, by considering freedom to be an instrument for achieving whatever it is valued for, one can say that the value of freedom is always instrumental. We have, however, used the term "instrumental value" in what we believe to be a more conventional sense.
8. We are using the terms "ranking" and "ordering" interchangeably.
9. The individual's considered evaluation of the options need not necessarily coincide with her preference ordering over those options. For example, an individual may *prefer* to eat unhealthy fast food though she *values* and has reasons to value healthier food much more (see Sen 1985, 1987 and Pattanaik 2009, among others, for a discussion between an individual's preference and her valuation).
10. Through a very different type of reasoning, Steiner (1973) arrives at a conclusion which has close intuitive links to (4.4).

11. The example is due to Pattanaik and Xu (1998).
12. See also Dowding and van Hees (2009) for some perceptive comments on the role of diversity in the assessment of freedom.
13. "Functionings" are the "beings" and "doings" that humans value. Being well nourished, being educated, and interacting with family and friends are some examples of functionings.

REFERENCES

Arrow, K. J. (1995). "A Note on Freedom." In K. Basu, P. K. Pattanaik, and K. Suzumura (eds.), *Choice, Welfare and Development: A Festschrift in Honour of Amartya K. Sen*. Oxford: Oxford University Press, 7–16.

Barberà, S., and B. Grodal. (2011). "Preference for Flexibility and the Opportunities of Choice." *Journal of Mathematical Economics* 47: 272–78.

Basu, K. (1987). "Achievements, Capabilities and the Concept of Well-Being." *Social Choice and Welfare* 4: 69–76.

Basu, K., and L. López-Calva. (2011). "Functionings and Capabilities." In K. Arrow, A. K. Sen, and K. Suzumura (eds.), *Handbook of Social Choice and Welfare*. Amsterdam: Elsevier, vol. 2, 153–88.

Berlin, I. (1958). *Two Concepts of Liberty*. Oxford: Oxford University Press.

Berlin, I. (1969). *Four Essays on Liberty*. New York: Oxford University Press.

Bervoets, S. (2009). "Freedom of Choice in a Social Context: Comparing Game Forms." *Social Choice and Welfare* 29: 295–315.

Bervoets, S., and N. Gravel. (2007). "Appraising Diversity with an Ordinal Notion of Similarity: An Axiomatic Approach." *Mathematical Social Sciences* 53: 259–73.

Debreu, G. (1959). *Theory of Value*. New York: John Wiley and Sons.

Dowding, K., and M. van Hees. (2009). "Freedom of Choice." In P. Anand, P. K. Pattanaik, and C. Puppe (eds.), *The Handbook of Rational and Social Choice*. Oxford: Oxford University Press, 374–92.

Feinberg, J. L. (1973). *Social Philosophy*. Englewood Cliffs, NJ: Prentice-Hall.

Foster, J. (1992). "Effective Freedom." Photocopy.

Foster, J. (2011). "Freedom, Opportunity, and Well-Being." In K. J. Arrow, A. Sen, and K. Suzumura (eds.), *Handbook of Social Choice and Welfare*, vol. 2. Amsterdam: North-Holland, 687–728.

Friedman, M. (1962). *Capitalism and Freedom*. Chicago: University of Chicago Press.

Gustafsson, J. E. (2010). "Freedom of Choice and Expected Compromise." *Social Choice and Welfare* 35: 65–79.

Hayek, F. (1944). *The Road to Serfdom*. London: Routledge.

Hobbes, T. (1952 [1651]). *Leviathan*. Ed. N. Fuller. In *Great Books of the Western World*, vol. 23. Chicago: Encyclopaedia Britannica.

Jones, P., and R. Sugden. (1982). "Evaluating Choices." *International Review of Law and Economics* 2: 47–65.

Kant, I. (2005 [1785]). *Groundwork for the Metaphysics of Morals*. Trans. T. K. Abbott. Ed. with revisions by L. Denis. Orchard Park, NY: Broadview Press.

Koopmans, T. C. (1962). "On Flexibility of Future Preference." Cowles Foundation Discussion Papers No. 150. Cowles Foundation for Research in Economics, Yale University.

Kreps, D. (1979). "A Representation Theorem for 'Preference for Flexibility.'" *Econometrica* 47: 565–77.
MacCallum, G. C. (1967). "Negative and Positive Freedom." *Philosophical Review* 76: 312–24.
Mill, J. S. (1962 [1859]). *On Liberty*. In M. Warnock (ed.), *Utilitarianism, On Liberty, Essays on Bentham, together with Selected Writings of Jeremy Bentham and John Austin*. New York: Penguin.
Nehring, C., and C. Puppe. (2002). "A Theory of Diversity." *Econometrica* 70: 1155–98.
Nussbaum, M. (1988). "Nature, Functioning and Capability: Aristotle on Political Distribution." In J. Annas and R. H. Grimm (eds.), *Oxford Studies in Ancient Philosophy: Supplementary Volume*. Oxford: Oxford University Press, 145–84.
Nussbaum, M. (2000). *Women and Human Development*. Cambridge: Cambridge University Press.
Oppenheim, F. (1981). *Political Concepts: A Reconstruction*. Chicago: Chicago University Press.
Pattanaik, P. K. (1994). "Rights and Freedom in Welfare Economics." *European Economic Review* 38: 731–38.
Pattanaik, P. K. (2009). "Limits of Utilitarianism as the Ethical Basis of Public Action." In P. Anand, P. K. Pattanaik, and C. Puppe (eds.), *The Handbook of Rational and Social Choice*. Oxford: Oxford University Press, 323–45.
Pattanaik, P. K., and Y. Xu. (1990). "On Ranking Opportunity Sets in Terms of Freedom of Choice." *Recherches Economiques de Louvain* 56: 383–90.
Pattanaik, P. K., and Y. Xu. (1998). "On Preference and Freedom." *Theory and Decision* 44: 173–98.
Pattanaik, P. K., and Y. Xu. (2000). "On Diversity and Freedom of Choice." *Mathematical Social Sciences* 40: 123–30.
Pattanaik, P. K., and Y. Xu. (2007). "Minimal Relativism, Dominance, and Standard of Living Comparisons Based on Functionings." *Oxford Economic Papers* 59 (2): 354–74.
Pattanaik, P. K., and Y. Xu. (2008). "Ordinal Distance, Dominance, and the Measurement of Diversity." In P. K. Pattanaik, K. Tadenuma, Y. Xu, and N. Yoshihara (eds.), *Rational Choice and Social Welfare*. Berlin: Springer-Verlag, 259–69.
Pattanaik, P. K., and Y. Xu. (2009). "Conceptions of Rights and Freedom in Welfare Economics: A Re-examination." In P. Dumouchel and R. Gotoh (eds.), *Against Injustice: Ethics, Economics and the Law*. Cambridge: Cambridge University Press, 187–218.
Pattanaik, P. K., and Y. Xu. (2012). "Some Foundational Issues in the Functioning and Capability Approach to the Concept of Well-Being." In UNESCO-EOLSS Joint Committee (ed.), *Social and Cultural Development of Human Resources*, in *Encyclopedia of Life Support Systems(EOLSS)*. Developed under the Auspices of UNESCO. Oxford: EOLSS Publishers.
Puppe, C. (1996). "An Axiomatic Approach to 'Preference for Freedom of Choice.'" *Journal of Economic Theory* 68: 174–99.
Sen, A. K. (1985). *Commodities and Capabilities*. Amsterdam: North-Holland.
Sen, A. K. (1987). "The Standard of Living." In G. Hawthorn (ed.), *The Standard of Living*. Cambridge: Cambridge University Press, 1–38.
Sen, A. K. (1990). "Welfare, Freedom, and Social Choice: A Reply." *Récherches Economiques de Louvain* 56: 451–85.
Sen, A. K. (1991). "Welfare, Preference and Freedom." *Journal of Econometrics* 50: 15–29.
Steiner, H. (1983). "How Free: Computing Personal Liberty." In A. P. Griffiths (ed.), *Of Liberty*. Cambridge: Cambridge University Press, 73–89.
Sugden, R. (1985). "Liberty, Preference, and Choice." *Economics and Philosophy* 1: 213–29.

Tadenuma, K., and Y. Xu. (2010). "The Walrasian Distribution of Opportunity Sets: An Axiomatic Characterization." Global COE Hi-Stat Discussion Paper Series No. gd 10-158. Institute of Economic Research, Hitotsubashi University, Japan.

Van Hees, M. (2004). "Freedom of Choice and Diversity of Options: Some Difficulties." *Social Choice and Welfare* 22: 253–66.

Weikard, H.-P. (2002). "Diversity Function and the Value of Biodiversity." *Land Economics* 78: 20–27.

Weitzman, M. (1992). "On Diversity." *Quarterly Journal of Economics* 107: 363–405.

CHAPTER 20

VALUE IN NATURE

DAVID SCHMIDTZ

At a conference in 1973, Richard Sylvan (then known as Richard Routley) proposed a science fiction thought experiment that helped to launch environmental ethics as a branch of academic philosophy. It came to be known as the "Last Man" argument.

Imagine that you are the last human being. You shall soon die. When you are gone, the only life remaining will be plants, microbes, invertebrates. For some reason, this thought runs through your head: Before I die, it sure would be fun to blow up the last remaining redwood.

Sylvan's audience was left to ponder. What, if anything, would be *wrong* with destroying that redwood? Destroying it won't hurt any person, or even any sentient creature. It won't *hurt* anything. So, what's the problem?

Environmental philosophers have been trying to answer that question ever since.

20.1. What to Expect from Moral Theory

Perhaps the most fundamental question in environmental ethics is: What should be our attitude toward nature? No environmental ethicist says we should regard nature as merely a repository of natural resources, but we are divided over what *kind* of respect nature commands, or what kind of value we should regard nature as having.

First, a word of caution: this is a field where making things look easy is hard work. The ground may appear solid, but beneath a (relatively!) simple surface lies a knot of philosophical issues that smart people spend careers trying to untangle with only partial success. Not everyone will describe the terrain as I do, but here is a fact of life: if you assign two cartography students to draw maps of any terrain, the maps they draw will not be identical. (If the maps are identical, you will know that someone cheated.) Moreover, there is no all-purpose correct way to draw a map, so differences between maps do not entail that someone made a mistake.[1] There is no reason why all maps should be identical. They would not give better guidance by virtue of being identical. Indeed, maps may be more illuminating by virtue of being different. For example, if you are confused after checking one map, uncertain about signs you find ambiguous at best, a different map sometimes clears up rather than adds to your confusion.

Even among people who have the same underlying view of, say, the essence of what makes a human life valuable (as evidenced by, for example, their all recognizing the same intuitive counterexamples to any theory other than their own) there will be disagreement about which of their theories best describes that essence. It says something about the point of theorizing. Theorizing does not aim at consensus so much as at understanding. Neither does theorizing result in consensus, but consensus is overrated.[2] Nor can even the best of maps render it unnecessary for drivers to exercise good judgment, and the same is true of even the best moral theory. Good judgment is a core virtue. There is no such thing as a map, a theory, or a consensus that makes judgment unnecessary.

I see the terrain in a particular way, for more or less weighty reasons, but there is enough objectivity in cartography and in moral theorizing that I sometimes learn from experience and change my mind. Moreover, human nature being what it is, my perspective may not work for you. Setting my map alongside yours may help you triangulate on a deeper understanding, but it may not. Differences between us are real, and it will not do to ignore them.

Indeed, to ignore our differences is to ignore a feature of the moral terrain itself. It is an objective fact that we see things differently, and this is a fact that *matters*. It bears heavily on how we need to treat each other if we are to live in peace as the separate persons that we are.[3]

Further, I have no good reason to think that in a more rational world, everyone would see things as I do. At one end of a continuum of thought is a dogmatic delusion that there is only one good map. At the other end is an indefensible relativism that shirks responsibility for evaluating the pros and cons of alternative perspectives. Each extreme in its own way manifests cowardice. In the middle is where we find the courage to seek truth, knowing that any raw data we collect will underdetermine the best way of extracting lessons from which we build our theory of value. However powerful or elegant our theory may be, it need not be the best way of seeing things. Even if it is best, it need not remain so. Occasionally having reason to change one's mind goes with the territory, so long as we are still learning.

20.2. Valuing Nature

20.2.1. Instrumental versus Intrinsic

We have more than one way of valuing redwoods. Many objects are useful as means to further ends. We value such objects as tools or instruments. In environmental ethics, we refer to this sort of usefulness as an object's *instrumental* value. Instrumental value is value we attribute to something by virtue of how it can function, which seems straightforward. But is that all there is?

Consider the difference between an excellent paintbrush and an excellent painting. A brush is literally an instrument. Such value as it has to a user is instrumental. Is the painting, too, nothing more than an instrument? Not necessarily. The painting has, or can have, a different kind of value, not just a different amount. We can mark the difference by saying an object has *noninstrumental* value to me when it has a value to me apart from any usefulness it has as a means to my further ends.[4]

Lumber, like a paintbrush, is something I may regard as a mere instrument. That last redwood could have value to me as an instrument, insofar as it could be made into lumber. But apart from any interest I may have in that last redwood as lumber, I may also value it simply because it is the majestic living thing that it is. If I value the last redwood in that way, then I am seeing it as good independently of what it is good *for*. I see it as more like the painting than like the paintbrush.

One of our tasks in environmental ethics is to be more precise about noninstrumental value, but greater precision is elusive. Much of environmental value theory is animated by a contrast between instrumental and intrinsic value, that is, a contrast between what we value as a means to further ends and what we value for its own sake.[5] But when used in that way, intrinsic value is a more specific notion and a proper subset of noninstrumental value, which leaves us with a contrast between instrumental and intrinsic value that is not jointly exhaustive.[6] Even so, the contrast is real and environmental philosophers who use it are not making a mistake. We value a tree instrumentally when we cherish what we can use or exchange the tree for; by contrast, we value a tree intrinsically when the tree itself is what we cherish.

Another possible misunderstanding: we are tempted to read "intrinsic" as a synonym for "really important" and to read "instrumental" as "merely" instrumental, as if instrumental values are necessarily small. Not so. A souvenir postcard from the Grand Canyon can have a small intrinsic value, while a kidney transplant has a huge instrumental value. The systematic difference between intrinsic and instrumental is a matter of quality rather than quantity. What distinguishes the two is the *type* of respect they command, not the amount.

A related point: it is not quite right to say, as Steven Kelman says, that "selling a thing for money demonstrates that it was valued only instrumentally" (Kelman 1981: 39). Suppose I sell a painting. The price I receive is the painting's instrumental value to me, but that does not entail that its instrumental value is its only value. Suppose I adore the painting, but I need to raise a large sum of money to save my life, so I sell. This implies not that the painting has no intrinsic value but rather that the instrumental value of selling it outweighs the intrinsic value of keeping it.

20.2.2. Relative versus Instrumental

To avoid another kind of misunderstanding, we also need to avoid assuming that all value must be instrumental by virtue of being relative. For example, the paintbrush matters *to me*; the painting matters *to me*. Therefore, this argument hastily concludes, both matter instrumentally.

On the contrary, the purpose of philosophical distinctions is to sort things out. When everything (paintbrushes and paintings alike) falls on one side of a distinction and nothing on the other, then we have failed to draw a distinction. The same problem arises when we say every motive is selfish, all value is instrumental, or all value is relative. Compared to what?

The kernel of truth in relativism is this: the fact that an object is valued does, after all, presuppose that some subject is doing the valuing. *Valuing* is a relation between valued object and valuing subject. Even so, instrumental value is one relation; intrinsic value is another. An object has instrumental value *to me* when I have a use for it. It has intrinsic value *to me* when I value it simply for being what it is. Both are values to me, and in that limited sense both values are relative. But that does not mean I value both instrumentally. A genuine distinction between instrumental and intrinsic marks a difference in the kind of value I see in them.

20.2.3. Valuing for a Reason

To treat valuing as a relation between valuing subject and valued object is *not* to say value is subjective. For example, when I say vitamin C has instrumental value to me, my judgment can be correct or incorrect. It can be objectively true that vitamin C serves the purpose I think it serves, thus objectively true that vitamin C has that value to me. To some degree, I choose whether to care about my health, but given that I do care, my valuing vitamin C is grounded in reality in a way it would not be if my beliefs about vitamin C were inaccurate.

The objectivity of intrinsic values is less obvious. On one hand, it is objectively (and in this case verifiably) true that redwoods have the properties that inspire me to regard them as intrinsically valuable. I could be wrong; fallibility goes with the territory when we judge objective value. But unless I am mistaken, redwoods really are alive. They really are as old and as huge as I think, and so on. Yet, people reasonably can remain unconvinced that a redwood's aesthetic (intrinsic) value is as objective as vitamin C's nutritional (instrumental) value.

I said valuing is a relation between valued object and valuing subject. Sometimes, when we value an object, we seem to *create* the relationship. (When I decide to start collecting stamps, stamps suddenly acquire a value to me that they lacked before my decision.) Other times, we seem to be discovering a relationship rather than creating one. The existing relationship consists of the fact that, given our nature and the object's nature, we have reason to value the object even if we do not know it. Thus, ascorbic acid had value to us even before we discovered that it is an essential vitamin (i.e., vitamin C). Given what ascorbic acid is, and given what we are—beings who want to be healthy and who need ascorbic acid to remain healthy—it is an objective fact that we have reason to value ascorbic acid. (So, there is a second way in which fallibility goes with objective value. If I have my facts wrong, then something could have value to me without my knowing it. That would not be true of subjective value.)

What about the last redwood? Is it like ascorbic acid? Is it an objective fact that we have reason to value redwoods? If I fail to value redwoods, am I missing something? If I do have reason to value redwoods, is my reason something I discover, or something I create?

20.3. VALUE WITHOUT VALUERS

Suppose, when the last person is gone, nothing will be left that needs ascorbic acid. Will it remain an objective fact that ascorbic acid has value? No. Ascorbic acid has value here and now, but in a world without persons (or any other animals) that need it, there is nothing to whom it could have value.

Again, what about that last redwood? Would it command respect? In a world devoid of sentient beings, whose respect would it command? Are redwoods the sort of thing that have value to us here and now, but would not have value in a mindless world? Some theorists would say yes, and would add that we should not find this troubling. What matters is whether the last redwood commands the last person's respect, which is independent of whether the tree will have intrinsic value after the last person is gone. Others will say something is missing from this picture: namely, redwoods have value, period. Somehow, it feels right to insist that the world would be a better place with that last redwood in it, regardless of whether anyone is left to appreciate it.[7] But why insist? What difference does it make?

There is no easy way to settle this debate. The problem, in part, is that we use the word "value" in more than one way. Sometimes, we use the word as a verb. We say, "I value redwoods." In that sense, value clearly presupposes a valuer; objects are valued only if valued by a valuing subject. Other times, we use the word as a noun, and then the relation between value and valuer is less clear. When I say, "Redwoods have value," that may be another way of saying, "I value redwoods." Or, I may be saying something different: namely, "I have reason to value redwoods. If I failed to value them, I would be missing something." When I say redwoods are intrinsically valuable, I seem to be saying the latter. When I say the mindless planet would be better with that last redwood in it, I am saying I have reason (as do you) to value the last redwood. I cannot be saying the last redwood would be valued by beings on *that* planet, because in the thought experiment, mindful valuers no longer exist on that planet. For the same reason, I cannot mean anything on that planet has reason to value the last redwood: the thought experiment stipulates that subjects capable of having reasons no longer exist. Presumably, what I am trying to say, whether I realize it or not, is that valuing subjects—you and me, here and now—have reason to value redwoods (even when they have no instrumental value), and therefore, in the world we are imagining, we *would* have reason to value the last redwood.

Where does that leave us? We are in deep and treacherous philosophical waters here, but the upshot appears to be twofold. First, when I say the last redwood has intrinsic value, I am not saying anyone actually is there to respect it. But I am saying that if we *were* there, it *would* be true that we have reason to respect it. When the last person is gone, there will be no perspective in that world from which the last redwood would have value, yet it remains true that, from my perspective here and now, the last redwood would have value. So if you ask me whether the last redwood would have value, you are asking for my view here and now on the hypothetical redwood's value. That is what I give you here and now when I answer, yes, it would have value.

Suppose the last person is a painter who reasons as follows: My paintbrushes are useful. After I am gone, there will be no one to use them. Therefore, they will no longer be useful, and therefore will no longer have instrumental value. My paintings, though, are different. They are beautiful. After I am gone, they will still be beautiful. (They are beautiful to me. After I am gone, they will be the kind of thing I *would* find beautiful if I were still around.) So, won't they still have value after I am gone? To answer yes is to see the paintings as having intrinsic value.[8]

If this still seems too abstract, then consider an everyday analog of the same problem. I tell my insurance agent I want my family to be financially secure when I die. Imagine my agent saying, "You're confused. When you're dead, you're dead. You will no longer be a sentient valuing creature. You won't care. So why not spend the money on something you care about?"

If my agent said that, I should reply, "You're the one who is confused. I am not saying that after I die, it will matter to me *then* what happens to my family. What is relevant is that I care right now. I am imagining a world in which I no longer exist, so when I say I value my family's financial security in that world, I'm not saying I value it from a perspective existing in *that* world. I value it right now. Here and now, I see my family's security as having a value that will survive my death. In other words, my attitude toward my family is: *their value does not depend on my attitude.* From my perspective, they are *worthy* of my love, and the worth I see in them is something that my death won't change."

Needless to say, some people feel like this about their family. Some feel like this about redwoods. In neither case is the feeling obviously mistaken. In a way, then, valuing does presuppose a valuer. The second upshot, then, is that intrinsic valuing presupposes a special kind of valuer, capable of respecting a valued object in a robust way. One need not see the value as eternal but neither does one see it as random. Again, my history with that souvenir postcard from the Grand Canyon makes my reasons for cherishing it reasons of a persistent kind. If I spill coffee on it, I do not simply forget about it as if it were nothing more than a blank sheet of paper sitting by my printer. Instead, I mourn for a bit, as if a tiny piece of me just died. Such cherishing may not outlive me. But I will tend to cherish the postcard for as long as I am around to cherish anything. And there are other entities—my loved ones, say—whose value to me is more robust than that. I see them as beings to be cherished so long as *they* exist, not only so long as *I* exist.

20.4. MORAL STANDING

A fundamental question is, as we said earlier: what should be our attitude toward nature? In particular, many theorists ponder whether nonhumans can have the sort of moral standing that humans have. As we understand the term, a being has *moral standing* just in case it is something to which we can have duties. By contrast, there are objects that we ought to treat with respect, but not because we owe it to the objects themselves. Arguably, for example, we can have duties regarding a painting, but not to a painting. We ought to treat paintings with respect because they are beautiful (or because their owners have rights), not because we think paintings have rights in the way that human beings do.

What about plants, then? Does a redwood command respect in the way excellent paintings command respect, or in the way persons command respect? Is it enough for us to have duties regarding redwoods, or must we see ourselves as having duties *to* redwoods as well? If we destroy that last redwood for fun, would that be like destroying a person for fun, or like destroying a beautiful painting for fun?

Perhaps we should seek an intermediate position. Could moral standing come in degrees? There are serious thinkers who view moral standing as a switch with only two settings: on or off. You either respect an entity or not. Other thinkers, equally serious, see moral standing as coming in degrees. Trees have some standing; people have more. Fish have some standing; dolphins have more. Mice have some; chimpanzees have more. Accordingly, if it seems preposterous that a mouse could have the same moral standing as a chimpanzee, it might be possible to argue that a mouse has a lesser, yet still real, moral standing.

20.4.1. What Kinds of Things Have Moral Standing?

Anything we can use is a potential bearer of instrumental value. Anything we can value simply because of what it is, independently of what it can be used for, is a potential bearer of intrinsic value. Paintings can have intrinsic value. Plants can have intrinsic value. Persons can have intrinsic value. However, being a bearer of value is a long way from having moral standing.

Almost everyone agrees that persons have moral standing, although theorists explain that obligation in different ways. Quickly put, some would say what separates plants from paintings is that plants have *lives*. What separates animals from plants is that animals have *perspectives*. What separates humans from other animals is that humans have *principles*. Humans have a unique or virtually unique capacity for self-conscious moral agency. (Do all humans have this capacity, though? Do all nonhumans lack it? A more holistic view—see section 20.5.1 below—may imply that organisms command respect not solely by virtue of properties they possess as individuals but also by virtue of properties characteristic of their species.)[9]

What is the connection between having the capacity for self-conscious moral agency and having moral standing? That capacity is the paradigm of what most theorists consider sufficient for moral standing, but is it necessary?

20.4.2. Anthropocentrism

Suppose we say it is. Would that imply that only humans have moral standing? (Again, be forewarned: these are issues on which consensus may never be achieved.) *Anthropocentrism* is a view that the answer is yes. *Nonanthropocentrism*, by contrast, is a view that some nonhuman life has moral standing, either because some nonhumans have a capacity for self-conscious moral agency, or because such capacity is not the only basis for moral standing. (*Weak* anthropocentrists say that while only humans have a full-blown right to be treated with respect, certain nonhumans should be treated with respect not because they have rights but because they have intrinsic value.)

Nonanthropocentrists say at least some nonhuman life has a full-blown right to be treated with respect, but they do not agree on which nonhuman life has such standing, or why. Animal liberationists like Peter Singer and Tom Regan depart from anthropocentrism in one direction. Rejecting the view that self-aware moral agency is the only proper basis for claiming moral rights, animal liberationists say sentience—the ability to feel pain and pleasure—would be a more properly inclusive basis. They say the realm of moral standing extends to all sentient animals. Further, everything within that realm has equal standing.

Other thinkers would extend the realm of moral standing farther, to include literally all living things. Animal liberationists accuse anthropocentrists of being "speciesists." Animal liberationists are in turn accused of their own brand of speciesism—sentientism—by *biocentrists* who see sentience as an arbitrary cutoff and endorse an even more radically inclusive view that simply being alive is the proper basis for moral standing.

Among biocentrists, Paul Taylor says not only that the realm of moral standing extends to all living things, but that everything in that realm has equal standing (Taylor 1981). Gary Varner agrees that all living things have standing—commanding *some* respect—but denies that they command *equal* respect (Varner 2011). Thus, Taylor and Varner are both biocentrists, but only Taylor is a *species egalitarian*.

20.5. Species Egalitarianism

Paul Taylor says all living things are equal because they all have lives of their own, but allows that we can systematically privilege animals over plants because animals are sentient: sentience gives animals, in effect, a superior kind of life. Where does this leave us?

What Taylor sensibly concedes here is that when it is time actually to live our lives, we give up on saying living things are *equal*, and acknowledge that the point is to treat living things with *respect*.

Taylor, moreover, sees a connection between self-respect and respect for the world in which one lives.[10] Our coming to see members of other species as commanding respect is a way of transcending our animal natures. It is ennobling. It is part of our natures unthinkingly to see ourselves as superior, to feel threatened by that to which we are not obviously superior, and to try to dominate accordingly; as noted, our capacity to see ourselves as equal is part of what makes humans unique. It may be part of what makes us superior. When the Cincinnati Zoo erected a monument to the passenger pigeon, Aldo Leopold reflected that, "We have erected a monument to commemorate the funeral of a species. . . . For one species to mourn the death of another is a new thing under the sun. . . . In this fact . . . lies objective evidence of our superiority over the beasts" (Leopold 1966 [1949]: 116–17).

Trying to see all life as equal may not be the best way of transcending our animal natures, but it is one way. Another way of transcending our animal natures and expressing due respect for nature is simply to not bother with keeping score. This way is more respectful of our reflective natures. It does not dwell on rankings. Neither does it insist on seeing equality where a more reflective being would see what is there to be seen and would not shy away from respecting what is unique as well as what is common. Someone might say we need to rank animals as our equals to be fair, but that appears to be false: I can be fair to my friends without ranking them. Until fate forces us to rank them (see the discussion below of *Sophie's Choice*), it is better to let them remain the unique and priceless friends that they are. Sometimes, respect is simply respect. It need not be based on a pecking order. (Leopold's reflection on the passenger pigeon implies not that every species is equal so much as that every species is worthy of acknowledgment.)

Children rank their friends. It is one of the things children do before they are old enough to understand friendship. Sometimes, the idea of ranking things, even as equals, is a child's game. It is beneath us.

Equality is not the real issue. It never was. There is a real issue, and there always was, but the real issue is this: Wouldn't the world be a better place if we stopped seeing ourselves as superior, and acknowledged that we live in a world of value extending far beyond humanity? The plea implicit in this rhetorical question is the intuition underlying biocentrism—nothing more, nothing less. This intuition is best grounded not in some tortured argument that everything is equal, but in the simple and plausible thought that the goods of trees and chimpanzees (and humans) are not comparable. They have goods of their own, and their goods are incomparably valuable. Period.

Therefore, a broad respect for living, beautiful, or well-functioning things need not translate into *equal* respect. Neither must it translate into *universal* respect. Part of our responsibility as moral agents is to be somewhat choosy about what we respect. I can see why people shy away from openly accepting that responsibility, but they still have it.

20.5.1. Individualism and Holism

We distinguished anthropocentrism from nonanthropocentrism. We also can distinguish individualism from holism. *Individualism* is a view that only individual living things can have moral standing. Gary Varner calls himself a biocentric individualist. Opposed to individualism is *holism*, a view that it is not only individual living things that can have moral standing. Can species have moral standing? Why not fragile ecosystems? Biocentric holists such as Aldo Leopold and Holmes Rolston III say the most serious environmental issues concern not the suffering of individual animals but the preservation of species and whole ecosystems: in a word, the environment (Leopold 1966 [1949]; Rolston 1991). Clearly, holism and individualism are real options. Each should be taken seriously by those who seek to understand the world and their place in it. Likewise, anthropocentrism and nonanthropocentrism are real options. You may be more attracted to one perspective than the other, but each captures key insights in its own way.

When we commit to one view or the other, we risk losing sight of what is valuable in opposing views. We are tempted to distort, reducing opposing views to cartoon caricatures. For example, we could have defined anthropocentrism as the view that only humans have intrinsic value and that anything nonhuman must have merely instrumental value at best. But that would be a caricature, not a serious theory. No one should deny that many objects, including redwoods, are intrinsically valued, and that our world is richer for it. The genuine division between anthropocentrists, animal liberationists, and biocentrists—the question that leaves us with serious thinkers on each side—is the question of whether (or which) nonhumans command respect in the same way (if not to the same degree) that self-aware moral agents do. If certain nonhumans command respect, is it because certain nonhumans (dolphins, chimpanzees) *are* self-aware moral agents, or because self-aware moral agency is not necessary for moral standing?

We are human, of course. Therefore, our values are human values. But that does not make us anthropocentric, for anthropocentrism does not say merely that we are human. Anthropocentrism properly understood is a theory about which *objects* have moral standing. In particular, it says nonhumans do not belong in that category. Should we be anthropocentric? Perhaps, but the bare fact that we are human does not make us anthropocentric. It does not commit us to thinking that only human beings have moral standing. We have a choice.

When we are alone in a forest and wondering whether it would be fine to blow up a tree for fun, our perspective on what happens to the tree is, so far as we know, the only perspective there is. The tree does not have its own. Therefore, explaining why we should care about trees requires us to explain caring from our point of view, since that (we are supposing) is all there is. We do not have to satisfy trees that we are treating them properly; rather, we have to satisfy ourselves. Again, can we have reasons for caring about trees separate from their instrumental value as lumber and such?

One reason to care (not the only one) is that gratuitous destruction is a failure of self-respect. It is a repudiation of the kind of self-awareness and self-respect that we can achieve by repudiating wanton vandalism. So far as I know, no one is puzzled by the idea that we have reason to treat our lawns or living rooms with respect. Lawns and living rooms have instrumental value, but there is more to it than that. Most of us can sense that taking reasonable care of our lawns and living rooms is somehow a matter of self-respect, not merely a matter of preserving their instrumental value. Do we have similar reasons to treat forests with respect? I think we do. There is an aesthetic involved, the repudiation of which would be a failure of self-respect.[11]

Obviously, not everyone feels the same way about forests. Not everyone feels the same way about lawns and living rooms, either. However, our objective here is to make sense of respect for nature, not to argue that respect for nature is in fact universal or that failing to respect nature is irrational. If and when we identify with a redwood—if we find it inspiring, if we respect its size and age and so on—then as a psychological fact, we face questions about how we ought to treat it. When we come to see a redwood in that light, subsequently turning our backs on it becomes a kind of self-effacement, because the values we thereby fail to take seriously are *our* values, not the tree's.

So, the attitude we take toward gazelles, for example, raises issues of self-respect insofar as we see ourselves as relevantly like gazelles. Here is a complementary perspective. Consider that lions owe nothing to gazelles. Therefore, if we owe it to gazelles not to hunt them, it might be because we are *unlike* lions, not—or not only—because we are *like* gazelles.

Unlike lions, we have a choice about whether to hunt gazelles, and we are capable of reflecting on that choice. We are capable of caring about the gazelle's pain, the gazelle's beauty, the gazelle's hopes and dreams, such as they are. So, if we do care, then in a more or less literal way, something is missing—we are less than fully, magnificently human—if we cannot adjust our behavior in light of what we care about. Or, if we do *not* care, that too is a case where something is missing. For a human being, to lack a broad respect for living things and beautiful things and well-functioning things is to be stunted. One has failed to become as capable as a normal human being might reasonably aspire to become.

20.6. INCOMMENSURATE VALUES

Sometimes we have to decide what to do. When important values are at stake, one of the most obvious things we can do is to try to be systematic, and try to calculate the costs and benefits of acting in one way rather than another. We sometimes describe attempts to develop formal or institutional procedures for managing such calculation as *cost-benefit analysis* (henceforth CBA). Many critics of CBA seem driven by a gut feeling that CBA is heartless. They think that, in denouncing CBA, they are taking a stand against heartlessness. This is unfortunate. The fact is, weighing a proposal's costs and benefits does not make you a bad person. What makes you a bad person is *ignoring* costs—especially costs you impose on others.[12]

We sometimes put dollar values on things even when their value to us is essentially different from the value of dollars. Incommensurability of different values is not generally an insurmountable obstacle to CBA. Still, there often is no point in trying to convert a qualitative balancing into something that *looks* like a precise quantitative calculation and thus *looks* scientific but in fact remains the same qualitative balancing, only now its qualitative nature is disguised by the attaching of made-up numbers.

Policy decisions can be like that. We can try to institutionalize the idea of CBA, but formalized and bureaucratized procedures will have their own costs and benefits, and therefore there is a real question about how often such procedures pass self-inspection. We can make up numbers when assessing the value of a public library we could build on land that otherwise will remain a public park. Maybe the numbers will mean something, maybe not. More often, even when we can accurately predict a policy's true costs and benefits, there need not be any bottom line from which we simply read off what to do. When competing values cannot be reduced to a common measure without distortion, that makes it harder to know the bottom line. It may raise doubts about whether there is any bottom line to be known. Or sometimes the only bottom line is the simple fact that one precious and irreplaceable thing is gained while another precious and irreplaceable thing is lost. None of that suggests any problem with the bare idea of taking costs and benefits into account. It means only that we should not assume too much about what kind of bottom line we can expect to see.[13]

Consider an analogy. A computer program can play chess by algorithm. Human chess players cannot. Human chess players need creativity, experience, alertness to unintended consequences, and other skills and virtues that are not algorithmic. People who formulate policy need similar skills and virtues, and interpersonal skills too. Employing CBA cannot change that.

Here is another respect in which CBA must inevitably be an art as well as a science. Activities have a potential not only to satisfy preferences, but to transform preferences, for better or worse. Sometimes preferences are negatively transformed—corroded—as when we develop addictions. Andrew Brennan introduced the term "transformative value" to describe positive preference transformations. A girl grudgingly attends a concert. The performance grips her. She falls in love with classical music. Her preferences are transformed and she now inhabits a richer world, to her lasting benefit (Brennan 1992).

For many people, experiences in nature have this capacity to positively transform preferences. Sometimes, arguably, we overconsume natural resources. Other times, it is more illuminating to describe our mistake as underconsuming nature's transformative value. There arguably is nothing wrong with harvesting a few redwoods for lumber, but there is something wrong with failing to notice how wonderful redwoods are, just as they are. To make the right decision in cases like this, we must *reflect* on costs and benefits, not merely pick a number that creates a spurious appearance of an objective bottom line.

Critics of CBA think they capture the moral high ground when they say some things are beyond price. They miss the point. Even if Atlantic green turtles are a priceless world heritage, we still have to decide how to save them. We still need to look at costs and benefits of trying to protect them in one way rather than another, for two reasons. First, we need to know whether a certain approach will be effective, given available resources. Dollar for dollar, an effective way of protecting them is better than an ineffective way. Second, we need to know whether the cost of saving them involves sacrificing something else we consider equally priceless.

If baby Jessica has fallen into an abandoned well in Midland, Texas, and it will cost nine million dollars to rescue her, is it worth the cost? It seems somehow wrong even to ask the question; after all, it is only money. But it is not wrong. If it would cost nine million dollars to save Jessica's life, what would the nine million dollars otherwise purchase? Would it have been sent to Africa where it might have saved nine thousand lives? Consider an even more expensive case. If a public utility company in Pennsylvania (in the wake of a frivolous lawsuit blaming its high-voltage power lines for a child's leukemia) calculates that burying its power lines underground will cost two billion dollars, in the process maybe preventing one or two deaths from leukemia, is it only money? If the two billion dollars could have been sent to Africa where it might have saved two million lives, is it obvious we should *not* stop to think about it?

Critics like to say not all values are economic values. They are right, but no values are purely economic values. Even money itself is never only money. In a small town in Texas in 1987, millions of dollars were poured into saving a baby's life—money that took lifetimes to produce. It was not only money. It did after all save a baby's life. It also gave a community a chance to show what it stands for. These are not trivial things. Neither are the other hopes and dreams for the sake of which people earned and saved all that money in the first place.

Some things are so valuable to us that we see them as beyond price. What does this imply? When we must make trade-offs, should we ignore items we consider priceless or take them into account?[14] The hard fact is that priceless values can come into conflict. When they do, and when we rationally weigh our options, we put a price, in effect, on something priceless. In such cases, CBA is not the problem. It is a response to the problem. The world hands us painful choices. Weighing our options is how we cope.[15]

Note that although critics often speak of incommensurable values, incommensurability is not quite the issue, strictly speaking. Consider the central dilemma of the novel *Sophie's Choice* (Styron 1979). Sophie's two children are about to be executed by a concentration camp commander. He will kill both children unless Sophie picks one of the two to be killed, in which case the commander will spare the other. To Sophie, each child is beyond price. She does not value one more than the other. In some sense, she values each more than anything. Nevertheless, she does in the end pick one for execution, thereby saving the other one's life. The point is, although her values were incommensu*rate*, she was still able to rank them in a situation where failing to rank would have meant losing both. The values were incommensu*rate*, but not incommensur*able*.[16] To Sophie, both children were beyond price, but when forced to put a price on them, she could.

Of course, the decision broke her heart. As the sadistic commander foresaw, the process of ranking her previously incommensurate values was devastating. At some level, commensuration is always *possible*, but there are times when something (our innocence, perhaps) is lost in the process of commensurating. Perhaps that explains why some critics want to reject CBA; they see it as a mechanism for ranking values that should not be ranked.

Elizabeth Anderson voices this concern when she says human life and environmental quality "are not properly regarded as mere commodities. By regarding them only as commodity values, cost-benefit analysis fails to consider the proper roles they occupy in public life" (Anderson 1995: 190). Anderson may be right—and yet, blaming Sophie for treating her children as commodities would be blaming the victim. Sophie's treating her children this way is, as Anderson says, a horrifying failure properly to honor the value of her children. But Sophie's choice is not *causing* the horror so much as acknowledging and coping with it.

We can hope people like Sophie will never need to rank their children and can instead go on treating each child as of infinite value. We can wish we never had to choose between worker safety and environmental quality, or between different aspects of environmental quality. But life tends to require trade-offs, some of which will be tragic.

20.7. CONCLUSION

Whether we should be holists or individualists, and why, is an ongoing matter of hot debate. Whether we should be anthropocentric, or how far beyond humanity the realm of moral standing should extend, is likewise a matter of hot debate. However these debates are resolved, the fact remains that there is much to be gained from cultivating a more biocentric appreciation of nature. Simply appreciating nature—cherishing it for what it is, treating it with respect—is how most of us begin to develop an environmental ethic. We learn that we live—and learn how to live—in a world of things worth appreciating.

The conclusion that all living things have *moral standing* is unmotivated. There is no evidence for it, and believing it would serve no purpose. By contrast, for human beings, viewing apes as having moral standing is motivated, for reasons just described. One further conjecture: Like redwoods and dolphins, apes capture our imagination. We identify with some animals, perhaps even some plants. We feel gripped by their stories. Now, in a way, this is a flimsy thing to say. If we were talking about reasons to see charismatic species as *rights-bearers* rather than about reasons simply to cherish them, it might be too flimsy. I offer this remark in a tentative way. It is not the kind of consideration that moral philosophers are taught to take seriously, yet it may be closer to our real reasons for valuing charismatic species than are abstract philosophical arguments. Our finding a species inspiring, or our identifying with beings of a given kind, implies that if we fail to care about how their stories turn out, our failure is a failure of self-respect, a failure to care about *our* values.

Viewing viruses as having moral standing is not the same thing. It is good to be vividly aware of how amazing living things are, but being able to marvel at living things is not the same as thinking that all living things have moral standing. Life as such commands respect only in the limited but important sense that for self-aware and reflective creatures who want to make sense, deliberately killing something is an act that does not make sense unless we have good reason to do it. Destroying something for no reason is, at best, the moral equivalent of vandalism.[17]

Notes

1. This is not to imply that the terrain is not real but simply that maps are not terrain. Maps *represent* terrain for a purpose, and purposes vary even when terrain is unchanging. At the risk of being misled by a metaphor, I allow that this could be true of moral terrain as well. *If* there is a fact of the matter about whether a theory is helping agents to track reality, then which theory helps most could vary with circumstance and user capability. The reality that makes it possible to guide badly also makes it possible that there is more than one way to guide well.
2. As might be expected, I do not worry about whether this is a consensus view. But see James Surowiecki (2004).
3. For more on diversity as a matter of central importance, see Gerald Gaus (2011).
4. One could think a value is instrumental insofar as my further end is to get pleasure from it. The fundamental distinction here is this: Do I get pleasure from some further end that a paintbrush, for example, helps me to achieve? Or do I get pleasure from, say, a painting itself, apart from any further end that the painting helps me to achieve? This is what we need to ask if we aim to succeed in drawing a real distinction between instrumental and noninstrumental. (Admittedly, there are people who think being unable to see this distinction is somehow clever.)
5. Schmidtz (1994) characterizes four classes of ends, explaining how even final ends can be rationally chosen by virtue of how embracing them as items to pursue serves a further end of coming to have ends that make life worth living. *Choosing* them served a purpose, but one subsequently *pursues* them as ends in themselves. One of the payoffs of this theory is that, within it, rational choice does not presuppose that chains of reasons terminate in something for which no further reason can be given.
6. As a (difficult!) aside, if it were important to have jointly exhaustive categories, one approach is to define *extrinsic* as the logical complement of intrinsic, and then treat that as a contrast between valuing X by virtue of how X relates to other things versus valuing X apart from how X relates to other things. The other approach is to treat noninstrumental as the logical complement of instrumental. Either way, the chosen categorization scheme should not affect examples of what can lie in the gap between instrumental and intrinsic. Suppose I value salt cedars because I regard them as a keystone species in the Sonoran Desert ecosystem. Do I value them *instrumentally*? Not exactly. I have no use for salt cedars so far as I know, so their value to me is noninstrumental as I just defined

that term. (Neither am I thinking of the ecosystem as the kind of entity that could have a use for salt cedars. I simply see salt cedars as an integral part of that larger whole.) Nor do I value salt cedars *intrinsically*, for when I learn that they are an invasive species, they fall hard in my estimation, revealing that I never did value them apart from how I saw them relating to other species in the Sonoran ecosystem, and neither did I value them as ends in themselves. Thus I value salt cedars noninstrumentally, but not intrinsically. Alternatively, I value salt cedars extrinsically, but not instrumentally. I have put Toni Rønnow-Rasmussen's entry on intrinsic and extrinsic value (chapter 2 in this volume) to good use in in my seminar on moral theory and practice. On the multiple contrasts that in different ways use the term 'intrinsic', see also Korsgaard 1983.

7. G. E. Moore's commonsense argument to this effect has influenced philosophers ever since.

8. Among the "Doubts about Intrinsic Value" capably described by Jonas Olson (chapter 3 in this volume) is this: Once I say that I regard redwoods as beautiful and I add that even after I am gone, they will still be something I would regard as beautiful, I have given a complete account of how I value them. If I then add, "Oh, another thing! They have intrinsic value!" it sounds as if I am giving a further reason but in fact what I have added is redundant. I am not listing two properties—beauty and intrinsic value—that lead me to cherish redwoods. I am just groping for a different way of conveying the depth of my feeling. Olson is not denying that my feeling is real, indeed well grounded. Olson's point is simply that I can say all I want about the value I find in redwoods without the language of intrinsic value.

9. See Valerie Tiberius's "Prudential Value," chapter 9 in this volume. Tiberius notes that according to eudaimonist theories, a good life for a human being involves fulfilling our natural telos: our characteristically human function. This sounds adequate as an account of a good tool or even a good plant. (Gardeners might refer to a lemon tree as happy, meaning the tree is thriving, healthy, and doing what lemon trees do under favorable conditions.) But something is missing in this as a description of a good life for humans: namely, acknowledgment of characteristically human subjectivity. A human might have everything on which happiness supervenes in a typically happy human life (health, family, career) and still be unspeakably depressed. In that case, something crucial is lacking.

My response on behalf of eudaimonists would be to acknowledge that our subjectivity is an objective fact about our characteristically human telos. That is to say, a characteristically well-functioning human being is, among other things, *whole-hearted*. Whole-heartedness is an achievement, not to be taken for granted. Yet, it is an achievement within human reach. Having a mission with which one whole-heartedly identifies, which makes it a joy to get up in the morning with work to do, is part of what goes with fully realizing one's functional potential as a human being. Some apparent counterexamples to eudaimonist conceptions of happiness dissolve when we acknowledge the centrality of whole-heartedness in a fully realized human telos.

10. Taylor 1986: 42–43. Note: I have said little about rights, but on Taylor's theory it is impossible for nonhumans to have rights. To have rights, on Taylor's theory, a being must be capable of self-conscious self-respect. Yet, although Taylor denies that nonhumans can have moral rights, he grants that there can be reason to treat trees and animals as having legal rights (1986, 246). Although not exactly called for on metaphysical grounds, it would be a way of treating them with respect. I will not argue the point here, but I doubt that this is true of trees. If higher primates and perhaps many other animals have interests in a literal sense, then lawyers can represent them in the same way that a lawyer might represent

a human baby. However, I can't see trees as having interests to be represented in the same robust way. A lawyer who claims to represent trees is metaphorically representing people's interest in trees. I thank Dan Shahar for the citation and for helpful discussion.
11. See Hill (1983). Hill observes that sometimes the most relevant question is not whether an act lacks utility or violates rights so much as, "What kind of person would do that?"
12. See Mathew Adler's "Value and Cost-Benefit Analysis," chapter 17 in this volume.
13. Andrew Brennan has a superb essay titled "Moral Pluralism and the Environment." Brennan's first sentence says, "Cost-benefit analysis makes the assumption that everything from consumer goods to endangered species may in principle be given a value by which its worth can be compared with that of anything else, even though the actual measurement of such value may be difficult in practice." Brennan and I both reject the assumption, but I also reject the idea that cost-benefit analysis must make this assumption. We all sometimes weigh particular costs against particular benefits without assuming that *all* values present themselves as comparable weights. I thank Dan Shahar for the thought that a true value pluralist acknowledges that CBA sometimes (although of course not always) has a place. The idea that *nothing* is comparable is no smarter than the idea that *everything* is.
14. Hargrove (1989, 211) notes that quantitative analysis may be inappropriate when dealing with intrinsic values. Fair enough, but quantitative analysis often is inappropriate with purely instrumental values too. Not all instrumental values are reducible to monetary values. For example, seat belts are of purely instrumental value, yet when the car hits the ditch and begins to roll over, no amount of money would be a reasonable substitute for having our seat belts fastened.
15. Readers who grant the point that trade-offs are sometimes requires should nevertheless heed Alan Holland's (2002) warning against viewing choices *in general* as trade-offs.
16. See also Ruth Chang's chapter 11 in this volume on incomparability and incommensurability.
17. My work on this essay was supported by a grant from the John Templeton Foundation. The opinions expressed here are mine and do not necessarily reflect the views of the John Templeton Foundation. I'm also grateful to the Property and Environment Research Center in Bozeman for welcoming me as Julian Simon Fellow in the summers of 2012 and 2013, and to the Earhart Foundation for support in the fall of 2013.

References

Anderson, E. (1995). *Value in Ethics and Economics*. Cambridge: Harvard University Press.
Brennan, A. (1992). "Moral Pluralism and the Environment." *Environmental Values* 1: 15–33.
Gaus, Gerald. (2011). *The Order of Public Reason*. Cambridge: Cambridge University Press.
Hargrove, E. (1989). *Foundations of Environmental Ethics*. Denton, TX: Environmental Ethics Books.
Hill, Thomas E. Jr. (1983). "Ideals of Human Excellence and Preserving Natural Environments." *Environmental Ethics* 5: 211–24.
Holland, Alan. (2002). "Are Choices Trade-Offs?" In D. Bromley, D. Paavola, and J. Paavola (eds.), *Economics, Ethics, and Environmental Policy: Contested Choices*. Oxford: Blackwell, 17–34.
Kelman, Steven. (1981). "Cost-Benefit Analysis: An Ethical Critique." *Regulation* 5: 33–40.
Korsgaard, C. (1983). "Two Distinctions in Goodness." *Philosophical Review* 92: 169–95.

Leopold, A. (1966 [1949]). *A Sand County Almanac*. New York: Oxford University Press.
Rolston, Holmes III. (1991). "Values in and Duties to the Natural World." In F. Bormann and S. Kellert (eds.), *Ecology, Economics, Ethics: The Broken Circle*. New Haven: Yale University Press, 73–96.
Schmidtz, D. (1994). "Choosing Ends." *Ethics* 104: 226–51.
Styron, W. (1979). *Sophie's Choice*. New York: Random House.
Surowiecki, J. (2004). *The Wisdom of Crowds*. New York: Random House.
Taylor, P. (1981). "The Ethics of Respect for Nature." *Environmental Ethics* 3: 197–218.
Taylor, P. (1986). *Respect for Nature*. Princeton, NJ: Princeton University Press.
Varner, G. (2011). "Biocentric Individualism." In D. Schmidtz and E. Willott (eds.), *Environmental Ethics: What Really Matters, What Really Works*, 2nd ed. New York: Oxford University Press, 90–101.

CHAPTER 21

POPULATION AXIOLOGY

M. A. ROBERTS

21.1. INTRODUCTION

POPULATION ethics represents the efforts of theorists who are happy to accept many consequentialist tenets but worry that traditional formulations—for example, classical utilitarianism—miss the mark when it comes to cases that involve distinct populations.

Such theorists may well accept that acts can be evaluated entirely by reference to an evaluation of their *effects* or *consequences*. They also accept that that latter evaluation might itself consist of nothing more than a determination of how the particular outcome, or possible future, or *world*, at which the act is performed and its consequences materialize *compares against* alternative worlds at which alternative acts are performed and alternative consequences materialize. And they accept that one world is *morally better than* another if it contains *more of* the good—*more of*, that is, that which itself is considered to have moral value. But they worry that the traditional formula for determining just when one world contains more of the good—more of that which has moral value—than another is inherently flawed. That formula defines the good at a given world as just the *aggregation*, or *summation*, or *total*, of the individual well-being levels of all the people who do or will exist at that world. Moral betterness, under the traditional formula, thus need not be a matter of making things *better for any particular person*, and we should instead, applying the traditional formula, think of it (somewhat metaphorically) as a matter of making things *better for the world*.

For purposes here, we leave open whether well-being is itself to be defined as pleasure, happiness, preference satisfaction, capability or something else entirely; for purposes here, we just say that well-being is whatever it is that can make life so precious to those who live. But as we shall see, even given that flexibility, the proposal that the *moral betterness* of a given world is the same thing as that world's containing *additional aggregate well-being* raises serious concerns when applied to cases involving different numbers of people and cases involving distinct people. The question, then, is whether any still better formula can be identified.

Two candidates seem most prominent. One is a *person-affecting*, or *person-based*, approach. That approach accepts that there is a relation between the morally better world and that world's containing more of the good. But it relocates the test for *more good* from the *world at large* to the *person*. The morally better world, then, is not always the world that contains more *aggregate* well-being or indeed more good simpliciter. It's rather the world that, for at least some member of a given collection of people, contains more good *for that person*.

The other candidate is *pluralism*. That view considers the *overall* good of a given world as constituted by more than just aggregate well-being. Thus, one world might be morally better than another in virtue of the fact that it contains more aggregate well-being. But its moral betterness might also be a matter of equality, human flourishing, and improvements in the plights of the least well-off.

21.2. Problems with the Traditional Formula

To see what we might want from any alternate formula for determining when one world is morally better than another, it is critical to understand the population problems that the traditional formula itself stumbles on. As noted, the traditional approach evaluates a given world by aggregating the individual well-being levels—net, of course, of any ill-being—of all the people who have existed, or do or will exist, at that world. On one variation on the traditional approach, we end our calculation there. We consider aggregate well-being at a given world to be identical to its moral value and one world to be morally better than another just in case its aggregate—or total—well-being is greater. The *total* view thus considers each individual well-being level at a given world to represent a quantum of *individual* moral value that itself directly contributes to the value of the *world*.[1] On the other variation on the traditional approach, we take the calculation one step further. We divide total well-being by the size of the relevant population—that is, by the number of people who do or will exist at that world—on the thought that how thinly well-being is distributed is a critical factor in determining moral value. The *average* view thus considers the moral value of a world to be determined by the average of all of the individual well-being levels—past, present and future—represented at that world.

As Sidgwick noted, whether we take the total or the average view makes a difference to how we analyze the cases (Sidgwick 1907: book 4, ch. 1). But either way the view we are left with seems implausible. Thus the total view leads to clearly problematic results in many cases in which the worlds being compared vary in population size. For example, a world that contains billions of people all of whom have lives only barely worth living might, on the total view, turn out to be morally better than a world that contains fewer (though still a great many) people all of whom have lives well worth living. Most philosophers agree with Parfit that such a "repugnant" conclusion is "hard to accept" (Parfit 1987: 388).

It may seem that the deficiency in the total view is its failure to take into account the number of people well-being is distributed across and thus that the average view holds more promise. But in still other sorts of cases the average view generates results that seem just as implausible. Here as well Parfit puts things succinctly: "research in Egyptology cannot be relevant to our decision whether to have children" (Parfit 1987: 420). Temkin's "Hell Three" also underlines a serious problem: the world that includes one person at a well-being level of (say) negative 1,000 and another person at a well-being level of negative 999 surely is not *morally better* than the world that includes just the one person (Temkin 2012: 319–20). The better world is the world in which at least one of these two anguished persons—even if the better off of the two—is never brought into existence to begin with.

Problems with the total and average views may lead us to become pluralists and take the view that the *overall* good of a world cannot be defined entirely by reference to aggregate well-being. We might also recognize human flourishing in the sense of fulfilling one's full potential as a human being—of becoming not the ordinary schoolchild taking piano lessons but the child prodigy—as a factor (Temkin says "value," or "ideal") in determining the overall good of a given world. Still a third factor might be improvements in the plights of the least well off. Recognition of the second factor seems potentially useful in dealing with the repugnant conclusion and recognition of the third with Hell Three.

It is easy, then, to see how pluralism may have the potential to avoid some versions of the repugnant conclusion and Hell Three. The world that contains *more* overall good, even if it contains *less* aggregate well-being, might still turn out to be the better world. But it is hard to see how pluralism might manage to avoid them all. We can always imagine cases in which a low degree of human flourishing at a given world is whitewashed away by vast amounts of aggregate well-being.

Pluralism thus, it seems, would need to be complicated by some further view—a view that enables us to say that even the smallest quantities of goods of one sort contribute more to the overall value of a world than even the largest quantities of goods of another sort. Parfit himself accordingly suggests the *lexical ordering* of certain values, while Temkin proposes a *capping* strategy, according to which—after reaching a certain limit—we no longer count additional aggregate well-being toward the value of a given world if that additional aggregate well-being can be achieved only at a cost to such "higher" goods as (for example) human flourishing.

The person-based approach addresses the population problems, not by *extending* the range of what has moral value beyond aggregate well-being, but rather by *restricting* it. A world isn't morally better because it contains more *aggregate* well-being—or because it contains more *overall* good. Rather, a world is morally better because it contains, for at least one person in a given collection of people, more well-being *for that person*.

We need to be more specific. On the total and average views, and even pluralism, one world can be *worse than* another even if it is *worse for* no one *who does or will exist at that world* at all. The person-based position, in contrast, insists that one world can be worse than another *only if* it makes things worse *for at least one such person* (Parfit 1987: 363). To invert Sidgwick's own language, this would be to take consequentialism to "prescribe, as the ultimate end of action," not "happiness on the whole," but rather happiness for each individual (Sidgwick 1907: book 4, ch. 1). It's to reconstruct consequentialism, not as an *impersonal* view, or indeed a *world*-based view, but rather as a *person*-based view.

To reference Narveson: what makes a world morally better isn't a matter of *making happy people* but rather of *making people happy* (Narveson 1976: 71–73).

These two proposals—pluralism and the person-based approach—can be combined into still a third approach, one we can call *radical pluralism*. Radical pluralism recognizes the moral betterness of a given world to be in part determined by how much overall good (including aggregate well-being, equality, human flourishing, and so on) that world contains. But it also considers the moral betterness of a given world to be in part determined in accordance with a person-based approach—an approach that itself gauges moral betterness on the basis of how much good is created *for people*.

21.3. Clarifications of the Person-Based Approach

The more common term is "person-affecting." But "person-based" is more concise to say and think. Moreover, the terminology invites us to draw the useful distinction between the person-based approach and the various impersonal, or world-based, approaches. One focuses on how things unfold for *particular individuals*; the others focus on how the *world itself* unfolds independently of what it does for any particular person.

As noted above, a defining feature of the person-based approach is the following necessary condition: one world is *worse than* another *only if* the one world is *worse for* at least one person who does or will exist at that world.[2] (In terms of acts: a "bad" act must be "bad for" *someone*, that is, for someone who *does or will exist* at the world at which the "bad" act is itself performed [Parfit 1987: 363].)

Person-based theories call this necessary condition the *person-affecting intuition* (we can say person-*based* intuition) and make it their core. But it's also been a primary point of contention. Many theorists otherwise taken with Narveson's make-people-happy-not-happy-people witticism thus have felt compelled to reject the person-based approach out of hand because they have felt compelled to reject the person-based intuition.

As it happens, however, formulating the person-based intuition is a surprisingly delicate task. We shouldn't reject the intuition just because the text we happen to be examining articulates that intuition badly. Four points of clarification (A)–(D) are in order.

(A) It may be tempting to think that the person-based approach will endorse a necessary condition on *betterness* that perfectly parallels its necessary condition on worseness. It may be tempting, that is, to think that the principle that one world is *better than* another *only if* the one world is *better for* at least one person who *does or will exist at that one world* is part of the person-based approach. But that temptation should be resisted. To give into it would put the person-based view out of compliance with the following principle: a world X is better than a world Y *if and only if* Y is worse than X. According to that principle, once we've figured out that one world is worse than another world, we've automatically also figured out that the other world is better than the one; talk of worseness and talk of betterness between worlds are just two ways of talking about the very same relation. That principle seems true by definition. For purposes here, what is important to note is that there is no reason at all to think that the person-based approach defies it.

An example helps make this point. Consider the anguished child p. This child is left out of existence altogether in world A but has an anguished life—a life that is *less* than worth living—in world B. I will take for granted here that on the basis of these facts we can reach certain conclusions about the individual well-being levels p has in each of A and B—namely, that p, who has no burdens and accrues no benefits at A, has a zero well-being level at A, and that p, whose life is nothing but anguish at B, has a negative well-being level at B.[3] These relative levels are represented in figure 21.1.

While we don't yet have the necessary apparatus to see just how the person-based approach analyzes this case, we can, looking ahead, simply note that that analysis will generate the—plausible—result that B is *worse than* A. (It's the fact that the anguished child p exists in B and is worse off in B than p is in A that satisfies the relevant necessary condition on worseness—that is, the person-based intuition itself.) But there's no reason at all to think that the person-based approach does not also consider A *better than* B *notwithstanding the fact that p never exists in A*. It's not that the person-based approach abandons its focus on *persons* in favor of an impersonal focus on *worlds* when we shift from talk of worseness to talk of betterness. Rather, it's that we can't *mechanically* rewrite the necessary condition on worseness into a necessary condition on betterness. Thus, the person-based approach must be understood to include not a necessary condition on betterness that simply tracks its condition on worseness but rather the following: one world is *better than* another *only if* the *other* world makes things *worse for* at least one person who does or will exist in that *other* world.

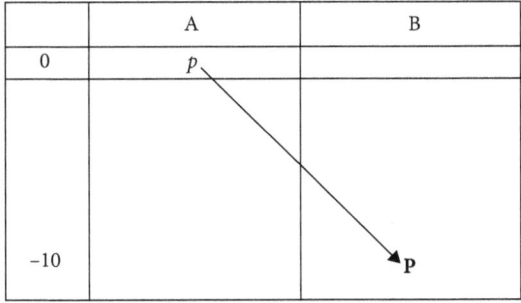

FIGURE 21.1 Anguished Child Case. Bold-faced name indicates individual does or will exist at the indicated world; italicized name indicates individual never exists at the indicated world.

(B) The person-based intuition as presented so far includes a critical ellipsis. We say that a world Y is worse than a world X *only if* Y makes things worse for a person p who does or will exist in Y. But "worse for a person p" than *what*? It's *not* that Y must be worse for p *than X is*, but *rather* that Y is worse for p *than some alternate world Z is*, where Z itself *may* be but *need not* be identical to X.

The *Compound Addition Case* makes the necessary point. Consider a person q who never exists in world C, has a life clearly worth living in world D, and has a still better life in E (figure 21.2).

It is assumed that E is a world *accessible* to agents from D—a world, that is, that agents aren't barred by metaphysics or the laws of nature from bringing about. As such, E reveals a moral defect in D. What E shows is that q's lower well-being level in D is perfectly *avoidable*—it's a *loss* (we might say) that q need never have been made to incur at all.[4] And on the basis of that loss—and here again we are anticipating the person-based result we can expect to obtain once we have the necessary apparatus in hand—D can be considered worse than C notwithstanding the fact that D is obviously *not* worse *for q* than C is. The person-based theorist, in short, is free to say that D's being worse for q *than E* is a perfectly legitimate way of satisfying the necessary condition on D's being worse *than C*.

To dispense, then, with the potentially misleading ellipsis, an adequate formulation of the person-based intuition can include the following detail:

Person-based intuition. Y is morally worse than X *only if* there does or will exist a person p in Y such that Y is worse for p than some Z is for p (where Z may but need not be identical to X).

An adequate comparison between two worlds will thus sometimes need to go beyond those two worlds.

That point constitutes a central tenet of what Temkin calls the "essentially comparative view" (Temkin 2012: 364–400). Indeed, Temkin's objection to Broome's argument against the person-based approach rests on that very point. The principle that Broome actually argues against—which he calls the "neutrality intuition" and associates, arguably mistakenly, with the person-based view—states that adding well-off people is morally "neutral"—does not, that is, make things either better or worse. Temkin notes,

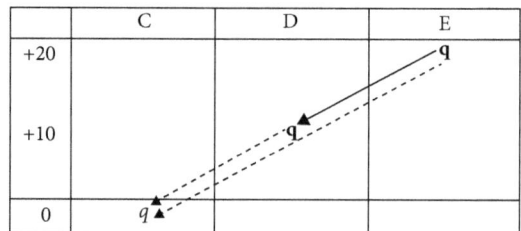

FIGURE 21.2 Compound Addition Case

however, that Broome's argument does not go through if we revise the neutrality intuition along essentially comparative lines. Consider, again, the Compound Addition Case. If, in comparing C and D, we ignore E altogether, then we ignore factors "relevant and significant" for the comparison between C and D. But Temkin thinks that would be a mistake. Taking those factors into account, we can instead say that D is worse than C (Temkin 2012: 433–34; see also Broome 2004: 146–48; 2012: 169–83).

Temkin's essentially comparative view is a refreshing change to formulations of the person-based approach that disable themselves from seeing the moral defects in a given world by blinding themselves to morally relevant facts about still other worlds. Such formulations include, of course, the neutrality intuition itself, explored and rejected by Broome, and also the "prior existence view," which Singer explores and ultimately rejects (Singer 2012: 88–89).

But Temkin's formulation is not unique. At this stage, it seems clear that *any* well-formulated statement of the person-based approach must recognize that, while adding a well-off person can't make things better, it can make things worse (Roberts 2010: 79–85; see also Roberts 2003b; 1998: 49–54 and generally ch. 2). Only where it's part of the case that only two alternative worlds are accessible to agents at the relevant time—only where what we are dealing with is itself a *two-*, rather than a *three-*, alternative case—can we be sure that adding a person whose life is worth living does not make things worse.[5]

(C) As noted, person-based theories focus on *particular* people. Also as noted, the particular people they focus on are the members of a certain collection of people. Specifically, they are the people who do or will exist at a given world and are there made worse off *if* that world is to be declared worse than some other.

This way of putting things might suggest that the person-based approach takes an *exclusive* position on the question of who matters morally, deeming some people—for example, *existing* and *future* people—to matter morally and others not to matter at all. In fact, however, the better view is that the person-based approach takes an *inclusive* position, deeming all people in all worlds—or at least in all *accessible* worlds—to have exactly the same moral status, whether they happen to be *existing* or *future* people or *merely possible* people, or *actual* or *nonactual* people, or *overlapping* (or *necessary*) people (people who exist whether the act under scrutiny is performed or not; that is, people who exist in all the worlds being compared) or *contingent* (or *dependent*) people (people whose existence depends on whether the act under scrutiny is performed).

To say that the person-based approach is inclusive is not to undo the prior point that the people who are made worse off at a given world if that world is itself to be declared worse are people *who do or will exist at that world*; we still must reference that *specific collection of individuals*; not just any person (e.g., a merely possible person whose life, had it been led, would have been worth living) will do for purpose of satisfying that necessary condition. The point is, rather, that the *specific collection* will itself vary, such that our focus will sometimes be on *actual* people and whether they are made worse off at a given world, and sometimes on *overlapping* people and whether they are made worse off, and sometimes on *merely possible* people and whether those people have been made worse off at some alternate world (one, that is, where they do or will exist).

It may seem surprising that the person-based approach would take an inclusive position on who matters morally. After all, if it takes that position, how can the person-based approach then turn around and insist that *failing* to bring a merely possible person into existence—a person whose existence would be worth having—cannot make things *worse*? For this reason, it is critical to take some time to see just why the person-based approach must be considered inclusive in nature. But we also need to show how the person-based approach can be both inclusive and yet remain true to its root idea that bringing additional happy people into existence does not make things better. Both those discussions are deferred to section 21.4 below.

(D) Person-based theories concern themselves with how well worlds unfold for people *as individuals* and *not* how well they unfold for people en masse or in the aggregate. Determinations of *personal identity*, in other words, will be critical.[6]

Thus: under either a person-based or an impersonal approach, that a world Y is worse for a given person than a world X is for that *same* person is, in some cases, enough to show that Y is worse than X. But: that Y is worse for a given person than X is for a *distinct* person may not be enough to show, under a person-based approach, that Y is worse than X. In contrast, impersonal theories will be indifferent to whether any *particular* person is worse off in one world than *that same person* is in another. Impersonal theories, in other words, bless two distinct equally effective ways of producing the better future: (A) substituting a high well-being person in for a distinct low well-being person, and (B) creating additional well-being for a particular person.[7]

21.4. INCLUSION AND THE BASIC PERSON-BASED RESULT

In part because formulating the person-based approach is, as noted earlier, a surprisingly delicate task and in part because of the *nonidentity problem*, the person-based approach has devolved into a minority position in recent years. But for just a fleeting moment a few decades ago the person-based approach, which claimed to offer a new and sensible reconstruction of traditional utilitarianism, captured the attention of a number of moral philosophers. Thus, the very core of the person-based approach—the person-based intuition itself—generates the following result:

Basic person-based result: Where two worlds X and Y have all their potentially morally relevant features in common except that a particular person never exists at all in X and has an existence worth having in Y, X is *at least as good as* Y is even though Y is *better for* that person than X is.

At the same time, the person-based intuition can be put together with a handful of consequentialist tenets that few philosophers sincerely dispute. Consistent, then, with the basic person-based result, and given a handful of such further tenets, we can also anticipate that the person-based approach will support the following:

Basic maximizing result: Where two worlds X and Y have all their potentially morally relevant features in common except that a particular person, who does or will exist in both worlds, has more well-being in Y than that same person has in X, Y is morally better than X is.

These are useful results. They mean that the person-based approach avoids the position that more aggregate well-being is always better. Instead, the person-based approach implies that sometimes the world that contains more aggregate well-being, as a matter of coincidence, is the better world, as when one person is made better off at no cost to anyone else, and sometimes it isn't, as when an additional well-off person is brought into existence and things are otherwise left unchanged. And that, in turn, is going to mean that bringing an additional well-off person into existence cannot on its own—whatever the situation in respect of aggregate well-being—wallpaper over the fact that a distinct person who exists in both worlds has been left badly off.

Consider, then, the *Simple Addition Case* (figure 21.3).[8] In that case, worlds C and D are exactly alike except that D contains the additional happy person q—a person who does not exist at all in C but exists and is well-off in D. There is no third world E accessible to agents.

The traditional aggregative formula—in both its total and average forms—implies that D is morally better than C—that the addition of q to D makes D *morally better than C*.[9] In contrast, the person-based approach discerns within that result a troubling commitment—a commitment whose difficulties to be sure may not become apparent until we turn to more complicated cases but are nonetheless significant. It hence takes steps to avoid that result from the start.

Thus, on the person-based approach, we don't make things worse—we don't get into trouble morally—by failing to produce additional well-off people. Instead, we make

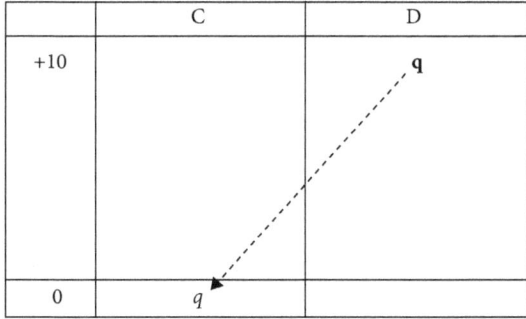

FIGURE 21.3 Simple Addition Case

things worse—get into trouble morally—by failing to produce additional well-being for existing and future people. "[W]e are in favour of making people happy, but neutral about making happy people" (Narveson 1976: 71–73).

In contrast, the traditional aggregative approach implies that we do sometimes make things worse by failing to produce an additional person, even in cases in which we have, for *every existing* and *every future* person, *maximized* well-being for that person. We *can*, that is, get into trouble, morally, by *not* getting into trouble, colloquially. But that implication is at least questionable.

It is widely thought that the basic person-based result—and indeed the person-based intuition itself—must be rooted in some deeper principle or insight. Given, moreover, the connection that the person-based approach makes between things being *worse* and things being *worse for people who do or will exist*, it may seem that that deeper principle must surely function by (somehow) using the property of *existing* to divide people up between those who matter morally and those who don't.[10]

As noted earlier, however, any *exclusive* position on who matters morally is going to be problematic. On analysis, it seems that the plight of *no one*—at least, no one who does or will exist in any *accessible* world—can be plausibly disregarded or set aside. (See Holtug 2010: 263–77; see also Roberts 2010: 41–92, and Hare 2007.)

Here, we'll examine three different ways of articulating the exclusive position and show why each one fails.

Consider, first, the view that the people who matter morally are just those who *do or will exist* at the world we are scrutinizing for its worseness relative to some alternate world. That this view fails is demonstrated by the *Two Anguished Children Case* (see figure 21.4).

Here, a person p never exists at all in world A but exists in world B and there has a life less than worth living. A person p' never exists in B but exists in A and there has a life less than worth living. Suppose that what we want to know is whether A is worse than B. Then, the view under consideration here implies that p' matters morally and p matters not at all, which result would seem in turn to lead us to conclude that the fact that p is better off in A has no moral significance—that it does not count in favor of A. We seem left then to conclude that A is worse than B. But that conclusion seems false. Moreover, suppose that we also happen to want to know whether B is worse than A. Then the

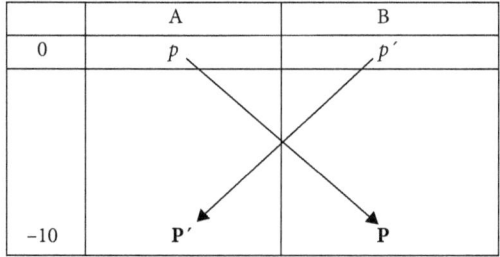

FIGURE 21.4 Two Anguished Children Case

parallel analysis implies that it is. Surely, however, moral worseness is not a symmetrical relation. It's not possible for A to be worse than B and B to be worse than A.[11]

Consider, then, the view that only *actual* people—people, that is, who exist at the uniquely *actual* world—matter morally. That view fails as well. Reconsider the *Anguished Child Case* (figure 21.1). Let's stipulate that A is the actual world. We want to say that B, where the anguished child exists and suffers, is worse than A. But we can't. For, on the present view, since p is nonactual—is, that is, merely possible relative to the *actual* world A—p doesn't matter morally.

Moreover, this view comes with a conceptual problem. Had B been the actual world, we would have grounds to say that B is worse than A. But surely (as Rabinowicz's principle of normative invariance instructs) B's being worse than A is independent of the incidental question whether A or B happens, in the end, to constitute the actual world (Carlson 1995: 100, citing Rabinowicz).

A third attempt at an exclusive position fails as well. On this third view, the people who matter morally are just the *overlapping* people, sometimes called the *necessary* people. These are the people who do or will exist in both the worlds being compared (the people who do or will exist, whatever the agents choose). Broome has shown, as noted before, that this view (which, if restricted in certain ways, itself implies the neutrality intuition) will not work. Singer makes the point as well (Singer 2011: 87–90). Consider, for example, the Anguished Child Case (figure 21.1). On this third view, since p exists in B but not in A, p does not matter morally for purposes of comparing A against B—leaving us, again, with no basis on which to conclude that B is worse than A (see Roberts 2010: 41–92; Holtug 2010: 265–67).

Now, at first glance, what emerges from this discussion is a powerful objection against the person-based approach. Simply put, the objection is just that however we try to ground the person-based approach in any deeper principle—any principle, that is, that explains and motivates both the person-based intuition itself and the basic person-based result—what we come up with is a view that we cannot accept. In fact, however, it seems that this first glance is too quick. It assumes that the person-based approach is *exclusive* in nature. But that assumption is itself without ground. As noted earlier, we should instead think of the person-based approach as *inclusive* in nature.

Now, to make that thought viable, we must show just how the person-based approach can be both inclusive in nature *and* generate the basic person-based result. If all people, including the merely possible, matter morally, how can adding happy people *not* make things better?

But before turning to that question and replying to the objection one more note is in order. As it happens, at least one way of answering that question will be invaluable in helping the person-based theorist reply to a second, related objection. The idea behind this second objection is that we can successfully deny that D is morally better than C in the Simple Addition Case only on pain of taking the clearly false position that B is just as good as A in the Anguished Child Case. If we say that adding the happy child doesn't make D *better* than C in the one case, then consistency requires that we also say that adding the anguished child doesn't make B *worse* than A in the other case. After all, we don't want to say that the anguished child p has moral status but the happy child q does not; or that anguish has a moral weight that happiness lacks; or that the comparison against nonexistence makes sense when our focus is p's anguished existence but not when it is q's happy existence; or that, while *existence* might be better or worse for a person, *nonexistence* can't be worse or better for that person (surely, if existence is better for a given person, nonexistence is worse for that same person). *Symmetry* seems the only consistent and plausible way to go.

McMahan labeled the intuitive idea that adding q doesn't make D better than C even though adding p makes B worse than A *the Asymmetry* decades ago. It's fair to say that, at this point, the argument against the Asymmetry has been widely accepted and that the Asymmetry itself has been rejected—along with any theory, including any person-based theory, that implies it—in favor of *Symmetry* (McMahan 1981; McMahan 2009; Persson 2009).

The person-based approach now faces two demands. First, it must be rooted in a principle that takes an inclusive position on who matters morally but still preserves the basic person-based result. And, second, the objection from Symmetry must be addressed.

Can both those demands be met? I've elsewhere argued that they can (Roberts 2010, 2011a, 2011b). To see how, we start with the Asymmetry itself. We compare, that is, the Anguished Child Case against the Simple Addition Case (aka the Happy Child Case).

Thus, we might note that the lower well-being level incurred by p at B—p's *loss* at B—is incurred by p at a world where p in fact exists, while the lower well-being level incurred by q at C—q's *loss* at C—is incurred by q at a world where q does not and will not exist. Having noted that fact, we can then naturally say—not that the anguished child has a moral status that the happy child lacks; or that anguish but not happiness has moral weight; or that comparisons against nonexistence can be made in some cases but not in others; or that only existence, never nonexistence, can cogently be said to be better or worse for a given person—but rather that p's lower well-being level at B has full moral significance for purposes of calculating the worseness of B (or indeed the betterness of A), while q's lower well-being level at C has no moral significance at all for purposes of calculating the worseness of C (or, again, the betterness of D). How can we say that? What's the difference? Simply that in one case the loss is incurred at a world where the subject exists, and in the other case the loss is incurred at a world where the subject never exists.

The principle at play here—which we can call *variabilism*—is as follows:

Variabilism. A person's having a lower well-being level at a given world X than that same person has at some alternate world Y—that person's *loss*, that is, at X relative to Y—has moral significance for the purpose of evaluating X against Y or X against any other accessible alternative to X *if and only if* that person does or will exist at X.

And we can now just note a key to the figures: downward-sloping solid arrows indicate what variabilism considers moral significant losses, while the losses indicated by broken arrows have no moral significance whatsoever.

Variabilism is *inclusive* in nature; *all* people matter morally and in exactly the same way. Thus, for *none* of us do *all* our losses have moral significance: just as your parents leaving you out of existence would not have made the world morally worse (but for, it goes without saying, all the good that you have done) *and yet* your parents bringing you into existence and treating you badly *would* have made things worse, so it is for the merely possible as well. Moreover, variabilism is *liberal* in terms of what it considers a *loss*: anyone who might have had an existence worth having at Y but never in fact exists at all at X incurs a loss at X relative to Y. And, finally, variabilism is highly intuitive: it's only the *instantiated* loss at a given world that can have moral significance. The loss that is, at a given world, *uninstantiated* in contrast, is devoid of any moral significance whatsoever.

Variabilism also can be used to ground the basic person-based result itself—*without* resorting to the problematic idea that some people matter morally and other people don't. Reconsider the Simple Addition Case. We concede that q matters morally, whether our question is whether D is worse than C or vice versa, and even if C is the actual world (and hence even if relative to that world q is merely possible), and even though q does not exist in both C and D. And we concede as well that q's well-being level at C is lower than at D—that q incurs a loss at C. But we reject the idea that that loss counts against C or in favor of D. According to variabilism, to say that q matters morally is just to say that some instances of q's being made worse off have moral significance while others do not. Specifically: the loss q incurs in C, where q never exists at all, has no moral significance whatsoever. As such, it cannot count against C and cannot make C worse than D. Notably, we say exactly the same things about the Compound Addition Case. But there we add that q's loss in D relative to E has full moral significance (since q exists in D); it counts against D and provides a basis on which to say that D is worse than not just E but C as well.[12]

At the same time, variabilism faces some serious challenges. First, variabilism relies on the assumption that comparisons between a person's well-being level at a world where that person does or will exist and that same person's well-being level at a world where that person never exists are cogent. It's that assumption—the assumption of *comparability*—that allows us to say (for example) that *both* children in the Two Anguished Children Case incur losses at the worlds where they exist. The assumption of comparability is, however, itself controversial (Holtug 2010: 131–34; Bykvist 2007; Roberts 2003a).

Second, it might be objected that variabilism is ad hoc. An ad hoc distinction is one that has no good reason behind it or that seems arbitrary or baseless. The question, then, is whether it is ad hoc to say that the lower well-being level displayed by a person at a world where that person *does or will exist* matters morally whereas the lower well-being level displayed by a person at a world where that person *never exists* doesn't. Or is that instead a reasoned a distinction, a distinction that we intuitively think might have moral weight? Whether we consider variabilism to provide a plausible foundation for the person-based approach may ultimately rest on how we answer that question.

21.5. THE PERSON-BASED INTUITION AND THE NONIDENTITY PROBLEM

We noted earlier the *person-based intuition*:

Person-based intuition. Y is morally worse than X *only if* there does or will exist a person p in Y such that Y is worse for p than some Z is for p (where Z may but need not be identical to X).

The person-based intuition itself implies the basic person-based result. Adding q to produce D in the Simple Addition Case won't make D better than C (make, that is, C worse than D) since C can't be worse than D unless some person does or will exist in C for whom D is worse, and q never exists at all in C. And variabilism, in turn, explains the person-based intuition. It concedes that q matters morally for purposes of determining whether C is worse than D and whether D is worse than C, regardless of whether q is actual and despite the fact that q doesn't exist in both C and D. It concedes as well that C is worse for q than D is. But it still insists that the fact that q has a lower well-being level in C is without moral significance: it can't make C worse than D (or the choice of C wrong).

The person-based intuition itself, however, faces a well-known objection—an objection independent of the conceptual issues that have heretofore been our focus—in the form of the *nonidentity problem*.

A classic version of the nonidentity problem is this. Consider the act α of pausing to take a teratogenic "pleasure pill" prior to conceiving a child (Kavka 1981). And imagine that a child Amy is brought into existence at a world A as a consequence of α's being performed at A and that, though worth having, that existence, also as a consequence of α, is flawed.

The act α can thus be seen as (loosely) procreative in nature; it is part of what causes Amy to come into existence. Now, the uninitiated might question—given that the pleasure pill isn't also a fertility drug—how that could be. At play here is the idea of the "precariousness" of existence (Kavka 1981: 93): the identity of the person who happens to be conceived on a given occasion is exquisitely sensitive to the timing and manner of the conception itself and all that has come before (Parfit 1987: 351–52, 361). "Which particular future people will exist is highly dependent upon the conditions under which we and our descendants procreate, with the slightest difference in the conditions of conception being sufficient, in a particular case, to insure the creation of a different future person" (Kavka 1981: 94). Thus conceiving a child moments earlier—*without*, that is, pausing to take the pill; call that act β—may well have caused a perfectly healthy child to have been conceived at an alternate world B. However, with hundreds of millions of sperm released per ejaculation, the odds that any such child would have been identical to *Amy* are vanishingly small. And in fact it's part of the case that Amy would never have existed at all at B, where β is performed in place of α, and that a healthy but distinct child, say, Ben, would have existed at B in her stead.

At the same time, it is no worse, and may well be better, for Amy to have the flawed existence she has at A than never to exist at all at B. The agents' choice of α thus seems not to *harm* Amy, or impose any *loss* on her, at least not in any morally relevant sense (Parfit 1987: 374); it doesn't make Amy worse off than Amy otherwise would have been. And yet we insist that A is worse than B. The implication—the argument concludes—is that the person-based intuition is false: A is *worse than* B even though A doesn't make things *worse for* anyone who does or will exist in A.

But this fairly cursory statement of the nonidentity problem is open to objection. After all, to decide whether A makes Amy worse off—whether Amy is harmed, or incurs a loss, at A—it isn't enough to look at just A and B. To avoid a false dilemma, we must look at *all* the alternative futures, or worlds, accessible to agents at the relevant time. One such accessible world is C, where agents, say, pause to take a sip of water prior to conceiving a child rather than pausing to take the pleasure pill—they perform γ, let's say, in place of α—and where Amy ends up existing despite this variation in the causal chain that gets her there. There's nothing in metaphysics or the laws of nature that rules C out as an accessible alternative. But now the argument against the person-based intuition has been derailed. Instead, we say that A is worse than B *and* that someone who does or will exist in A, namely Amy, has indeed been harmed in A—harmed relative not, of course, to B but rather relative to C.[13]

The nonidentity theorist may try to reply to this objection by simply underlining the truth of the stipulated counterfactual: had the agents, contrary-to-fact, not performed α at world A, they would have performed β at B and Amy would never have existed at all. We can have no objection to that stipulation; there will be plenty of cases where such a stipulation will hold, and all that is needed to disprove the person-based intuition is a single counterexample.

But this reply isn't adequate. For it fails to establish that Amy is not harmed in A. Indeed, it would seem that the only way to use the stipulation to obtain the no-harm-done result would be to rely on the following counterfactual test for *harm*: α performed at world A harms Amy *only if*, had α not been performed, Amy would have been better off. But that test is problematic. Suppose I shoot Sam in the arm for no good reason. Suppose, moreover, that, if I hadn't shot Sam in the arm, I would have shot him in the head instead (anger issues). It doesn't follow that my shooting Sam in the arm doesn't *harm* him in the intuitive, comparative, worse-off sense of harm. I harm Sam in virtue of the fact that I *could* have just stood there—in virtue, that is, of the fact that the future in which I don't shoot him at all is perfectly accessible to me.[14]

Similarly, the truth of the stipulated counterfactual in the nonidentity case—that, had agents not performed α at A, Amy would never have existed—doesn't mean that, all the sudden, there is something in metaphysics or the laws of nature that renders C inaccessible. It's what agents *could* have done—what they in fact do at C—not what they *would* have done—at B—that must be measured against what they have done—at A—to determine whether what they have done at A *harms*, or *makes things worse for*, Amy (Roberts 2009, 2007).

But the nonidentity theorist might offer a second and more interesting reply. The idea here is that, while the counterfactual test for harm may well be too narrow, the analysis

I have replaced it with—call it the *possibilist*, or *modal*, *analysis*—is far too broad. Specifically, that analysis ignores the very insight that the nonidentity problem itself rightly trades on—that any individual's coming into existence is itself highly precarious. This second reply concedes that it is *possible* for Amy to have had an unflawed existence— that C is *accessible* to agents—but reminds us that the *odds against* Amy's coming into existence if α isn't performed and if A itself doesn't obtain are overwhelming. Had agents done *anything* other than α—even if they had avoided β and had instead done something that mimicked α, such as γ—the probability of Amy's ever coming into existence at all would have been virtually nil. And such facts are often very important. The physician doesn't harm us, or make things worse for us, when he (say) gives us drug number 1 and induces in us something slightly less than perfect health, when his only other options were to give us drug number 2, which comes with a 0.0001 probability of perfect health and a 0.9999 probability of death, or to do nothing and make our death a certainty.

By taking into account the relevant probabilities, we may thus seem to have secured a result that challenges the person-based intuition. We may seem, that is, after all to face a case in which A is morally worse than B is even though A isn't worse for Amy than B is or, taking probabilities into account, worse for Amy than C is.

This, however, is not the straightforward result we would like to see. Indeed, it's highly contestable and a literally false result: whatever we say about the *probabilities*, A *is* worse for Amy than C is.

We can't, though, just dismiss the second reply. We should instead understand it as aiming to get us to agree, not that the *outcome* A isn't worse for Amy than the *outcome* C is, but rather that the act α isn't worse for Amy than any alternative to α is. In other words: even though γ performed at C (against all odds) produces a better outcome for Amy, because the performance of γ in place of α makes it highly improbable that Amy will ever exist at all, γ is if anything worse for Amy than α is

On this more sophisticated construction of the second reply, we are asked to shift our focus from how Amy fares in the various *worlds* to how she will probably fare under the various *acts*. Specifically: we are asked to shift from a focus on the *actual* value γ produces for Amy at C to the *expected value* γ produces for Amy (whether at C or anywhere else).

But even on this construction the second reply faces difficulties. After all, we should agree that the expected value γ generates for Amy is extremely low since we should agree that, given γ, Amy very probably will never exist at all. But against what *other* value are we to compare that expected value to? The answer cannot be that we compare it against the *actual* value of α, the value, that is, that α in fact has for Amy at A. While the latter is clearly the greater number, that test for determining betterness-for-Amy is unsound. No sound betterness result can be based on a comparison between actual and expected values. To think otherwise invites results of the form X is better than Y for p *and* Y is better than X for p in some cases (Roberts 2009, 2007) and to construct what is in effect an instance of post hoc ergo propter hoc.

The only remaining alternative, then, is to compare the expected value of γ against the expected value of α. The problem for the argument is that that latter value is itself going to be very low. Calculating probabilities as of that moment just prior to performance, which we must, we should quickly appreciate that Amy is indeed *no more likely to exist given α than she is given γ*. Her existence remains highly precarious, whether the agents pause to take a pleasure pill prior to conception or pause to take a sip of water. The upshot—given that the outcome for Amy if she does exist is better under γ than under α—is that the expected value of α for Amy isn't, after all, greater than the expected value of γ for Amy. But that means that the second reply fails as well. Like the first, it fails to establish that α doesn't make things worse for, or harm, Amy.

Not all variations on the nonidentity problem involve mistakes in assessing the relevant probabilities. Some do not involve probabilities at all. Those cases, which include Parfit's "two medical programmes" case, constitute unresolved challenges against the person-based intuition (Parfit 1987: 367–68; 2011: 221–23). Such cases constitute two-alternative cases; there is no plausible basis for the claim that agents could have created additional well-being for the person whose existence is flawed. Some theorists consider such cases on their own sufficient to warrant abandoning a purely person-based approach in favor of an approach that is impersonal at least in part. Still others have modified the person-based approach itself to accommodate the two-alternative cases. Holtug thus shifts from a "narrow" person-based view to a specific variety of the "wide" person-based view (Holtug 2010: 160–62, 247–52; 2009). Heyd, in contrast, remains convinced of the merits of the original ("narrow") intuition and specifically the critical role that matters of personal identity seem to play in moral analysis (Heyd 2009, 1992).

21.6. THE REPUGNANT CONCLUSION AND THE IMPERSONAL APPROACH

The analysis suggested above shows only that the person-based approach cannot easily be dismissed and that an impersonal approach may not be our only option. But it obviously does not show that the impersonal approach is false. Moreover, as noted, the person-based approach continues to face important challenges.

But so, however, does the traditional aggregative formula. Imagine that world A contains a very large population whose members have lives that are well worth living. In contrast, world Z contains a much larger population—an

> enormous population whose members have lives that are not much above the level where life ceases to be worth living.... But if the numbers are large enough, this is the outcome with the greatest total sum of happiness (Parfit 1987: 388).

The traditional formula implies—provided just that "the numbers are large enough"—that Z is morally better than A. Most philosophers agree with Parfit that "this conclusion is hard to accept" (Parfit 1987: 388).

As the case is normally presented, there is no overlapping population—there is no one, that is, who exists in both A and Z (Parfit 1987: 385). That fact may seem to suggest that the person-based approach cannot immediately avoid the result that Z is morally better than A, there being no person p who does or will exist in Z who is worse off in Z than in A. A more immediately fruitful proposal for solving the repugnant conclusion would be a form of *pluralism*, a view that, though impersonal in nature, recognizes that moral betterness involves a plurality of values. Thus, aggregate well-being might be one factor in determining whether one world is better than another, while equality, human flourishing, and improvements in the plights of the least well-off might be still others (Temkin 1993: 221–27; 2012: 313–62). Taking this view, we might protest the result that Z is better than A on the ground that, while Z does a better job of maximizing aggregate well-being, A does a better job of promoting human flourishing.

But as Temkin recognizes the discussion can hardly end there. If, on balance, A is better than Z in virtue of the human flourishing that A displays, we can always imagine yet another case in which the population of Z swells still further to produce some Z′ such that the level of aggregate well-being in Z′ dwarfs the level of human flourishing in A and the balance of value shifts in favor of Z′. To make pluralism function effectively, the individual values need to be understood to add to the overall good of a given world *only up to a certain point*. Once, in other words, a world displays *enough* aggregate well-being, additional well-being no longer makes things better (Temkin 2010: 328–29, 350–51).

The most obvious difficulty with the capped position Temkin describes is that it is unclear just how aggregate well-being is to be balanced against human flourishing and any other values that we think should be incorporated into a theory of the overall good. How do we graph aggregate well-being against human flourishing? When and how fast does the contribution aggregate well-being makes toward the overall good decline against the contribution human flourishing makes toward overall moral value?

An alternative proposal for solving the repugnant conclusion, described by Parfit, takes a lexical view of value. According to that view, certain types of values will always simply trump others. Whatever the value of the life of an oyster or a pig, no amount of that value "could be as good as the value in the life of Socrates" (Parfit 1987: 414).

A more black-and-white form of pluralism, the lexical view avoids the difficulty of saying just how much aggregate well-being is enough. But the lexical view faces challenges as well. It seems to suggest, for example, that the world containing many billions of happy pigs and no Socrates is morally worse than the world containing those very same pigs but in a perfectly miserable state and a single Socrates. And that result is surely questionable.

A third proposal suggests that the value of a given person's well-being level does not contribute to the overall good of the world on a one-to-one basis but rather must first be adjusted on the basis of *desert*. When the person's life is only barely worth living, we could then say that his or her undeservedly low well-being level does not contribute to, but rather detracts from, the value of the world (Feldman 1995: 567–85). On that basis we could say—depending on the actual numbers and the adjustment factor itself—Z is not better than but rather worse than A.

It is unclear, however, that desert itself can be defined in terms that go beyond an equal, positive, and maximal distribution of well-being. But if desert goes no further than that, there will be no adjustment to be made to the individual well-being levels displayed in Z and no basis for declaring Z worse than A.

A fourth proposal asks us to reassess where the dividing line between the existence worth having and the existence less than worth having falls. Parfit wants us to consider the case in which Z is populated entirely by lives that are worth living though only barely so. But if we *think* we have in mind a case in which the Z lives are only barely worth living and yet we immediately find the conclusion that Z is better than A *repugnant*, we may *in fact* have in mind a case that has crossed the line and involves lives that are *less* than worth living. We may *think* the existence consisting of Muzak and potatoes, in combination with an average dose of pain and suffering, is worth having though barely so. The more realistic (and perhaps more humane) view might instead be that such a life is actually *less* than worth living.

But if that's so, then the description of the Z population as containing lives "uniformly of poor quality"—not lives where the ecstasies are nearly counterbalanced by the agonies but rather "drabber" lives—isn't possible (Parfit 1987: 388). After all, it's a stipulation of the case that the lives of the Z population are worth living. However, on a revised and less Pollyannaish view of the life worth living, the lives of the Z population cannot be lives of "uniformly poor quality" but rather lives more or less like our own. Once the description of the case is corrected accordingly, the implication that Z is better than A becomes far less objectionable. If Z is populated by the sort of people "who live to read this," we may be perfectly happy and indeed approve the result that Z is better than A (Tännsjö 1997: 250–51; Ryberg 1996: 163).

It might be felt that, consistent with this view, the repugnant conclusion will simply reemerge at a level farther up the well-being hierarchy. That objection seems weak. The deeper objection is, instead, that it is just not plausible that a life has to be more or less like our own to be worth living. (For a counterargument, see Benatar 2006.)

The idea that a correction in our initial assessment of the lives of the Z people may be in order is put to work in a fifth proposal as well, one that brings to bear the concept of vagueness. The claim, specifically, is that the dividing line between existences worth having and those *less* than worth having is imprecise. The implication that Z is better than A can thus hold only in cases in which the Z lives fall above, not some mythical line marking the distinction between lives worth living and lives less than worth living, but rather some "neutral" range of valuations none of which themselves are capable of marking that distinction. Thus Broome writes that "[i]t is in the nature of betterness that it is vague" (Broome 2004: 179). The upshot for the repugnant conclusion is that the life worth living may not be "mediocre" at all—indeed that it might be a "reasonably good level of life," in which case "the repugnant conclusion may not be unattractive" (Broome 2004: 212).

Here again, however, it seems implausible to think that only the "reasonably good level of life" can be considered worth living. I might anticipate a hard last year of my life—a year that isn't "reasonably good" by any stretch—yet still be able to eke out enough that is good as to make it better for me to continue to live that year rather than to die now.

Broome offers a sixth way of addressing the repugnant conclusion. We think it is clear that the result that Z is better than A is repugnant—that that result is without doubt false. But we also understand that our intuitions about cases involving "large numbers" sometimes fail us (Broome 2004: 212). "Homely intuitions" should be set aside in such cases (Broome 2004: 212).

But why? What Broome says may well apply to some questions involving large numbers—the question whether, for example, the (infinite) power set of the set of natural numbers is larger than the (infinite) set of natural numbers. But there seems no basis for thinking that similar conceptual difficulties arise in the context of the repugnant conclusion. Even assuming, however, that he is correct, the antidote he offers is puzzling. If the numbers are too large for us to manage, what we should do is refrain from judgment. Broome, however, suggests that we should instead rely on "theory" (Broome 2004: 212). But what theory is it we are to rely on? Whether something very like the traditional aggregative formula—which Broome himself in the end favors—is correct is just the question we are trying to decide. To say that we'll say about the repugnant conclusion whatever *that* theory tells us to say is no answer at all.

As a final effort, one might simply argue that the conclusion that Z is better than A is not really so repugnant after all, even in the case where the Z lives remain incontrovertibly drab. Holtug argues that such a response is at least viable (Holtug 2010: 283–87; see also Huemer 2008: 899–933). Even if, however, we are convinced that it's an overstatement to call the conclusion *repugnant*, we might still be convinced that it is highly *implausible* that Z is better than A.

I noted earlier that, given that between A and Z there is no overlapping population, it might seem that the person-based approach cannot easily avoid the result that Z is morally better than A. After all, there exists no person p in Z who is better off in A than that person is in Z. But it should be clear by now that that fact alone does not mean that the person-based view has nothing to say about the case. At least, as the person-based approach has been presented here, to determine whether Z is worse than A it is not enough to consider just whether Z is worse for some person p than A is. We may instead end up finding Z worse than A provided that there does or will exist a person p in Z such that p is better off in *any accessible world* than p is in Z.

The question, then, becomes whether there exists *any* such accessible world Z′—not just A—such that at least some person p in Z is better off at Z′ than p is in Z. But the answer to that question seems on the face of things obvious—and made especially so by Parfit's presentation of the repugnant conclusion as a case of "overpopulation" (Parfit 1987: 384). A simple *reduction* in the size of the population at Z that preserves the existence of at least one person who does or will exist in Z, together with a corresponding better quality of life for that person, is not *inaccessible* to agents at the critical time.

A fractional increase in the well-being available to be distributed across the population does not mean that none of that increase can go to any of the people who do or will exist in Z. There's nothing in metaphysics or the laws of nature that bars a person p who exists in Z from existing in Z′ as well. If Z is accessible to agents, so, it seems, is Z′.

Now, one might resurrect the logic of the nonidentity problem at this point and try to argue that, while such a Z′ is possible and indeed accessible, the *probability* that any person p who does or will exist in Z will exist if agents do anything other than what they in fact do is very small. But in the end taking probabilities into account does no more to undermine the person-based analysis in the context of the repugnant conclusion than it does in the context of the pleasure pill case. Once we move to an evaluation of acts and a calculation of expected well-being, we must keep in mind that the coming into existence of any person p is very small whether agents do opt for a slight reduction in population or they don't. Indeed, in the end, taking steps to make more resources available to a future population may well make p's coming into existence fractionally *more* probable, and certainly will not make it less probable, than not taking such steps.

21.7. Conclusion

Few conclusions can be clearly drawn in this area. The basic issues still line up as Parfit suggested in 1984. The person-based view, while intuitive, remains vulnerable to certain types of nonidentity problems. But modest progress may lie in the fact that we seem able to (*a*) put still other types of nonidentity problems to the side at this point and (*b*) escape the charge that the person-based view itself fails basic conceptual tests. Moreover, the traditional aggregative formula still must face the repugnant conclusion.

Our best options at this juncture, then, seem to be the following:

(A) to pursue a well-articulated version of the person-based approach;
(B) to develop a form of pluralism (or perhaps Temkin's radical pluralism, which considers the overall good of a world to be determined by a combination of impersonal and person-based values); or
(C) to conclude that the problems of population ethics are indicative of an underlying inconsistency in our moral thinking (Arrhenius 2000, 2009).

One last note. If there is a moral to this story, it is this. When it comes to population problems, we must be willing to do not just ethics but *modal* ethics. We must recognize that the *moral landscape* determines the accessible worlds that exist for agents in a given case even if the case *as presented* asks us to focus just on how one such world compares against one other. We've seen that that's so as we've struggled both to articulate the person-based approach and to address at least some forms of the nonidentity problem as well as the repugnant conclusion. Further alternatives may not be relevant, but we shouldn't, absent evaluation, put blinders on and make the assumption that they don't or can't bear on the moral analysis we aim to give.

Acknowledgments

I am immensely grateful to Iwao Hirose and to Jonas Olson, as well as to Nils Holtug and Larry Temkin, for their comments on prior drafts of this chapter.

Notes

1. For further discussion, see Holtug, chapter 14 in this volume, section 14.2.
2. The difference between the two approaches isn't that the one cares about all sentient creation and the other only about human beings. *People*—including, perhaps, cats, dolphins, horses, etc.—may have a critical moral status under a world-based approach just as they have a critical moral status under a person-based approach.
3. Both these assumptions are controversial. It might seem, for example, that just as it is somehow not right, or misleading, to say that an individual is zero inches tall at a world where that individual never exists, or that the temperature in a world where there exists nothing at all is zero degrees Celsius, we also go off-track when we assert that a person—Barack Obama, say—has a zero well-being level at a world where that person never exists. On the other hand, it might also seem that we surely can agree that the anguished child who exists and suffers would have been better off never existing at all—and indeed that the child who, on balance, benefits (on a net basis) in even the smallest way from a particular existence would have been worse off never existing at all. If we then elect to designate that "line in the sand"—that dividing line between the existence that is less than worth having and the existence that is worth having and not merely neutral—a zero well-being level for reasons of convenience, it is not obvious that that choice is problematic. Moreover, it's unclear that well-being and such things as height and temperature are analytically on par. Well-being might be more like money. Thus, while it's misleading and odd to say that my grandmother, who has never been to China and who does not exist in China, has a temperature of zero degrees Celsius in China or is zero inches tall in China, it seems perfectly natural to say that that same grandmother has zero money in China. (She has no debts there and no income there and no assets there—she has zero money in China.) This response might trigger the further objection that the concern is really a matter of reference: because my grandmother does exist in Fort Worth (or, at least, did), we can cogently attribute to her the property of having zero money in China, but since in the Simple Addition Case p never exists in A we have no subject to attribute the property of having zero well-being to. But that further objection seems questionable on its face: by hypothesis, p does exist in B and our claim about that person p is just that p has significant negative well-being in B and zero negative (or positive) well-being in A, and hence that A is better for p than B is. For further discussion, see Arrhenius and Rabinowicz, chapter 22 in this volume; for a summary of the current debate, see Roberts (2010), 48–49 and n. 45. For purposes here, however, the position (*comparability*) that a person has a zero well-being level at any world

where that person never exists and, more generally, that it can be better (or worse) for a person never to exist at all are cogent and can be true must remain an assumption. See part 4 below (discussion of *variabilism*).

4. For discussion of *accessibility* and related concepts useful to the analysis of problems in population ethics, see Feldman 1986.
5. It bears noting that this same clarification of the person-based intuition—in effect, this same tactic for limiting the scope of the necessary condition on one world's being worse than another—can be productively applied to Parfit's Tom, Dick, and Harry case (Parfit 2011: 224–25; Temkin 2012: 431–32). It also has implications for the mere addition paradox (Parfit 1987: 419–41; Roberts 2010: 111–12; Roberts 2014).
6. Velleman (2008) suggests that the bare fact that person-based theories require determinations of identity is alone enough to force us to reject such theories. While personal identity is a challenging area, Velleman's assessment seems unduly pessimistic.
7. This fourth clarification means that the sort of view that Holtug (for example) describes as "person-affecting" in nature will not count as person-affecting, or person-based, in my sense here (Holtug 2009; see also Holtug, chapter 14 in this volume). Perhaps Holtug's is the sort of view Parfit had in mind when he distinguished the *wide* from the *narrow* person-affecting view. But for purposes here it is strictly the *narrow* view that is under investigation—the view that complies with the person-based intuition itself and makes facts about personal identity critical to a determination whether that necessary condition on worseness has been satisfied.
8. The Simple Addition Case may look just like the Compound Addition Case except that the former is "missing" option C. In fact, however, an important issue arises at this point. For it is not clear that the option we label "D" in figure 21.3 can be the very same option we label "D" in figure 21.1. It seems, for example, that the world with respect to which it is possible that I reach out and save the child from drowning in the pond cannot be identical to the world with respect to which it's not possible for me to reach out and save the child from drowning in the pond. Here we touch on issues relating to the Axiom of the Independence of Irrelevant Alternatives. For purposes here, though, keeping such cross-case identifications in place helps to simplify the graphs and does not do any immediate (or I think ultimate) damage to the argument.
9. Moreover, it's hard to see how pluralism, or indeed radical pluralism, can avoid generating that same result. For pluralism and radical pluralism as well consider additional aggregate well-being a plus. In any case in which no other values are at stake—and they're not, in the Simple Addition Case—the result that D is morally better than C seems unavoidable.
10. We can see how the argument from that deeper principle to the basic person-based result is supposed to go. After all, what is supposed to make things better is making things better for *existing* people and *future* people, not making things better for the *merely possible*. Why not, then, just say that existing people matter morally and the merely possible matter not at all? There's some intuitive strength in that idea (even if, as I believe, we must in the end reject it). Why should the interests of people who never exist at all be of any concern at all to us? Why shouldn't we focus exclusively on *real* people, on those who do, or at least will, exist? See generally Heyd 1992.
11. Connecting worseness with wrongness, we can make the point a different way: agents must choose between D and E; E's being worse than D implies that the act that generates E is wrong; D's being worse than E implies that the act that generates D is wrong; whatever agents do, then, they are bound to do wrong. Deontic axioms require, however, that agents

must always have some permissible choice or another. While such axioms may be controversial, that a view is able to comply with them is significant since failure to comply raises important issues.

12. Variabilism suggests plausible analyses as well for the Mere Addition Paradox (Roberts 2014), the Addition Plus case (Roberts 2010: 64–59; 2011a) and Parfit's Tom, Dick, and Harry case (Parfit 2011: 224–25), among others.

13. Here, clarification (B) on the person-based intuition presented in section 21.3 above is at play.

14. At least in any ordinary case, I clearly harm Sam when I shoot him in the arm. I only escape the charge of harm if it somehow happens that *there's nothing more for Sam I could have done*. But in ordinary case there is something more for Sam I could have done. I could have not shot Sam at all.

References

Arrhenius, G. (2000). "An Impossibility Theorem for Welfarist Axiologies." *Economics and Philosophy* 16: 247–66.

Arrhenius, G. (2009). "Can the Person Affecting Restriction Solve the Problems in Population Ethics." In M. A. Roberts and D. T. Wasserman (eds.), *Harming Future Persons: Ethics, Genetics and the Nonidentity Problem*. London: Springer, 289–314.

Broome, J. (2004). *Weighing Lives*. Oxford: Oxford University Press.

Broome, J. (2012). *Climate Matters: Ethics in a Warming World*. New York: Norton.

Bykvist, Krister (2007). "The Benefits of Coming into Existence." *Philosophical Studies* 135: 335–62.

Carlson, E. (1995). *Consequentialism Reconsidered*. Boston: Kluwer.

Feldman, F. (1986). *Doing the Best We Can: An Essay in Informal Deontic Logic*. Boston: Reidel.

Feldman, F. (1995). "Adjusting Utility for Justice." *Philosophy and Phenomenological Research* 55: 567–85.

Hare, C. (2007). "Voices from Another World: Must We Respect the Interests of People Who Do Not, and Will Never, Exist?" *Ethics* 117: 498–523.

Heyd, D. (1992). *Genethics: Moral Issues in the Creation of People*. Berkeley: University of California Press.

Heyd, D. (2009). "The Intractability of the Nonidentity Problem." In M. A. Roberts and D. T. Wasserman (eds.), *Harming Future Persons: Ethics, Genetics and the Nonidentity Problem*. London: Springer, 3–25.

Holtug, N. (2009). "Who Cares About Identity." In M. A. Roberts and D. T. Wasserman (eds.), *Harming Future Persons: Ethics, Genetics and the Nonidentity Problem*. London: Springer, 71–92.

Holtug, N. (2010). *Persons, Interests and Justice*. Oxford: Oxford University Press.

Huemer, M. (2008). "In Defence of Repugnance." *Mind* 117: 899–933.

Kavka, G. (1981). "The Paradox of Future Individuals." *Philosophy and Public Affairs* 11: 93–112.

McMahan, J. (1981). "Problems of Population Choice." *Ethics* 92 (1): 96–127.

McMahan, J. (2009). "Asymmetries in the Morality of Causing People to Exist." In M. A. Roberts and D. T. Wasserman (eds.), *Harming Future Persons: Ethics, Genetics and the Nonidentity Problem*. London: Springer, 49–68.

Narveson, J. (1976). "Moral Problems of Population." In M. Bayles (ed.), *Ethics and Population*. Cambridge, MA: Schenkman, 59–80.
Parfit, D. (1987). *Reasons and Persons*. Oxford: Oxford University Press.
Persson, I. (2009). "Rights and the Asymmetry between Creating Good and Bad Lives." In M. A. Roberts and D. Wasserman (eds.), *Harming Future Persons: Ethics, Genetics and the Nonidentity Problem*. London: Springer, 29–47.
Roberts, M. A. (1998). *Child versus Childmaker: Future Persons and Present Duties in Ethics and the Law*. Lanham, MD: Rowman and Littlefield.
Roberts, M. A. (2003a). "Can It Ever Have Been Better Never to Have Existed at All? Person-Based Consequentialism and a New Repugnant Conclusion." *Journal of Applied Philosophy* 20: 159–85.
Roberts, M. A. (2003b). "Is the Person-Affecting Intuition Paradoxical?" *Theory and Decision* 55 (1): 1–44.
Roberts, M. A. (2007). "The Nonidentity Fallacy: Harm, Probability and Another Look at Parfit's Depletion Example." *Utilitas* 19: 267–311.
Roberts, M. A. (2009). "The Nonidentity Problem and the Two Envelope Problem." In M. A. Roberts and D. T. Wasserman (eds.), *Harming Future Persons: Ethics, Genetics and the Nonidentity Problem*. London: Springer, 201–28.
Roberts, M. A. (2010). *Abortion and the Moral Significance of Merely Possible People: Finding Middle Ground in Hard Cases*. London: Springer.
Roberts, M. A. (2011a). "The Asymmetry: A Solution." *Theoria* 77: 333–67.
Roberts, M. A. (2011b). "An Asymmetry in the Ethics of Procreation." *Philosophy Compass* 6 (11): 765–76.
Roberts, M. A. (2014). "Temkin's Essentially Comparative View, Wrongful Life and the Mere Addition Paradox." *Analysis* 74 (2): 306–26.
Ryberg, J. (1996). "Is the Repugnant Conclusion Repugnant?" *Philosophical Papers* 25: 161–77.
Ryberg J., and T. Torbjorn, eds. (2004). *The Repugnant Conclusion: Essays on Population Ethics*. Boston: Kluwer.
Sidgwick, H. (1907). *The Methods of Ethics*. London: Macmillan).
Singer, P. (2011). *Practical Ethics*, 3rd ed. Cambridge: Cambridge University Press.
Tännsjö, T. (1997). "Doom Soon?" *Inquiry* 40: 243–53.
Temkin, L. (1993). *Inequality*. Oxford: Oxford University Press.
Temkin, L. (2012). *Rethinking the Good: Moral Ideals and the Nature of Practical Reasoning*. Oxford: Oxford University Press.
Velleman, D. (2008). "Persons in Prospect." *Philosophy and Public Affairs* 36 (3): 221–322.

CHAPTER 22

THE VALUE OF EXISTENCE

GUSTAF ARRHENIUS AND WLODEK RABINOWICZ

22.1. INTRODUCTION

CAN it be better or worse for a person to be than not to be, that is, can it be better or worse for her to exist than not to exist at all? This old and challenging philosophical question, which we can call *the existential question*, has been raised anew in contemporary moral philosophy. There are roughly two reasons for this renewed interest. First, traditional "impersonal" ethical theories, such as utilitarianism, have paradoxical and very counterintuitive implications for procreation and our moral duties to future not yet existing people. Second, it has seemed evident to many that an outcome can be better than another only if it is better for someone, and that only moral theories that are in this sense "person affecting" can be correct. The implications of this so-called *Person Affecting Restriction* will differ radically, however, depending on which answer one gives to the existential question. Hence, many of the problems regarding our moral duties to future generations turn around the issue of whether existence can be better or worse for a person than nonexistence.

Some think so, others adamantly deny it. Thus, for example, Nils Holtug (1996, 2001), Melinda Roberts (1998, 2003), and Matthew Adler (2009) have defended an affirmative answer to the existential question. Contrariwise, Derek Parfit (1991 [1984]), John Broome (1999), Krister Bykvist (2007), and others have worried that if we take a person's life to be better for her than nonexistence, then we would have to conclude that it would have been worse for her if she did not exist, which is absurd: Nothing would have been worse or better for a person if she had not existed.

We shall start by explaining in more detail why the existential question has in recent years moved to the forefront of moral philosophy. We shall then discuss some of the proposed answers in the literature and our own suggestion. On our view, one can plausibly claim that it is better or worse for a person to exist than not to exist without thereby implying any absurdities. Finally, we shall consider some objections to our position and consider some of its implications in population ethics.

22.2. THE PERSON-AFFECTING RESTRICTION AND THE EXISTENTIAL QUESTION

The Person-Affecting Restriction, put as a slogan, states that one outcome can be better than another only if it is better for someone. The restriction has a strong intuitive appeal and it has been suggested that it is presupposed in many arguments in moral philosophy, political theory, and welfare economics.[1] Moreover, several theorists have argued that the counterintuitive implications in population ethics of "impersonal" welfarist theories arise because such theories violate this restriction. This applies in particular to the well-known repugnant conclusion, which—as has been pointed out by Parfit—is entailed by classical utilitarianism.[2]

It is not easy to discern what exactly the distinction between "impersonal" and "person affecting" theories amounts to in the literature, partly because different authors have had a different take on the distinction and partly because other ideas have been conflated or combined with the Person-Affecting Restriction. One can interpret the restriction in a weak way that makes it perfectly compatible with impersonal welfarist theories such as classical utilitarianism (see Arrhenius 2003, 2009, 2015). For example, it could be understood as the idea that moral goodness exclusively supervenes on facts concerning individual well-being. We are, however, interested in a stronger reading of the restriction which stresses the individualist aspect of value even more by claiming that axiology is essentially *person comparative*:

The Person-Affecting Restriction: If an outcome A is better (worse) than B, then A is better (worse) than B for at least one individual in A or in B.

In cases involving only the same people in the compared outcomes, this restriction is, we surmise, widely accepted by theorists with welfarist inclinations.[3] In comparisons between outcomes involving different people, for example in cases involving people whose existence is contingent on our choices, the restriction however becomes ambiguous. An outcome A is better than B for Peter if Peter has a higher welfare in A as compared to B. We can assume that much. But what if Peter exists in outcome A but not in outcome B? Is A then better than B *for Peter*? More generally, can existence be better or worse for a person than nonexistence?[4] Depending on the answer to the existential question, the Person-Affecting Restriction has very different implications regarding how to morally evaluate different possible futures.

22.3. NEITHER BETTER NOR WORSE TO BE THAN NOT TO BE

A popular answer is to claim that existence cannot be better or worse for a person than nonexistence, nor equally as good for that matter, since existence and nonexistence are, in some sense, incomparable in value for a person. Thus, David Heyd argues that the view according to which existence could be worse than nonexistence "is inconsistent with a person-affecting theory as it presupposes the comparability of non-existence with life of a certain quality."[5]

In his early pioneering work in population ethics, Narveson seems to share Heyd's concern regarding comparability, although he formulates it in terms of happiness comparisons rather than comparisons in value:

> If you ask, "whose happiness has been increased as a result of his being born?", the answer is that nobody's has. [. . .] Remember that the question we must ask about *him* is not whether he is happy but whether he is happier as a result of being born. And if put this way, we see that again we have a piece of nonsense on our hands if we suppose the answer is either "yes" or "no." For if it is, then with whom, or with what, are we comparing his new state of bliss? Is the child, perhaps, happier than he used to be before he was born? Or happier, perhaps, than his alter ego? Obviously, there can be no sensible answer here. (Narveson 1967: 67; emphasis in original)

Similarly, John Broome states that " . . . it cannot ever be *true* that it is better for a person that she lives than that she should never have lived at all."[6] Cf. also Dasgupta (1995: 383):

> Recall our definition of the zero level of well-being. This isn't a standard arrived at through a comparison with "non-existence." Such comparisons can't be made. The "unborn" aren't a class of people. It makes no sense to attribute a degree of wellbeing, low or high or nil, to the "state of not being born."

Likewise, Alan Buchanan and coauthors (2000: 234) claim that "when the alternative is nonexistence, there is no individual who is made worse off by being conceived and born. Nonexistence is not a condition that is better for an individual only in rare cases like having Lesh-Nyhan or Tay Sachs disease; it is no condition at all, and so it is not better or worse than any other condition."

The negative answer to the existential question in combination with the Person-Affecting Restriction has such counterintuitive conclusions that it is hard to believe that anyone would seriously endorse the conjunction of these two views. Consider the Future Bliss or Hell case represented in figure 22.1. The blocks in the diagram represent populations. The width of each block represents the number of people, whereas the height represents their welfare. This welfare is positive (or, as we could also put it, people have lives worth living) when the block is above the horizontal line, and negative when the block is below the line. Assume that we can

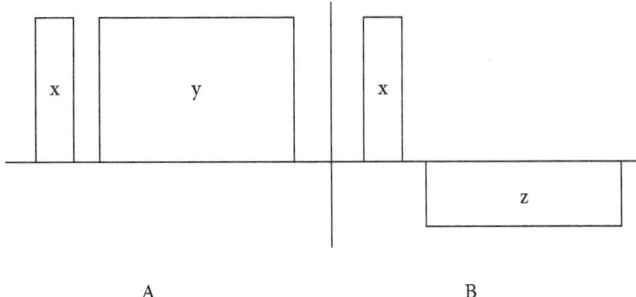

FIGURE 22.1 Future Bliss or Hell

either see to it that all the people in the future have excellent lives (the y-people in outcome A) or that they have hellish lives (the z-people in outcome B). Assume further that these two possible future populations are of the same size but consist of different people, and that these two outcomes are equally good for us, the currently existing x-people.

We take it that outcome A is clearly superior to outcome B. However, since the y- and z-people don't exist in both outcomes, the negative answer to the existential question implies that outcome A is neither better nor worse for the y- and z-people as compared to B. Moreover, the two outcomes are equally good for the x-people. Hence, according to the Person-Affecting Restriction, A cannot be better than B since it is not better for any individual. Nor is of course B better than A. In other words, if combined with the negative answer to the existential question, the Person-Affecting Restriction ranks these outcomes as either equally good or as incomparable in value. But that is clearly the wrong diagnosis of the Future Bliss or Hell case.

This and other counterintuitive implications of the Person-Affecting Restriction in combination with the negative answer to the existential question have led philosophers to abandon the restriction (the majority) or to accept not only that existence can be better or worse for a person than nonexistence but also that (1) a nonexistent person has a certain welfare level (namely, zero welfare, *pace* Dasgupta) and that, consequently, (2) nonexistence can be better or worse for that nonexistent person than a life at some specified level of welfare. As we shall show, we neither need to give up the restriction nor make moves (1) and (2). However, we shall also point out that the restriction and the affirmative answer will still have certain implications in population ethics that some might find counterintuitive.

22.4. THE ARGUMENT FROM ABSURDITY

One worry that seems to motivate the negative answer to the existential question is the following: If the question were given an affirmative answer, that is, if we took a person's life to be better or worse for her than nonexistence, then we would have to conclude that *it would have been worse or better for her if she did not exist* (henceforth, the Absurd

Conclusion). Clearly, this is unacceptable: Nothing would have been worse or better for a person if she had not existed. Parfit puts this worry as follows: "in being caused to exist, someone can be benefited. . . . [W]e need not claim that this outcome is *better* for this person than the alternative. This would imply the implausible claim that, if this person had never existed, this would have been worse for this person."[7] The absurdity of the conclusion is well brought out by Broome:

> [I]t cannot ever be *true* that it is better for a person that she lives than that she should never have lived at all. If it were better for a person that she lives than that she should never have lived at all, then if she had never lived at all, that would have been worse for her than if she had lived. But if she had never lived at all, there would have been no her for it to be worse for, so it could not have been worse for her.[8]

However, the Absurd Conclusion does not follow. A triadic relation consisting in one state (having a certain life) being better for a person p than another state (non-existence) cannot hold unless its three relata exist. Now, the states in question are abstract entities and thus can be assumed to exist even if they do not actually obtain. Consequently, the triadic relation in question can indeed hold as long as also the third relatum, person p, exists. However, if persons are concrete objects, which is the received view (and, we surmise, the correct one), a person exists only insofar as she is alive. Therefore, this relation could not hold if p weren't alive, since the third relatum, p, would then be missing.[9] Consequently, even if it is better for p to exist than not to exist, assuming she has a life worth living, it doesn't follow that it *would have been worse* for p *if she did not exist*, since one of the relata, p, would then have been absent.[10] What does follow is only that nonexistence *is* worse for her than existence (since "worse" is just the converse of "better"), but not that it *would have been* worse if she didn't exist. Hence, Broome's argument is a non sequitur and the Absurd Conclusion doesn't follow from the idea that existence can be better or worse for a person than nonexistence.[11]

It might be that Broome assumes that the following general principle is true:

> *Subjunctive Connection 1 (SC1)*: An outcome A is better (worse, equally as good) for p than (as) another outcome B only if outcome B would be worse (better, equally as good) for p than (as) A if B came about.[12]

Krister Bykvist has suggested a similar principle which he calls *Accessibility*: "If A is better (worse) for S than B, then A would be better (worse) for S than B even if A obtained."[13] However, as we pointed out above, it doesn't follow logically from "it is better for p to exist than not to exist" that "it would have been worse for p if she did not exist" since in the latter case one of the relata, p, would be absent.[14] So it is not clear to us why one should go for SC1 rather than for the following connection between "better for" and "would be worse for":

Subjunctive Connection 2 (SC2):

(i) If a person *p* exists in both outcomes A and B, then A is better (worse, equally as good) for *p* than (as) B only if B would be worse (better, equally as good) for *p* than (as) A, if B obtained.
(ii) If a person *p* exists in A but not in B, then A can be better (worse, equally as good) for *p* than (as) B although B would not be worse (better, equally as good) for *p* than (as) A, if B obtained.

Of course, one might find SC1 more attractive than SC2, perhaps because one finds it more in line with our common way of thinking and reasoning: If we consider one outcome as better for someone than another outcome, then we usually are prepared to conclude that the other outcome, if it obtained, would be worse for that person (and not just that it *is* worse). This, however, might simply have to do with the fact that we are accustomed to compare outcomes in both of which the affected person exists. If this habitual presupposition is given up, the old ways of thinking have to be adjusted accordingly. Note that we do not simply reject SC1 in order to avoid the Absurd Conclusion; we explain what's wrong with this condition in the context where people's existence is at stake.

22.5. The Argument from Welfare Level Comparisons

To save the Person-Affecting Restriction from cases like the Future Bliss or Hell case, Melinda Roberts has suggested that we should accept not only that existence can be better or worse for a person than nonexistence, but also the apparently absurd conclusion that in cases like this it would have been better or worse for a person not to exist than to exist. The reason is that according to Roberts a nonexisting person has a certain welfare level, namely, zero welfare:[15]

> Nora does not have any properties at all at any alternative at which she does not exist and . . ., where Nora has no properties at all, all the properties that she does have—that empty set—add up to a zero level of wellbeing. [. . .] It would have been better for Nora not to have any wellbeing at all—to have zero wellbeing—than to have the negative level of wellbeing that she in fact has. It would have been [better] for Nora . . . never to have existed at all than it is for Nora to exist.[16]

However, in our view it is quite nonsensical to ascribe any well-being level at all to a person in a state in which she does not exist. Well-being presupposes being. Having a zero degree of well-being is arguably the kind of property the instantiation of which requires the existence of property bearers.[17] Indeed, Roberts's view seems contradictory: While she ascribes to the nonexistent Nora the property of having zero degree of well-being, she states that the nonexistent Nora "has no properties at all."[18]

As we have shown above, one can endorse an affirmative answer to the existential question without affirming that nonexistence could have been better or worse for a person and without assigning any welfare levels to persons who don't exist.

Yet one might insist that the suggestion we make still doesn't make sense: that we cannot make sense of one state, A, being better for p than another state, B, if we cannot compare the well-being levels of p in the two states in question. This might be what Buchanan and coauthors and Heyd had in mind in the quotes above. Likewise, when Bykvist claims that SC1 (his Accessibility principle) is true about any "interpretation of 'better for' that is conceptually linked to well-being . . .," it seems that his idea is that "better for" claims are analyzable in terms of comparisons between well-being levels possessed by a given individual in different outcomes.[19] This would entail SC1 given that no individual has any level of well-being in an outcome in which she does not exist.[20] The idea is that there is a necessary connection between "better for" and "has a higher welfare than":

Welfare Level Connection (WLC): An outcome A is better for a person p than another outcome B if and only if p would have higher welfare in A than in B.

However, as we shall argue in the following section, "better for" comparisons can be made without comparisons of welfare levels. Consequently, one should reject the suggested tight connection between "better for" and comparisons of welfare levels as expressed by WLC.

22.6. Guardian Angels and Fitting Attitudes

Instead of relying on WLC, one might explicate "better for" in terms of what a benevolent impartial observer would prefer for a person when she is only considering what is in the interests of the person in question, or—better—in terms of what that person's guardian angel would prefer.[21] According to this view, an outcome A is better for a person than another outcome B if and only if this is what her guardian angel would prefer for her sake. If a person exists in the two compared outcomes, then trivially the guardian angel will prefer the state in which her charge has the highest welfare level. However, if the guardian angel compares a state in which her charge has a life with negative welfare with a state in which that person does not exist at all, she prefers the latter. Moreover, if the guardian angel compares a state in which her charge has a life with a positive welfare with the state in which her charge does not exist, she prefers the former.

We can think of this idea of a guardian angel as just a *criterion* for the "better for" relation. On this criterial interpretation, we can try to find out what is better for a person by putting ourselves, in imagination, in her guardian angel's shoes and then try to determine what our preferences would be in that hypothetical position. Additionally, on a view that is philosophically more far-reaching, the idea of a guardian angel can also be seen as a metaphor for a certain *analytical* proposal. More precisely, on this reading, we should take it as an application to "better for" of the so-called *fitting attitude analysis of value*. Along the lines of this format of analysis, we could say that

> A is better for p than B if and only if one ought to prefer A to B for p's sake.[22]

This analytic proposal could be made to work provided we can make some sense of locutions such as "preferring A to B for p's sake."[23] Again, it seems reasonable to say that in the choice between bringing p into existence with negative welfare or not bringing her into existence at all, one ought to prefer the latter for p's sake. Likewise, in the choice between bringing p into existence with positive welfare or not bringing her into existence at all, one ought to prefer the former for p's sake.

On both these interpretations, the criterial and the analytic one, if a person p has higher welfare in an outcome A as compared to another outcome B, then A is better for p than B, but the reverse doesn't always hold. Hence, there is a connection between "better for" and "has higher welfare than," but this connection isn't as tight as WLC would have it.

22.7. The Issue of Value Bearers

The affirmative answer to the existential question faces a serious problem, however. We have assumed that the "better for" relation obtains between abstract states and a person. One might object, however, that what is better for a person is not an abstract state itself but the *obtaining* of that state.[24] To assume that states and not just their obtainings are better for a person seems counterintuitive, since the existence of such abstract states doesn't make things better for a person in any way. It is only the obtaining of such states that can make things better for a person. Now, it is clear that we cannot claim that the obtaining of the state of a person p's existence is better for p than the obtaining of p's nonexistence since these two obtainings and the person under consideration do not coexist. Indeed, they cannot coexist and hence they cannot stand in any relation to each other. As we have assumed throughout, a relation cannot obtain without the existence of all the relata.

Actually, this is a general problem in axiology. It concerns not only "better for" but also "better" (and "good," "good for," etc.). We quite often want to say that a state, S, is better than another state, T, when S and T are incompatible with each other. Yet we cannot reduce this relation between abstract states to a relation between the obtainings of those states. We cannot say that if S were to obtain, this would be better than if T were to obtain, if this is meant to state a relation between the obtainings of S and T, respectively. For if S and T are mutually incompatible, then if one of them obtains, the other does not.

So the two obtainings cannot coexist and consequently cannot stand in any relation to each other.

As this is a general problem in axiology, which isn't specific to the comparisons of existence and nonexistence, we might ignore it in the present context. As an objection to the affirmative answer to the existential question, it has too wide a reach to be convincing. Most of our thinking in axiology, both in philosophy and everyday life, presupposes that we can meaningfully say that a certain state is better than another state even when the obtainings of these states are mutually incompatible.[25]

Let us, however, say a bit about how we believe this issue could be dealt with. One might simply take the view that not only obtainings of states of affairs can be good or better, but also those very states themselves. On this reading, S is literally better than T and this claim is not reducible to a claim about the relationship between the obtainings of these states.

How can one then deal with the objection that the world is not made any better by the existence of such states? Well, a simple and straightforward answer is to say that abstract states can be valuable but they don't contributive any value to the world. As Michael Zimmerman puts it: "One might ... contend that the way to avoid having to declare that our world is better simply for the *existence* in it of the state of affairs of everyone being happy is to say that what counts in the evaluation of a world is not what valuable states of affairs *exist* in it but what valuable states of affairs *obtain* in it" (Zimmerman 2001: 48, emphasis in original).

Zimmerman himself rejects the view we have just suggested as inadequate: "Perhaps it is reasonable to say that a world's parts consist of those states of affairs that obtain in it, rather than of those that exist in it, so that it's no surprise that *its* final value derives only from the former. But this still leaves us with the problem of saying that states of affairs (including worlds) themselves have final value, even when *they* don't obtain" (Zimmerman 2001: 48, emphasis in original) He doesn't explain however, why the latter problem he mentions is a problem to begin with. It seems to us that the view in question is tenable provided we allow for the possibility of valuable entities that do not contribute in value to the actual world. More precisely, a state of affairs S *can* contribute in value to a world understood as a possible way things might be, that is, to a world understood as a maximal consistent abstract state of affairs, if that world contains S. However, when we talk about "the world" or "the actual world," we normally mean the totality of what obtains and an abstract state of affairs that *doesn't* obtain cannot, of course, contribute in value to that totality. To assume otherwise would be to confuse distinct ontological categories.[26]

That abstract states can be valuable is supported by the fitting attitude analysis of value. This point was already noted by Lemos (1994: 24): "The weightiest reason for an affirmative answer [to the question whether states of affairs are intrinsically valuable] arises from thinking of intrinsic value in terms of correct or fitting emotional attitudes. ... Whether a state of affairs is worthy of love or a pro-attitude does not depend on whether it obtains or is a fact."[27] In fact, it seems to us that both abstract states and their obtainings can be fitting objects of pro-attitudes. For states it might be fitting to, say, contemplate them with pleasure or desire them to obtain, whereas for obtainings it might be fitting to be pleased with them or to welcome their existence.

22.8. THE PERSON-AFFECTING RESTRICTION REVISITED

As for the connection between "better" and "better for," the Person-Affecting Restriction remains an attractive option. It does seem plausible to claim that, to the extent we only focus on welfare, an outcome cannot be better than another outcome without being better for someone. While this restriction would lead to counterintuitive implications if combined with the negative answer to the existential question (see the case of Future Bliss or Hell above), we have argued that the existential question can be given an affirmative answer.

It should be noted, however, that even coupled with the affirmative answer to the existential question, the Person-Affecting Restriction, as we have stated it above, leads to counterintuitive implications, unless it is appropriately weakened. The reason is that the betterness relation between outcomes does not require the actual existence of the affected persons. Persons enter as relata in the triadic "better for" relation and therefore must exist for that relation to obtain, but they are not relata in the dyadic betterness relation that obtains between outcomes. This contrast between the triadic and the dyadic relations of betterness explains why the Person-Affecting Restriction cannot be correct as it stands.

Thus, to give an example, consider a variant of the Future Bliss or Hell case above in which only the x-people exist in outcome A (i.e., in this variant, outcome A does not contain any future y-people) while outcome B still in addition contains z-people that lead hellish lives, and suppose that outcome A is the one that actually obtains. The Person-Affecting Restriction implies, counterintuitively, that A is not better than B, since—as things actually are—there exists no one for whom A is better than B: The added z-people in the hypothetical outcome B, for whom A would have been better, do not actually exist. Intuitively, however, if A would have been better than B had B obtained (and B is not better than A if A obtains, as in our case), then A *is* better than B irrespective of whether A or B obtains.[28] To solve problems like this, Holtug (2004) has argued that we should replace the restriction with a weaker version, which in our formulation runs as follows:

The Wide Person-Affecting Restriction: If an outcome A is better than B, then A would be better than B for someone that would exist if A were to obtain *or* if B were to obtain.

In the example above, it is the second disjunct of this weaker restriction that is applicable. Clearly, it is only this wide, disjunctive version of the restriction that deserves serious consideration.[29]

Another problem is that it might seem that the restriction doesn't have much bite given the affirmative answer to the existential question. If one compares two outcomes A and B, then the restriction won't exclude any rankings of A and B as soon as A contains

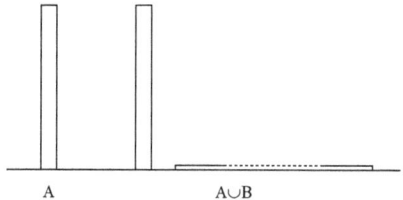

FIGURE 22.2 Mere Addition

some persons with positive well-being that don't exist in B and B contains some persons with positive well-being that don't exist in A.

However, the appearances are misleading. The wide restriction does have some force, irrespectively of whether it is coupled with a positive or negative answer to the existential question. For example, it rules out all welfarist theories which imply that a mere addition of lives with positive welfare can make a population worse. Prominent examples of such theories are Average and Critical-Level Utilitarianism.[30] To see this, consider the case shown in figure 22.2 (dashes indicate that the block in question should be much wider than shown, that is, the population is much larger than shown). According to Average Utilitarianism, A∪B is worse than A since the average welfare is lower in A∪B as compared to A. According to Critical-Level Utilitarianism, the contributive value of a person's life is her welfare minus a positive critical level, and the value of a population is calculated by summing these differences for all individuals in the population. Assuming that the B-people are below the critical level, Critical-Level Utilitarianism reaches the same verdict as Average Utilitarianism. The addition of B-people has a negative contributive value given that their welfare is below the critical level.

However, A∪B would not be worse than A for anyone, irrespectively of whether A or A∪B were to obtain. Consequently, the Wide Person-Affecting Restriction rules out theories such as Average and Critical-Level Utilitarianism.

Nevertheless, even if we deny that A∪B is worse than A, we are not yet forced to say that A∪B is better than or equally as good as A. The wide restriction is compatible with theories that declare these outcomes incommensurable. Consider, however, the following condition:

Subjunctive Weak Pareto: If A would be better than B for everyone who would exist if A were to obtain, and for everyone who would exist if B were to obtain, then A is better than B.

This condition is a weaker version of the Pareto condition adjusted for the context in which it can be better for someone to exist than not to exist. It might seem to be an irresistible condition in the present setting, as long as we disregard other values apart from welfare. Consider now the outcomes shown in figure 22.3. Assume that A and A′ consist of the same people, namely the α-people. Assume further that A is the case. Then A′∪B is better than A for all the people that exist since the α-people enjoy higher welfare in A′ as compared to A. Assume now that A′∪B is the case. Since the B-people have

FIGURE 22.3 Pareto Addition and Inequality Aversion

positive welfare, A'∪B is better for them than A given the affirmative answer to the existential question. As before, A'∪B is better than A for α-people. Thus, A'∪B is better than A for everybody irrespective of whether A or A'∪B were to obtain. It follows from Subjunctive Weak Pareto that A'∪B is better than A. Hence, the affirmative answer to the existential question in conjunction with Subjunctive Weak Pareto rules out theories which imply that A'∪B and A might be incommensurable.

Moreover, it follows from weak and intuitively compelling conditions of inequality aversion (or priority to the worse off) that one can always find a B-population such that C, which consists of the same people as A'∪B but at a very low positive welfare level just slightly higher than that of the B-people, is at least as good as A'∪B. It follows, given transitivity, that C is better than A. Hence, the affirmative answer to the existential question together with a couple of weak additional conditions yield the repugnant conclusion.

Some will find this implication and the earlier one above unsettling and as reasons to resist the affirmative answer to the existential question or the Wide Person-Affecting Restriction. However, it can also be taken as a new argument in favor of accepting the repugnant conclusion *or* as a reason to be cautious with seemingly irresistible conditions such as Subjunctive Weak Pareto.[31]

Before we finish, we should say more about ordinary language formulations of value comparisons between outcomes. The reader might have got an impression that, on our view, counterfactual claims such as "Not to exist would have been better/worse for *p* than to exist" are absurd. But are such claims really so unpalatable? Think of Melinda Roberts's statement about Nora: "It would have been better for Nora never to have existed at all than it is for Nora to exist." This doesn't sound absurd at all. But, if not, then perhaps the Argument from Absurdity doesn't even get started?

However, how should a counterfactual statement like the one about Nora be understood? Here is what we'd like to suggest. When we use ordinary language formulations of the form "A would have been better/worse for *p* than B" what we do is something along these lines: (1) we state that the relevant triadic relation obtains between A, B, and *p*; *and* (2) we imply that A does not obtain. If we instead of "would have been" use "would be," (2') we only imply that it is not settled that A obtains.

On this analysis of "A would have been better/worse for *p* than B," or "A would be better/worse for *p* than B," when we use such formulations, we don't take a stand on what relation would obtain between A, B, and *p* under counterfactual or potential circumstances, that is, if A did obtain. It is this feature that explains the absence of absurdity in

Nora-type statements. However, we do take such a stand when we expressly state that "A would have been better/worse for p than B, *if C had been the case.*" Thereby we do state that the betterness/worseness relation would have obtained between A, B, and p under the counterfactual circumstance C. Consequently, the following *is* absurd: "Not to exist would have been better/worse for p than to exist, *if p had not existed.*" It is this kind of statements that the Argument from Absurdity focuses on. Therefore, if that argument is to be invalidated, it has to be met head on, as we have done, rather than rejected on the grounds that there is no absurdity in what is being claimed to begin with.

Acknowledgments

We would like to thank Matthew Adler, Staffan Angere, Johan Brännmark, John Broome, Krister Bykvist, Erik Carlson, Marc Fleurbaey, Ingvar Johansson, Christian Piller, Melinda Roberts, and Toni Rønnow-Rasmussen for their helpful comments. Thanks also to the Collège d'Études Mondiales and to the Swedish Collegium for Advanced Study for being such generous hosts during some of the time when this chapter was written and revised. Financial support from the Swedish Research Council as well as from Riksbankens Jubileumsfond and Fondation Maison des Sciences de l'Homme through the Franco-Swedish Program in Economics and Philosophy is gratefully acknowledged..

Notes

1. See Temkin 1993a, 1993b. The label "Person-Affecting Restriction" was introduced by Glover (1977: 66), but see also Narveson 1967.
2. See Parfit 1991 [1984]: 388. For an overview of these counterintuitive implications, see Arrhenius, Ryberg, and Tännsjö 2006 and Arrhenius 2000, 2015. The repugnant conclusion is the claim that for any world inhabited by people with very high welfare, there is a *better* possible world in which everyone has a life that is barely worth living, other things being equal. Imposing the Person-Affecting Restriction might block the derivation of the repugnant conclusion if it is conjoined with a negative answer to the existential question. Then it is arguable that a world in which everyone has a life barely worth living cannot be better than a world in which all individuals have a very high quality of life, since the former is not better for anyone, not even for the people who exist in the former but not in the latter world. Since we are going to argue that the existential question should be answered in the affirmative, however, we are skeptical about this maneuver. For more on this, see Arrhenius (2014).
3. Three qualifications: (1) The label "Person Affecting" might be misleading, since many theorists would, sensibly we think, weaken the restriction so as to also cover other sentient beings. Cf. Holtug 1996. (2) Since the Person-Affecting Restriction is formulated without a *ceteris paribus* clause, value pluralists are not likely to accept it since it leaves little room for other values apart from welfarist ones. Clearly, one might embrace nonwelfarist values such as virtue, reward in accordance to desert (cf., for example, Feldman 1995a, 1995b,

1997), beauty (cf. Moore 1966 [1903]: § 50), variety of natural species, or what have you (for a general discussion of value pluralism, see Rabinowicz and Rønnow-Rasmussen 2004; for a discussion of this issue in connection with the Person-Affecting Restriction, see Arrhenius 2003, 2009, 2015). We shall, however, only discuss implications of the restriction in cases where one can assume that nonwelfarist values are not at stake. Hence, the arguments below also apply to the *ceteris paribus* version of the restriction, that is, the version that is of interest also to the value pluralists. (3) Certain welfarist theories are ruled out by the restriction already in the same people cases, such as some extreme versions of welfarist egalitarianism (Arrhenius 2009, 2015).
4. To forestall possible misunderstandings, the question we are interested in is not whether *mere* existence, or life *as such*, can be better or worse for a person than nonexistence. Instead, the question is whether having a life of a certain quality can be better or worse for a person than not having a life at all.
5. Heyd 1988: 161. See also Heyd 1992: 124–25. Heyd states that his view is "grounded in an 'anthropocentric' conception of value according to which value is necessarily related to human interests, welfare, expectations, desires and wishes—that is to say to human volitions" (1988: 164).
6. Broome 1999: ch. 10, p. 168; emphasis in original. See also Parfit 1991 [1984]: 395, 489. However, these two authors, unlike Heyd and Narveson, do not endorse the restriction.
7. Parfit 1991 [1984]: 395; emphasis in the original; cf. also p. 489. He asserts, however, that causing someone to exist still can be *good* for the person in question. Good, but not better. It seems to us that Parfit needn't have been so cautious. His discussion of the matter contains all that is needed for the bolder betterness claim (see below).
8. Broome 1999: ch. 10, p. 168; emphasis in original. Note that this argument, if correct, would also work against the idea that existence could be worse for someone than nonexistence: If it were worse for a person that she exists than that she should never have existed, then it would have been better for her if she had never existed. But if she had never existed, then there would have been no her, so it could not have been better for her. Thus, it cannot be true that it could be worse for a person to exist than not to exist.
9. On the other hand, if persons were viewed as collections of (abstract) states of affairs, which can exist without "obtaining," then there would be nothing absurd in claiming that if a person did not obtain, this state could have been worse for her than her actual state, since all three relata would then exist as abstract objects. However, this interpretation of persons as abstract objects is a view that no philosophers we know of would be prepared to accept. Abstract objects cannot have the kind of properties we ascribe to persons: they have no temporal existence, they have no bodies, they cannot be happy or sad, nor can they make any decisions.

   It should be noted that in this chapter we presuppose that relations require the existence of relata. This presupposition could, of course, be questioned. (We are indebted to Staffan Angere for pressing this point.) Thus, for example, it could be argued that intentional attitudes are best interpreted as relations between a subject and an intentional object, which would mean that a relation can obtain even if one of the relata (the intentional object) happens not to exist. On our view, such a relational account of intentional attitudes is unsatisfactory. An ontology that allows obtaining of the relations without existing relata leads to a whole host of problems, but the discussion of these issues would take us too far afield.
10. Another approach to this issue has been suggested by Tim Williamson (2013). On his "necessitist" view, everything that exists does so necessarily, in all possible worlds.

Consequently, a person *p* exists even in a possible world in which she never has lived at all and will never live in the future. She still does exist, as a merely possible person. (As such, she is according to Williamson neither a concrete nor an abstract object.) This would mean that even if *p* is a merely possible person, all three relata of the "better for" relation exist. However, one might still question whether anything could be better or worse for a merely possible person and whether such a person could be assigned any level of well-being. Williamson himself leaves this possibility open pending further philosophical investigation (cf. 2013: 29). We are skeptical on this point. Even if mere possibilia do exist (which is a huge "if," of course), they can hardly be assigned more than a merely possible level of well-being (or rather a whole range of such possible levels). And it can hardly be claimed that being merely possible is worse (or better) for that merely possible person than having a life. A philosopher who actually was prepared to make this seemingly preposterous claim was Richard Hare, but his proposal, when it was made, fell on deaf ears (cf. Hare 1988, 1993, 1993 [1975], 1998).

11. Rabinowicz suggested this argument back in 2000 in personal conversation with Arrhenius, Broome, Bykvist, and Erik Carlson at a workshop in Leipzig; and he has briefly presented it in Rabinowicz 2003: n. 29, and in more detail in Rabinowicz 2009a: n. 2. For a similar argument, see Arrhenius 1999: 158, who suggests that an affirmative answer to the existential question "only involves a claim that if a person exists, then she can compare the value of her life to her non-existence. A person that will never exist cannot, of course, compare 'her' non-existence with her existence. Consequently, one can claim that it is better . . . for a person to exist . . . than . . . not to exist without implying any absurdities." In fact, even though he accepted the negative answer to the existential question (and instead went for the view that it can be good but not better for a person to exist than not to exist), Parfit (1991 [1984]) came very close to making the same point as we are making when he observed that there is nothing problematic in the claim that one can benefit a person by causing her to exist: "In judging that some person's life is worth living, or better than nothing, we need *not* be implying that it would have been worse for this person if he had never existed.—Since this person *does* exist, we can refer to this person when describing the alternative [i.e., the world in which she wouldn't have existed]. We know who it is who, in this possible alternative, would never have existed" (487–88; emphasis in original; cf. n. 8 above). See also Holtug 2001, Bykvist 2007, and Johansson 2010.
12. As we have seen, this principle is assumed by Parfit (1991 [1984]: 395, 489).
13. Bykvist 2007: 348. Symbols have been changed in this quotation, for the sake of consistency.
14. Moreover, it seems clear that SC1 is false, mutatis mutandis, for related concepts, such as "considered better by" / "would be considered worse by" and "preferred by" / "would be dispreferred by." This is acknowledged by Bykvist (2007: 349). Bykvist (2014) considers the possibility that subjunctive connection obtains specifically for values even though it doesn't hold for preferences and the like. In particular he considers what he calls the principle of Axiological Invariance: "If [A] has absolute or comparative value for a person, it would have this value, no matter whether [A] were to obtain or not." He points out, however, that this principle is untenable: A person's existence might be good (or bad) for that person but it couldn't be good (bad) for her if she did not exist.
15. Adler (2009: 1506) tentatively embraces a similar position: "Existence can be better or worse for an individual than nonexistence. Nonexistence can be better or worse for an individual than existence. Where an outcome set contains potential nonexistents, their

interests should be taken into account by assigning them a utility level of zero in the outcomes where they do not exist."

16. Roberts 2003: 168–69. Moreover, Roberts (1998: 64) writes: "I am thus supposing that it is at least possible that *s* has more well-being in a world in which *s* does not exist than *s* actually has. Suppose *s*'s existence in X is unavoidably *less* than one worth living... and that *s* has, in any world in which *s* does not exist, a zero level of well-being. Under these conditions, *s*'s level of well-being at zero is actually *greater* than *s*'s well-being in X" (emphasis in original). See also Roberts, chapter 21 in this volume.
17. Of course, it isn't evident that all properties are of this kind, for example, properties of fictional objects or tropes (that is, concrete property-like particulars whose existence is supposed to be ontologically independent of the existence of property bearers).
18. We are indebted to Jonas Olson for this last point.
19. See Bykvist 2007: 348. Adler (2009: 1503) considers a similar conceptual connection, which he presents as the connection between "worse for" and "worse off than." However, unlike Bykvist, Adler's discussion leads him to reject, at least tentatively, this supposed conceptual link (cf. 2009: 1505).
20. This seems to hold even if we were to construct persons as abstract objects that can obtain or not obtain. A specific welfare level is something an abstract person can possess only in a world in which she obtains. Unless, of course, we bring in that level in the abstract specification of the person in question. But then this need not be the zero level; it can be any level.
21. This passage on guardian angels draws on Arrhenius and Rabinowicz (2010) but has now been re-formulated. The original formulation, which was in terms of pairwise choices a guardian angel would make, invited an unfortunate misinterpretation of our view, as we have become aware after reading a forthcoming paper by Fleurbaey and Voorhoeve (forthcoming).
 Rabinowicz suggested the guardian angel approach in 2000 (see n. 11) and Arrhenius (2003) proposes the benevolent impartial observer approach. See also Bykvist 2007. Broome (2004: 63) credits Rabinowicz with a suggestion that is simpler but less plausible: A history (or a world) X is better for *p* than a history Y if and only if *p* prefers X to Y. As Broome points out: "A person may prefer one history to another even if she does not exist in both of them" (2004: 63). Obviously, however, this simple proposal is not satisfactory as it stands. The advantage of appealing to the preferences of the guardian angel rather than to those of the benevolent impartial observer is that the latter are supposed to track what is impersonally good (good, period) rather than what's good for the person under consideration. A benevolent impartial observer tracks impersonal goodness even when she only focuses on the interests of that person and of no one else. There is a conceptual distinction between how good a prospect that only concerns the interests of a given person is for the person in question and how good that prospect is from an impersonal perspective. And, at least for prioritarians, that distinction makes a difference: It affects the ordering of prospects. (Cf. Rabinowicz 2001, 2002.) The task of a guardian angel is different in that respect: His responsibility is to track goodness for the person in his care.
22. Cf. Darwall (2002) for this proposal. As Darwall puts it: "[W]hat it is for something to be good for someone *just is* for it to be something one should desire for him for his sake, that is, insofar as one cares for him" (8). See also Toni Rønnow-Rasmussen (2007, 2011), where this fitting attitude account of value-for is elaborated and defended. That this account can

be used to clarify comparisons between existence and nonexistence has been suggested in Rabinowicz (2009a: n. 2).

23. The challenge here is whether the "for p's sake" locution can be independently understood, without presupposing the notion of "better for" as already given. If preferring something for p's sake just means "preferring it insofar as one only cares for what is better for p," then the analysis becomes circular. On the other hand, if "for p's sake" is given an independent interpretation, then it is not obvious that all that one ought to prefer for p's sake *is* better for p. In particular, perfectionist considerations complicate matters at this point. Thus, for example, it might be argued that one is a better person if one experiences sorrow at the thought of others' suffering and that one ought to desire this for p's own sake. Yet it is not obvious that such a state of mind would be good for p. (We are indebted to Johan Brännmark for pressing this point.) Maybe, therefore, a circular analysis of "sake" would, after all, be preferable. It should be noted that even circular analyses can be instructive to some extent: They can used to exhibit structural connections between concepts appearing in the analysans and the analysandum. Thereby, they can provide relevant information to those who already possess the concepts involved but are not clear about their mutual relationships. Thus, to take an example, David Wiggins adheres to the sentimentalist version of the fitting attitude account even though he explicitly recognizes the charge of circularity. Still, as he argues, the account is informative in its "detour through sentiments" (see Wiggins 1987: 189). Cf. Rabinowicz and Rønnow-Rasmussen (2004, 2006). The circularity Wiggins has in mind is different from the one mentioned here, though. He thinks that it might be essential to the fitting sentiments with regard to objects that these attitudes themselves already involve evaluations.

24. We are grateful to Erik Carlson for pressing this point. A somewhat similar point has subsequently been made by Bykvist (2014). Following Sven Danielsson, Bykvist writes: "to say that a state of affairs [A] is good for you is to say that you are such that it is possible that the world ... would be good for you (at least to some extent), if it exemplified [A].—The slogan is: states of affairs that are good for you could rate the universe a plus for you [if they were exemplified by the universe, that is, if they obtained]."

25. A caveat: There is a way of dealing with this general problem. We could argue that statements of the form "The obtaining of S would be better (for p) than the obtaining of T" should be read as "The obtaining of S would have a higher degree of goodness or lower degree of badness (for p) than the obtaining of T." Unlike obtainings, degrees of goodness and badness are abstract objects and there is therefore nothing that hinders their coexistence.

While this proposal would solve the general problem of value comparisons between obtainings of states of affairs, it would lead to the negative answer to the existential question: The obtaining of the state consisting in p's nonexistence could not have any level of goodness or badness *for p*, since p would not exist if that state had obtained. Consequently, the obtaining of that state could not be compared in its degree of value for p with the obtaining of p's existence.

However, a serious weakness of the proposal under consideration lies in its reduction of comparative value notions (such as 'better' and 'worse') to the noncomparative ones ('good', 'bad'). On the view taken by many philosophers, not least those who have been influenced by measurement theory, the order of conceptual priority is precisely the opposite one: We arrive at such notions as levels of goodness and badness only by making value comparisons; thus, betterness is prior to goodness and not the other way round. See, e.g., Broome 1999: ch. 10, p. 164. Cf. also Chisholm and Sosa 1966.

26. We are indebted to Jonas Olson for pressing us on this point.
27. Nevertheless, Lemos rejects the suggestion that nonobtaining states of affairs possess intrinsic value and draws the conclusion that there might be something wrong with the fitting attitude account of value: "if some nonobtaining states of affairs are worthy of love, then we should say that being intrinsically good implies being worthy of love, but being worthy of love does not imply being intrinsically good" (1994: 24).
28. This counterfactual invariance of the dyadic betterness relation is possible only because its relata (outcomes) can be assumed to exist even if they do not obtain. By contrast, the triadic relation of "better for" can only satisfy a weaker condition of counterfactual invariance: If A would have been better for p than B if B obtained, then A is better for p than B even if B does not obtain, *provided that p exists*.
29. In fact, even this disjunctive version of the restriction might be too strong. In principle, it is conceivable that A is better than B because it would be better for some individual who only exists in the actual outcome but not in A or B. For example, suppose that C is the actual outcome and p exists in C but not in A or B. Suppose further that p in C devotes her whole life to a certain goal x. For p, this goal is categorical: she wishes it to be realized even if it weren't her goal in the first place. The realization of p's categorical goals is of one of the things that determine how good an outcome is for p. Although p wouldn't exist in A or B, let us suppose that x would be better realized in the former outcome than in the latter. It then might well be the case that A is better for p than B, even though—as it happens—there would be no one in either A of B for whom the former outcome would be better than the latter. However, note that this would make better-for comparisons outcome relative, which one might find problematic. For example, if in outcome D p would have not-x as her categorical goal, B could be better than A relative to D whereas A is better than B relative to C.
30. For the latter theory, see Blackorby, Bossert, and Donaldson 1997, 1995, 2005 and Blackorby and Donaldson 1984. For a discussion of both theories, see Arrhenius 2015: chs. 3 and 5.
31. For more on the implications in population ethics of the affirmative answer to the existential question and the Wide Person-Affecting Restriciton, see Arrhenius (2014, 2015).

References

Adler, M. D. (2009). "Future Generations: A Prioritarian View." *George Washington Law Review* 77 (5–6): 1478–1520.

Arrhenius, G. (1999). "Population Axiology." Ph.D. diss., Department of Philosophy, University of Toronto.

Arrhenius, G. (2000). *Future Generations: A Challenge for Moral Theory*. F.D. diss. Uppsala: University Printers.

Arrhenius, G. (2003). "The Person Affecting Restriction, Comparativism, and the Moral Status of Potential People." *Ethical Perspectives* 10, 3–4: 185–95.

Arrhenius, G. (2009). "Can the Person Affecting Restriction Solve the Problems in Population Ethics?" In M. A. Roberts and D. Wasserman (eds.), *Harming Future Persons*. Aldershot: Ashgate, 289–314.

Arrhenius, G. (2014). "The Affirmative Answer to the Existential Question and the Person Affecting Restriction." In I. Hirose and A. Reisner (eds.), *Weighing and Reasoning*. Oxford University Press, forthcoming.

Arrhenius, G. (2015). *Population Ethics*. New York: Oxford University Press, forthcoming.

Arrhenius, G. and W. Rabinowicz. (2010). "Better to Be Than Not to Be?" In H. Joas and B. Klein (eds.), *The Benefit of Broad Horizons. Intellectual and Institutional Preconditions for a Global Social Science*, Festschrift for Björn Wittrock, Brill: Leiden, 399–421.

Arrhenius, G., J. Ryberg, and T. Tännsjö. (2006). "The Repugnant Conclusion." In E. N. Zalta (ed.), *Stanford Encyclopaedia of Philosophy*, Spring 2014 ed. http://plato.stanford.edu/archives/spr2014/entries/repugnant-conclusion/.

Blackorby, C., and D. Donaldson. (1984). "Social Criteria for Evaluating Population Change." *Journal of Public Economics* 25: 13–33.

Blackorby, C., W. Bossert, and D. Donaldson. (1995). "Intertemporal Population Ethics: Critical-Level Utilitarian Principles." *Econometrica* 65: 1303–20.

Blackorby, C., W. Bossert, and D. Donaldson. (1997). "Critical-Level Utilitarianism and the Population-Ethics Dilemma." *Economics and Philosophy* 13: 197–230.

Blackorby, C., W. Bossert, and D. Donaldson. (2005). *Population Issues in Social Choice Theory, Welfare Economics, and Ethics*. Cambridge: Cambridge University Press.

Broome, J. (1999). *Ethics out of Economics*. Cambridge: Cambridge University Press.

Broome, J. (2004). *Weighing Lives*. Oxford: Oxford University Press.

Bykvist, K. (2007). "The Benefits of Coming into Existence." *Philosophical Studies* 135: 335–62.

Bykvist, K. (2014). "Being and Well-Being." In I. Hirose and A. Reisner (eds.), *Weighing and Reasoning*, Oxford University Press, forthcoming.

Buchanan, A., D. W. Brock, N. Daniels, and D. Wikler. (2000). *From Chance to Choice: Genetics and Justice*. Cambridge: Cambridge University Press.

Chisholm, R. M., and E. Sosa. (1966). "On the Logic of 'Intrinsically Better.'" *American Philosophical Quarterly* 3: 244–49.

Darwall, S. (2002). *Welfare and Rational Care*. Princeton, NJ: Princeton University Press.

Dasgupta, P. (1995). *An Inquiry into Well-Being and Destitution*. Oxford: Oxford University Press, 1995.

Feldman, F. (1995a). "Adjusting Utility for Justice: A Consequentialist Reply to the Objection from Justice." *Philosophy and Phenomenological Research* 55 (3): 567–85. Reprinted in Feldman 1997.

Feldman, F. (1995b). "Justice, Desert, and the Repugnant Conclusion." *Utilitas* 7 (2): 189–206. Reprinted in Feldman 1997.

Feldman, F. (1997). *Utilitarianism, Hedonism, and Desert: Essays in Moral Philosophy*. Cambridge: Cambridge University Press.

Fleurbaey, M., and A. Voorhoeve.(Forthcoming). "On the Social and Personal Value of Existence." In I. Hirose and A. Reisner (eds.), *Weighing and Reasoning: A Festschrift for John Broome*. Oxford University Press.

Glover, J. (1977). *Causing Death and Saving Lives*. New York: Penguin.

Hare, R. (1988). "Possible People." *Bioethics* 2: 279–93.

Hare, R. M. (1993). "When Does Potentiality Count?" In R. M. Hare (ed.), *Essays on Bioethics*. New York: Oxford University Press, 84–97.

Hare, R. M. (1993 [1975]). "Abortion and the Golden Rule." In R. M. Hare (ed.), *Essays on Bioethics*. New York: Oxford University Press, 147–67.

Hare, R. M. (1998). "Preferences of Possible People." In C. Fehige and U. Wessels (eds.), *Preferences*. Berlin: de Gruyter, 399–405.

Heyd, D. (1988). "Procreation and Value: Can Ethics Deal with Futurity Problems?" *Philosophia* (Israel) 18 (July): 151–70.

Heyd, D. (1992). *Genethics: Moral Issues in the Creation of People*. Berkeley: University of California Press.
Holtug, N. (1996). "In Defence of the Slogan." In W. Rabinowicz (ed.), *Preference and Value: Preferentialism in Ethics*. Studies in Philosophy, vol. 1. Lund: Department of Philosophy, Lund University, 64–89.
Holtug, N. (2001). "On the Value of Coming into Existence." *Journal of Ethics* 5: 361–84.
Holtug, N. (2004). "Person-Affecting Moralities." In J. Ryberg and T. Tännsjö (eds.), *The Repugnant Conclusion: Essays on Population Ethics*. Dordrecht: Kluwer, 129–61.
Johansson, J. (2010). "Being and Betterness." *Utilitas* 22: 285–302.
Lemos, N. M. (1994). *Intrinsic Value: Concept and Warrant*. Cambridge: Cambridge University Press.
Narveson, J. (1967). "Utilitarianism and New Generations." *Mind* 76 (January): 62–72.
Moore, G. E. (1966 [1903]). *Principia Ethica*. Cambridge: Cambridge University Press.
Parfit, D. (1991 [1984]). *Reasons and Persons*. Oxford: Clarendon Press.
Rabinowicz, W. (2001). "Prioritarianism and Uncertainty: On the Interpersonal Addition Theorem and the Priority View." In D. Egonsson, J. Josefsson, B. Petersson, and T. Rønnow-Rasmussen (eds.), *Exploring Practical Philosophy: From Action to Values*. Aldershot: Ashgate, 139–65.
Rabinowicz, W. (2002). "Prioritarianism for Prospects." *Utilitas* 14: 2–21.
Rabinowicz, W. (2003). "The Size of Inequality and Its Badness: Some Reflections around Temkin's Inequality." *Theoria* 69: 60–84.
Rabinowicz, W. (2009a). "Broome and the Intuition of Neutrality." *Philosophical Issues* 19: 389–411.
Rabinowicz, W. (2009b). "Values Compared." *Polish Journal of Philosophy* 3: 73–96.
Rabinowicz, W., and T. Rønnow-Rasmussen. (2004). "The Strike of the Demon: On Fitting Pro-attitudes and Value." *Ethics* 114: 391–423.
Rabinowicz, W., and T. Rønnow-Rasmussen. (2006). "Buck-Passing and the Right Kind of Reasons." *Philosophical Quarterly* 56: 114–20.
Roberts, M. A. (1998). *Child versus Childmaker: Future Persons and Present Duties in Ethics and the Law*. Lanham, MD: Rowman and Littlefield.
Roberts, M. A. (2003). "Can It Ever Be Better Never to Have Existed at All? Person-Based Consequentialism and a New Repugnant Conclusion." *Journal of Applied Philosophy* 20 (2): 159–85.
Rønnow-Rasmussen, T. (2007). "Analyzing Personal Values." *Journal of Ethics* 11: 405–35.
Rønnow-Rasmussen, T. (2011). *Personal Value*. Oxford: Oxford University Press.
Temkin, L. S. (1993a). *Inequality*. Oxford: Oxford University Press.
Temkin, L. S. (1993b). "Harmful Goods, Harmless Bads." In R. G. Frey and C. W. Morris (eds.), *Value, Welfare, and Morality*. Cambridge: Cambridge University Press, 291–324.
Wiggins, D. (1987). *Needs, Values, Truth: Essays in the Philosophy of Value*. Oxford: Blackwell.
Williamson, T. (2013). *Modal Logic as Metaphysics*. Oxford: Oxford University Press.
Zimmerman, M. J. (2001). *The Nature of Intrinsic Value*. Lanham, MD: Rowman and Littlefield.

Index

abstract values 206–12, 215–6
actual desire theory 62–4, 140, 164–6
additive separability 5–6, 251–2, 269
additivity 230, 234–5, 290–1
agent-neutrality 3, 96–112
    of reasons 96, 104–5
    of value 96–112, 211
agent-relativity 3, 96–112, 211
    and consequentialism 3, 97, 100–5, 108–12
    of reasons 96, 104–5
    of value 96–112, 211
aggregation 4, 6, 225–31, 249–64, 267–83, 290–1, 300–14
    and the separateness of persons 280–1, 306–8
    aggregative principles 267–83, 302–3
    argument from counterexamples 304–6
    definition 301–4
    in utilitarianism 226–7, 229, 249–64, 267–82
    intrapersonal aggregation 227–8, 253–9, 267, 269, 301–2, 306–7
    of subject-relative values 65–7
    skepticism about 269–73, 280–3, 300–14
affective concepts. *See* thick concepts
anthropocentricism 388
archimedean property 225–33, 288
associativity 288–9, 292–3
atemporal goods 121–2
attitude-dependence 60–7, 75–6, 158–9, 164–70
attributive goodness 13–14, 21, 23, 37
axiological egalitarianism 252, 273–83, 303

basic person-based result 406–12
basic value relations 208–14
betterness relations 5, 177–200, 225–64, 293, 302, 329–30, 399–441
    among worlds 399–441
    and the dualism of practical reason 177–200
    and discontinuity 225–46
    general 5, 250–60
    personal 5, 250–60
biocentrism 388–91, 394–5
    biocentric holism 390–1
    biocentric individualism 390–1
buck-passing view 22, 40, 56, 113, 171

capabilities approach 140–1, 160–2, 172, 351, 356, 375
cardinal measurement 205–7, 213–5, 221, 262–3, 298
collapsing principle 214–5
commutativity 288–9, 292–3
comparability 142–3, 150–3, 177–85, 188–91, 205–22
    and justified choice 205–6, 216–20
    and pluralism 150–3, 177–85, 188–91
    definition 205–9
    of abstract values 207, 209–11
    of value-bearers 207, 211–2
comparativism 216–20
comparison function 210–12
completeness 5, 7, 177–97, 232–43, 258–9, 288, 301, 317–25, 344–53
conditional value 4, 175–7, 184–97, 276
consequentialism 1, 3–4, 15–20, 97, 100–14, 171, 175, 300, 303–5, 399, 401–2
    and aggregation 300, 303–5
    and relative-value 97, 100–14
contextualism 294–5
continuity 225–48, 302–3, 312, 322
contractualism 310–2
contributive value 228–38, 253–9, 269–71, 277, 331, 432
cost–benefit analysis 2, 6–7, 206–7, 317–34, 391–4
    agency interpretation of 318–9
    and desire-satisfactionism 318–28
    and interpersonal comparisons 7, 318, 325–331
    and nature 325, 391–4
    distributive weighting of 330–1
counterfactual test for harm 412–4
covering value 180–5, 208–16

defective desires 62–4, 67
deontic constraints 18, 97, 101–3, 108, 195, 304
desire 3, 22, 35, 60–78, 83, 118–21, 140, 146–7, 151–3, 164–71, 322–8
desire-satisfactionism 62–6, 118–21, 129, 140, 146–7, 164–71, 322–8, 365
diminishing marginal value 230, 236, 254–6, 269–71, 277–8
discontinuity 5, 225–46, 302–3, 312–3, 322
    strong 5, 225–6, 232–7
    weak 5, 225–6, 232–4, 237–8

discounting 128–9, 258
distribution-sensitivity 269–77
duration of a good 3, 117–9, 125–6
duties 1, 15–20, 45, 47–8, 137, 175–7, 185–200, 206, 387, 424
dynamic inconsistency 118, 130–1

egalitarianism 5–6, 121, 129, 142, 252, 267–8, 273–83, 303
emotions 3, 71, 76, 80–93, 168–9
    perceptual theory of 81, 85, 90
equality 5–6, 121, 126–9, 142, 250, 252, 256–8, 267–83, 308–9, 388–9, 435
    and personal good 256–8, 276
    between species 8, 388–9
    and time 121, 126–9
    and utilitarianism 269–73
essentially comparative view 404–5, 425
eudaimonism 160–2, 168–9
existential question 424–41
expected utility theory 2, 5, 206–7, 250–4, 258–62, 321–4
experience machine 146–7, 163–4, 168
extended preferences 327–8
extrinsic value 2, 14, 29–41, 46–7, 286, 294

fairness 252, 256–8, 260, 273, 281
final extrinsicalism. *See* nonintrinsicalism
final value 2, 14–26, 32–41, 46–7, 117, 133–4, 286, 294–6, 432
fitting-attitude analysis 21–6, 35, 48–9, 53–4, 61, 67–73, 81–85, 98–108, 110–2, 135, 430–2
    challenges to 21–5, 48, 54, 69–70, 84, 90
    and population axiology 430–2
    and relative value 98–108
fittingness 2–3, 21–6, 35, 48–9, 53–4, 61, 67–73, 83–5, 89–90
    representational notion of 69–73, 83–5, 89–90
formal values 179–80, 185–9
freedom 7, 136, 233, 338, 351–2, 356–78
    constraints on 357–64, 367–9
    definition 357–64
    instrumental value of 364–6
    interpersonal comparisons of 374–5
    intrinsic value of 364, 366
    measurement of 367–77
    and preferences 359, 365–6, 370–3
full-information theory 63–4, 164–5
future-orientedness 118, 129–31

goodness *simpliciter* 4, 13–26, 37–8, 44–61, 64–7, 88, 137–9, 141–2, 145–6, 153, 250–60, 301, 308–9, 313, 400
    fundamentality of 13–26, 44–9
    nonnaturalism about 45–6, 48
    skepticism about 14, 37–8, 49–54, 139, 308–9, 313

happiness 4, 108, 140, 167–8, 175–200, 409–10
    Kantian conditionalism about 4, 175–200
    and well-being 108, 140, 167–8
Harsanyi's theorem 5, 249–65
    and fairness 257–8, 260
    objections to 256–64
    and prioritarianism 252, 254–7, 264
health 7, 141, 161, 319, 324, 338–54
    and capability 141, 161, 350–2
    definition 338–44
    interpersonal comparisons of 344–53
    measurement of 344–53
    and opportunity 338, 345–6, 348–52
    and preferences 346–8
hedonism 3–4, 136, 140, 143–5, 162–4, 167, 229–30, 287, 305

impartial spectator 107–9, 306–7
impartiality 107–9, 180, 256, 264, 268, 302, 309, 312
incommensurability 4–5, 151, 171, 177–85, 205–7, 211, 322, 392–4, 434–5
incomparability 4–5, 142–3, 150–3, 177–85, 188–91, 205–22
    of abstract values 207, 209–11
    definition 205–9
    and justified choice 205–6, 216–20
    and pluralism 150–3, 177–85, 188–91
    of value-bearers 207, 211–2
incompleteness 189–91, 258–9, 344–53
independence axiom 235, 260–1
indeterminacy. *See* vagueness
inequality aversion 256–8, 435
instrumental value 2, 33–6, 45, 138, 147, 382–7, 390–1
internalism 166–71
interpersonal comparisons 7, 258–9, 309, 325–34, 344–53, 367, 374–5
    of freedom 367, 374–5
    of health 344–53
    of utility 7, 258–9, 309, 325–34
intransitivity 7, 189–91, 327–9
intrapersonal repugnant conclusion 226–8
intrinsic value 1–4, 14, 16–20, 29–41, 44–58, 88, 117, 121, 123, 133–4, 138–51, 176–97, 285–96, 382–97, 432
    analysis of 21–6, 45, 48, 53–4, 432
    basic vs derivative 138–51
    conditional intrinsic value 176–97
    unanalyzability of 45–49, 53
    versus final value 2, 14, 32–3, 35–6, 46–7

finality sense 30–3
and nature 382–96
skepticism about 3, 14, 37–8, 49–54, 308–9, 313
supervenience sense 30–3
and time 117, 121
intrinsicalism 14, 36–7, 46–7, 286, 294–6
isolation test 30–1, 45, 53

Kaldor-Hicks criterion 7, 318, 328–31
Kantian value dualism 4, 175–200

levelling down objection 275–6, 278–80
lexical ordering 178, 186, 278–9, 282, 401, 416
leximin 5–6, 272, 274, 278–9, 282–3, 303
life worth living 8, 226–8, 275, 400–1, 403–5, 415–8, 428

marginal value. *See* contributive value
maximalism 217, 219–20
maximin 5, 272, 303, 307
momentary well-being 118–21, 127
monetary equivalents 318–31
inferring of 323–4
monotonicity 235, 288–94
monism 3–4, 136–55, 177–8, 197
arguments against 145–50
arguments for 147–8, 150–3
about goodness simpliciter 143–7
about value-properties 138–9
about well-being 140–1, 143, 146–7
Moore's additivity principle 290–1
Moorean holism 294–5
moral standing 8, 387–95

neutrality intuition 404–5
nominal-notable comparisons 152, 184–5, 210
non-aggregative principles 6, 272, 274, 278, 282–3, 300–1, 303–5, 307, 309–13
nonanthropocentricism 388–90
non-archimedeanism 225–43
nonidentity problem 8, 275–6, 406, 412–5, 419
noninstrumental value. *See* final value
nonintrinsicalism 14, 32–4, 36–7, 46–7, 134, 286, 294–6
noncomparability 5, 188–91, 205, 211, 215–6, 322
normative reasons 2, 13, 23–4, 35, 48–54, 69–70, 84, 90, 96, 99–100, 104–5, 109–11, 135, 159, 181–96, 217–20
normative redundancy argument 49–52
normativity 2, 13–26, 159, 161, 163–71, 176, 182–8
number problem 6, 309–13

objective list theory 140–1, 160, 163, 166–8, 170–1, 238
objective value 34, 61, 65–76, 106–7, 140, 160–71, 308, 384–6

objectivism 4, 34, 61, 65–76, 160–71, 384–6
opportunity sets 7, 357–77
organic unities 6, 46–7, 88, 118, 127–9, 251, 285–99, 301, 308–9
and aggregation 301, 308–9
bonum variationis case 289, 292, 295–6
criteria for organicity 287–96
nonidentity definition 287–90
nonproportionality definition 287–90
and time 118, 127–9
outcomism 17–9, 47

paretian egalitarianism 273–5, 278–9, 282–3
Pareto principle 5–6, 188, 269, 273–5, 278, 281, 302–3, 309, 312, 320, 328–30
parity 5, 205, 212–4
person-affecting view 8, 275–6, 279, 400–15, 418–20, 425
inclusivity of 405–12
narrow versus wide 275–6, 279, 415
and the nonidentity problem 412–5
personal good 5–6, 249–64
Pigou-Dalton principle 5–6, 272–8
pleasure 3–4, 14, 54, 117–20, 123, 136, 140–53, 160, 162–4, 206, 225, 229–31, 234, 287, 300–2
definitions of 162–4
and non-archimedeanism 225, 229–31, 234
and time 117–20, 123
pluralism 4, 8, 136–55, 177–85, 193–4, 400–2, 416, 419
arguments against 147–8, 150–3
arguments for 145–50
about goodness simpliciter 141–5
in population axiology 8, 400–2, 416, 419
and practical reason 177–85, 193–4
about value properties 138–9
about well-being 140–5
possibilist analysis of harm 413–15
practical reason 4–5, 136–7, 153, 205–8, 213–4, 216–20
dualism of 4, 153, 175–200
predicative goodness. *See* goodness *simpliciter*
preferences 7, 35, 62–5, 75–6, 102–3, 110–2, 129, 131–2, 164–7, 249, 318–28, 331, 338, 345–8, 350, 359, 365–6, 370–3, 430–1
idealizing conditions on 7, 63–5, 164–5, 318, 321–4
non-remoteness conditions on 318, 324–5
and time-bias 131–2
and well-being 164–7, 249, 318–28, 350, 365–6
preferentialism. *See* desire-satisfactionism
principle of personal good 250–4, 261–2

prioritarianism 5–6, 252, 254–7, 260, 262–4, 267, 272–83, 302–3, 330–1
   and aggregation 282–3, 302–3
   arguments against 262–4, 280–3
   arguments for 278–80
prudential value. *See* well-being

quality weights 347–8

radical pluralism 142–3, 148–50, 152–3, 402, 419
rational regret 137, 148–50, 195
realism 3, 60–2, 67–76
   axiological 3, 61, 70–7
   normative (*see* fitting-attitude analysis)
   representational 61, 70–7
remoteness problem 318, 324–5
repugnant conclusion 8, 226–9, 231, 236, 400–1, 415–20, 425, 435
rescue case. *See* number problem
respect 383, 387–91, 394–5
rights 20, 206, 387–8, 394
risk aversion 254–7, 264
risk neutrality 255–6

separateness of persons 6, 280–1, 301, 306–8
silencing 184–6, 192–7
social welfare functions 7, 318, 330–1
species egalitarianism 8, 388–9
strong separability 6, 269, 274, 277–8
subject-relative values 61–7, 96–114, 158–69
subject-relativity requirement 158–69
subjectivism 33–4, 61–6, 136, 140, 146–7, 158–60, 164–7, 169–70
super-value 152–3, 178–9, 183–6
superiority. *See* discontinuity
supervenience 2, 30–4, 50, 192, 250

telic egalitarianism. *See* axiological egalitarianism
temporal bias 129–35
temporal location 3, 117–25
thick concepts 3, 81–90
   variability argument 87–90

transformative value 392
trichotomy thesis 208, 212–4

uncompensability 142–3, 148–50
utilitarianism 1, 5–6, 65, 108, 163, 226–7, 229, 249–64, 267–82, 300, 302–4, 306–7, 330–1, 399, 406, 424–5, 434
utility 2, 5, 7, 251–64, 270–2, 319–31, 365–6, 371
utility functions 5, 250–64, 269–72, 319–331, 365

vagueness 214–5, 417
Value Appearance Thesis 71–6
value-bearers 3, 4, 31–3, 100, 111, 207, 210–2, 286–7, 292–6, 431–2
value-emotion equivalences 3, 81–5, 89–91
value idealism. *See* attitude-dependence
valuer-dependence 168–9, 385–6
variabilism 410–2
virtue 117, 126, 140, 146–7, 160–1, 177, 193–5, 225, 231

welfare. *See* well-being
welfare economics 7, 317, 331, 425
welfarism 108, 170–1, 236, 276, 302, 425, 434
well-being 4, 7–8, 14, 61–5, 117–29, 137–43, 146–9, 158–72, 175–200, 226–38, 249–83, 302–3, 308–9, 318–31, 338–52, 356, 366, 375, 399, 420
   aggregation of 226–38, 249–83, 302–3, 308–9, 399–420
   and cost–benefit analysis 318–31
   and freedom 356, 366, 375
   and health 338–52
   Kantian conditionalism about 175–200
   normativity of 163–71
   theories of 62–5, 118–21, 140–1, 146–8, 158–72
   and time 117–29
world-based approaches 399–402, 406–8, 415–20
wrong kind of reason problem 23–4, 48, 54, 69–70, 84, 90. *See also* fitting-attitude analysis, objections to

www.ingramcontent.com/pod-product-compliance
Ingram Content Group UK Ltd.
Pitfield, Milton Keynes, MK11 3LW, UK
UKHW011508160425
457382UK00015B/105